THE INSTITUTE FOR POLISH–JEW.

The Institute for Polish–Jewish Studies in Oxford and its sister organization, the American Association for Polish–Jewish Studies, which publish *Polin*, are learned societies that were established in 1984, following the International Conference on Polish–Jewish Studies, held in Oxford. The Institute is an associate institute of the Oxford Centre for Hebrew and Jewish Studies, and the American Association is linked with the Department of Near Eastern and Judaic Studies at Brandeis University.

Both the Institute and the American Association aim to promote understanding of the Polish Jewish past. They have no building or library of their own and no paid staff; they achieve their aims by encouraging scholarly research and facilitating its publication, and by creating forums for people with a scholarly interest in Polish Jewish topics, both past and present.

To this end the Institute and the American Association help organize lectures and international conferences. Venues for these activities have included Brandeis University in Waltham, Massachusetts, the Hebrew University in Jerusalem, the Institute for the Study of Human Sciences in Vienna, King's College in London, the Jagiellonian University in Kraków, the Oxford Centre for Hebrew and Jewish Studies, the University of Łódź, University College London, and the Polish Cultural Institute and the Polish embassy in London. They have encouraged academic exchanges between Israel, Poland, the United States, and western Europe. In particular they seek to help train a new generation of scholars, in Poland and elsewhere, to study the culture and history of the Jews in Poland.

Each year since 1987 the Institute has published a volume of scholarly papers in the series *Polin: Studies in Polish Jewry* under the general editorship of Professor Antony Polonsky of Brandeis University. Since 1994 the series has been published on its behalf by the Littman Library of Jewish Civilization, and since 1998 the publication has been linked with the American Association as well. In March 2000 the entire series was honoured with a National Jewish Book Award from the Jewish Book Council in the United States. More than twenty other works on Polish Jewish topics have also been published with the Institute's assistance.

Further information on the Institute for Polish–Jewish Studies can be found on their website, <www.polishjewishstudies.pl>. For the website of the American Association for Polish–Jewish Studies, see <www.aapjstudies.org>.

THE LITTMAN LIBRARY OF
JEWISH CIVILIZATION

Dedicated to the memory of
LOUIS THOMAS SIDNEY LITTMAN
who founded the Littman Library for the love of God
and as an act of charity in memory of his father
JOSEPH AARON LITTMAN
and to the memory of
ROBERT JOSEPH LITTMAN
who continued what his father Louis had begun
יהא זכרם ברוך

'*Get wisdom, get understanding:*
Forsake her not and she shall preserve thee'
PROV. 4: 5

The Littman Library of Jewish Civilization is a registered UK charity
Registered charity no. 1000784

POLIN

STUDIES IN POLISH JEWRY

VOLUME TWENTY-SEVEN

Jews in the Kingdom of Poland,
1815–1918

Edited by

GLENN DYNNER, ANTONY POLONSKY

and

MARCIN WODZIŃSKI

Published for
The Institute for Polish–Jewish Studies
and
The American Association for Polish–Jewish Studies

Oxford · Portland, Oregon
The Littman Library of Jewish Civilization

The Littman Library of Jewish Civilization

Chief Executive Officer: Ludo Craddock
Managing Editor: Connie Webber

PO Box 645, Oxford OX2 0UJ, UK
www.littman.co.uk

———

Published in the United States and Canada by
The Littman Library of Jewish Civilization
c/o ISBS, 920 NE 58th Avenue, Suite 300
Portland, Oregon 97213-3786

A catalogue record for this book is available from the British Library

Library of Congress Cataloging-in-Publication data applied for
ISSN 0268 1056

ISBN 978-1-906764-21-0 (cloth)
ISBN 978-1-906764-22-7 (pbk)

Publishing co-ordinator: Janet Moth
Copy-editing: George Tulloch
Proof-reading: Mark Newby and Joyce Rappaport
Index: Bonnie Blackburn
Design, typesetting and production: Pete Russell, Faringdon, Oxon.
Printed in Great Britain on acid-free paper by
TJ International Ltd, Padstow, Cornwall

Articles appearing in this publication are abstracted and indexed in
Historical Abstracts and America: History and Life

This volume is dedicated to the memory of
ROBY LITTMAN
director of the
Littman Library of Jewish Civilization,
who took great pride in the achievements of Polin
and died, aged 60, while this volume was in press

———

This volume benefited from grants from
THE MIRISCH AND LEBENHEIM CHARITABLE FOUNDATION
THE LUCIUS N. LITTAUER FOUNDATION

Editors and Advisers

Preface

THIS VOLUME investigates the situation of the Jews in the Kingdom of Poland, the autonomous, constitutional state, in dynastic union with the Romanovs, created at the Congress of Vienna to satisfy, at least in part, the national aspirations of the Poles. Although its autonomous status was severely restricted and nearly done away with by the tsars after the unsuccessful Polish uprisings of 1830–1 and 1863–4, and despite its comparatively small territorial size, the Kingdom of Poland played a disproportionately great role in both Polish and Polish Jewish history. During the course of the nineteenth century it emerged as the most important centre of Polish cultural and political life and the setting for key social, political, economic, and cultural transformations, including those deeply affecting the Jewish population. The kingdom contained the largest urban centres in the Polish lands and some of the major Jewish metropolises of Europe. Moreover, it gave shape to Polish–Jewish relations in modern times, both within and beyond its borders.

The specific features of Jewish life in the Kingdom of Poland have not, by and large, been recognized in the scholarship on this area and this volume, with contributions from leading scholars in Poland, Israel, and the United States, seeks to fill this gap and provide a clear picture of what made the Kingdom of Poland different from the other areas of partitioned Poland and from the centres of Jewish life in central Europe.

Polin is sponsored by the Institute of Polish–Jewish Studies, which is an associated institute of the Oxford Centre for Hebrew and Jewish Studies, and by the American Association for Polish–Jewish Studies, which is linked with the Department of Near Eastern and Judaic Studies, Brandeis University. As with earlier issues, this volume could not have appeared without the untiring assistance of many individuals. In particular, we should like to express our gratitude to Professor Frederick Lawrence, president of Brandeis University, to Mrs Irene Pipes, president of the American Association for Polish–Jewish Studies, and to Andrzej Szkuta, treasurer of the Institute for Polish–Jewish Studies. These three institutions all made substantial contributions to the cost of producing the volume. A particularly important contribution was that made by the Mirisch and Lebenheim Foundation, and the volume also benefited from a grant from the Lucius N. Littauer Foundation. As was the case with earlier volumes, this one could not have been published without the constant assistance and supervision of Connie Webber, managing editor of the Littman Library, Ludo Craddock, chief executive officer, Janet Moth, publishing co-ordinator, Pete Russell, designer, and the tireless copy-editing of George Tulloch and Joyce Rappaport.

Plans for future volumes of *Polin* are well advanced. Volume 28 will analyse aspects of Jewish writing in Poland, volume 29 will examine the historiography of Jews in the Polish lands, and volume 30 will investigate Jewish education in eastern Europe. Future volumes are planned on a comparison of the situation over the *longue durée* of Jews in Poland and Hungary, on Jewish musical life in the Polish lands, and on recent research on the Holocaust in Poland. We should welcome articles for these issues. We should also welcome any suggestions or criticisms. In particular, we are always grateful for assistance in extending the geographical range of our journal to Ukraine, Belarus, and Lithuania, both in the period in which these countries were part of the Polish–Lithuanian Commonwealth and subsequently.

We have long felt concerned at how long it takes to publish reviews in an annual publication. We now therefore post all our reviews on the website of the American Association for Polish Jewish Studies (<aapjstudies.org>) instead of publishing them in hard copy, which enables us to discuss new works much nearer to their date of publication. We welcome the submission of reviews of any book or books connected with the history of the Jews in Poland–Lithuania or on Polish–Jewish relations. We are happy to translate reviews submitted in Polish, Russian, Ukrainian, Lithuanian, Hebrew, or German into English. They should be sent to one of the following: Dr Władysław T. Bartoszewski, Forteczna 1A, 01-540, Warsaw, Poland (email: wt@wtbartoszewski.pl); Professor ChaeRan Freeze, Department of Near Eastern and Judaic Studies, Brandeis University, Waltham, Mass. 02254-9110 (email: cfreeze@brandeis.edu); Professor Antony Polonsky, Department of Near Eastern and Judaic Studies, Brandeis University, Waltham, Mass. 02254-9110 (email: polonsky@brandeis.edu); Professor Joshua Zimmerman, Yeshiva University, Department of History, 500 West 185th Street, New York, NY 10033-3201 (email: zimmerm@yu.edu).

We note with sadness the deaths of the following colleagues: Professor Yisrael Gutman, Warsaw ghetto fighter and Auschwitz survivor, a great historian, one of the pioneers of Polish–Jewish understanding and a member of the editorial board of *Polin*; Professor Geza Vermes, a fellow of the Oxford Centre for Hebrew and Jewish Studies whose work gave new impetus to the quest for the historical Jesus in the context of Jewish history and theology; Alexandra Hawiger, a devoted member of the board of the American Association for Polish-Jewish Studies; and Roby Littman, director and trustee of the Littman Library and a strong supporter of our yearbook.

POLIN

We did not know, but our fathers told us how the exiles of Israel came to the land of Polin (Poland).

When Israel saw how its sufferings were constantly renewed, oppressions increased, persecutions multiplied, and how the evil authorities piled decree on decree and followed expulsion with expulsion, so that there was no way to escape the enemies of Israel, they went out on the road and sought an answer from the paths of the wide world: which is the correct road to traverse to find rest for their soul? Then a piece of paper fell from heaven, and on it the words:

Go to Polaniya (Poland)!

So they came to the land of Polin and they gave a mountain of gold to the king, and he received them with great honour. And God had mercy on them, so that they found favour from the king and the nobles. And the king gave them permission to reside in all the lands of his kingdom, to trade over its length and breadth, and to serve God according to the precepts of their religion. And the king protected them against every foe and enemy.

And Israel lived in Polin in tranquillity for a long time. They devoted themselves to trade and handicrafts. And God sent a blessing on them so that they were blessed in the land, and their name was exalted among the peoples. And they traded with the surrounding countries and they also struck coins with inscriptions in the holy language and the language of the country. These are the coins which have on them a lion rampant from the right facing left. And on the coins are the words 'Mieszko, King of Poland' or 'Mieszko, Król of Poland'. The Poles call their king 'Król'.

And those who delve into the Scriptures say: 'This is why it is called Polin. For thus spoke Israel when they came to the land, "Here rest for the night [*Po lin*]." And this means that we shall rest here until we are all gathered into the Land of Israel.'

Since this is the tradition, we accept it as such.

S. Y. AGNON, 1916

POLIN
Studies in Polish Jewry

Contents

Note on Place Names

POLITICAL connotations accrue to words, names, and spellings with an alacrity unfortunate for those who would like to maintain neutrality. It seems reasonable to honour the choices of a population on the name of its city or town, but what is one to do when the people have no consensus on their name, or when the town changes its name, and the name its spelling, again and again over time? The politician may always opt for the latest version, but the hapless historian must reckon with them all. This note, then, will be our brief reckoning.

There is no problem with places that have accepted English names, such as Warsaw. But every other place name in east-central Europe raises serious problems. A good example is Wilno, Vilna, Vilnius. There are clear objections to all of these. Until 1944 the majority of the population was Polish. The city is today in Lithuania. 'Vilna', though raising the fewest problems, is an artificial construct. In this volume we have adopted the following guidelines, although we are aware that they are not wholly consistent.

1. Towns that have a form which is acceptable in English are given in that form. Some examples are Warsaw, Kiev, Moscow, St Petersburg, Munich.

2. Towns that until 1939 were clearly part of a particular state and shared the majority nationality of that state are given in a form which reflects that situation. Some examples are Breslau, Danzig, Rzeszów, Przemyśl. In Polish, Kraków has always been spelled as such. In English it has more often appeared as Cracow, but the current trend of English follows the local language as much as possible. In keeping with this trend to local determination, then, we shall maintain the Polish spelling.

3. Towns that are in mixed areas take the form in which they are known today and which reflects their present situation. Examples are Poznań, Toruń, and Kaunas. This applies also to bibliographical references. We have made one major exception to this rule, using the common English form for Vilna until its first incorporation into Lithuania in October 1939 and using Vilnius thereafter. Galicia's most diversely named city, and one of its most important, boasts four variants: the Polish Lwów, the German Lemberg, the Russian Lvov, and the Ukrainian Lviv. As this city currently lives under Ukrainian rule, and most of its current residents speak Ukrainian, we shall follow the Ukrainian spelling.

4. Some place names have different forms in Yiddish. Occasionally the subject matter dictates that the Yiddish place name should be the prime form, in which case the corresponding Polish (Ukrainian, Belarusian, Lithuanian) name is given in parentheses at first mention.

Note on Transliteration

HEBREW

An attempt has been made to achieve consistency in the transliteration of Hebrew words. The following are the key distinguishing features of the system that has been adopted:

1. No distinction is made between the *alef* and *ayin*; both are represented by an apostrophe, and only when they appear in an intervocalic position.

2. *Veit* is written *v*; *ḥet* is written *ḥ*; *yod* is written *y* when it functions as a consonant and *i* when it occurs as a vowel; *khaf* is written *kh*; *tsadi* is written *ts*; *kof* is written *k*.

3. The *dagesh ḥazak*, represented in some transliteration systems by doubling the letter, is not represented, except in words that have more or less acquired normative English spellings that include doublings, such as Hallel, kabbalah, Kaddish, rabbi, Sukkot, and Yom Kippur.

4. The *sheva na* is represented by an *e*.

5. Hebrew prefixes, prepositions, and conjunctions are not followed by a hyphen when they are transliterated; thus *betoledot ha'am hayehudi*.

6. Capital letters are not used in the transliteration of Hebrew except for the first word in the titles of books and the names of people, places, institutions, and generally as in the conventions of the English language.

7. The names of individuals are transliterated following the above rules unless the individual concerned followed a different usage.

YIDDISH

Transliteration follows the YIVO system except for the names of people, where the spellings they themselves used have been retained.

RUSSIAN AND UKRAINIAN

The system used is that of British Standard 2979:1958, without diacritics. Except in bibliographical and other strictly rendered matter, soft and hard signs are omitted and word-final -й, -ий, -ый, -ій in names are simplified to -*y*.

PART I

Jews in the Kingdom of Poland
1815–1918

The Kingdom of Poland and her Jews

An Introduction

GLENN DYNNER AND MARCIN WODZIŃSKI

THE KINGDOM OF POLAND, also known as the Congress Kingdom or Russian Poland, was created in 1815 by a decision of the Congress of Vienna, which set up a new post-Napoleonic European order. The new map's eastern European portion turned out to be exceptionally durable and the post-Napoleonic disposition of its frontiers, including those of the Kingdom of Poland, survived almost one hundred years with only minor changes (an exceptional state of affairs in European history), shaping not only the basic nineteenth-century political divisions but also the social and cultural ones.

The Kingdom was created from most of the territory of the Napoleonic Duchy of Warsaw; just two of its districts, Poznań and Bydgoszcz, were returned to Prussia. The area of the newly created Kingdom amounted to 127,321 square kilometres, with, at the moment of its creation, a population of 3.3 million inhabitants, mainly ethnic Poles (75 per cent), Jews (10 per cent), Germans (7.5 per cent), Lithuanians (5 per cent), and Ruthenians (2.5 per cent). This semi-autonomous Polish state was one of the smallest political creations in nineteenth-century eastern Europe.

During the Congress of Vienna the Kingdom's shape and form of government were the subject of a sharp dispute between the European powers, resulting in a face-off in January 1815 between the armies of England, Austria, and France, on the one side, and Russia and Prussia on the other. However, the conflict was defused without the use of force and with Tsar Alexander I emerging triumphant. For the next hundred years, the Kingdom was subordinated to the tsars. Admittedly, the Kingdom was joined by a personal union with the Russian empire, so that each tsar in turn was also king of Poland; however, the constitution granted by Alexander I limited the tsar's authority. This created a paradoxical situation whereby in the Kingdom of Poland the autocratic ruler of Russia was a constitutional monarch with limited powers controlled by Polish state institutions. The rights of the king (never called the tsar in official documents) were limited by the prerogatives of the parliament (the Sejm) and the government (the Administrative Council and the viceroy), as well as a truly independent judiciary. Admittedly, the Sejm had quite limited authority (for instance it could not propose legislation). But it did have governmental oversight and immunity for its members, which in the Europe of the day was a new and significant prerogative. The government in its entirety was appointed by the king and was answerable to him, but the constitution also introduced the principle of ministers' legal responsibility, while royal decrees had to be countersigned by the appropriate minister in order to become law.

The Kingdom also possessed most of the attributes of an independent state: its own territory and borders, separate state and administrative bodies, an independent judiciary, its own educational system, its own post office, central bank, and currency, even its own army, distinct from the Russian one. Government service was theoretically open only to citizens of the Kingdom, and thus closed to officials from Russia. Polish was the sole official language, while French—the language of international diplomacy—was used in correspondence with the king. Additional indications of the Congress Kingdom's genuine independence in certain areas were the existence of a legal opposition and the independence of the judicial branch, which was demonstrated, for example, at the Sejm trial of 1827 when, despite pressure from Grand Duke Konstantin and Tsar Nicholas I, the court acquitted the leaders of the conspiratorial Patriotic Society (Towarzystwo Patriotyczne). Such marks of autonomy were found nowhere else in the Empire.[1]

The Kingdom of Poland's relatively extensive independence did not last very long, however. The tsar's first attempts to curtail these constitutional freedoms occurred almost at the Kingdom's very creation, especially through the appointment of Senator Nikolay Novosiltsev as the Kingdom's Imperial Commissioner—a post designed to reconcile the interests of the Kingdom with those of the Empire. A broader retreat from this 'liberal experiment' came after 1831. Nevertheless, up until the collapse of yet another uprising in 1864, the Kingdom remained a state with a distinctive Polish character, a considerable degree of autonomy, and quite broad powers in internal affairs; while up to its dissolution in the First World War it was separate from the tsarist empire in terms of structure, politics, society, and culture. For Poles, the Kingdom of Poland felt tantalizingly close to a sovereign Polish state.

The durability of the new map of Europe drawn by the Congress of Vienna impacted the Jewish community, too. The Kingdom's autonomous status, in contrast to other areas of the former Commonwealth, caused the Jewish community relatively quickly to develop distinctive regional characteristics vis-à-vis Jews living in the remaining lands of the former Commonwealth. The stereotypical, and

[1] A good introduction to this subject is to be found in A. Chwalba, *Historia Polski, 1795–1918* (Kraków, 2000), 257–87, 319–84; A. Ajnenkiel, B. Leśnodorski, and W. Rostocki, *Historia ustroju Polski, 1764–1939* (Warsaw, 1970); S. Kieniewicz, *Historia Polski, 1795–1918* (Warsaw, 1976); S. Kieniewicz (ed.), *Polska XIX wieku: Państwo, społeczeństwo, kultura* (Warsaw, 1982); J. Zdrada, *Historia Polski, 1795–1914* (Warsaw, 2005), 94–137. For an overview in English, see P. S. Wandycz, *The Lands of Partitioned Poland, 1795–1918* (Seattle, 1974).

sometimes grotesque, categories of the German, Russian, Galician, or Polish Jew corresponded to those post-1815 divisions, equating a 'Polish Jew' with a Jew living in the Kingdom of Poland. Indeed, Israeli and Jewish American historiography even today refers only to Jews from the Kingdom as Polish Jews, contrasting them, for instance, with Russian Jews (e.g. from Białystok), Galician Jews (e.g. from Kraków), or German Jews (e.g. from Poznań).[2] This can be a source of misunderstanding among Polish historians, for whom the category 'Poland' is an umbrella term that includes 'Galicia', the 'Seized Lands' (*ziemie zabrane*—the territories incorporated directly into the tsarist empire, roughly coterminous with the Pale of Settlement), and the 'Congress Kingdom', despite divisions which are valid to this day within the Jewish community (a 'Polish hasid' is a follower of the *tsadik* of Ger (Góra Kalwaria) or Alexander (Aleksandrów), but not of Galician Bełz or of Trisk (Turzysk, Turiisk) in Volhynia). Applying these American and Israeli conceptions of the east European Jewish world, we could very well claim that this is the first volume of *Polin* entirely devoted to Polish Jews!

But in all seriousness, the aim of this volume is to deepen the state of knowledge on the subject of the Jewish community living in a state that for many decades was the most important centre of Polish politics, finance, science, education, and culture, and which for many people then, and for some now, was and is the embodiment of 'Polishness'. This was obvious up to 1831 and after 1905, when the Kingdom of Poland's extensive autonomy assured it a key role in the development of the Polish lands. However, even after the partial loss of autonomy in 1831 and the radical curtailment of home rule in 1863–4, the Kingdom of Poland continued to be a centre of 'Polishness', and not just for geographical reasons: it was the most ethnically and linguistically Polish area. In so far as legitimate doubts could be raised as to the Polish status of Galicia (especially its eastern part) and the territories directly incorporated into the tsarist empire, which were home to aspiring stateless nations such as Ukrainians and Lithuanians, the dominance of the ethnically Polish population within the Kingdom was indisputable. It was in the Kingdom, moreover, that the most important public debates were held, and that the most important political programmes and dominant cultural events were developed (western Galicia only began to rival the Kingdom in this respect at the end of the nineteenth century). Finally, in the realm of symbols, the Kingdom bore the strongest features of Polishness: despite the fact that after the 1863 uprising the term 'Kingdom of Poland' (Rus. Tsarstvo Polskoe) was replaced by the phrase 'Vistula Land' (Rus. Privislinsky Kray) in administrative usage, these lands continued officially to be called the Kingdom of Poland, and the tsar still bore the title of King of Poland. Warsaw, the capital of the former Commonwealth and of the hoped-for reborn

---

[2] On the problems of defining both the 'Polishness' of Polish Jews and what was and is called nineteenth-century 'Poland', and on the implications of this for the historiography of those Jews, see S. Ury, 'Who, What, When, Where, and Why Is Polish Jewry? Envisioning, Constructing, and Possessing Polish Jewry', *Jewish Social Studies*, NS, 6/3 (2000), 205–28.

Poland, was its capital. This meant that the Kingdom of Poland emerged as the embodiment of 'Poland', at least of what had survived into the nineteenth century.

THE LEGACY

The Kingdom of Poland also displayed a significant degree of independence from Russia in its policies towards the Jewish community. The best-known examples of this were the rejection of a plan to organize the Jews in Poland, drawn up by Senator Novosiltsev at the personal request of Tsar Alexander, the rejection of a plan to conscript Jews following the Russian conscription model (eventually carried out when Polish autonomy was diminishing after the 1831 uprising), failed attempts to standardize Polish and Russian legislation dealing with the Jews, and the rejection of a plan to introduce the Russian 'May Laws' of 1882 into the Kingdom.[3]

This autonomy in Jewish policy derived not just from the scope of the Kingdom's independence, but also from the specific composition of the new state's political elite and its views on the so-called 'Jewish question' in Poland. In the tense situation accompanying the creation of the Kingdom, Tsar Alexander was eager to win over Polish public opinion, including, above all, the nation's political elite, and to convince it that the Kingdom was a continuation of Polish national sovereignty and even a harbinger of Poland's future rebirth within its (more or less) pre-partition borders. Hence, in the first years of the Kingdom's existence many of its most senior appointees were drawn from the politicians, writers, and activists of the Polish Enlightenment, who had been on the political stage since the days of the Four Year Sejm (1788–92) and during the Kingdom's immediate predecessor state, the Duchy of Warsaw. They included, for instance, Julian Ursyn Niemcewicz, a delegate to the Four Year Sejm, co-author of the Third of May Constitution, Senate Secretary in the Duchy of Warsaw and the Kingdom of Poland, and an active participant, too, in discussions on the Jewish question; Stanisław Kostka Potocki, a member of the Four Year Sejm, President of the Council of State and the Council of Ministers in the Duchy of Warsaw, and Senate President and Minister of Public Education in the government of the Kingdom of Poland, administratively co-responsible for Jewish reforms among others; and Stanisław Staszic, author of Enlightenment treatises during the Four Year Sejm, Minister of

---

[3] A critical analysis of Novosiltsev's project and the Polish politics in this matter is given in A. Eisenbach, *Emancypacja Żydów na ziemiach polskich 1785–1870 na tle europejskim* (Warsaw, 1988), 179–93; English version, A. Eisenbach, *The Emancipation of the Jews in Poland, 1780–1870*, ed. A. Polonsky, trans. J. Dorosz (Oxford, 1991). On attempts to standardize the laws after 1840, see ibid. 316–31 (Polish edn.). A complete collection of reports on the Novosiltsev project is stored in the Archiwum Główne Akt Dawnych, Warsaw (hereafter AGAD), I Rada Stanu Królestwa Polskiego, 283. On the issue of the possibility of introducing the May Laws into the Kingdom, see A. Eisenbach, 'Raport o położeniu i strukturze ludności żydowskiej w Królestwie Kongresowym w latach osiemdziesiątych XIX wieku', in id., *Z dziejów ludności żydowskiej w Polsce w XVIII i XIX wieku: Studia i szkice* (Warsaw, 1983), 254–302.

State and adviser to the Duchy of Warsaw, Deputy Minister of Education in the Kingdom, and the de facto author of its Jewish policy.

This continuity in government personnel meant that the newly created Kingdom's policies were in many aspects a continuation of the traditions of the Four Year Sejm and the Duchy of Warsaw, including the basic policies towards the Jewish community. As Richard Butterwick shows in this volume in his chapter tracing the Enlightenment genealogy of Polish discourses on the Jews, ideas formulated in the time of King Stanisław August Poniatowski (including Staszic's views) became a lasting legacy in the Kingdom of Poland. Butterwick's study is thus part of the more general trend of contemporary research seeking in the Enlightenment the genealogy of nineteenth-century anti-Jewish attitudes in the Kingdom of Poland, and—more generally—the sources of nineteenth-century Polish–Jewish relations.[4]

Somewhat different, but by no means less important for an understanding of the Kingdom's Jewish policy, is the legacy of the Duchy of Warsaw. The liberal constitution granted to the Duchy of Warsaw in 1807 had conferred full civil rights on all of the state's inhabitants, including the Jews. However, the Duchy's authorities, under the influence of Napoleonic laws limiting the rights of the Jewish population in France, soon introduced similar restrictions on the Jews of the Duchy of Warsaw. These restrictions were to be only temporary and abolished after ten years, contingent upon the Jews' achieving a satisfactory level of 'civilization' over this trial period. However, the ten-year trial period was cut short by Napoleon's defeat and the occupation of central Poland by Russian forces. This striking disjuncture between the Duchy's enlightenment rhetoric of egalitarianism and its contradictory anti-Jewish policies remains the best-remembered, indeed practically the only, element of the Duchy's Jewish policy that historiography has addressed.[5] However,

---

[4] See e.g. G. D. Hundert, *Jews in Poland–Lithuania in the Eighteenth Century: A Genealogy of Modernity* (Berkeley and Los Angeles, 2004), 211–31; I. Bartal, *The Jews of Eastern Europe, 1772–1881*, trans. C. Naor (Philadelphia, 2005), 30–7; M. Wodziński, '"Civil Christians": Debates on the Reform of the Jews in Poland, 1789–1830', in B. Nathans and G. Safran (eds.), *Culture Front: Representing Jews in Eastern Europe* (Philadelphia, 2008), 46–76; A. Polonsky, *The Jews in Poland and Russia*, 3 vols. (Oxford, 2010–12), i. 200–8, 210–20. Eisenbach also begins his study of the emancipation of the Jews in the Polish lands with an analysis of the debates in the Great Sejm: Eisenbach, *Emancypacja Żydów na ziemiach polskich*, 26–124.

[5] The classic texts on the situation of the Jews in the Duchy of Warsaw are Yu. Gessen, 'V efemernom gosudarstve: Evrei v Varshavskom gertsogstve (1807–1812)', *Evreiskaya starina*, 1910, no. 1, pp. 3–38; S. Askenazy, 'Z dziejów Żydów polskich w dobie Księstwa Warszawskiego i Królestwa Kongresowego', *Kwartalnik Poświęcony Badaniu Przeszłości Żydów w Polsce*, 1/1 (1912), 1–14; A. Eisenbach, 'Yidn in varshaver firshtntum', *YIVO-bleter*, 10 (1936), 91–9; J. Stanley, 'The Politics of the Jewish Question in the Duchy of Warsaw', *Jewish Social Studies*, 44/1 (1982), 47–62; R. Mahler, *A History of Modern Jewry, 1780–1815* (New York, 1971), 347–68. Strikingly little has been published in recent years about any aspect of the life of the Jews in the Duchy. There is a good summary of knowledge on the Duchy of Warsaw, also to a certain extent taking into account the history of the Jewish population there, in the work of J. Czubaty, *Księstwo Warszawskie, 1807–1815* (Warsaw, 2011).

as Aleksandra Oniszczuk shows in her chapter on the subject of the Duchy's policies towards the Jewish community, of greater importance was the long-term influence of the Duchy's general administrative and legal changes not directly affecting Jews but linked rather to the overall professionalization of the civil service and the universalization of law (even if still only partial), i.e. what Max Weber called the state's modernization, which in the Duchy of Warsaw found its supreme expression in the Napoleonic Code. Oniszczuk shows that the picture that emerges from administrative sources is actually a relative improvement in the situation of the Duchy's Jewish subjects. Notwithstanding the limitations on Jewish civil rights, the Duchy's assurances of basic equality before the civil service and its legal code significantly improved the Jews' political and legal status. In addition, despite blatant anti-Jewish prejudice among the state's highest officials, the Duchy's administration in essence did not discriminate against Jewish petitioners (at least not openly), and honestly discharged its basic responsibilities towards them. This fundamental change in the relationship between the state and the citizen was bequeathed to the Kingdom of Poland, and determined the nature of relations between the state and the Jewish population in the Kingdom. In the middle of the nineteenth century, it became a crucial instrument for the political mobilization of Polish Jews, of both their liberal and conservative wings.[6]

FROM WORDS TO DEEDS

Despite some clear continuity, the Polish political elite's views and attitudes towards the so-called Jewish question had of course evolved since the time of the Four Year Sejm, while the first years of the Kingdom, 1815–22, saw the largest upsurge in discussion on this question within Polish public opinion.[7] Despite the divergence of views expressed and the often violent disputes it engendered, one can point to a common direction in the changes taking place. During the period of Stanisław August Poniatowski reform assumed—in the well-known words of a member of the Four Year Sejm, Mateusz Butrymowicz—the turning of the Jews into 'citizens

---

[6] M. Wodziński, *Hasidism and Politics: The Kingdom of Poland, 1815–1864* (Oxford, 2013), chs. 5–6; id., 'Haskalah and Politics Reconsidered: The Case of the Kingdom of Poland, 1815–1860', in D. Assaf and A. Rapoport-Albert (eds.), *Let the Old Make Way for the New: Studies in the Social and Cultural History of Eastern European Jewry Presented to Immanuel Etkes*, 2 vols. (Jerusalem, 2009), ii. 163–197; G. Dynner, *Yankel's Tavern: Jews, Liquor, and Life in the Kingdom of Poland* (New York, 2013), ch. 3; id., *Men of Silk: The Hasidic Conquest of Polish Jewish Society* (New York, 2006), 35–7, 59–64.

[7] The classic works on the debate and reforms of this period are M. Wischnitzer, 'Proekty reformy evreiskogo byta v Gertsogstve Varshavskom i Tsarstve Pol'skom (po neizdannym materialam)', *Perezhitoe*, 1 (1909), 164–221; N. M. Gelber, 'She'elat hayehudim bepolin bishenot 1815–1830', *Tsiyon*, 13–14 (1948–9), 106–43; id., 'Di yidn-frage in kongres-poyln in di yorn 1815–1830', *Bleter far geshikhte*, 1/3–4 (1948), 41–105; R. Mahler, *Divrei yemei yisra'el: dorot aḥaronim*, v (Merhavia, 1970), 153–72; id., *History of Modern Jewry*, 303–13; Eisenbach, *Emancypacja Żydów na ziemiach polskich*, 164–212.

useful to the country',[8] and so above all an economic and social reform in which the principal obligation of the Jews was to demonstrate their utility—a basic category in Enlightenment ideology. The fall of the Commonwealth, the partitions of Poland, and a series of drastic political changes had contributed to a general reformulation within the Polish public discourse, including discussion of the Jewish issue. The nation, now defined by its soul and its culture rather than politically (for obvious reasons), became the principal concept, while society became a rather vague notion, set more within the nation's cultural life than in its state structure. The assumption that the Jews were meant to become 'citizens useful to the country' was now seen as inadequate. The Jews were now to adopt not only social and political reforms that would render them purportedly useful, but in addition were expected to become 'civilized', i.e. to abandon Jewish culture and adopt Polish culture.

Polish reformers assumed that the Jews possessed a primitive culture, no match for the culture of Enlightenment Europe, and thus doomed to extinction. This civilizing mission was typical of cultural imperialism, and could justify any measure imposed on Jews. As the Minister of Public Education Stanisław Kostka Potocki wrote, his proposed actions 'only appear to be harsh towards the Jews, but in fact will be most salutary for them'.[9] Thus, reform came to mean not simply complete linguistic, cultural, and national assimilation, but dragging the Jews out of barbarism.

This was put most bluntly by one of the key politicians of the day, Adam Jerzy Czartoryski. In his view, what was needed was 'to transform the Jews from unproductive and harmful members of society into good citizens attached to the country, to give them more enlightenment, in other words morality, which they lack; in a word to turn them into civil Christians, that is people who would develop Christian feelings for their neighbours, the monarch, and their country'.[10] Other writers celebrated Jews who were 'surrogate Christians', or identical to Christians 'in terms of customs and their way of life'. These statements should not be seen as embodying crypto-missionary aspirations. In line with the linguistic norm of the day, 'civil' meant both 'secular, non-religious' as well as 'civilized'. This ambiguity enabled Polish reformers after 1795 to express the Jews' future place in Polish society: Jews were to cease being Jews and become identical to Christians in everything except their professed religion, narrowly defined. The perceived failure of Jews to civilize themselves was readily used to justify the disadvantaged political and legal status of the Jewish population (and of other disadvantaged segments of the population). In contrast to the optimistic, Enlightenment plans for civic reform, subsequent politicians made eventual emancipation dependent on ever more numerous and far-reaching limitations and ideals.

Stanisław Staszic, an exceptionally active figure in the Polish Enlightenment,

---

[8] M. Butrymowicz, 'Sposób uformowania Żydów polskich w pożytecznych krajowi obywatelów', in *Materiały do dziejów Sejmu Czteroletniego*, vi, ed. A. Eisenbach et al. (Wrocław, 1969), 78–93.

[9] AGAD, Centralne Władze Wyznaniowe (hereafter CWW), 1418, p. 71.   [10] Ibid. 40–1.

embodied this discursive transformation. Staszic had denounced the Jews as a contaminating, destructive influence in his earliest writings, including his political tract *Przestrogi dla Polski* ('Warnings for Poland') published during the sessions of the Four Year Sejm in 1790: Jews are 'our country's summer and winter plague of locusts', since they 'impoverish industrious folk, destroy the most productive pastures, bring poverty to the villages, and fill the air with putrefaction. Jewry impoverishes our villages and fills our towns with stench.'[11] However, it was only after 1815 that Staszic's views on the Jewish question took on an obsessive aspect. He wrote now that among the three greatest misfortunes to have befallen the former Commonwealth—the lack of a hereditary sovereign, the lack of a standing army, and the influx of Jews—it was in fact the last that represented the greatest and most lasting threat, for 'even if the body [i.e. the Polish–Lithuanian state] had not been divided, even if after this division it were to be re-formed, with such an internal flaw [as the presence of the Jews] it could never regain strength and robustness'.[12] The culprit was contemporary Jewish religion. In his view, the splendid Jewish religion of biblical times had been deformed by the disastrous influence of the Talmud, which had nothing in common with the real Mosaic religion: 'Moses neither gave nor knew any Talmuds; he would not even have been able to understand them. For the whole of today's faith rests on the Talmud and that is its principal source of contamination.' From this he drew the simple conclusion that 'the Talmud needs to be removed from the present-day Jews' religion'.[13] Staszic's agenda came down to replacing rabbinic Judaism with 'Mosaism', which was to be based on the Pentateuch. The state was to impose Mosaism and prevent it from becoming a new basis of Jewish separatism and fanaticism, which is what in his view had happened to rabbinic Judaism.

However absurd such a plan may seem, Staszic was in no way alone in holding such ideas. In fact, his views shortly became the Congress Kingdom's official policy. In 1825, the Jewish Committee (Komitet Starozakonnych)—a state body created to reform Poland's Jewish population—was formed under Staszic's decisive influence. Julian Ursyn Niemcewicz propagated similar views in an attractive literary form (e.g. in *Lejba and Sióra*, the first novel in Polish literature with a Jewish theme), arguing that the Jewish people had abandoned the religion of Moses and had 'drunk deeply of the prejudices of its wild zealots'.[14] By the 1820s, the idea of the complete degeneration of the Jewish religion and the resulting difficulty of integrating the Jewish community with the Polish population had become a staple of Polish political thought. Together with the supposed threat of a 'Jewish infestation of Poland', thus turning her into 'Judaeo-Polonia', this view of Jew-

[11] S. Staszic, *Przestrogi dla Polski* (Warsaw, 1790), 523.

[12] S. Staszic, 'O przyczynach szkodliwości żydów i środkach usposobienia ich, aby się społeczeństwu użytecznemi stali', in id., *Dzieła*, iv (Warsaw, 1816), 218.

[13] AGAD, CWW, 1418, p. 16.

[14] J. U. Niemcewicz, *Lejbe i Sióra; czyli, Listy dwóch kochanków* (1821; Kraków, 1931), p. v.

ish isolationism entered the canon of Polish antisemitic thought and influenced successive generations.[15]

Wincenty Krasiński, first a Napoleonic general and then an important figure in the Congress Kingdom's conservative politics, has gone down in history as the author of a virulently antisemitic pamphlet claiming that 'the Jews represent an insurmountable obstacle for each government, which would need to turn them into something other than Jews', owing to their secret conspiracies. Polish Jews were 'dependent on unknown leaders, run to a certain extent by an unseen hand, sacrificing everything to the interests of the masses, devoted only to trade, scorning farming, citizens of the world, tied to no country, recognizing no homeland, protecting none, they thwart all government plans to nationalize them and turn them into citizens'.[16] Krasiński's conspiracy theories shaped the political imagination of his son Zygmunt, a famous Romantic poet and the author of the visions of Jewish converts conspiring to subvert the Christian world.

Gerard Witowski, an official in the government of the Congress Kingdom, endorsed Krasiński's ideas but went further and proposed petitioning Tsar Alexander I to allocate to the Jews 'an area of land on the borders of greater Tartary, or somewhere else in the southern reaches of his own extensive country, so that they may live comfortably and let their tribe multiply comfortably'.[17] He developed his plan into very specific proposals: after an appropriate province had been allocated on the southern borders of the Russian empire all the Kingdom's Jews should be transported there as speedily as possible in 300 columns of 1,000 people each, which would cover on foot the distance between central Poland and the steppes of southern Russia. In his view, 'isolating the Jews from the Christians is the only way to allow Poland to flourish'.[18]

These projects can be seen as drawing dangerously close to eliminationist ideas, although these writers could not yet sense just where such views would lead in the following century. The whole debate was evolving very clearly from civic and inclusive Enlightenment projects to ever more xenophobic projects, which excluded Jews from the domain of Polish social life, with exile as the best option. In addition, phobias and stereotypes, which the men of the Enlightenment were unable to resist,

---

[15] The literary reception of antisemitic stereotypes in late-Enlightenment writing and their life beyond the grave have recently been studied by, in particular, M. Janion, 'Mit założycielski polskiego antysemityzmu', in J. Hensel (ed.), *Społeczeństwa europejskie i Holocaust: Poszerzona dokumentacja konferencji w Żydowskim Instytucie Historycznym w Warszawie 30 września 2004 r. z okazji 75. urodzin Feliksa Tycha* (Warsaw, 2004), 11–48 (German version, M. Janion, 'Der Gründungsmythos des polnischen Antisemitismus', in J. Hensel (ed.), *Europäische Gesellschaften und der Holocaust* (Warsaw, 2004), 13–55); ead., *Bohater, spisek, śmierć: Wykłady żydowskie* (Warsaw, 2009). See also M. Wodziński, 'Reform and Exclusion: Conceptions of the Reform of the Jewish Community during the Declining Years of the Polish Enlightenment', *Polin*, 24 (2012), 31–48.

[16] [W. Krasiński], *Aperçu sur les Juifs de Pologne par un officier général polonois* (Warsaw, 1818), 3–4.

[17] [G. Witowski], *Sposób na Żydów; czyli, Środki niezawodne zrobienia z nich ludzi uczciwych i dobrych obywateli: Dziełko dedykowane posłom i deputowanym na Seym Warszawski 1818 roku* (Warsaw, 1818), 13.   [18] Ibid. 20.

paradoxically turned out to be one of the most durable elements of their legacy, moulding the Kingdom of Poland's policy towards its Jewish population.

The first expression of this was the Kingdom's constitution, which despite being extremely liberal in certain areas, guaranteed civil liberties only to the Christian population and thus excluded a handful of Muslims and the whole Jewish population, which composed more than 10 per cent of the Kingdom.[19] Individual Jews could still petition for special legal status, but were only granted such status on condition that they abandon their traditional Jewish appearance and language, with the final decision resting arbitrarily with the authorities. The number of Jews to whom such special status was accorded remained very low.[20]

The attempted reform of the Jewish population was pursued most actively between 1820 and 1826, when the authorities of the Kingdom of Poland liquidated those institutions which, in the opinion of the reformers, reinforced Jewish separatism. In 1822, the basis of the Jews' former autonomy in the Kingdom, Jewish communal self-administration (embodied in the *kahal*s) was eliminated. Some of the religious functions of the *kahal*s were transferred to so-called synagogue administrations (*dozory bóżnicze*), which had in fact been formed in 1821. Then it was the turn of all types of confraternities (*ḥevrot*), especially the burial confraternity (*ḥevra kadisha*), to be eliminated. Finally, in 1825 the Jewish Committee was formed, whose task it was to prepare and supervise the comprehensive reform of all aspects of Jewish social life, and a year later the Rabbinical School (Szkoła Rabinów) was established, an institution intended to lead to a radical reform of the rabbinate and local communal organization.[21]

[19] Article 11 of the constitution that Alexander I granted in 1815 stated: 'The Roman Catholic religion, professed by the majority of the Kingdom of Poland's citizens, will be an object of special protection on the part of the Government, which cannot, however, harm the freedom of other faiths, all of which, with no exceptions, may practise all their rituals in public under the protection of the Government.'

[20] A. Eisenbach, 'Prawa obywatelskie i honorowe Żydów (1790–1861)', in W. Kula (ed.), *Społeczeństwo Królestwa Polskiego: Studia o uwarstwieniu i ruchliwości społecznej*, i (Warsaw, 1965), 237–300. Research into this issue was one of the favourite topics of historians inspired by Marxist methodology and ideology, since it fitted perfectly into the Marxist model of a capitalist state persecuting underprivileged social classes. Such research, especially popular during the inter-war years and developed post-war particularly by Artur Eisenbach, has become less popular over the last few decades, with an obvious loss for the integral development of our knowledge on the subject. Among the classic works on the subject are Eisenbach, 'Prawa obywatelskie i honorowe Żydów'; id., *Kwestia równouprawnienia Żydów w Królestwie Polskim* (Warsaw, 1972); id., *Emancypacja Żydów na ziemiach polskich*.

[21] Much has been written about the dissolution of the *kahal*s and the introduction of synagogue supervision, but the best study of this so far is F. Guesnet, *Polnische Juden im 19. Jahrhundert: Lebensbedingungen, Rechtsnormen und Organisation im Wandel* (Cologne, 1998), 223–50; see it too for the dissolution of the confraternities and other elements of the reform. The Jewish Committee and its Advisory Board (Izba Doradcza) still await their scholar, the most recent works on the subject being D. Kandel, 'Komitet Starozakonnych', *Kwartalnik Poświęcony Badaniu Przeszłości Żydów w Polsce*, 1/2 (1912), 85–103, and a master's thesis written at Professor Majer Bałaban's seminar: R. Szmulewicz, 'Dzieje Komitetu Starozakonnych w Warszawie, 1825–1837' (Warsaw, n.d.) (a copy is in the Archiwum Żydowskiego Instytutu Historycznego, Warsaw, 117/1).

Efforts were also made simultaneously to change the Jews' economic structure by attracting them to agriculture.[22] Yet, as allowing Jews to hold land outright caused considerable unease, the favoured form of Jewish farming was the agricultural colony.[23] In 1823, the regime declared that Jews were now free to settle on state land and on empty or uncultivated areas, provided that they 'work the land they lease and not engage in the production and sale of liquor'.[24] However, the inducement was loaded with conditions: only small amounts of church or state-owned land could be leased for a limited period, and only by wealthy Jews. Anything Jewish tenants built would pass into the landowners' hands at the expiration of their lease. Jewish farmers were to be temporarily exempted from certain taxes, but were still responsible for both agricultural and kosher meat taxes. The failure of these plans was the result of deep ambivalence in the attitude of the Kingdom's politicians towards the Jews, who saw agriculture as the magic solution to the Jewish problem yet baulked at giving Jews land or funding such activities.[25]

Another arena where publicist demands seem to have influenced governmental policy was state-sponsored education. In 1818, Jacob Tugendhold was commissioned to establish the first elementary schools for Jewish boys and girls in Warsaw. Similar schools were established over the next decades in other towns too. Jewish enrolment in public schools, including elementary and secondary schools, amounted to 1,672 pupils by 1842.[26] As we have mentioned, a Rabbinical School whose language of instruction was Polish was opened in Warsaw in 1826 to train modern-oriented rabbis. Enrolment rose to 305 students by 1843. It was hoped that graduates would form a cadre of enlightened rabbis who would lead the Jewish communities out of darkness, but the school was closed in 1863 without having graduated a single rabbi who proved acceptable to a Jewish community.[27] It seems that those controlling the school, especially Antoni Eisenbaum, had hoped to Polonize the Jewish population (seen as increasingly dangerous by tsarist authorities themselves) at the expense of the traditional Jewish canon, especially the Talmud, which was unacceptable to the vast majority of Polish Jewry, including several maskilim.[28] Thus the Rabbinical School became a battleground for the

---

[22] J. Shatzky, 'An Attempt at Jewish Colonization in the Kingdom of Poland', *YIVO Annual of Jewish Social Science*, 1 (1946), 44–63; Eisenbach, *Emancypacja Żydów na ziemiach polskich*, 52–4, 287–9; M. Wodziński, 'Clerks, Jews and Farmers: Projects of Jewish Agricultural Settlement in Poland', *Jewish History*, 21 (2007), 279–303.

[23] Such colonies had been formed as early as the late eighteenth century. For an overview of colonization initiatives, see Shatzky, 'Attempt at Jewish Colonization in the Kingdom of Poland'.

[24] AGAD, CWW, 1419, pp. 2–5 (decreed by Tsar Alexander I on 12 March 1823).

[25] Wodziński, 'Clerks, Jews and Farmers'; Dynner, *Yankel's Tavern*, ch. 6.

[26] Eisenbach, *Emancipation of the Jews in Poland*, 242–4; S. Levin, 'Batei sefer livnei dat mosheh bevarshah be-1818–1830', *Gal-ed*, 1 (1973), 63–100. See also Z. Borzymińska, *Szkolnictwo żydowskie w Warszawie, 1831–1870* (Warsaw, 1994).

[27] Eisenbach, *Emancipation of the Jews in Poland*, 242–4.

[28] Levin, 'Batei sefer', 88. For maskilic critics of the Rabbinical School, see E. Tahlgrin, *Tokhaḥat musar: hasefer tehilim* (Warsaw, 1854), 'First Introduction', 9; 'Second Introduction', 28; and the memo

greatest conflict affecting the Kingdom of Poland's Jewish population in the nineteenth century, that is—put simply—the conflict between modernizing and conservative tendencies. The school has been the subject of a number of historical studies, and is without a doubt the best-researched element of the Jewish educational system in the Kingdom of Poland.[29] Interesting studies have also focused on other aspects of Jewish education in the Kingdom in the first half of the nineteenth century.[30]

The objectives of policy makers in the Kingdom of Poland did not always align with those of the Polish publicists, however. The cameralistic desire on the part of policy makers to maximize state revenue by dissolving ethnic economic niches and productivizing the populace melded with publicist aspirations to a point, but policy makers were not willing to pursue this at the expense of order and stability.[31] This ambivalence can be demonstrated in the case of policies aimed at curtailing the Jewish liquor trade, a veritable obsession in Polish public debate from at least the early eighteenth century.[32] Rye-based vodka, produced and sold on monopolistic

by Moses Jerozolimski in AGAD, Komisja Rządowa Spraw Wewnętrznych (hereafter KRSW), 6630, fos. 84–9. See also Dynner, *Yankel's Tavern*, ch. 6.

[29] See also M. Bałaban, *Historya projektu Szkoły Rabinów i nauki religii mojżeszowej na ziemiach polskich* (Lwów, 1907); A. Sawicki, 'Szkoła Rabinów w Warszawie (1826–1862) (na podstawie źródeł archiwalnych)', *Miesięcznik Żydowski*, 3/1 (1933), 244–74; Z. Borzymińska, 'Przyczynek do dziejów szkolnictwa żydowskiego w Warszawie w XIX w., czyli jeszcze o Szkole Rabinów', *Biuletyn Żydowskiego Instytutu Historycznego*, 131–2 (1984), 183–96; ead., 'Wpływy Szkoły Rabinów na przemiany kulturowe Żydów warszawskich w drugiej połowie XIX wieku', in K. Pilarczyk (ed.), *Żydzi i judaizm we współczesnych badaniach polskich*, ii (Kraków, 2000), 251–66; S. Levin, 'Beit-hasefer lerabanim bevarshah bashanim 1826–1863', *Gal-ed*, 11 (1989), 35–58; A. Polonsky, 'Warszawska Szkoła Rabinów: Orędowniczka narodowej integracji w Królestwie Polskim', in M. Galas (ed.), *Duchowość żydowska w Polsce: Materiały z międzynarodowej konferencji dedykowanej pamięci Profesora Chone Shmeruka, Kraków, 26–28 kwietnia 1999* (Kraków, 2000), 287–307; id., *Jews in Poland and Russia*, i. 294–9, 302–6, 311–13; L. Finkelstein, 'History of the Rabbinical School of Warsaw from its Establishment in 1826 to its Closure in 1863', Ph.D. thesis (Open Univ., 2006).

[30] See above all S. Levin, *Perakim betoledot haḥinukh hayehudi bepolin bame'ah hatesha-esreh uvereshit hame'ah ha'esrim* (Tel Aviv, 1997); Borzymińska, *Szkolnictwo żydowskie w Warszawie*. On educational projects for Jews in the Kingdom, see most recently Polonsky, *Jews in Poland and Russia*, i. 291–9. See also J. Shatzky, *Yidishe bildungs-politik in poyln fun 1806 biz 1866* (New York, 1943), esp. 13–48. On the differences between reform initiatives in the Russian and Polish cases, see Y. Petrovsky-Shtern, *Jews in the Russian Army, 1827–1917: Drafted into Modernity* (Cambridge, 2009), 26–7.

[31] On the origins of cameralism, see J. Karp, *The Politics of Jewish Commerce: Economic Thought and Emancipation in Europe, 1638–1848* (New York, 2008), 101–4. On Russian Minister of Finance Egor Kankrin's version of cameralism, see W. M. Pintner, *Russian Economic Policy under Nicholas I* (Ithaca, NY, 1967), 22–3. On cameralism and Habsburg Jewry, see L. C. Dubin, *The Port Jews of Habsburg Trieste: Absolutist Politics and Enlightenment Culture* (Stanford, Calif., 1999), 69. On the internalization of cameralist ideals by maskilim, see D. Penslar, *Shylock's Children: Economics and Jewish Identity in Modern Europe* (Berkeley, 2001), 68–84.

[32] Jewish dominance in the liquor trade may have emerged from increasing competition between the petty nobility and the major aristocratic landowners: while the former attempted to push out Jews from competition for leases, the latter perceived Jews as the most desirable leaseholders. See *Sejmy i*

terms by the nobility in taverns leased predominantly to Jews, accounted for the majority of estate revenues after the decline of the grain export trade. The nobility's preference for Jewish lessees in a trade that was at once so lucrative, addictive, and socially harmful provoked an energetic anti-Jewish campaign by Polish publicists, who attempted to blame Jews for peasant drunkenness and ruin. Government officials throughout the Polish lands seemed to share their concern, placing bans and restrictions on Jewish innkeeping and occasionally expelling Jews from the countryside. At the same time, however, many of those same officials recoiled at the disorder caused by their own bans and expulsions, and often repealed or stopped enforcing them, especially when political conditions became unstable.[33]

In the Kingdom of Poland, the tsar upheld the lucrative policy inherited from its predecessor, the Napoleonic Duchy of Warsaw: increasingly expensive liquor concessions as a prelude to outright expulsions, repeatedly deferred.[34] The policy was intended gradually to squeeze Jews out of the liquor trade, a humane alternative to the expulsions occurring in other partitions, while providing a handsome revenue for the state. It was pursued despite the repeated protests of publicists, who would be satisfied with nothing less than immediate expulsions.[35] During the 1830–1 uprising against the tsar and after its suppression, each respective regime continued to dole out liquor concessions as a way of garnering or rewarding Jewish support. However, in 1844, as part of a general crackdown on drunkenness in the Kingdom, a ban was finally placed on Jewish liquor sales in rural areas. The rural ban merely enlarged the underground Jewish liquor trade. With the full knowledge and complicity of local landowners, who tended to resent the state's attempts to meddle

sejmiki koronne wobec Żydów: Wybór tekstów źródłowych, ed. A. Michałowska-Mycielska (Warsaw, 2006), index. For the parallel conflict in Belarus, see B. Stępniewska-Holzer, *Żydzi na Białorusi: Studium z dziejów strefy osiedlenia w pierwszej połowie XIX w.* (Warsaw, 2013), 45–57.

[33] On the role of Jews in the Polish liquor trade and efforts to drive them out of it, see most recently G. Dynner, 'Legal Fictions: The Survival of the Rural Jewish Liquor Trade in the Kingdom of Poland', *Jewish Social Studies*, NS, 16/2 (2010); id., *Yankel's Tavern*, esp. ch. 2.

[34] On 30 October 1812, an all-out ban on Jewish innkeeping was decreed for the Duchy of Warsaw, effective 1 July 1814. In the two-year interim, Jewish innkeepers were required to purchase a liquor concession (*konsens*). See Stanley, 'Politics of the Jewish Question', 57; J. Hensel, 'Żydowski arendarz i jego karczma: Uwagi na marginesie usunięcia żydowskich arendarzy ze wsi w Królestwie Polskim w latach 20. XIX wieku', in M. Meducka and R. Renz (eds.), *Kultura Żydów polskich XIX–XX wieku* (Kielce, 1992), 89; Wischnitzer, 'Proekty reformy evreiskogo byta', 170–1; Mahler, *History of Modern Jewry*, 358.

[35] A memo of 1818 from the secretary of state Ignacy Sobolewski to the viceroy Józef Zajączek states: 'Were the Jewish payments for permission to sell liquor in taverns gradually to increase, the number of those making a living from this pursuit would continually diminish and they would be forced to support themselves from other kinds of occupations': Gelber, 'She'elat hayehudim bepolin', 35. This strategy was reiterated a decade later by Mateusz Muszyński, a clerk in the Consumption Tax Office: see AGAD, KRSW, 1849, fos. 152–9. See also Hensel, 'Żydowski arendarz i jego karczma', 92, and id., 'Polnische Adelsnation und jüdische Vermittler, 1815–1830: Über den vergeblichen Versuch einer Judenemanzipation in einer nicht emanzipierten Gesellschaft', *Forschungen zur osteuropäischen Geschichte*, 23 (1983), 71–93.

with their local economies, many rural Jews installed Christian fronts in their rural taverns and continued to run them.[36]

Jewish urban residential restrictions, which also originated in the prior, Duchy of Warsaw, era, were also at cross purposes with the aims of many publicists, who demanded an end to Jewish separateness. Neither the Duchy of Warsaw nor the Kingdom of Poland contained anything akin to the Pale of Settlement, but both instituted Jewish residential restrictions in economically advanced urban centres. In 1809, Frederick August, as duke of Warsaw, labelled a handful of Warsaw streets 'restricted' (*egzymowany*), meaning off-limits to Jewish residences and businesses, citing the 'indecent state of affairs' resulting from so many Jews living on main or narrow streets, and the accompanying dangers, such as conflagrations, epidemics, lack of cleanliness, lawlessness and disorder, and, finally, the nature of the economic activities in which Jews typically engaged.[37] Only members of Jewish families who possessed at least 60,000 zlotys, removed their beards and other distinguishing marks, enrolled their children in Polish schools, and fitted a desired professional profile (factory owners, large-scale merchants, doctors, and so on) could obtain exemptions. Similar residential restrictions were extended to several other towns and cities in the Duchy of Warsaw over the next few years, and were eventually adopted and expanded in the Kingdom of Poland.

When the Kingdom of Poland was formed, Warsaw's Christian residents sent a delegation to Józef Zajączek, the viceroy, demanding the reimplementation of the segregation policy, while Jewish mercantile elites approached Novosiltsev with an eloquent appeal to Enlightenment principles and with a sizeable financial gift.[38] Novosiltsev saw to it that the residential decree was suspended for the next six years.[39] In 1821, however, the Christian townspeople prevailed. That year, Tsar Alexander I re-enacted the 1809 decree and added new restricted streets, creating a restricted zone in the centre of Warsaw.[40] In addition, the tsar reinstated older, originally Prussian, decrees requiring non-resident Jews who wished to do business in Warsaw to pay a sojourner's tax (*bilet*) and an escort fee (*Geleitzoll*).[41]

In contrast to the Duchy of Warsaw, the regime in the Kingdom of Poland rigorously enforced residential restrictions, expelling Jews from homes and businesses in Warsaw in 1824, with the exception of a handful of qualifying wealthy and

---

[36] Dynner, *Yankel's Tavern*, chs. 2–3.

[37] In issuing that decree, Frederick August had been responding to complaints from the Warsaw municipality that Jews were leasing apartments from nobles in 'the most profitable neighbourhoods and best houses'. See E. Bergman, *'Nie masz bóżnicy powszechnej': Synagogi i domy modlitwy w Warszawie od końca XVIII do początku XXI wieku* (Warsaw, 2007), 58. The original decree is reprinted in Tsar Alexander's decree of 10 July 1821 in *Dziennik Praw*, 7 (1821), 155 n. *a*.

[38] AGAD, Akta Kancelarii Senatora Nowosilcowa, 206, pp. 14–18. The same delegation made a similar request of the Grand Duke Konstantin: see ibid. 25.   [39] Ibid. 103–4.

[40] Decree issued on 10 July 1821 and published in *Dziennik Praw*, 7 (1821), 155–73.

[41] A somewhat similar policy obtained in Warsaw during the Prussian occupation, initiated in 1799.

acculturated Jews.[42] Jewish quarters were also established or reinstated in thirty other towns and cities.[43] An additional kind of Jewish quarter, called a 'compass' (*obręb*), was established or reinstated in twenty-four towns possessing age-old *de non tolerandis Judaeis* status.[44] By 1833, the year in which the creation of further Jewish quarters was halted, fifty-five Jewish quarters had been established in the Kingdom of Poland.[45] The very next year, in an effort to curtail smuggling (most smugglers were believed to be Jews), Jewish settlement was limited in towns along the Prussian and Austrian borders, bringing the total number of restricted towns to 166. Jews were also expelled from state mining towns in an attempt to undercut the black market. Some restrictions were repealed, but on the eve of the 1862 liberalizing decrees, Jewish settlement was still restricted or banned in a total of 121 towns in the Kingdom.[46]

Officials justified Jewish residential restrictions along Enlightenment lines, stressing their benefits for society at large. Residential restrictions, according to the governor of Mazovia, functioned 'not only to cleanse the main streets of Jewish slovenliness, but to give Christians a fair chance to make profits and become more industrious'.[47] By preventing Jews from driving Christian townspeople into poverty, as they were wont to do, another report explained, residential restrictions reduced inter-ethnic conflicts and hence disorder.[48] Several publicists protested against the residential restrictions as perpetuating Jewish isolation and poverty.[49] Even the Polish reformers on the Jewish Committee of 1826, usually quite critical of the Jewish population, argued that expelling Jews from their homes and forcing them to live in new, separate quarters did not foster their moral reform, a point echoed by the 1858 Jewish Committee.[50] Nevertheless, the restrictions remained in place until 1862.

---

[42] By 1836, 124 Warsaw Jewish families possessed exemptions, and an additional seven families did so by 1842. See A. Wein, 'Żydzi poza rewirem żydowskim w Warszawie (1809–1862)', *Biuletyn Żydowskiego Instytutu Historycznego*, 41 (1962), 45–70. On 1842, see AGAD, KRSW, 5752.

[43] AGAD, KRSW, 188, fos. 96–7; AGAD, Protokoły Rady Administracyjnej Królestwa Polskiego, vols. 11–16.

[44] Compasses were established in fifteen out of forty such royal towns; in one out of thirty such clergy-owned towns; and in eight out of twenty such noble-owned towns.

[45] AGAD, KRSW, 188, fos. 223–6. See also ibid. 98, and AGAD, KRSW, 6632, fo. 68; and E. Bergman, 'The *Rewir* or Jewish District and the *Eyruv*', *Studia Judaica*, 5/1–2 (2002), 86.

[46] Border towns lay within three Polish miles (i.e. 21 km) of one of those borders. Decree issued on 29 May 1834, published in *Dziennik Praw*, 16 (1834).

[47] AGAD, KRSW, 187, fo. 175.   [48] Report of 1852, in AGAD, KRSW, 188, fos. 87^v, 95^v.

[49] Jean [Jan] Czynski, *An Enquiry into the Political Condition of the Polish Jews, Considered in Relation to the General Interests of Europe* (London, 1834), 18; A. Ostrowski, *Pomysły o potrzebie reformy towarzyskiéy w ogolności, a mianowiciéy co do Izraelitów w Polszcze, przez założyciela miasta Tomaszowa Mazowieckiego* (Paris, 1834), 45.

[50] AGAD, KRSW/Komisja Rządowa Przychodów i Skarbu, 1849, fo. 328; AGAD, KRSW, 6632, fos. 72–6.

NEW MOVEMENTS

The Polonizing and integrating Jewish groups in the Kingdom of Poland in the first half of the nineteenth century were represented by supporters of the Jewish Enlightenment, or Haskalah. Owing to the strong connection of the maskilim and other Jewish reformers to the Polish late-Enlightenment public debate (1815–31), the Haskalah in the Kingdom of Poland did, however, develop somewhat differently than in neighbouring Galicia or the Russian Pale of Settlement. Just about all the leading maskilim of the Kingdom of Poland—Abraham Jakub Stern (1762–1842), Abraham Buchner (1789–1869), Abraham Paprocki (1813–52), Jakub Centner-szwer (1797–1880), Jan Glücksberg (1782–1858), and others—served in various governmental agencies, especially in their 'Jewish' sections, whereas comparatively fewer of their Russian and Galician counterparts held governmental posts. This link between the Kingdom's maskilim and government agencies turned out to have important consequences. Above all it had a decisive influence on the strength and social position of maskilim there, who took advantage of the authority emanating from their close relationship with governmental agencies, which not only allowed them to implement elements of a maskilic programme more easily than in other countries in eastern Europe, but also gave it a specific character, geared very prag-matically towards the realization of social and political aims. Especially significant was the fact that the close co-operation with institutions and representatives of the government of the Kingdom of Poland bore fruit in the Polish Haskalah's specific linguistic profile. By contrast with the situation in Russia or Galicia, where the great majority of maskilic work was written in Hebrew, the maskilim of the Kingdom of Poland to a great extent wrote and published in Polish, a language in which they could communicate with their strategic partner—the government.[51] Among such writers, one could mention Jan Glücksberg, who strongly criticized the policy of half-measures carried out by the authorities of the Kingdom of Poland towards the Jews. Other, non-maskilic, representatives of the liberal camp among Polish Jews joined them. The radical activist for religious reform Antoni Eisenbaum was the author of a great many articles in the press devoted to the burning political issues, including the rabbinate, the confraternities, the *kahal*, and excommuni-cation (*ḥerem*). The appearance of such a large and well-informed group of Jewish polemicists, who clearly stated their views in the language of the land, was a new phenomenon not just for Polish culture of the time.

At the same time Warsaw was a strong centre of maskilic publishing. Between the end of the eighteenth century and 1862 close to one hundred titles in Polish or German by Polish maskilim and other integrationists appeared there, and close to two hundred Hebrew titles propagating Enlightenment ideology (around 20 per

[51] On this, see M. Wodziński, *Haskalah and Hasidism in the Kingdom of Poland: A History of Conflict*, trans. S. Cozens (Oxford, 2005), ch. 2; id., 'Good Maskilim and Bad Assimilationists: Toward a New Historiography of the Haskalah in Poland', *Jewish Social Studies*, NS, 10/3 (2004), 87–122.

cent of all the books in Hebrew published there), including classic Haskalah works. Maskilic titles also found numerous subscribers in the smaller towns of the Kingdom.[52]

Despite the fact that in recent years the Haskalah in the Kingdom of Poland has been the object of some interest, the subject continues to be insufficiently recognized, and maskilic works in Polish—unlike ones in German or French—have still not entered the canon of texts studied by scholars of the eastern European Haskalah.[53] Expanding research on the Polish Haskalah, analysing its links to other regional versions of the movement, researching epigones of Haskalah in the second half of the nineteenth century, studying the maskilic Hebrew press and ties between maskilim and other movements of liberal Jews seems today to be one of the most important research imperatives, in terms of developing both a better understanding of the history of the Jews in the Kingdom of Poland, and a better understanding of the phenomenon of the Haskalah itself.

The state of research into the second of the great nineteenth-century movements, hasidism, appears much healthier, although here too a great many of the basic issues continue to be the subject of debate, while scholars—including the authors of this introduction—continue to be far from a consensus. This is above all an issue of the dynamics, and thus of the thrust and speed, of hasidism's development, and even the point of departure at which it entered the history of the Kingdom of Poland.[54] Thanks to this debate, the state of our knowledge on the development of hasidism is, however, much greater today than two decades ago, while the area of issues which have been analysed has greatly expanded. Not just the thrust and pace of its expansion, but also the typology of hasidic leadership, its social base, the hasidic book, political activity, as well as the ties between hasidism and other social movements have become objects of research.[55] In recent years a

[52] S. Werses, 'Hasifrut ha'ivrit bepolin: tekufot vetsiyunei derekh', in I. Bartal and I. Gutman (eds.), *Kiyum veshever: yehudei polin ledoroteihem*, 2 vols. (Jerusalem, 1997–2001), ii. 161–90.

[53] For an overview of the state of knowledge on the Polish Haskalah, see M. Zalkin, 'Hahaskalah hayehudit bepolin: kavim lediyun', in Bartal and Gutman (eds.), *Kiyum veshever*, ii. 391–413; Wodziński, 'Good Maskilim and Bad Assimilationists'. For a classic view, see R. Mahler, *Hasidism and the Jewish Enlightenment: Their Confrontation in Galicia and Poland in the First Half of the Nineteenth Century*, trans. E. Orenstein, A. Klein, and J. M. Klein (Philadelphia, 1985), 203–43.

[54] M. Wodziński, 'How Many *Hasidim* Were There in Congress Poland? On the Demographics of the Hasidic Movement in Poland during the First Half of the Nineteenth Century', *Gal-ed*, 19 (2004), 13–49; G. Dynner, 'How Many *Hasidim* Were There Really in Congress Poland? A Response to Marcin Wodziński', *Gal-ed*, 20 (2006), 91–104; M. Wodziński, 'How Should We Count *Hasidim* in Congress Poland? A Response to Glenn Dynner', *Gal-ed*, 20 (2006), 105–21. For new analyses of the geographical tendencies and parameters of the hasidic expansion, including Congress Poland, see G. Dynner, 'Hasidism and Habitat: Managing the Jewish–Christian Encounter in the Kingdom of Poland', in id. (ed.), *Holy Dissent: Jewish and Christian Mystics in Eastern Europe* (Detroit, 2011), 104–30; P. Radensky, 'The Rise and Decline of a Hasidic Court: The Case of Rabbi Duvid Twersky of Tal'noye', ibid. 131–69; M. Wodziński and U. Gellman, 'Toward a New Geography of Hasidism', *Jewish History*, 27/2–4 (2013).

[55] A summary of the state of research two decades ago was provided by D. Assaf, 'Ḥasidut polin

great many important works have appeared on hasidic leaders active in the Kingdom of Poland, including the Seer of Lublin, Simhah Bunim of Przysucha, Isaac of Warka, and the *tsadikim* from the Izbica–Radzyń dynasty.[56] The source material for research into hasidism has also expanded dramatically, incorporating extensive archival material, the nineteenth-century press, memoirs, belles-lettres, iconography, and other sorts of material, alongside more traditional sources such as hasidic literature. These sources have also become more and more accessible.[57] Agnieszka Jagodzińska, in her chapter in this volume on the value and limitations of the reports of the London Society for Promoting Christianity amongst the Jews, suggests, however, that there still exist valuable and underutilized sources that throw new light on aspects of hasidism that are invisible in other sorts of historical narrative, including issues of daily life, social structure and stratification, and the popular perception of hasidism among the broad masses of Jewish people in Poland. Missionary ethnographical, or para-ethnographical, reports, analysed by Jagodzińska, appear to be even more valuable, given that the latest research on hasidism in the Kingdom of Poland is ever more frequently asking questions about the popularity of the hasidic movement, definitions, categories of belonging to and barriers separating hasidim from non-hasidim, and above all questioning the binary division of the world of Polish Jews into hasidim and their opponents. As Shaul

bame'ah ha-19: matsav hamehkar usekirah bibliografit', in R. Elior, I. Bartal, and C. Shmeruk (eds.), *Tsadikim ve'anshei ma'aseh: mehkarim bahasidut polin* (Jerusalem, 1994), 357–79. In addition to that volume, works published on the subject in the last two decades include T. M. Rabinowicz, *Bein peshisha lelublin: ishim veshitot behasidut polin* (Jerusalem, 1997); Dynner, *Men of Silk*; Wodziński, *Haskalah and Hasidism in the Kingdom of Poland*; id., *Hasidism and Politics*. See also U. Gellman, 'Hahasidut bepolin bamahatsit harishonah shel hame'ah hatesha-esreh: tipologiyot shel hamanhigut ve'edah', Ph.D. thesis (Hebrew Univ. of Jerusalem, 2011). A special case is the work written by Ignacy Schiper in the Warsaw ghetto, which miraculously survived and was published in 1992: I. Schiper, *Przyczynki do dziejów chasydyzmu w Polsce*, ed. Z. Targielski (Warsaw, 1992).

[56] On the Seer of Lublin, see Gellman, 'Hahasidut bepolin'; Dynner, *Men of Silk*, esp. 68–70. On Simhah Bunim of Przysucha, see M. Rosen, *The Quest for Authenticity: The Thought of Reb Simhah Bunim* (Jerusalem, 2008); A. Brill, 'Grandeur and Humility in the Writings of R. Simhah Bunim of Przysucha', in Y. Elman and J. S. Gurock (eds.), *Hazon Nahum: Studies in Jewish Law, Thought, and History Presented to Dr. Norman Lamm* (New York, 1997), 419–48; Dynner, *Men of Silk*, 183–95. On Isaac of Warka, see M. Wodziński, 'Hasidism, Shtadlanut, and Jewish Politics in Nineteenth Century Poland: The Case of Isaac of Warka', *Jewish Quarterly Review*, 96/2 (2005), 290–320. On the *tsadikim* of Izbica and Radzyń, see M. M. Faierstein, *All Is in the Hands of Heaven: The Teachings of Rabbi Mordecai Joseph Leiner of Izbica* (Hoboken, NJ, 1989); S. Magid, *Hasidism on the Margin: Reconciliation, Antinomianism, and Messianism in Izbica/Radzin Hasidism* (Madison, 2003); id., *Hasidism in Transition: The Hasidic Ideology of Rabbi Gershon Henoch of Radzin in Light of Medieval Jewish Philosophy and Kabbala* (Ann Arbor, 1998).

[57] See e.g. *Hasidism in the Kingdom of Poland, 1815–1867: Historical Sources in the Polish State Archives / Źródła do dziejów chasydyzmu w Królestwie Polskim, 1815–1867, w zasobach polskich archiwów państwowych*, ed. M. Wodziński (Kraków, 2011). For an archival guide to the most significant collection of documents on the Jews in the Kingdom of Poland, also taking into account extensive hasidiana, see M. Wodziński, *Judaica w aktach Centralnych Władz Wyznaniowych Królestwa Polskiego Archiwum Głównego Akt Dawnych: Informator archiwalny* (Wrocław, 2010).

Stampfer has put it so well, there were in the Jewish community of eastern Europe, besides hasidim and their opponents, also 'neutral (*parve*)' Jews, who were ambivalent or indifferent towards hasidism and its opponents.[58]

The forms of religious life of this considerable majority of Polish Jews were evolving slowly, together with modernizing changes, but were in many regards outgrowths of traditions inherited from the eighteenth century. The *kahal*, for example, continued to play a very important role in the community's religious life and, despite its formal liquidation in the Kingdom of Poland in 1822, retained a religious significance for a sizeable part of the Jewish community, even if it was now informal. The *kahal* continued to organize the daily rhythm of religious observances and exercised control over the religious life of a local community's inhabitants, a control to which a considerable majority of the Jewish community willingly submitted. The basic places of worship in most local communities continued to be the synagogue, open to all, and the *beit midrash*. The basic organizational form of religious studies conducted in the *beit midrash*, as of a great many other religious activities, was still the religious confraternity (*hevra*), even if delegitimized by the government. For a great many Jews, the basic religious concepts still derived from eighteenth-century notions of practical kabbalah, supplemented by a large dose of folk customs, beliefs, and superstitions. It appears that this segment of Jewish society in Poland remains the most poorly researched.[59]

THE PERIOD 1830–1863

The liberal and Enlightenment character of the Kingdom did not last. The autocratic ruler of Russia, who as the constitutional king of Poland had granted an extremely liberal constitution, was surprised and dismayed by the 'unrestrained' use of its guaranteed freedoms. The growing conflict between Alexander and then Nicholas, on the one hand, and part of the political elite on the other, represented especially by the parliamentary opposition known as the Kaliszanie (the men from Kalisz), inclined Alexander to harden his political line. The infamous personification of this policy was the tsar's official plenipotentiary, Senator Nikolay Novosiltsev, and also—to no less a degree—the tsar's brother Grand Duke Konstantin Pavlovich, backed up by his secret police, the institution of the censorship, and other repressive measures. Both Novosiltsev and Konstantin, commander-in-chief of the Polish army, carried out their duties as legally and professionally as possible. However, both the way in which they discharged their assigned duties and the reach of their authority generated much controversy, while the political system became ever less transparent. Of course, the ambiguity of the hierarchy and the occasionally

[58] As recorded in Y. Petrovsky-Shtern, 'Hasidism, Havurot, and the Jewish Street', *Jewish Social Studies*, NS, 10/2 (2004), 45.

[59] On the whole, the best-identified aspects of this issue are institutional, mainly thanks to the study by Guesnet, *Polnische Juden im 19. Jahrhundert*, 333–446.

extra-legal arrangements did not encourage efficiency on the part of the state administration. With the death of the first viceroy, General Józef Zajączek, in 1826, the Kingdom's administration fell into ever deeper lethargy and crisis.

On 29 November 1830, Polish cadets staged an attack on Konstantin's residence at the Belvedere Palace. Armed rioters filled the streets of Warsaw, massacring, among others, Jews in the poor house for allegedly spying for the Russians, until order was finally restored by a Polish revolutionary dictatorship.[60] During the first weeks of what would become a year-long uprising against the tsar, regional synagogue council representatives came forward with offers to double the Jewish recruitment tax in order to prevent their constituencies from being drafted. In contrast, Józef Berkowicz, son of Berek Joselewicz, Synaj Hernisz, a student at the Warsaw Rabbinical School, and several other acculturated Jews proposed a voluntary Jewish Unit of the Polish National Guard composed of Jews who were willing to shave their beards, against traditional Jewish proscriptions. Eventually, Jews were given a role in the revolutionary regime as national and civic guardsmen (the latter permitted to retain their beards).

This kind of Jewish participation was permitted reluctantly. Prominent members of the Polish revolutionary regime mistrusted the Jewish population, whom they sometimes accused of spying on behalf of Russian forces (Jewish tavern-keepers, owing to their strategic locations, were particularly singled out).[61] At the same time, insurrectionist leaders such as Antoni Ostrowski, commander of the Warsaw National Guard, advocated full emancipation for Jewish military volunteers.[62] Several publicists similarly urged Sejm representatives to allow Jews to earn citizenship by fighting for the national cause, noting as well the positive effects such toleration would have on European public opinion. Nevertheless, the Minister of War Franciszek Morawski and the Minster of the Treasury Alojzy Biernacki argued that the time was not ripe for radical reforms. Morawski felt, moreover, that it would be 'unpleasant' for a Pole to have to admit that he could not have prevailed in battle 'without the help of the Israelite people'.[63] Under their influence, the Sejm passed a bill exempting Jews from military service in exchange for a quadrupled recruitment tax.

After the collapse of the uprising, Tsar Nicholas I abrogated the constitution, replacing it with an Organic Statute, and abolished the Kingdom's autonomy, formally recognizing it as part of the Russian state. In subsequent years a great many agencies and additional symbols of sovereignty, such as a separate currency and an army, were abolished. Most former politicians and officials with an Enlightenment background either went into exile, reinforcing the ranks of the so-called Great Emigration, or were removed from any kind of influential administrative position.

---

[60] I. Schiper, 'Z instytutu badań spraw narodowości', *Sprawy Narodowościowe*, 5–6 (1930), 696.

[61] See Dynner, *Yankel's Tavern*, ch. 4.

[62] I. Schiper, *Żydzi Królestwa Polskiego w dobie powstania listopadowego* (Warsaw, 1932), 111–16.

[63] Ibid. 168–9.

Many of the most senior posts were filled with officials from Russia, often bureau-crats with low morale and few abilities. This signified a radical and final break with Enlightenment plans for reform, including reforms of the Jewish population. Nicholas's appointees were sent to implement a policy of integrating the Kingdom into the Russian empire, which in some areas was in fact achieved. Nevertheless, the Kingdom retained a distinctive identity, around 90 per cent of officials continued to be Poles, the government continued to be run in Polish, and most importantly, the Kingdom's legal and political systems remained independent of the Empire's and Polish law still applied.

The personification of such ambiguity was the viceroy himself, General Ivan Paskevich, the very same figure who, at the head of a tsarist army, had defeated Polish insurrectionary forces and had taken Warsaw. As a tsarist general appointed viceroy of the Kingdom, his task was gradually to integrate the Kingdom into the Empire. At the same time, however, implementing this policy would have curtailed his own authority in the Kingdom, and so was not to his personal advantage. Despite his unquestioned loyalty to the emperor, therefore, Paskevich in fact failed to implement such integration and, instead, worked to maintain the Kingdom's separate identity.

All this created an exceptionally unclear and tangled political, legal, and social situation, in which the policy of the Kingdom of Poland in general, and its policy towards the Jews in particular, became hostage to the country's incoherent strategic goals, the progressive collapse of its civil service, its conflicting aims and interests, the self-interest, ignorance, frustrations, and incompetence of officials at every level, but above all, the apparently conflicting and chaotic actions from the very highest level of Nicholas and Viceroy Paskevich right down to the lowest level of gendarme or town councillor. What is more, after the abandonment of Enlighten-ment reform projects, the government had nothing to offer in their stead, and so most strategic policies ceased to exist. The only real macro-political goals were cam-eralist: ensuring public law and order, containing radical and pro-independence movements, and increasing the state's revenues. There was little place in these plans for most kinds of Jewish social reform, since integrating the Jewish population with that of the Kingdom, that is, a Polish population hostile to Russian rule, was now seen as counter to the Empire's interests. The civil service was to a large extent reduced to managing rather than governing the Kingdom.

However, the Kingdom's government, urged on by the tsar's somewhat chaotic actions, could not completely abandon Jewish policy, especially given that post-Enlightenment reform rhetoric was still the country's sole language. The most ambitious reform projects implemented at this time were the introduction of compulsory military service for the Kingdom's Jews (1843), as well as the prohibi-tion of traditional Jewish dress (1846–50). Both resulted from a more general move towards importing policies from the tsarist empire proper, where Jews had been subject to compulsory military service since 1827, and dress reform had been introduced in 1845. Paradoxically, both reflected a lingering Polish autonomy, high-lighting the fundamental differences between the situation of the Jews in the King-dom and in Russia. In comparison with military service in the Empire, for example, the Jews' terms of service in the Kingdom were relatively modest and caused nothing like the deep communal crisis they had engendered in Russia.[64] The Kingdom's clothing reform—very similar to the one implemented in the Empire—met initially with a very strong reaction from the Orthodox population and caused a serious social crisis, but was resolved by adopting one of the officially accepted fashions, the 'Russian style', which in the Kingdom eventually became more or less identical to the previous Jewish style, fulfilled halakhic requirements (it permitted the use of headgear and beards), and most importantly was Russian and therefore distinct from the dress of the surrounding Polish population, preventing a dilution of differences between the Jewish and Christian communities.[65] Despite the initial vigour of the dispute, the conflict more or less fizzled out.

The difference between the Kingdom and the Empire could be seen even more clearly in a series of minor actions, such as the attempt to introduce the Empire's policy on Jewish printing presses and books. An investigation in 1833–4, which in Russia had led to the closure of Jewish printing presses and the subjection of the two remaining ones in Vilna and Zhytomyr to close government supervision, was rejected in the Kingdom by the viceroy as a 'pretext to take over on advantageous terms, either indirectly or directly, the whole printing industry'.[66] The education of a network of crown rabbis, which had had such weighty consequences for the Russian Jewish population, was never implemented in the Kingdom. Finally, the attempted educational reform of Russian Jews of the 1840s, feared by the Jewish masses as another Christianization scheme, completely bypassed the Kingdom. As a result, what was a period of great changes in the Empire proper was, in the Kingdom of Poland, a period of relative stagnation. A fuller comparison of the situation of Polish and Russian Jews at that time still awaits a definitive analysis, while the scope of research into the history of the Jews in the Kingdom of Poland between 1831 and 1863, especially their political and legal status, is particularly poor.[67] The absence of works in our volume devoted specifically to this period and to the subjects mentioned here is, in our view, a good illustration of this.

[64] Petrovsky-Shtern, *Jews in the Russian Army*, esp. 28–9.

[65] For the reform of dress in the Kingdom, see above all A. Jagodzińska, *Pomiędzy: Akulturacja Żydów Warszawy w drugiej połowie XIX wieku* (Wrocław, 2008), 86–102; ead., 'Overcoming the Signs of the "Other": Visual Aspects of the Acculturation of Jews in the Kingdom of Poland in the Nineteenth Century', *Polin*, 24 (2012), 71–94. For the reform of dress in Russia, see E. M. Avrutin, *Jews and the Imperial State: Identification Politics in Tsarist Russia* (Ithaca, NY, 2010), 39–50; I. Klauzner, 'Hagez-erah al tilboshet hayehudim, 1844–1850', *Gal-ed*, 6 (1982), 11–26.

[66] AGAD, CWW, 1871, pp. 251–79. For an analysis of these events, see Wodziński, *Hasidism and Politics*, 133–9.

[67] Of course, the subject of the period between the uprisings is tackled by numerous works focusing on longer cycles, as do textbooks and surveys. However, there have been almost no new works devoted specifically to this period since the 1930s.

FRATERNIZATION, INTEGRATION, AND REFORM

The death of Nicholas I brought hope for an improvement of conditions in the Kingdom. The new tsar, Alexander II—known as the tsar-liberator—came to the throne intending to implement deep reforms in a Russian state sunk in crisis after its defeat in the Crimean War of 1853–5. However, the tsar baulked at Polish independence. 'Pas de rêveries, messieurs', Alexander warned the crowd during his visit to the Kingdom of Poland in 1856. His warning against indulging in daydreams might easily have applied also to those Jewish subjects displaying integrationist tendencies and hoping for wholesale emancipation and social acceptance.

Changes in the Jewish community that were gathering strength in the middle of the nineteenth century—developing economic and social modernity, the appearance of new social classes, including the new intelligentsia, as well as ever-strengthening acculturation—did lead at the end of the fifties to the emergence in the Kingdom of a somewhat extensive and influential group of Jewish intelligentsia with a strongly integrationist ideology and an ambitious social agenda. Apart from post-Haskalah assumptions about the defence of Jewish identity, religion, group solidarity, and the unique nature of Jewish culture, the Polish integrationists' ideology laid emphasis on political and cultural Polonization, as well as social integration. The change had, in addition, a dimension of identity: the Polish language and culture became not just neutral carriers of modernization and European secular culture, but also conduits of emotional values. Having arrived in 1858 in Warsaw from Prussia, the preacher Marcus Jastrow (1829–1903) wrote after not quite three years in that city: 'I saw it as a new obligation to speak to my fellow believers who were recognized as Poles in the Polish tongue and to introduce into the house of the Hebrew God this treasure, which was so dear to all those who had not yet forgotten Poland's past and who still did not doubt that she would be reborn.' Later, explaining the circumstances in which he and the chief rabbi of Warsaw, Ber Meisels (1798–1870), were arrested for patriotic activities and deported from the Kingdom, he wrote: 'After three months of suffering, together with my esteemed friend Meisels, I had to bid farewell to the country whose threshold I had crossed as a stranger and which I was leaving as a native!'[68]

The events described by Jastrow have gone down in history as the era of 'Polish–Jewish fraternization'. The revolutionary events of 1861–3, when a rapprochement was achieved between a significant portion of the Polish and Jewish intelligentsia, as well as mass gestures of solidarity between these communities, accompanied by the participation of relatively great numbers of 'progressive' Jews in preparations for, and armed action in, the January uprising of 1863, shaped a whole generation of Polish Jewish intelligentsia in the Kingdom (and partly also in Galicia), who were active from the end of the fifties until the end of the century. These communities published journals, worked with the Polish Positivists, the dominant intellectual

---

[68] M. Jastrow, *Kazania miane podczas ostatnich wypadków w Warszawie r. 1861* (Poznań, 1862), 9.

group in the Kingdom in the decades following the insurrection, actively influenced local community affairs, set up social programmes, did charitable works, and published important literary, historical, and journalistic texts.

Fortunately, both the actual incidents of fraternization and broader integrationist processes are among the better-known issues in the history of nineteenth-century Polish Jewish society, mainly thanks to several exhaustive studies published in the last two decades. Full-length monographs analyse the phenomenon of Polish–Jewish fraternization and its influence on the subsequent attitudes of liberal Polish and Jewish communities.[69] Polish–Jewish fraternization was not only a transformative event and a defining generational experience for Polish integrationists, but a symbolic, watershed moment when Jews became more involved in the Polish pro-independence movement. Studies on this subject were especially popular in traditional Polish and Polish Jewish historiography, given that they were meant, apologetically, to supply proof of Jews' Polish patriotism. Newer studies indicate, however, some rather more complex mechanics behind Jews' pro-Polish patriotism and their attitudes towards Poland and Polishness.[70] A great deal of attention has also been devoted to the journals published by these circles, especially the Warsaw weeklies *Jutrzenka* and *Izraelita*, although we still await a full account of the latter.[71] The same is true of *Hatsefirah*, a maskilic, epigonic journal produced in Warsaw by Chaim Zelig Słonimski.[72] Valuable works analyse the social base of the integrationist movement, as well as the actual scope of the acculturation process, compar-

[69] M. Opalski and I. Bartal, *Poles and Jews: A Failed Brotherhood* (Hanover, NH, 1992). See also Theodore Weeks's chapter in the present volume.

[70] G. Bacon, 'Messianists, Pragmatists and Patriots: Orthodox Jews and the Modern Polish State', in Y. Elman, E. B. Halivni, and Z. A. Steinfeld (eds.), *Neti'ot Ledavid: Jubilee Volume for David Weiss Halivni* (Jerusalem, 2004), 15–30; I. Bartal, 'Giborim o mogei lev: yehudim bitsevaoteiha shel polin (1794–1863)', in Bartal and Gutman (eds.), *Kiyum veshever*, i. 315–36; see also Wodziński, *Hasidism and Politics*, 258–65. The issue definitely requires further study. The most recent review of Jews' participation in Polish liberationist movements is S. Rudnicki, 'Żydzi w walce o niepodległość Polski', in id., *Równi, ale niezupełnie* (Warsaw, 2008), 10–28.

[71] On *Jutrzenka*, see B. Daniłowicz, 'Jutrzenka — tygodnik Izraelitów polskich', in S. Walasek (ed.), *Studia o szkolnictwie i oświacie mniejszości narodowych w XIX i XX wieku* (Wrocław, 1994), 23–62. On *Izraelita*, see M. Fuks, *Prasa żydowska w Warszawie, 1823–1939* (Warsaw, 1979), 85–102; A. Jagodzińska, '"Izraelita" (1866–1915)', in J. Nalewajko-Kulikov with G. P. Bąbiak and A. J. Cieślikowa (eds.), *Studia z dziejów trójjęzycznej prasy żydowskiej na ziemiach polskich (XIX–XX w.)* (Warsaw, 2012), 45–60; Z. Kołodziejska, '"Izraelita" (1866–1915): Znaczenie kulturowe i literackie czasopisma', Ph.D. thesis (Univ. of Warsaw, 2012); ead., '"Środowisko "Izraelity" wobec antysemityzmu', in Nalewajko-Kulikov, Bąbiak, and Cieślikowa (eds.), *Studia z dziejów trójjęzycznej prasy żydowskiej*, 299–316; *Izraelita, 1866–1915: Wybór źródeł*, ed. A. Jagodzińska and M. Wodziński, forthcoming; Polonsky, *Jews in Poland and Russia*, i. 317–19.

[72] E. Bauer, '"Ha-cefira" (1862–1931)', in Nalewajko-Kulikov, Bąbiak, and Cieślikowa (eds.), *Studia z dziejów trójjęzycznej prasy żydowskiej*, 31–44; ead., *Between Poles and Jews: The Development of Nahum Sokolow's Political Thought* (Jerusalem, 2005); Fuks, *Prasa żydowska w Warszawie*, 103–23; O. Soffer, 'Iton "Hatsefirah" vehamodernizatsyah shel hasiah hapoliti-ḥevrati ha'ivri', Ph.D. thesis (Hebrew Univ. of Jerusalem, 2001); id., 'Antisemitism, Statistics, and the Scientization of Hebrew Political Discourse: The Case Study of *Ha-tsefirah*', *Jewish Social Studies*, NS, 10/2 (2004), 55–79.

ing the integrationists' ideological declarations with the form that this process in fact took.[73] Recent works have also brought us closer to understanding the maskilic roots of the integrationist movement, and the ideological transition, affecting a whole generation, from the Haskalah to pro-Polish integrationism. In addition, these works have introduced terminological and conceptual clarity about the relationship between integration as the principal social goal, acculturation as a tool in this social integration, and secularization, modernization, and assimilation. Fortunately, current studies no longer treat the concept of assimilation as a primary term and as the name for the whole integrationist thrust. Quite the opposite—they point to the polemical function of this term in the writings of Zionist critics of the integrationist ideology, who accused their ideological opponents precisely of assimilation, understood by them as a betrayal of Jewish identity.[74]

One of the less well-researched dimensions of integration, however, is competition from non-Polish paths of acculturation. François Guesnet addresses this theme in our volume, focusing on a profile of Louis Meyer, a liberal Jew from Włocławek, who spent his whole life under the influence of German acculturation. As Guesnet demonstrates, Meyer was a typical representative of the Polish Jewish bourgeoisie attempting to link Polish Jewish traditions (as well as a positive view of the traditions of the former Commonwealth) in a harmonious way with modern European culture, represented by its German version. Meyer's history illustrates in an interesting way the more general process of the erosion of these pro-German sympathies, linked to the expansion of Prussian militarism. We hope that Guesnet's interesting study on the subject of Louis Meyer will nudge research into acculturation in a comparative direction, and will help to explain better the joint efforts of and competition between variants of integration among the Jews of the Kingdom of Poland and other lands of the former Commonwealth.

Another issue, which in recent years has seen a renewal of interest, is the reform of Judaism in the Polish lands, a subject that for many years was treated as nonexistent. Classic studies of the religious reform of Judaism, deriving from a German and American model, have rightly questioned the similarity of changes in Polish Judaism in the nineteenth century to the phenomenon called Reform Judaism in central Europe and America. An additional problem has, of course, been the inaccessibility of sources, overwhelmingly in Polish, which has prevented scholars of the German or American reforms of Judaism from incorporating the Polish case into their research interests. Current research, carried out mainly, but not exclusively, in Poland, challenges the universality of the German–American model. It emphasizes too the scale of the changes in the Judaism of liberal Polish

---

[73] Jagodzińska, *Pomiędzy*. On the Warsaw intelligentsia, see H. Datner, *Ta i tamta strona: Żydowska inteligencja Warszawy drugiej połowy XIX wieku* (Warsaw, 2007). See also A. Cała, *Asymilacja Żydów w Królestwie Polskim, 1864–1897: Postawy, konflikty, stereotypy* (Warsaw, 1989).

[74] See above all A. Jagodzińska, 'Asymilacja, czyli bezradność historyka: O krytyce terminu i pojęcia', in K. Zieliński (ed.), *Wokół akulturacji i asymilacji Żydów na ziemiach polskich* (Lublin, 2010), 15–31.

Jews, correctly pointing to German, and above all Viennese, models, even if those who promoted changes of this type have managed to camouflage the extent and radicalism of these German influences. The chapter in this volume by Benjamin Matis, which analyses the High Holiday prayer book (*maḥzor*) of the Warsaw preacher Izaak Cylkow, points exactly to this strategy of linking daring theological innovations derived from Abraham Geiger's circle to very conservative liturgical changes that seek to retain the values of traditional forms of prayer. Matis suggests that perhaps Cylkow's strategy exemplified a more general line of development and the *differentia specifica* of the Polish brand of reform-oriented Judaism, which was theologically daring, liturgically conservative, and highly sensitive to the values of tradition. If that is so, it perhaps indicates the existence of a distinctly Polish model for reform-oriented Judaism. Matis's study, together with other published works on the views and activities of the Warsaw preachers Marcus Jastrow and Izaak Cylkow, as well as on the history of reform-oriented synagogues (the principal institutions of reform in the Kingdom of Poland), extends the scope of our knowledge on the subject in the Kingdom of Poland and, more generally, in the Polish lands.[75] A topic which still awaits its scholar, however, is that of the fundamental and still unexplained genealogy, links, and relations of the three liberal trends working jointly in the Kingdom of Poland (as in other areas of eastern Europe)—the Haskalah, integrationism, and the reform of Judaism—in terms of ideas, personal connections, and the whole spectrum of institutional links.

EMANCIPATION, URBANIZATION, AND INDUSTRIALIZATION

Alexander II introduced substantial improvements in the status of Jews in the Kingdom of Poland, beginning on 24 May 1862, a process which almost warrants the designation *równouprawnienie* ('equality of rights'), or emancipation. These liberalizing decrees are usually understood as a response to growing Polish demands for autonomy and to impending insurrection. The tsar's new viceroy, Aleksander Wielopolski, regarded the emancipation of peasants and Jews as the best way to win over these important elements. However, the liberalizing decrees were also a

---

[75] For a general overview, see M. Galas, 'The Influence of Progressive Judaism in Poland', *Shofar*, 3 (2011), 55–67. For good examples of contemporary research into the field, see especially Guesnet, *Polnische Juden im 19. Jahrhundert*, 281–302; M. Galas, *Rabin Markus Jastrow i jego wizja reformy judaizmu: Studium z dziejów judaizmu w XIX wieku* (Kraków, 2007); id. (ed.), *Izaak Cylkow (1841–1908): Życie i dzieło* (Kraków, 2010); A. Maślak-Maciejewska, *Rabin Szymon Dankowicz (1834–1910): Życie i działalność* (Kraków, 2013). On institutional aspects, see also older publications, especially S. Zilbersztejn, 'Postępowa synagoga na Daniłowiczowskiej w Warszawie (przyczynek do historii kultury Żydów polskich XIX stulecia)', *Biuletyn Żydowskiego Instytutu Historycznego*, 74 (1970), 31–57; A. Guterman, *Mehitbolelut lile'umiyut: perakim betoledot beit-hakeneset hagadol hasinagogah bevarshah* (Tel Aviv, 1993); id., 'The Origins of the Great Synagogue in Warsaw on Tłomackie Street', in W. T. Bartoszewski and A. Polonsky (eds.), *The Jews in Warsaw: A History* (Oxford, 1991), 181–211.

product of debates stimulated by new kinds of Jewish political activism around the mid-century, of which the British Jewish philanthropist Sir Moses Montefiore's criticisms during his visit to the Kingdom in 1846 are a good example. Even more importantly, the death of Nicholas I and the Russian defeat in the Crimean War in 1855 led to what has been described as the 'post-Sevastopol détente' and a liberalizing shift in state policy.

The lengthy report of the 1858 Jewish Committee provides considerable insight into the evolution of official thinking.[76] It begins almost pharaonically: 'In the Kingdom, out of a total population of 4,733,000 inhabitants, there are close to 580,000 Jews, which constitutes practically one-eighth of the general populace.' This disproportionate presence could be contrasted with the situation in countries such as Austria (where one person in forty-five was a Jew) and even the Russian Pale of Settlement (one in fifteen). Furthermore, the Kingdom's Jewish population was disproportionately urban and oriented towards trade, crafts, and 'speculation', which prevented it from merging with the rest of the nation and hence posed a threat to social stability. The only way that Jews could be reformed, the authors concluded wearily, was by equalizing their legal status with that of other inhabitants, i.e. granting them emancipation. This, however, could happen only by rewarding those Jews who had already shaken off their religious superstitions, learned to read and write Polish or Russian, and ceased to separate themselves from other inhabitants, while punishing those numerous fanatical Jews who belonged to the hasidic sect by refusing to admit them to positions of communal leadership. Until now, the hasidic sect had 'paralysed every great effort by the regime to repair the moral and material condition of members of the Mosaic persuasion'.[77]

A key figure in these debates was the margrave Aleksander Wielopolski, who was by turns pragmatic and idealistic when it came to the Jewish question. Instead of insisting that Jews become civilized before they were granted equal rights, Wielopolski argued that legal restrictions and fiscal burdens on Jews hindered their integration and was confident that emancipation and compulsory secular education would transform them into good citizens. Ultimately, Wielopolski sought the Polonization of Jews. While such an aspiration was obviously at odds with the tsar's, the rising instability in the Kingdom compelled the tsar to compete with the Polish insurrectionists' promises. On 5 June 1862, he appointed Wielopolski to the post of head of the Kingdom's civil administration and signed a series of liberalizing decrees based on Wielopolski's proposals.[78] Jewish residential restrictions were abolished. The prohibition on Jewish land purchases was annulled. Jews were now allowed to act as witnesses in legal proceedings and were to be treated on a par with Christians in criminal suits. With the exception of the production and sale of liquor, restrictions on Jewish economic activity were removed. A second decree in October 1862 repealed all special Jewish taxes, including the burdensome kosher

---

[76] AGAD, KRSW, 6632, fos. 26–80.   [77] Ibid. 28–32.
[78] Eisenbach, *Emancipation of the Jews in Poland*, 444–69.

meat tax. In 1868, Jews were permitted to move freely between the Kingdom of Poland and the Russian Pale of Settlement—a boon to merchants.

Still, the 1862 decrees retained significant restrictions. Jews were prohibited from holding offices in local government, such as that of *wójt* (mayor). Nor could they employ Christians as domestics.[79] Jewish languages were still forbidden in bookkeeping and other economic transactions. Even more importantly, despite formal legislation, a number of discriminatory practices continued. Jews could now theoretically purchase landed property, but such real-estate purchases by Jews and other non-noble classes remained subject to restrictions and were limited in number.[80] In 1866, Jewish university graduates were theoretically permitted to hold positions in the central government administration, but this rarely occurred.

Yet the change in legal status had enormous consequences for the Jews in the Kingdom of Poland. As Theodore R. Weeks points out in his survey chapter on change and continuity in the situation of the Jews in the Kingdom of Poland in the post-emancipation period, after 1862 the Kingdom's Jews found themselves in a privileged legal position in comparison to other Jews in the Russian empire. Indeed, a memo from the Pahlen Commission in the 1880s observed that Jews in the Pale 'look with envy upon the Jews in the adjacent provinces of the Kingdom of Poland, who are almost entirely emancipated'.[81] It should be remembered that beyond the Kingdom of Poland, the Jews of the Russian empire were not legally emancipated until the February revolution of 1917. This meant, among other things, severe legal restrictions, above all restrictions on freedom to settle. Furthermore, the May Laws of 3 May 1882, introducing further limitations on the already meagre Jewish rights in the Empire, were not introduced in the Kingdom, which only accentuated the legal difference between these two territories and turned the Kingdom into a safe and relatively attractive haven. As Weeks demonstrates, in concert with the social transformations accompanying Polish–Jewish fraternization, this fundamentally contributed to the industrial and demographic, and indirectly the social and cultural, development of the Kingdom of Poland's Jews.

Perhaps the most spectacular expression of these changes was the growth of the great metropolises and their Jewish districts. Although the Jewish population in the Polish lands had always been disproportionately urban, in the second half of the

[79] Eisenbach, *Emancipation of the Jews in Poland*, 477. On Jews in the administration of the Kingdom of Poland, see K. Latawiec, 'Kariery urzędnicze Żydów w administracji ogólnej imperium rosyjskiego na przełomie XIX i XX stulecia (na przykładzie Królestwa Polskiego)', in Zieliński (ed.), *Wokół akulturacji i asymilacji Żydów na ziemiach polskich*, 45–68.

[80] The process of land acquisition by Jews was slowed down by prohibitions on Jews purchasing estates that had not yet established fixed rents for the peasantry, a process that could drag on for years. To an even greater degree, it was retarded by the real, rather than the imagined, financial state of most of the Kingdom's Jews. By 1887, non-nobles still owned a mere 15.2% of the Kingdom's private estates. It is not known how much of this modest percentage was accounted for by Jews.

[81] M. J. Ochs, 'St. Petersburg and the Jews of Russian Poland, 1862–1905, Ph.D. thesis (Harvard Univ., 1986), 25.

nineteenth century significant numbers of Jews moved from small semi-urban settlements, the shtetls, to the then-growing metropolises of eastern Europe, both to those developing in the Polish lands and to those beyond their borders. At this time Warsaw became the greatest Jewish centre in the Polish lands, and also home to the largest Jewish community on earth. Up to the end of the previous century Jews had in principle been forbidden from living in Warsaw. Nevertheless, in 1781 about 3,500 Jews lived in the so-called *jurydyki* (zones in which city law did not apply) in Warsaw, representing less than 4 per cent of the city's population. The lifting of the restrictions on settlement and the simultaneous development of the city after 1815 rendered Warsaw an especially attractive destination of migration for Jews both from the Kingdom of Poland and from other areas of the Russian empire, and the percentage of Jewish inhabitants began to rise dramatically. By 1816, Jews already represented 19 per cent of Warsaw's population; a hundred years later, in 1910, despite the very dramatic rise in the city's Christian population, the proportion of Jews peaked at 39.2 per cent, that is 306,000 people. The pace of the Jewish population's growth worried a great many inhabitants of Warsaw, who feared that Jews might soon become a majority in Poland's capital. This was an especially touchy issue in the years leading up to the First World War, when the introduction of urban autonomy was being discussed in the Kingdom, since it potentially meant the ethnic Polish population's loss of political control over the capital.[82]

Equally spectacular was Łódź's urban growth. In the 1820s, this small town was transformed into a centre of the textile industry. Together with a number of surrounding places Łódź grew very quickly and attracted an ever-growing number of Polish, German, and Jewish settlers. At the time when Łódź was being set up as a textile centre, Jews there represented as much as 36 per cent of the population, but this was no more than 288 people out of a total population of 799. Jews were represented relatively poorly in the first phase of Łódź's development, when mainly unskilled Polish workers, as well as German investors and textile craftsmen, flocked to the city. Hence, the proportion of Jews had fallen to 11.7 per cent by 1856. Soon, however, Łódź also became the 'promised land' for Jews. In 1897, they again represented over 30 per cent of the population and in 1910 they even reached 40.7 per cent, meaning as many as 166,628 Jews in a city of over 400,000. By the first decade of the twentieth century, one in four Jews in the Kingdom of Poland lived either in Warsaw or in Łódź. In both cities, great and diverse Jewish districts sprang up, developing in Łódź around poor, working-class Bałuty, while in Warsaw they congregated in a somewhat better-located north-western district. No urban centre outside the Kingdom of Poland became a Jewish metropolis to rival Warsaw and Łódź.

---

[82] See D. Engel, 'Hashe'elah hapolanit vehatenuah hatsiyonit: havikuah al hashilton ha'atsmi be'arei polin hakongresa'it, 1910–1911', *Gal-ed*, 13 (1993), 59–82. For the debates on urban autonomy and the attendant Polish–Jewish conflict, see T. R. Weeks, *Nation and State in Late Imperial Russia: Nationalism and Russification on the Western Frontier, 1863–1914* (DeKalb, Ill., 1996), 152–71.

The basic engine of this process of urbanization was, of course, dramatic industrial expansion. The Kingdom of Poland became the most modern, the most industrialized, and the fastest-developing area in the Russian empire. This had an enormous significance, especially after the lifting of the customs barrier between the Kingdom and the Empire in 1858, since this allowed the free expansion of trade throughout the vast expanse of the Romanov empire, and also influenced the intensification of industrial growth in the Empire itself by the last decades of the nineteenth century. The basic branch of industry which benefited from the opening of the eastern market was the textile industry, and it was precisely on it that the economic success of Łódź was based, as well as of a number of smaller satellite towns that also lived off textiles, such as Aleksandrów, Zgierz, Pabianice, and Zduńska Wola. From the middle of the nineteenth century the participation of Jewish investors in the textile industry of Łódź was considerable (although far from dominant). By the end of the century, Izrael Poznański (1833–1900) was seen as one of the three 'kings of Łódź cotton', and alongside him a great many other Jewish entrepreneurs were now active in the city.

From the beginning of the nineteenth century, the Jewish population had participated in the process of capitalist transformation in other sectors of the country's economy. In Warsaw throughout the greater part of the century most of the banking houses belonged to Jews or to people of Jewish ancestry, for instance the wealthy Frankel, Epstein, and Wawelberg families. Leopold Kronenberg (1812–78) and Jan Bloch (1836–1902), who had both converted to Christianity, competed fiercely in the railway industry, financing among other things the Vistula railway and the Łódź factory line, as well as a great many other lines. Jewish involvement was also clearly evident in the sugar, machine tool, and mining industries.

Urbanization and industrialization affected the Polish and Jewish populations' social stratification and stimulated the emergence of new social classes. Perhaps the most interesting new social class was the Jewish intelligentsia, which was particularly active after the 1850s. It was precisely then that, in the circle of young converts to the Haskalah—pupils of the Warsaw Rabbinical School or members of the new professions of the professional intelligentsia—there arose a camp that from the mid-sixties became the dominant formation of the modernizing trend among Polish Jews. As one participant in these events, the writer and social activist Hilary Nussbaum, wrote:

The noblest manifestation, the most obvious feature of this period has without a doubt been the breaking into the world of the first-born cohort of young Israelite doctors, lawyers, naturalists, and philologists, who, having devoted themselves to special, prestigious professions, have become brave citizens, breeding grounds for general education, and the most effective engines of progress in the broader circles of their co-religionists.[83]

---

[83] H. Nussbaum, *Szkice historyczne z życia Żydów w Warszawie od pierwszych śladów pobytu ich w tem mieście do chwili obecnej* (Warsaw, 1881), 174.

Although this pompous statement ignores the Jewish intellegentsia's relatively limited scope, this group did become the most significant secularist culture-forming factor in Jewish society in the Polish lands, and its significance grew in subsequent decades. The growth in demand for a professional (especially technical) intelligentsia, as well as the traditional respect for learning in the Jewish community, meant that acquiring a secular education and joining the ranks of the new Jewish intelligentsia in the second half of the century became a way to escape the 'Jewish ghetto' for those who desired to do so. At least up to the eighties, it appeared that Polish Christian society might greet such refugees with open arms.

The processes of emancipation, urbanization, industrialization, and new stratification belong, of course, to the historiographical canon of the twentieth century and as such have become the object of interest on the part of scholars of the history of the Polish Jews, especially those of a Marxist bent.[84] Yet, intensive research into these subjects has slackened off considerably with the end of the dominance of Marxist historiography sponsored by the communist state and the departure of a generation of inter-war Jewish historians. In their place have appeared some interesting studies employing the tools of historical demography, touching on some, but not all, of the issues raised here,[85] and work is continuing on newly emergent social classes, especially the bourgeoisie and the intelligentsia (the history of the Jewish worker continues—rather surprisingly—to be studied the least).[86]

[84] Among the most important works in the field of socio-economic history we should mention above all the studies by Artur Eisenbach on the emancipation, and those by Filip Friedman and Bernard Weinryb, e.g. Eisenbach, *Kwestia równouprawnienia Żydów w Królestwie Polskim*; id., *Emancypacja Żydów na ziemiach polskich*; F. Friedman, *Dzieje Żydów w Łodzi od początków osadnictwa Żydów do r. 1863: Stosunki ludnościowe, życie gospodarcze, stosunki społeczne* (Łódź, 1935); S. B. Weinryb, *Neueste Wirtschaftsgeschichte der Juden in Russland und Polen*, i: *Das Wirtschaftsleben der Juden in Russland und Polen von der 1. polnischen Teilung bis zum Tode Alexanders II., 1772–1881* (Breslau, 1934). Significant later works are B. Garncarska-Kadary, *Ḥelkam shel hayehudim behitpateḥut hata'asiyah shel varshah bashanim 1816/20–1914* (Tel Aviv, 1985); ead., 'Hayehudim behitpateḥutah hakalkalit shel polin bame'ah hayod-tet', in Bartal and Gutman (eds.), *Kiyum veshever*, i. 315–36; W. Puś, *Żydzi w Łodzi w latach zaborów, 1793–1914* (Łódź, 2001), 50–104. For a good recent overview of the economic developments in the Kingdom of Poland, see Guesnet, *Polnische Juden im 19. Jahrhundert*, 95–176.

[85] See above all A. Markowski, *Między Wschodem a Zachodem: Rodzina i gospodarstwo domowe Żydów suwalskich w pierwszej połowie XIX wieku* (Warsaw, 2008); Guesnet, *Polnische Juden im 19. Jahrhundert*, 29–86. There is a good overview of the state of knowledge on the demography of the Polish Jews in the nineteenth century, although dealing rather poorly with the specific issue of the Kingdom of Poland, in S. Stampfer, 'Gidul ha'okhlosyah vehagirah beyahadut polin-lita be'et haḥadashah', in Bartal and Gutman (eds.), *Kiyum veshever*, i. 263–85.

[86] See R. Kołodziejczyk, *Jan Bloch (1836–1902): Szkic do portretu 'króla polskich kolei'* (Warsaw, 1983); I. Ichnatowicz, *Obyczaj wielkiej burżuazji warszawskiej w XIX wieku* (Warsaw, 1971); J. Hensel, *Burżuazja warszawska drugiej połowy XIX w. w świetle akt notarialnych* (Warsaw, 1979); E. Bauer, 'Jan Gottlieb Bloch: Polish Cosmopolitism versus Jewish Universalism', *European Review of History*, 17/3 (2010), 415–29. On the intelligentsia, see above all Datner, *Ta i tamta strona*, as well as a splendid three-volume synthesis of the history of the Polish intelligentsia that also takes into account the history of the Polish Jewish intelligentsia: *Dzieje inteligencji polskiej do roku 1918* (Warsaw, 2008), vol. i: M. Janowski, *Narodziny inteligencji, 1750–1831*; vol. ii: J. Jedlicki, *Błędne koło, 1832–1864*; vol. iii: M. Micińska,

A return to the major topics of emancipation, urbanization, industrialization, and the history of emergent classes is, however, much needed, both on account of their importance and because of the ever more evident imbalance in fields of interest, together with the growing dominance of postmodernist historiography.

ANTISEMITISM

The last two decades of the nineteenth century in the Kingdom of Poland were marked by all the tensions of the modernized, capitalist world. An outburst of ethnic xenophobia and inter-ethnic violence on the one hand, and new forms of political and cultural activism on the other, radically changed Polish–Jewish relations within the Kingdom and beyond. Modern, ideological antisemitism, present from the 1870s in Polish and European public life, nourished itself on traditional antisemitic attitudes and a growing fear of social change in the industrial age. Its best-known representative in the Kingdom of Poland was Jan Jeleński (1845–1909), the author of numerous pamphlets and newspaper articles and, from 1882, the editor and principal (initially the sole) author of the first specifically antisemitic Polish-language journal, *Rola*. Jeleński was a somewhat typical representative of the frustrated, quasi-intellectual members of urban communities threatened by modernization and in search of culprits. His aggressive journalism, using the cheapest rhetorical techniques, met initially with opposition from all opinion-making circles in Poland. However, it soon turned out that anti-Jewish anxieties also affected other groups, including even eminent liberal ideologues of Positivism. In the twentieth century, the 'pope' of Polish Positivism, Aleksander Świętochowski, moved to an openly antisemitic stance. This period also saw the development of the odd phenomenon of 'progressive antisemitism'. Representatives of this line of thinking, above all Andrzej Niemojewski, sharply attacked the Jewish community from left-wing and anticlerical positions.[87]

The epicentre of antisemitic ideology was the new, nationalist political right, which soon came to dominate the National Democracy (Narodowa Demokracja (ND), also known as the Endecja). In the first years of existence of the nationalist circles—the Polish League (Liga Polska) and the Union of Polish Youth (Związek Młodzieży Polskiej; 'Zet')—antisemitic ideology played no significant role in their activities. However, with the appearance of Roman Dmowski (1864–1939) as a leader, in 1893 the National League (Liga Narodowa) was formed, quickly becoming the tribune of political, and soon racial, antisemitism. Dmowski's initial

---

Inteligencja na rozdrożach, 1864–1918. See also R. Czepulis-Rastenis, *'Klassa umysłowa': Inteligencja Królestwa Polskiego, 1832–1862* (Warsaw, 1973). On the civilizational discourses of the Polish intelligentsia, see J. Jedlicki, *A Suburb of Europe: Nineteenth-Century Polish Approaches to Western Civilization* (Budapest, 1999); id., *Świat zwyrodniały: Lęki i wyroki krytyków nowoczesności* (Warsaw, 2000).

[87] T. R. Weeks, 'Polish "Progressive Antisemitism", 1905–1914', *East European Jewish Affairs*, 25/2 (1995), 49–68.

antisemitism was, apparently, first of all strategic in nature, calculated to win over those circles nurturing traditional, pre-modern anti-Jewish attitudes; but in later years it undoubtedly evolved into an obsessive hostility towards Jews. The final years of the Kingdom's existence saw a dramatic escalation in the Polish–Jewish conflict, aggressive antisemitic propaganda, and growing social polarization. Its final stage on the eve of the First World War was the political conflict caused by elections to the Russian parliament (the Duma) in 1912, as a result of which ND politicians announced a boycott of Jewish businesses that lasted up to the start of the war.[88] As Yedida Kanfer points out in this volume in her analysis of events and debates in Łódź, the 1912 boycott was in fact the second one called in the Kingdom, after the boycott of German goods in 1907, and was a sign of a broader process of the spread of economic nationalism at the turn of the century, especially after the revolution of 1905.[89] Kanfer's study examines the hitherto poorly known context of the development of modern antisemitism, especially so-called economic patriotism, and the invoking of economic arguments in a growing ethnic conflict in Łódź whose three sides were the Poles, the Germans, and the Jews, in addition to the Russian authorities and Russian industrial competition coming from Moscow. Kanfer's work supplements in a valuable way the state of knowledge on the spread of antisemitism and on Polish–Jewish and Christian–Jewish relations in the Kingdom of Poland at the turn of the twentieth century. Her study complements a number of recent works offering both narrower and broader analyses of these attitudes.[90] Numerous studies dealing with antisemitic threads in Polish literature might also be mentioned.[91]

---

[88] On the boycott, see R. Blobaum, *Boycott! The Politics of Anti-Semitism in Poland, 1912–1914* (Washington, 1998): <http://www.ucis.pitt.edu/nceeer/1998-812-19g-3-Blobaum.pdf>; S. Corrsin, *Warsaw before the First World War: Poles and Jews in the Third City of the Russian Empire, 1880–1914* (Boulder, Colo., 1989); T. R. Weeks, *From Assimilation to Antisemitism: The 'Jewish Question' in Poland, 1850–1914* (DeKalb, Ill., 2006), 163–9; id., 'Fanning the Flames: Jews in the Warsaw Press, 1905–1912', *East European Jewish Affairs*, 28/2 (1998–9), 63–81.

[89] See Kanfer's chapter for an extensive bibliography of the subject.

[90] The most important works on this subject are Weeks, *From Assimilation to Antisemitism*; K. Lewalski, *Kościoły chrześcijańskie w Królestwie Polskim wobec Żydów w latach 1855–1915* (Wrocław, 2002); A. Cała, *Żyd — wróg odwieczny? Antysemityzm w Polsce i jego źródła* (Warsaw, 2012), chs. 5–6; F. Golczewski, *Polnisch-jüdische Beziehungen, 1881–1922: Eine Studie zur Geschichte des Antisemitismus in Osteuropa* (Wiesbaden, 1981); R. Blobaum (ed.), *Antisemitism and its Opponents in Modern Poland* (Ithaca, NY, 2005). On Roman Dmowski's antisemitism, see G. Krzywiec, *Szowinizm po polsku: Przypadek Romana Dmowskiego (1886–1905)* (Warsaw, 2009). On Bolesław Prus and—partly—other Positivists, see A. Friedrich, *Bolesław Prus wobec kwestii żydowskiej* (Gdańsk, 2008); more broadly on the Warsaw Positivists, see M. Iwańska, *Prasa pozytywistów warszawskich wobec Żydów i kwestii żydowskiej* (Łódź, 2006); see also Stanislaus A. Blejwas's classic piece 'Polish Positivism and the Jews', *Jewish Social Studies*, 46/1 (1984), 21–36. On accusations of ritual murder in the Polish lands in the nineteenth and twentieth centuries, including the Congress Kingdom, see J. Żyndul, *Kłamstwo krwi: Legenda mordu rytualnego na ziemiach polskich w XIX i XX wieku* (Warsaw, 2011), esp. 62–86, 168–90.

[91] See in particular G. Borkowska and M. Rudkowska (eds.), *Kwestia żydowska w XIX w.: Spory o tożsamość Polaków* (Warsaw, 2004); M. Domagalska, 'The Image of the Jews in the Anti-Semitic

One of the classic subjects of studies on the manifestations of antisemitism is the pogrom. However, this literature tends to focus on pogroms in Russia rather than in the Kingdom of Poland. The best-known pogroms in the Kingdom are those that took place in Warsaw over Christmas 1881 and in Siedlce in September 1906.[92] Artur Markowski's chapter in this volume greatly supplements our knowledge of pogroms in the Kingdom, describing their geography, typology, chronology, Jewish and non-Jewish behaviours, and the reactions of the authorities. Thanks to Markowski's exhaustive research, it is possible to challenge a number of basic assumptions of studies of pogroms, above all assumptions about so-called waves of pogroms, that is, the sequencing of successive pogroms. Markowski also confirms and strengthens the findings of other scholars who question the tsarist authorities' direct responsibility for the pogroms. Perhaps of greatest importance, in describing the little-known pogroms in Warsaw in 1829 and Kalisz in 1878 Markowski radically extends the chronology of nineteenth-century pogroms in the Kingdom and challenges the dominant conviction that pogroms were the product of modern antisemitism at the end of the nineteenth century. In fact, as Markowski demonstrates, pogroms—at least those in the Kingdom of Poland—were more a form of pre-modern violence of a popular nature, and their chronology was closely linked to the Christian religious calendar rather than to the waves of pogroms of 1881–4, 1903–7, and 1917–21.

REACTIONS

Jews in the Kingdom of Poland—as elsewhere—were not of course passive observers, or mere victims of the crisis at the end of the nineteenth century and the rising tide of antisemitism. One of the Jewish responses was mass emigration, although this was not that widespread within the Kingdom of Poland. In fact, the waves of migration after 1881 led to an increase, not a decrease, in Jewish settlement in the Kingdom. The reasons for this were, first, that the Kingdom had become an attractive area for the Jews of the Russian empire to settle, owing to its relatively privileged political and legal status. This brought large numbers of Russian Jews, known in the Kingdom as Litvaks, to Poland. The true dimensions of Litvak settlement are not known; however, there is no doubt that at the turn of the century they had become a significant and clearly visible social group, often accused of Russifying tendencies, and vigorously combated not only by ethnic Poles, but by the local

Popular Novel in Poland at the Beginning of the 20th Century', *Iggud*, 2 (2009), 59–66; ead., '"Looking for the Jew": The Image of Assimilated Jews in Polish Anti-Semitic Novels at the Turn of the 20th Century', in A. Molisak and S. Ronen (eds.), *Polish and Hebrew Literature and National Identity* (Warsaw, 2010), 129–39.

[92] On the Warsaw pogrom, see Cała, *Asymilacja Żydów w Królestwie Polskim*, 268–78. A recent work on the pogrom in Siedlce is S. Rudnicki, 'Pogrom siedlecki', *Kwartalnik Historii Żydów*, 233 (2010), 18–39.

Jewish population too.[93] Secondly, it appears that emigration among the Jews of the Kingdom of Poland was somewhat weaker than in the case of the Jewish population living in the Pale of Settlement, especially from the north-western provinces.[94] This does, however, require verification, and a comprehensive comparison of the extent, directions, and type of migration, including the overseas emigration of Jews from the Kingdom and other areas of the Empire, remains an unfinished task.

Another Jewish response to the crisis was modern politics, seen especially in the emergence of national Jewish movements whose development was stimulated by modern antisemitism's challenge to integrationist ideology and, even more importantly, by a parallel national and cultural revival experienced by a great many ethnic groups in central and eastern Europe. However, the Zionist movement—somewhat surprisingly—was not especially strong in the Kingdom of Poland. Out of the twelve or thirteen members of the Zionist Organization's executive no more than two were from the Kingdom, while the shekels collected from the Jews of the Kingdom of Poland (financial proof of membership in the organization) represented merely 10 per cent of those raised in the Russian empire, although one in four Jews in the Empire lived in the Kingdom.[95] It does appear that standing in the path of the spread of Zionism in central Poland were both the newly politicized Orthodox communities and the still-significant, though declining, integrationist influence.[96] Despite the image projected by the Zionists, the Jewish community in the Kingdom of Poland was not politically undeveloped, but its involvement in politics in the Kingdom was quite different in nature from that in the Pale of Settlement, where neither hasidic *shtadlanut* (intercession) nor integrationism (together with its political forms) achieved comparable influence. While groups of the proto-Zionist Hibat Tsiyon organization were active from the eighties in Warsaw and Łódź, it appears that their members were for the most part Litvaks, immigrants from the Russian Pale of Settlement. The policy of the Russian authorities forbidding Zionist activities, aggressively enforced in the Kingdom, also contributed to the decrease in the Zionists' influence.

The 1905 revolution transformed this state of affairs. In the words of a witness to

[93] On the Litvaks, see F. Guesnet, 'Migration et stéréotype: Le Cas des Juifs russes au Royaume de Pologne à la fin du XIXe siècle', *Cahiers du monde russe*, 41 / 4 (2000), 505–18; id., *Polnische Juden im 19. Jahrhundert*, 61–4. However, the issue is still poorly understood and requires further study.

[94] See S. Stampfer, 'The Geographic Background of East European Jewish Migration to the United States before World War I', in I. A. Glazier and L. De Rosa (eds.), *Migration across Time and Nations: Population Mobility in Historical Contexts* (New York, 1986), 220–30; see also L. P. Boustan, 'Were Jews Political Refugees or Economic Migrants? Assessing the Persecution Theory of Jewish Emigration, 1881–1914', in T. J. Hatton, K. H. O'Rourke, and A. M. Taylor (eds.), *The New Comparative Economic History: Essays in Honour of Jeffrey G. Williamson* (Cambridge, Mass., 2007), 267–90.

[95] See J. Goldstein, 'The Beginnings of the Zionist Movement in Congress Poland: The Victory of the Hasidim over the Zionists?', *Polin*, 5 (1990), 114–30.

[96] On the political activities of the Orthodox, mainly the hasidim, in the last years of the Kingdom of Poland, see G. C. Bacon, *The Politics of Tradition: Agudat Yisrael in Poland, 1916–1939* (Jerusalem, 1996), 22–46. On political organizations of integrationism and so-called neo-assimilation, see K.

these events, Bernard Singer, 'Between 1905 and 1906, there was a change in the life of my district, which would have been unthinkable even a year before. Lightning struck God-fearing Nalewki.'[97] During the revolutionary period of 1905–7, radical parties—the Polish Socialist Party (Polska Partia Socjalistyczna; PPS), Social Democracy of the Kingdom of Poland and Lithuania (Socjaldemokracja Królestwa Polskiego i Litwy), the General Jewish Labour Union in Lithuania, Poland, and Russia (the Bund), Po'alei Tsiyon, and others—quickly swelled their ranks with numerous Jewish members.[98] Admittedly, detail on the scope of this phenomenon is not available, while recent scholarship suggests that the attempts to assess numerically the Jews' participation in radical parties have been unreliable and misleading.[99] Yet there is no doubt that the 1905 revolution caused a dramatic increase in political commitment by the whole of society in the Kingdom of Poland, including the Jewish community, and greater freedom of speech facilitated political expression. An analysis of the political biography of one of these radical political activists, a co-founder of the most important left-wing Polish party, the PPS, and the author of its platform, Feliks Perl, is presented in this volume by Joshua Zimmerman. Zimmerman's study demonstrates the effects of the penetration of nationalist ideas on the socialist movement, and the growing divisions between the Polish and Jewish workers' movements, which are most clearly expressed in Perl's writings. Of even greater importance, an analysis of Perl's statements shows that even for a fully acculturated member of the Polish—not Jewish—workers' movement who was hostile to the recognition of the Jews as a nation, Jewishness was a key element of identity, and that discussions on the subject of solving the so-called Jewish question still constituted a key reference point. Comparing the biographies of Perl and Bronisław Grosser, one of the leaders of the Bund, Zimmerman also shows that belonging to one of the two sides in the debate between the Bund and the PPS on the subject of the Jewish minority's status and its rights did not follow simple lines. Thus, Zimmerman's thesis corresponds to the newest trends in research into Jewish politicization at the start of the twentieth century, according to which the dramatic increase in Jewish membership of all political organizations, including radical parties, was tied more to a crisis of life in the great metropolises and the crisis in public order than to ideological motivations.[100]

Newer research also emphasizes that the politicization of the Jewish street was

Zieliński, 'Neoasymilacja: Przyczynek do badań nad myślą polityczną Żydów polskich', in id. (ed.), *Wokół akulturacji i asymilacji Żydów na ziemiach polskich*, 69–84.

[97] B. Singer (Regnis), *Moje Nalewki* (Warsaw, 1993), 119.

[98] Among more recent studies, see J. D. Zimmerman, *Poles, Jews, and the Politics of Nationality: The Bund and the Polish Socialist Party in Late Tsarist Russia, 1892–1914* (Madison, 2004). See also the controversial study by P. Śpiewak, *Żydokomuna: Interpretacje historyczne* (Warsaw, 2012).

[99] A good summary of estimates quantifying Jews' participation in communist movements is given in S. Rudnicki, 'Pawła Śpiewaka droga przez mękę: Od "Żydokomuny" do żydokomuny', *Kwartalnik Historii Żydów*, 244 (2012), 603–19.

[100] See S. Ury, *Barricades and Banners: The Revolution of 1905 and the Transformation of Warsaw Jewry* (Stanford, Calif., 2012), 91–140.

part of a more general process of the birth of a modern consciousness among Polish Jews, in which politics was simply one, and not necessarily the most important, form of participation. The new culture created in the Kingdom of Poland both in Yiddish and, to a lesser degree, in Hebrew and in Polish has turned out perhaps to be even more important.[101] The best-known symbol of it is Isaac Leybush Peretz (1852–1915), an outstanding individual in many respects who contributed greatly to the development of a self-aware Jewish culture in its modern form. Peretz, as the Kingdom's first major Yiddish writer, introduced into Yiddish literature in Poland contemporary artistic trends, contesting what he saw as provincialism, and, more powerfully than any writer before him, introduced current political debate into this culture. He assembled around him a circle of followers who would be counted among the most famous writers of the succeeding generation, and through them made an enormous mark on the development of Jewish culture in Poland. His ethnographical interests also contributed to the subject throughout the Polish lands.[102] After 1905, the Yiddish theatre, which had been hobbled by an official ban in 1893 against theatrical performances in Yiddish, also developed splendidly. After the ban was lifted in 1905, Warsaw became the locus of a singularly rich growth of Yiddish theatres, including the popular open-air theatres and unrefined vaudeville of low artistic merit, called *shund*. However, in addition to *shund*, an artistic theatre developed, and the most distinguished individual of the day in Jewish theatre in the Polish lands was Esther Rachel Kamińska (1870–1925), a famous actress and a driving force in Warsaw's theatrical life.[103]

The most important exemplar of the new Jewish culture was the press. New papers in Yiddish—*Yidishes tageblat* (1906–11), *Haynt* (from 1908), and *Der moment* (from 1910)—many times exceeded the print runs of all other Jewish periodicals, and were the dominant daily fare of the Jewish readership in the Kingdom of Poland and beyond. While maskilic journals rarely reached print runs in the thousands, *Yidishes tageblat* shortly after its debut reached 70,000 copies. In her chapter devoted to the beginnings of the Yiddish press in the Kingdom of Poland, Joanna Nalewajko-Kulikov points to the revolutionary changes introduced by the new press. As she shows, many, perhaps most, of the periodicals founded at

---

[101] There is an important study analysing *inter alia* the development of theatres, the press, and public life at the turn of the century in Warsaw in Ury, *Barricades and Banners*, 141–71. Cf. also Polonsky, *Jews in Poland and Russia*, ii. 379–403.

[102] On Peretz, see above all R. R. Wisse, *I. L. Peretz and the Making of Modern Jewish Culture* (Seattle, 1988); see also M. W. Kiel, '*Vox Populi, Vox Dei*: The Centrality of Peretz in Jewish Folkloristics', *Polin*, 7 (1992), 88–120; N. Ross, *Ahuvah usenuah: zehut yehudit modernit ukhetivah neo-ḥasidit befetaḥ hame'ah ha'esrim* (Beer Sheva, 2010); B. Kraut (ed.), *The Enduring Legacy of Yitzchok Leybush Peretz* (New York, 2006).

[103] Of newer work on the theatre, see M. C. Steinlauf, 'Polish-Jewish Theater: The Case of Mark Arnshteyn. A Study of the Interplay among Yiddish, Polish, and Polish-Language Jewish Culture in the Modern Period', Ph.D. thesis (Brandeis Univ., 1988); id., 'Jewish Theatre in Poland', *Polin*, 16 (2003), 71–91; *Teatr żydowski w Polsce do 1939*, special issue of *Pamiętnik Teatralny*, 41 (1992); A. Kuligowska-Korzeniewska and M. Leyko (eds.), *Teatr żydowski w Polsce* (Łódź, 1998).

the time were not guided by any social mission, but by a desire for profit. On the other hand, the possibility of making money publishing a paper demonstrates an enormous and continually growing need for a press in Yiddish and of a more general cultural and social transformation. Revolutionary changes introduced especially by Shmuel Yankev Yatskan's (1874–1936) *Haynt* and Tsevi Prylucki's (1862–1942) *Der moment*, such as printing stories in instalments, aggressive marketing, and tabloid-style content, also radically expanded their readership, which included women and part of the Orthodox community, thus bringing these groups into a continually expanding public sphere. These new developments permanently shaped popular culture, the readership, and the public domain of Jews in the Kingdom of Poland. Nalewajko-Kulikov also points to the significance of the abolition of censorship in 1905 and the revolution as turning points in the history of the Yiddish press, and of the whole public domain in the Kingdom.[104]

THE GREAT WAR

The outbreak of the First World War, the collapse of the tsarist regime, and the eventual Allied victory over Germany and Austria brought the question of Polish independence to the fore. While the rebirth of Poland seemed finally in sight, however, other ethnic nationalities throughout the territories that once comprised the Polish–Lithuanian Commonwealth—above all Lithuanians, Ukrainians, and Belarusians—by this time harboured territorial aspirations of their own. Thus, what was elsewhere a conflict between the Allied and Central powers became a simultaneous, bitter struggle for nationhood on several fronts, with Jews caught as ever in the middle. The next few years were to see the most lethal pogroms to date at the hands of Polish, Ukrainian, and a variety of Russian troops, with death tolls approaching 70,000 or more.[105] Only the territories of the Kingdom of Poland seemed relatively certain to remain Polish (now consisting of a German-ruled General Government in the north and west and an Austrian section in the south-east, these territories were vaguely declared an 'independent' Polish state). This did not, however, do much to ease Polish–Jewish tensions.

The outbreak of war interrupted the rapid development of the spread of the Yiddish press in the Kingdom, as well as just about everything else. The invasion

[104] Among the most recent work on the Yiddish press in the Kingdom of Poland, see Nalewajko-Kulikov, Bąbiak, and Cieślikowa (eds.), *Studia z dziejów trójjęzycznej prasy żydowskiej*; K. Weiser, *Jewish People, Yiddish Nation: Noah Prylucki and the Folkists in Poland* (Toronto, 2011); S. A. Stein, *Making Jews Modern: The Yiddish and Ladino Press in the Russian and Ottoman Empires* (Bloomington, Ind., 2004).

[105] On this period's anti-Jewish violence, see H. Abramson, *A Prayer for the Government: Ukrainians and Jews in Revolutionary Times, 1917–1920* (Cambridge, Mass., 1999); W. Hagen, 'The Moral Economy of Popular Violence: The Pogrom in Lwów', in Blobaum (ed.), *Antisemitism and its Opponents in Modern Poland*, 124–47; Polonsky, *Jews in Poland and Russia*, vol. iii, esp. pp. 32–55.

of the Kingdom of Poland by German and Austrian forces brought widespread material damage and massive resettlement. Admittedly, the German authorities brought about a change in the legal status of Jews; however, the economic situation was very difficult, given that the Russian authorities had shipped a great many factories and just about all the banks and their assets out of the Kingdom. In addition, almost half a million Jews had been expelled to the east for fear that they might co-operate with the advancing Germans. Those who returned often found their houses and places of work plundered and became dependent on public assistance. Masses of refugees both suffered from poverty themselves and worsened the economic situation for the rest of the population. The inhabitants of the Kingdom of Poland, including the Jews, found themselves on the edge of an economic precipice.

Political and social relations between Jews and the rest of Polish society were no better. Jewish attitudes here were decidedly anti-Russian, given the recent tenor of the tsarist government's attitudes towards its Jewish subjects. The replacement of Russian rule by German and Austrian rule was thus greeted with some enthusiasm by Jews, some of whom served in Józef Piłsudski's Polish legions and joined the fight for Polish independence. At the same time, however, right-wing Polish nationalists led by Roman Dmowski held Jews responsible for food shortages and other aspects of the wartime crisis, and called for a boycott of Jewish businesses.

A major irritant was the growth of national aspirations on both sides. The activities of the citizens' committees, which during the period of preparations for the evacuation of Russians from the Kingdom took over the civilian administration, were a prime source of conflict. Although formally responsible for the whole population of the Kingdom, these committees often ignored the needs of the Jewish community and did not admit its representatives as members. This evoked a wave of suspicion, mistrust, and protests from the Jewish side, whose representatives charged that the Poles had not shown themselves to be capable of home rule and thus capable of running the country in the future. This conflict also had repercussions beyond the borders of the Polish lands, escalating tensions between representatives of the Polish and Jewish communities abroad. Furthermore, neither side spoke with one voice. On the Polish side, in addition to the conciliatory Central Citizens' Committee (Centralny Komitet Obywatelski) there was the antisemitic press dominated by the ND, whose aim was to strengthen its own political position rather than resolve the conflict. On the Jewish side, in addition to the conciliatory board of the Warsaw Jewish community, representatives of the German and Russian Jewish communities fought for their own respective interests, which were often at variance with the aims of the local Jewish population. The German Committee for Eastern Affairs (Komitee für den Osten), averse to the notion of an independent Polish state, also deeply complicated matters. The growing conflict hindered agreement even between the most conciliatory communities on both sides and poisoned relationships far beyond circles of competing politicians. The conflict moved to the street, and the anti-Jewish boycott spontaneously revived.

Relations between the Polish and Jewish communities improved only temporarily after the German occupation of the Kingdom. During the first elections to the Warsaw city council in 1916, despite the protests of radical political groups on both sides (especially the ND on the Polish side, and the Folkists on the Jewish side), an agreement was reached between the Polish and Jewish electoral commissions leading to the creation of a joint electoral list. The Central Powers' worsening material position meant that conflicts of an economic nature once again began to divide the Polish and Jewish communities. The crisis on all the sides of the armed conflict towards the end of the war only stiffened the positions of Polish and Jewish politicians, who proved unwilling to make any concessions. The Regency Council (Rada Regencyjna) and the Provisional Council of State (Tymczasowa Rada Stanu) formed in Warsaw refused to deal with Jewish national rights and consistently defined this community as a religious minority. On the other hand, the Jewish nationalist parties—the Folkists, the Zionists, and the Bund—antagonized Polish public opinion by waging aggressive propaganda campaigns and increasingly involving international public opinion. None of the key conflicts between the Polish and Jewish communities was solved, and tension and suspicion grew.

Our state of knowledge on the situation of Jews in the Kingdom of Poland during the First World War appears very good, especially when compared with a great many other poorly understood chapters of the history of the long nineteenth century. Polish–Jewish relations, and the growing Polish–Jewish conflict in the context of the policies of the occupation authorities, initially Russian, then German and Austro-Hungarian, have received extensive treatment.[106] An illustration of this good state of knowledge are two chapters devoted to this issue in our volume. Marcos Silber's study discusses disagreements on the status of the Yiddish language and the Jewish minority's language rights in the Kingdom. Analysing the case of language policies in Łódź and Warsaw, Silber demonstrates that they were a key tool in the German occupation authorities' colonization policies. The German authorities, he shows, used the Yiddish language as a tool to neutralize Polish demands for independence. The status of Yiddish changed, however, after the creation of the Provisional Council of State. As Silber claims, invoking the theoretical models of Miroslav Hroch and Pierre Bourdieu, the Polish political elite saw in the Jews, much more than in the Lithuanian, Belarusian, and Ukrainian rural populations, dangerous rivals in the struggle for dominance in the new governmental structures, and thus rejected all demands for the use of Yiddish in schools, as well as

---

[106] Of the most recent works, see F. Schuster, *Zwischen allen Fronten: Osteuropäische Juden während des Ersten Weltkrieges, 1914–1918* (Cologne, 2004); K. Zieliński, *Stosunki polsko-żydowskie na ziemiach Królestwa Polskiego w czasie pierwszej wojny światowej* (Lublin, 2005); id., *Żydzi lubelszczyzny, 1914–1918* (Lublin, 1999); id., *W cieniu synagogi: Obraz życia kulturalnego społeczności żydowskiej Lublina w latach okupacji austro-węgierskiej* (Lublin 1998); P. Wróbel, 'Przed odzyskaniem niepodległości', in J. Tomaszewski (ed.), *Najnowsze dzieje Żydów w Polsce w zarysie (do 1950 roku)* (Warsaw, 1993), 104–39. See also M. Sobczak, *Stosunek Narodowej Demokracji do kwestii żydowskiej w latach 1914–1919* (Wrocław, 2008); E. Zechlin, *Die deutsche Politik und die Juden im Ersten Weltkrieg* (Göttingen, 1969).

any official status for the language. Paradoxically, the Jewish population's comparatively advantageous circumstances, with its relatively good social position (as an urban population), as well as its good economic situation (as a population concentrated in commerce and industry), proved to be the very cause of its unfavourable political situation in the new Polish state vis-à-vis Polish social classes, who felt keenly threatened.

While the war did bring a definitive end to the Kingdom of Poland, the reborn Polish Republic inherited all its conflicts and problems in Polish–Jewish relations in an enhanced form. Much may be ascribed to unintended consequences. The German authorities' commitment to equal rights for Jews by the end of 1916, for example, was praiseworthy. However, these benign promises compelled the Allies to respond, and the Polish question thus became intimately tied to the Jewish question. Jewish lobbyists such as Lucien Wolf and Louis Marshall were able to see to it that Poland's minorities, including the Jews, received guarantees of their civil rights and (more controversially) cultural autonomy as part of any Allied initiative for Polish statehood. Poland was to be reborn with a Minority Treaty clutching its ankle.[107]

The problems and tensions accompanying the Minority Treaty are discussed here by Szymon Rudnicki. In describing the attitudes of various groups in the Jewish community towards Polish projects for regaining independence during the First World War and its aftermath, Rudnicki presents a generally positive attitude on the part of almost every Jewish party to the idea of Polish independence. However, that support for Polish independence did not mean withdrawing from the battle over the future state's shape, including national, cultural, or linguistic autonomy for the Jewish population. In Rudnicki's view, the factor that specifically antagonized the Polish and Jewish political elites was the internationalization of the issue of minority rights that compelled Poland to sign the Minority Treaty of Versailles, perceived by the Poles as a Jewish plot. Paradoxically, too, the greatest diplomatic success of the Zionists, who were seriously engaged in imposing the Minority Treaty on the countries of eastern Europe, poisoned relations between Polish and Jewish politicians in inter-war Poland and beyond. Both Marcos Silber's and Szymon Rudnicki's contributions thus show clearly that the end of the First World War did not bring a solution to any of the conflicts between the Polish and Jewish communities, and even inflamed some of them.

CONCLUSION

The Jewish experience in the Kingdom of Poland may be said to have paralleled the Jewish experience in other parts of partitioned Poland, but in a more intensified

---

[107] Polonsky, *Jews in Poland and Russia*, iii. 11–32. Cultural autonomy included the right to Yiddish language institutions, including state-funded Yiddish schools, with funds allocated at the discretion of local Jewish leaders.

way. This may have been the consequence of the Kingdom's atmosphere: a higher level of industrialization, a greater degree of Polish autonomy, a more fervently activist Polish patriotic movement, and a larger concentration of Jews. The latter were sometimes able to benefit from the Kingdom's anomalous status, which made it a kind of laboratory for liberal experiments, such as the liberalizing decrees of 1862. However, the Jews of the Kingdom were also to feel more pressured to support the Polish cause for independence, thereby inviting tsarist reprisals against those Jews who did participate and bitter recriminations against those who did not. To add to the pressure, the Kingdom's Jewish population was periodically the target of state experiments in social engineering, which resulted in debilitating restrictions with few tangible gains.

Notwithstanding such pressures, Jewish cultural and eventually political movements did flourish in the Kingdom. Hasidism was given an unusual degree of latitude, and several of its *tsadikim* defied the logic of modernization by creating vital courts near major urban centres such as Warsaw and Łódź and houses of prayer (*shtiblekh*) within them, all the while producing some of the movement's freshest and most innovative homiletic literature down to the First World War and beyond. Maskilim, for their part, were employed as government officials to a greater degree than elsewhere, and were given the opportunity to establish several educational institutions and periodicals and to influence the course of the development of the Jewish community in the Kingdom. Their immediate successors, the Jewish integrationists, managed to gain considerable power within the Jewish community and to create a vibrant Polish Jewish culture, which continued to influence the Jewish community in Poland until the end of the inter-war period. Proponents of these older movements were increasingly joined by advocates of Zionism, Jewish socialism, and cultural autonomy towards the end of the nineteenth century. The relative strength of each movement on the eve of the rebirth of Poland is extremely difficult to measure. But the ferment of so many potent, competing movements undoubtedly helps to explain the disproportionate influence of the relatively small Kingdom of Poland on the modern Jewish experience.

Jews in the Discourses of the Polish Enlightenment

RICHARD BUTTERWICK-PAWLIKOWSKI

THE OLD-FASHIONED TERM 'genealogy' has gained in popularity among historians, as it conveys a sense of where things came from, without the teleology implied by 'origins', 'roots', or 'genesis'. From common ancestors come diverse descendants.[1] The varieties of antisemitism experienced in the Polish–Lithuanian lands and encountered in Polish discourses since the later nineteenth century derive some, but by no means all, of their genetic code, as it were, from discourses about Jews in the later eighteenth century. However, the intellectual and cultural formation known as the Polish Enlightenment scattered many seeds, not all of which came to fruition, but which included the potential for philosemitism as well as antisemitism. The discourses in question are found in a range of sources, including treatises, pamphlets, correspondence, projects for legislation, and resolutions and instructions passed by the local assemblies of the Polish–Lithuanian nobility—the *sejmiki*. I focus in particular on the period of the Four Year Sejm. The 'Polish Revolution' of 1788–92 precipitated unprecedented debate on political, fiscal, economic, social, cultural, and religious affairs in the Polish–Lithuanian Commonwealth. Many of these strands had relevance for the Commonwealth's Jews, even if Jews were only rarely the principal objects of polemical exchanges.[2]

*

Earlier versions of this chapter were presented to the seminar run by Professor Susanne Marten-Finnis at the University of Portsmouth in 2008 and the annual conference of the Institute for Polish–Jewish Studies at the Polish Embassy in London in 2009. It draws on my monograph *Polska rewolucja a Kościół katolicki, 1788–1792* (Kraków, 2012), of which a shorter and more tightly focused version has been published as *The Polish Revolution and the Catholic Church, 1788–1792: A Political History* (Oxford, 2012). I am particularly grateful to Professor Antony Polonsky for his comments and encouragement, as well as for allowing me to read the first six chapters of his *The Jews in Poland and Russia*, i: *1350–1881* (Oxford, 2010) before its publication.

[1] A prominent example of this usage is G. D. Hundert, *Jews in Poland–Lithuania in the Eighteenth Century: A Genealogy of Modernity* (Berkeley and Los Angeles, 2004).

[2] See especially J. Lukowski, *Disorderly Liberty: The Political Culture of the Polish–Lithuanian Commonwealth in the Eighteenth Century* (London, 2010), chs. 9–11.

The first half of the eighteenth century saw the apogee of harassment by the Roman Catholic Church of the Commonwealth's Jews, 'heretics', and 'schismatics'.[3] This trajectory is only partly explained by reaction to the traumatic wars of 1648–1721, and still less so in the case of Jews, who were fellow victims rather than foes. It needs to be seen in the context of a revival of interest, beginning towards the end of the seventeenth century, in implementing the reforms of the Council of Trent. For example, the last diocesan synod held in the pre-partition diocese of Wilno, called by Bishop Michał Zienkowicz in 1744, passed resolutions hostile to Jews and Protestants in the context of regulations aiming at tighter discipline and higher pastoral standards among the clergy. This synod also increased the degree of episcopal control over exorcisms and the trial of suspected witches.[4] This fits into a wider picture. The post-Tridentine renewal of the Church was a very long-term process across Catholic Europe. In its later stages, it shaded almost imperceptibly into what has been called 'Enlightened Reform Catholicism'.[5]

Politics continued to absorb most bishops, but many paid greater attention to administering their dioceses. These men were well educated. Post-Tridentine Catholicism even began to acquire an 'enlightened' sheen by the 1740s, guided by the courteous and scholarly Benedict XIV. But Pope Benedict also issued edicts against Freemasons and, at the request of the Polish episcopate, an encyclical repeating centuries-old prohibitions against Christians mixing with, and serving, Jews.[6]

Several bishops attempted to ensure that Jewish worship and social and business

---

[3] See, among others, M. Teter, *Jews and Heretics in Catholic Poland: A Beleaguered Church in the Post-Reformation Era* (Cambridge, 2006); W. Kriegseisen, *Ewangelicy polscy i litewscy w epoce saskiej (1696–1763): Sytuacja prawna, organizacja i stosunki międzywyznaniowe* (Warsaw, 1996); id., 'Between Intolerance and Persecution: Polish and Lithuanian Protestants in the 18th Century', *Acta Poloniae Historica*, 73 (1996), 13–27; B. Skinner, *The Western Front of the Eastern Church: Uniate and Orthodox Conflict in Eighteenth-Century Poland, Ukraine, Belarus, and Russia* (DeKalb, Ill., 2009).

[4] J. Kurczewski, *Biskupstwo wileńskie od jego założenia aż do dni obecnych, zawierające dzieje i prace biskupów i duchowieństwa djecezji wileńskiej, oraz wykaz kościołów, klasztorów, szkół i zakładów dobroczynnych i społecznych* (Vilna, 1912), 137–40.

[5] See, among others, N. Aston, *Christianity and Revolutionary Europe, c.1750–1830* (Cambridge, 2002), 14–15, 41, 57–61, 77–82, 111–12; O. Chadwick, *The Popes and European Revolution* (Oxford, 1981), 193, 198–203, 391–5; P. Hersche, 'Der österreichische Spätjansenismus: Neue Thesen und Fragestellungen', in E. Kovács (ed.), *Katholische Aufklärung und Josephinismus* (Vienna, 1979), 180–96.

[6] See J. Dygdała, 'Episkopat rzymsko-katolicki doby saskiej: Aktywność w życiu publicznym Rzeczypospolitej', in A. Sucheni-Grabowska and M. Żaryn (eds.), *Między monarchą a demokracją: Studia z dziejów Polski XV–XVIII wieku* (Warsaw, 1994), 332–76; id., 'U początków katolickiego oświecenia w Polsce? Z działalności kościelnej biskupów Andrzeja Stanisława Załuskiego i Adama Stanisława Grabowskiego', in K. Stasiewicz and S. Achremczyk (eds.), *Między barokiem a oświeceniem: Nowe spojrzenie na czasy saskie* (Olsztyn, 1996), 181–7; Chadwick, *Popes and European Revolution*, 17, 30, 32, 111, 138, 166, 173–4, 184, 238, 295–8, 316, 398–401, 557; M. Rosa, 'The Catholic *Aufklärung* in Italy', in U. L. Lehner and M. Printy (eds.), *A Companion to the Catholic Enlightenment in Europe* (Leiden, 2010), 224–9. Benedict XIV's encyclical *A Quo Primum* (1751) is discussed by Teter, *Jews and Heretics in Catholic Poland*, 89–90.

contacts between Jews and Christians did not lead to the 'corruption' or even 'apostasy' of the latter, and that Jews knew their subordinate place. This was of great theological import, for it was held that the Jews, having failed to recognize the Messiah, still bore 'blind' witness to the Old Testament in their accursed exile, and that their conversion would be part of the Apocalypse. They were commanded, for example, to seek permission to repair their synagogues, to stay indoors on major Christian feasts, and to wear distinctive clothing.[7]

Such repressions had a more sinister impact when episcopal objectives found common ground with popular myths. In Żytomierz in 1753, the coadjutor/bishop of Kiev, Kajetan Sołtyk, initiated the trial of thirty-three Jews for alleged ritual murder. Following confessions obtained by torture, thirteen were sentenced to torments and death. Two abjured their religion and were spared at his request; five who only did so at the last minute were beheaded, and then solemnly buried by him in the Catholic cemetery. Sołtyk gave the affair wide publicity. His motives may have been partly pecuniary, as he was said to have threatened other Jews with similar trials in order to extort money.[8] Even the learned Andrzej Załuski (whom Sołtyk would later succeed as bishop of Kraków) denounced Jews as a 'species of lizard' in a pastoral letter of 1751. They committed, he claimed, endless blasphemies, sacrileges, treacheries, deceits, thefts, seductions, and adulteries on the Catholics they inebriated, as well as murders, attested by 'public echo and a strong presumption, and still more frequent and recent examples, [of] innocent Christian children for their superstitions'. If this was the conviction of one of the most enlightened bishops of his time (who banned exorcisms without written episcopal approval, and for whom the word 'superstition' was especially pejorative), then the extent of belief in the blood libel among the clergy and laity may be imagined.[9]

Admittedly, economic forces often frustrated episcopal wishes to exclude Jews from positions of authority over Christians. The exhortations of Cardinal Jan Lipski failed to persuade the Kraków cathedral chapter to remove Jews from leases on the chapter's properties.[10] Nevertheless, even the most powerful magnates hesitated before defying a bishop in defence of 'their' Jews. As Adam Kaźmierczyk has observed, one reason for the denser settlement of Jews in the private towns

[7] Teter, *Jews and Heretics in Catholic Poland*, passim; Hundert, *Jews in Poland–Lithuania*, ch. 3; A. Kaźmierczyk, 'Polscy biskupi wobec Żydów w XVIII wieku', in A. Kaźmierczyk et al. (eds.), *Rzeczpospolita wielu wyznań* (Kraków, 2004), 349–56.

[8] M. Czeppe, 'Sołtyk, Kajetan Ignacy', in *Polski słownik biograficzny*, xl (Kraków and Warsaw, 2001), 387, 390. Cf. K. Rudnicki, *Biskup Kajetan Sołtyk, 1715–1788* (Kraków and Warsaw, 1906), 15–18; Z. Guldon and J. Wijaczka, *Procesy o mordy rytualne w Polsce w XVI–XVIII wieku* (Kielce, 1995), 60–4.

[9] Quoted after Kaźmierczyk, 'Polscy biskupi wobec Żydów', 355. Cf. B. Kumor, *Dzieje diecezji krakowskiej*, iv (Kraków, 2002), 622. See Guldon and Wijaczka, *Procesy o mordy rytualne w Polsce*, passim; eid., 'The Accusation of Ritual Murder in Poland, 1500–1800', *Polin*, 10 (1997), 99–140.

[10] Teter, *Jews and Heretics in Catholic Poland*, 85.

of the eastern reaches of the Commonwealth may have been the weaker influence of the Latin-rite clergy there.[11]

The restrictions and permissions imposed by bishops anxious to retain a proper theocratic hierarchy irked Jews. So did the bouts of trying to convert them to Christianity. Although the cause of conversion was not helped by Judaeophobic rhetoric, many among the Catholic clergy took it seriously.[12] The Mariavite nuns were founded by the charismatic Father Szczepan Turczynowicz in the diocese of Wilno in 1737 to educate and care for converted Jewish (and Karaite and Tatar) girls, and to integrate them into Christian society. The congregation was confirmed by Bishop Zienkowicz in 1744, and noted by Benedict XIV in 1752. They soon had eighteen houses, and their own converts began to swell the ranks of the sisters.[13] Some evangelists were legendary. One Dominican, Wawrzyniec Owłoczyński, who died in 1763, was said to have convinced sixty-six Jews that Jesus of Nazareth was their true Messiah.[14] The tireless Franciszek Kobielski, bishop of Łuck, ordered Jews to attend a weekly sermon by a Catholic priest, delivered in their synagogue.[15]

However, after about 1760, episcopal attitudes towards the Jews grew significantly milder. A report written by Cardinal Lorenzo Ganganelli, the future Pope Clement XIV, condemning belief in the ritual murder of Christian children by Jews, helped to end such trials.[16] In 1775, a court of the Sejm confederacy, presided over by the bishop of Poznań and grand chancellor of the Crown, Andrzej Młodziejowski, found thirty Jews not guilty of the ritual murder of a 3-year-old girl from the Mazovian village of Grabie, because their (mutually contradictory) confessions had been obtained by torture.[17]

Episcopal permission to build synagogues and schools became easier to obtain.

---

[11] A. Kaźmierczyk, *Żydzi w dobrach prywatnych w świetle sądowniczej i administracyjnej praktyki dóbr magnackich w wiekach XVI–XVIII* (Kraków, 2002), 170–5.

[12] See J. Goldberg, 'Żydowscy konwertyci w społeczeństwie staropolskim', in A. Izydorczyk and A. Wyczański (eds.), *Społeczeństwo staropolskie: Studia i szkice*, iv (Warsaw, 1986), 195–214, 226; M. Teter, 'Jewish Conversions to Catholicism in the Polish–Lithuanian Commonwealth of the Seventeenth and Eighteenth Centuries', *Jewish History*, 17/3 (2003), 257–83.

[13] M. Borkowska, 'Dzieje zgromadzenia *Mariae Vitae* czyli mariawitek', *Nasza Przeszłość*, 93 (2000), 107–52; ead., *Zakony żeńskie w Polsce w epoce nowożytnej* (Lublin, 2010), 118, 218–21, 348–55.

[14] K. Górski, *Zarys dziejów duchowości w Polsce* (Kraków, 1986), 260. If this was considered notably high, conversions were hard to come by. According to statistics from 1718–55 (cited by Teter, 'Jewish Conversions to Catholicism', 259–61), the number of Jews converted by the Jesuits (usually 20–30 a year) was significantly less than than the number of Lutherans and Orthodox, although more than the number of Calvinists—who were much less numerous than Jews in the eighteenth-century Commonwealth.

[15] On Kobielski's activities, see G. D. Hundert, 'Identity Formation in the Polish–Lithuanian Commonwealth', in K. Friedrich and B. M. Pendzich (eds.), *Citizenship and Identity in a Multinational Commonwealth: Poland–Lithuania in Context, 1550–1772* (Leiden, 2009), 131–47.

[16] Guldon and Wijaczka, *Procesy o mordy rytualne w Polsce*, 95.

[17] S. Waltoś, 'L'Abolition de la torture et des procès contre les sorcières en Pologne', *Archiwum Iuridicum Cracoviense*, 11 (1978), 109–11.

Zienkowicz's successor as bishop of Wilno, Ignacy Massalski, rarely refused such requests. He would, however, generally attach caveats, such as those stating that the synagogue should not resemble a church, be located next to it, or exceed one in size. Funeral processions should be discreet. He also gave permission for Jews to settle in ecclesiastical towns, where they were not already present. Michał Poniatowski, the king's brother, took a similar line in the diocese of Płock, and later in the dioceses of Kraków and Gniezno.[18] In the diocese of Kujawy in 1783, the Jews of Izbica were permitted to build a synagogue provided its dimensions were appropriate to their number, that it was located thirty paces beyond the town, and that an annual quota was payable to the parish church. Moreover, the Jews were expected to live harmoniously and 'honestly' with the Christians of the town.[19]

The phenomenon of Jewish conversions to Catholicism underwent a significant change. The research undertaken to date seems to indicate that the mass conversion by followers of Jakub Frank in 1759 contributed significantly to a lasting reluctance among the Commonwealth's increasingly enlightened ecclesiastical elite to prioritize conversions. On the other hand, the accelerated growth of towns and commerce in the late eighteenth century and the particularly rapid increase in the Jewish urban population gave rise to social and economic conditions that encouraged Jews in desperate personal straits to seek baptism. The resources required to help these neophytes to adjust to their new lives and discourage their return to Judaism were considerable. As most bishops distanced themselves from the cause of conversion, some of the religious orders stepped in.[20]

Massalski tried—with mixed results—to suppress the Mariavites in 1773, apparently in response to Jewish complaints, although it should also be stressed that the congregation consisted of just sixty sisters and very few material resources.[21] The bishop of Wilno evidently thought conversions not worth the trouble they involved, such as furious protests from relatives. In 1787 he wrote to the parish priest of Troki:

---

[18] T. Kasabuła, *Ignacy Massalski, biskup wileński* (Lublin, 1998), 477–84; M. Grzybowski, 'Kościelna działalność Michała Jerzego Poniatowskiego biskupa płockiego', *Studia z Historii Kościoła w Polsce*, 7 (1983), 46, 154.

[19] J. Wysocki, *Józef Ignacy Rybiński, biskup włocławski i pomorski, 1777–1806: Zarys biograficzny na tle rządów diecezją* (Rome, 1967), 230–1.

[20] P. Zarubin, 'Zjawisko konwersji w stanisławowskim Krakowie', in A. Jagodzińska (ed.), *W poszukiwaniu religii doskonałej? Konwersja a Żydzi* (Wrocław, 2012), 49–53, 59–66, 70–4, 76–7. On Frank and Frankism, see P. Maciejko, *The Mixed Multitude: Jacob Frank and the Frankist Movement, 1755–1816* (Philadelphia, 2011).

[21] Goldberg, 'Żydowscy konwertyci w społeczeństwie staropolskim', 212–13. Seven of the eight houses located beyond the pre-partition boundary of the Commonwealth survived, as well as four of those remaining in Poland–Lithuania, following a dramatic journey to Rome by the order's visitor. The Holy See refused to recognize the suppression. In 1788, Massalski finally gave permission to the congregation to renew its activity within his diocese (with a greater emphasis on work in hospitals). Borkowska, 'Dzieje zgromadzenia *Mariae Vitae*', 124–33; ead., *Zakony żeńskie*, 348–55.

There is very little to be gained from these neophytes, and for the most part we see in them idlers unwilling to work, and occupying themselves with roguery . . . Such eagerness is the result of misunderstood zeal, which, in imprudently increasing the number of sons of the Mother Church, also increases, as experience teaches, the ranks of those unworthy of her womb.[22]

Conversions, usually by young and indigent persons, were a disorienting, even traumatic process, and many were unable to adjust to the excommunication imposed on them by their own communities. Fear of violent reprisals was not unknown. In 1783, Massalski ordered that all Jews (and Muslims) wishing to be baptized had to be examined on their knowledge of the Catholic faith and their motivations by the parish priest or auditor, acting on express episcopal authority. Sometimes these examinations would take place in the presence of representatives of the Jewish community. Fourteen standard questions were to be asked. Following Benedict XIV, several bishops issued clear instructions forbidding the baptism of Jewish children against the wishes of their parents.[23]

In an incident from 1791, the Jews of Opatów alleged that a Jewish woman from Sandomierz, engaged to another Jew of the town, had been violently abducted and placed in a convent by soldiers. The suffragan bishop of Sandomierz in the diocese of Kraków, Wojciech Radoszewski, investigated the incident, and heard testimony that she had felt a vocation for a year, and wished to become a nun. At her examination by, among others, 'two respectable priests', the woman said that she felt a strong desire to accept the Catholic faith, and to live and die in it. She said this to the Jews at the convent gate and was baptized. Her engagement gifts were to be sorted out by the courts. Admittedly, the testimony cited is that of the suffragan bishop. But he did claim to have observed all the procedures in order to make sure the conversion was genuine. He does not seem to have been a zealous proselytizer.[24]

The diminishing scale of episcopal objectives can be gauged from their negotiations with the Sejm in 1790: in the course of a complaint against disruption of the Christian sabbath, the bishops objected to taverns opening and Christians serving Jews on Sundays and holy days. But they did not raise the question of Christians serving Jews as a general point of principle.[25]

Bishops had not entirely shed their prejudices. During debates on clerical taxation in 1789, the historian, poet, and bishop Adam Naruszewicz exclaimed: 'Is our clerical estate such an erroneous, arbitrary, and merely tolerated estate? So that arbitrary tributes should be thrown on us, as on Jews, in whose lewd company we

[22] Quoted after Kasabuła, *Ignacy Massalski*, 484.

[23] Ibid. 484–91. See, in general, Goldberg, 'Żydowscy konwertyci w społeczeństwie staropolskim', 218–29.

[24] Wojciech Radoszewski to Ignacy Potocki, Sandomierz, 6 Dec. 1791: Archiwum Główne Akt Dawnych, Warsaw (hereafter AGAD), Archiwum Publiczne Potockich, 279b, vol. vi, pp. 459–60.

[25] 'Przełożenia Collegii Episcoporum Prześwietney Deputacyi, do traktowania z niemi w Interessach Duchownych wyznaczoney podane': Archiwum Archidiecezji Gnieźnieńskiej, Gniezno, Archivum Capituli, B84, fos. 92–3.

have been insultingly reckoned, or on Gypsies, or on some other despicable mob?' He used the derogatory forms *żydy* and *cygany*, rather than the correct *Żydzi* and *Cyganie*.[26] His colleague Kacper Cieciszowski, a paragon of gentleness and holiness, asked why ministers of the dominant religion were singled out for worse treatment than dissidents, 'and even the infidel Jews themselves?'[27] The same point was made by a Reformed Franciscan friar, Karol Surowiecki, in a polemical exchange in print: 'We tax them almost triple; we strip them as if they were Jews, and excepting the appearances of politeness and respect, as regards civil existence, we put them almost in the same rank as Jews, because we decide about them without them, as sovereigns, and when it pleases us we oppress them, and extort from them.'[28]

By the later eighteenth century, Jews were generally regarded by better-educated Christians, from the clergy and laity alike, as a socio-economic, not a religious problem. Above all, they were blamed for mass alcoholism among the enserfed peasantry. The alcohol monopoly, the *propinacja*, was probably the most morally and physically corrupting factor affecting the relationship between lord and peasant. Lords distilled vodka from surplus grain, and sold it to the peasants. In some years this could account for a third or a half of the revenues of magnates' latifundia. Peasants were obliged to buy—and therefore consume—fixed amounts of beer and vodka in the lords' taverns. Other items and commodities could also be obtained there, as could credit. Peasant resentments were borne by the tavern-keeper and usurer, who was traditionally a Jew.[29]

Clergymen also blamed the indifference of lords. For example, in 1784 the parish of Kowarsk (Kavarskas) in the diocese of Wilno contained four Catholic-run taverns (including the parish priest's own) and eight Jewish ones, not to mention fifteen Jews who illegally sold alcohol 'on the side'. These points of sale, we read in the visitation records, led the 'simple folk' (*prostota*) to 'every kind of drunkenness, theft, Jewish superstition, and the neglect of every Divine and Church command-ment'. The parish priest asked for the bishop's advice on how to prevent such opportunities, 'because the lords do not listen to the Word of God, although they know the damage to their own interests'.[30] We may also note residual fears of the Judaization of the (not so) faithful.

If we are to believe the bishop of Livonia, Józef Kazimierz Kossakowski, some

[26] *Głos Adama Naruszewicza, biskupa smoleńskiego, za duchowieństwem na sessyi seymowej roku 1789 dnia 16 marca* (n.p., n.d.).

[27] *Mowa jaśnie wielmożnego jmci Xiędza Cieciszowskiego, biskupa kijowskiego, miana na sessyi seymowey dnia 16 marca r. 1789* (n.p., n.d.).

[28] [Karol Surowiecki], *Gandżara prawdy niecnotliwego cygana chłoszcząca, czyli na paszkwil pod tytułem cygan cnotliwy gandżarą prawdy nie chłoszczący odpowiedź, dedykowana temuż cyganowi przez autora U.N.P.P.S.* (Warsaw, 1792), 76–7.

[29] See J. Lukowski, *Liberty's Folly: The Polish–Lithuanian Commonwealth in the Eighteenth Century, 1697–1795* (London, 1991), 29–30, 47–8.

[30] *Ukmergės dekanato vizitacija 1784 m.*, ed. S. Jegelevičius (Vilnius, 2009), 42.

clergymen were their own worst enemies in this regard. Among the anti-heroes of his novel *Xiądz pleban* ('The Parish Priest') we find a choleric preacher of fire and brimstone, who publicly thrashed his parishioners for 'drinking with foreign Jews ... the enemies of Christ, wizards and blasphemers, despite the parish priest's own tavern, in which the drinks, although dearer, in smaller measures, and not so good, were at least free of all suspicion'.[31] In this case the residual Judaeophobia is among the objects of satire.

Be that as it may, growing criticism of Jewish tavern-keepers for inebriating the peasantry did seem to have had an effect, especially in the areas touched by the massive Cossack and peasant revolt of 1768, known as the Koliyivshchyna: it appears that more than half of the taverns and inns in Polish Ukraine were transferred from Jewish to Christian leaseholders between 1778 and 1784.[32] The rebellion scare of 1789[33] spurred further calls to deprive Jews of taverns and inns.

Discussions of the condition of the Commonwealth's Jews were especially abundant during the Four Year Sejm, or the Polish Revolution, of 1788–92. When many burning political and social questions were discussed, it was not surprising that enlightened minds turned also to what appeared to be the disordered and anomalous state of Jewish affairs. I shall focus first on three prominent political thinkers.[34]

At the time, the most important of this trio was Hugo Kołłątaj, a politically ambitious clergyman with an unorthodox personal theology which leaned towards deism, although it acknowledged an active Divine Providence. The subject of Jews was given a separate chapter in his *Prawo polityczne narodu polskiego* ('Political Law of the Polish Nation'), published at the end of 1789, reflecting their status as a social as well as a religious group. It was a separateness which Kołłątaj wished to end as soon as possible. Although toleration for all non-Christians had been assured, he wrote, the Jews were too numerous, and were like a privileged estate, insufficiently subject to governmental authority. They should therefore be ordered to shave their beards and dress as Christians did. Jewish courts would be reduced and subjected to supervision by local government, and in cases of appeal would be subordinated to the central ecclesiastical commission he wished to establish. Kołłątaj particularly wanted to eradicate rabbinical excommunications. All official documents and court proceedings were to be in Polish, and nobody could become a rabbi or other minister of religion without a certificate of proficiency in Polish and Latin from the

---

[31] [Józef Kazimierz Kossakowski], *Xiądz pleban* (Warsaw, 1786), 33.

[32] D. Stone, *The Polish–Lithuanian State, 1386–1795* (Seattle, 2001), 304. On the Koliyivshchyna, see B. Skinner, 'Borderlands of Faith: Reconsidering the Origins of a Ukrainian Tragedy', *Slavic Review*, 64/1 (2005), 88–116.

[33] On this panic, see R. Butterwick, 'Deconfessionalization? The Policy of the Polish Revolution towards Ruthenia, 1788–1792', *Central Europe*, 6/2 (2008), 102–6.

[34] They are discussed by, amongst others, A. Eisenbach, *Emancypacja Żydów na ziemiach polskich 1785–1870 na tle europejskim* (Warsaw, 1988), 82–4, 88–9, 106–10; Polonsky, *Jews in Poland and Russia*, i. 200–2.

Commission for National Education (Komisja Edukacji Narodowej). Four years would be allowed to implement the law. All *kahal*s would be abolished, and local government would supervise a modest tax to maintain Jewish ministers, until the *kahals'* debts were paid off. No further debts would be permitted. Jews would be banned from brewing, distilling, and selling alcohol, within a year of the law's passage. Other trades and occupations would be open to them, subject to the towns' privileges, and Kołłątaj did not wish them to be coerced into any particular occupation. However, within a year, no vagrancy would be tolerated, and alms could only be given to the old and infirm. This far-reaching programme of assimilation for the hundreds of thousands of the Commonwealth's Jews was certainly ambitious.[35]

Comments on Jews by Stanisław Staszic, a burgher who had unwillingly taken lower orders to please his mother, exceeded Kołłątaj's in their hostility. In his *Przestrogi dla Polski* ('Warnings for Poland') of 1790, he compared Jews to a plague of locusts—economically and morally disastrous for burghers and peasants alike. But the measures he proposed were similar: a ban on their selling alcohol, their subjection to the urban authorities, and the supervision of their schools by the Commission for National Education. He was under the mistaken impression that Jews conducted religious rites not in Hebrew, which he thought they had forgotten, but in 'corrupted German'. They should learn Polish forthwith.[36]

Józef Pawlikowski, a layman whose ancestors had gone from being nobles to burghers, was more sensitive to Jewish cultural and religious distinctiveness, and was well aware of the poverty in which most Jews lived. He wanted their 'civilizing' (*ucywilizowanie*), but he refused to countenance coercive methods. The one breach he was prepared to make in their 'natural liberty' was a temporary bar on them leasing taverns, in order to break their economic dependence on inebriating the peasantry. But they would equally temporarily be freed from recruitment into the army. Otherwise, he looked to reformed schooling in the Polish language to make Jews into 'Poles'—without interfering in their 'religion', in which he comprehended not only theology, worship, and prayer, but also sumptuary and dietary requirements. The tone was that of a passionate but well-informed and practical campaigner against injustice. Peasant, burgher, Jew, and clergyman: all were vulnerable to the licence of the nobility.[37]

Pawlikowski's tone was unusual among Christian burghers. The anonymous

---

[35] H. Kołłątaj, *Listy Anonima i Prawo polityczne narodu polskiego*, ed. B. Leśnodorski and H. Wereszycka, 2 vols. (Warsaw, 1954), ii. 328–33.

[36] S. Staszic, *Przestrogi dla Polski*, in id., *Pisma filozoficzne i społeczne*, ed. B. Suchodolski, 2 vols. (Warsaw, 1954), i. 298–303.

[37] [Józef Pawlikowski], *Myśli polityczne dla Polski* (Warsaw, 1789), 106–27. See E. Rostworowski, '"Myśli polityczne" Józefa Pawlikowskiego', in id., *Legendy i fakty XVIII wieku* (Warsaw, 1963), 195–264. Cf. J. Goldberg, 'Żydzi polscy XVIII wieku w pracach Jerzego Michalskiego i Emanuela Rostworowskiego', in Z. Zielińska and W. Kriegseisen (eds.), *W kręgu badaczy dziejów politycznych XVIII wieku: Józef Feldman, Emanuel Rostworowski, Jerzy Michalski* (Warsaw, 2010), 164.

author of *Starych uprzedzeń nowe roztrząśnienie, do reformy rządu kraiowego służącego* ('A New Discussion of Old Prejudices, Serving the Reform of the Country'), published at the beginning of 1790, denounced the prejudices of the nobility—'absolute lords' and 'despots' over the enslaved peasants, 'the most useful part of the people'. But in denouncing some prejudices, he revealed others, especially towards 'loathsome Jewry, banished from other states . . . these people, devious by nature, and hateful to Christianity'. Burghers, he claimed, were driven to desperation by usurious Jews selling drink—many had to leave their own towns. He warned that neophytes had often converted for material advantage, exploited true Christians like Jews, and sent money abroad to their patriarch, Jakub Frank.[38]

Frank also featured in an exchange between two or three pamphleteers in April– May 1790. The first two pamphlets accused neophytes of using Catholicism to mask undesirable economic activities, while remaining Frankist sectaries at heart. By sending their 'patriarch' money, they damaged the economy further.[39] The author of the second pamphlet, *Dwór Franka* ('The Court of Frank'), who himself claimed to be a neophyte (of his own free will), having prefaced his remark with 'although I am and always shall be for toleration', declared that he would if necessary establish a 'Spanish Holy Inquisition', with 'investigators and spies' to ask neighbours about the neophytes' activities. He also recalled, approvingly, the burning of the nobleman Kazimierz Łyszczyński for atheism in 1689.[40] A riposte accused him of coveting the fortunes of others, defended the honesty of neophyte traders, and claimed that the knowledge of human souls should be left to God.[41]

Although the warnings that Frankist neophytes continued to behave like Jews might seem to anticipate late nineteenth-century antisemitic discourses, in most respects this exchange only reinforces the point that during the Four Year Sejm the Jewish question was overwhelmingly regarded not as a religious but as a social, economic, and cultural problem, with political and fiscal ramifications.[42] It should be added, however, that many of the topics which to noble supporters of reform appeared to be empty rituals, or even superstitions, were, even for the small number of maskilim, an integral part of the Jewish religion.[43]

---

[38] *Starych uprzedzeń nowe roztrząśnienie, do reformy rządu kraiowego służącego* (Warsaw, 1790), 34–5.

[39] *List przyjaciela Polaka, niegdyś w Warszawie, a teraz w Wrocławiu mieszkającego, do obywatela warszawskiego, wyjawiający sekreta neofitów, poprawy rządu wyciągające, pisany dnia 2 miesiąca kwietnia roku 1790*, in *Materiały do dziejów Sejmu Czteroletniego* (hereafter *MDSC*), vi, ed. A. Eisenbach et al. (Wrocław, 1969), 175.

[40] *Dwór Franka, czyli polityka nowochrzeńców odkryta przez neofitę jednego dla poprawy rządu roku 1790*, in *MDSC*, vi. 181–2.

[41] *Odpowiedź zazdrosnemu cudzego dobra i szukającemu sławy dla siebie z pokrzywdzenia honoru bliźniego przez wydane o neofitach i dworze Franka pisma* (1790), in *MDSC*, vi. 182–7.

[42] I draw this conclusion both from the documents collected in *MDSC*, vol. vi, and from the historiography.

[43] M. Wodziński, '"Civil Christians": Debates on the Reform of the Jews in Poland, 1789–1830', in B. Nathans and G. Safran (eds.), *Culture Front: Representing Jews in Eastern Europe* (Philadelphia, 2008), 48–53, 66–8.

The impetus for reform of the Jews at the Four Year Sejm owed much to tensions between nobles and Christian burghers. From the very beginning of the Sejm, Jewish and burgher lobbying had taken place in an atmosphere of mutual rivalry and hostility, aggravated by those members of the Sejm who were ill disposed to the burghers. A group of Jewish merchants which, as Jakub Goldberg has shown, later developed into an organized group of plenipotentiaries asked for permission for three hundred Jewish traders to reside permanently in Warsaw, and for the right to unrestrained economic activity in royal and ecclesiastical towns, offering substantial contributions in return.[44] The Christian population of Warsaw for its part was becoming increasingly angered by the extended suspension (for the duration of the Sejm) of the city's privilege *de non tolerandis Judaeis*. Many Jews settled in the city and took up employment in such areas as crafts, trade, and brewing. Among them were also diverse criminals, especially traders in stolen goods, who benefited from the plague of pickpockets (most of whom were Christians).[45]

Feeling the competition, Christian traders and craftsmen put pressure on the corporation for their expulsion, threatening violence. Michał Jerzy Mniszech, the grand marshal of the Crown, promised to do this in March 1790, although it was another month before the Jews were moved out. By mid-May, however, the city again contained many Jewish traders, and tensions rose. The spark came on 16 May, when a Christian tailor clashed with a Jew carrying cloth, and a (false) rumour spread that the Jews had killed the tailor. The mob, composed mainly of apprentices and their masters, attacked the Jews and their property, and stoned the marshal's guard, before finally being pacified by additional troops. Many nobles were outraged, seeing the attack on the Jews as a threat to themselves. Although the (non-fatal) tumult offended enlightened sensibilities, most nobles treated Jews as a convenience. The following day in the Sejm, several speakers demanded exemplary punishment not just of those guilty of assault, but of the Warsaw burghers as a whole. For a while, the Jewish question now received more attention than the urban one.[46]

Mateusz Butrymowicz, the envoy from Pińsk, the predominantly Jewish town at the gentle confluence of the rivers Prypyats and Pina, reminded the Sejm of a project he had submitted the previous November. In many respects, his would have been a highly enlightened reform, granting full freedom of worship, forbidding the conversion of Jews to Christianity by coercion or trickery ('namową podstępną'), and equalizing the economic status and civic rights of Jews and Christians within

[44] J. Goldberg, 'Pierwszy ruch polityczny wśród Żydów polskich: Plenipotenci żydowscy w dobie Sejmu Czteroletniego', in J. Michalski (ed.), *Lud żydowski w narodzie polskim* (Warsaw, 1994), 45–63.

[45] M. Majewski, 'Przestępczość żydowska w Warszawie doby Sejmu Wielkiego', *Kwartalnik Historii Żydów*, 234 (2010), 143–56.

[46] See Eisenbach, *Emancypacja Żydów na ziemiach polskich*, 70–113; Polonsky, *Jews in Poland and Russia*, i. 210–14; K. Zienkowska, '"The Jews Have Killed a Tailor": The Socio-Political Background of a Pogrom in Warsaw in 1790', *Polin*, 3 (1988), 78–101.

royal towns. It was also typical of the Enlightenment in that it expected Jews to lose all external signs of cultural distinctiveness ('wishing to adapt Jewry living in the territories of the Commonwealth to the laws of the country and national customs'). Polish was to be used in all transactions, and only strictly religious books would be permitted in 'Jewish', which probably referred to both Hebrew and Yiddish. Likewise, the *kahals* would lose all powers except in purely religious matters. Jews were to be removed from taverns and distilleries, and were expected to take up useful trades and agriculture.[47]

This package generally satisfied the postulates of a small number of reform-minded Jews, and a section of the nobility. Essentially, it was in the same assimilationist spirit as Kołłątaj's prescriptions and the partial emancipation imposed by Joseph II in the Habsburg territories.[48] However, as Krystyna Zienkowska has argued, such a reform would have practically eliminated any chance of the admission of the burghers to political rights. Both its author, for all his sincere convictions in favour of toleration, and some of its supporters probably intended it to have just such an effect.[49]

In the Sejm on 19 June 1790, Jacek Jezierski, castellan of Łuków and the prime example of an enterprising noble in economic competition with burghers, called for the establishment of a deputation to reform the Jews, which would take Butrymowicz's project as its starting point. He hailed Butrymowicz as 'a friend of the human race, of whatever religion', and reminded the Sejm that the Jews, unlike the towns, did not threaten rebellion, but humbly asked for their affairs to be put in order. The Sejm appointed a deputation, including Jezierski and Butrymowicz.[50]

By 16 August, the deputation's project was ready. It largely followed Butrymowicz's concepts, with the first article guaranteeing religious toleration for all, except apostates from Catholicism, and even providing that all public acts should refer to 'the people of the Old Covenant' (*lud starozakonny*) rather than 'infidels' (*niewierni*). The title of rabbi (*rabin*) would be replaced by that of 'teacher' (*nauczyciel*), who was to play a similar role in enlightening his congregation as the Catholic *pleban*. The anti-clericalism manifest towards Christian clergy was also

---

[47] Mateusz Butrymowicz, *Reforma Żydów* (1789), in *MDSC*, vi. 119. The project followed up his pamphlet of February 1789, *Sposób uformowania Żydów polskich w pożytecznych krajowi obywatelów*, in *MDSC*, vi. 78–93. See J. Michalski, 'Sejmowe projekty reformy położenia ludności żydowskiej w Polsce w latach 1789–1792', in id., *Studia historyczne z XVIII i XIX wieku*, ed. W. Kriegseisen and Z. Zielińska, 2 vols. (Warsaw, 2007), i. 305–22; Lukowski, *Disorderly Liberty*, 214–16; Wodziński, '"Civil Christians"', 50–1.

[48] K. Zienkowska, 'Reforms Relating to the Third Estate', in S. Fiszman (ed.), *Constitution and Reform in Eighteenth-Century Poland: The Constitution of 3 May 1791* (Bloomington, Ind., 1997), 344–5. Cf. D. Beales, *Joseph II*, 2 vols. (Cambridge, 1987–2009), ii. 196–213, 600–3.

[49] K. Zienkowska, 'Obywatele czy mieszkańcy? Nieudana próba reformy statusu Żydów polskich w czasie Sejmu Czteroletniego', in J. Kowecki (ed.), *Sejm Czteroletni i jego tradycje* (Warsaw, 1991), 158–60.

[50] Ibid. 158, 165 n. 29. See also K. Zienkowska, *Jacek Jezierski, kasztelan łukowski, 1722–1805: Z dziejów szlachty polskiej XVIII wieku* (Warsaw, 1963).

apparent in the various provisions to prevent rabbinical extortions. In order to have an 'industrious and polite' and 'informed and enlightened' Jewish population, the Commission for National Education was to bring forward means by which 'the youth of the Jewish people and the teachers who are to teach that youth could improve themselves in all that is useful and necessary to civil life', within two months. The organs of local government, Civil-Military Commissions, would ensure that Jews used 'the language of the country', although a degree of Hebrew and Polish bilingualism would be acceptable in official documents.[51]

However, the Sejm did not find time to consider the deputation's project, and the question slipped down the political agenda. Attempts to present it were opposed by some members of the deputation (from the province of Małopolska) on 16 August 1790 and on 24 May 1791. A rival project was presented by one of those members and read out on the latter date, but it was not discussed either.[52] I would again stress the low level of interest aroused by what was considered to be the purely religious element of the Jewish question. We should also note that the postulate of subjecting Jews to municipal authority was unwelcome to the Jews themselves.[53]

At least eleven local assemblies of the nobility, or *sejmiki*, held in November 1790, favoured some kind of reform of the Commonwealth's Jews.[54] None of these instructions, however, shared the relatively humanitarian tone of Butrymowicz's project. The Wilno *sejmik* simply highlighted 'the need for a new law to reform completely their estate and condition',[55] and most other Lithuanian instructions were also laconic. The exception was that of Wołkowysk, which pronounced the 'Jewish nation' to be the 'most damaging part of our state . . . a people engaged in fraud and living off the work of industrious peasants . . . the evident cause of the impoverishment of the country'.[56] It called for Jews to be excluded from the production and sale of alcohol, and to be forced to work in agriculture and craft.

In Mazovia, the Wyszogród instruction recommended an improved version of Butrymowicz's project because 'the most particular aim of every state is that no part of the inhabitants should remain in inactivity, useless to the country, and moreover harmful to the fortunes of citizens'.[57] The Czersk *sejmik* wanted to

---

[51] *Reforma Żydów: Projekt od deputacji do tego wyznaczonej*, in *MDSC*, vi. 217, 228. See Michalski, 'Sejmowe projekty reformy położenia ludności żydowskiej', *passim*.

[52] Michalski, 'Sejmowe projekty reformy położenia ludności żydowskiej', 305; Ignacy Chołoniewski, *Projekt względem Żydów i długów kahalnych żydowskich*, in *MDSC*, vi. 269–71.

[53] Polonsky, *Jews in Poland and Russia*, i. 216.

[54] In Mazovia: *Ciechanów*: Biblioteka Polskiej Akademii Umiejętności i Polskiej Akademii Nauk w Krakowie (hereafter BPAU), MS 8318, pp. 363–73; *Czersk*: BPAU, MS 8320, pp. 492–503; *Różan*: BPAU, MS 8337, pp. 635–42; *Wyszogród*: BPAU, MS 8352, pp. 373–80. In the Grand Duchy of Lithuania: *Grodno*: Lietuvos mokslų akademijos Vrublevskių biblioteka, Vilnius (hereafter LMAVB), F233-126, fos. 23–34; *Kowno*: LMAVB, F233-126, fos. 52–6; *Orsza*: LMAVB, F233-126, fos. 124–30; *Pińsk*: LMAVB, F233-126, fos. 137–42; *Upita*: AGAD, Archiwum Roskie, publica XCV/4/5, fos. 6–8; *Wilno*: LMAVB, F233-125, fos. 37–40; *Wołkowysk*: LMAVB, F233-126, fos. 240–50. See also Lukowski, *Disorderly Liberty*, 218–19.   [55] LMAVB, F233-125, fo. 39.

[56] LMAVB, F233-126, fo. 244.   [57] BPAU, MS 8352, p. 374.

reduce Jewish autonomy and alterity. Jewish children were to be taught the Polish alphabet, for use in contracts, while *kahals* would record religious decisions in Polish, and rabbis would no longer have powers to judge civil cases between Jews. *Kahals* would also lose all powers of taxation.

It is striking that demands for Jewish reform came only from Lithuania and Mazovia (although even there, only from a minority of *sejmiki*). Despite their numbers, Jews evidently were not felt to be a pressing problem in the south-east of the Commonwealth. Perhaps the shared trauma of the 1768 massacre and a shared prosperity since then had led to less antipathy towards the Jews there. Or perhaps the key was in the economic interdependence of Jews and magnates in the region. The Volhynian *sejmik* demanded that, on private estates at least, Jews continue to be able to trade in alcohol.[58]

The Law on Royal Towns, passed on 18 April 1791 and incorporated into the Constitution of 3 May 1791, opened urban citizenship to Christians of all denominations. We have already seen how intense was the rivalry between Christian and Jewish inhabitants in many towns. Many nobles employed Jews, but they could never imagine them as equals. The exclusion—for the moment at least—of Jews from urban citizenship was also motivated by the conviction that they were a separate and largely unassimilated 'nation' that required coherent and separate legislation. Moreover, given that the overwhelming majority of Jews lived in private towns, it would have caused great complications to treat Jews equally with Christians in royal towns, effectively cutting them off in legal terms from most other Jews.[59] Nevertheless, Reverend Surowiecki worried that 'newly educated youngsters, who think in the French way . . . even whisper in Warsaw about priests' wives and citizenship for Jews. And what else is needed? Are these not French steps?'[60]

The Sejm never got around to considering the projects for Jewish reform. But the Police Commission of the Two Nations, established after the Constitution of 3 May, did deem that the medieval noble privilege of no incarceration without trial, *neminem captivabimus nisi iure victum*, applied to urban Jews on the same basis as it applied to Christian burghers—who had received it by the Law on Royal Towns. In this way, one of the defining features of Polish citizenship was extended to some Jews. Jews in royal towns, now renamed 'free towns', generally benefited from being put under the authority and protection of the Police Commission, rescuing them from the newly autonomous municipal corporations. Some of the commission's interventions protected Jews from disproportionate burdens of taxation and quartering. But the leaders of *kahals* were not always pleased; ordinary Jews began

---

[58] For the Volhynian *sejmik*, see Lukowski, *Disorderly Liberty*, 218–19.

[59] Zienkowska, 'Reforms Relating to the Third Estate', 340–1.

[60] Karol Surowiecki, *Python: Lipsko-warszawski diabeł. Kontr-tragedya na tragedyą Saul wyjęta z Pisma Świętego, grana przez aktorów tamtego świata w roku 1789; a w roku 1792 światu ziemskiemu obiawiona* (n.p., 1792), 104–5.

to appeal against oppressive practices, and the commission responded by forbidding excommunications.[61]

The tone among the social élite in the spring of 1792 was expressed by the presence of the king and other leading Catholics at the wedding party of the daughter of the Jewish financier Szmul Zbytkower. Foreign Jews appeared in 'French' costume —a breach with tradition. The dances were held in the king's own gardens at Łazienki. A newsletter recorded: 'The Jews and others are inexpressibly content that the king was there in his own person for the breaking down of prejudices.'[62]

The monarch was an interested party. On the eve of the first anniversary of the Constitution of 3 May, having received death threats and fearing his assassination during the festivities, he wrote a testament to the marshal of the Sejm, in which he asked for his debts to be paid. This, he explained, could be done by the Jews in return for 'such internal arrangements in their nation, which cannot harm the Polish nation'.[63] Let us note that however Stanisław August may have understood the 'Polish nation', he considered the Jews to be a separate 'nation'.

It was in expectation of such arrangements that Jews participated in the celebrations of 3 May 1792—separately from Christians, it should be added, in services at synagogues. The *Gazeta Narodowa i Obca* published the Polish translation of a hymn 'sung by Jews in Warsaw and other towns of the Commonwealth by all communities of the Jewish nation' in the synagogues and 'offered', presumably to the king and Sejm, by the Jewish delegates in the capital. Although according to Majer Bałaban the language (in the original Hebrew) is essentially Pentateuchal,[64] some of the lines, when translated from Polish into English, are also reminiscent of Alexander Pope's epitaph for Isaac Newton:

> God, the father of all people, shall crown this work.
> He said: let there be light, and there was light.
> He said again: let there be light; Stanisław came forth,
> who by enlightenment saved the nation from death.[65]

---

[61] A. Zahorski, *Centralne instytucje policyjne w Polsce w dobie rozbiorów* (Warsaw, 1959), 158–60; J. Gordziejew, *Komisje Porządkowe Cywilno-Wojskowe w Wielkim Księstwie Litewskim w okresie Sejmu Czteroletniego (1789–1792)* (Kraków, 2010), 127–33. Cf. Polonsky, *Jews in Poland and Russia*, i. 219–20.

[62] Newsletter, 31 Mar. 1792: Biblioteka Narodowa, Warsaw, Akc. 9830, fos. 39–40.

[63] E. Rostworowski, *Maj 1791–maj 1792: Rok monarchii konstytucyjnej* (Warsaw, 1985), 15–16; Stanisław August to Stanisław Małachowski, 2 May 1792, in *MDSC*, vi. 335.

[64] M. Bałaban, *Z historji Żydów w Polsce: Szkice i studja* (Warsaw, 1920), 119–24.

[65] *Hymn . . . dnia 3 maja 1792 r. . . . śpiewany . . . od wszystkich narodu żydowskiego zgromadzeń*, in *MDSC*, vi. 480–3. Two quadrilingual editions were published (Hebrew, Polish, French, and German). The Polish version, the basis of my translation, appeared in *Gazeta Narodowa i Obca* on 19 May 1792. The Hebrew version is printed on plates in *MDSC*, vol. vi, between pp. 480 and 481. See also K. Maksimowicz, *Poezja polityczna a Sejm Czteroletni* (Gdańsk, 2000), 238–40. Cf. 'Nature and nature's laws lay hid in night. / God said: "Let Newton be", and all was light': Alexander Pope, 'Epitaph. Intended for Sir Isaac Newton, in Westminster-Abbey', in *The Works of Alexander Pope, Esq.*, 10 vols. (London, 1824), iii. 378.

The lines also made a humanitarian plea. Although such hopes were undoubtedly limited to a small, metropolitan, prosperous, and well-educated circle, the striking Enlightenment rhetoric of the hymn shows that the Haskalah cannot be ignored altogether in discussions of Jews in the late eighteenth-century Commonwealth.

However, despite such optimism, and the king's hopes that grateful Jews would pay off most of his debts, it proved impossible for supporters of a general reform of the Jews to initiate a debate on the measure in the Sejm. Even if such a reform had been passed, it would probably have contained fewer rights for Jews, and more interference from the state and municipal authorities, than the deputation's final project, which was agreed to by a majority of its members on 20 May 1792, and presented to the Sejm by its chairman, Hugo Kołłątaj, on 29 May. As this was the last day of the Sejm's deliberations, before it was adjourned in the early hours of the following morning, the project was lost in the mass of other business and was not discussed.[66]

This final project, largely as a result of the resistance mounted by the plenipotentiaries of the burghers, would have given the Jews less self-government than earlier versions. On the other hand, largely as a result of lobbying by Jews, the assimilationism so evident in Butrymowicz's project and the deputation's project of 1790 was toned down. Jews were to be given more time to abandon their traditional dress, beards were to be permitted, and more understanding was shown towards the observance of dietary laws and the sabbath. Similarly, rather less emphasis was put on using the Polish language in business and in schools.[67]

In contrast, a general reform of the Orthodox Church in the Commonwealth, granting it an autonomous or 'autocephalous' hierarchy, was passed in the last days of the Sejm. This occurred, however, only as a result of the evident and urgent need, in the face of the Russian invasion, to curtail the control hitherto exercised over the Commonwealth's Orthodox communities by the Holy Synod in St Petersburg. A comparable geopolitical imperative was lacking in the case of Polish–Lithuanian Jews.[68]

[66] The chances of passing a reform were assessed as unlikely by Eisenbach, *Emancypacja Żydów na ziemiach polskich*, 113–22, but as probable by Zienkowska, 'Obywatele czy mieszkańcy?', 164. Michalski, 'Sejmowe projekty reformy położenia ludności żydowskiej', 323, established that Eisenbach (on p. 121) had misread a key piece of evidence (a letter from Hugo Kołłątaj to Stanisław Małachowski, dated 23 May 1792, in *MDSC*, vi. 337), confusing a discussion at Małachowski's house with a session of the Sejm. Michalski concluded that the reform might well have been passed, albeit in a modified form, had the Sejm lasted longer. Polonsky's conclusion is decidedly more pessimistic: *Jews in Poland and Russia*, i. 215–19.

[67] Michalski, 'Sejmowe projekty reformy położenia ludności żydowskiej', 306–8, 321, compares the various projects. The final draft of the deputation's final project, *Urządzenie ludu żydowskiego w całym narodzie polskim*, is published, alongside indications of changes from the initial draft (dating from January 1792), in *MDSC*, vi. 491–515. According to the editors, this project owed more to the 'Mémoire pour servir de projet à l'établissement des Juifs', in *MDSC*, vi. 358–72, drawn up by Scipione Piattoli for King Stanisław August in September–October 1791, than it did to the deputation's earlier project, *Reforma Żydów*.

[68] On the reform of the Orthodox Church in the Commonwealth, see E. Sakowicz, *Kościół*

In the laws and projects of the Four Year Sejm, all non-Catholic confessions, Christian and Jewish alike, were expected to conduct their non-liturgical affairs at least partially in the Polish language. There was no trace of modern ethnic nationalism here, but nor was there in the misguided efforts of Joseph II to impose German on his territories. In addition, according to the relevant paragraphs of the Project for the Form of Government, which, again, the Sejm did not manage to consider, other churches and religions were to submit their schools to the Commission for National Education. Without touching articles of faith and rites, the commission's visitors would ensure that the same instruction was given as in other schools, 'so that the tolerated difference of opinion should in no way spoil the uniformity of civic spirit, and attachment to the constitution'.[69] To this end the commission was to draw up a 'constitutional catechism', which was to be taught in all schools. These provisions were repeated in the project for the Commission for National Education, which—like the Jewish reform—the Sejm did not in the end find time to consider. In essence, members of all creeds would worship freely in their own way, but a common civic morality was to be taught by all religions.[70]

Reverend Kołłątaj was exceptionally rigorous in his determination to forge a single 'Polish' nation out of Ruthenians and Jews, Lithuanians and Germans, using the Polish language, and preaching the same civic and moral virtues regardless of confession. Most discourse referred to a 'Jewish nation'. But Kołłątaj exemplified a trend. Traditional hatred of Jews, founded in religion, undoubtedly abated among the enlightened elite. At the same time, however, economic and social rivalries between Jews and Christian burghers were worsening, and some nobles were prepared to exploit the Jewish question in their own rivalry with the burghers. Most enlightened minds—even the relatively realistic and humane Pawlikowski—believed the solution lay in pushing Jews out of their 'substantially Jewish universe'[71] and giving them similar burdens and rights as Christian inhabitants of towns. With minds concentrated by a rebellion scare in Ukraine, they also wished to defuse tension in the countryside by moving Jews out of the production and sale of alcohol.

*

prawosławny w Polsce w epoce Sejmu Wielkiego, 1788–1792 (Warsaw, 1935), 182–226; K. Paździor, 'Polityka Sejmu Czteroletniego wobec kościołów wschodnich', Ph.D. diss. (Univ. of Silesia in Katowice, 2000), ch. 4; Butterwick, 'Deconfessionalization?', 115–18.

[69] 'Komisja Edukacji Narodowej' (1791), in *Ustawodawstwo szkolne za czasów Komisji Edukacji Narodowej: Rozporządzenia, ustawy pedagogiczne i organizacyjne (1773–1793)*, ed. J. Lewicki (Kraków, 1925), 421–2.

[70] See K. Paździor, 'Edukacja jako narzędzie polityki wyznaniowej Sejmu Wielkiego wobec innowierców', *Nasza Przeszłość*, 100 (2003), 329–66. Cf. R. J. W. Evans, *Austria, Hungary, and the Habsburgs: Essays on Central Europe, c.1683–1867* (Oxford, 2006), 134–69; Beales, *Joseph II*, ii. 366–70. [71] Hundert, *Jews in Poland–Lithuania*, 31.

Guarding against the temptations of teleology, where in enlightened discourses might we locate the genealogy of subsequent attitudes to Jews in Poland? On the one hand, Enlightenment discourses recoiled from persecution of religious minorities, and emphasized the common humanity of all inhabitants of the Commonwealth. On the other hand, the enlightened expectation that compelling Jews to assimilate into Christian society would solve rising economic and social tensions, for which the Jews were blamed, often in abusive language, both underestimated Jewish reluctance to abandon much of those things which made them distinctively Jewish (which grew under the influence of hasidism), and the intractability of rural and urban social problems. Moreover, unsympathetic foreign regimes imposed their own solutions in the nineteenth century. Perhaps the concept of a Pole of the Mosaic faith, implicit in some (but not all) Enlightenment discourses, was an impossible dream for more than a minority of Jews, and was unacceptable to most Christian peasants or petty-bourgeois. The disappointment of that dream after the crushing of the 1863 uprising would encourage racist and ethnic nationalist antisemites.

The Jews in the Duchy of Warsaw

The Question of Equal Rights in Administrative Theory and Practice

ALEKSANDRA ONISZCZUK

IN INVESTIGATING the history of the Kingdom of Poland, one must bear in mind that this history did not emerge in a vacuum or as a complete negation of the state organism that preceded it—the Duchy of Warsaw. A number of issues that the new authorities took upon themselves were continuations of problems that had earlier confronted the Duchy of Warsaw, and hence the construction of the new state rested on some pre-existing legal arrangements. For while the establishment of new state borders and the replacement of the highest government authorities could be accomplished in a matter of months, radical changes, and the development of a comprehensive new legal and political system and a relatively coherent ideological vision, did not take place automatically. The Kingdom's authorities as well as its inhabitants (including those of the Jewish faith) often appealed to laws and regulations from the period of the Duchy of Warsaw,[1] and a large number of laws did indeed remain in force. Clear continuity could also be seen at the level of personnel: some of the senior officials from the Duchy period joined the ranks of the government of the Congress Kingdom,[2] just as most lower-level functionaries found employment in the administration and judiciary of the newly established state.[3] Their experience and views, formed in the period of the Duchy, were thus

---

[1] For example, the decision of the viceroy (*namiestnik*) of the Kingdom to send copies of decrees of 1808 and 1809 to courts, attorneys, notaries, and voivodeship commissions to remind them of the obligation to apply them: A. Eisenbach, 'Dobra ziemskie w posiadaniu Żydów', in W. Kula (ed.), *Społeczeństwo Królestwa Polskiego: Studia o uwarstwieniu i ruchliwości społecznej*, iii (Warsaw, 1968), 213. An individual example is the case of the Jewish petitioner from Kalisz who quoted the 1809 decrees when seeking a favourable decision from the authorities in the 1820s: see Archiwum Główne Akt Dawnych, Warsaw (hereafter AGAD), Komisja Rządząca Spraw Wewnętrznych, 1123, fos. 142–4.

[2] For example, the office of viceroy was bestowed on Józef Zajączek, one of the commanders of the period of the Duchy of Warsaw.

[3] W. Rostocki, *Pochodzenie społeczne, kwalifikacje i przebieg kariery urzędników Komisji Województwa Mazowieckiego w czasach Królestwa Polskiego, 1816–1830* (Warsaw, 2002), 32, calculates that as many as half of the functionaries holding managerial and mid-level executive positions in the Mazovian Voivodeship Commission had begun their careers in the time of the Duchy of Warsaw; taking into

transplanted to the Kingdom.[4] Another tangible example of the links between the two state organisms was bureaucratic practice: a great number of administrative, economic, and property matters continued to be supervised by the same offices, in accordance with the same laws, and often by the same functionaries. The change of the country's name and ruler had little bearing on the interests of individuals: tenants wanted to keep their right to tenancy, creditors expected the enforcement of debt payments, notaries continued their business by entering new records in the same books, and it was deemed that many issues left unresolved under the previous administration—such as the tax collected by Austria for the repayment of *kahal* (Jewish community council) debts[5]—must necessarily be settled. Elements of continuity could be observed in many areas.

Among the laws—and the established views—transplanted to the Kingdom of Poland were those regarding the Jewish population. Just as had happened at the time of the formation of the Duchy of Warsaw, a comprehensive regulation of Jewish affairs was put off till later. Instead, previously existing legislation was modified according to current needs and used ad hoc.[6] The regulation of Jewish affairs in the Duchy drew on the traditions of three legal systems—those of the Rzeczpospolita (the pre-partition Polish–Lithuanian Commonwealth) and Prussia, and the Napoleonic laws[7]—while in the Kingdom the legislation of the Duchy remained for many years one of the main points of reference. A telling example is the granting of citizenship, in accordance with article 10 of the Organic Statute of 1 December 1815, exclusively to those persons who had held the status of citizen in the preceding state system, which had the effect of depriving Jews of citizenship. The significance of 'inherited legislation' in Jewish affairs manifested itself also in the fact that when new circumstances arose, in which there were no pre-existing legal regulations for the authorities to rely on, the result was a chaos of indecision.[8] Therefore, while taking 1815 as a turning point, it is worth bearing in mind that

account all categories of functionaries, 28.3% had started their careers in that period. On continuities in the sphere of the organization of administration, see M. Kallas, *Organy administracji terytorialnej w Księstwie Warszawskim* (Toruń, 1975), 157.

[4] As noted by D. Vital, *A People Apart: The Jews in Europe, 1789–1939* (Oxford, 1999), 79.

[5] See AGAD, Rada Ministrów (RM) II, 22, *passim*.

[6] One example of such modification of policies is provided by the fees for licences to produce and sell liquor, which were introduced in the Duchy of Warsaw and were raised several times during the period of the Kingdom of Poland. Another was the attempt to create Jewish districts (*rewiry*), although these were also reminiscent of the medieval concept of the ghetto. In the Kingdom of Poland, these regulations were based upon the decree of 16 March 1809, which prohibited Jews in Warsaw from living in certain 'exempted' streets (*egzymowane ulice*).

[7] Austrian legislation did not become a source of inspiration for the government of the Duchy because of the late incorporation of the Austrian partition into its territory (1809). Those legal solutions were additionally used only in four previously Austrian departments.

[8] M. Wodziński, 'How Modern is an Antimodernist Movement? The Emergence of Hasidic Politics in Congress Poland', *AJS Review*, 31 (2007), 230. The lack of pre-existing legislation concerned, among other things, the issue of hasidic Jews.

many of the problems and proposed solutions relating to the position of Jews were not only manifestations of the lasting impact of the Four Year Sejm,[9] but were also a continuation (as well as an extension and modification) of the legislation and policies of the Duchy of Warsaw.

This chapter explores an issue that has not previously been studied: the realization in the years 1807–15 of legal equality for Jews in practice, particularly at the local level. My discussion is based on material gathered during an investigation of community records (*akta gminne*) in the collection of the Jewish Historical Institute (Żydowski Instytut Historyczny) in Warsaw, and of official records in the collections of local state archives in eight Polish cities: Bydgoszcz, Kalisz, Kraków, Lublin, Płock, Poznań, Radom, and Siedlce. The great majority of these documents have not previously been the subject of research. They constitute a record of local cases in which Jews were involved, and allow us to grasp the nature of everyday relations with the state authorities. Owing to limitations of space, I shall make use of only a small portion of the material, in order to illustrate the characteristic tendencies. Before presenting the practical dimension of the status of the Jewish population, however, I would like briefly to review the state of previous research on the legal situation of this category of inhabitants of the Duchy of Warsaw.

LEGISLATION AND ITS CONTEXT

Acts regulating the legal status of Jews in the Duchy of Warsaw have been the object of many studies. Most of these analyses were undertaken by Artur Eisenbach,[10] but the works of other authors should not be ignored.[11] These studies

---

[9] As noted by M. Wodziński, *Władze Królestwa Polskiego wobec chasydyzmu: Z dziejów stosunków politycznych* (Wrocław, 2008), 21; English version: *Hasidism and Politics: The Kingdom of Poland, 1815–1864* (Oxford, 2013).

[10] A. Eisenbach, 'Yidn in varshaver firshtntum', *Yivo-bleter*, 10 (1936), 91–9; id., 'Struktura ludności żydowskiej w Warszawie w świetle spisu 1810 r.', *Biuletyn Żydowskiego Instytutu Historycznego*, 13–14 (1955), 73–121; id., 'Prawa obywatelskie i honorowe Żydów (1790–1861)', in W. Kula (ed.), *Społeczeństwo Królestwa Polskiego: Studia o uwarstwieniu i ruchliwości społecznej*, i (Warsaw, 1965), 237–300; id., 'Dobra ziemskie w posiadaniu Żydów', 201–94; id., *Kwestia równouprawnienia Żydów w Królestwie Polskim* (Warsaw, 1972); id., *Z dziejów ludności żydowskiej w Polsce w XVIII i XIX wieku: Studia i szkice* (Warsaw, 1983); id., *Emancypacja Żydów na ziemiach polskich 1785–1870 na tle europejskim* (Warsaw, 1988); English version: *The Emancipation of the Jews in Poland, 1780–1870*, ed. A. Polonsky, trans. J. Dorosz (Oxford, 1991).

[11] W. Tokarz, 'Z dziejów sprawy żydowskiej za Księstwa Warszawskiego', *Kwartalnik Historyczny*, 16 (1902), 262–76; M. Wishnitzer, 'Proekty reformy evreiskogo byta v Gertsogstve Varshavskom i Tsarstve Pol'skom', *Perezhitoe*, 1 (1909), 164–72; Yu. Gessen, 'V efemernom gosudarstve: Evrei v Varshavskom Gertsogstve', *Evreiskaya starina*, 1910, no. 1, pp. 3–38; S. Askenazy, 'Z dziejów Żydów polskich w dobie Księstwa Warszawskiego i Królestwa Kongresowego', *Kwartalnik Poświęcony Badaniu Przeszłości Żydów w Polsce*, 1/1 (1912), 1–14; D. Kandel, *Żydzi w roku 1812* (n.p., [1910]): <http://www.dbc.wroc.pl/dlibra/docmetadata?id=6763&from=publication> (repr. in *Biblioteka Warszawska*, 1910, vol. 2, pp. 157–75); J. Kirszrot, *Prawa Żydów w Królestwie Polskiem: Zarys*

usually address a similar set of issues. Typically, they start off by stating that article 4 of the constitution of 1807 granted legal equality to all citizens regardless of their religion. Immediately following that comes the observation that this particular article was never actually enforced, because of two decrees that were issued soon afterwards, in September and October 1808; modelled on Napoleon's *décret infâme*, these suspended the political and civil rights of Jews for ten years. Here it is usually noted that affluent and 'enlightened' Jews made efforts to improve this legal status. Next follows a catalogue—in a variable order—of the legal restrictions that discriminated against Jews. The subjects considered have included taxes levied exclusively on Jews (the tax on kosher meat, the 'ticket tax' paid on entering Warsaw, the *Geleitzoll* levied on a foreigner of the Mosaic faith when crossing the Duchy's border); the limitation of Jews' freedom to reside on 'exempted' streets in Warsaw; and the extension of the general military draft to Jews, and its subsequent repeal in exchange for a new tax (the recruitment tax). Sometimes emphasis is placed on the question of acquisition of real property and the limitations in that area, such as a ban on the purchase of rural land and of brick buildings in towns. Another topic is the debate on the reform of Jewish life. Previous research supports the conclusion that the legislation of the Duchy of Warsaw did indeed contain a significant number of regulations that created particular difficulties for Jews. These were broadly related to the fact that the Duchy's legal order had not achieved a consistent break with feudal principles, and the law continued to distinguish between the old social strata of medieval origin: the privileged strata—the nobility (*szlachta*) and the aristocracy; the Christian and Jewish bourgeoisie; and the peasantry. This meant that a social order based on estate was maintained.[12] That being so, the general

historyczny (Warsaw, 1917); S. Hirszhorn, *Historja żydów w Polsce od Sejmu Czteroletniego do wojny europejskiej (1788–1914)* (Warsaw, 1921); I. Schiper, 'Dzieje Żydów na ziemiach Księstwa Warszawskiego i Królestwa Polskiego (od 1795 do 1863 r. włącznie)', in I. Schiper, A. Tartakower, and A. Hafftka (eds.), *Żydzi w Polsce Odrodzonej: Działalność społeczna, gospodarcza, oświatowa i kulturalna*, 2 vols. (Warsaw, 1932–3), i. 426–32; id., *Żydzi Królestwa Polskiego w dobie powstania listopadowego* (Warsaw, 1932); id., *Dzieje handlu żydowskiego na ziemiach polskich* (Warsaw, 1937); J. Shatzky, *Yidishe bildungspolitik in poyln fun 1806 biz 1866* (New York, 1943); W. Sobociński and M. Senkowska-Gluck, 'Księstwo Warszawskie', in J. Bardach and M. Senkowska-Gluck (eds.), *Historia państwa i prawa*, iii: *Od rozbiorów do uwłaszczenia* (Warsaw, 1981), 87–8, 120; J. Stanley, 'The Politics of the Jewish Question in the Duchy of Warsaw', *Jewish Social Studies*, 44/1 (1982), 47–62. Also worth mentioning are the unpublished master's theses written at Warsaw University under the guidance of Majer Bałaban in the inter-war period. Copies are kept in the Archive of the Jewish Historical Institute: Miriam Litwin, 'Sprawa reformy Żydów za czasów Księstwa Warszawskiego i w pierwszych latach Królestwa Polskiego' (Warsaw, n.d.), and Freida Zimmerspitz, 'Podatek "koszerne" i jego dzierżawcy w Księstwie Warszawskim i Królestwie Polskim (1809–1862)' (Warsaw, n.d.). The latter study in particular deserves attention owing to its detailed analysis of taxation, which had not previously been comprehensively examined. See also Raphael Mahler's study *A History of Modern Jewry, 1780–1815* (New York, 1971), 347–68.

[12] M. Kallas, *Historia ustroju Polski* (Warsaw, 2005), 199; W. Sobociński, *Historia ustroju i prawa Księstwa Warszawskiego* (Toruń, 1964), 63–5, 297.

equality before the law stipulated in article 4 of the constitution was simply *not given effect*—and not only with respect to Jews. However, when the Christian bourgeoisie acquired certain new rights, decrees were issued that limited these constitutionally granted rights as applied to Jews and peasants. Thus it is possible to talk of the discriminatory character of state legislation, as compared with that concerning the privileged strata and the Christian bourgeoisie.

It was primarily the attitudes of the ruling elites towards Jews that shaped legislation. According to the dominant view among those elites, Jews still constituted a foreign group undeserving of equality, set apart in many ways by clearly perceptible differences that had existed for centuries.[13] In this respect, the ruling strata of the Duchy did not differ significantly from those of other countries.[14] Without the French Revolution and Napoleon's triumphs, ideas of equality, completely at odds with the traditional estate-based social order of the time—the only social order known to most people—would probably have had to wait much longer for realization. That is why, at the outset of the nineteenth century in the Duchy of Warsaw, emancipatory and egalitarian ideas were met with a lack of understanding and with opposition from members of the Council of Ministers, who were hoping for the restoration of the constitution of 3 May 1791 and did not accept all the provisions of the new charter imposed by Napoleon in 1807.[15] A thoroughgoing transformation of the existing social structure, which the equality of all and the granting of citizenship and political rights to Jews and peasants would necessarily lead to, was beyond their imagination. The rulers of the Duchy had been raised in a world in which barriers separating Christians and Jews were 'eternal'; they believed that the radical social changes imposed by Napoleon were simply not suited to Polish conditions. Postponing the looming spectre of equality by at least ten years was an attempt to salvage the world they knew.

[13] There were, however, other opinions, even among the highest government officials. By way of example, it is worth mentioning the views of Feliks Łubieński, the Minister of Justice. He expressed the opinion that Jews had been denied only political and citizenship rights; on the strength of the civil rights to which they were entitled, however, acquisition of property was generally to be permitted. He argued that in order to dispel any doubts in that regard the king should make it explicit in his decree that the prohibition on property acquisition (decree of 19 November 1808) was to be understood as relating exclusively to landed (rural) property. Approving a proposal by Jan Paweł Łuszczewski, the Minister of Internal Affairs, to regulate this issue, he expressed reservations concerning one article, arguing that '[this article], prohibiting the incurring of mortgage debt on property acquired by Jews, is too strict and offends against property law, contradicting the spirit of the Law in whose eyes *all are equal*, all are equally bound by it, and all hold an equal right to manage their property': AGAD, Rada Ministrów (RM), 167, fo. 71 (emphasis added). Łubieński pointed out thereby that in principle one should not create regulations in civil law that distinguish the situation of Jews relative to other subjects of law, or at least not regulations excessively infringing upon the 'spirit' of Napoleonic law.

[14] As Stanley reminds us, in Europe at that time, the differentiation of political status according to religion was the norm: Stanley, 'Politics of the Jewish Question in the Duchy of Warsaw', 60,

[15] For more on this subject, see Jarosław Czubaty's highly valuable work *Księstwo Warszawskie, 1807–1815* (Warsaw, 2011), 137–40.

It must be emphasized, however, that even if some individuals among the ruling group *had* stipulated the introduction of the principle of equality, it seems that it would have been a risky political move, threatening to provoke strong opposition from the nobility and magnates as well as to cause serious internal destabilization. These social strata had quickly regained their previous significance and power: as early as the end of 1806, still before the official establishment of the state, several key elements of collective life from the time of the Polish–Lithuanian Common-wealth were being restored on the ground. Thus, the 'symbols, institutions, and style of political action' were reinstated, and public space was to a great extent permeated with noble habits and traditions in which the old political language and the Sarmatian model of patriotism reigned supreme.[16] This situation did not change after the official foundation of the state; then too it was the nobility and magnates that assumed higher posts in the administration, the judiciary, and the Polish army.[17] In light of their unquestionable political dominance and their initial disillusionment with the design of the new state,[18] any attempts by the government to carry out revolutionary changes, as envisioned by the constitution, would have spawned a very real threat of discontent on the side of the elites. A test of their readiness to accept in-depth social transformations (in the form of equality of all social groups) was their reaction to what the consequences of the constitution would be on the status of peasants. The privileged strata decidedly opposed con-sistent implementation of the provisions of the constitution and its extension to the Duchy's largest social group; the reason was fear of social revolution and loss of their position, particularly in the face of a serious crisis in agricultural produc-tion.[19] The nobility, therefore, managed to attain what amounted to an annulment, under the December Decree, of all rights previously granted to peasants under the Napoleonic legislation.[20] To press for equally revolutionary regulations regarding

[16] Czubaty, *Księstwo Warszawskie*, 112. A telling example is provided by the rallying slogans used in the army of the Duchy, which sometimes called it 'the Polish knighthood': Archiwum Państwowe w Bydgoszczy, Akta Podprefektur, 2, fo. 39: order of Maurycy Hauke, 2 Jan. 1807. For more on estate-specific terminology used for military mobilization, see also J. Jedlicki, *Klejnot i bariery społeczne: Przeobrażenia szlachectwa polskiego w schyłkowym okresie feudalizmu* (Warsaw, 1968), 230–1.

[17] Czubaty, *Księstwo Warszawskie*, 119; C. A. Blackburn, *Napoleon and the Szlachta* (New York, 1998), 4.

[18] For more on the effects of the provisions of the treaty of Tilsit (Tylża) and the granting of a con-stitution, see Czubaty, *Księstwo Warszawskie*, 153–78.

[19] The gentry, which drew its income from landed properties, was in a severe financial crisis owing to the permanent presence of billeted troops, the requisitioning of food, the continental blockade, tax liabilities, and a serious decline in manpower caused by disease, military recruitment, or the desertion of peasants; for details, see Blackburn, *Napoleon and the Szlachta*, 51–66. They were therefore seriously concerned by the consequences that article 4 of the constitution could have for relations in the country-side: 'The possibility of a radicalization of feelings in the countryside or a cementing of the landlords' aversion to the new order put the king and the ministers in a difficult position': Czubaty, *Księstwo Warszawskie*, 162–3.

[20] Blackburn, *Napoleon and the Szlachta*, 87; Sobociński, *Historia ustroju i prawa Księstwa War-szawskiego*, 67–76; H. Grynwaser, *Pisma*, 3 vols. (Wrocław, 1951), i. 54–6.

Jews—who were also undeserving, in the gentry's view, of the rights proper to the nobility and the Christian bourgeoisie—could simply be 'too much'. The Duchy was already struggling with tremendous difficulties related to the construction of the administrative apparatus and judiciary. Money was constantly short, especially in view of the colossal financial obligations to Napoleon (*sumy bajońskie*). Nearly half of all state revenue was needed for the maintenance of the army—and here too shortages were constant, even for the purchase of necessary armaments, or footwear for all soldiers. In consequence, the priority of the authorities had to be to build lasting support from 'familiar and trusted' social groups. Such co-operation was a condition of even minimal internal stability. The Duchy's highest authorities, even if they had wished to force through the principle of real political equality, would not have had sufficient liberty and power to act.[21]

The opposition to granting legal equality, and especially political rights, to Jews could also have been grounded in practical considerations.[22] It would, after all, be necessary to subject them to rigid control in order to distinguish between those eligible for these rights—for example by virtue of birth or residence for ten years or more within the borders of the Duchy of Warsaw—from those who were not, such as foreign Jews. Maintaining the separate status of Jews as a quasi-estate was far easier. Otherwise, it would have been necessary to create a wholly new division of state administration to supervise births and deaths and issue appropriate certificates, or to employ an entire army of additional bureaucrats who would take on the burden of the affairs of the 200,000 Jewish inhabitants. First and foremost, there was not enough money. In addition, the public criticism of the already existing administration—which was reproached on account of the proliferation of official bodies (a situation often likened to that of pre-partition Poland)—was already strong enough for the authorities to have no desire to let it grow even more.[23]

Finally, we may raise the question whether the Duchy's Jewish inhabitants themselves were interested in achieving equality. The Jewish population, living in accordance with the old model and accustomed to following its own rules, different from those of the rest of the country, may have expected the same in the Duchy period. An example of this may be the petition put forward by an Aron Szmulowicz of Warsaw, who, as the representative of the Jews of the Łomża department

---

[21] If this reasoning is correct, it would not be the only time that the authorities had refrained from implementing equal rights for Jews out of anxiety that other citizens might react negatively. A similar situation arose in Gdańsk in 1817, when the town council refused to implement the regulations of the Prussian emancipation edict. 'It cited . . . anti-Jewish sentiment in the town as the factor regulating the implementation of the new laws. In the council's opinion the introduction of the new law on emancipation should be dependent on the reaction it would provoke among the citizens of the town. If it were the case that, owing to adverse sentiments towards Jewish merchants, an approval of the new regulations would risk the outbreak of riots, it would be advisable to postpone their implementation': M. Szulc, 'Rozruchy antyżydowskie w Gdańsku w 1821 roku i ich polityczno-prawny kontekst oraz konsekwencje', in K. Pilarczyk (ed.), *Żydzi i judaizm we współczesnych badaniach polskich*, v (Kraków, 2010), 227.   [22] I thank Professor Leszek Ziątkowski for drawing my attention to this point.
[23] Czubaty, *Księstwo Warszawskie*, 167.

(*departament*), applied to the authorities for confirmation of the hitherto existing privileges.[24] Maybe Yuly Gessen was right when he pointed out that the idea of extending a uniform legislation to the Jews was met with surprise on their side;[25] similarly, John Stanley observes that the majority of the Jewish population were supporters of a traditional world for whom moves towards legal equality brought with them the threat of assimilation.[26] Although, undoubtedly, limitations on the freedom of settlement and travel, as well as restrictions in the realm of property acquisition or special taxes, were certainly perceived by many as a burden[27] and caused discontent and a sense of disadvantage, we may ask whether the ministers' decision to suspend citizenship and political rights for a period of ten years was as important for the majority of Jews as traditional historiography—with Artur Eisenbach—used to claim. It is possible that it disappointed mainly a group of affluent bankers, industrialists, royal court suppliers, and merchants who had been sending memoranda and petitions to the government. There is, however, no source material that could resolve the issue and we can only leave it as an open question.[28]

To summarize, it must, however, be restated that, regardless of the probability of the principle of equality actually being implemented and regardless of the extent of the Jews' own interest in this, the legislation of the Duchy of Warsaw did not introduce equal rights for all its inhabitants. Even though one may point to a large collection of norms that applied to all irrespective of their religion (in most articles of civil and criminal law), there did exist a category of laws pertaining specifically to Jews, usually putting them in a situation of legal disadvantage (in regulations concerning citizenship and political rights, as well as certain civil rights). The latter category leaves no doubt that Jews continued to be treated—in accordance with the centuries-old European practice—as a separate social category of specific and inferior social status somewhere between citizens and foreigners; their legal status clearly differed *in theory* from that which the constitution and other acts granted to the privileged Christian social strata.

ADMINISTRATIVE PRACTICE

The above characterization, based almost exclusively on documents created by the highest authorities (the ministers and the monarch), has not previously been

[24] Gessen, 'V efemernom gosudarstve', 6. [25] Ibid.

[26] Stanley, 'Politics of the Jewish Question in the Duchy of Warsaw', 58–9. On the lack of support for the reform of Jewish life among Jews themselves and the need to take into account the differences between the situations in Poland and in France, see Litwin, 'Sprawa reformy Żydów', 53.

[27] See a similar remark in F. Guesnet, *Polnische Juden im 19. Jahrhundert: Lebensbedingungen, Rechtsnormen und Organisation im Wandel* (Cologne, 1998), 189.

[28] Guesnet has pointed out that in the nineteenth century proponents of reforms among Polish Jews were a 'quantité négligeable': ibid. 252. Taking into consideration also that there were large numbers of hasidim throughout the century, we could reason that maybe achieving citizenship and political rights was not the main objective of the majority of Jews. Unfortunately, this cannot serve as a solid proof. The issue, however, seems very interesting.

confronted with local sources showing the operation of 'law in action'.[29] Although huge numbers of local documents from the Duchy period were destroyed during the First and Second World Wars, the remaining holdings of the provincial archives are so numerous and so valuable that, in order to gain a full picture of the issue of the legal status of Jews, it is important to turn to them as well. My investigation of sources has focused on town and prefecture records[30] in the archives of former department capitals (*siedziby departamentów*)—that is, those archives potentially containing the largest number of entries from the period of the Duchy of Warsaw. The records of the Jewish community in Kraków are a unique and extremely valuable supplement, chiefly containing correspondence with the Christian municipal authorities. Additionally, documents held in the Central Archives of Historical Records (Archiwum Główne Akt Dawnych) in Warsaw will be referred to, primarily with a focus on the particular cases they describe. I omit cases of the kind much discussed in the existing literature—those which deal with attempts to obtain individual privileges in spite of the restrictions applying to Jews.

An analysis of the sources listed above complements our previous knowledge about the situation of Jews. Legal discrimination at the level of the central authorities turns out to be less clear in practice; as usual, the reality prescribed in regulations does not completely match the practice of everyday life. Turning to sources at the grass-roots level allows us to sketch new areas of analysis.

Legality of Administrative Actions and Procedures

In countless instances, one can see that the representatives of the state were concerned over the legality of the actions taken towards individual Jewish petitioners. In this regard, there is hardly any difference to be found between the treatment of Christians and Jews. This is well illustrated by the problems relating to the requisition of private property by the state—typically food for the army and construction materials. When Samuel Szaj, an inhabitant of the town of Płock, applied to the authorities in mid-1808 for compensation for merchandise seized for the needs of the French troops, the response of the prefect of the department was quite assertive: the town's former mayor, Jędrzejewicz, was summoned to give an

---

[29] To a certain extent, differences between the statutory law and law in action have been noted by researchers investigating earlier periods. Examples of such discrepancies are offered by, amongst others, J. Goldberg, 'Poles and Jews in the 17th and 18th Centuries: Rejection or Acceptance', *Jahrbücher für Geschichte Osteuropas*, NF, 22/2 (1974), 248–82. Obstacles (especially of a social nature) standing in the way of the implementation of laws in the Duchy of Warsaw are mentioned in Grynwaser, *Pisma*, i. 37–66, and in K. Sójka-Zielińska, *Kodeks Napoleona: Historia i współczesność* (Warsaw, 2008), 199–203, while discrepancies between law and administrative practice with regard to Jews in the Kingdom of Poland are noted by Wodziński, *Władze Królestwa Polskiego wobec chasydyzmu*, 175–220.

[30] These are usually documents originating from the state; letters sent by Jews are also present, but make up on average only 5% of the corpus. Given the significant disproportion in the amount of surviving material, I will only reference sources from selected archives.

account.[31] An identical procedure was followed again later that year, in December 1808, when another Jew, Józef Moszkowicz, submitted a request to the authorities for recompense for wood requisitioned for the repair of ferries for the French army to cross the river Vistula.[32] In these cases, all the procedures that applied to Christian petitioners were adhered to.[33] Several people were involved in the effort to resolve the issue: the former and incumbent mayors, as well as the prefect of the department. In both cases the heart of the matter was whether the requisition of goods was legal.

If the administration infringed the law in individual cases, it was possible, in accordance with the general principles obtaining, to take legal action in order to assert the civil claims of the injured parties. This procedure, which was open also to Jews, was sometimes invoked by state officials themselves. For example, the prefect of the Radom department called upon the mayor of Radom to reopen local Jewish breweries—which had been shut down by the mayor a few weeks earlier because the Jews had infringed local agreements—and to permit their owners to produce beer without restriction; he concluded with a reminder that 'if the owners of the breweries should suffer any damage as a consequence of this closure, they shall have the right to seek compensation in court'.[34] In another case, the mayor pointed out the possibility of a later prosecution of claims against the administration.[35] It is worth mentioning that the right to take legal action in disputes with the administration was significant from the point of view of regulating the rights belonging to Jews; in Prussia the enforcement of this principle became 'an important element facilitating the undertaking and achievement of the emancipation of the Jews, because the assessment of any possibly contentious issues that arose could be subjected

---

[31] Archiwum Państwowe w Płocku (hereafter APP), Akta miasta Płocka (AmP), 415, fo. 2^{r–v}: prefect of the Płock department to the chief of the Płock police, 11 Aug. 1808. This letter shows an engaged approach to the issue: '[With regard to] the request of Samuel Szaj in respect of recompense for the merchandise taken from him by the Municipality as requisition for the benefit of the French army . . . the police authorities of the town of Płock are instructed to summon the former mayor Jędrze-jewicz and obtain from him a detailed elucidation of this complaint by requiring that he present supporting evidence. Once they are assured that the complaint is genuine, a satisfactory recompense to the supplicant should be calculated . . . as the Municipality was instructed to do by the Chamber of Administration on the 17th day of October, and furthermore a detailed report on this circumstance must be made out to the Prefect within fourteen days.'   [32] APP, AmP, 415, fos. 3^{r–v}, 5^{r}–6^{r}.

[33] In Moszkowicz's case, the petitioner himself was heard first, after which the former mayor was urged in writing to inform the municipality 'as promptly as possible' about 'who authorized, during the passage of the French army, the requisition from the Jew Józef Moszkowicz of 325[?] planks of 1½-inch timber and eight pieces of unwrought timber 8 inches wide and 30 feet long, and what the said planks and timber were used for, as no information in this respect can be obtained from the files left behind by the previous office of the municipality': ibid. 3^{v}. The former mayor sent a written explanation, and the whole case was resubmitted to the prefect of the department. See ibid. 3^{r–v}, 5^{r}–6^{r}.

[34] Archiwum Państwowe w Radomiu (hereafter APR), Akta miasta Radomia (AmR), 182, fo. 8^{r}.

[35] Ibid. 11^{v}.

to rational legal judgement by qualified judicial personnel'.[36] In the Duchy of Warsaw, which did not exist long enough for the effects of the principles it introduced to become apparent, one could not speak of such far-reaching consequences.

It is worth asking why the representatives of the state authorities were so anxious to have issues thoroughly clarified and to make sure that the population, in this case Jews, did not suffer loss. Considering the condition of the Duchy at the time—a state still in the process of formation and contending with numerous problems—it seems that, from the government's point of view, the care shown towards petitioners was of key importance. It was after all incumbent on the government to ensure that the Duchy's inhabitants did not doubt the justice of its actions; otherwise, it could risk losing the trust of the people, and even greater difficulties might arise with future requisitions of goods. Although these were made under duress, without seeking the citizens' consent, their co-operation and their belief that they would be compensated financially made the acquisition of the necessary goods far easier. It was thus pragmatic concerns that determined that the authorities behaved in this way rather than in any other.

That standard administrative procedures were followed with respect to Jewish petitioners is further confirmed by the content of a letter sent by the town council of Radom to the mayor regarding a plan proposed in 1814 by the Supreme Provisional Council (Rada Najwyższa Tymczasowa). The plan envisaged the compulsory removal of the town's Jewish inhabitants from its centre and their relocation to the outskirts by 1 July 1815. The town council reminded the mayor of the indispensability of informing the Jewish population about the plan, 'lest they, at a later time and under the pretext of ignorance, inconvenience the Honourable Mayor, the Council, and the Most Honourable Prefect with unnecessary letters, and lest they, owing to such delay, continue from time to time to attempt to force their way into the town, thus violating its privilege and law'.[37] The very idea of a compulsory resettlement was clearly linked to the attempts, of medieval origin, to separate the Christian and Jewish populations in the public space, and the town council's reasoning—calling on the privilege *de non tolerandis Judaeis*—had an equally feudal provenance. All this was a manifestation of the persistent aversion of the authorities to the presence—excessive in their eyes—of Jews in the urban space.[38] At the same time, however, the council's letter confirmed that appeals submitted by Jews, like the appeals of any other petitioners, would result in the suspension of the administrative process.

Although requisitions of goods for military use had taken place before, as had pleas by Jews to local authorities to refrain from certain activities, this had occurred on a less formalized basis; the old Commonwealth simply did not have a state administration (in the modern meaning of the term). It was only towards the end of

---

[36] L. Ziątkowski, *Między niemożliwym a koniecznym: Reformy państwa pruskiego w końcu XVIII i na początku XIX wieku a proces równouprawnienia Żydów ze szczególnym uwzględnieniem sytuacji na Śląsku* (Wrocław, 2007), 38.   [37] APR, AmR, 467, fos. 4–5.   [38] Ibid.

the eighteenth century that the first attempts to modernize were initiated through the establishment of government offices running a state-wide administration, especially for the treasury,[39] though a bureaucracy had not yet been created; there was still a division between the manorial and the royal territories, each operating according to its own rules. In the Duchy of Warsaw, on the other hand—as in the period of Prussian rule, and following the French model—there was an attempt to construct an administrative apparatus according to new rules and to base it on uniform procedures, seeking a professionalization of administrative posts[40] and requiring that civil servants and officials abide strictly by the law under threat of disciplinary, criminal, or compensational liability for any violations, including, to a limited degree, cases of infractions against the interests of petitioners.[41] And although these new rules of operation for the administration encountered countless obstacles when implemented and were far from consistently followed,[42] they did constitute a space of contact with public authorities different from what had obtained in the time of the Commonwealth, a space in which a pragmatic outlook and new principles led to the imposition of bureaucratic solutions and to a greater rigour in the application of the law.

Positive Decisions in Cases Involving Jews

Reading analyses of the legislation regulating the status of Jews, and examining attempts made by individuals or groups to have prohibitions and impediments lifted, one may be left with the impression that in nearly all cases Jews received only negative decisions. It is true that requests submitted by Jews for legal restrictions to be waived were indeed usually denied, but the documents that contain such decisions do not, however, constitute the entirety of the surviving source material. Examples of cases in which religion did not play a role are numerous. Provided that circumstances allowed, such cases were decided in favour of Jewish petitioners,

[39] See R. Rybarski, *Skarbowość Polski w dobie rozbiorów* (Kraków, 1937).

[40] This was to be achieved, for example, by introducing examinations to certify that civil servants were qualified to carry out their functions and by creating a higher educational establishment to train cadres for the administration. As noted by Barbara Grochulska, 'for the first time, the professionalism of civil servants was foregrounded': B. Grochulska, *Księstwo Warszawskie* (Warsaw, 1991), 118, 134–6. For more on the functioning of the administration in the Duchy, see Kallas, *Organy administracji terytorialnej w Księstwie Warszawskim*, *passim*; M. Krzymkowski, *Rada Stanu Księstwa Warszawskiego* (Poznań, 2011), 178–228; id., *Status prawny urzędników Księstwa Warszawskiego* (Poznań, 2004), *passim*; Sobociński, *Historia ustroju i prawa Księstwa Warszawskiego*, 125–291.

[41] Krzymkowski, *Status prawny urzędników Księstwa Warszawskiego*, 113–29. The sought-after ideal bureaucrat and ideal way of organizing the administration corresponded with the vision described over a century later by Max Weber in *Economy and Society: An Outline of Interpretive Sociology*, ed. G. Roth and C. Wittich, 2 vols. (Berkeley and Los Angeles, 1978), ii. 956–1005.

[42] Especially because of the initially poor preparation of civil servants, the lack of sufficiently detailed rules governing the mutual relations between the different powers, and the uncertainties arising from the application of newly introduced laws. See Grynwaser, *Pisma*, i. 37–53; Kallas, *Organy administracji terytorialnej w Księstwie Warszawskim*, 157–8.

with consideration being given to their individual situations; sometimes the supplicant was even offered exemption from the general rules that applied to everyone, including Christian citizens, on account of special difficulties experienced by him. As an example, we may take cases when the municipal authorities approved the suspension of the quartering of troops. A favourable decision on this matter was given to the Jewish inhabitants of Przytyk, who asked that billeting in their homes be suspended for Passover. A similar privilege was sought on behalf of 'the entire community of the Mosaic faith in Radom' by four Jews who argued that such a privilege had already been granted more than once in Radom.[43] They obtained approval without further ado. Particular difficulties were also taken into account when a local mayor granted to a Jewish man by the name of Kierzbaum an extension of a time limit for collecting liquor from the local customs warehouse, because a means of transport could not be found.[44] Despite the initially sharp tone of the official letters sent to him by the authorities, Kierzbaum's request was eventually approved. A few days later, he again wrote a formal request to the mayor, this time asking for permission to sell liquor in amounts smaller than required by the regulations (because he 'could find no purchaser' for such great amounts of liquor), and he was again granted a favourable decision.[45]

The reason for some of the authorities' positive decisions, which sometimes waived restrictive regulations that applied to all, may have been an awareness of the objective difficulties experienced by everyone in equal degree: war damage, billeting, and requisitions were ubiquitous in the Duchy of Warsaw.[46] That small state came into being in 1807, at a time when for months on end the French army was on the move; and subsequently the need arose to maintain a Polish military force. Nor did the following years bring about stabilization. In 1809 a long-lasting struggle took place in the territories of the Duchy against an Austrian offensive, and three years later another war was unleashed. The movements of armies continued for another two years, until the state was officially abolished. Only a handful of its most entrepreneurial individuals (such as court suppliers and industrialists) could benefit; for the great majority of the population, the lack of stabilization and the

---

[43] APR, AmR, 779, fo. 1$^{r–v}$. Approval for the suspension of billeting for personal reasons was granted to Christians as well, for example on the grounds that they had borne the burden of that duty for many years; see ibid. 2^{r}–5^{r}.

[44] The mayor granted the extension 'in view of . . . the passage of troops and therefore the impossibility of obtaining a wagon or settling a sale': APR, AmR, 182, fo. 17.   [45] Ibid. 20$^{r–v}$.

[46] The quartering of all the troops stationed in a given area in private houses, farm buildings, and neighbouring villages was the only solution, as army barracks were virtually non-existent; and such billeting gave rise to complaints everywhere. See Czubaty, *Księstwo Warszawskie*, 113–16, 127–8, who points out the scale of the related problems, reminding us that the war of 1807, 'conducted in extremely difficult conditions, was not just a war over strategic goals but also over food and quarters' (p. 122). From the point of view of those on the other side (the owners of the dwellings), constant quartering, aside from reducing living and utility areas, caused a severe decline in rental income, which is why they were 'remembered as the most burdensome plague': Grochulska, *Księstwo Warszawskie*, 52.

recurring state of war caused hardship and, as Jarosław Czubaty has noted, created an atmosphere of general despondency.[47] Many of the requests found in local sources were motivated by war damage, as in the case of a Jewish inhabitant of Płock, whose one house in Radziw was left in ruins by the French army, and his other one, in Płock, was standing half-demolished as a result of damage caused by billeting.[48] In these circumstances the sympathy shown by the state authorities is understandable, as is the liberal treatment they offered to all categories of people. Favourable administrative decisions could also have been the result of attempts to expedite the work of the bureaucracy. Faced with a multitude of tasks, the officials might reasonably use uniform criteria to hasten the processing and issuing of decisions in order not to give petitioners cause to submit further appeals.[49]

It is worth mentioning in passing that among the officials themselves there was often no agreement as to how a given case should be settled, which led to conflicts between them. Such was the situation, for example, in the case of the mayor of Radom's decision to shut down breweries owned by Mendel Szmul and Mosiek Herszkowicz. These were soon unlawfully reopened by a certain Choiński (on the initiative of a third person, a plenipotentiary of the holder of the eldership in which the breweries were located), which in turn prompted the mayor to impose a fine of 30 zlotys on the Jews for not notifying the appropriate authorities. At the same time, he intended to punish Choiński. The latter's consequent complaint against the mayor led to a sharp reaction from the prefect, and soon afterwards the mayor wrote back saying that he felt offended by Choiński's complaint 'and even more by the pronouncements delivered by the Most Honourable Prefect'.[50] The mayor's feelings were clearly not taken into consideration by the prefect, who soon called on him to reopen the Jewish-owned breweries.[51] Instances when officials of different ranks took divergent positions on a given case were frequent, just as they were in cases instituted in connection with the activities of Christians. The question of religion was not significant in this context: at issue was whether a given official had the authority to make a ruling and whether regulations were being applied appropriately.

The State's Relationship to 'Useful' Jews

The examples above pertain to the situations of what one might call 'average' Jews, whose favourable treatment could have resulted from such circumstances as the administration's efforts to expedite and automate the processing of a backlog of cases. It is also worthwhile, however, to look at situations in which favourable decisions may have derived from the authorities' conviction that certain categories of Jews had a greater utility to the state—a sentiment not unknown during the

---

[47] Czubaty, *Księstwo Warszawskie*, 151–2. [48] APP, AmP, 14, fos. 16ᵛ–17ᵛ.

[49] W. Rostocki, *Korpus w gęsie pióra uzbrojony: Urzędnicy warszawscy, ich życie i praca w Księstwie Warszawskim i Królestwie Polskim do roku 1831* (Warsaw, 1972), 22–3. [50] APR, AmR, 182, fo. 9ʳ.

[51] For the entire case of Mendel Szmul and Mosiek Herszkowicz, see ibid. 1ʳ–10ʳ.

period of the Commonwealth too. Such categories included, first and foremost, merchants and bankers engaged in large-scale financial operations. For the government of the Duchy of Warsaw, a state constantly struggling with a fiscal deficit, people who stimulated the economy had significant value. Caring for the interests of this category of people was, in essence, a sign of caring for the interests of the state treasury, in which respect the Duchy was similar to neighbouring states, such as Prussia, which had created a separate category of protected Jews, or Austria, which made efforts to abolish the imposition of customs dues on its Jewish merchants.[52]

The Duchy of Warsaw, too, felt the need to create conditions to attract people of this category to conduct their activities. This goal was to be achieved by, among other measures, the Moratorium Act introduced early in 1807, which was intended to assist people struggling to repay debts resulting from loss of assets caused by the movements of armies, billeting, military requisitions, increased public levies, and other burdens arising from the current situation. However, moratorium letters were issued on the condition that the recipient held capital of such an amount that, in peacetime, he could have discharged his entire indebtedness without exhausting all his available means. Of particular interest here are the conditions laid down for merchants and bankers: to be granted a moratorium, they were expected to prove that, besides the losses they had suffered, they had also lost their trade connections and 'sources of credit, foreign or domestic, from which they could seek aid'.[53] Evidently, the purpose of the act was to prevent merchants and industrialists from declaring bankruptcy or a suspension of economic activity, which would have had a strong impact on the supply capacities of the state. Archival materials relating to particular merchants' efforts to obtain moratorium letters, which allowed delay of payment for six months, are an invaluable source of information about the material situation of merchants, including Jews, and about the conditions in which they had come to operate at the outset of the Duchy of Warsaw's existence.[54]

Both Jews and Christians applied for moratoriums. Most were inhabitants of Warsaw who engaged in international trade. The sources of their financial difficulties were requisitions imposed not only within the borders of the Duchy but also

[52] Austria sought to protect the good financial condition of its 'useful' Jewish subjects engaged in international trade by appealing to the authorities of the Duchy of Warsaw to waive customs dues on its border with the Duchy. A request to this end was made by the emperor's envoy to the court of Frederick Augustus, citing privileges enjoyed by Jewish subjects in Austria irrespective of whether they came from Saxony or the Duchy: AGAD, RM, 168, fos. 1–3. On the 'rehabilitation' of the merchant profession and the perception of trade as the best way of increasing the state's wealth, see Grochulska, *Księstwo Warszawskie*, 122–3: 'The problem of a merchant's professionalism was recognized to be so important that it was stipulated for the first time that there should be co-operation between trade councils and Jewish merchants as the finest experts.'

[53] *Gazeta Warszawska*, 10 Feb. 1807, pp. 176–81.

[54] In applying for a moratorium letter the petitioner had to provide a detailed description of his situation, attaching a list of debtors and a detailed account of his assets. See the thorough examination of the material situation of the Kalisz merchant Salomon Stange, whose application was accepted, in AGAD, Komisja Rządząca (KR) II, 8, fos. 29–34.

during their travels to German markets, as was the case with the Warsaw merchants of Brabant goods Wigdor and Reysa, a married couple 'whose merchandise, along with the wagoner and horses, was seized [in Leipzig] upon the arrival of French troops, and on which merchandise they were forced to pay a sizeable levy, as well as other similar fees they incurred on their journey, which they have witnesses' testimonies to support'.[55] People involved in economic activity also lost their sources of income because of quartering and war damage, as happened to the couple just mentioned, who 'maintained billets during the passage of the army',[56] or to Lipman Markus Lewita, one of whose seven(!) houses was 'first made to serve as a French and Polish military hospital, and now as barracks for the troops'; two of his other houses were vacant because of the war.[57] Another difficulty for those involved in trade was caused by the embargo on English products, a problem that affected the Warsaw merchant Kacper Hirsch Janków. A source of considerable financial difficulty for him—as for many others—was high public levies, raised even further during the war; the moneys collected were spent on wages for men recruited to build fortifications and 'on hospital needs, advances to the war fund, and contributions to the *kahal* elders'.[58] These difficulties were cited as arguments in favour of obtaining a moratorium on debt repayment.

Positive decisions—in the form of a moratorium letter—were made as often for Christians as for Jews; it is hard to find any differences in this respect. It is also interesting that an initially negative ruling by a moratorium committee did not necessarily result in the granting of a letter being automatically refused by the Justice Directorate (Dyrekcja Sprawiedliwości), which reviewed applications before they were sent for final decision to the Government Committee (Komisja Rządząca). Referring again to the case of Wigdor and Reysa, when the moratorium committee established that a portion of the assets that they listed did not qualify for approval (they were deemed not to constitute sufficient security for the debts), the director of justice did not confine himself to providing an opinion on the moratorium application but sought to verify its legitimacy by scrutinizing the reasons why certain assets had not been approved and requesting that the body responsible for refusing the application provide a more detailed account of the rationale.[59] The body responsible for issuing moratoriums would itself sometimes take the Jewish petitioners' side, as for example when the issuing of a moratorium letter for Wigdor and Reysa was challenged by one of their creditors, a certain Zawadzki. After hearing both sides, the moratorium committee concluded that 'to the best of its com-

---

[55] AGAD, KR II, 7, fo. 69. The case of Wigdor and Reysa is particularly interesting because of the multiplicity of issues connected with their petition, and I shall therefore return to it again below. At this point, it is worth recalling that in the early years of the nineteenth century Jews still comprised the majority (approximately 90%) of merchants coming to markets from the Duchy of Warsaw: see B. Grochulska, *Handel zagraniczny Księstwa Warszawskiego: Z badań nad strukturą gospodarczą* (Warsaw, 1967), 168. Hence their greater significance from the point of view of the economy.

[56] AGAD, KR II, 7, fo. 69.   [57] AGAD, KR II, 8, fo. 312.

[58] AGAD, KR II, 7, fos. 69, 115–18.   [59] Ibid. 72.

petence, it cannot find any fault on the part of the persons accused, because the matter is not of a kind that could, in the eyes of the law, be understood as deception or fraud'.[60] Pressing traditional charges of fraud against the Jews did not suffice in this particular case. In the view of the committee, Zawadzki had provided insufficient proof of his contention. In any event, surviving documents suggest that decisions to grant or deny a moratorium were based on the merits of the case rather than on the petitioner's religion. In the face of the state's economic paralysis, one had to take care of all entrepreneurs.

Such attempts to care for those categories of Jews whose activities were crucial to the economic life of the state can also be discerned at the level of central state legislation. One manifestation of that was the establishment within the structure of the Jewish tax, the *Geleitzoll*, of both a special lower rate for traders in cattle or 'other necessities of life' and a privilege in the form of permission to cross the border several times without incurring additional fees, provided this was done within the four-week stay in the Duchy which was permitted to all.[61] It was a sign of the government's pragmatic approach and its differentiation of Jews in different situations according to their utility.

Similar considerations seem to have determined the position of the Minister of Internal Affairs, Jan Paweł Łuszczewski, when he issued his proposal to establish special conditions for the purchase by Jews of brick houses. He argued that 'because also among Jews there are people who by their enterprise and their wealth bring benefit to the country, it would be not only unwise to deny them special protection, but indeed it is advisable to grant certain privileges to them, in order to encourage others to use their funds to establish factories and other undertakings'.[62] This shows proof of a willingness to grant certain benefits to a narrow category of Jews —a willingness shown several times over the course of a two-year period, during which the minister sent repeated requests to the Council of Ministers for the matter to be regulated and even openly proposed a decree that would, with certain conditions, allow Jews to acquire urban real property. The Council of Ministers failed to respond.[63] He substantiated his position with pragmatic arguments: after the pronouncement by the king on 30 October 1811 of a decree prohibiting Jews from producing and trading in alcoholic beverages, he took the view that it would be advisable to allow Jewish capital to enter the domestic market in order to prevent it from being transferred abroad. Furthermore, considering that the decree was intended to encourage Jews to take up occupations requiring greater stability, it was fitting to facilitate longer-lasting residence in one place. Another argument was that, in light of the very poor condition of the bourgeoisie (as a result of the ravages of war), bringing a new category of buyers to the market would lead to an increase in the price of real estate.[64] These actions undermine Eisenbach's depiction of Łuszczewski: it turns out that the minister—for all that he treated Jews as an

---

[60] Ibid. 73.   [61] AGAD, RM, 168, fo. 5.   [62] AGAD, RM, 167, fos. 4, 9.
[63] See ibid. 5–8, 74–6, 80–4, 93–4.   [64] Ibid. 84–5.

inferior category requiring many years of 'civilizing' and as a group unworthy of legal equality—at the same time showed a pragmatic approach and proposed rewards for selected individuals particularly useful to the state.[65]

It is worth parenthetically correcting here an error in Eisenbach's work. Referring to the fiasco of the proposed decree that would conditionally allow the purchase of urban real property by Jews, he mistakenly argued that the project failed because of the ministers' negative attitude towards the purchase of landed property. Eisenbach's view was that, after the king had turned down the decree proposal and had suggested that this issue be regulated by a police order rather than a law, 'the ministers of the Duchy did not accept the king's suggestion and insisted that a complete ban on the purchase of *rural landed property* by Jews be maintained. The council did not discuss this question again.'[66] Eisenbach refers to a letter of 25 April 1812 from Łuszczewski to the Council of Ministers. In reality, the conclusions to be drawn from that letter are far broader. Although the minister in his long letter did indeed oppose granting Jews the right to purchase rural property,[67] its essence was to draw attention to the *need* to *entitle* Jews to buy *urban* property and the *benefits* that this would bring. Among the reasons he listed were the difficult situation of Christian town-dwellers, who were often forced to 'abandon their homes, which they are not allowed to sell to Jews, but cannot find other purchasers',[68] as well as the proclamation in Prussia of the Edict of Toleration of 11 March 1812, which granted Jews rights equal to those of all other citizens. Łuszczewski claimed that

This law, granting Jews extensive liberties without hindering foreign Jews from settling in the Prussian states, will likely arouse in our Jews—who are burdened with higher taxes, deprived of political rights, and are so greatly limited in their scope to properly enjoy freedoms *granted to them by nature*—an irresistible urge to move abroad, where they might conduct their lives without restrictions. Such an event should be feared most in the case of the more affluent Jews, particularly in departments located in greater proximity to Prussia, who, as both more enlightened and wealthier, would find their reception in the Prussian lands less difficult. The prefect of Poznań has already informed me of the great impression this law has made on our Jews. This is not the place . . . for me to expatiate on the consequences that the departure of the most enlightened and most wealthy Jews would have for the country . . .

---

[65] Interestingly, this argument was adopted by Jewish petitioners themselves. The vodka distiller Samuel Moses Muscat, for example, asking the minister to approve the issue by the prefect of the Warsaw department of a licence for the purchase of a brick house in Warsaw, cited his utility to the state treasury and to the merchants and citizens of the state: ibid. 15–16, 26.

[66] Eisenbach, *Kwestia równouprawnienia Żydów w Królestwie Polskim*, 128 (emphasis added).

[67] As reasons, he cited fears that these properties would soon become the object of frequent exchange (which threatened a loss of economic stability); the fact that the Jews were not accustomed to farming; and the Jews' financial domination over Christians, which would make the latter uncompetitive and unable to introduce equally important improvements in farming. See AGAD, RM, 167, fo. 92. It should be noted that the second and third arguments are mutually exclusive since the third implies the Jews' potential proficiency in farming.   [68] Ibid.

It only befits me to add that, when one cannot be prohibited by force from moving abroad along with one's riches, there remains no way of *retaining in our country the most useful Jews* other than by unknotting the bonds that are choking them at present.[69]

The reason why the council 'did not discuss this question again' was not, in fact, a negative attitude on the part of the ministers, which pertained only to the question of rural landed property. The Minister of Justice and Minister of Police,[70] as well as the Minister of Internal Affairs, were in favour of regulating this matter in accordance with the requests of the state's wealthier Jewish inhabitants, as it was in the interest of both citizens and the state treasury (and—as indirectly implied in the letter—in accord with the rights inherently given to Jews by nature). Although this positive attitude to the interests of wealthy Jews ultimately failed to produce a separate law, it found practical expression in the issue by Frederick Augustus of personal licences for the purchase of real property in Warsaw to two Jewish entrepreneurs, Tobiasz Michałowicz and Salomon Mojżesz Muscat, a fact ignored by Eisenbach.[71] The Minister of Internal Affairs and the deputy mayor of Warsaw, as well as, indirectly, the prefect of the Warsaw department, who advocated granting Muscat the licence, all emphasized his extraordinary utility to the state and its citizenry.[72]

The Kahal *as a Quasi-State Organ of the Administration*

Another interesting area of research concerns the relationship between Jewish community councils and the state—and here too we are brought back to the question of the authorities' pragmatism. As has been emphasized in the historiography, already in medieval times '*kahal*s were drawn into the orbit of the state-wide treasury administration' and formed a kind of 'Jewish department'.[73] Requiring the *kahal*s to act as taxing bodies, which entailed that they be entrusted with a number of supervisory powers, influenced the development of Jewish autonomy in Poland.[74] By comparison with earlier times, Jewish autonomy weakened in the eighteenth century at all three levels—local, regional, and central—particularly in noble towns,

---

[69] Ibid. 93–4 (emphasis added).

[70] For the position of these two ministers, see ibid. 63–4, 69–72.

[71] Eisenbach, *Kwestia równouprawnienia Żydów w Królestwie Polskim*, 127, did mention petitions by several Jews, including Muscat, but omitted to say that two of them achieved positive outcomes, although he did point out other such cases in the period of the Kingdom of Poland.

[72] The deputy mayor of Warsaw described him as 'one of the richest and most honest Jews' and stated that, as the founder of the largest distillery, he was 'of utility to the country and the treasury', and as such was 'deserving of the government's favourable attention': AGAD, RM, 167, fo. 13.

[73] I. Schiper, 'Samorząd żydowski w Polsce na przełomie wieku 18 i 19-go (1764–1831)', *Miesięcznik Żydowski*, I/I (1931), 514.

[74] Ibid. See also G. D. Hundert, 'Kahał i samorząd miejski w miastach prywatnych w XVII i XVIII w.', in A. Link-Lenczowski and T. Polański (eds.), *Żydzi w dawnej Rzeczypospolitej* (Wrocław, 1991), 72, who points out that in private towns the *kahal* was included in the administrative structures and its members were sometimes given instructions by the magnate as if they had been appointed by him.

owing to increasing interventions by feudal lords seeking a fuller realization of their interests.[75] The demand for the abolition or restriction of the *kahal*'s autonomy, promoted in the last years of the Commonwealth by both Christian and Jewish reformers,[76] found fertile soil in the Prussian partition. In 1797 the Judenreglement led to the abolition of the autonomy of the *kahal*, stripping it of most of its powers. It soon turned out, however, that the new model of state management of its Jewish subjects' affairs, while in accord with Enlightenment views, had serious limitations. It was much easier to rely on the mediation of *kahals*, especially when it came to the collection of special taxes levied on Jews. Consequently, a number of their fiscal prerogatives had already been restored by 1799.[77] In the Duchy of Warsaw, too— despite the strong centralizing tendencies and the creation of the administrative structure from scratch—the authorities accepted, tacitly, the existence of Jewish autonomy and consented to the convenient mediation of *kahals*, which relieved them of the necessity of dealing with the internal matters of the communities.

This is illustrated by correspondence with the leaders of the Kraków Jewish community. They mediated in issues of taxation, the military, and other matters concerning Jewish inhabitants. Community elders were therefore treated by the local branches of state administration in an official manner: in correspondence with the *kahal*, all honorific forms of address were maintained, and requests (recommendations) conveyed to the elders were accompanied by justifications.[78] It was clear that the authorities' intention was to make the purpose and the essence of

---

[75] G. D. Hundert, *The Jews in a Polish Private Town: The Case of Opatów in the Eighteenth Century* (Baltimore and London, 1992), 134–55; id., *Jews in Poland–Lithuania in the Eighteenth Century: A Genealogy of Modernity* (Berkeley, 2004), 99–118; A. Leszczyński, 'Metoda kontroli władzy państwowej i dominialnej nad autonomią Żydów Korony od połowy XVII w. do 1795 r.', *Biuletyn Żydowskiego Instytutu Historycznego*, 147–8 (1988), 21–7; A. Polonsky, *The Jews in Poland and Russia*, 3 vols. (Oxford, 2010–12), i. 66; M. J. Rosman, *The Lords' Jews: Magnate–Jewish Relations in the Polish–Lithuanian Commonwealth during the Eighteenth Century* (Cambridge, Mass., 1990), 186–7.

[76] This demand was usually justified by the necessity for a closer integration of Jews with the state's other inhabitants. See I. Schiper, 'Wewnętrzna organizacja Żydów w dawnej Rzeczypospolitej', in Schiper, Tartakower, and Hafftka (eds.), *Żydzi w Polsce Odrodzonej*, i. 108–9. The demand to abolish the autonomy of the *kahal* first began to appear more widely with the rise of new socio-political ideas. As Samuel Hirszhorn correctly observed almost a century ago, in earlier periods the norm was a mosaic of nationalities, and 'for all the hatred felt for Jews, no one in the former Polish state ever accused them of "separatism", or of the creation of "a state within the state", because to the Poles the notion of internal autonomy was perfectly well understood. The idea of forcing a motley heterogeneity of nationalities into one Polish nationality was completely foreign to Poles. Nothing could seem more alien to the Polish gentry than attempting to assimilate the Jews in order to grant them legal equality in return': Hirszhorn, *Historja Żydów w Polsce*, 20. See also the interesting discussion in S. Volkov, *Das jüdische Projekt der Moderne: Zehn Essays* (Munich, 2001), 13–31, on the non-existence of the notion of a minority in pre-modern societies lacking in homogeneity.

[77] Schiper, 'Samorząd żydowski w Polsce', 517–18.

[78] See e.g. Archiwum Żydowskiego Instytutu Historycznego (hereafter AŻIH), Gmina Wyznaniowa Żydowska w Krakowie (GWŻK), 57/1, 1001, mayor of Kraków to leaders of the *kahal*, 1 Feb. 1812.

these recommendations understandable to the community leaders; the goal was probably to ensure their co-operation in the conducting of administrative business. The state authorities, rather than trying to reach the city's Jewish inhabitants directly, sent letters to their elders about all sorts of matters—for example, when the need arose to disseminate information about a law already in force,[79] or to introduce a new law,[80] to collaborate against crime,[81] to help a Jewish inhabitant of Kazimierz find a site to build a new brick house,[82] to recruit Jewish tailors for the preparation of uniforms for the military,[83] to ensure that an overdue liquor tax (*podatek czopowy*) was paid,[84] or to engage Jews in attempts to achieve common goals, such as protecting the city from flooding.[85] Sometimes internal communi-

[79] AŻIH, GWŻK, 55, 989, Frederick Augustus's comments of 17 Apr. 1810 on the decree introducing a consumption tax, sent to the Jewish community, among others.

[80] AŻIH, GWŻK, 56, 997, mayor of Kraków to the *kahal* elders, 26 Mar. 1811: 'I am sending to the honourable leaders of the *kahal* an announcement regarding the introduction of a patent tax, in order that they might apply themselves to publicize it forthwith; and, at the same time, in accordance with the announcement, for the tax to be implemented they . . . should without delay draw up an attested register of all persons liable to payment, according to the scheme attached under A., and assign to them their appropriate tax class according to the tariff attached under B.; they should exercise careful judgement in [allocating appropriate people to] the categories of artists, professionals, and craftsmen in the classification, and be attentive to securing a simpler revenue so that neither the treasury nor those liable to payment suffer. The honourable leaders are to present to me within eight days three identically worded copies of the said register, drawn up as conscientiously and accurately as possible, and bearing their signatures.' What they were charged to do represented a time-consuming undertaking, requiring the individual listing of both natives of the Duchy and foreigners, and of the concessions to which each was entitled.

[81] As in the case of a stolen diamond ring, in which the *kahal* was called on to co-operate with the state: AŻIH, GWŻK, 57/1, 1015, mayor of Kraków to the *kahal*, 7 Apr. 1812.

[82] AŻIH, GWŻK, 57/2, 1031, mayor of Kraków to the *kahal* of Kazimierz, 20 Aug. 1812: 'In response to the request of the Jew Jonas Auerfeld . . . submitted to the Most Honourable Prefect regarding the designation of a location for building his brick house in the Jewish Town, [the mayor] states that the supplicant is to apply to the *kahal* of Kazimierz, which with the help of the honourable gentleman Dobrzański, the local intendant, and the honourable gentleman Drachny, the municipal inspector of works, will indicate an appropriate place in accordance with the royal decree of 19 March of this year, enacted with a view to the enhancement of the town.' The plans, along with the affidavits provided by the elders confirming that he would be able to erect the building, were then to be submitted by Auerfeld to the mayor so as to let the matter proceed.

[83] See AŻIH, GWŻK, 55, 990, garrison commander to Kazimierz municipality, letter delivered to the elders of the Jewish synagogue, 5 May 1810; AŻIH, GWŻK, 57/2, 1029, mayor of Kraków to the *kahal* of Kazimierz, 15 Aug. 1812. In the latter case, the letter to the *kahal* reads: 'By the express order of the Most Honourable Prefect, the honourable leaders of the Jewish *kahal* of Kazimierz are instructed that tomorrow . . . at 8 o'clock in the morning they are strictly bound to deliver without fail all Jews who are tailors or clothiers . . . to the Most Honourable Prefect's office; this is in order to make uniforms for the army, in return for immediate compensation as they will have contracted. In view of the urgent need the country is in, if the honourable elders of the *kahal* fail to carry out this instruction, they will be held strictly responsible.'

[84] AŻIH, GWŻK, 57/2, 1032, mayor of Kraków to the *kahal* elders, 20 Aug. 1812.

[85] For example, the mayor of Kraków called on the *kahal* elders 'immediately to issue instructions' for eight Jews with appropriate equipment to report to work in order to safeguard the bridge against ice

cations of the state administration were copied to the *kahal* for its information.[86] Thus, the *kahal* was continually obliged to carry out tasks proper to the public administrative authorities, such as implementing laws and government decisions. There is no reason to doubt that similar practices were also in place in other cities; this is corroborated by one of the few letters to a *kahal* that has survived in urban records—a letter from the commissioner of the Lublin department. In connection with information obtained by him regarding the Jewish cemetery located in the centre of the town of Bełżyce, the commissioner calls on the *kahal* leadership immediately to submit a formal request to the state authorities to designate a new site for the cemetery. 'A report on the outcome of the directive must be delivered within twelve days, as otherwise the police commissioner will have to dispatch someone to effectuate his order, which proceeds from the will of the government.'[87]

Kahal elders were sometimes also treated as an advisory body and called on to take positions on an issue regarding a Jewish town-dweller. This happened, for example, when the authorities in Kraków needed to issue a ruling on a private complaint against the city lodged with the prefect by two Jewish leaseholders of the liquor tax.[88] It should be emphasized that opinions and suggestions offered by the Jewish community council were sometimes regarded as having force. For example, when elders petitioned for the payment of debts owed by tax leaseholders to be enforced, the mayor ordered this to be carried out; when the *kahal* requested soon afterwards that the order be suspended, the mayor again complied with the *kahal*'s suggestion.[89] Interestingly, the *kahal* itself treated the municipal authorities as an ally in administrative matters—for instance, when one of the *kahal*'s subjects, Sara Goldman, threatened to move away from Kazimierz without first settling her tax arrears.[90] In other words, requests could be exchanged in both directions, although it was decidedly much less common for the *kahal* to initiate action. It is also hard to speak of an equal relationship here, as only the state authorities could threaten to compel the fulfilment of obligations in the event that the *kahal* failed to carry them out.[91]

---

damage. Thus it is not the mayor, officially the local representative of state power, but the *kahal* that is supposed to issue the instructions; this is evidently to ensure greater effectiveness. AŻIH, GWŻK, 57/1, 1004, mayor of Kraków to the *kahal* of Kazimierz, 18 Feb. 1812.

[86] As happened in the case of the leaseholders of Jewish taxes, when the prefect informed the mayor that the leaseholders were free to invest the taxes, and urged that the city intendants be instructed to offer the leaseholders any help they might need. AŻIH, GWŻK, 57/1, 1007, vice-prefect of the Kraków district to the mayor of Kraków, for the attention of the *kahal* leaders, 24 Feb. 1812.

[87] Archiwum Państwowe w Lublinie, Akta miasta Bełżyce, 18, fo. 1.

[88] AŻIH, GWŻK, 57/1, 1016, mayor of Kraków to the *kahal* leaders, 20 Apr. 1812.

[89] AŻIH, GWŻK, 57/1, 1021, mayor of Kraków to the *kahal* of Kazimierz, 22 May 1812; ibid., 1022, *kahal* leaders to mayor, 5 June 1812, and mayor to *kahal* leaders, 7 June 1812.

[90] AŻIH, GWŻK, 57/1, 1002, minutes of Sara Goldman's hearings, 2 Feb. 1812.

[91] See e.g. AŻIH, GWŻK, 57/2, 1035, vice-prefect of the Kraków district to the *kahal*, 22 Dec.

It is interesting that the *kahal* performed such functions in ways essentially similar to the model familiar from the times of the Commonwealth. The authorities of the Duchy of Warsaw did not follow the French example of organizing non-traditional institutional structures on the basis of new principles and objectives.[92] Minor modifications were made: the state entrusted the collection of the kosher tax to leaseholders, not to *kahal*s, and *kahal*s themselves (particularly the Warsaw *kahal*) came to act as representatives of Jews at large.[93] However, *kahal*s still participated in the collection of taxes (for example the recruitment tax) and in 'preserving order, and exercising authority over part of the population', so they fulfilled a number of functions which made them 'an extension of [state] administration',[94] at the same time keeping a considerable degree of autonomy. A more pronounced integration of Jewish communities into the state administration—despite their continuing independence—took place in the Kingdom of Poland.[95]

CONCLUSION

Historical research based primarily on laws regulating the status of Jews in the Duchy of Warsaw has rightly pointed out that there was no equality between Jews and other categories of the population. However, neither did principles of legal equality apply to other inhabitants of the state. Each group (Jews, nobles and magnates, the Christian bourgeoisie, the peasantry) had its own particular rights based not only in the egalitarian constitution, but also in later royal decrees, as well as in Prussian law or old Polish customary law. In effect, in many areas of the law, mutually contradictory provisions were in force. The Duchy continued to be a political entity based on the estate order, still only embarking on the path to modernization. The feudal legal system and the elite outlooks that went back to medieval times coexisted with modern conceptions according to which certain rights and

---

1812. Documents from the period of war mobilization in 1812 seem somewhat more stern in tone; during peace, categorical demands occurred more rarely.

[92] The competencies of the consistories were not as broad as those of the *kahal*s. Among the objectives of the consistories claimed by the Jews themselves were, for example, a guarantee that the principles of equality won during the revolution would be implemented, and a greater integration of Jewish communities into the state. For more on the creation and functioning of consistories, see P. C. Albert, *The Modernization of French Jewry: Consistory and Community in the Nineteenth Century* (Hanover, NH, 1977), 45–61.   [93] Schiper, 'Samorząd żydowski w Polsce', 519–20.

[94] As Rosman wrote in regard to the eighteenth-century situation: *The Lords' Jews*, 186.

[95] The closer integration of *kahal*s and state administration in the Kingdom of Poland was conditioned by, for example, increased control over elections and finances of Jewish communities by the state and the entrusting to rabbis of additional functions concerning the issuing of documents on births, marriages, and deaths. The broad range of autonomy still enjoyed by the Jewish communities, despite the changes of 1821, was pointed out by Schiper in 'Samorząd żydowski w Polsce', 520–9. On the competencies of congregational boards (*dozory bóżnicze*), see also J. Walicki, 'Dozory bóżnicze w teorii i działaniu: Polska środkowa, 1821–1866', in S. Pytlas and J. Kita (eds.), *Historia, społeczeństwo, gospodarka* (Łódź, 2006), 110–21. See also Guesnet, *Polnische Juden im 19. Jahrhundert*, 202–22.

freedoms belonged to all, including Jews, by nature. Limiting those rights some-times raised doubts whether that did not constitute a breach of the very essence of the new legislation. It was a period full of contradictions and inconsistencies, which, incidentally, would last throughout the nineteenth century.[96]

For this reason, no significant change occurred in the legal status of Jews during the years of the Duchy of Warsaw's existence; what was lacking was will on the part of those who governed, who believed that the differences between Christians and Jews remained an obstacle in the way of achieving a consistent equality of the two groups. In the Duchy of Warsaw, and for a long time to come, Jews were considered a special category of the population, unsuited to be labelled as citizens. Nor does it seem justifiable to believe that the Jewish community itself viewed its relations with the authorities much more positively. Individual administrative cases that had favourable outcomes did not automatically lead to an improved perception of the state authorities, or induce a sense of being treated fairly and equally with, for example, the Christian bourgeoisie.

However, although one cannot speak of the legal equality of Jews in the realm of state law regulating their status, one still can perceive the *germs* of equal treatment regardless of religion in the realm of everyday matters decided by local admini-strative practice. The state administration, seeking to follow completely new, centrally defined, and mechanically applied rules, produced a space of a peculiar kind of equality among the state's inhabitants, referred to uniformly as petitioners or 'supplicants'. As a result, in ordinary situations, in which there existed no special regulations pertaining specifically to Jews, the administration treated them like any other petitioners, which in the context of a hefty backlog of cases expedited their settlement. Care in following the rules and a legalistic approach seem to stem from the authorities' vested interest in promoting co-operation among all the inhabitants of the state. It also seems that certain manifestations of equality extended towards a few groups of Jews considered 'useful' to the state—merchants involved in large-scale trade, entrepreneurs, court suppliers—were simply the result of pragmatic concerns, as were cases of co-operation with *kahal*s. In other words, the state auth-orities accepted equality in those spheres in which it was advantageous to the state itself and in which the benefits were immediate and obvious.

This duality initiated in the Duchy of Warsaw endured also in the Kingdom of Poland. On the one hand, there would continue to exist, especially up to 1862, a number of special laws regulating Jewish affairs, a consequence of a strong reluc-tance in the ruling circles and among people involved in political life to grant Jews unconditional equality.[97] On the other hand, particular individuals were 'rewarded'

[96] On the continuity of the feudal *ancien régime* in Poland, see Blackburn, *Napoleon and the Szlachta*, 127–8; and in France or Germany till as late as the end of the nineteenth century, D. W. Allen, *The Institutional Revolution: Measurement and the Economic Emergence of the Modern World* (Chicago, 2012), 45.

[97] On the Kingdom of Poland's policy towards Jews, see Polonsky's overview in *Jews in Poland and Russia*, i. 288–99.

with broader rights, and in countless instances universal administrative procedures were applied. Formally, at least, decisions made in individual cases involving Jews were independent of civil servants' views; what mattered more was the 'formalized and impersonal collection of laws' and the official review procedure. The ability of individuals or groups to navigate these procedures often resulted in favourable rulings, sometimes contrary to the intentions of legislators or civil servants.[98] At the same time, this 'equality in practice' should not be overestimated; the old estate divisions remained very evident until the last days of the Kingdom of Poland.

Translated from the Polish by Grzegorz Sokół

[98] See Marcin Wodziński's interesting analysis 'Hasidism, Shtadlanut, and Jewish Politics in Nineteenth-Century Poland: The Case of Isaac of Warka', *Jewish Quarterly Review*, 95/2 (2005), 290–320, and Wodziński, *Władze Królestwa Polskiego wobec chasydyzmu*, 216–20.

'English Missionaries' Look at Polish Jews

The Value and Limitations of Missionary Reports as Source Material

AGNIESZKA JAGODZIŃSKA

'I WILL NOW ENDEAVOUR to give you some further account of my conversation with Jews',[1] Ferdinand Wilhelm Becker promises the reader, in the opening words of one of the reports devoted to missionary work in the Kingdom of Poland in 1851. Becker belonged to the London Society for Promoting Christianity amongst the Jews, the oldest and largest nineteenth-century British organization conducting this type of ministry. Just like other missionaries working for the Society, for many years he conducted religious discussions with Jews, distributed missionary literature, and offered religious instruction. The official purpose of contact with Jewish society was, of course, to propagate the Christian faith and encourage Jews to abandon 'the superstitions of Judaism', rather than to engage in secular matters such as, for instance, ethnographic observation. However, while carrying out these activities in various towns and shtetls of the Kingdom, the missionaries observed Jews' behaviour and customs, noted processes and events taking place in that society, and wrote down their reflections on its dynamics and so on. Their reports, both held in archives and widely disseminated in the missionary press, have hitherto not aroused any great interest among scholars as sources for the history and culture of Jews in the Kingdom of Poland.

In this chapter I should like, on the one hand, to discuss the specifics of this type of source material and its limitations, factors which the reader of it must confront, and, on the other, to indicate its potential value. I shall also offer comments and pointers which might be of help in reading as well as in understanding these reports,

I would like to thank the editors of this volume for their helpful comments and suggestions on an earlier version of this chapter. I am also grateful to the Church's Ministry among Jewish People (formerly the London Society for Promoting Christianity amongst the Jews) for granting me permission to use their archive deposited at the Bodleian Library, University of Oxford.

[1] *Jewish Intelligence*, 1851, no. 10, p. 377.

especially when dealing with a rhetorical analysis of the missionary discourse. Among many important historical issues present in the reports, I shall focus in particular on the subject of hasidism. An analysis of selected threads of this subject will serve to illustrate the value of missionary reports as source material. Before moving on to a more detailed discussion, I shall outline briefly the history of the London Society's mission in the Polish lands, describe the source material I have used, and discuss (and interpret) the current state of research. This will allow, I hope, for my subsequent analysis to be put in an appropriate context. The basic questions which I should like to answer are: how does the way in which the English missionaries (English often only in name)[2] looked at Polish Jews influence *our* ability to see that past reality, and what, thereby, do we learn about the Jews of the Congress Kingdom?

THE LONDON SOCIETY

The London Society for Promoting Christianity amongst the Jews was founded in 1809. It was formed under the influence of the so-called Evangelical revival and millenarian expectations, which drew Protestant England's attention to the issue of converting Jews to Christianity.[3] Thanks to highly placed patrons as well as an efficient method of collecting contributions, the Society grew and quite soon was able to send its agents overseas. Its activities encompassed not only the area of Great Britain's imperial influence, but also countries outside its colonial orbit. The Polish lands, containing the numerically largest Jewish community, very quickly attracted the attention of English proselytizers as an important strategic area for missionary work.

The London Society began to operate in the Kingdom of Poland in the early 1820s. In addition to its main base in Warsaw, satellites sprang up in other places as the missionary structure developed. Over and above the regular work conducted in these outposts, missionaries would deploy several times a year on missionary visits to towns and villages inhabited by Jews. Both while in residence and on the move, they worked to spread Christianity among the Jews, a process which consisted of holding religious discussions with them and distributing or selling missionary

[2] On its missions to Polish Jews, the London Society employed people of various nationalities and Christian denominations, not just Englishmen and Anglicans. For example, in 1834 out of eight 'English missionaries', as they were popularly called, as many as six were German: Archiwum Główne Akt Dawnych, Warsaw (hereafter AGAD), Centralne Władze Wyznaniowe (CWW), 1454, fo. 241. Furthermore, it should be noted that the Society's employees were recruited among both 'Christians from birth' and Jewish converts. Those missionaries who were 'outsiders' in the religious and national sense (British and German non-Catholics) viewed the Kingdom's ethnic, social, and religious diversity, as well as local relations between Jews and Christians, from an external perspective.

[3] For a detailed examination of nineteenth-century and earlier Christian millenarian expectations, and of their influence on the situation of the Jews in Great Britain, see M. Scult, *Millennial Expectations and Jewish Liberties: A Study of the Efforts to Convert the Jews in Britain, up to the Mid Nineteenth Century* (Leiden, 1978).

Figure 1. Chapel of the Institute for Jewish Converts at Warsaw
From Jewish Intelligence, 1846, no. 2, image before p. 33
(Bodleian Library, University of Oxford, Dep. CMJ e. 44, reproduced by courtesy of the
Church's Ministry among Jewish People)

tracts and bibles. They also prepared catechumens for baptism and conducted religious services. In addition, for some time a school for children operated in Warsaw,
as did the Operative Jewish Converts' Institution (also known as the Institute for
Jewish Converts; see Figure 1), where some of the catechumens and converts found
employment printing and binding books.[4]

Missions were carried out in the Kingdom until 1855, when, as a result of the
outbreak of the Crimean War in 1853 and conflict between Great Britain and
Russia, the Society's employees shared the fate of other foreigners who were
considered political *personae non gratae*, and were expelled from the Kingdom.
Official missionary work ceased for two decades and was revived only in 1875.
Excluding the period of hostilities during the First World War, it continued
uninterrupted until the outbreak of the Second World War.

THE SOURCE MATERIALS

An exceptionally extensive amount of primary source material exists for studying
the London Society's missions to Polish Jews. The Society's principal archive, the
Papers of the Church's Ministry among the Jews, consisting of more than five

[4] AGAD, CWW, 1456, fo. 50; *Jewish Intelligence*, 1846, no. 2, pp. 33–5.

hundred boxes with various types of documents covering the missions' worldwide activities in the nineteenth and twentieth centuries (including those in Poland),[5] have been deposited in the Bodleian Library in Oxford (Dep. CMJ).[6] In Poland the largest collection of source material dealing with the missions is held in the Central Archives of Historical Records (Archiwum Główne Akt Dawnych; AGAD) in Warsaw, where altogether seven volumes have survived in the collections of the Central Religious Authorities (Centralne Władze Wyznaniowe; CWW) and the Government Commission for Internal Affairs (Komisja Rządowa Spraw Wewnętrznych; KRSW),[7] covering the period from the beginning of the Society's work in the Kingdom to the moment of its expulsion. Fortunately, these records escaped the fate of the many Polish archives that were partly or completely destroyed during the Second World War, as the Society's papers had been carried off to Russia in 1871, and until 1962 were kept in the Central State Historical Archive in Leningrad.[8] Documents dealing with the missions can also be traced in other Polish archives, most notably the Archiwum Miasta Stołecznego Warszawy, the Archiwum Akt Nowych in Warsaw, and the Archiwum Państwowe in Lublin. These collections are varied in terms of both content and language, featuring Polish, English, German, Russian, French, Hebrew, and Yiddish.

The sources forming the basis of this analysis are reports of the missionaries' activities which they were obliged to supply to their head office in London. Additionally, from 1834 those present in the Kingdom of Poland had to present these reports for approval first to the General Consistory of Evangelical Churches, and then to the civil authorities. Only thereafter could they send them to England. Reports for London were submitted in English,[9] while the authorities of the Kingdom of Poland received them in German until 1846, and thereafter in Polish. The German and Polish translations are kept today in the collections of the CWW in AGAD. I have been unable to find the original reports sent to England in the first half of the nineteenth century; it is likely that they did not survive.[10] However, they

---

[5] By Poland I mean initially the Kingdom of Poland and subsequently the Second Polish Republic.

[6] The material is available as part of the Special Collections of the library. Two smaller English collections of relevant documents are kept in the University of Southampton (the Parkes Collection) and University College London (Special Collections).

[7] AGAD, CWW, 1454–9, and AGAD, KRSW, 7126. The volume CWW, 1459, deals only partly with the Society.

[8] M. Wodziński, *Judaica w aktach Centralnych Władz Wyznaniowych Królestwa Polskiego Archiwum Głównego Akt Dawnych: Informator archiwalny* (Wrocław, 2010), 8–9.

[9] I have in mind the final form of the reports in which they were sent to London. It sometimes happened that the missionaries would make notes for these reports in the European language which they knew best (e.g. German) and only later would they be translated into English.

[10] I have been able to locate only one such report, stranded among government papers in AGAD, CWW, 1458, fos. 761a–761h. Most probably the missionaries did not have a chance to send it before they were expelled from the country in 1855. The original English reports from the Polish missions of this period are not to be found in the collections of either the Bodleian or University College London, though some are preserved from the later period.

were reprinted in edited form in the missionary publications issued by the Society. The basic source material for the present study consists of reports from the first phase of the activities of the 'English missionaries' in the Kingdom of Poland, i.e. up to 1855. I refer both to the unbroken and complete collection of reports for the years 1834–54 housed in AGAD, and to their reprints in the English-language missionary press covering these and the earlier years. In the second phase of the Society's activities in Poland, after 1875, missionaries' reports to London were no longer passed to the local administration, and the only known versions are the partially preserved originals and their reprints in the Society's missionary press, which have survived in England.[11]

To understand the character of the missionary reports, it is worth quoting the guidelines that were prepared for the missionaries. It was the duty of each missionary to keep a journal, which automatically became the property of the Society and was to be sent to England whenever an opportunity arose. The Society recommended thus: 'In these Journals you will record, not only the events and transactions in which you are engaged, but the feelings of your mind, and your reflections upon various objects around you, and in the great work upon which you are occupied, its difficulties, and the means of its advancement.'[12] Additionally, the missionaries were obliged to send monthly reports with passages from these journals which might be of interest to friends and patrons of the Society. The missionaries were instructed 'not to withhold any unpleasant truths, nor to exaggerate appearances, but to state every thing as it really is; mentioning discouragements as well as favourable events, that the Committee may be in possession of the true state of circumstances around you'.[13] Furthermore, not only in their journals, but also in their general missionary work, they were requested not to engage in politics and to avoid commenting on local customs which they might find odd.[14] As I shall show later, this prohibition on commenting on odd local customs did not extend to Jewish customs, which the missionaries mentioned frequently and remarked upon particularly.

The material on the English missions, or on foreign Protestant missions to the Polish Jews in general, is of course much richer than the reports I examine in the present study. However, I focus on this source because my purpose is to study the unmediated accounts of missionaries whose dealings with the Kingdom's Jews were long-lasting and whose reports were written fresh after their encounters.

[11] I cover more fully the issue of the London Society's missionary periodicals in two articles: 'For Zion's Sake I Will Not Rest: The London Society for Promoting Christianity among the Jews and its Nineteenth-Century Periodicals', *Church History: Studies in Christianity and Culture*, 82/2 (2013), 381–7; and 'The London Society and its Missions to the Polish Jews, 1814–1855: The Gospel and Politics', in F. Jensz and H. Acke (eds.), *Missions and Media: The Politics of Missionary Periodicals in the Long Nineteenth Century* (Stuttgart, 2013), 151–65.

[12] *General Instructions by the Committee of the London Society for Promoting Christianity amongst the Jews, to their Missionaries* (London, 1824), 19 (Bodleian Library, Dep. CMJ e. 3).

[13] Ibid. 19–20.   [14] Ibid. 14, 19–20.

Hence, I do not take into account the observations of foreign missionaries on Polish Jews that crop up in travel reminiscences, works of a biographical nature, historical sketches on Jewish history or on Judaism, or other missionary literature.[15] The analysis suggested here can serve as a basis for comparison with the reports preserved from earlier Protestant missions conducted on this territory by the Pietists from Halle, which are too extensive to be considered here.[16]

THE STATE OF RESEARCH

Despite such rich and varied source material, the subject of the English missions to the Polish Jews in general, and of the London Society in particular, has not hitherto been adequately identified and examined. Amongst historians writing in Polish, Krzysztof Lewalski and Elżbieta Alabrudzińska have drawn attention to it; their work can be recognized de facto as the first critical studies of the history of these missions based on archival material.[17] The subject has also received passing mention in German-language works dealing with the history of Protestantism and Protestant missions in Poland.[18] We also have at our disposal earlier studies, which, however, require comment in view of the positions of their writers. As Yaakov Ariel has remarked in the context of Protestant missions to American Jews, 'Most works on the subject have been hagiographic accounts by members of the missionary community, or antagonistic Jewish ones that vehemently attacked the missions' work. Neither genre does justice to the complex history of the movement.'[19] The same could apply to our case. Robust apologetics are a feature also of works by the

[15] Amongst other works of this nature, I draw the interested reader's attention to E. Henderson, *Biblical Researches and Travels in Russia* (London, 1826) (Henderson was connected with other English organizations, such as the British and Foreign Bible Society, the Religious Tract Society, and the British Society for the Propagation of the Gospel among the Jews); A. McCaul, *Sketches of Judaism and the Jews* (London, 1838); W. Becker, *Ferdinand Wilhelm Becker: Eine Heldengestalt in der Judenmission des 19. Jahrhunderts* (Berlin, 1893).

[16] Parts of the journals of missionaries from Halle been translated into Polish and edited by Jan Doktór; this is still the only primary material from this extensive documentation to have been published: J. Doktór, *W poszukiwaniu żydowskich kryptochrześcijan: Dzienniki ewangelickich misjonarzy z ich wędrówek po Rzeczypospolitej w latach 1730–1747* (Warsaw, 1999). For the Halle Pietists, as well as the image of Jews and Judaism in their writings, see also C. M. Clark, *The Politics of Conversion: Missionary Protestantism and the Jews in Prussia, 1728–1941* (Oxford, 1995), ch. 3, esp. pp. 66–71.

[17] K. Lewalski, *Kościoły chrześcijańskie w Królestwie Polskim wobec Żydów w latach 1855–1915* (Wrocław, 2002); E. Alabrudzińska, 'Misje chrześcijańskie wśród Żydów w Polsce w latach 1918–1939', *Studia Judaica*, 5–6 (2002–3), 117–29.

[18] A. Gerhardt, 'Die Judenmission in Polen', in *Ekklesia: Eine Sammlung von Selbstdarstellungen der christlichen Kirchen*, v: *Die osteuropäischen Länder: Die evangelischen Kirchen in Polen* (Leipzig, 1938), 196–211; E. Kneifel, *Geschichte der Evangelisch-Augsburgischen Kirche in Polen* (Niedermarschacht über Winsen an der Luhe, 1964), 156–9, 238–40.

[19] Y. Ariel, *Evangelizing the Chosen People: Missions to the Jews in America, 1880–2000* (Chapel Hill, NC, 2000), 2.

Society's most important English historian, William Thomas Gidney,[20] as well as of historians writing from the perspective of the Jewish community, such as Yitshok Fein[21] or Raphael Mahler.[22] The trauma and threat which the conversion of Jews to Christianity represented for the Jewish community meant that these last two historians' aversion to the missions and the missionaries translates into an aversion towards the missionary sources, which were treated tendentiously and selectively. For example, Fein, knowing the missionary reports solely from reprints in the Society's periodicals, accused the missionaries of falsifying reality in their accounts, while at the same time drawing on the reports himself in order to prove the validity of one or another complaint made against the missionaries. Mahler, in turn, made quite extensive use of archival material, but basically relied only on files then available in AGAD (mainly those of the KRSW). I conclude from an examination of his sources that he did not study the reports, either those forming part of the CWW collection or their reprints in the missionary press.[23] Although his scholarship is more balanced than Fein's, his knowledge of the historical context of the missions in the Kingdom and his attention to the precision of the conclusions are immeasurably greater, and he shows a clear aversion to the Society and its missionaries.

Works written on this subject in recent years are marked by a more balanced approach to the missions among Jews, and also by the knowledge that the outcome of missionary activities for the Jewish community could be other than exclusively negative. This is exemplified by Yaakov Ariel's study *Evangelizing the Chosen People*, in which he notes not only the threat posed to American Jews by the missions, but also that missionary communities in America became advocates of Jewish national interests and supported first Zionism and later the State of Israel.[24] Adam Mendelsohn has in turn proved that Jewish merchants managed to turn contact with the missionaries to advantage for themselves and the Jewish communities with which they maintained business relations. In his article 'Trading in Torah' he shows that by picking up inexpensive or free bibles distributed by missionaries with the object of evangelizing Jews in Palestine, Lebanon, and Syria and transporting them further east, these merchants were able to supply their own ethnic market with scarce goods. He demonstrates also that Christian translations

[20] e.g. W. T. Gidney, *At Home and Abroad: A Description of English and Continental Missions of the London Society for Promoting Christianity amongst the Jews* (London, 1900); id., *The History of the London Society for Promoting Christianity amongst the Jews: From 1809 to 1908* (London, 1908).

[21] Y. Fein, 'Di londoner misionen-gezelshaft far yidn: ir arbet in poyln un rusland bemeshekh fun 19-tn j"h', *YIVO-bleter*, 24 (1944), 27–46.

[22] R. Mahler, 'Hamediniyut kelapei hamisyonerim bepolin hakongresa'it bitekufat "haberit hakedoshah"', in M. Handel (ed.), *Sefer shiloh* (Tel Aviv, 1960), 169–81.

[23] As noted above, the CWW collection was until 1962 kept in Leningrad; Mahler, who published his article in 1960, does not refer to these documents at all. As regards the reports published in the missionary press, he does not have a first-hand acquaintance with them, but simply quotes them from Fein.

[24] Ariel, *Evangelizing the Chosen People*, 288, 290.

of the Bible were adapted and used to satisfy the needs of the Jewish communities that they found their way into.[25] Likewise, Yaron Perry, writing about the significance of the London Society's mission in Palestine in the nineteenth century, has demonstrated first the value of the missionary texts as source material for Jewish history, and secondly the positive role that British missions to the Jews played in preparing the ground for later Zionist activities.[26] An extract from an endorsement of Perry's book on the back cover by Professor Alex Carmel is characteristic. He writes:

Although the London Mission . . . was only one among scores of missionary societies, some quite short-lived, which were active in the country during the nineteenth century, the Jewish community considered it the most dangerous. For this reason, it has received hardly any mention in Israeli historiography, being proscribed by a general feeling of aversion. It is therefore to his credit that the historian Yaron Perry was not deterred from choosing this particular subject for his research. His fascinating account reveals for the first time, without bias or partiality, the story of the Society and its unique contribution to the restoration of the Holy Land.

Carmel's view, though laudatory, illustrates both the Zionist paradigm of the literature on missions to the Jews and the (r)evolution taking place within it.

Ariel's, Mendelsohn's, and Perry's studies have shown that, in examining the Christian missions to the Jews, one can find something more than simply a perspective on the destructive influence of the former on the latter, and that the effects of the missions on the Jewish community can be measured not just by the numbers of converts. Furthermore, these works show that missionary sources can be a valuable supplement to those created by local communities. The earlier historical analyses by Fein and Mahler teach us an important lesson. We understand today that a selection of just the negative aspects of missionary contacts with Jews was a consequence of the specific metahistory of both researchers, which led to the one-sided and sometimes tendentious character of these works. We see, too, that a refusal to perceive the positive aspects of a broader spectrum of interactions at the Christian–Jewish religious, cultural, or social interface really translates into an impoverishment of our perception and understanding of these societies, or leads even to a falsification of their image.

In the case of missions carried out specifically in the Kingdom of Poland, Glenn Dynner and Marcin Wodziński have pointed out the value of the missionary reports as well as their limitations, both having used them in their studies of hasidism. Dynner has noted that, although the results of the missions were rather meagre, 'the missionaries performed an indispensable service as amateur anthropologists

---

[25] A. Mendelsohn, 'Trading in Torah: Bootleg Bibles and Secondhand Scripture in the Age of European Imperialism', in G. Reuveni and S. Wobick-Segev (eds.), *The Economy in Jewish History: New Perspectives on the Interrelationship between Ethnicity and Economic Life* (Oxford, 2011), 187–201.

[26] Y. Perry, *British Mission to the Jews in Nineteenth-Century Palestine* (London, 2003).

and ethnographers'.[27] Wodziński emphasizes that 'the British[28] missionaries were possibly the only educated non-Jewish observers who took an interest in Jewish religious life in Poland, and they left a relatively large number of reports on the subject. For this reason, their reports are an invaluable source of knowledge, despite their obviously partisan character.'[29] Their conclusions show that, although this source has its limitations, it can, if critically assessed, not only be used in research on the history of Polish Jews, but can also contribute significantly to filling gaps in this research. I should like in the present study to analyse this issue a little further.

METHODOLOGICAL CHALLENGES

The rehabilitation of missionary texts, especially the reports, as source materials for investigating the history of the Jews in the Kingdom of Poland does not imply an uncritical approach to them. Furthermore, in order for this analysis to be truly critical, the scholar undertaking it must be aware of the pitfalls lying in wait and be methodologically prepared for them. The reports can have ethnographic and historical value, if they are approached with the appropriate set of research tools. They can also lead us astray if we try to force from them answers to questions which, owing to their limitations, they are in no position to provide. What follows is a sketch of the principal methodological challenges facing the scholar of the missionary texts.

The most important factor one needs to take into account is the apologetic and polemical nature of the missionary accounts. The researcher should remember that the missionaries' goal was not to give an ethnographic description of the local Jewish communities they encountered, but to provide a report on progress in spreading Christianity among them. Thus the reports chiefly contain accounts of debates held with Jews and of the distribution of missionary publications. It is precisely in these religiously oriented accounts that we are forced to seek passages which might hold historical or ethnographic value. The patronizing attitude of the missionaries (whether Christians by birth or converts) towards the Jewish community, stemming from a conviction of the superiority of the Christian faith to the Jewish one and often too from a conviction of the superiority of the culture of Christian Europe over Jewish culture, reveals itself in the manner in which this society is described. What could be seen as ethnographic description in its proper sense (disregarding the postmodernist critique of ethnographic description and the calling into question of any such thing as ethnography in a proper sense) appears sporadically in its 'purest form', but even so is usually of a polemical nature. This polemical side reveals itself, for example, in the classification of Jewish religious

[27] G. Dynner, *Men of Silk: The Hasidic Conquest of Polish Jewish Society* (New York, 2006), 166.
[28] Cf. n. 2 above.
[29] M. Wodziński, *Haskalah and Hasidism in the Kingdom of Poland: A History of Conflict*, trans. S. Cozens (Oxford, 2005), 98.

customs as superstitions of one kind or another. The scholar must take care not to fall under the spell of this judgemental narrative and not to adopt the source's language and, along with it, its built-in attitudes. Examining blood libels, Joanna Tokarska-Bakir has warned of this: 'Ignoring the specificity of ethnographic source material, a lack of distance from the source material's inner categories . . . leads one to repeat the text's point of view. This is facilitated by the source material's specific rhetorical mimesis, in other words an unconscious adaptation of the historian's account to the narrative of the text under review.'[30]

The question which suggests itself in the light of this discussion is: can the missionaries' reports, despite their polemical nature, be a trustworthy source? Or were historians such as Fein perhaps correct when they assumed from the outset that they were untrustworthy—untrustworthy because missionary? To provide an answer to this question, I should like to refer to the results of Yaacov Deutsch's research.[31] Despite the fact that the subjects of his investigation are ethnographic descriptions of Jewish life, Jewish festivals, and Jewish traditions in modern Europe recorded in the sixteenth to eighteenth centuries, many of his conclusions and lines of inquiry are also methodologically useful in studying the nineteenth-century London missions. Deutsch has demonstrated that those ethnographies, whose aim was basically a polemic with Judaism, are in a significant majority of cases trustworthy, which he has proved by authenticating them on the basis of contemporaneous Jewish sources. Deutsch has coined a term for this body of texts, calling them 'polemical ethnographies'. His brilliant analysis, which creates an important precedent, has proved that the polemical nature of these texts does not invalidate their trustworthiness; they can simultaneously be polemical and trustworthy.

As regards the missionary reports, it does, however, seem to me to be legitimate to refine the term suggested by Deutsch and indicate that in their case it is more legitimate to speak not of polemical ethnographies but of ethnographicizing polemics included in the reports. Such a modification of the term is dictated by the different character of Deutsch's corpus and mine. That is, in Deutsch's case what we are dealing with are descriptions of the life, customs, and traditions of the Jews, descriptions which had covert or overt polemical overtones: in other words, the official, declared object was ethnography, from which polemic followed. In my case, by contrast, we are dealing with polemics which happened to take into account ethnographic elements.

Let us examine some passages that show how polemic is linked with ethnographic description in the missionary reports. These passages deal with two Jewish festivals: Pesach and Yom Kippur. Parts that we can classify as either historical or ethnographic information have been indicated in bold type, and polemical parts by italic.

[30] J. Tokarska-Bakir, *Legendy o krwi: Antropologia przesądu* (Warsaw, 2008), 70.

[31] Y. Deutsch, *Judaism in Christian Eyes: Ethnographic Descriptions of Jews and Judaism in Early Modern Europe*, trans. A. Aronsky (New York, 2012).

Pesach, Lublin 1844

20 March . . . We spoke also of Easter. **He complained that festivals like that were a great burden to them, because unleavened bread was very expensive.** *I reminded him that they bore such a yoke by choice, since God had in no way put it on them. I stated that there were two paths before them in order for them to free themselves of this, or at least to lighten the burden, for if they were to examine Holy Scripture it would show them another Easter lamb, which had freed us from the burden of the law. However, if they did not want to accept him, they should at least return to God's ways and learn how they should observe his festivals.*[32]

Yom Kippur, Lublin 1842

13 September. **Today the Jews begin observing the Day of Atonement. I went to the synagogue in Wieniawa. I saw a large gathering of Jews, raising their arms and voices to heaven, dressed in penitential garments**; in a word: *everything superficial, having the semblance of a deep confession of sin and meriting God's wrath.* This made a great impression on my heart, which hurt me greatly, since it was abundantly clear that this was all simply an external act, an 'opus operatum'.

14 September. Today I went to the synagogue here in Lublin. **The building is large and it was full, and many Jews besides stood outside the doors. While some were reciting their penitential prayers on this most important day,** *others, at the same time and in this same place, were laughing, and yet others were quarrelling, coming almost to blows.* I met two Jews heading for the synagogue and I engaged them. However, they replied disdainfully and continued on their way.[33]

Of these examples, the last is of particular interest, since it contains an element that is simultaneously ethnographic and polemical. The polemic does not have to be expressed in the form of separate value judgements added to the ethnographic descriptions, criticizing Judaism from the Christian point of view. As Deutsch has already shown, it can actually lie in the decision as to which details of observed reality are to be noted and which omitted:

Most of the scholars that view the circumstances in which accounts were written to be an effective barometer of their credibility have overlooked a significant methodological issue: the question of what material the authors chose to include in their ethnographic descriptions. In many cases, the very decision to include certain subjects and leave out others can point to a bias, even if the information is trustworthy.[34]

It would appear obvious that, by including in the above account a description of noisy behaviour which, in the missionaries' opinion, was unworthy of the dignity of the festival of Yom Kippur, the writer intended to criticize the Jews' demeanour. However, at the same time he provided information about a spectrum of Jewish behaviours in the synagogue during the festival of Yom Kippur. Of course, if being polemical does not automatically exclude trustworthiness, neither does it

[32] AGAD, CWW, 1457, fo. 60.   [33] AGAD, CWW, 1456, fo. 396.
[34] Deutsch, *Judaism in Christian Eyes*, 11.

automatically guarantee it. As when we work with any other source, we are obliged to confront the reports with other contemporary sources, the current state of knowledge, a critical analysis of linguistic rhetoric, and so on. The precedent set by Deutsch's research has, however, led me to question the assertion that the polemical missionary texts are by definition untrustworthy on account of their polemical nature.

The reports, mainly those which are accounts of missionary travels, have an additional feature which in Deutsch's classification places them beyond the bracket of ethnography in the proper sense. This is the random nature and lack of continuity of the observations of Jewish society made during such travels, which sometimes do not allow us to judge the character of the phenomena described, which are, like most festivals and religious customs, cyclical in nature. In other words, missionaries arriving at a given location observe only part of this cycle. Thus the question arises, can one draw general conclusions on the basis of these fragmentary observations? The following passage from an account by Alexander McCaul of a visit to hasidim in Ostrowiec in 1826 serves to illustrate this problem:

We soon visited the rabbi, a Chassid. We found an old man so deaf that we could not carry on a regular conversation: he was reading in the book of Zohar when we entered. In the next room were three Jews lying on a bed, one was singing and clapping his hands and feet, making a most barbarous noise. This is what the Chassidim call the joy of the Sabbath שמחה שבת.[35] They came out soon after we entered. One, the rabbi's son-in-law, when he saw the Prophets and the New Testament which we had brought for the rabbi, said 'Wares that are hawked at a house for sale are never good.' To the rabbi he said, 'It stinks; fui, fui, throw it on the earth', and then again to us, 'Go to the synagogue and darshan (preach), perhaps you may pick up some crazy fellows.' I replied that if it were our intention to pick up crazy fellows, we need not go so far.[36]

This description too carries the hallmark of a polemic whose intention is to demonstrate the odd behaviour of the hasidim. It is after all not only the manner of the narration that may be polemical, but also the choice of specific elements to include in the narrative. However, a greater problem here is the random nature of this observation of Jewish customs: does it record the typical and recurrent, or only an isolated event? What does this passage tell us, except that the hasidim were making the missionaries the butt of jests? What do we learn about their observance of the sabbath? Was what McCaul observed the rule, or perhaps an exception to the rule? The source is unfortunately unable to tell us if the Ostrowiec hasidim lay on their beds *every* Saturday clapping their hands and feet.

---

[35] Correctly שמחת שבת. The error may go back to the original missionary report.

[36] *Jewish Expositor and Friend of Israel*, 11 (1826), 63. This description was first quoted by Glenn Dynner, who gives a longer extract showing how the missionaries' meeting with the hasidim developed: Dynner, *Men of Silk*, 168–9.

MISSIONARY REPORTS AND THE PROBLEM OF THE
WRONG RESEARCH QUESTIONS

In testing the value of missionary reports as source material, we must recall the problem that arises from asking the wrong questions, to which the sources are unable to provide an answer. In my view, the question that seeks Jews' motivation for converting is an example. All we can learn from the missionary reports are the stated motives for conversion, but confusing those with the real ones can turn out to be a serious mistake. If we analyse the Jews' statements, as submitted by the missionaries, concerning their interest in Christianity, or indeed their desire to convert, we simply arrive at what constitutes a public declaration of motivation (or what the missionaries interpreted as such), whereas our ability to corroborate it remains limited.

Incidentally, the missionaries' own abilities in this area were similarly limited. They frequently expressed uncertainty whether the motives for conversion were 'proper', by which they generally meant spiritual and non-material. A case in point is that of a Jew called Grünfeld, who visited a missionary post in Warsaw in 1835; passages expressing the missionary's doubt about the motives for Grünfeld's visit are italicized:

I was giving instruction at home to the aforementioned Jew, Grünfeld, who came regularly, almost daily. Since he is not from Warsaw, he must have a certificate that he has paid for an entry permit, which given his poverty is very difficult for him . . . We have the same problems with him as we usually do with outsiders, but in his case even more so, since he has mastered no trade. *It is difficult in such cases to know whether the motives inclining someone to Christianity are sincere and serious, or whether worldly reasons are leading him to us, namely exemption from paying for an entry permit . . .*

I had a serious conversation with him today to get him to make up his mind what he wants to do and to examine what inclines him to come over to us. *I do not know what I am to think of him, whether he is serious or not. In his overall behaviour there is nothing which would allow one to divine the true state of his heart. He comes regularly for instruction, he is attentive when we read the New Testament, and he understands the meaning. But as for a sense of sin and a thirst for the Saviour—neither sight nor sound.*[37]

Only in a subsequent report do we learn that Grünfeld turned out to be a fraud.[38] Sometimes the missionaries are in a position to be able to make a negative assessment, to uncover the inconsistency between reality and declared motives (their 'inappropriateness', as they put it), as early as the first meeting;[39] sometimes, however, as in the above example, it takes them longer.

---

[37] AGAD, CWW, 1454, fos. 455, 456.   [38] Ibid. 494.

[39] Ibid. 375: 'On 29 May I had a long conversation with a Jew who had indicated a desire to become a Christian. He knew nothing about Christianity and his motivation was inappropriate.'

Figure 2. The first encounter: a missionary preaching to a Jewish pedlar
From *Jewish Records*, 1867, no. 1, p. 1
(Bodleian Library, University of Oxford, Dep. CMJ e. 24, reproduced by courtesy of the
Church's Ministry among Jewish People)

A positive assessment is a rather more complicated matter, which neither the missionaries nor those studying their reports are able to make solely on the basis of this kind of material. To pronounce on the sincerity or insincerity of motives that cannot definitely be discounted as feigned is in my view to oscillate between the Scylla of scholarly naivety and the Charybdis of a researcher's scepticism. The problem with this issue appears to stem partly from one of the cardinal differences between Christianity and Judaism. Whereas the Christian is defined first and foremost by faith in the Christian truths, from which religious practice flows as a consequence, Judaism is defined by practice—the performance of *mitsvot*. If in the case of Christianity the description and assessment of external religious practices is possible, to judge the sincerity of someone's faith is practically impossible in the absence of any external factors that show it to be false. Thus, in working with the missionary reports one should not force questions upon them which they cannot answer. Rather than seeking the real motives for conversion—which are usually beyond our reach—we should discuss the declared motives recorded by the missionaries. This distinction is also suggested by the results of the rhetorical analysis of the language of the reports, to which I now turn.

THE LANGUAGE OF THE REPORTS AS A CHALLENGE AND A SOURCE OF INFORMATION

The language which the missionaries use, and the world view contained within it, is of itself a valuable source and a challenge. It is through the language of their accounts that we get at the events which they witnessed, the stories which they heard, and their judgements and opinions on the world around them. In Edward Sapir's words, it is a 'guide to [the] "social reality"' of that time.[40] Thanks to a rhetorical analysis of the language of the reports, we are able to obtain additional information, often left unexpressed by the missionaries, concerning their attitude towards the subjects of their accounts.

Pursuing further the question of motivation for conversion, we should note that in their reports the missionaries serve as a medium for transmitting information on the Jews' motives for becoming interested in Christianity. But although it does happen that the missionaries really do believe in the sincerity of the declarations (even when they lack the means to exclude their insincerity), it happens also that they prefer to distance themselves from such a responsibility with the aid of rhetorical devices, chief among which are distancing expressions known as 'hedges'.[41] These can take the form of an epistemic modality, which qualifies correspondingly the content of a sentence. Thus, epistemic phrases such as 'it is possible that . . .', 'it appears that . . .', 'I believe that . . .' define the speaker's attitude towards the content of a sentence, distancing him from the truth contained in it and weakening his commitment to it.[42]

We can discover in the missionary reports various types of device that serve this purpose. It is achieved, for example, by the use of distancing phrases, whether epistemic phrases, or indirect speech or its equivalent. Thus, the missionaries write that 'other Jews too *made it understood* that they were sympathetic to Christianity',[43] or '*it appears that* the Jews here are much desirous of New Testaments'.[44] Let us consider this in greater detail using a later example, which juxtaposes, respectively, the German-language report, my translation of it into English, and the version published in the Society's missionary press. Distancing expressions are italicized:

[40] E. Sapir, *Selected Writings in Language, Culture and Personality*, ed. D. G. Mandelbaum (Berkeley and Los Angeles, 1985), 161–2.

[41] Distancing expressions are especially widely used in English. For more on this subject, see A. Hübler, *Understatements and Hedges in English* (Amsterdam, 1983).

[42] E. Closs Traugott and R. B. Dasher, *Regularity in Semantic Change* (Cambridge, 2002), 106. Referring to other studies in this field, they continue: 'If the proposition is thought of as an expressed world (the "described event") which is related to an actual referenced world, then epistemic modality can be said to index the degree of distance from the actual world' (p. 107).

[43] AGAD, CWW, 1455, fo. 273. In the original: 'Auch andere Juden deuteten ihre Geneigtheit für das Christenthum an.'

[44] Ibid. 109. In the original: 'Es scheint hier ein großes Verlangen nach Neuen Testamenten vorhanden zu sein.'

Spät am Abend kam ein jüdischer Schuhmacher, 60 Jahre alt, welcher des Tages hier gewesen war, wieder. Er *bekannte* alles zu glauben, was wir den Tag gesprochen hätten, und *erklärte* von der Wahrheit der christlichen Religion völlig überzeugt zu sein, indem er fragte, was er thun solle. Da er begierig *schien* die Wahrheit kennen zu lernen, so gaben wir ihm ein jüdisches Neues Test., wofür er *sich* sehr dankbar *bezeigte*. Möge der Herr ihn recht aufrichtig machen.[45]

[Late in the evening a Jewish shoemaker, a man of sixty, who had been here during the day, came back. He *confessed* that he believed everything that we had spoken about during the day, and *declared himself* to be completely persuaded of the truth of the Christian religion, asking us what he should do. Since he *seemed* to be desirous of learning the truth, we gave him a New Testament in Jewish, for which he *expressed himself* very thankful. May the Lord make him truly sincere!]

Late at night, a Jewish shoemaker, a man of sixty, who had been here today, returned and *expressed himself* as fully convinced of the truth of the Christian religion, asking what he should do. *Appearing* desirous to know the truth, we supplied him with a New Testament in Jewish, for which he *expressed himself* thankful. May the Lord make him truly sincere![46]

Let us compare how this same passage would sound if its distancing phrases were removed:

Late in the evening, a Jewish shoemaker, a man of sixty, who had been here during the day, came back. He believed everything that we had spoken about during the day and was fully persuaded of the truth of the Christian religion, asking what he should do. Since he wished to know the truth, we supplied him with a New Testament in Jewish, for which he was very grateful. May the Lord make him truly sincere!

We see that the character of the narration changes dramatically. Shorn of its distancing expressions, the text lays full responsibility on the narrator for the veracity of the account and strengthens his commitment to the truth of the words. However, when these expressions are present in the text, the missionaries indicate their distance from an unconditional acceptance of the truth of the Jews' declaration of their interest in Christianity. The conclusion of this passage ('May the Lord make him truly sincere') also points indirectly to the fact that in this case the missionary is unable to verify the declaration.

On the one hand, the distance that the missionaries maintain from the declarations of others recorded in the reports, expressed by 'hedges', indicates the post-Enlightenment nature of the language used by them. As Helen Bromhead has shown, in confirmation of Anna Wierzbicka's hypothesis,[47] after the seventeenth century there was an epistemic shift in the English language. It consisted of a transition from 'certainty' to 'doubt' in the expression of our knowledge of the world and in formulating judgements on it: 'I know' was supplanted by 'I assume'. This shift was caused by much more general changes in the social and intellectual

---

[45] AGAD, CWW, 1454, fo. 434. [46] *Jewish Intelligence*, 1836, no. 3, p. 52.
[47] A. Wierzbicka, *English: Meaning and Culture* (Oxford, 2006).

climate of British Enlightenment culture, by the development of empiricism and the particular role played in it by John Locke's philosophy.[48] I think that although this change expressed itself especially strongly in the English language, the Enlightenment's rationalist and empiricist legacy was not without its influence on other European languages.[49] Missionaries living in a post-Enlightenment world were involuntary beneficiaries of this epistemic shift.

On the other hand, however, the language of the missionaries preserves fossils of earlier stages of Christian–Jewish polemic, some dating back even to the Middle Ages. This is especially evident in their manner of describing Jews. A case in point is this extract from a report by Ludwik Hoff: 'We found many of the Christian writings which we had distributed torn up in the streets. How could these *poor blind people*, tearing up these writings, have destroyed the eternal truths of Christianity contained in them? May God have mercy on these *poor* Jews, who reject Our Lord, reject their real Messiah, their own real salvation!'[50] The concept of 'blind Jews' was already popular in medieval polemics. The reason for this was the conviction that, unlike the pagans, Jews had proofs of the Christian truths in their own writings yet despite this were unable to perceive their value. This juxtaposition of the exalted and dominant Church with the blind Synagogue heading for perdition was also reflected in medieval iconography.[51] The missionaries' reports, continuing the theological vein of earlier polemics, also copy the linguistic stereotypes which expressed it. The epithet 'blind', used in Christian polemical discourse to describe Jews, survived from the Middle Ages right up to modern times, and occurs, for example, in the polemical ethnographies noted earlier. An illustrative use of it can be seen in the title of the polemical anti-Jewish work written by the convert Johannes Pfefferkorn, *In disem buchlein vindet yr ein entlichen furtrag, wie die blinden Juden yr Ostern halten* ('In this Little Book You Will Find a Conclusive Exposition, How the Blind Jews Celebrate their Easter'), published in Cologne in 1509. However, beyond the linguistic and theological fossil of the 'blind Jews', in the passage

[48] H. Bromhead, *The Reign of Truth and Faith: Epistemic Expressions in 16th and 17th Century English* (Berlin, 2009), 1–4, 280. As Bromhead emphasizes, this does not mean that before the British Enlightenment users of the English language did not express doubt, but rather that after the period of the sixteenth and seventeenth centuries, a time which she calls 'the reign of truth and faith', they began to emphasize more strongly their recognition of the limits of their own knowledge.

[49] Modern English may be given as an example of a language which displays both an exceptionally large diversity of forms of epistemic modality and a high incidence of their use. In particular, as Wierzbicka writes: 'English appears to be unique in its wealth of verbs analyzing in great detail the *speaker's* own attitude to the proposition, in particular, of first-person "epistemic" verbal expressions': Wierzbicka, *English*, 206; examples of this are given throughout her work. In turn, Jan Nuyts has pointed out the large class of comparative epistemic adverbs and adjectives in English, German, and Dutch: J. Nuyts, *Epistemic Modality, Language, and Conceptualization: A Cognitive-Pragmatic Perspective* (Amsterdam, 2001), 56. See too, however, Wierzbicka's reservations on his position: Wierzbicka, *English*, 206–7.
[50] AGAD, CWW, 1454, fo. 306 (emphasis added).

[51] For more on this, see W. S. Seiferth, *Synagogue and Church in the Middle Ages: Two Symbols in Art and Literature*, trans. L. Chadeayne and P. Gottwald (New York, 1970).

from Hoff there also appears an innovation indicating a change in the attitude towards them: 'poor Jews' (*die armen Juden*). Although it is admittedly patronizing, at the same time it expresses a compassionate attitude towards the Jews on the part of the speaker.

We can reconstruct the missionaries' attitude not only through their use of a specific set of metaphors, but also by other means. As Teun van Dijk demonstrates when describing the persuasive strategies present in discussions on ethnic minorities, frequent characteristics of such language are, amongst others, generalizing comments referring to all the members of a specific minority, the drawing of contrasts between oneself and them, exaggeration, a distancing of oneself from them, and condescension.[52] We can find many of these features in the discourse of the missionary reports too. A detailed analysis is beyond the scope of this chapter, as is also a study of specific missionaries' individual styles. What I wish to draw attention to above all is the diversity of the discourse of the reports, the variety of the rhetorical repertoire in them, and the presence of various world views— sometimes very different from one another.

THE VALUE OF THE REPORTS AS HISTORICAL SOURCES: THE EXAMPLE OF HASIDISM

Despite their limitations, the reports are a source which augments or corroborates our historical knowledge of the Jewish community of the Kingdom of Poland. The information contained in them can be valuable for a number of topics. For example, they expand our knowledge of the Jews' social, religious, and ideological diversity. They provide material for our understanding of hasidism, of the messianic expectations among the Jews, and of the religious negotiation of Jewish identity. They are a record of the modernizing processes taking place among the Jews, expressed in acculturation or secularization—seized, as it were, *in statu nascendi*. They substantiate our knowledge of the implementation of state reforms dealing with Jews (e.g. the reform of Jewish clothing[53]), and of the attitude of the government towards Jews as seen from an external perspective. They show how the censorship and the demise of Jewish printing presses had an influence on the life of the Jewish community, and in what way the missionaries exploited this community's 'hunger for books' with the distribution of their own publications. They contain statistical data,

[52] T. A. van Dijk, *Prejudice in Discourse: An Analysis of Ethnic Prejudice in Cognition and Conversation* (Amsterdam, 1984), 133–41. Various approaches to studying the discourse of linguistic and visual discrimination are compared in M. Reisling, 'Discrimination in Discourses', in H. Kotthoff and H. Spencer-Oatey (eds.), *Handbook of Intercultural Communication* (Berlin, 2007), 365–94. I have made use of a revised version of this article published in Polish: M. Reisling, 'Dyskryminacja w dyskursach', trans. D. Przepiórkowska, *Tekst i Dyskurs*, 3 (2010), 27–61.

[53] I have written more on this subject in 'Overcoming the Signs of the "Other": Visual Aspects of the Acculturation of Jews in the Kingdom of Poland in the Nineteenth Century', *Polin*, 24 (2012), 71–94.

taken from local sources, on the size of the Jewish population in specific parts of the Kingdom of Poland. They show in a new light well-known institutions of Jewish life, such as the Rabbinical School in Warsaw,[54] or famous figures from the pages of Jewish history such as Antoni Eisenbaum, Abraham Buchner, and Stanisław Hoge. But above all they give a voice to those who in the first half of the nineteenth century were 'mute souls', in other words women and ordinary Jewish men whose opinions or points of view no other source—Christian or Jewish—has preserved in such great numbers.[55] Here I shall focus on only one of these strands, demonstrating the usefulness of this type of source for research on the history of hasidism. As I have already mentioned, Glenn Dynner and Marcin Wodziński have used the reports for this purpose, showing both the kind of information they can provide on the hasidim, and their limitations, for instance in determining the numbers of hasidim in the Kingdom of Poland and the extent of their influence.[56] Here I should like to propose an analysis of other aspects of this subject.

As emerges from the reports, hasidim were that segment of the Jewish community most resistant to missionary activities and opposing them the most vehemently. In general, though, the descriptions of active resistance to the London missionaries preserved in these reports do not corroborate the stereotype of the weak and defensive Jew. As Elliott Horowitz has shown, the nineteenth-century missions, which threatened the basic values of Jewish communities, led them to react violently. Irrespective of geographical dispersion—whether in Jerusalem or Brooklyn—faced with such a threat the Jews knew how to defend themselves: 'When their religion was on the line, and not only in situations of potential martyrdom, mild Jews could become wild Jews . . . attacking Christian missionaries with such weapons of the weak as dead cats and hot soup.'[57]

The missionaries working in the Kingdom of Poland at different times during the first half of the nineteenth century invariably reported on obstacles placed in their path by hasidim. Amongst these they mentioned the provocation of other Jews that were listening to the missionaries, breaking up or interrupting meetings, isolating the Jewish community from the missionaries,[58] destroying or profaning

[54] See A. Jagodzińska, 'Szkoła Rabinów w świetle źródeł misyjnych', *Kwartalnik Historii Żydów*, 1 (249) (2014),142–61.

[55] Writing on quite another matter, Geoffrey Oddie has also drawn attention to a comparable value of this type of source. Studying Protestant missions in India, Oddie points out that missionary texts are priceless material for 'history written from below', directing our attention to 'the underdog—the under-privileged classes and eventually also on women'. See G. A. Oddie, 'Missionaries as Social Commentators: the Indian Case', in R. A. Bickers and R. Seton (eds.), *Missionary Encounters: Sources and Issues* (Richmond, 1996), 198, 210.

[56] Dynner, *Men of Silk*, 47, 49, 67, 95–6, 165–9; Wodziński, *Haskalah and Hasidism in the Kingdom of Poland*, 98–100, 128–30.

[57] E. Horowitz, *Reckless Rites: Purim and the Legacy of Jewish Violence* (Princeton, 2006), 188–203, quotation at p. 203.

[58] This also included pronouncing a *ḥerem* for maintaining contact with the missionaries, or for reading their literature. Dynner mentions such a case: *Men of Silk*, 168.

distributed missionary materials, insulting and deriding the missionaries, poking
fun at them or their religion, and using vehement language or physical force. In the
reports we come across so many passages describing the hasidim's negative reaction
to the missions that when the missionaries encounter a hasid and there is *no* unpleasant incident, they mark this as a noteworthy event. In 1825 Ferdinand Wilhelm
Becker recorded a discussion with some Jews, one of whom was a hasid, *but* despite
this he behaved correctly.[59] In 1844 his colleague Fryderyk Jan Rosenfeld, dealing
with a prominent Jew in the small town he was visiting, recorded with similar
astonishment that he had never met such a gentle hasid.[60] However, the two
extracts from reports given below present more typical hasidic reactions to contact
with the missionaries:

We travelled to Białobrzeg—a very small town. Since we were staying at a Jewish inn,
various Jews soon came round. However, since most of them were hasidim, they were ill-
tempered and rowdy; they tore up one of our tracts and spoke roughly. The other Jews
were calm and, as long as the hasidim did not cause a disturbance, willingly listened to the
Gospel.[61]

Or: 'Later, we tried to strike up conversations with Jews on the street, but there too
we were accosted by a troublemaker in the form of a hasid, who used words to try to
draw people away from us and, when words failed, had recourse to his fists.'[62] Such
an unwilling or openly hostile attitude towards the missionaries on the part of the
hasidim, who resorted at times to crude means of persuasion that extended even to
violence, must be seen, however, against the background of a broader hasidic policy
of using similar means even within the Jewish community itself. As Wodziński
points out when examining the hasidim's political activities, 'confrontation was the
prime feature of hasidic politics at the community level. Moreover, the level of
aggression in some incidents suggests that conflicts were easily divorced from their
original political contexts and took on lives of their own.'[63] However, what is interesting here is that open confrontation was usually risked only within the confines
of the Jewish community, whereas in the event of a conflict with a non-Jewish
antagonist, hasidim preferred to resort to non-confrontational methods. Perhaps
their attitude towards the missionaries was caused to a certain extent by an incorrect
interpretation of their status, for they were not infrequently taken for Jews. This
was a result of the London Society's strategy of also recruiting converts from the
local community as missionaries. Hence they could be seen as Jewish, and in con-
flictual situations were treated accordingly. Missionaries who were Christian by
birth, but who made use of Yiddish or Hebrew, were also initially mistaken for
Jews.[64]

[59] *Jewish Expositor and Friend of Israel*, 10 (1825), 392: 'One of them was of the sect of the Chassidim but he behaved well.' [60] AGAD, CWW, 1457, fo. 173.
[61] AGAD, CWW, 1454, fo. 285. [62] Ibid. 509.
[63] M. Wodziński, *Hasidism and Politics: The Kingdom of Poland, 1815–1864* (Oxford, 2013), 240.
[64] I dealt with this in more detail in 'To the Jews and by the Jews? Missions of the London Society

The hostility which the missionaries continually encountered from the hasidim could lead to the stereotyping and demonization of the image of the hasid.[65] One also encounters in the reports another popular stereotype, that of the hasidim's overindulgence in alcohol. The observations of the missionaries, who were able— perhaps more than any other Christians in the first half of the nineteenth century— to get into such close and frequent contact with the Jewish community, provide an interesting assessment of this stereotype. Below I examine some passages that concern this.

It must be conceded that the missionaries, apprehensive of obstacles placed in the path of the missions by the hasidim, were especially sensitive to contact with them and looked on them exceptionally critically. Thus some of the passages from the reports dealing with them are characterized by a highly polemical tone. This is exemplified by a passage from a report by Jan Waschitschek, who, when trying to convince his Jewish interlocutors that Christians are more pious and charitable than Jews, uses as an example the founding by Christians of various charitable organiz- ations, including temperance societies. The object of such societies was to restrain 'the vice of drunkenness and its terrible consequences', and to prevent it by getting people to renounce alcohol and to warn others of its effects—all of which, as the missionary remarks, 'may also be recommended to the hasidim in particular'. It turns out that mentioning temperance societies is for Waschitschek merely a point of departure for open criticism of the hasidim:

However, it would doubtless be very difficult for them to agree to this, since in general they like nothing better than intoxicating beverages. They would probably prefer to shoulder the burden of yet another 613 superficial commandments than give up their moonshine and other spirits. It appears that they hold that strong spirits are an essential element in current Jewish hasidism.[66]

Commentaries of this type tell us more about the missionaries than about the hasidim, revealing as they do the stereotypical way in which the former imagine the latter. These are stereotypes which, with Walter Lippmann, I understand as 'pictures in our heads'.[67] However, the motif of alcohol abuse by the hasidim was not just part of how the missionaries saw the hasidim. It was a permanent element in criticism of the Jews, which the maskilim used in their anti-hasidic policies and of which the authorities in the Congress Kingdom took advantage.[68] Missionary sources attest an additional context in which accusations of drunkenness were

to the Jewish Communities in 19th-Century Poland', a paper read at the AJS conference in Boston in 2010.

[65] I am grateful to Marcin Wodziński for this observation.   [66] AGAD, CWW, 1455, fo. 93.

[67] W. Lippmann, *Public Opinion* (New Brunswick, NJ, 1991), esp. 11–34, 71–132. Van Dijk remarks that Lippmann 'shows that our culturally defined stereotypes of other people bias our perception of their actions. Given one single trait, we tend to fill in the details about others according to the stereotyp- ical picture in our head': Van Dijk, *Prejudice in Discourse*, 14.

[68] Wodziński, *Haskalah and Hasidism in the Kingdom of Poland, passim.*

made against the hasidim, reflecting not only the religious but also the social and political fever of the first half of the nineteenth century.

However, in addition to passages which are critical and polemical in relation to hasidim, we also find accounts of a different nature. Let us see what the missionary Ludwik Hoff, who was staying in Radzyń Podlaski, observed in 1839:

Last night we received further proof of the corruption of the hasidim's morals, which is all the more painful since it is taking place under the guise of religious respectability. After we had gone to bed late in the evening, *we were disturbed by continual noise, singing, running, and shouting. We saw a number of hasidim, who—judging by their behaviour—were already drunk, but who were encouraging one another to drink more.* The noise continued until two in the morning, and since we had reason to fear that for religious reasons they might subject us to indignity too, it was far into the night before we fell asleep. This morning we heard that *they cause such trouble nearly every Friday night; they insult the rabbi and others who do not belong to their sect, they break other people's windows, roll logs up against their doors, and so on. This is how this sect of fanatics observes the peace and joy of the sabbath. Furthermore, the saddest part is that they believe that they are in this way serving God.* That which is contained in the description of the cult of the golden calf—'and the people sat down to eat and to drink, and rose up to play'—could apply equally to these people. May the Lord have mercy on them![69]

Hoff's description of incidents on the night of the sabbath involving drunk hasidim (like the testimony of other missionaries describing similar events) is an interesting piece of evidence, since it describes events which could indeed provide a real basis for developing such a stereotype. By contrast with the description quoted above of the sabbath joy of the Ostrowiec hasidim—where there was a lack of information as to whether this was a common occurrence or merely a one-off incident observed by the missionaries—in this passage we find in addition a report of a local source that confirms the regularity of such behaviour. Of course, just as in the earlier passages from missionary reports, here too ethnographic information is not devoid of a polemical tone. It comes out clearly in the comparison of the behaviour of the hasidim to the biblical story of idolatry. Recalling Yaacov Deutsch's observation that the very choice of what one includes in and omits from an ethnographic description may have a polemical character, we cannot exclude the possibility that we may also be dealing with a similar situation in this case. The dual nature of the polemic, expressed explicitly or implicitly, does not, however, diminish the ethnographic value of the missionaries' observations. Interestingly, alongside the accusations of drunkenness made against the hasidim, they also record attempts to defend such hasidic customs. Perhaps an example of this is the voice of a Jew from Łuków who tries to persuade the missionaries that 'alcohol stimulates inspiration, intensifies the Jews' rocking at prayer, and thus translates into praise of God'.[70]

In the missionaries' accounts, positive (from the Jewish point of view) aspects of the stereotype of the hasidim also emerge. In shtetls visited by the emissaries of the

---

[69]   AGAD, CWW, 1455, fo. 405 (emphasis added).   [70]   Ibid. 409.

London Society, local Jewish communities very often designated precisely the hasidim as suitable interlocutors for the missionaries, as for instance in 1834 in Opoczno: 'Today we had a great many visits from Jews. One group chose a hasid as its spokesman and the group spent several hours with us.'[71] Hasidim were considered educated and pious, but above all zealous enough to rebut Christian teaching as well as attacks on Judaism, and it fell to them to stand at the head of groups of local Jews to represent them in discussions. This can be seen perfectly in a situation that arose in Gniewoszów in 1838:

As we were thus talking to some Jews in our lodgings, one of them called out through the window to another Jew who happened to be passing by in the street to come in, saying that that man would be capable of talking to us. Not long afterwards a large group of hasidim came into our room and one of them took the floor with a proud and supercilious expression. He began to dispute with us in an argumentative and angry manner . . . Several times we allowed him to speak uninterruptedly for a quarter of an hour, even though he kept repeating himself. However, whenever we began to reply to one of his assertions, he quickly interrupted us, shouting and sneering. When we asked why he was so impatient and why he could not stop shouting, he would reply that he was filled with great love for his religion and a great determination, and thus he was unable to speak dispassionately about it.[72]

This scene well illustrates the positive dimension of the stereotype of a hasid operating in the Jewish community who, thanks to his piety and zeal, developed into its defender against the missionaries' designs. Against a quite extensive background of comparable testimonies repeated at different times, another confrontation between hasid and missionary, which took place in 1846 in the village of Sroki, is startling. In the report we read that a local Jew brought a hasid to the missionaries so that *they* could defeat *him* in a debate. When the Jew judged that the missionaries had won the argument, he was delighted, because—as we read in the report—'he appeared to be a great opponent of the hasidim'.[73] This incident demonstrates the flexibility of social and religious cultural norms at the Jewish–Christian interface and reveals too the mechanisms of local intra-Jewish conflicts. In order to resolve them, as we learn from this account, missionaries turned out to be as good an 'implement' as any other that various elements of the Jewish community could avail themselves of.

The missionary reports show that agents of the London Society were well acquainted with hasidic customs. In 1835 missionaries visiting the rabbi in Stoczek, who was a hasid, found him at prayer, and explained to the recipient of the report: 'The hasidim say their prayers later than do others, thus the rabbi was still busy with his.' A knowledge of hasidic practices (or more broadly of Jewish ones) was for the missionaries an important element of their strategy of making contact with the Jews. This is how the missionaries accosted local Jews in the same town of Stoczek: 'In the afternoon we again engaged Jews in conversation on the market square. There were some hasidim there whom we asked whether they had already had a

---

[71] AGAD, CWW, 1454, fo. 298.   [72] AGAD, CWW 1455, fos. 93–4.
[73] AGAD, CWW 1457, fo. 508.

bath, since the sabbath would shortly begin, and how did they intend to cleanse their souls? One of them replied that the soul is cleansed by studying the Talmud, by prayer, and so on.'[74]

Scenes of Jewish life in the shtetls observed by the missionaries also have value in preserving the voices of those who have left no trace of themselves in any other source. This applies specifically to the *am ha'arets*—ordinary Jewish men and the majority of women, who, not belonging to the rabbinical, economic, or political elites, had no means of appearing within the compass of written texts of Jewish culture. For example, a voice from this sphere is that of an old hasid from Kałuszyn recorded by missionaries in 1844: speaking of his devotion to the *tsadik* of Kock, 'he stated that just seeing his face was for him a great joy'.[75]

In the reports we also find important information for reconstructing the cult of *tsadikim* on the territory of the Kingdom of Poland. In addition to the pronouncements, both positive and negative, that ordinary Jews made about this cult (which sometimes, in the case of hasidim, described their own experience of it), other aspects of the cult also appear in the missionary narratives, such as the issue of hasidic cult iconography. The work of Richard Cohen and Maya Balakirsky Katz has uncovered new dimensions of Jewish iconography and has explained the role that portraits of a religious leader, and even items used by him, could play among the masses of the faithful.[76] Balakirsky Katz has observed that 'a complex dialectic evolved as Hassidim struggled to reconcile the perceived profanity of the mass-produced medium with the ascribed sacredness of the subject'.[77] Although her study deals with the visual culture of mainly twentieth-century Habad, some of her observations could quite well apply to other hasidic iconography.

Attentively observing the hasidim of the Kingdom of Poland, the missionaries also preserved in their accounts the history of 'hasidic devotional items', which is all the more valuable for reaching back to the beginning of the nineteenth century, and thus to a time when such items were not yet mass-produced as they would be in the second half of the century. We read in a report of 1829 by Ludwig Hoff:

Rabbi of the Chasidim in Lipsko, travelled through, but we could not get to speak with him. He came from a pilgrimage to the grave of the late Rabbi in Gratow [Opatów]. The next morning a Chasid brought a picture of this deceased Rabbi to show us. Underneath was written in Hebrew and Polish 'Likeness of the Holy Rabbi Meir in Gratow [Opatów]'. Rabbi-idolatry, pilgrimage, and image-worship appear to assume a tangible shape amongst the Chasidim. They bought this picture, but would not buy the word of God, which we offered at a low price.[78]

Hoff's observation linking a pilgrimage to the *tsadik*'s grave with 'rabbi idolatry' can be explained by the connection described by Balakirsky Katz between the

---

[74] Both quotations are from AGAD, CWW 1454, fo. 339.   [75] AGAD, CWW, 1457, fo. 134.

[76] R. Cohen, *Jewish Icons: Art and Society in Modern Europe* (Berkeley, 1998); M. Balakirsky Katz, *The Visual Culture of Chabad* (Cambridge, 2010).   [77] Balakirsky Katz, *Visual Culture of Chabad*, 21.

[78] *Jewish Expositor and Friend of Israel*, 14 (1829), 95.

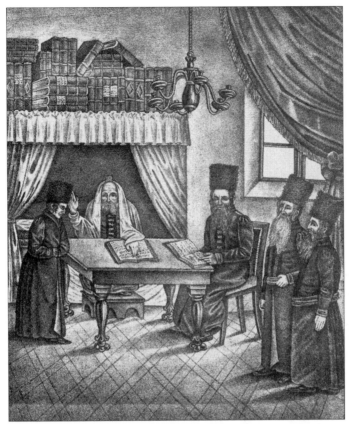

Figure 3. The Maggid of Kozienice portrayed with his son and followers
An illustration from a fascicle of documents of the late Father Stanisław Żuchowski
(Biblioteka Diecezjalna w Sandomierzu, AKKS 739, reproduced by permission of the library)

usually short opportunity to spend time with a rabbi (or, in this case, his grave) and an activity that substituted for regular contact with him, namely the contemplation of his likeness: 'Hassidim might lower their eyes in the presence of their master, but they could intently study the portrait of their rebbe's face in private. Rebbe-portraits convert mysterious charisma into a tangible object and offer stable visual experiences of teachers whose accessibility is otherwise limited.'[79] The bilingual inscription on the portrait of Meir of Opatów mentioned in the report is interesting too. It suggests, perhaps, that this image was directed not only at Jews (compare the passage quoted below on the Christian cult of the Maggid of Kozienice). I know of no extant copy of the image seen by the missionaries. However, others have been preserved from what must have been a series of portraits of hasidic leaders and rabbis printed with a bilingual Hebrew–Polish caption (see Figure 3).

[79] Balakirsky Katz, *Visual Culture of Chabad*, 21.

In this account, one other matter is also of interest. The identification of the travelling rabbi as the 'Rabbi of the Chasidim in Lipsko', in other words R. Yehudah Pesach of Lipsk, and of the grave which was visited as the burial place of R. Meir of Opatów,[80] finally allows us to solve the disparity, noted in the literature, over the dates given for Meir Rotenberg's death. Since Yehudah Pesach of Lipsk was travelling to the site of the grave in 1829, we can be certain that of the two dates given in the literature, the correct one is 1827 and not 1831.[81] Yet another passage from this report testifies to the fact that the *tsadik* of Opatów was no longer alive in 1829. On the occasion of a visit to Ożarów, and during conversation with local Jews, the missionaries noted the rapid development of hasidism there. This was the result, as they relate, of the fact that the local *tsadik*, who 'is now coming into celebrity, as one of their most famous wonder-workers', had no strong local competition, since the *tsadikim* of Przysucha, Opatów, and Międzybóż had all died within a short space of time.[82] Here the name Opatów, owing to the missionaries' source of information, is given in turn in the Jewish version (Abt, actually Apt) and leaves no doubt that in 1829 Meir Rotenberg was no longer alive. Thus, the missionary sources can serve to corroborate or supplement basic facts of hasidism.

The motif of the pilgrimage to the grave of a deceased *tsadik*, which is taken up in the reports, also provides a closer view of the customs accompanying this form of

[80] The place name is printed as 'Gratow'. What is it that leads us to read this as 'Opatów', and to identify the *tsadik* whose grave and image are under discussion here as Meir Rotenberg of Opatów? The possibility that the journal's editors incorrectly read the name of the town from the missionary's manuscript, misreading an unclear 'Op' as 'Gr', is suggested by other distorted place names in the same report: 'Osorow' instead of 'Ożarów', or 'Zamrose' instead of 'Zamość'. If the first example could be an attempt by the missionaries to adapt a foreign-sounding name to English orthography, in the second we are dealing with distortions resulting from an incorrect reading of letters in the original report. Since the original manuscript has not been preserved, we cannot decide the question by graphological analysis. However, some important circumstantial evidence suggests an interpretation of the above passage in favour of Opatów. First, the town in which the missionaries' path crossed that of the 'Rabbi of the Chasidim in Lipsko', Yehudah Pesach, was Sienno (Sienne as printed), which does indeed lie on the road connecting Lipsk with Opatów. Second, we know that this *tsadik* was a pupil of Meir of Opatów: see C. M. Rabinowicz, *Bein peshisha lelublin: ishim veshitot baḥasidut polin* (Jerusalem, 1997), 381. Furthermore, he is not known to have any connections with a town called Gratów; and indeed no place of this name is known in the Kingdom. Finally, the rabbi's pilgrimage to the site of the grave took place around the *yortsayt* of Meir, if we accept the date of his death as 25 Tamuz 5587, as given by Y. Alfasi, *Entsiklopedyah laḥasidut*, iii (Jerusalem, 2000), col. 56. The missionaries left Radom on 5 July, while the final part of the report written in Zamość bears the date of 30 July. In 1829, *yortsayt* would have fallen on 26 July, and from the report it appears that the missionaries arrived at Sienno probably around mid-July.

[81] Dynner, *Men of Silk*, 28, and Wodziński, *Haskalah and Hasidism in the Kingdom of Poland*, 79, are among those who give 1831 as the date of Meir's death. A dual dating is given by, for example, J. Meir, 'Me'ir ha-Levi Rotenberg of Apt', in *The YIVO Encyclopedia of Jews in Eastern Europe*, <http://www.yivoencyclopedia.org/article.aspx/Meir_ha-Levi_Rotenberg_of_Apt>.

[82] The missionaries write that they had died 'within a year', which is correct in the case of Meir of Opatów and Simhah Bunim of Przysucha, who died in 1827; however, Abraham Joshua Heschel had died earlier, in 1825.

cult. As the missionaries note when writing about the grave of Izrael Hapstein (known as the Maggid of Kozienice), it was not only the Jews that believed in the power of the *tsadik*'s miracle-working, but also the Christians, who like the Jews sought his help.[83] The following passage describes a visit to the Kozienice cemetery in 1844:

About thirty years ago, a celebrated *magid* lived here and his grave is still to this day visited by many Jews. Since the Christians no less than the Jews believe that he had the power to work miracles while alive and still has even now, though he has been dead quite some time, they seek help from him for various problems. We went to the cemetery hoping to see his grave. But a small building has been erected around it and its windows and door are always shut. A candle burns day and night. If a Jew wishes to bring to the *magid* some request and beg him to help, he writes down his wish on a piece of paper. Then the door is opened and he is admitted to the grave, where he lays his request. From time to time all these pieces of paper are burnt. Since the Jews lay great store by charity—for they believe that they can buy salvation for themselves with it—there is no lack of jars by the grave into which the petitioner throws money to add weight to his request.[84]

Despite this account's polemical character, in which *tsedakah* is interpreted as 'buying salvation', it is still a rare account for the first half of the nineteenth century—a view from outside, but first-hand—providing a glimpse into the world of hasidic practices and customs.

CONCLUSION

Summing up these considerations of the usefulness of the reports for research into hasidism, it should be said that they are an ambiguous source. On the one hand, in their descriptions of behaviour or events they confirm the stereotypes known to us from that period (e.g. the drunken hasid). On the other hand, given their polemical nature they emphasize those features of the image of hasidism which are in line with the aim of their narrative. Yet even from this crooked mirror we can learn a great deal about hasidic customs, the cult of the *tsadik*, and also how hasidim were viewed in the Jewish community and what status they were accorded. Furthermore, the missionaries bear witness to internal tensions observed in the Jewish local communities which they visited. Their writings show that not only did they generate controversies and quarrels between Christians and Jews, but at times they themselves became a tool used in local Jewish conflicts.

As I have demonstrated in this chapter, missionary reports have their pros and cons as source material. David Arnold and Robert A. Bickers have noted that 'uncritically viewing the world through the mission prism can be profoundly

---

[83] Several works have already been written about the Christian cult of the *tsadikim*. For the literature on the subject, see A. Cała, 'The Cult of Tzaddikim among Non-Jews in Poland', *Jewish Folklore and Ethnology Review*, 17/1–2 (1995) 16–19; Wodziński, *Haskalah and Hasidism in the Kingdom of Poland*, 113 n. 118.   [84] AGAD, CWW, 1457, fo. 157.

misleading, and can often be a cause of disappointment to the researcher'.[85] So can be the search in the missionary sources for answers to a question which, by their very nature, they are in no position to provide (e.g. the motivation of converts). Moreover, to the historian who has received a secular training, missionary discourse can seem obscure and obviously partisan,[86] and overcoming its limitations requires the use of carefully selected research tools. However, as I believe I have been able to demonstrate in this study, the language of the reports written by missionaries not only constitutes a challenge for a researcher but can also be a source of information itself. The curse of the bias clearly present in this type of source can turn into a blessing: 'the biases of missionary reporters are often much more clearly acknowledged and better known than those of other writers, which adds to their usefulness'.[87]

Thus, to be aware of the shortcomings of the missionary source material and to approach it critically is already one half of success. The other half lies in corroborating the material with other historical sources, remembering that no single type of source can grant us full understanding of the subject under study. This chapter has shown that reports of the London Society's agents can be both polemical *and* trustworthy, but it has also emphasized the need to study them in context. After all, missionaries, like other authors of historical texts, were only humans with limited or imperfect knowledge, as capable of making mistakes as anyone else. Thus, only careful and critical reading of the missionary reports contributes to our knowledge of the past reality they describe, and only then can looking at Polish Jews through the eyes of the 'English missionaries' be truly rewarding.

Translated from the Polish by Jarosław Garliński

[85] D. Arnold and R. A. Bickers, 'Introduction', in Bickers and Seton (eds.), *Missionary Encounters*, 3.

[86] Ibid.

[87] Ibid. 4. Arnold and Bickers refer here to the research of Geoffrey Oddie, who later in that volume observes: 'in the case of missionaries we already know something about their ultimate aims and what their biases are likely to be. Whereas in some other sources the writers' aims and agenda are not always so clearly apparent, in the cases of the missionary material, missionaries seldom tried to hide their objectives or particular point of view': Oddie, 'Missionaries as Social Commentators', 204.

'Languishing from a Distance'

Louis Meyer and the Demise of the German Jewish Ideal

FRANÇOIS GUESNET

FOR SEVERAL DECADES, the merchant Louis Meyer (1796–1869) lived and worked in Włocławek, a commercial centre on the Vistula near the border between Congress Poland and Prussia. Meyer was born in the small town of Służewo, likewise in the border area and near the city of Toruń.[1] He evidently received a traditional Jewish education in Hebrew and the Holy Scriptures. From the start, the aim of his education appears to have been a career in commerce or banking. In 1810 he was sent at the young age of 14 to serve as an apprentice in Berlin. We have no information about the specific circumstances of his life or training there, where he spent eight years. These years in Berlin had a major formative impact on him, creating the basis for his later professional activity and laying the foundation for his high level of proficiency in German, both spoken and written. In the decades after his return to Poland and down to his death, writing in German satisfied his apparently strong need to maintain some link with German culture. His collected works in German were published in 1871, two years after his death, edited by an anonymous group of friends.[2]

These texts by a Jewish merchant document in a unique way the complex cultural situation and intellectual and religious environment of the Jews living in the western regions of Congress Poland at the time. This area was situated in the broad transitional zone between German and Polish culture, extending from Pomerania across Wielkopolska to the western and northern reaches of Mazovia, a

---

The quotation in the title of this chapter is taken from the poem 'Erinnerung an Berlin' (1819), which is included in translation in the Appendix below, item 1.

[1] Służewo had little further claim to distinction aside from the fact that the well-known rabbinical family of Caro from Wielkopolska was long resident there. See N. Lippmann, *Biographie des David Caro* (Posen, 1840), 2.

[2] L. Meyer, *Hinterlassene deutsche Schriften eines polnischen Juden* (Berlin, 1871), and the new edition L. Meyer, *Hinterlassene deutsche Schriften eines polnischen Juden*, ed. F. Guesnet (Hildesheim, 2010). Unless otherwise noted, all references below are to the new edition.

zone that over centuries was characterized more by fluid cultural transitions than by solidly fixed borderlines.[3] The western boundary of Congress Poland near Włocławek had been established only a short time before by the partitioning of Poland. The fact that a Polish Jewish merchant, trained in Berlin, who spent his later life in Poland, nonetheless continued to write literature and letters in German, documents Louis Meyer's capacity and readiness to perceive and remain open to the culture beyond the border.[4] Building on the basis of his traditional Polish Jewish education, Meyer absorbed both German and German Jewish culture in an intense manner during his years in Berlin. The educational and cultural institutions of the young Prussian metropolis and the dynamic character of the German Jewish culture there in the era of the Wissenschaft des Judentums exercised a strong attractive force on Meyer. His early writings, in particular, reflect his ambition to absorb the innovative potential of Berlin, a major centre of the spiritual and intellectual renewal of central European Jewry, to fuse it with the world of Polish Jewish tradition so familiar to him, and to disseminate this fusion of two powerful cultures. The impact of non-Jewish Polish culture—above all literature—is much weaker, even if Polish historical and political contexts are referred to constantly. His stance of mediation avoided the simplistic positive and negative excesses typical of many of the east European Jewish authors, especially of a later generation.[5] Meyer's later writings reflect a growing scepticism about the positive role of Prussia, resulting from its transformation from a beacon of the sciences and the Enlightenment to an overly militarized society striving for political hegemony. Although he continued to hold German Jewish culture in high esteem, his later writings express a growing concern for the coexistence of Poles and Jews and raise questions about the nature and the future of their relations. Perhaps Meyer's inter-weaving of German and Polish Jewish traditions, based on personal perception and avoiding simple stereotypes, is one reason why he has largely been forgotten as a writer.

*

After his return to the Kingdom of Poland newly established after the Congress of Vienna, Meyer settled in 1818 as a businessman in the small commercial and

---

[3] This also led to less clearly delineated boundaries between the various central European Jewish communities. See I. Bartal, 'The Image of Germany and German Jewry in East European Jewish Society during the Nineteenth Century', in I. Twersky (ed.), *Danzig, between East and West: Aspects of Modern Jewish History* (Cambridge, Mass., 1985), 4.

[4] On the programmatic introduction of a comparative consideration of border regions and their cultural and political dynamics, see M. Baud and W. van Schendel, 'Toward a Comparative History of Borderlands', *Journal of World History*, 8/2 (1997), 211–42. For an excellent example of a comparative historical perspective on border regions, see É. François, J. Seifarth, and B. Struck (eds.), *Die Grenze als Raum, Erfahrung und Konstruktion: Deutschland, Frankreich und Polen vom 17. bis zum 20. Jahrhundert* (Frankfurt am Main, 2007).

[5] Compare, for example, the hymn of praise to Berlin by Yehudah Leib Gordon; see Bartal, 'Image of Germany and German Jewry', 8.

administrative town of Włocławek on the Vistula, where members of his family had lived since 1803. A list of Jewish families in the city in 1825 indicates that Meyer continued to reside in a part of the town outside that area specifically set aside for Jewish settlement; this fact points to his more elevated social standing.[6] Over the course of several decades, he earned 'a very respected position in the entire district' by dint of his personality and high degree of education.[7] He married, but there is no information about the name and background of his spouse in the *Hinterlassene deutsche Schriften*. His only child, Herman, was born in 1824. His wife died early, in 1834.[8] Shortly after that, in 1835, he moved to Warsaw, the capital of the Kingdom of Poland, and took up a position in the bank of Simon Rosen, a Jew from Prussia.[9] A number of noteworthy letters survive, written from Warsaw to his sister and son. They provide a remarkable window onto the social life of the Jewish elites in the Polish capital. After a few years in Warsaw, Meyer returned to Włocławek, where he seems to have led a peaceful life. There are no extant texts by him from the 1840s, suggesting that this was a period of intensive professional activity, which did not allow him sufficient time and leisure for writing in a foreign language. In the 1850s his writing resumes, both prose and poetry, and his creativity was heightened during the last decade of his life.[10] Meyer's writing in German focuses on special occasions, political events, or incidents noteworthy for some other reason, as well as the recurrent high points in the Jewish calendar of festivities and family life. In addition, it is clear that Meyer considered it important to practise and demonstrate his competence in German, and, as is evident from his letters to his son, to instruct and guide his own family.[11]

Meyer owed his 'respected position' not only to his education and activity as a merchant and businessman, about which unfortunately we know only very little. In addition, he distinguished himself by active participation in the political, religious, social, and cultural developments of his time. According to the preface to the

[6] M. Gruszczyńska, 'Początki osadnictwa żydowskiego we Włocławku', in *Zapiski Kujawsko-Dobrzyńskie*, 13: *Mniejszości narodowe na Kujawach wschodnich i w ziemi Dobrzyńskiej* (Włocławek, 1999), 327. Meyer's address is given in the list as 81 Szeroka Street at the house of a certain Przedowieski; his profession is given as merchant.

[7] 'Vorrede', in Meyer, *Hinterlassene deutsche Schriften* (1871), p. vi.

[8] In a letter dated 27 December 1835, Meyer wrote to his son from Warsaw that a year of mourning had now passed: Meyer, *Hinterlassene deutsche Schriften*, 179.

[9] On the Rosen family, see my entry 'Rosen, Mathias', in G. D. Hundert (ed.), *The YIVO Encyclopedia of Jews in Eastern Europe*, 2 vols. (New Haven, 2008), ii. 1591.

[10] For the essential stages and events of Meyer's life, see *Jewish Encyclopedia*, 12 vols. (New York, 1901–16), viii. 526; *Evreiskaya entsiklopediya*, 16 vols. (St Petersburg, 1906–13), x. 811; *Polski słownik judaistyczny: Dzieje, kultura, religia, ludzie*, 2 vols. (Warsaw, 2003), ii. 145; J. Trunk, 'Toledot hayehudim bivelotsvavek', in *Velotslavek vehasevivah: sefer zikaron* (Jerusalem, 1967), 9–12; see further J. Shatzky, *Geshikhte fun yidn in varshe*, 3 vols. (New York, 1947–53), ii. 132.

[11] Diaries and private correspondence were obvious places for him to practise his knowledge of German. On this, see S. Lässig, *Jüdische Wege ins Bürgertum: Kulturelles Kapital und sozialer Aufstieg im 19. Jahrhundert* (Göttingen, 2004), 224–5.

original edition of his writings, he was an 'outstanding son of his fatherland', and his 'glowing enthusiasm for Judaism' was palpable everywhere.[12] His social engagement is reflected in the fact that in 1861, when the first municipal elections were held in the Kingdom of Poland, he was elected to the county assembly in Włocławek. However, after the uprising of 1863, these councils were dissolved by the Russian administration, and no traces survive of his activity as a member of this local diet.

Meyer clung for a long time to his image of Prussia as the homeland of an enlightened and liberal citizenry. Soon after his return to Poland, he began to idealize his years spent in the ambitious Prussian metropolis of Berlin, which he regarded as a stronghold of the arts, science, architecture, and hard work, as well as of bourgeois social intercourse in the best sense and of the simple enjoyment of life. That view is reflected in a concentrated form in the poem 'Erinnerung an Berlin' ('Memory of Berlin'), written a year after his return to Poland. Against the backdrop of the 'bare open fields' which the lyrical 'I' gazes upon, there unfolds the vision of 'your towers, your houses, magnificent in number', the 'hubbub of your brave and decent people', the 'visual arts and science', and 'the flock of Muses and the Graces'. These 'pleasures lost' fill his heart with longing, comparable only to 'love's ardour' in which, 'languishing from a distance', a youth 'longs for an embrace with his beloved'.[13] Meyer long cherished the hope for a 'favourable stroke of luck' that would allow him to return once again to the place where he had spent his youth. In 1838, in a letter to his sister from Warsaw, he reflected on his displeasure with the forms of social intercourse in Warsaw, and he wondered: 'Would it be the same for me with the social life of Berlin? I would like some day to be able to find a practical answer to that question.'[14] At this point in his life, he appeared to have a strong desire to move to Berlin. In a melancholy mood in 1839, he wrote:

Once again, for a time a dull quiet entered the chamber of my soul. Then an old pet idea stirred once more within me: the scene of my golden age, my unforgettable *Berlin*, re-emerged into view, like a shadow from a better world, and beckoned to me in a luring shape. It seemed to me as if my past was unveiling herself before my eyes and wished to invite me to wed my future onto her.[15]

His desire to return would not be fulfilled until some fifty years after his stay in the city. Suffering from a disease threatening his eyesight, Meyer decided in 1868 to have an operation in Berlin. He seemed impressed by the changes he discovered there: 'Yet we saw enough of this metropolis to find it colossal. I recognized my old Berlin again, but it's been joined by ten new ones.' Nonetheless, the city appeared to him to be a 'wasteland bustling with human life', one in which he did not now wish to live. 'Basically the Berliners are good people at heart. It's just that they don't have the time to *be* so.' Doubtless a must for the visitor was the New Synagogue on

[12] 'Vorrede' (1871), p. vi.   [13] Meyer, *Hinterlassene deutsche Schriften*, 93–4.
[14] Ibid. 172.   [15] Ibid. 179.

Oranienburger Strasse, which had been opened in 1866, and was considered the emblem of the metropolitan and dynamic Jewish ommunity there: 'From among Berlin's new creations, we viewed the synagogue with its magical sabbath illumination, and heard the prayers. The effect of the new form is overpowering, and the religious service is exalted.' He cited the critical view of an acquaintance—'You don't know what religion this is unfolding before you'—commenting that 'a character that absorbs into itself the best parts of all characters is also a character'.[16]

Meyer educated his son fully in the sense of an Enlightenment attuned to the needs of civil society, and in the spirit of a religiosity conscious of tradition and aware of its responsibilities. Herman Meyer became a merchant like his father, dealt in grain, and after his relocation to Warsaw was active in the cotton trade and leather goods trade, items he exported to Austria and the German Reich. As the business partner of Leopold Kronenberg, one of the most successful entrepreneurs in the Kingdom of Poland, who had converted to Christianity as a young adult, Louis Meyer's son was involved in banking and commercial transactions, and became active as an industrialist. Herman Meyer was more outspoken than his father in support of Polish–Jewish rapprochement at the time of the January uprising. He served for an extended period on the board of the Reform-oriented Tłomackie Street synagogue, and was for a short time a board member of the Jewish community and on the executive board of the Jewish Home for the Poor and Aged maintained by the Warsaw Jewish community. In addition, Herman Meyer furthered the establishment of institutions for Jewish adult education.[17] He died in 1898.

WŁOCŁAWEK—A TYPICALLY ATYPICAL JEWISH URBAN COMMUNITY

What did Włocławek look like in the years immediately after the establishment of the Kingdom of Poland, or the Congress Kingdom, as it is also called? Meyer tells us little about that in his *Hinterlassene deutsche Schriften*. A certain picture is conveyed by an older contemporary of his, the well-known writer Julian Ursyn Niemcewicz (1758–1841), who visited the town while on a trip through Polish Prussia in 1817. His first-hand description makes clear just what activities a merchant might pursue in that town:

Włocławek is favourably located as a centre for commerce. It has quite an agreeable appearance as a town, although it lacks prominent buildings. It is clean and illuminated by street lights. It exhibits that traffic that can only be generated by commerce and industry. Thanks to its location on the Vistula, Włocławek has become a grain depot. It is first and foremost storehouses that are being constructed . . . In the spring, when many of these boats are being loaded with cargo and come and go, the numerous masts and sails give the town the character

---

[16] Ibid. 202.   [17] 'Herman Meyer', in *Polski słownik judaistyczny*, ii. 145.

of a small port. The presence of the district superintendent and the court commissioner have been advantageous for the town, which now boasts four thousand inhabitants.[18]

Contrary to the widespread assumption that the lands of the former Polish crown were marked by a strong hasidic orientation in Orthodox observance, there were a whole series of medium-size and large towns where the local Jewish community showed a high degree of differentiation and diversity. In the western areas of the Kingdom of Poland, in particular, there were a number of towns where advocates of a Jewish enlightenment largely attuned to a Prussian paradigm undermine the image of an unrestricted triumphal march by hasidic communities. Such friends of the Enlightenment, and later of the Wissenschaft des Judentums, were present in all metropolitan areas of eastern Europe from the late eighteenth century, or at the latest from the first quarter of the nineteenth, in the form of socio-religious networks: in Warsaw as in Lviv (Lwów, Lemberg), in Odessa as in Moscow.[19] The closer we come to one of the centres of gravity of this Jewish enlightenment, such as Königsberg, Breslau, or Berlin, the smaller are the towns in which one finds advocates of a secular education for the younger generation, of a rapprochement (variously defined) with the surrounding culture, and of reform in Jewish religious practice. It is not surprising that such innovations were consequent on the mobility of Jewish merchants in particular. In parallel with the vicissitudes of their paths, concentrations of advocates of the Enlightenment emerged in new sites where commerce and traffic led them: for example, in Brody in Galicia, a free-trade town on the Austrian–Russian border, in Odessa, the heart of the international grain trade, or in Shklov, the residence of a wealthy and influential supporter of the Prussian Enlightenment, Nota Notkin.[20]

In Włocławek too there was a group of leading community members actively working for moderate reform in Jewish religious services and a rapprochement with the non-Jewish environment. Louis Meyer was one of them. What characterized the development of the Jewish community in this small town? There was not any appreciable Jewish settlement in Włocławek until the end of the eighteenth century. Among the first Jewish families to settle there were those from territory that had come under Prussian administration in the first Polish partition, areas from which

---

[18] J. U. Niemcewicz, 'Podróż do Prus Polskich i książęcych w roku 1817', quoted in *'Do ziemi naszej': Podróże romantyków*, ed. J. Kamionka-Straszakowa (Kraków, 1988), 260.

[19] An overview can be found in R. Mahler, *Hasidism and the Jewish Enlightenment: Their Confrontation in Galicia and Poland in the First Half of the Nineteenth Century* (Philadelphia, 1985), and more recently M. Wodziński, *Haskalah and Hasidism in the Kingdom of Poland: A History of Conflict*, trans. S. Cozens (Oxford, 2005). On Warsaw, see F. Guesnet, *Polnische Juden im 19. Jahrhundert: Lebensbedingungen, Rechtsnormen und Organisation im Wandel* (Cologne, 1998), 281–303. On Lviv, see T. Grill, 'Ein Märtyrer für Licht und Wahrheit? Das Wirken Rabbiner Abraham Kohns in Lemberg (1844–1848)', *Jahrbücher für Geschichte Osteuropas*, 56/2 (2008), 178–220. On Odessa and Moscow, see S. Zipperstein, *The Jews of Odessa: A Cultural History, 1794–1881* (Stanford, Calif., 1985), and B. Nathans, *Beyond the Pale: The Jewish Encounter with Late Imperial Russia* (Berkeley, 2002).

[20] D. Fishman, *Russia's First Modern Jews: The Jews of Shklov* (New York, 1995).

thousands of needy Jewish families were expelled.[21] From 1823, Jewish settlement was restricted to a designated district in the town.[22] As elsewhere in the Kingdom of Poland, with the granting of far-reaching civil equality in May 1862, restrictions on freedom of settlement in particular were abolished. The closeness to Prussia and commerce along the Vistula also facilitated intellectual exchange. In a development not typical in the circumstances of Congress Poland, Reform-oriented forces in Włocławek took over the leadership of the community at an early point; they did not allow adherents of traditional rabbinical observance (so-called mitnagedim) to assume honorary offices until the 1850s.[23] It is possible that this institutional opening-up of community leadership to these declared adversaries of hasidism was due to the conflict over the establishing of a private house of prayer, as recently described by Marcin Wodziński.[24]

An informative account of the history of the Jewish community in Włocławek appeared in Warsaw in the Reform-friendly, Polish-language journal *Jutrzenka*, a weekly edited by Daniel Neufeld.[25] The article was published anonymously in two instalments in the summer of 1861, during the brief period of Polish–Jewish 'fraternity', which ended with the January 1863 uprising and the subsequent political repression.[26] The fact that this article appeared reflects the special position of the Jewish community in Włocławek and the significant role played by individual members oriented to ideas of religious reform. The article stresses at the beginning that the community in Włocławek, which had been established only seventy years before, is the youngest in the country, but in regard to the level of its 'civilization'— meaning here a penchant towards Reform Judaism—it is in fact the community with the oldest such liberal tradition. The article recounts that ten families from a number of surrounding smaller localities, including Służewo, Louis Meyer's birthplace, decided to settle in Włocławek, among them four cloth merchants. It relates that an employee of the community stemming from Prussia fulfilled the multiple

[21] E. Bergman, *Nurt mauretański w architekturze synagog Europy Środkowo-Wschodniej w XIX i na początku XX wieku* (Warsaw, 2004), 111. For an overview of the harsh measures taken by the new Prussian regime against the local Jewish population, see M. Jehle, '"Relocations" in South Prussia and New East Prussia: Prussia's Demographic Policy towards the Jews in Occupied Poland, 1772–1806', *Leo Baeck Institute Year Book*, 52 (2007), 23–47.

[22] On the dynamics of settlement in Jewish neighbourhoods in Polish towns, see A. Eisenbach, 'Mobilność terytorialna ludności żydowskiej w Królestwie Polskim', in W. Kula (ed.), *Społeczeństwo Królestwa Polskiego: Studia o uwarstwieniu i ruchliwości społecznej*, ii (Warsaw, 1966), 212.

[23] Bergman, *Nurt mauretański*, 111.

[24] M. Wodziński, 'State Policy and Hasidic Expansion: The Case of Włocławek', *Jewish Studies at the CEU*, 5 (2006–7), 171–85. He posits the plausible thesis that the founders of the prayer house, despite their claim to the authorities that they were part of a hasidic association, were first and foremost concerned to avoid paying taxes to the Jewish community.

[25] On Neufeld, see Guesnet, *Polnische Juden*, 21–2.

[26] 'O zawiązanie się i wzrost Gminy Izraelskiej miasta Włocławek', *Jutrzenka*, 1861, no. 9, p. 68, and no. 11, p. 85. For an authoritative account of this period of Polish–Jewish brotherhood, see M. Opalski and I. Bartal, *Poles and Jews: A Failed Brotherhood* (Hanover, NH, 1992).

duties of teacher, cantor, and ritual slaughterer. He also introduced the young community to the Bible translation by Moses Mendelssohn, and their progeny were later educated in Leszno in Wielkopolska (Prussian Poland), Poznań (Posen), and Berlin (possibly a reference to Louis Meyer). The author contends that this early familiarity with the Prussian Jewish Enlightenment was the source of the moral advancement of this young community.[27] That had also been encouraged by the favourable geographical location of the town: its position on the commercial routes between Toruń, Danzig, Poznań, Stettin, Frankfurt an der Oder, Berlin, and Leipzig permitted a pronounced stimulation of the economy and an upturn, especially in banking, after difficult periods during the time of the Duchy of Warsaw, which was marked by a burden of high taxes and other hardships. The author notes that the Jews of Włocławek, through their involvement in international commerce, had 'acquired European dress and customs, and adopted modern languages, including the language of this country'. The latter was 'widespread in the more well-to-do, respectable families'. At the time, there were some 315 Jewish families living in the town, among them about seventy artisans and two owners of chicory factories. The author describes the construction of the synagogue, referring to the dedicatory address given in German by the Warsaw preacher Dr Abraham Goldschmidt, adding that he himself had on this occasion given a speech in Polish at another gathering. As a further important date in the history of this community, he mentions the appointment of Dr Joseph Caro as rabbi.[28] In keeping with the spirit of the times, the author notes the fact that on the initiative of the local bishop, Tadeusz Lubieński, in 1850 the district hospital was given its own ward for Jewish patients, after plans for a Jewish hospital had to be abandoned owing to a lack of support from the Jewish communities in the area. Finally, he discusses in detail the merger of the Jewish and Christian associations of merchants: the Jewish club Harmonia disbanded at the request of Christian merchants and merged with a Polish Jewish club called Konkordia.[29] The amicable relations between prominent Jewish and Polish figures were also reflected in the fact that one of the most important public construction initiatives in Włocławek at the time, the bridge over the Vistula that was opened in 1865, was supervised by a construction committee on which three Christians and four Jews worked together.[30] In the overview of institutions of Jewish welfare that closes the two-part article, the traditional fraternities are mentioned, including the burial fraternity, and its activity in the sphere of provision of medical care. One of the community's leading members, Selig Neuman, who died in Warsaw in 1879, established the first Jewish cemetery in the town in 1832 on land he had purchased, and was also centrally active in establishing the Jewish ward at the hospital in 1850 and a Jewish elementary school in 1859.[31]

---

[27] 'O zawiązanie się i wzrost Gminy Izraelskiej miasta Włocławek', 68.   [28] I return to this below.
[29] This event was also reported in the Russian-language Jewish press: see *Sion*, 1861, no. 12, p. 191.
[30] Meyer, *Hinterlassene deutsche Schriften*, 186 (letter to his son, 18 Oct. 1865); see the Appendix below, item 6.   [31] 'Wspomnienie pośmiertne', *Izraelita*, 1879, no. 39, p. 324.

This picture of life in Włocławek, whose author was possibly Hirsz Osser, a teacher at the Jewish elementary school, is in accord with insights from other sources on the history of the Jewish community in Włocławek and its 'Western orientation'. Osser headed a school for Jewish boys and girls, which the author claims was founded in 1859.[32] In the late 1850s, leading members of the community were successful in seeking to appoint Joseph Caro (1800–95), then living in Wielkopolska, as rabbi, and this upset community members who were more tradition-minded. Towards the end of the 1850s, an opponent of the Prussian candidate for the rabbinate stated in a petition to the relevant ministry that in the town

there are between ten and twenty adherents of the Old Testament [a term then used for Jews], among them some Prussian subjects, who have adopted foreign civilization and customs—more with the aim of strengthening their position than strengthening religion—and who in co-operation with the synagogue sextons are appointing a foreign rabbi in keeping with these principles. By doing so they wish to alter the ancient principles of the adherents of the Mosaic faith, and to introduce their own new ones.[33]

To bolster his argument, Markus, the author of the petition, warned about the risks of engaging a rabbi trained abroad and not knowledgeable about the local law, who would one-sidedly represent the interests of the wealthy Jewish families, and whose appointment in the community would inevitably lead to conflicts 'the likes of which have never been seen here or anywhere'.[34] Despite this initial resistance, Joseph Caro served as rabbi in Włocławek for some thirty-five years. He enjoyed great respect as a scholar and judge, but at the same time showed clear sympathies for the Polish independence movement. In that he resembled his friend Dov Ber Meisels (1798–1870), one of the outstanding figures of Polish Jewish history.[35] Joseph Caro took great care in arranging the education of his two sons. The older, Jacob (1836–1904), initially became a teacher, but later studied history and took a doctorate in 1860 at the University of Leipzig. One of the most prominent experts on Polish medieval history, he was appointed to a chair in history at the University of Breslau.[36] Joseph's younger son, Yehezkel (1844–1915), received a doctorate in theology and philosophy at the University of Heidelberg in 1866, and after several positions as a rabbi was appointed chief rabbi in Lviv.[37]

[32] 'Kronika', *Izraelita*, 1875, no. 39, p. 314. In its first few years, some four dozen pupils attended the school, which had its own association of friends and supporters, and by the mid-1870s the number of pupils had soared to more than 250.   [33] Bergman, *Nurt mauretański*, 111 n. 35.   [34] Ibid.

[35] F. Guesnet, 'Meisels, Dov Berush', in Hundert (ed.), *YIVO Encyclopedia of Jews in Eastern Europe*, i. 1148.

[36] G. Rhode, 'Jüdische Historiker als Geschichtsschreiber Osteuropas: Jacob Caro, Adolf Warschauer, Ezechiel Zivier', in id. (ed.), *Juden in Ostmitteleuropa: Von der Emanzipation bis zum Ersten Weltkrieg* (Marburg, 1989), 100–5.

[37] M. Brocke and J. Carlebach (eds.), *Biographisches Handbuch der Rabbiner*, Teil 1: *Die Rabbiner der Emanzipationszeit in den deutschen, böhmischen und großpolnischen Ländern, 1781–1871*, Bd. i, rev. C. Wilcke (Munich, 2004), 223–4.

The way in which leading members of the community in Włocławek sought early on to identify with the broader sphere of a European Jewish culture oriented to Enlightenment was reflected in the ambitious project to build a new synagogue. The blueprint for this synagogue was drafted by Franciszek Tournelle, the officially appointed architect of the Warsaw province. The building, with a basilica ground-plan, reflected the Moorish style, especially in the design of its façade.[38] It was built in accordance with these plans in the years 1848–54.[39] The form and interior of the new synagogue were in strong contrast with the Polish traditions of synagogue construction. Four small decorative towers framed the structure at the corners of the square ground-plan, and the *bimah*, centrally placed beneath a high dome, had no covering. It was spacious, with seating for nearly a thousand, including accommodation for three hundred in the women's gallery. Both the Jewish and the non-Jewish press praised its beauty and perfection.[40] The festivities on the occasion of the opening of the synagogue reflect the specific religious orientation closely bound up with its construction. Dr Abraham Goldschmidt, a Warsaw-based preacher of Prussian origin, led the religious service.[41] Along with Goldschmidt, the cantor from his Warsaw congregation and its choir also participated in the opening of the new synagogue: this was indeed a notably strong presence of Reform-minded Jews from Warsaw, which suggests a considerable religious and cultural affinity between this Warsaw congregation and those responsible for the construction of the new synagogue in Włocławek. Later comments by Meyer are instructive, such as those made in a letter to his son in June 1867 on the occasion of a thanksgiving service.[42] He called the synagogue a 'temple', a common term among adherents of Reform Judaism.[43] As is clear from another letter to his son, Meyer identified closely with this tradition of progress. Referring to an evening of drama organized for the celebration of Purim, he noted in March 1865: 'The most pleasant thing is that our little town, after a period of decline, has resumed its former position in the

---

[38] An illustration can be found in Bergman, *Nurt mauretański*, 270–1. On the Moorish style quite popular in synagogue architecture in the nineteenth century, see I. D. Kalmar, 'Moorish Style: Orientalism, the Jews, and Synagogue Architecture', *Jewish Social Studies*, 7/3 (2001), 68–100.

[39] For details of the construction process, see Bergman, *Nurt mauretański*, 112–16. The writings of Louis Meyer contain no reference to the construction of the synagogue in Włocławek.

[40] Bergman, *Nurt mauretański*, 114.

[41] On Goldschmidt, who lost his post in Warsaw in 1859 and became rabbi in Leipzig, and on the so-called 'German synagogue', see J. Hensel, 'Wie "deutsch" war die "fortschrittliche" jüdische Bourgeoisie im Königreich Polen?', in H. Hecker and W. Engel (eds.), *Symbiose und Traditionsbruch: Deutsch-jüdische Wechselbeziehungen in Ostmittel- und Südosteuropa (19. und 20. Jahrhundert)* (Essen, 2004), 135–72.

[42] On 6 June 1867, a young supporter of the Polish independence movement attempted to assassinate Tsar Alexander II in Paris. Neither the tsar nor Napoleon III, who was accompanying him, were injured in the incident. The following weekend, across the entire Russian empire, including Włocławek, thanksgiving services were held in churches and synagogues. The London *Times* reported that the angry mob wanted to hang the assassin on the spot: 'Attempt to Assassinate the Czar in Paris', *Times*, 6 June 1867, p. 9.   [43] Meyer, *Hinterlassene deutsche Schriften*, 199.

vanguard of progress.'[44] His robust call for the abolition of the *shofar*, a ram's horn blown on various occasions in the synagogue, was also part of that religious approach: 'It is high time we abolished this disgusting music, and replaced the bizarre horn-blowers with competent oboists.'[45] In the later course of the nineteenth century, visitors to the town complained that this very promising tradition of progress had lost influence and the construction of the synagogue had also failed to achieve the effect hoped for: 'None of these expectations have been realized,' wrote Maxymilian Cohn in 1876; 'right down to the present, the service is full of disorder and shouting, just as in the good old days, while the chanting of the cantors defies description.'[46]

A POLISH JEWISH AUTHOR AND HIS POSTHUMOUSLY PUBLISHED WRITINGS IN GERMAN

Meyer's *Hinterlassene deutsche Schriften* constitute a noteworthy monument to Jewish religious self-assurance in a phase of extensive shifts in self-perception and identity among Jews. They document reflections by the author on religion, the place of the Jewish religious community in its non-Jewish surroundings, and the internal character of the community. Włocławek lay in a region that was clearly classifiable both geographically and culturally as part of the traditional Polish Jewish world. On the other hand, there were distinct external influences discernible here, coming especially from Prussia, not least for the geographical reasons discussed earlier. In substantial measure, Meyer's great longing for what he recalled as happy years spent in Berlin provides a reason for his strong inclination to identify with religious attitudes that—to simplify crudely—could be considered part of a German Jewish current that had strong sympathies with Reform Judaism. Meyer's statements on the Jewish community, religion, and Orthodoxy in a number of texts in the *Hinterlassene deutsche Schriften* provide a rich ensemble of references pointing to this.

Not untypically for a member of the numerically small number of adherents of reform in religious services and other aspects of Jewish religious life, Meyer did not champion drastic change. He responded to the staunch enlighteners of his time: 'If you run too fast with a lantern, it doesn't shine. Moderator lamps ensure that oil flows only in small drops to the light, not in large quantities; such lamps provide the best light.'[47] His attitude towards formal institutions of religious practice is

---

[44] Ibid. 184 (letter to his son, 14 Mar. 1865). The tradition of amateur theatrical evenings continued in Włocławek in subsequent decades too, as is evident from regular reports; see e.g. A. W-n, 'Korrespondencja', *Izraelita*, 1900, no. 7, p. 80.

[45] Meyer, *Hinterlassene deutsche Schriften*, 185 (letter to his son, 20 Sept. 1865 / 29 Elul 5625).

[46] Max. Cohn, 'Korrespondencja', *Izraelita*, 1876, no. 17, p. 134.

[47] Meyer, *Hinterlassene deutsche Schriften*, 161. Moderator oil lamps, which controlled the flow of oil, were an innovation in lighting in the mid-nineteenth century.

strikingly distant, if not downright sceptical. In his view, a religiosity grounded on trust in God and observance of the religious commandments was more important than traditional authorities and those installed in office. In one observation that Meyer made on his times, he notes that 'an excess of religion from the pulpit, in synagogues, leads to a passion that is destructive'.[48] As early as 1819, in a letter to the Berlin journalist Isaak Lewin Auerbach, from whom he had hoped to obtain some support in publishing his poems, he expressed himself to be among those who 'have not uttered a ḥerem against reason, and wish to conduct their devotions with sincerity, with spirit and sense', in so doing erecting an obstacle to the 'self-empowering rabbinical guild':

Who could remain indifferent to what we have to put up with today, when a tiny group of isolated pietists, living in a self-created world of fantasy filled with their own empty illusions, with no idea whatsoever of the real world—when these dreamers, who only in their ignorance believe themselves full of knowledge, dare to claim for themselves sole authority over our entire people, and to toss about *authoritative rulings* almost akin to thunderbolts of anathema?[49]

Rather, in Meyer's view, an inward concern for the needy and a charity and benevolence towards them are the real expression of an attitude pleasing to God. In a letter from Warsaw, Meyer told his son to mark the anniversary of his mother's death in the following way:

Celebrate it with prayers of devotion in the Lord's house and pious vows at *her* grave, where you can distribute alms directly to the needy, paid for by the funds I have given you. May this action of yours, undertaken in a sense of piety, stand as a worthy monument for your mother, as solid as one made of stone and metal, because benevolence was your mother's dearest activity.[50]

In addition, we see in these instructions a continuing familiarity with traditional customs observed in a Jewish cemetery at the time. Meyer assumed that his son would meet people in need at his mother's grave-site, who on this occasion could expect to receive by tradition some gift of alms, and indeed did receive this. This was a custom that more resolute representatives of reform in Jewish religious customs had begun to struggle against systematically at this time.[51] Unlike these reformers, Meyer sees the core of Judaism in a community recreated ever anew. His poem 'Die Weihe durch Kinder' ('Consecration by Children'), the first of the poems grouped under the programmatic heading 'Jüdisches' ('Jewish Matters'),

---

[48] Meyer, *Hinterlassene deutsche Schriften*, 132.

[49] Ibid. 208 (letter from Włocławek to I. L. Auerbach in Berlin, 31 July 1819). With his remarks critical of the rabbinate, Meyer espoused a key line of argumentation of the Reform-oriented Wissenschaft des Judentums, which—as for example in the person of the Prussian Jewish writer Eduard Gans (1798–1839)—welcomed legislative measures to reduce traditional rabbinical judicial powers in Poland too. See Guesnet, *Polnische Juden*, 90.

[50] Meyer, *Hinterlassene deutsche Schriften*, 180 (letter to his son, 27 Dec. 1835).

[51] Guesnet, *Polnische Juden*, 303–25.

provides us with an idyllic picture in this connection: the newborn infant is welcomed by the schoolchildren of the locality with song and prayer immediately after its birth, and is accepted into the Jewish community even before circumcision, which for Jewish males marks the religious entry into the Jewish covenant with God.[52]

For Meyer, a vital community is grounded on religious practice and overcomes differences of class and wealth by means of ritual. This becomes clear in the poem 'Die Peßach-Feier' ('Celebrating Passover'), with its hints of the Biedermeier period, which describes in warm colours the family celebration at the beginning of this holiday, in which the needy whom the father brings home from the synagogue, as also the domestic servants, all take part.[53] The drama of 'Der Vorabend des Versöhnungstages' ('The Evening before the Day of Atonement') equally invokes the nexus between religion and community: a wealthy man, a member (*parnas*) of the board of the community, has insulted the rabbi, and is lying alone at home, sick, on the evening before Yom Kippur. He is thus excluded from the ritual of this solemn day, where in the synagogue transgressions are confessed, penance is done, and reconciliation with God is sought. Yet in keeping with the lofty character of this cycle of poems, this sinner also is able to relieve his soul, because the rabbi visits the sick man at home and allows him to atone.[54] The cycle follows the annual calendar of holidays, repeatedly invoking the covenant and community of the Jews. In the poem 'Das Laubhütten- oder Freudenfest' ('The Festival of Tabernacles or Festival of Joy'), Meyer describes how the congregation disperses after the service, proceeding to the *sukot* or booths constructed all around the synagogue:

> Wie im Gotteshause die Gemeinde
> Sich vereint zum großen weiten Bund,
> Bilden Bundes-Ringe hier die Freunde
> In den Hütten, an der Tafel Rund.
>
> (As in the house of God the congregation
> unites in a great broad covenant,
> the friends here form rings of bonding
> in the booths, around the table.)

Here too the theme of the equalizing effect of ritual appears: 'Arme reih'n an Reiche sich als Gäste | Bei dem festlich schönen Freudenmahl' ('The poor sit down with the rich as guests at the festive, beautiful meal of joy'). This poem, didactic in tone, is marked by the description of a world that is indisputably whole. One can clearly discern here Meyer's desire to acquaint his readers with key features of the Jewish religion, and to convey a positive image of Jewish community.[55] This raises the question: for what audience was this and similar poems intended?

---

[52] Meyer, *Hinterlassene deutsche Schriften*, 218–19.   [53] Ibid. 219–20.
[54] Ibid. 222–6.   [55] Ibid. 227–9.

A quite different mood prevails in the literary reworking of the biblical legend 'Die Mutter mit den sieben Söhnen' ('The Mother with Seven Sons').[56] It is not surprising that the reworking of this theme of martyrdom stems from the time of the so-called Hep-Hep riots (1819), and it is likely that Meyer seized on the story of the martyrdom described in 2 Maccabees 7 as a reaction to those events.[57] Meyer also worked with the figure of the martyr in 'Palästinische Elegie' ('Palestinian Elegy'), which has a number of striking similarities to the early Zionist hymn of the 1880s by Isaak Feld, 'Dort, wo die Zedern' ('There Where the Cedars'), so that it is possible to argue that Feld may have used this text as a template.[58] Meyer links the traditional motif of the sanctification of God's name (Hebrew *kidush hashem*, i.e. martyrdom) with a patriotic perspective: both the historical tragedy of the decline of Israel ('Judäas Ruhm und Fall': 'Judah's fame and fall') and the contemporary misery of dispersion ('dumpf'ger Kerker . . . wo Juda's Helden schmachten': 'musty dungeon . . . where Judah's heroes languish') appear here to be awaiting their dissolution, made void by a new generation of 'heroes'. Salvation will be the consequence on the one hand of the deeds of the martyrs, and on the other of the actions of the 'new rulers of the world', those who administer 'eternal justice'.

The texts contained in the short cycle 'Gebete und Lieder' ('Prayers and Songs') heighten further the high tone of the previous poems, bringing them to a new level in a series of declamatory festive religious texts circling around the themes of prayer, loyalty to the Law, faith in God, and religious community.[59] Among these texts, the poem 'Höre, Israel!' ('Hear, O Israel!'), seeking to make comprehensible the importance of this prayer (the Shema) as a Jewish confession of faith, harks back to the didactic character of the previous poems. It was published in 1861 in the periodical *Hamagid*, a Hebrew weekly for the east European Jewish public issued in the small East Prussian town of Lyck (Ełk), rendered in a literal Hebrew translation; Meyer is named as author with his Jewish first and middle name, Yehudah Leib. The poem appeared not much later in a translation into Polish in the Warsaw periodical *Jutrzenka*.[60] The Polish version of 'Hear, O Israel!' is, like its original, an

---

[56] Meyer, *Hinterlassene deutsche Schriften*, 229–33.

[57] On the anti-Jewish riots that began in Würzburg and surged into a wave of bloody violence against Jews across a wide region of southern Germany and in some northern German cities, see R. Erb and W. Bergmann, *Die Nachtseite der Judenemanzipation: Der Widerstand gegen die Integration der Juden in Deutschland, 1780–1860* (Berlin, 1989).

[58] Meyer, *Hinterlassene deutsche Schriften*, 233–5. See F. Guesnet, 'Chanukah and its Function in the Invention of a Jewish-Heroic Tradition in Early Zionism, 1880–1900', in M. Berkowitz (ed.), *Nationalism, Zionism and Ethnic Mobilization of the Jews in 1900 and Beyond* (Leiden, 2004), 227–45.

[59] Meyer, *Hinterlassene deutsche Schriften*, 236–44.

[60] Y. L. Meyer, 'Shema yisra'el', *Hamagid*, 14 May 1861, p. 101, and *Jutrzenka*, 1863, no. 1, pp. 1–2. As in the later German edition, in *Jutrzenka* the title is given in Hebrew first ('Shema yisra'el'), followed by the Polish translation. The name of the translator appears only in initials, as Al. K. A likely candidate would be Aleksander Kraushar, whom Meyer appreciated as an author (see n. 86 below), and with whom he may have been in contact.

almost literal translation of the Hebrew of the Shema.[61] This cycle, which concludes the section 'Jüdisches', ends with a poem in German and Hebrew versions. This solemn poem, 'An die heilige Bruderschaft!' ('To the Holy Fraternity!'), is addressed to members of the burial society (see the Appendix below, item 4). According to the editors of the first edition of Meyer's writings, it was written at the beginning of Meyer's last year of life, and deals with the work of the members of the burial society (*hevra kadisha*), who traditionally care for the dead in the community.[62] The familiar tone in which Meyer addresses the members of the burial society suggests that he may well have been one of them himself. In a series of images, the German version mentions the actual activities performed by the members of the *hevra kadisha*: cleaning and preparing the body (*tohorah* or purification), closing the eyes, enclosing the corpse in a simple linen shroud, prayers and chants, and the preparation of the burial site. Meyer even added an assumed year of death to the poem: 'ca. 1870'. The Hebrew version is more connected with the spiritual-religious bond between the lyrical 'I' and the brothers in the *hevra kadisha*, and chants, prayers, and the wake are evoked here too. In both versions the tribulation and joy of a long life lead to a similar longing for eternal rest. The comrades in the burial society function as guarantors of this transition to the realm of rest.[63] Ultimately, the community of the *hevra kadisha* embodies the certainty of salvation, the highest expression, also manifest in other poems, of the extremely great importance that Meyer attached to the Jewish community (*kehilah*) in his religious-spiritual world view.

Beyond treatment of these directly religious topics, Louis Meyer's *Hinterlassene deutsche Schriften* contain a broad spectrum of literary and occasional texts, observations on events of personal and general importance, commentaries, letters, carefully composed poems, dramatic works, and philosophical and religious reflections. Some of these works have a distinctly amateurish character. A studied and often pretentious manner is conspicuous, and many of his texts are indisputably imitative. Yet precisely this desire to emulate sheds light on the broad spectrum of the *musée sentimental* of a Jew living in Poland in the mid-nineteenth century, which appears unique in its totality.

[61] In the last verse, the neutral German expression 'vom Anbeginne bis zur heut'gen Stunde', i.e. from the beginning of Jewish history until today, is enriched with a more patriotic formula, 'gdy już ojczyste stracił ołtarze' ('when [the Jews] had already lost their fatherland's altars'), very much in tune with the Polish patriotic fervour of the period. Also, the German words 'Israelit' and 'Israel', in lines 3 and 6 of the last stanza, are translated as 'Żyd'.

[62] Meyer, *Hinterlassene deutsche Schriften*, 243–4. On the role of the burial societies in Poland, see Guesnet, *Polnische Juden*, 357–86. A general interpretation and description of the *hevra kadisha* can be found in S. A. Goldberg, *Crossing the Jabbok: Illness and Death in Ashkenazi Judaism in Sixteenth-through Nineteenth-Century Prague* (Berkeley, 1997).

[63] As in the conceptions of death and the world beyond in other cultures, Jewish legend also knows a river, the Yabok, which divides the living from the dead, and death is seen as a crossing of this river. Correspondingly, the manual of the burial societies is called *Ma'avar yabok*, 'the one who crosses the river of death'.

The first part of his *Hinterlassene deutsche Schriften* offers a broad array of poetic, humorous, dramatic, and didactic works. It begins with a section 'Landmanns- und Handwerkerlieder' ('Songs of Farmers and Artisans'). They are marked by a post-Romantic longing for nature, an enthusiasm for simple village life distant from civilization and religion, and by an effort to achieve an energetic yet at the same time sensuous tone. Instead of Christian or Jewish philosophical views of the world, there is a naive earthiness and joy in living, whose rhythms are those of planting and harvest, desire and dying. This world of imagery is exemplified in the bucolic hymn 'Beim Mähen' ('Reaping'): the 'true sons of the earth' are the farmers who at 'an early morning hour' harvest the 'luxuriant bursting fields'.[64] Concrete references to a real-life world remain stereotypical, such as a verse about 'the crazy dance of the Poles' in the poem 'Beim Ernte-Fest' ('Harvest Festival'). The basic current running through this group of poems is a desire to harmonize, and it does not hesitate to overstep the boundary into kitsch, ending up on occasion in the realm of what is involuntarily funny—as in 'Beim Ernte-Fest':

> Jetzo räumet für die Alten
> Einen hohen Ehrensitz;
> Denn, wo Ordnungssinn soll walten,
> Muß das Alter an die Spitz.[65]
>
> (Now clear the way for the old
> to sit on a high seat of honour;
> because where a sense of order should prevail,
> Age must lead the way.)

The romanticizing references to rural life are in obvious contrast to the realities of traditional Jewish life, whether in Germany or in Poland, as are those to the life of artisans, celebrated for their 'spirit of freedom'. In the 'Maurer-Lied' ('Song of the Mason'), industriousness, cheerfulness, and fraternity in artisan life underpin social peace and political freedom: 'So wird der Arbeits-Kreis zum schönen Bund, | Der Geist der Freiheit thut in ihm sich kund' ('Thus the fellowship of work becomes a beautiful alliance, the spirit of freedom makes itself known there'). And it goes on: 'Der Ordnungsgeist gleicht selbst Ungleichheit aus, | Er baut die Staaten wie er baut ein Haus' ('The spirit of order evens out inequality by itself; it builds states just as it builds a house').[66] While most of the 'Handwerker-Lieder' ('Songs of Artisans') contain the ideal of a traditional social order external to history, whose members are bound together by simple piety and co-operative egalitarian solidarity, giving the poems in this section an unusually conservative undertone, in the 'Buchdrucker-Lied' ('Printer's Song') Meyer takes a far clearer and more unambiguous position in favour of press freedom and enlightenment, calling its enemies the 'black, bleak priests of Baal', doubtless a reference to the Roman Catholic clergy. The comparatively simple juxtaposing of night, darkness, and

---

[64] Meyer, *Hinterlassene deutsche Schriften*, 46.   [65] Ibid. 49–50.   [66] Ibid. 54.

religious fanaticism to day, light, and enlightenment, as the saviour of which Guten-berg is lauded, is especially instructive for understanding Meyer's basic position on the relation between religion, knowledge, and society. It was the invention of printing as an 'intellectual spear' that made possible the spread of the 'general light' of the Enlightenment, whose adversaries are the (above all Catholic) clergy.[67]

The cycle 'Geschichtliche Lieder' ('Historical Songs') begins with two poems that Meyer, then just turned 21, most certainly composed while still in Berlin. Napoleon's final defeat is interpreted by Meyer in his 'Nach dem Pariser Frieden (1815)' ('After the Peace of Paris, 1815') as an end in particular to armed hostili-ties and war. War is termed 'humanity's demon', which 'separates peoples from peoples'. It is evident that Meyer cannot and does not want to interpret the victory over Napoleon's France in patriotic terms and does not idealize military confron-tation. He appeals to the 'German bosom' to welcome once again the Graces and the Muses, and thus to return to intellectual heroic deeds—instead of seeking to prove oneself on the field of battle. A 'comely girl' promises to be waiting for the 'brave horseman' and to reward him with 'faithful love' for proven valour in the field. The faster the German nation of culture so revered by Meyer can disarm, the better.[68] A comparable empathetic and observant stance also marks the second early song, 'Die Weichsel und die Pleiße' ('The Vistula and the Pleisse'), in which the death by drowning of Prince Józef Poniatowski (1763–1813), a Polish statesman and military leader of the Napoleonic era, is structured as an antiphony between two rivers: the Polish Vistula and the Saxonian Pleisse. The song celebrates the hero as such, whose death is worthy of regret in both Poland and Germany.[69] The two songs 'Auf dem Rhein (1850)' ('On the Rhine, 1850') and 'Auf der Elbe (1850)' ('On the Elbe, 1850'), river poems with their date of composition in the title, suggest how large rivers in Europe can shape identity.[70] Whereas the Rhine stands for the—compre-hensible—longing of the Germans for unity, the Elbe reflects rather the diversity of peoples, languages, trades, and religions on its banks. It ends with a hymnal praise for the city of Hamburg, which stands 'in Pracht und wunderbarer | Tausend-jähr'ger Blüthe prangt' ('resplendent in its magnificence and wondrous florescence of a thousand years').[71] The poem 'Der Pariser Congreß (1856)' ('The Paris Con-gress, 1856') is more a satirical commentary on political developments of the day, and on a congress at which, after the Crimean War, the western European great powers tried to arrange a balance of interests among themselves, seeking a lasting control of Russia and the Ottoman empire and a weakening of their power.[72]

In his noteworthy synopsis 'Wettgesang der Hauptflüsse Europa's (1855)' ('Sing-ing Match between Europe's Main Rivers, 1855'), Meyer commented on the

---

[67] Ibid. 59.   [68] Ibid. 60.   [69] Ibid. 64.

[70] Ibid. 65. It is interesting that Meyer distances himself here from his possible paradigm Heinrich Heine, in particular Heine's *Deutschland: Ein Wintermärchen*. In contrast with Heine, Meyer finds a longing for the unity of the Reich comprehensible.

[71] Meyer, *Hinterlassene deutsche Schriften*, 66–9.   [72] Ibid. 70.

tension between aspiration and reality, between the potentials of European culture and the sobering realities of his time. It is not difficult to see, despite the lightly encrypted formulation, that he regards Roman Catholicism as one of the main impediments to the development of the European potential for peace and culture. Thus, the Tiber complains that 'gift'ge Schlangenarten um den Lebensbaum [nisten]' ('poisonous snakes lurk round the Tree of Life') and it issues the call: 'Auf, Ihr Gärtner, treibet sie heraus | Treibt die Schlangen aus Italia's Haus!' ('Arise, ye gardeners, drive them out, drive the snakes from Italia's house!'). In Spain, the 'spirits of the night' rule, and in France 'streben noch auch hier die Dunkeln zu tödten | Jeglichen Geist' ('here too dark powers strive to extinguish any and all intellect)'. By contrast, the English Thames flows in a land that respects human dignity. But there is a reservation: 'Denn es heget engherzig der Britte | Stets nur die Freiheit in eigener Mitte' ('Because the petty Briton cherishes always and only freedom in his own setting'). The greatest German cultural achievement was the Reformation, the 'Sieg gegen röm'schen Lug und Geisteszwang' ('victory over Roman mendacity and intellectual coercion') of which the Elbe sings, and 'Höher glänzen Deutschlands kühne Denker | Als die Helden, als die Schlachtenlenker' ('Germany's bold thinkers sparkle more than all the heroes, the leaders of battles'). Meyer sees Poland too as part of Europe, and he has high regard for the fact that Poland 'nicht mit anderen Mächten kämpfte, | Um Völker unter sich zu knechten' ('did not fight against other powers in order to subjugate other peoples under its yoke'). Rather, 'brach der Strom asiatischer Barbaren | An dem Schutzdamm seiner Heldenschaaren' ('the river of Asiatic barbarians broke against the protective dam of its hordes of heroes'). But Europe by contrast proved ungrateful for this: 'Doch Europa — welche Schmach und Schande! | Dankte ihm durch Theilung seiner Lande' ('Yet Europe—what shame and disgrace!—thanked Poland by partitioning its lands').[73]

Political undertones are even clearer in his 'Wiegenlied (1856)' ('Lullaby, 1856'), where he bitterly complains about the prevailing censorship and police control, in surprisingly clear and unambiguous terms: 'Was man heißt, das *thue*; | Widerstand der frommt dir nicht' ('What they say, *obey*; resistance is of no use'). Resigned to the situation, he goes on: 'Freiheit ist nur Grille. | Auf die Freiheit thu' Verzicht, | *Ruhe* ist die *schönste* Pflicht' ('Freedom is but a whim. Renounce freedom, *peace and quiet* is the duty *most beautiful*').[74]

In heavily encoded verse, Meyer comments on the massive and violent suppression of the Polish independence movement in his poem 'Der Winter im Frühling (1861)' ('Winter in the Spring, 1861'). The connection with political events of the time is evident only from the indication of month (in the first stanza) and year (in the title): in March 1861, five demonstrators were shot down in Warsaw, slain by Russian police. Among them were two Jewish students, and these

---

[73] Meyer, *Hinterlassene deutsche Schriften*, 72–7. Several other texts express his critical view of Roman Catholicism, such as 'Drei Isabela's', ibid. 135.   [74] Ibid. 77; see the Appendix below, item 2.

victims and the 'shared blood shed', often voiced as a slogan in the subsequent period, are considered the myth of origin of a short-lived period of Polish–Jewish solidarity and fraternity.[75] Again making a political comment, Meyer looks back in his 'Das neue Jahr (1867)' ('New Year, 1867') to the Austro-Prussian war of 1866. He notes that every year starts peacefully, but soon 'begins to hum songs of war', and then degenerates into a 'wild brawl'.[76] Meyer's humanistic attitude is clear here, rejecting war as a means for solving political, social, or religious conflicts. Rather, he viewed war as the principal evil of his era, destructive of intellectual greatness and creativity.

A group of poems under the label 'Lyrisches' ('Lyrical') stems partly from Meyer's Berlin years, and partly from the 1850s and 1860s. Rapture, a deep feeling for nature, euphoria, and melancholy mark these lyrical pieces. Meyer also preserved this elevated tone in the poems he wrote in the final years of his life, in which he elaborates on feelings of loss and sorrow: in 'Zur Ruhe' ('To Sleep') he takes a lullaby for a little child and places it in parallel with the preparations of an old man for death, and in 'Am Sterbetage meiner Schwester Blümchen (1867)' ('On the Day of the Death of my Sister Blümchen, 1867') Meyer expresses his sorrow at the loss of his sister.[77] Even decades after returning to Poland, Meyer still writes with a quite smooth and supple diction. The extent of his awareness that his time in Berlin was a unique and limited period in his life emerges clearly, and nowhere more so than in his poem 'Erinnerung an Berlin' ('Memory of Berlin'), written a year after his return to Włocławek.[78] The leitmotif of this poem is Meyer's admiration for the magnificence of Berlin and Prussia, and for the urbanity, quality of life, fine arts, education, and science there. Finally, noteworthy are two poems from his Berlin years that are strongly charged with eroticism.[79]

Many of Meyer's songs, poems, and texts are addressed to members of his family, but alongside the family man a picture emerges of him as the host, or at least an organizer, of social events of a cultural nature. Some of the works were evidently the occasional products of cultural life in a small town, such as a quite large number of short prose texts, perhaps best described as *causerie*: brilliant observations, but largely devoid of substantial content.[80] Precisely when commenting on serious topics, Meyer adopted an imaginative, almost burlesque, tone. His 'Selbstbiographie eines Flohes' ('Autobiography of a Flea') targets religious fanaticism in general and the excesses of the Catholic religion in particular. The flea leaves Eastern Pomerania with its parents, when the 'despised progressive economy

---

[75] Ibid. 79; see also Opalski and Bartal, *Poles and Jews*, 44–8.

[76] Meyer, *Hinterlassene deutsche Schriften*, 81.

[77] Ibid. 101, 102.   [78] Ibid. 93–4; see the Appendix below, item 1.

[79] Ibid. 90, 'An einen erwarteten Abend' ('To an Awaited Evening'); 94–5, 'Symptome' ('Symptoms').

[80] Ibid. 116, 'Apologie des Auges' ('Apology of the Eye'); 119, 'Der Kuckuck und der Baum' ('The Cuckoo and the Tree'); 121, 'Der Aufstand der Flüsse' ('Revolt of the Rivers'); or 136, 'Die Hand' ('The Hand').

begins to expand there', and in its wanderings arrives in Rome. Here the flea listens to the Pope, subsequently biting the pontiff as he delivers a sermon directed, amongst others, 'against the Jews, who dare to demand the return of their infants, taken by pious wet nurses into the bosom of the Church'. This evident allusion to the Mortara affair, triggered by the secret baptism and abduction of a Jewish child in Bologna, suggests that the poem can be dated to sometime after 1858.[81] In 'Messias' ('Messiah') Meyer bemoans the general decay of morals, manifested in war, brutality, and violence. A murder in Włocławek, apparently the occasion for writing the text, leads to a conversation with a Polish 'gentleman', who attributes the violent act to a lack of religion. Meyer quotes his interlocutor as saying in Polish: 'Przez brak religii' ('through a lack of religion'), to whom he retorts, also in Polish: 'Owszem przez zbytek religii' ('on the contrary, through an excess of religion'). He goes on: 'In actual fact, there is too much religion in the world and too little morality. Religion has its synagogues, churches, mosques, and pagodas everywhere—but where are the temples to morality?'[82] In other texts, Meyer's thoughts are marked by efforts to argue convincingly over and beyond religious boundaries. The topics and viewpoints that he chose and the events that inspired him to write show clearly just how broad his horizon was, and how great were his efforts to integrate a multitude of religious and philosophical views into his understanding of a diverse society more friendly to human interests and sentiments.[83]

Meyer's dramatic works contained in his *Hinterlassene deutsche Schriften* are of very uneven quality. They may have been written for reading or use at home or in some local framework. On 14 March 1865, Meyer described in a letter a local theatrical performance in the course of which 'a cloverleaf of three comedies' was staged, and he added: 'The actors and actresses were our relatives and friends.'[84] Deserving of special mention among his plays is *Die Schöpfung* ('Creation'), a humoresque about the creation of the world. The rather nonchalant and somewhat bored proclamation by God of the creation of the earth and man leads to intensive discussions between Satan, the archangels, and the Creator. Satan says: 'I am opposed as a matter of principle to the annexation and integration of new bodies. It will be much too much work for us, and to organize these recalcitrant new parts will create much ill will.' This assessment, not least a reflection of Meyer's thinking about the injustice of the partition of Poland, is echoed by the archangels, who think that 'this time, Satan is right', while the Creator contends: 'I, the Eternal and Everlasting One, must know better what I am doing, since *l'Empire, c'est Moi!*' At the conclusion of the successful creation of the world, Adam and Eve welcome the sabbath together with the other dramatis personae.[85]

---

[81] Further allusions to this cause célèbre can be found in Meyer's letters to his son, *Hinterlassene deutsche Schriften*, 180 (15 Sept. 1860) and 182 (30 Sept. 1864), as well as in a letter to an anonymous Warsaw acquaintance, ibid. 214 (24 Dec. 1858).   [82] Ibid. 131–3.

[83] Ibid. 120–1, 'Andacht' ('Devotion'); 134–5, 'Religion' ('Religion'); 135, 'Religion der Zukunft' ('Religion of the Future').   [84] Ibid. 184.   [85] Ibid. 140–7.

More clearly and pointedly than in the songs and poems, his attentive and critical view of his times is contained in a great number of sayings and short commentaries that were gathered together under the heading 'Allerlei Kleinigkeiten' ('Assorted Trifles') in the first edition of *Hinterlassene deutsche Schriften*. Among them are numerous reflections on Jewish history, Jewish religion, and the Jewish present, and he was inspired here by both the German Jewish and Polish Jewish historiography of his time.[86] Thus, he regularly reflects on the similarities and differences between Poles and Jews. Even though his remarks are generalizing and aphoristic in nature, Meyer sought to avoid any negative stereotype. Rather, he tried to recognize the one in the other, and bring out their shared features. In reference to the Jewish patriarchs Shem, Ham, and Japheth, he noted: 'These three principal races of humankind appear to be strongly represented in Poland. The Polish nobleman is the true type of one descended from the refined Japheth. He calls the farmer literally "Cham",[87] and this class really does have something of its scruffy progenitor. The Polish Jew is the incarnate bench-warmer Shem, as described in the Talmud.'[88] He has similar comments on the January uprising: 'The Poles are Jews with sabres, the Jews are Poles without sabres. Two tough nationalities, amongst whom sublimity walks side by side with insanity. Thus, today's Polish movement (1863) is a sublime insanity.'[89] In these observations on his times, Meyer did not limit himself to just the Polish horizon. He very attentively followed developments in Prussia and Austria. To an appreciable degree, it was sympathy for the Polish independence movement, which sought to undo the consequences of the partitioning of Poland, that made the two great powers Prussia and Austria look similar to him: 'The Austrian saying "divide et impera!" is similar in sense to the Prussian dictum "suum quique"—both love to *divide things up*.'[90] He repeats this assessment in the context of the Austro-Prussian war of 1866, when he weighs the historical burdens of the two states one against the other. Gradually, his initially boundless admiration for Prussia receded, to be replaced by a more sober evaluation: 'In Prussia, Germany is now rising *up*—and going *under*', was his comment on the situation after the Austro-Prussian war.[91]

Meyer's songs, poems, and prose texts provide a differentiated impression of his literary, religious, and cultural horizon. In addition, his *Hinterlassene deutsche Schriften* contain a large number of letters in German, in which he reports to his sister and son about everyday life in Warsaw or in Włocławek. The letters from

[86] Apart from references in passing to the Jewish press of his day, Meyer only rarely mentions authors he has read. Among those noted are the author of the 'magnificent twelve lectures on Jewish history', whom he does not name (it was Abraham Geiger, 1810–74), and Aleksander Kraushar (1843–1931) and his book on Jewish history in the Polish medieval period, *Historya Żydów w Polsce*: Meyer, *Hinterlassene deutsche Schriften*, 189–90 (letters to his son, 15 May 1866).

[87] In Polish, *cham* is a derogatory word for a boorish, uncouth man.

[88] Meyer, *Hinterlassene deutsche Schriften*, 150.   [89] Ibid. 160.   [90] Ibid. 151.

[91] Ibid. 154; and 194–6 (letter to his son, 22 June 1866).

Warsaw were written mainly to his sister in Włocławek during the period 1835–9. They describe life in the Polish capital in vivid colours and with a richness of detail. In the second group of letters, in the main composed at a later date, Louis Meyer wrote from Włocławek to his son Herman, describing life in the provincial town. There are three longer letters, to Isaak Lewin Auerbach in Berlin,[92] to a Russian military doctor probably stationed in Włocławek, and to an unidentified acquaintance in Warsaw. It is clear from the letters to his sister that when Meyer was working in the Warsaw bank of Simon Rosen, he often stayed on in Warsaw during the Jewish high holidays, although not always. He liked to compose letters on the occasion of such holidays, and combined them with wishes and pious admonitions. His everyday life emerges in the proud description of new garments he has acquired: 'Just take a look at my long, sky-blue greatcoat—the colour is divine, the tailoring English. And now behold this broad, dark blue overcoat, with its black velvet collar and green lining.'[93] Among the accounts of everyday life, there is also Meyer's witty description of his employer, the banker Simon Rosen: 'Despot to the highest degree, he is nonetheless no tyrant in his own field of activity, and when he does radiate a beam of friendliness, he appeases those around him.' Of his influential son, Mathias Rosen, he wrote: 'On the railway track of my life, Mathias by himself would be enough to reconcile me with human society. I don't know anyone else who is so full of sheer goodness.'[94] He did not much like, as he revealed in his letters, what he found in the social life of the capital, in which he participated as a senior bank official. Since people were evidently trying to find a new spouse for him, it is clear that he was perceived as part of this society.[95] He describes in some detail outstanding social events in Warsaw, such as a soirée given in 1836 to introduce the Breslau-born husband-to-be of a daughter of one of the leading Warsaw families. Meyer regretted that the evening meal was not served until after card games and dancing, in the small hours of the morning, and not seated at a table, but rather as a cold buffet:

Alas, fresh misfortune! People did not sit down in an orderly fashion around a table, as our good fathers used to. No, instead people rushed like mad things to a table full of all sorts of food, grabbed a plate and a fork, piled the plate high with their choice, and made off to a corner. And then they devoured the stuff they'd managed to grab, rather in the way that V—nese *merchants' wives* consume their lunch at the shop. In the sophisticated world, this is called dining 'à la fourchette', in German—'fork-dinner'![96]

Just as graphically, Meyer describes the wedding festivities in one of the prominent Jewish families in Warsaw:

[92] Isaak Lewin Auerbach (1791–1853) was one of the pioneers of the German Jewish Reform movement and a founding member of the Verein für Kultur und Wissenschaft des Judentums (Association for the Culture and Science of Judaism).

[93] Meyer, *Hinterlassene deutsche Schriften*, 166 (letter to his sister, 7 Nov. [1835]).

[94] Ibid. 174–5 (letter to his sister, 27 May 1838).   [95] Ibid. 178 (letter to his sister, 23 Dec. 1839).

[96] Ibid. 168 (letter to his sister, 4 Jan. 1836); see the Appendix below, item 5.

We enter the first room. The resplendence of a multitude of candelabra glitters to welcome us. We greet people with a slight nod of the head right and left, shake the hands of acquaintances as we pass, and congratulate the feted couple. We proceed further. In the room to the right, the good old days seem to tarry. Sable coats and long beards are a vivid reminder that here a wedding of 'our people' is being celebrated. In the room to the left it's all quite different. No trace of Judaism is to be seen here. A Babylonian confusion of languages predominates: Polish, French, and German intermingle.[97]

By contrast, his sister in Włocławek learned very little about the life of the broader circles of the Jewish community in Warsaw, then growing very rapidly. Meyer does not mention anywhere that he himself enjoyed a prominent place among the adherents of Enlightenment and Jewish reform in Warsaw, as Jacob Shatzky, the chronicler of the Warsaw Jewish community, reports.[98] The lower status of Jewish residents in the Polish capital is barely touched upon. The 'wretched head tax' ('erbärmlicher Tag-Zettel') demanded from Jews to permit entry to the capital, which people regarded as a great affront and one of the worst forms of discrimination, is mentioned only once by Meyer.[99] He did not comment on conflicts between Jews and non-Jews, aside once from several remarks regarding the lack of proper recognition for a rising Jewish actor:

The Jewish actor *Davidsohn*, whom you find so interesting, did a good job of playing his third inaugural role, and is already active in the theatre. There is no doubt he's one of the best local actors, and maybe some day will become the best of all. But he still faces difficult challenges, and people still cannot stomach the idea that a son of Israel should be a hero on the stage.[100]

Meyer's letters to his son follow the rhythms of the Jewish holidays and describe the quiet, comfortable life in the province, but are no less informative for that. For example, it becomes clear how the railway had significantly changed small-town life, and had itself become a metaphor for cultural innovation. Thus, Meyer commented on the Mortara affair as it developed that it was a 'Nemesis now riding the rails', and at Jewish New Year 1864 he summarized the year after the January 1863 uprising and its suppression in a vivid formulation:

The railway cars rolling by in opposite directions can indeed provide us with a graphic image of the turn of the year: the long, dark train of coaches of the past year, we know what it contains. We know the heavy cargo of bitterness it brought to the country in general and to each person in particular. May this funeral train of sorrow roll off into time's abyss, into the gorge of the past. And may the mire it brought with it never again appear![101]

[97] Ibid. 170 (letter to his sister, 1836), 170.   [98] Shatzky, *Geshikhte fun yidn in varshe*, ii. 132.
[99] Meyer, *Hinterlassene deutsche Schriften*, 173 (letter to his sister, 27 May 1838).
[100] Ibid. 172 (letter to his sister, undated). While Meyer was still alive, a similar case of insufficient recognition of artistic performance was to develop into a scandal that kept the public in suspense for many weeks, the so-called 'Jewish war' of 1859. On this, see *Der Fremde als Nachbar: Polnische Positionen zur jüdischen Präsenz: Texte seit 1800*, ed. F. Guesnet (Frankfurt am Main, 2009), 129–57.
[101] Meyer, *Hinterlassene deutsche Schriften*, 181–2 (letter to his son, 30 Sept. 1864).

And in this same letter, he notes with alarm that the members of the hasidic community of the Gerer Rebbe are also using the railway in order to travel at New Year to their leader:

During these days we have experienced the sight of something totally new for our rational part of the world: the open coaches of the fourth class filled with those physically and morally wretched figures who call themselves hasidim, and who go on pilgrimage in groups to their Rebbe on the holy Mount Calvary. Whence do these children of the steppes of the spirit come to us? Did Hell spit them out and hurl them in our direction? They came from the other side . . . of the Vistula, from out of the caves of backwardness, in order to use the railway here, the pathway of progress, for their pilgrimages.[102]

In the period after the quashing of the January uprising, Meyer often turned to look towards the West, interested in observing and commenting in some detail on Prussia's bid for predominance in Germany. There is no doubt that the Prussian victory over Catholic Austria in 1866 gave him a certain satisfaction ('no sympathies for the great divider of the races, with the slogan on its banner: divide and rule!').[103] Yet Bismarck's politics had little in common with the cultural radiance of the Prussia of his youth that he admired so much. In the approach to the 1866 war, he bemoaned the 'disgusting German sabre-rattling',[104] and two years later he wrote: 'a spirit of conquest of blood and iron has sprung from the moral conquests'.[105] Meyer did not wish to overlook, nor could he, that nationalism and militarism were increasingly overshadowing the Prussian achievements he admired in the realm of enlightenment, education, culture, and science.

In his final years, Meyer's correspondence dealt mainly with comments on political developments that he followed from afar, various Jewish holidays, the death of his sister (for whom he wrote a moving obituary), and a trip by his son to western Europe to visit Paris and London. In the summer of 1868, his dream for many decades to return to Berlin was finally realized. Full of love for the city, he observed the profound changes that had taken place there since the time of his youth. The New Synagogue on Oranienburger Strasse was a source of great fascination for Meyer. In his eyes, it was the realization of his desire for a Jewish religious community solidly attached to its religious principles, while also strongly integrated into the city in aesthetic, cultural, and social terms. While Prussia as a state was growing ever more distant from his ideals, he thought that Berlin Jewry had succeeded in finding a good balance between independence and integration. His confrontation with hasidic Jews back home appeared in significant measure to strengthen that perception. In a letter to a Warsaw acquaintance written in 1858, he developed a vision of the expulsion of the hasidim:

First, we should send off the whole blooming tribe of the hasidim, the Kotzker dynasty, the Zychliner hasidim, the Lutomiersker hasidim, and all that bunch, along with their matrons,

---

[102] Meyer, *Hinterlassene deutsche Schriften*, 182.   [103] Ibid. 192 (letter to his son, 4 June 1866).
[104] Ibid.   [105] Ibid. 205 (letter to his son, 30 Dec. 1868).

who wear half-bonnets à la mode, covering their *empty skulls* with dirty rags instead of hair. We shall place these people in the steppes and forests of the Caucasus, where they can unite their wild *Sehmers* with those of the Chechens.[106]

In this caricature, Meyer expresses his deep sense of unease. In the same letter, he formulated his view as an 'assertion that the material and intellectual wellbeing of the Jews can only prosper where they do not form a compact mass among themselves but mingle more with the Christians'. In a tone of slight resignation, Meyer saw his own place as being in Poland: 'We shall remain in this country, and intend to get along with our Poles, because "Co się kłóci, to się kocha" (teasing is a sign of affection) and Polak and Jew have a certain soft spot for one another, despite all the feuding of the insipid journalists.'[107]

CONCLUSION

In a unique way, Meyer's *Hinterlassene deutsche Schriften* document the intellectual, aesthetic, and religious *musée sentimental* of a Jewish businessman from provincial Poland. Although he felt a deep bond with Polish Jewish tradition, he had great admiration for the world of European modernity that he had come to know as a young man in Berlin. His texts in German are an expression of his attempt to harmonize these two shaping elements in his life. They also stand symbolically for his wish not to let his ties to Berlin and to everything this metropolis signified for him be sundered in Polish provincial life. Among the lasting influences of his years spent in the Prussian capital was a powerful affinity for the German language and literature, and for education, science, and middle-class bourgeois culture. Meyer retained a loyal affection for the German language all his life, as eloquently attested by his numerous literary texts. In addition, his letters to his family document Jewish life in both Warsaw and the provinces. There are numerous observations on the relationship between Poles and Jews. Their life together over centuries was in his eyes the guarantee of resilient and lasting Polish–Jewish relations based less on mutual affection and more on the recognition of difference. He regarded the partitioning of Poland by Prussia, Austria, and Russia as an ever-present injustice, and he harboured undisguised sympathies for the struggle against partition. It is noticeable that Meyer's enthusiastic identification with Prussia as an ideal embodiment of German culture receded in the last decade of his life, overshadowed by his growing scepticism regarding Prussian ambitions for political and military hegemony. He did not regard war as politics by other means, but rather as the very epitome of the failure of human community, the raw defeat of Reason. The 'soft spot' Poles and Jews had for one another because of centuries of cohabitation seems to have offered only limited solace to Louis Meyer, this orphan of the Enlightenment.

---

[106] Ibid. 213 (letter from Włocławek to Mr H. K. in Warsaw, 24 Dec. 1858). *Sehmers* are musicians.
[107] Ibid.

APPENDIX

(1) MEMORY OF BERLIN (1819)

I think of You, Berlin, O Princess of the Cities,
when my eye, roaming o'er bare open fields,
    longs for the environs of cities delightful;

then am I reminded of your towers, your houses,
magnificent in number, rising up in rows well formed,
    rich in artistic creation.

When in the solitude of lonely hours
my heart melancholic sighs in vain for pleasures lost,
    I see You in my mind's eye,
        Crown of the Cities!

I see the busy hubbub of your brave and decent people,
blessed in number and grandeur,
    a pleasant feast for the eye,
        joyful in motion.

Of You I think when my spirits, cast down here,
far from the visual arts and science, lie languishing,
    dying of thirst at the fountain of life;

then I recall with respectful remembrance
your consecrated place, O splendid royal city!
    where in hallowed sites and temples

industry and art and science bear golden fruit;
—where the flock of Muses and the Graces gathered,
    familiar in a beautiful bond
        are eternally united.

I send greetings to You from afar, O Princess of the Cities!
As a youth, languishing from a distance and burning with love's ardour,
    longs for an embrace with his beloved;

so do I bear your image wrapped in my heart.
Here on the Vistula, I pay no heed to its noisy roar,
    I hearken to the silver beat
        of a more distant river.

And when some day, with a favourable stroke of luck,
Fortune shall lead me again to your level plain,
    then will I sing with highest rapture once more
      a song to You!

ERINNERUNG AN BERLIN (1819)

Dein gedenk' ich Berlin, o Fürstin der Städte,
Wenn mein Auge, schweifend auf nackte Fluren, sich
    Sehnt nach ergötzender
      Städte Umgebung;

Dann gedenk' ich der Thürme und deiner Häuser
Prächtige Anzahl, die sich in wohlgebildeten
    Reihen mit künstlicher
      Schöpfung erheben.

Wenn in einsamen bangen Stunden die Brust voll
Wehmuth nach den verlornen Genüssen vergeblich seufzt,
    Seh' ich im Bilde dich,
      Krone der Städte!

Sehe das rege Getümmel deines wackern
Volkes, das gesegnet an Anzahl und Herrlichkeit,
    Lieblich zur Augenweid',
      Froh sich beweget.

Dein gedenk' ich, wenn niedergedrücket mein Geist hier,
In der Entfernung von bildender Kunst und Wissenschaft,
    Schmachtend verdürstet am
      Brunnen des Lebens;

Dann gedenk' ich mit ehrfurchtsvoller Erinn'rung
Deines geweihten Platzes, o herrliche Königsstadt!
    Wo in geheiligten
      Sitzen und Tempeln

Fleiß und Kunst und Wissenschaft goldene Früchte
Tragen; — wo der Musen Schaar und der Grazien
    Traulich im schönen Bund
      Ewig vereint sind.

Sei mir gegrüßt in der Entfernung, o Fürstin der Städte!
Wie sich der Jüngling, ferne schmachtend vor Liebesgluth,
    Nach der Umarmung sehnt
      Seiner Geliebten;

So auch trag' ich dein Bild im Herzen verwahret.
Hier am Weichsel-Strom acht' ich sein lärmendes Rauschen nicht
   Horch' ich dem Silberschlag
     Ferneren Stromes.

Und wenn einst in günstiger Schickung das Glück mich
Wieder führet zu deinen Eb'nen, dann sing' ich mit
   Höh'rer Begeisterung
     Wieder ein Lied dir!

(2) LULLABY (1856)

    Quiet! Quiet! Quiet!
    Sleep in your cradle;
Even if you are lacking much—
Rest is the citizen's solemn duty.
    Close your eyes;
    Sleep in quiet peace!

    Quiet! Quiet! Quiet!
    If your shoes are tight,
Don't wear a sour frown;
Rest is the first duty.
    Close your eyes;
    Sleep in quiet peace!

    Quiet! Quiet! Quiet!
    What they say, *obey*;
Resistance is of no use.
Rest is the greatest duty.
    Close your eyes;
    Sleep in quiet peace!

    Hush! Hush! Hush!
    Just don't shout;
Even if some scoundrel upsets you—
Rest is the highest duty.
    Close your eyes;
    Sleep in quiet peace!

    Hush! Hush! Hush!
    Do your *duty*!
As the wise proverb says:
Rest is the first duty.
    Close your eyes;

Hush! Hush! Hush!
Freedom is but a whim.
Renounce freedom,
Peace and quiet is the duty *most beautiful.*
Close your tiny eyes,
Sleep in sweet peace!

WIEGENLIED (1856)

Ruhe! Ruhe! Ruhe!
Schlaf in deiner Truhe;
Wenn dir manches auch gebricht,
Ruhe ist des Bürgers Pflicht.
Drück' die Augen zu;
Schlaf' in guter Ruh'!

Ruhe! Ruhe! Ruhe!
Drücken dich die Schuhe,
Mach' dazu kein sau'r Gesicht;
Ruhe ist die erste Pflicht.
Drück' die Augen zu;
Schlaf in guter Ruh!

Ruhe! Ruhe! Ruhe!
Was man heißt, das *thue*;
Widerstand der frommt dir nicht,
Ruhe ist die größte Pflicht.
Drück' die Augen zu,
Schlaf in guter Ruh!

Stille! Stille! Stille!
Mach nur kein Gebrülle;
Kränkt dich auch so mancher Wicht,
Ruhe ist die höchste Pflicht.
Drück' die Augen zu,
Schlaf' in guter Ruh'!

Stille! Stille! Stille!
Deine *Pflicht* erfülle!
Wie das weise Sprichwort spricht:
Ruhe ist die erste Pflicht.
Drück' die Augen zu,
Schlaf in guter Ruh'!

Stille! Stille! Stille!
Freiheit ist nur Grille.
Auf die Freiheit thu' Verzicht,
Ruhe ist die *schönste* Pflicht.
Drück' die Aeuglein zu,
Schlaf in süßer Ruh!

(3) FROM 'ALLERLEI KLEINIGKEITEN' ('ASSORTED TRIFLES')

Page references are to L. Meyer, *Hinterlassene deutsche Schriften eines polnischen Juden*, ed. F. Guesnet (Hildesheim, 2010).

Whoever despises his religion or denies his nationality, or does not love or even hates his fatherland, because of its many defects, is like a person who rejects his father and mother because they are deformed, old, or frail. (p. 150)

Shem, Ham, and Japheth
These three principal races of humankind appear to be strongly represented in Poland. The Polish nobleman is the true type of one descended from the refined Japheth. He calls the farmer literally 'Cham', and this class really does have something of its scruffy progenitor. The Polish Jew is the incarnate bench-warmer Shem, as described in the Talmud. (p. 150)

The Prussian 'suum cuique', one might think, articulates a *universal* law, but 'to each his own' is depicted in the Prussian coat of arms by two *wild animals*, the representatives of raw strength, who appear to be *dividing* their prey. (p. 151)

The word 'overstrung' should be recorded in the yellow book of the Polish nation as the principal debt and guilt. But the main debtors are its wives, whose exaltation causes calamity in every area, yet most especially in connection with their devotion to the priests. (p. 153)

In Prussia, Germany is now rising *up*—and going *under*. (p. 154)

It is the disastrous fate of the Poles to be disunited at the wrong time, and united at the wrong time. (p. 158)

The Jewish nation in its dual form of baseness and sublimity is the embodiment of the divine idea that a human being, climbing from the lowest standpoint, can ascend to the highest.

In the image of Jacob's ladder, to this patriarch was revealed the entire future of his descendants: *ascent* and *descent*. (p. 159)

Enlightenment without religiosity is like a light without a protective lantern on the open road. (p. 159)

The Poles are Jews with sabres, the Jews are Poles without sabres. Two tough nationalities, amongst whom sublimity walks side by side with insanity. Thus, today's Polish movement (1863) is a sublime insanity. (p. 160)

For those who spread light
If you run too fast with a lantern, it doesn't shine. Moderator lamps ensure that oil flows only in small drops to the light, not in large quantities; such lamps provide the best light. (p. 161)

(4) TO THE HOLY FRATERNITY!

Gather round about me, dear brothers!
My limbs sink wearily.
Sing to me the lullaby;
I'm exhausted—I'm so, so tired.

I felt so well, I felt so terrible,
Sometimes cheerful, sometimes sad;
Now I just long for quiet rest—
Oh, close my eyes!

Much that I did was crowned with success,
Much pain entered my heart;
Weary of joys and pains,
I'm so very tired, so exhausted and weary.

Lots of light, I always wished for that,
So don't be stingy with the sacred candles;
Undress me, remove any trumpery,
And clothe me in a gown of light.

Make my bed fine,
So that I can sleep for many a night;
Until that great day dawns,
And I awake in eternal light.

Farewell, farewell, my holy brethren!
Some day we will all see each other once again—
Oh, sing me the lullaby;
I'm so, so tired, very tired!

c.1870

AN DIE HEILIGE BRÜDERSCHAFT!

Versammelt Euch um mich, Ihr Brüder!
Ermattet sinken meine Glieder.
O singet mir das Wiegenlied;
Ich bin erschöpft, — ich bin so müd'.

Mir war so wohl, mir war so schaurig,
Ich war bald heiter und bald traurig;
Nun sehn' ich mich nach stiller Ruh, —
O drücket mir die Augen zu!

So manches Thun ist mir gelungen,
So mancher Schmerz in's Herz gedrungen;
Der Freuden und der Leiden satt,
Bin ich so müd', — so müd' und matt.

Viel Licht, — das lag mir stets am Herzen,
Drum sparet nicht die heil'gen Kerzen;
Entkleidet mich von jedem Tand,
Und hüllet mich in Licht-Gewand.

Und macht das Lager mir zurechte,
Daß ich durchschlumm're viele Nächte;
Bis einst der große Tag anbricht,
Und ich erwach' im ew'gen Licht.

Lebt wohl, lebt wohl, Ihr heil'gen Brüder!
Einst sehen wir uns Alle wieder. —
O singet mir das Wiegen-Lied;
Ich bin so müd', — so müd', — so müd'!

ca. 1870

LETTERS

(5) WARSAW

Thursday, 4 January 1836, evening
My dearest sister!

I didn't write to you with today's mail. So you'll have to spend the coming sabbath without me. But to have visited you on Friday evening, I would have had to make my toilet on Wednesday evening, i.e. I would have had to write yesterday evening, and that was impossible. Why? Because I was already very sleepy by 7 o'clock. Why?

Because I hadn't slept the night before. Why? Because I spent that night at a soirée. What's a 'soirée'? That's an evening party. What? Stretch an *evening* over the *entire night*? Yes, in the fashionable world, which may ordinarily set itself apart from the ordinary, it doesn't become real night until dawn. If only you could just sleep all day! But I cursed the soirée into the night of nights after I spent an eight-hour evening wide awake and had to go to work the next day. And I didn't even accept the invitation because I wanted to go, but rather just for the experience of having been at such an event. It was in the respectable residence of Mr L. He hosted the evening in honour of his sister, whose husband-to-be was a guest from Breslau. Those with pretensions to grandeur usually don't arrive till between 9 and 10 o'clock; those who cannot rise to such high-flown ambitions have already come by about 7. I gravitated to the 'happy medium', and arrived at 8 o'clock. I was dressed pretty much as was required, because making my toilet and preparations had taken four times as long as usual, i.e. a whole ten minutes. But to my horror, I noticed afterwards that almost all the gentlemen were wearing white gloves. And I, just imagine, was wearing a pair of yellow ones! Unfortunate wretch that I am, I knew that yellow gloves were the done thing during the day, but I didn't know that *white* ones were expected at night. What inexcusable ignorance! In the meanwhile, to my consolation I noticed that several new arrivals had also clumsily violated the same rule of etiquette. At that point I enjoyed the rapturous delight of the hunchback when he sees a fellow sufferer. I'd already spent an hour slowly sipping a glass of tea, paying compliments to acquaintances, and hiding an occasional yawn, when suddenly war was declared on boredom. The signal was given: dance music struck up in the hall; a solid, respectable polonaise was soon followed by a graceful contredanse, an animated waltz, and a lively mazurka. In the adjoining room, game tables were set up, pipes were stuffed with tobacco. But as for me, poor defeated soul, a man who doesn't dance, gamble, or smoke, what was I to do?! I looked around for a fellow sufferer to find some company, and noticed to my delight that, among others, the very king of the festive evening, the bridegroom himself, was not participating in any of these marvels either. Since he is a comely young man, I confessed to him my astonishment that he was not paying due homage to Terpsichore. He said he had no knowledge and experience when it came to Polish dances. Probably they seem to him, as a German, too wild, because the Germans tend to dance and gyrate in a manner refined and slow, always piano. But I took a fancy to the merry dancing girls, and feasted my eyes on their beautiful movements. Midnight had passed. The hands of the card-players and the feet of the dancers were still in motion, as if by clockwork. Lemonade and similar refreshments were repeatedly offered—but I searched in vain for what is commonly called 'dinner'. It was 2 o'clock, and dancing and card games were still going strong, for good or for ill. I was already preparing myself to leave the so-called 'evening' without an evening meal, when a friend whispered to me that I should wait until *after dinner*. To wait at 2 o'clock in the morning until *after dinner*! It sounded to me more than a little odd. Finally, at 3 o'clock the guests were summoned to the dining hall. Alas, fresh misfortune! People did not sit down in an orderly fashion around a table, as our good fathers used to. No, instead people rushed like mad things to a table full of all sorts of food, grabbed a plate and a fork, piled the plate high with their choice, and made off to a corner. And then they devoured the stuff they'd managed to grab, rather in the way that V—nese *merchants' wives* consume their lunch at the shop. In the sophisticated world, this is called dining 'à la fourchette', in German—'fork-dinner'!

Now it was time for the champagne. And the Lord saw that it was good, and he divided the Russian tea from the French wine, and it was evening, and it was morning.

End of the chapter on the soirée.

(6) WŁOCŁAWEK

18 October 1865
My dearest son!

As of yesterday our town can be called *Dreibrücken* [Three Bridges]. Up to now it has been possible to call it *Zweibrücken* [Two Bridges], because of the two bridges over the Glowiaczka [Zgłowiączka].

The bridge over the Vistula was opened yesterday without an actual ceremony, which has been postponed until later, when the governor will be paying a visit. It was striking that there was not the least element of festivity in yesterday's act of formal opening. By 2 o'clock the expanse near the castle was already crowded with members of the public. Members of the local nominal Bridge Committee, consisting of three Christians and four Jews, had taken up their positions in front of the garlanded turnpike. Soon members of the Warsaw Construction Committee arrived, transported in several carriages. They got out in front of the bridge, and General *Szuberski* then literally handed over the bridge to the president and the municipal committee, after which these gentlemen expressed their thanks for the important achievement, speaking in German. Then the General, speaking in his best German, replied: 'I cannot formally accept your words of gratitude, because these are properly meant for the governor, who will later inspect the work he has created.' Then, at a signal from the chief of police, the assembled military bands struck up the melody of the national anthem, for which all bared their heads. At another signal, there was a drum roll—and the garlanded turnpike shot up in the air. The gentlemen of the two committees then crossed over the bridge on foot or in carriage, after which a few of us lay people, including yours truly, also smuggled ourselves across—for the riff-raff, in other words the general public, was still not allowed to cross the bridge. Only after we had returned was permission granted. The police chief gave yet another nod, and the Polish national march 'Poszły panny' sounded out. Now from all points on the higher ground a great throng descended onto the bridge, and a huge crowd gushed across the majestic Vistula, which was a grand sight to behold.

Walking across the bridge is truly a delight; the view in all directions is indescribably beautiful. Before there was a bridge there, all of that could only be seen in a fragmentary way.

(Continuation)

As extremely important as yesterday's event was for us, it was nonetheless received coolly and with a certain passivity. Or rather just accepted; it lacked the patriotic character that stamps every achievement of progress as an occasion for a popular festival. How different it was here when the steamer *Włocławek* was commissioned! Then dignitaries came from far and wide to our fair town, which for two days took on a festive mien. Nothing like that now. These days are simply a time of passivity.

29 October 1865
(Continuation)

The conqueror of the revolutionary hydra, the royal governor, was royally received in the metropolis of Kujavia. Triumphal arches at every turn, garlands and tapestries hanging from all balconies and windows, deputations at various points, bells a-ringing, bishops, pastors, Capuchins, and rabbis.

It was a grand funeral reception for the revolution.

Because I did not feel too well, I only observed the spectacle from a distance, looking from our windows. At the same time, I served as a stenographer for several petitions from widows and orphans, whose relatives were languishing in exile. A speech and toasts also flowed from my pen; but they were somewhat modified.

Włocławek had never experienced so many dignitaries gathered together—all the top people from Warsaw. The gentlemen were charmed by all they saw, heard, and enjoyed. The words spoken had a great effect, and several transcripts were taken of what was said. The toast to the governor was roughly as follows:

A bridge can justifiably represent the symbol of transition. May the founder of our beautiful material bridge also be the creator of a spiritual bridge spanning the heart of the country and the heart of the sovereign. May he establish the transition from a sad past to a consoling future!

That was the basic idea; naturally it has been much abbreviated.

It was H. who proposed this toast, and on the whole he was the only one who put forward anything decent, and with whom the count and the other gentlemen conversed the most. At the bridge, the rabbi presented the latter with a song in Hebrew and German, which, like everything else, was very well received.

The governor formed a great impression of our little hamlet. Who knows what good that will do . . .

Translated from the German by Bill Templer

'Each for his Own'

Economic Nationalism in Łódź, 1864–1914

YEDIDA KANFER

MUCH HAS BEEN WRITTEN on the bitter Polish–Jewish conflict over the election to the Fourth Russian Duma from Warsaw in October 1912. What is not often realized is that the history of the 1912 boycott of Jews that followed that election begins with the development of economic nationalism in Poland and the rest of the Russian empire.

In the mid-nineteenth century, Friedrich List had articulated the notion of a 'national economy': the implementation of an economic policy that would serve the interests of the nation, narrowly construed.[1] With the rise of ethno-linguistic nationalism in the second half of the century, ethnic minorities across east-central Europe and the Polish partitioned lands came to adopt ideas of economic nation-alism and act upon them.[2] Economic self-sufficiency was not only regarded as the key to national advancement—but in effect defined the emergence of the nation itself.[3]

The case of the multi-ethnic city of Łódź, 75 miles west-south-west of Warsaw, enables us to take a close look at this process. Before the First World War, Łódź was

This study was made possible through the Title VIII funding of the Kennan Institute, Woodrow Wilson International Center for Scholars. Many thanks to Tim Snyder, Sarah Cameron, Vlad Alalykin-Izvekov, and Olga Litvin for their ideas, comments, and assistance.

[1] F. List, *National System of Political Economy* (1841), trans. S. S. Lloyd (Fairfield, NJ, 1991); R. Szporluk, *Communism and Nationalism: Karl Marx versus Friedrich List* (New York, 1988). Many thanks to Kenneth Moss for his insights on this issue.

[2] R. Jaworski, 'Nationalismus und Ökonomie als problem der Geschichte Ostmitteleuropas im 19. und zu Beginn des 20. Jahrhunderts', *Geschichte und Gesellschaft*, 8/2 (1982), 184–204. On boycotts in Habsburg Galicia, see J.-P. Himka, 'Ukrainian–Jewish Antagonism in the Galician Country-side during the Late Nineteenth Century', in P. J. Potichnyj and H. Aster (eds.), *Ukrainian–Jewish Relations in Historical Perspective*, 2nd edn. (Edmonton, 1990); I. Vytanovych, *Istoriya ukrayins'koho kooperatyvnoho rukhu* (New York, 1964).

[3] The literature on the rise of nationalism and ideas of the 'nation' is vast. This chapter focuses both on the origins of national ideas and on the form in which they were expressed; in exploring the relationship between nationalism and industrialization, it follows upon the work of Ernest Gellner and Alexander Gerschenkron.

the textile capital of Russian Poland, known to contemporaries as the Polish Manchester.[4] It was remarkably diverse ethnically and religiously, with populations of Poles (46 per cent), Jews (29 per cent), and Germans (21 per cent), among others.[5] For national leaders who increasingly identified the interests of the nation with those of the industrialized masses, the Łódź working population became the site of multiple projects in economic self-sufficiency.[6]

The case of Łódź, and the rise of economic nationalism in Russian Poland, sheds light on Jewish economic life and movements in the modern world.[7] Historians of Imperial Russia have documented the extent to which Jews contributed to and were involved in modernizing processes—whether via integration in an evolving social structure or through contributions to commerce and industry.[8] But modernity in Russian Poland can be defined by a much broader characteristic, one which Jews shared with others: it was the process by which distinct ethno-religious groups began to define a national identity specifically through a particularistic economic future. Jews were participants in this process, even as they were its victims. Ethnic Germans, to a somewhat lesser extent, were its victims as well.

[4] Among the rich resources available on Łódź Jewry before First World War are *Polin*, 6 (1991) and W. Puś, *Żydzi w Łodzi w latach zaborów, 1793–1914* (Łódź, 2003).

[5] J. K. Janczak, 'The National Structure of the Population in Łódź in the Years 1820–1939', *Polin*, 6 (1991), 24–5. The 1897 Russian census based ethnicity on native language. Though religion is not the subject of this chapter, it may be noted that Łódź also boasted a remarkably diverse religious population of Catholics (48%), Jews (32%), and Protestants (18%), among other groups. The 'Orthodox' category constituted 2% of the population. (This figure is slightly higher than the actual percentage of Russian Orthodox in the Łódź population because the Russian army, about 4,500 people, was included in the census.)

[6] A relatively large amount of material has been preserved in Łódź from the period before the First World War. Sources on the Łódź working population include archival and rare primary documents as well as the Polish-, Yiddish-, and German-language press. In addition to materials from the Łódź State Archive (Archiwum Państwowe w Łodzi), I make use of sources from the State Archive of the Russian Federation (Gosudarstvennyi arkhiv Rossiiskoi Federatsii) in Moscow, the Central Archives for the History of the Jewish People in Jerusalem, and the YIVO Archives in New York.

[7] The history of Jewish economic life in Europe was neglected for many years; disillusionment with Marxism rendered economic history both taboo and out of fashion. Recently, scholars of western Europe have begun to revive this question, addressed in the seminal work of S. W. Baron and A. Kahan et al. (eds.), *Economic History of the Jews* (Jerusalem, 1975). See the recent compendium G. Reuveni and S. Wobick-Segev (eds.), *The Economy in Jewish History: New Perspectives on the Interrelationship between Ethnicity and Economic Life* (New York, 2011); D. J. Penslar, *Shylock's Children: Economics and Jewish Identity in Modern Europe* (Berkeley, 2001); J. Karp, *The Politics of Jewish Commerce: Economic Thought and Emancipation in Europe, 1638–1848* (New York, 2008). Historians of Polish Jewry have also recently returned to the question of Jewish economic life, especially in Warsaw. See G. Dynner, *Men of Silk: The Hasidic Conquest of Polish Jewish Society* (New York, 2006); B. Garncarska-Kadary, *Ḥelkam shel hayehudim behitpateḥut hata'asiyah shel varsha bashanim 1816/20–1914* (Tel Aviv, 1985). Finally, in his many works, Jerzy Tomaszewski has bridged economic and Jewish history: see e.g. I. Kostrowicka, Z. Landau, and J. Tomaszewski, *Historia gospodarcza Polski XIX i XX wieku* (Warsaw, 1975); J. Tomaszewski (ed.), *Śladami Polin: Studia z dziejów Żydów w Polsce* (Warsaw, 2002).

[8] B. Nathans, *Beyond the Pale: The Jewish Encounter with Late Imperial Russia* (Berkeley, 2002); Y. Slezkine, *The Jewish Century* (Princeton, 2004).

The rise of ethnic nationalism in Poland began in the years of Russian repression that followed the Polish revolt of 1863. The Łódź strike of 1892, the first general strike in Russian Poland, marked a return to political activism after the revolt. A Polish socialist movement was founded later that year, with an independent Poland at the top of its programme. This was followed by the establishment of a rival socialist internationalist party, and, in 1897, both Polish and Jewish nationalist (Zionist) movements. At the turn of the century, the first Polish co-operatives were founded in Łódź: an attempt to improve the conditions of Polish workers through the establishment of co-operative stores. The leaders of the Łódź Jewish community strove to instil a competing ethos of economic self-sufficiency among Jewish workers by establishing factories with exclusively Jewish labour.

With the Russian revolution of 1905–7, these limited and short-lived efforts developed into much larger movements for economic self-sufficiency. In Poland, the revolution took the form of a third national uprising, with demands for Polish-language education, administration, and self-government.[9] Łódź became a centre of worker mobilization, with over two years of strike activity and sectarian violence. By October 1905, Tsar Nicholas II had yielded to popular demands, granting basic civil rights as well as an institution of popular representation, the Duma. Socialist and nationalist parties in Poland grew into mass political movements; in Łódź, union membership reached the tens of thousands. The Polish co-operative movement, too, flowered in Łódź, under the leadership of the radical Catholic priest Andrzej Rogoziński. Rogoziński envisioned Polish co-operative stores as not only raising the moral calibre of Polish workers but contributing to a larger economic struggle against Jews. The revolution of 1905–7 did indeed aggravate Polish–Jewish tensions throughout Russian Poland—and Polish nationalist disappointment in the reactionary period that followed gave rise to heightened antisemitism.[10]

In Łódź, however, the revolution contributed to an increase in national sentiments among the city's Polish, Jewish, *and* German populations.[11] National

[9] The historiography on the Russian revolution of 1905–7 is immense. Among urban accounts, see L. Engelstein, *Moscow, 1905: Working-Class Organization and Political Conflict* (Stanford, Calif., 1982). Recently, Charters Wynn and Faith Hillis have examined the question of worker mobilization in the imperial peripheries: see C. Wynn, *Workers, Strikes, and Pogroms: The Donbass–Dnepr Bend in Late Imperial Russia, 1870–1905* (Princeton, 1992); F. Hillis, 'Between Empire and Nation: Urban Politics, Community, and Violence in Kiev, 1863–1907', Ph.D. diss. (Yale Univ., 2009). On the revolution in Russian Poland, see e.g. R. Blobaum, *Rewolucja: Russian Poland, 1904–1907* (Ithaca, NY, 1995); S. Ury, 'The Generation of 1905 and the Politics of Despair: Alienation, Friendship, Community', in S. Hoffman and E. Mendelsohn (eds.), *The Revolution of 1905 and Russia's Jews* (Philadelphia, 2008), 96–110.

[10] Theodore Weeks has recently emphasized this point in his *From Assimilation to Antisemitism: The 'Jewish Question' in Poland, 1850–1914* (Dekalb, Ill., 2006). See also R. Blobaum, 'The Politics of Antisemitism in Fin-de-Siècle Warsaw', *Journal of Modern History*, 73/2 (2001), 275–306.

[11] As is discussed below, education in particular became a battleground for limited municipal resources and tax funding. Russian Poland was not unique in this regard. Historians have elaborated on the work of Eric Hobsbawm and Ernest Gellner in demonstrating the centrality of education to nationality struggles across east-central Europe. On the Moravian Compromise of 1905 and the question of

tensions were heightened by anti-Polish policy in eastern Germany, the lands of the Prussian partition. Since Bismarck, Germany's rulers had aimed for the Germanization of its Polish population and supported German colonization of Polish lands and estates.[12] In late 1907, the Polish nationalist press in Russian Poland responded to new anti-Polish legislation with an economic boycott against Germany, German goods, and 'German' firms. The term 'boycott' itself was a relatively new one, born in an age that witnessed the rise of mass consumption, along with movements for national, political, and social liberation.[13] The creation of a Polish parliamentary club (*koło*) following the Russian revolution had allowed Polish activists to pursue national concessions through legal means. Now, in declaring a boycott against all things German, these same leaders began to articulate their own foreign policy, and to act upon it in the economic realm.

Jews were pressured to choose sides. Jewish financial and intellectual elites in Poland, even those who advocated Jewish social integration, had often maintained the respect for German language and culture that dated back to the Berlin-based Jewish Enlightenment (Haskalah). Now, the Warsaw Jewish journal *Izraelita* chose to join the anti-German campaign, thereby supporting Polish commerce and industry. If maintaining an economic boycott was too difficult, *Izraelita* advised its readers, they should boycott German language and culture. This would not only demonstrate Jewish solidarity with Poles, a step towards earning equal rights, but would serve as a Jewish response to another sort of repression in Germany: antisemitism.[14]

The new geopolitical implications of economic nationalism provided the immediate background for the boycott of Jews in 1912. Russian parliamentary elections served as the direct impetus. With a Jewish electoral victory assured in Łódź,

German- and Czech-language education in Habsburg Bohemia, see J. King, 'Who Is Who? Separate but Equal in Imperial Austria', unpublished manuscript. See also R. Szporluk, 'Thoughts about Change: Ernest Gellner and the History of Nationalism', in J. A. Hall (ed.), *The State of the Nation: Ernest Gellner and the Theory of Nationalism* (Cambridge, 1998).

[12] J. Buzek, *Historya polityki narodowościowej rządu pruskiego wobec Polaków: Od traktatów wiedeńskich do ustaw* (Lwów, 1909); W. W. Hagen, *Germans, Poles, and Jews: The Nationality Conflict in the Prussian East, 1772–1914* (Chicago, 1980); R. Blanke, *Prussian Poland in the German Empire (1871–1900)* (Boulder, Colo., 1981).

[13] The term 'boycott' was coined in late nineteenth-century Ireland, in the context of the Irish Land League's campaign for fair rent practices. It derived from the protest action of tenant farmers in 1880 against their British land agent, Charles Boycott. The verb 'to boycott' was quickly taken up by the press and used in the general sense of 'cutting off relations', whether in the economic sphere (strikes, blacklisting) or in the political one. It was used especially in cases of non-state actors taking action against a state or country. See e.g. J. Marlow, *Captain Boycott and the Irish* (London, 1973). See also R. Rybarski, *Bojkoty ekonomiczne w krajach obcych* (Kraków, 1916) and W. Zwinogrodzka, 'Przypadki bojkotu w życiu teatralnym warszawy drugiej połowy XIX stulecia', in J. Maciejewski (ed.), *Z domu niewoli: Sytuacja polityczna a kultura literacka w drugiej połowie XIX wieku* (Wrocław, 1988), 81–2.

[14] 'W spawie [*sic*] bojkotu', *Izraelita*, 1907, no. 49, pp. 1–2; 'W sprawie bojkotu II', *Izraelita*, 1907, no. 50, pp. 1–2.

Jewish electors in Warsaw chose to defer to Polish interests and support the election of a Polish Duma delegate in the Polish capital. However, rather than giving their swing vote to a Polish nationalist leader, they backed instead a candidate who would support Jewish rights. In protest, the Polish nationalist press in Warsaw called for an economic struggle against Jews, under the slogan of 'each for his own' (*swój do swego*). Open antisemitism even among those intellectuals who had previously advocated Jewish integration led, in turn, to the radicalization of Jewish politics and further development of Jewish nationalism.[15]

Like the 1907–8 German boycott before it, the 1912 campaign against Jews never achieved full implementation. Nevertheless, discussions continued in the Łódź press regarding the concept of economic self-sufficiency. The Polish nationalist newspaper in Łódź rejected the term 'boycott', favouring instead the concept of 'nationalization' (*unarodowienie*) of industry and trade. The latter implied a continuous struggle for Polish self-sufficiency, one that had begun long before the 1912 campaign against Jews—and one waged, similarly, against all things 'German'.

THE ROLE OF ŁÓDŹ IN RUSSIAN ECONOMIC DEVELOPMENT

The history of Łódź as an industrial city began in the early years of Russian rule in Poland. The tsarist regime accorded the Congress Kingdom a large degree of financial autonomy, allowing its economic integration to proceed at a slower pace than its political incorporation into the empire.[16] The Polish administration, led by reformers from the pre-partition era, initiated a full-scale campaign of Polish industrial development. As a major landowner, the state administration invested directly in heavy metals, mining, and transportation.[17] In the realm of textiles, it gave incentives to entrepreneurs in Prussia, Silesia, and Bohemia to migrate and settle in the Congress Kingdom.[18]

---

[15] For accounts of the 1912 elections in Warsaw, see S. D. Corrsin, *Warsaw before the First World War: Poles and Jews in the Third City of the Russian Empire, 1880–1914* (Boulder, Colo., 1989); Weeks, *From Assimilation to Antisemitism*; Blobaum, 'Politics of Antisemitism in Fin-de-Siècle Warsaw'; F. Golczewski, *Polnisch-jüdische Beziehungen, 1881–1922: Eine Studie zur Geschichte des Antisemitismus in Osteuropa* (Wiesbaden, 1981). Golczewski in particular has made the point that the 1912 boycott was not new in the repertoire of Polish political activism: ibid. 106. On the implications of the boycott for Jewish politics, see A. Polonsky, *The Jews in Poland and Russia*, 3 vols. (Oxford, 2010–12), vol. ii.

[16] E. A. Pravilova, *Finansy imperii: Den'gi i vlast' v politike Rossii na natsional'nykh okrainakh, 1801–1917* (Moscow, 2006), 42.

[17] J. Jedlicki, 'State Industrial Economy in the Kingdom of Poland in the Nineteenth Century', *Acta Poloniae Historica*, 18 (1968), 221–37; id., *Nieudana próba kapitalistycznej industrializacji: Analiza państwowego gospodarstwa przemysłowego w Królestwie Polskim XIX w.* (Warsaw, 1964).

[18] In doing so, it continued policies initiated by the Polish administration of the Napoleonic Duchy of Warsaw (1807–15) to promote industry and urban development. On the settlement campaigns, see G. Missalowa, *Studia nad powstaniem łódzkiego okręgu przemysłowego, 1815–1870*, 3 vols. (Łódź,

In an age when borders were still fluid and the Polish partitions still a formative memory, individual initiative played a key role in economic growth and urban development. At the suggestion of the voivodeship commissioner Rajmund Rembieliński, the Polish administration named a series of promising towns and villages as future 'factory settlements', eligible for government sponsorship and support. The small agricultural town of Łódź, surrounded by forests and a bountiful water supply, received such a designation.[19] Once an old Polish trading post, Łódź was now conveniently located on a newly constructed road connecting two established manufacturing centres. Rembieliński, a champion of urban planning, converted the Łódź Old Town into a new textile district, quickly settled by German-speaking weavers and clothiers. Polish peasants were resettled in outlying districts; Jewish traders constituted about a third of the town's population.[20]

While towns surrounding Łódź produced mainly woollen fabrics, Rembieliński invested in Łódź in the manufacture of cotton—a branch of textiles relatively unknown in the region.[21] The lack of a tradition of industry in Łódź allowed for greater innovation in production, especially in the technology of cotton spinning.[22] Following the Polish revolt of 1830–1, the Russian regime took punitive measures against the Polish wool industry. While surrounding wool-producing towns were left impoverished and depopulated, Łódź, in its manufacture of cotton textiles, found itself without competition.[23] Łódź entrepreneurs rapidly mechanized the cotton-spinning process, bypassing the hand production characteristic of pre-

1964–75), i. 61–2; A. Rynkowska, *Działalność gospodarcza władz Królestwa Polskiego na terenie Łodzi przemysłowej w latach 1821–1831* (Łódź, 1951), 21–2. These policies resembled the tsarist settlement of ethnic German colonists in southern Ukraine and elsewhere. See A. Kappeler, *The Russian Empire: A Multiethnic History*, trans. A. Clayton (Harlow, 2001), 50–1; E. Amburger, *Die Anwerbung ausländischer Fachkräfte für die Wirtschaft Russlands vom 15. bis ins 19. Jahrhundert* (Wiesbaden, 1968).

[19] From the fourteenth to late eighteenth centuries, Łódź was a private town owned by the bishopric of Włocławek. During the brief period of Prussian rule following the Polish partitions, Łódź was converted into a royal town as the lands of the bishopric were secularized. See B. Baranowski and J. Fijałek (eds.), *Łódź: Dzieje miasta*, i: *Do 1918 r.* (Warsaw and Łódź, 1980), 74–145.

[20] About 262 out of 800. See P. Friedman, *Dzieje Żydów w Łodzi od początków osadnictwa Żydów do r. 1863* (Łódź, 1935), 45–52; A. Alperin, 'Żydzi w Łodzi: Początki gminy żydowskiej, 1780–1822', *Rocznik Łódzki*, 1 (1928), 170–1, 177–8. On urban planning in Łódź and population resettlement, see Rynkowska, *Działalność gospodarcza władz Królestwa Polskiego*, 16; K. Woźniak, 'Inicjatywy przemysłowe Rajmunda Rembielińskiego w Łodzi w latach 1820–1830', in A. Barszczewska-Krupa (ed.), *Rajmund Rembieliński: Jego czasy i jego współcześni* (Warsaw, 1989), 63–6.

[21] Missalowa, *Studia nad powstaniem łódzkiego okręgu przemysłowego*, i. 190–1; M. Ajzen, *Polityka gospodarcza Lubeckiego, 1821–1830* (Warsaw, 1932), 164–6.

[22] One of the first cotton-spinning mills in Poland was constructed in Łódź. The only other existing spinning mill in the Congress Kingdom in the mid-1820s was in the village of Lipków, near Warsaw; it produced yarn of a low quality. See Missalowa, *Studia nad powstaniem łódzkiego okręgu przemysłowego*, i. 191.

[23] An early historian of Łódź, Frida Bielschowsky, was one of the first to characterize the downturn in wool as favourable for Łódź. See F. Bielschowsky, *Die Textilindustrie des Lodzer Rayons: Ihr Werden und ihre Bedeutung* (Leipzig, 1912), 17–18. Gryzelda Missalowa has more recently expanded on the

industrialized countries.[24] Migration from both central and western Europe continued in the 1840s, including a significant wave of Jewish immigration from the Prussian and Austrian borderlands.[25]

Over the course of the nineteenth century—and, decisively, with the 1863 Polish uprising—the tsarist regime gradually eliminated Poland's financial autonomy. Nevertheless, thanks to Russian imperial modernization, industrialization in Łódź not only continued but accelerated. In 1850, Russia had dismantled the tariff barrier between the Congress Kingdom and the rest of the empire. Now, the construction of new railways opened up vast Russian markets to Łódź industrialists.[26] The emancipation of the Polish peasantry in 1864 contributed to ever more rapid demographic growth.[27] Thanks to the Russian conquest of Central Asia, Łódź industrialists began to cultivate and process their own cotton in Russian Turkestan.[28] Tariffs imposed upon German goods in the late 1870s enabled them to operate with minimal competition.[29] By the end of the century, as the Russian Finance Ministry sought to position itself as a world economic power, it identified cotton textiles as the first sector of industrial production.[30] Petrokov province (including Łódź and

same idea: Missalowa, *Studia nad powstaniem łódzkiego okręgu przemysłowego*, i. 16–17, 166–74. See also Baranowski and Fijałek (eds.), *Łódź*, i. 233.

[24] In 1842, England ended its ban on the export of spinning machines and therefore its monopoly on the mechanized production of cotton textiles. See W. O. Henderson, *Britain and Industrial Europe, 1750–1870: Studies in British Influence on the Industrial Revolution in Western Europe* (Liverpool, 1954), 5–7; S. Tompston [Thompstone] (ed.), *Rossiiskaya tekstil'naya promyshlennost': Tekhnologicheskii transfert, syr'e, finansy* (St Petersburg, 2006), 6–7; Rynkowska, *Działalność gospodarcza władz Królestwa Polskiego*, 90; Missalowa, *Studia nad powstaniem łódzkiego okręgu przemysłowego*, i. 179–95.

[25] The tsarist authorities, in an attempt to cut down on the smuggling trade, had expelled Jews from the areas closest to the Prussian and Austrian borders. See Friedman, *Dzieje Żydów w Łodzi*, 38 n.

[26] Baranowski and Fijałek (eds.), *Łódź*, i. 233.

[27] From the 1860s to 1914, the population of Łódź grew twelvefold; the Jewish population alone grew twentyfold. See Puś, *Żydzi w Łodzi w latach zaborów*, 22–3. While this demographic explosion topped the growth rates of European industrial centres, it was contemporaneous with the rise of non-European industrial cities. See W. Puś, 'The Development of the City of Łódź, 1820–1939', *Polin*, 6 (1991), 5–7; B. Ruble, *Second Metropolis: Pragmatic Pluralism in Gilded Age Chicago, Silver Age Moscow, and Meiji Osaka* (Washington, DC, 2001).

[28] The economic role of Jews such as the Łódź industrialist Izrael Poznański in the new Central Asian territories became an issue debated by the Russian Finance Minister Sergey Witte himself and then by the ministries of War and the Interior. See Central Archives for the History of the Jewish People, Jerusalem, RU 754 (copy of an original in the former Tsentral'nyi gosudarstvennyi arkhiv Uzbekskoi SSR, Tashkent, f. 1, op. 13, d. 347, fo. 33ᵛ).

[29] Rosa Luxemburg emphasized the importance of the tariffs of the 1870s in her *The Industrial Development of Poland*, trans. T. DeCarlo (New York, 1977), 95–9. See also S. Pytlas, *Łódzka burżuazja przemysłowa w latach 1864–1914* (Łódź, 1994), 66–80.

[30] *The Industries of Russia: Manufactures and Trade with a General Industrial Map. By the Department of Trade and Manufactures, Ministry of Finance, for the World's Columbian Exposition at Chicago*, ed. J. M. Crawford, 5 vols. (St Petersburg, 1893), i. 1. See also Ministerstvo Finansov, *Materialy dlya statistiki khlopchato-bumazhnogo proizvodstva v Rossii* (St Petersburg, 1901), p. i. By the eve of the First World War, half of Russian industrial production did indeed derive from consumer industries, with

its environs) had become the third producer of cotton textiles in the empire, following only Moscow and Vladimir.[31]

Łódź resembled Moscow in its fluid social structure: its large number of small and medium-sized plants, its migrant working population, and its high levels of female and child labour.[32] In one important respect, however, Łódź differed in character from the textile cities in the Russian centre. Whereas Moscow and Vladimir were predominantly Russian ethnically, Łódź was marked above all by its tri-ethnic population.[33] Its leading industrialists were first-, second-, and third-generation immigrants from Prussia, Silesia, and Bohemia; they were joined by Jewish merchants and factory owners.[34] The working population was ethnically Polish in the largest of industrial plants, and ethnic and social tensions inevitably overlapped in worker relations with German-speaking foremen and administrators.[35] Jewish workers, for their part, predominated in small weaving workshops in the northern slums of the city.

As a whole, the Łódź industrialist elite enjoyed relative freedom in shaping the city's economic and cultural life. While the Russian administration placed limits on Polish public life and publishing, it allowed for a thriving German-language press in Łódź, as well as German singing and hunting societies. Łódź Jewish elites, too, often spoke German—although by the end of the nineteenth century, they had increasingly begun to adopt Polish manners of speech and dress. Nevertheless, the continued predominance of a German-language public sphere in Łódź set it apart

textiles occupying the first place among them. See W. L. Blackwell, *The Industrialization of Russia: A Historical Perspective*, 3rd edn. (Arlington Heights, Ill., 1994), 42–3. The literature on the Russian turn towards industrialization in the 1890s is rich; see e.g. T. H. Von Laue, *Sergei Witte and the Industrialization of Russia* (New York, 1963); O. Crisp, *Studies in the Russian Economy before 1914* (London, 1976).

[31] I use here the Russian name of the province; the Polish form is Piotrków. On Russian textile production, see Ministerstvo Finansov, *Materialy dlya statistiki khlopchato-bumazhnogo proizvodstva v Rossii*, 1–9.

[32] On Moscow textiles, see Ruble, *Second Metropolis*; R. E. Johnson, *Peasant and Proletarian: The Working Class of Moscow in the Late Nineteenth Century* (New Brunswick, NJ, 1979); Engelstein, *Moscow, 1905*; V. Bonnell, *Roots of Rebellion: Workers' Politics and Organizations in St. Petersburg and Moscow, 1900–1914* (Berkeley, 1983); J. Bradley, *Muzhik and Muscovite: Urbanization in Late Imperial Russia* (Berkeley, 1985). On the social structure of Łódź and the composition of its working population, see S. Pytlas, 'The National Composition of Łódź Industrialists before 1914', *Polin*, 6 (1991), 37–56; A. Żarnowska, *Klasa robotnicza Królestwa Polskiego, 1870–1914* (Warsaw, 1974), 145–50, 187–8; M. Bandurka, *Początki i rozwój ruchu robotniczego w Łodzi do 1918 r.* (Łódź, 1973), 5; M. Sikorska-Kowalska, *Wizerunek kobiety łódzkiej przełomu XIX i XX wieku* (Łódź, 2001), 23, 35–7.

[33] On the religious diversity of the population of Łódź, see n. 5 above.

[34] On Łódź industrialists, see Missalowa, *Studia nad powstaniem łódzkiego okręgu przemysłowego*, i. 191–217; M. Budziarek, *Łodzianie* (Łódź, 2000), 79–106; A. Kempa and M. Szukalak (eds.), *Żydzi dawnej Łodzi: Słownik biograficzny łódzkich Żydów oraz z Łodzią związanych*, i (Łódź, 2001).

[35] On tensions between Polish workers and German foremen and their implications for the development of Polish nationalism in Łódź, see L. Crago, 'The "Polishness" of Production: Factory Politics and the Reinvention of Working-Class National and Political Identities in Russian Poland's Textile Industry, 1880–1910', *Slavic Review*, 59/1 (2000), 16–41.

from other industrial cities in the western territories of the empire—and from the textile cities in the Russian centre.[36]

By the mid-1880s, this ethnic difference, together with the competition posed by Łódź, prompted Moscow textile merchants to act upon burgeoning sentiments of economic nationalism. In the mid-nineteenth century, Moscow merchants, together with Slavophile activists, had fashioned a platform of Russian economic self-sufficiency: Russia could develop economically while avoiding the pitfalls of Western-style industrialization. Economic growth, they argued, was essential to the political advance of the Russian empire—and the state must serve to defend industrial interests.[37] With the advent of the pan-Slavist movement following the Russo-Turkish War, these ideas evolved into a concern with the role of 'foreigners' in Russian imperial industry.[38]

In 1885, the pan-Slavist and Moscow publicist Sergey Sharapov journeyed to Russian Poland. Upon his return, he commenced on a lecture tour, speaking on 'the industrial competition of Łódź and Sosnowiec with Moscow'. Sharapov argued that industrialists in Russian Poland enjoyed better credit, lower taxes, and more favourable customs conditions than Moscow merchants. In Łódź in particular, a German 'detachment' had 'fortified itself': 'three or four Polish factories are lost in a crowd of German and some Jewish ones . . . Polish and Russian can't even be heard any more'. Rather than providing healthy competition from fellow Slavs, this 'foreign' industry was 'paralysing the development of industry in our centre' and would lead to the 'ruin of the whole Slavonic tribe'.[39]

Sharapov's lectures intensified what one contemporary termed 'the battle between Moscow and Łódź'.[40] Moscow merchants sent petitions to the Finance Ministry, and a delegation travelled to St Petersburg to demand measures against competition from Łódź.[41] Łódź industrialists, in turn, submitted figures indicating

[36] Contemporaries compared Łódź on more than one occasion to Riga, also a centre of Russian industry with a high ethnic German population. See e.g. S. Gorski, *Niemcy w Królestwie Polskiem* (Warsaw, 1908).

[37] A. J. Rieber, *Merchants and Entrepreneurs in Imperial Russia* (Chapel Hill, NC, 1982), 135–45. See also T. C. Owen, *Capitalism and Politics in Russia: A Social History of the Moscow Merchants, 1855–1905* (Cambridge, 1981); id., *Dilemmas of Russian Capitalism: Fedor Chizhov and Corporate Enterprise in the Railroad Age* (Cambridge, Mass., 2005); V. Ya. Laverychev, *Krupnaya burzhuaziya v poreformennoi Rossii, 1861–1900* (Moscow, 1974), 115–21.

[38] Owen, *Capitalism and Politics in Russia*, 46–52, 64–70; Rieber, *Merchants and Entrepreneurs in Imperial Russia*, 171–2.

[39] S. Sharapov, 'Rech' o promyshlennoi konkurentsii Lodzi i Sosnovits s Moskvoyu', in his *Sochineniya* (St Petersburg, 1892), 70–2, 74–84.

[40] A. P. Subbotin, *Bor'ba Moskvy s Lodz'yu, v svyazi s istorichesko-ekonomicheskim obzorom promyshlennosti lodzinskogo raiona* (St Petersburg, 1889). Moscow merchants had first petitioned against Polish textiles in the 1820s. See Pravilova, *Finansy imperii*, 58–9; Luxemburg, *Industrial Development of Poland*, 125; Subbotin, *Bor'ba Moskvy s Lodz'yu*, 3; Rieber, *Merchants and Entrepreneurs in Imperial Russia*, 62–5.

[41] I. I. Yanzhul, *Iz vospominanii i perepiski fabrichnogo inspektora pervogo prizyva* (1907; St Petersburg, 1978), 118–19; Subbotin, *Bor'ba Moskvy s Lodz'yu*, 22.

that they enjoyed few advantages over their Moscow counterparts.[42] The local newspaper *Dziennik Łódzki*, financed by the Łódź German industrialist elite, further disputed the claims of Moscow merchants on economic grounds.[43] In 1886, the Finance Ministry sent an investigatory commission to Russian Poland, led by Ivan Yanzhul, the factory inspector of the Moscow region.[44] Largely on the basis of Yanzhul's recommendations, the Finance Ministry imposed a set of tariffs making it substantially more costly for Łódź industrialists to import raw materials.[45] Another decree prohibited 'foreigners' from owning Russian land or real estate.[46] When striking Łódź workers in 1892 complained of abuse from German-speaking foremen, the Russian administration instituted a set of Russian- and Polish-language exams for foremen in Petrokov province.[47] Many of the workers who had taken part in the 1892 strike were deported, together with their families.[48]

In an 1892 lecture, the St Petersburg merchant and activist Vasily Belov framed the debates of recent years in the following way: 'Do the interests of industry in Russian Poland coincide with state interests?—and if they don't coincide, as a last resort, can they be made to coincide through specific state policies?'[49] The relationship between Russia and Poland needed to be reformulated in an age when modern nationalism asserted its own visions of social and economic reform. As the

[42] Subbotin, *Bor'ba Moskvy s Lodz'yu*, 25–6. On the formation of associations of Łódź industrialists with fixed representation in St Petersburg, see Pytlas, *Łódzka burżuazja przemysłowa*, 141–5.

[43] Z. Gostkowski, *Dziennik Łódzki w latach 1884–1892: Studium nad powstawaniem polskiej opinii publicznej w wielonarodowym mieście fabrycznym* (Łódź, 1963), 21, 23; 'Podanie łódzkich przemysłowców do J.W.P. Gubernatora piotrkowskiego', *Dziennik Łódzki*, 1886, nos. 116–17; 'Z powodu polemiki o szerokość perkalu', *Dziennik Łódzki*, 1886, nos. 132 and 133.

[44] Yanzhul would go on to play a leading role in the development of Russian factory laws and legislation.

[45] *Otchet I. I. Yanzhula po issledovaniyu fabrichno-zavodskoi promyshlennosti v Tsarstve Pol'skom* (St Petersburg, 1888), 98. Looking back on the period in his 1907 memoirs, Yanzhul would characterize the claims of Moscow merchants as 'inflated and exaggerated'. There was 'no basis for expecting any great danger from the competition of Russian Polish factories'. See Yanzhul, *Iz vospominanii i perepiski fabrichnogo inspektora*, 152–3. On the punitive measures, see also K. Badziak, 'Podłoże gospodarczospołeczne "buntu łódzkiego"', in P. Samuś (ed.), *'Bunt łódzki' 1892 roku: Studia z dziejów wielkiego konfliktu społecznego* (Łódź, 1993), 30; Baranowski and Fijałek (eds.), *Łódź*, i. 249–50.

[46] Valid for Russian Poland, it was soon extended to the western province of Volhynia: V. D. Belov, *Lodz': Lodz'i Sosnovitsy. Lodz'i Moskva* (St Petersburg, 1892). See also 'Novyi zakon ob inostrantsakh', *Moskovskie vedomosti*, 26 Apr. 1892, p. 3.

[47] Those who did not pass the exams were deported. See A. Próchnik, 'Bunt łódzki w roku 1892', in his *Pisma: Studia i szkice, 1864–1918*, ed. K. Dunin-Wąsowicz (Warsaw, 1963), 454–61.

[48] A list of 134 'foreigners' who took part in the 1892 Łódź strike was compiled with a view to their deportation. Some of these workers were deported, others were deprived of Russian citizenship, and some left Łódź of their own volition. See Archiwum Państwowe w Łodzi (hereafter APŁ), Kancelaria Gubernatora Piotrkowskiego (KGP), 220, 223; APŁ, Starszy Inspektor Fabryczny, 2394; Gosudarstvennyi arkhiv Rossiiskoi Federatsii, Moscow (hereafter GARF), f. 996, d. 56, fos. 131–2.

[49] Belov, *Lodz'*, 2. Belov was a member of the St Petersburg Society for the Promotion of Russian Industry and Trade (Obshchestvo dlya sodeistviya russkoi promyshlennosti i torgovle); he would later become a member of the Imperial Duma: see <http://history.ntagil.ru/6_36.htm>.

economist Andrey Subbotin understood, this was inherently a question of empire and autocracy. To what extent, as Subbotin suggested, should Russian economic policy towards Poland be determined by considerations of 'fundamental laws', 'protection of all legal rights', and 'equal protection upon which all state taxpayers can depend'?[50] Or, rather, in an empire where both social and ethnic groups jockeyed for favour with an autocratic regime, to what extent did ideas of Great Russian nationalism specifically frame state economic goals and planning?

ECONOMIC SELF-SUFFICIENCY AND ETHNIC NATIONALISM

In Poland, ideas of economic reform and industrial development had their origins in the Polish–Lithuanian Commonwealth. In the late eighteenth century, Polish intellectuals began to envision a reformed government and social structure that would oversee the transformation of a largely agrarian system into one of industry and urbanization.[51] Even as a separate estate, Jews had long played a prominent role in Polish commercial life. As Polish reformers proposed to stimulate urban life and industry to modernize an unproductive feudal economy, the role of Jews within that structure came under renewed scrutiny. Foremost among reformers' concerns was the role of Jews in the production and sale of liquor, which accounted for well over half of estate revenues.[52]

In the years following the 1863 revolt, the Jewish question once again became intertwined with discussions of Polish economic progress. In the context of harsh Russification, Polish patriots sought to compensate for the loss of political activism with 'organic work', or socio-economic development. Influenced by Herbert Spencer and Auguste Comte, they adopted a vision of the nation as a social organism, whose growth was predicated on exchange and mutual co-operation. They began to understand the future of the 'nation' as based not only upon the intellectual but upon the 'people', especially the newly emancipated Polish peasantry.[53] In 1862, the Russian regime had granted Polish Jews their own 'emancipation': greater (although by no means equal) rights.[54] The necessity of Jewish social integration came to form part of the general positivist outlook of the times.[55]

[50] Subbotin, *Bor'ba Moskvy s Lodz'yu*, 71.

[51] J. Jedlicki, *A Suburb of Europe: Nineteenth-Century Polish Approaches to Western Civilization* (Budapest, 1999), 52–64.

[52] H. Rożenowa, *Produkcja wódki i sprawa pijaństwa w Królestwie Polskim, 1815–1863* (Warsaw, 1961).

[53] On the emergence of ethnic nationalism in Poland and shifts in ideas of the 'nation', see e.g. A. Walicki, 'Intellectual Elites and the Vicissitudes of "Imagined Nation" in Poland', in R. G. Suny and M. D. Kennedy (eds.), *Intellectuals and the Articulation of the Nation* (Ann Arbor, 1999), 259–87; Jedlicki, *Suburb of Europe*.

[54] A. Eisenbach, *The Emancipation of the Jews in Poland, 1780–1870*, ed. A. Polonsky, trans. J. Dorosz (Oxford, 1991).

[55] Weeks, *From Assimilation to Antisemitism*, 57–70; A. Cała, *Asymilacja Żydów w Królestwie Polskim,*

A circle of Warsaw Jewish intellectuals, grouped around the journal *Izraelita*, shared and propagated the same goal of Jewish social integration. The *Izraelita* group championed the adoption of Polish language and culture as a key to strengthening the Polish nation, conceived as a future multi-ethnic state.[56] *Izraelita* therefore sought to 'reform' the Yiddish-speaking 'Jewish masses', emphasizing, in the tradition of the Jewish Enlightenment, both education and economic productivity as the key to progress.[57] It additionally criticized the Russified habits of the so-called Litvaks who migrated to Poland from the Russian western territories. When it came to German language and culture, however, *Izraelita* was more ambivalent. It associated German with high culture as Jewish intellectuals had done since the Haskalah itself, yet it nevertheless criticized tendencies of Germanization among Polish Jews.[58]

While Warsaw positivists addressed the 'Jewish question' as a programmatic topic, they devoted less direct attention to the question of the ethnic German population in Poland.[59] When the Warsaw journalist Henryk Elzenberg created the first Polish-language newspaper in Łódź in 1884, *Dziennik Łódzki*, he was concerned primarily with the promotion of organic work and Jewish social integration. Yet by 1885 this newspaper was devoting the majority of its opinion pieces to the question of the city's German population. On the one hand, *Dziennik Łódzki* emphasized the imperial loyalties of Łódź industrialists in the face of attacks from Moscow; on the other hand, it asserted its programmatic commitment to Polish social integration. In this sense, its views on ethnic Germans mirrored those on the 'Jewish question': 'we believe . . . that the Jew can be a good citizen of the country and that the German is capable of assimilating and of fulfilling his civic obligations'.[60]

Such discussions in *Dziennik Łódzki* were interrupted by the Łódź strike of 1892. Intellectuals were taken aback by the fairly spontaneous action of Łódź workers, motivated by economic distress in a period of downturn.[61] Reports of

1864–1897: Postawy, konflikty, stereotypy (Warsaw, 1989); M. Iwańska, *Prasa pozytywistów warszawskich wobec Żydów i kwestii żydowskiej* (Łódź, 2006); S. Blejwas, 'Polish Positivism and the Jews', *Jewish Social Studies*, 46/1 (1984), 27–8.

[56] On *Izraelita*, see Cała, *Asymilacja Żydów w Królestwie Polskim*, 49–86; M. Fuks, *Prasa żydowska w Warszawie, 1823–1939* (Warsaw, 1979).

[57] Cała, *Asymilacja Żydów w Królestwie Polskim*, 56. On the views of Warsaw Jewish intellectuals regarding Yiddish-speaking Jews, see M. Wodziński, 'Jidysz a modernizacja: Język jidysz w myśli polskiej haskali i jej spadkobierców', in E. Geller and M. Polit (eds.), *Jidyszland: Polskie przestrzenie* (Warsaw, 2008), 243–62. On the views of Warsaw Jewish intellectuals regarding hasidism specifically, see M. Wodziński, *Haskalah and Hasidism in the Kingdom of Poland: A History of Conflict* (Oxford, 2005). [58] Cała, *Asymilacja Żydów w Królestwie Polskim*, 53–4.

[59] On the 'Jewish question', see Iwańska, *Prasa pozytywistów warszawskich*, 59–61. The far-right publicist Jan Jeleński was one of the few to directly address the question of both ethnic groups in his anti-Jewish, anti-German pamphlet *Żydzi, Niemcy i my*, 4th edn. (Warsaw, 1880).

[60] 'Z powodu polemiki o szerokość perkalu', *Dziennik Łódzki*, 1886, no. 132, pp. 1–2.

[61] On the response of Polish intellectuals to the strike, see F. Perl, *Dzieje ruchu socjalistycznego*

striking Polish workers marching to Polish patriotic songs, and of the Russian order to 'Shoot! No holding back!', left an indelible mark on the Polish consciousness. The strike contributed to a new, ethno-linguistic understanding of the 'nation', one that differentiated 'Polish' from 'German' workers—and one that was rooted in industrial workers in addition to peasants.[62] In late 1892, socialist leaders in exile founded a Polish socialist movement with an independent Poland at the top of its programme.

For Łódź workers, however, the pogrom that followed the strike illustrated that social and religious concerns still bridged ethnic divides. Of those arrested for the murder of the scholar Volf Nusenov Berger, four were listed as 'Poles' and 'Catholics' and three as 'Germans' and 'Lutherans'.[63] This was violence perpetuated for mercenary reasons—by blacksmiths, bricklayers, bakers, boot-makers, and weavers from small, middle-sized, and large enterprises.[64] Jews often recognized their assailants as neighbours. While Mendel Kapitulnik and his wife were distracted by the looting of their tavern, a neighbour by the name of Ekaterina Emilia Ingver (28 years old) dragged the iron bed out from their apartment, along with a pail, easily recognizable from a stain on the bottom.[65] Above all, victims were attacked because they were Jews. As the cab driver Izrael Steinholz testified, 'there was not one incident of a pogrom of a Polish or German tavern'.[66]

The Łódź working force was relatively slow to resume labour activism following the 1892 strike. While underground party life proliferated in Warsaw, Łódź workers were scarred by police repression and, in the case of Jews, by memories of the pogrom.[67] It was several years before a newspaper replaced the Polish–German

---

w zaborze rosyjskim do powstania PPS (Warsaw, 1958); L. Wasilewski, *Zarys dziejów Polskiej Partji Socjalistycznej w związku z historją socjalizmu polskiego w trzech zaborach i na emigracji* (Warsaw, 1925), 27; F. Tych, *Związek Robotników Polskich, 1889–1892: Anatomia wczesnej organizacji robotniczej* (Warsaw, 1974), 386–9; Próchnik, 'Bunt łódzki w roku 1892', 465. On the economic conditions of Łódź workers, see 'Raport inspektora fabrycznego okręgu piotrkowskiego G. Rykowskiego do gubernatora piotrkowskiego K. Millera o strajkach w fabrykach łódzkich', in 'Dokumenty buntu łódzkiego 1892 r.', *Rocznik Łódzki*, 31 (1982), 210–11.

[62] Perl, *Dzieje ruchu socjalistycznego*, 415; Walicki, 'Intellectual Elites', 277.

[63] Russian police protocols carefully noted the ethnicity, religion, and citizenship of each of those arrested. See APŁ, Sąd Okręgowy Piotrkowskiego (SOP), 6949.

[64] APŁ, SOP, 6859, 6878, 6949; 'Dokumenty buntu łódzkiego 1892 r.' Socialist histories of the 1892 strike, both Polish and Jewish, sought to portray the pogrom as the work of 'criminal elements', rather than of industrial workers. Some accused the tsarist police of inciting the pogrom. See Perl, *Dzieje ruchu socjalistycznego*, 320, 412; 'Lodzher flugblat tsum ondenkn fun 1 may 1892': YIVO Archives, New York, RG 1400, MG 9, F. 33; Y. Sh. Herts [J. S. Hertz], *Di geshikhte fun bund in lodzh* (New York, 1958), 47; Próchnik, 'Bunt łódzki w roku 1892', 412–13. For a Bundist history of the Jewish labour movement in Łódź, see A. Volf Yasni, *Geshikhte fun der yidisher arbeter bavegung in lodzh* (Łódź, 1937).

[65] APŁ, SOP, 6859.   [66] APŁ, SOP, 6858, p. 6.

[67] M. Mishkinsky, 'Wpływ pluralizmu etnicznego i religijnego na powstanie żydowskiego ruchu robotniczego w Łodzi (zarys)', in P. Samuś (ed.), *Polacy — Niemcy — Żydzi w Łodzi w XIX–XX w.: Sąsiedzi dalecy i bliscy* (Łódź, 1997), 234–7.

venture of *Dziennik Łódzki*, dissolved by the tsarist authorities after the strike. The new newspaper, *Rozwój* ('Progress'), soon began to display the sort of strident anti-Jewish and anti-German rhetoric that was now becoming typical of the Polish nationalist movement as a whole.[68] By the turn of the century, the Polish National Democratic Party (Stronnictwo Demokratyczno-Narodowe) had begun to organize in Łódź, alongside socialists of various stripes.[69] With the rise of Herzlian Zionism in 1897, Łódź emerged as one of the centres of Zionist organization in Poland, second in numbers only to Warsaw.[70]

Worker organization stimulated interest in worker poverty. The poor condition of Jews in the Russian Pale of Settlement had already attracted the attention of intellectuals, journalists, and activists of both liberal and socialist bent.[71] Economists such as Andrey Subbotin (the critic of Russian economic nationalism) conducted statistical analyses of Jewish poverty in the Pale in order to counter deeply rooted views of Jewish economic exploitation of Christians.[72] Other discussions concerned the problem of Jewish employment: in both the Pale of Settlement and Russian Poland, Jewish industrialists had traditionally hired Christian rather than Jewish workers. This was partly to avoid the problem of sabbath rest among a multi-religious working force (Jews rested on Saturdays; Christians on Sundays); partly due to a belief that Jews, lacking in technical training, could not operate mechanized plants.[73]

The issue of Jewish employment came to the forefront during the winter of 1899–1900, as an economic downturn hit the Russian western territories as well as Poland. Reports of worker starvation in Łódź reached St Petersburg: 'Jewish weavers, deprived of work, are going from house to house, holding out their hands

[68] The shift to anti-German rhetoric occurred within *Rozwój*'s first year of publication. Anti-Jewish rhetoric began to appear in 1902, with *Rozwój*'s increased coverage of the Zionist movement. See J. Sobczyk, 'Ruch syjonistyczny w Królestwie Polskim w świetle gazety "Rozwój", 1897–1907', master's thesis (Univ. of Łódź, 1993), 13–17.

[69] T. Monasterska, *Narodowy Związek Robotniczy, 1905–1920* (Warsaw, 1973), 15–16, 23, 26–8; S. Kozicki, *Historia Ligi Narodowej: Okres 1887–1907* (London, 1964), 216.

[70] On Zionism in Łódź, see Sobczyk, 'Ruch syjonistyczny w Królestwie Polskim'; J. Goldstein, 'The Beginnings of the Zionist Movement in Congress Poland: The Victory of the Hasidim over the Zionists?', *Polin*, 5 (1990), 114–15, 119–20; E. Popielarz, 'Żydzi w Łodzi w rewolucji 1905–7 w świetle "Rozwoju"', master's thesis (Univ. of Łódź, 1991), 18–22.

[71] For accounts by travellers of worker poverty in the Pale, see L. Soloweitschik, *Un prolétariat méconnu: Étude sur la situation sociale et économique des ouvriers juifs* (Brussels, 1898); I. Khorosh, 'Po promyshlennoi cherte osedlosti', *Knizhki Vostoka*, 1901, nos. 3–4, 7–8.

[72] Subbotin followed the example of the financier and economist Jan Bloch in his statistical approach to the legal, social, and economic situation of Jews in the Russian empire. See A. P. Subbotin, *Evreiskii vopros v ego pravil'nom osveshchenii: V svyazi s trudami I. S. Bliokha* (St Petersburg, 1903); id., *V cherte evreiskoi osedlosti*, 2 vols. (St Petersburg, 1888–90); id., *Nastoyashchee polozhenie evreiskogo voprosa* (Warsaw, 1906).

[73] On the question of Jewish labour, see E. Mendelsohn, *Class Struggle in the Pale: The Formative Years of the Jewish Workers' Movement in Tsarist Russia* (Cambridge, 1970).

for alms; many craftsmen and foremen . . . wander along the streets like madmen.'[74] When pressed by his superiors, the mayor of Łódź struggled to minimize the problem of the 'Jewish weavers'. However, statistics provided by the newly founded Jewish Philanthropic Society (Łódzkie Żydowskie Towarzystwo Dobroczynności) indicated that, of 898 Jews receiving assistance from the organization, 704 were weavers. As the Łódź factory inspector explained, large textile firms weathered the downturn through limited lay-offs and reductions in working hours. Many small workshops, in contrast, were pushed to bankruptcy.[75] Jewish weavers, who worked disproportionately in small workshops, suffered disproportionately from the crisis.

In late 1899, the Warsaw journal *Izraelita* joined discussions about Jewish poverty and employment with its own front-page article 'Work for Jews'. The resolution of the Jewish question, it argued, lay neither in the 'religious' nor in the 'racial' realm, but rather in the economic sector. In a vein typical of Jewish Enlightenment thought, *Izraelita* proposed the solution of 'productive labour': 'Let Jewish capitalists found new factories, and let them give jobs to the Jewish masses, eager for pay and suitable for work.' There was no reason, *Izraelita* declared, why 'non-Jewish public opinion' should object to this effort: 'It doesn't at all follow that non-Jewish masses would be excluded, boycotted—that is not our way . . . We only wish that Jewish workers, too, should be hired.'[76]

In the winter of 1899–1900, the Łódź Jewish Philanthropic Society founded a mechanized textile factory exclusively for Jewish workers in the heart of the city's industrial district. Although the enterprise seems to have soon collapsed for lack of funds, it was celebrated by the St Petersburg Jewish press as a 'model' of social welfare for Jewish workers.[77] In March 1901, a Łódź police agent reported that four factories in the city, mainly producers of kerchiefs, had committed themselves to hiring Jewish workers exclusively. 'There has been observed among them, that is, the Jewish hand-weavers, a strong solidarity in action—and it is without doubt that this circle of people, strongly intertwined, acts according to agreement, according to a deliberate programme. They support each other and defend the principle "one for all and all for one".'[78]

Such projects for Jewish economic self-sufficiency, though perhaps relatively limited in number, had their parallel in the Polish co-operative movement. Theorists such as Stanisław Wojciechowski envisioned the co-operative as the kernel of Polish nationalist activism: it would not only improve the material conditions of the people (*lud*) but facilitate a transition to a higher ethical system of economics, one based on co-operation and social justice.[79] Worker co-operatives were based in their

---

[74] APŁ, KGP, 1186, p. 4.

[75] Ibid. 168. On the crisis, see also APŁ, Akta Policmajstra, 1054, District I Report, 18 Dec. 1899.

[76] 'Praca dla Żydów', *Izraelita*, 1899, no. 41, pp. 459–60.

[77] 'Be'artsenu: lodz', *Hamelits*, 1899, no. 255, p. 2. This column in *Hamelits* cites an article on the Łódź factory in the Russian-language St Petersburg journal *Voskhod*.

[78] APŁ, Akta Policmajstra, 1054.

[79] S. Wojciechowski, *Historia spółdzielczości polskiej do 1914 roku* (Warsaw, 1939), 230. Following the

organization on the west European model: it was cheaper for several families to purchase in bulk than individually, 'through a [Jewish] middle-man'.[80] In Łódź, the first two worker co-operatives were founded in 1901.[81] The movement took off during the revolution of 1905–7, thanks to new freedoms of organization and the abolition of legislation requiring the exclusive use of Russian in accounting and record-keeping.[82] Łódź in particular led other cities in the number of co-operatives founded, and theorists envisioned Łódź as the 'helm' of the movement.[83] The National Democratic Party founded its own co-operatives in the city, as did Christian worker organizations.[84]

Among the leaders of the Polish co-operative movement in Łódź was the young Catholic priest Andrzej Rogoziński.[85] Rogoziński had arrived in Łódź in 1904, having been ordained as a priest two years earlier. He was assigned to the largest parish in the city, Holy Cross, which numbered 150,000 parishioners.[86] Highly charismatic by all accounts, Rogoziński envisioned himself as a modern-day Joshua, leading his people to their 'promised land'; he later called himself the 'Moses of Łódź'.[87] Of the Polish Catholic leaders engaged with workers' issues during the revolution, Rogoziński was the most radical: his Christian Democratic Association (Stowarzyszenie Demokracji Chrześcijańskiej) departed from the larger Christian workers' movement in organizing exclusively Catholic workers.[88] For Rogoziński, the establishment of worker co-operative stores constituted part of a larger effort to improve both the material and the moral conditions of Polish

Polish uprising of 1863, Polish patriots came to share a social-ethical belief system in which morality was both 'historical' and 'evolutionary' in nature: the 'conscious development of society required its moral development as well'. See B. Cywiński, *Rodowody niepokornych* (Paris, 1985), 68.

[80] E. Abramowski, *Kooperatywa jako sprawa wyzwolenia ludu pracującego* (Warsaw, 1912), 2–3.

[81] W. L. Karwacki, *Związki zawodowe i stowarzyszenia pracodawców w Łodzi do roku 1914* (Łódź, 1972), 19.

[82] Owing to restrictions on public life, the co-operative movement was slower to develop in Russian Poland than in the other partitions. See Wojciechowski, *Historia spółdzielczości polskiej*, 164–6, 234–5.

[83] W. L. Karwacki, *Łódź w latach rewolucji, 1905–1907* (Łódź, 1975), 287.

[84] Karwacki, *Związki zawodowe i stowarzyszenia pracodawców*, 277–8; id., *Łódź w latach rewolucji*, 287.

[85] Of the 160 co-operative stores founded in the city over the period 1905–7, an estimated one hundred were a product of Rogoziński's influence. See Karwacki, *Związki zawodowe i stowarzyszenia pracodawców*, 275. The relationship between Catholicism and Polish nationalism in Łódź would repay further investigation. On religion and nationalism in Poland, see e.g. Cywiński, *Rodowody niepokornych*; B. R. Berglund and B. Porter-Szűcs (eds.), *Christianity and Modernity in Eastern Europe* (Budapest, 2010); B. Porter, '*Hetmanka* and Mother: Representing the Virgin Mary in Modern Poland', *Contemporary European History*, 14/2 (2005), 151–70.

[86] A. W. Wóźniak, 'Rogoziński, Andrzej', in R. Bender et al. (eds.), *Słownik biograficzny katolicyzmu społecznego w Polsce*, 3 vols. (Warsaw and Lublin, 1991–5), iii. 21–2; Ks. Andrzej Rogoziński, *Karta mego życia w Łodzi* (Warsaw, c.1909), 15; Karwacki, *Związki zawodowe i stowarzyszenia pracodawców*, 93. [87] Rogoziński, *Karta mego życia*, 43.

[88] A. Wóycicki, *Chrześcijański ruch robotniczy w Polsce* (Poznań and Warsaw, 1912), 85–92; Rogoziński, *Karta mego życia*, 89; APŁ, Akta Policmajstra, 886.

workers. 'In the old days', he wrote, 'wives and mothers used to complain that they couldn't keep their husbands and sons at home, since they were always going out to the pub; now they're once again complaining, that all the men sit the whole evening in their shops.'[89] Polish entrepreneurship, in Rogoziński's mind, required the cultivation of both individual self-worth and group solidarity: 'This [worker] fashioned a cupboard, another a drawer, one a shelf, and another a box, and every [worker] created something, and each was content, because he made it for himself. There wasn't any "this is mine, and that is yours"; rather, everyone grasped and understood my teaching perfectly, and they worked as one for all and all for one.'[90]

From Rogoziński's arrival in Łódź, he had noted the 'preponderance of Jews and Germans' and characterized both as the source of the material and spiritual deprivation of Polish workers.[91] At the same time, he viewed the co-operative movement as a means of waging an economic struggle against Jews in particular. He instructed his workers not to buy from Jews and he sought to eliminate competition from Jewish private shops and traders. In the context of revolutionary unrest, Rogoziński saw his economic activism as an alternative to national warfare: 'The workers', he wrote several years later, 'became convinced that they didn't need to kill Jews, or torture them, but rather to struggle in a noble, higher fashion, worthy of civilized people, and by that means to take trade and industry into their own hands.'[92]

The Polish co-operatives in Łódź do not seem to have entirely lived up to the hopes of the movement's theorists. Wojciechowski himself wrote regretfully that the low education level of most of their members prevented worker co-operatives from developing financially; even the most active representatives of Łódź co-operatives suffered from illiteracy.[93] The leading historian of worker organization in Łódź has argued that the co-operative stores 'differed only in name from private enterprises' and rarely adopted a 'democratic form of management'.[94] Nevertheless, the establishment of worker co-operatives reflected a particular moment in Polish nationalist activism: the realization of ideas of Polish economic self-sufficiency in concrete organizational structures. As in Poland as a whole, Polish nationalist activists in Łódź were concerned primarily with the economic relationship between Poles and Jews; this would shortly change.

BOYCOTTS

In addition to the co-operative movement, the 1905–7 revolution opened up possibilities for socialist and nationalist activism among each of Poland's ethnic groups. The revolution led to a liberalization that enabled the formation of a public sphere through newspapers and other publications; the establishment of an

---

[89] Rogoziński, *Karta mego życia*, 60.   [90] Ibid.   [91] Ibid. 16, 21–2.
[92] Ibid. 60.   [93] Wojciechowski, *Historia spółdzielczości polskiej*, 245.
[94] Karwacki, *Łódź w latach rewolucji*, 286.

elementary-school system based on the principle of native-language education; and the formation of legal political parties that competed in parliamentary elections. In Łódź, Polish workers joined nationalist and socialist unions by the tens of thousands; Zionist parties proliferated.[95] In January 1906, a group of prominent German professionals and entrepreneurs in Łódź founded the Constitutional-Liberal Party (Constitutionell-Liberale Partei), the first German national party in Poland.[96] Among its other programmatic goals, it sought to promote German-language education.[97]

The question of education, in fact, had come to the forefront in the early days of the revolution, as university and gymnasium students across Russian Poland left the classroom in a wave of school strikes. The National Democratic Party, opposed to strikes on both ideological and tactical grounds, was forced to embrace the movement after the fact. It promoted the 'nationalization' (*unarodowienie*) of education and issued proclamations that called for an 'absolute boycott' of Russian schools.[98] Over the course of 1905–6, the Russian regime gradually extended the right to Polish-language education to Catholic religious classes, private schools, and, finally, to one-class public elementary schools.[99]

In Łódź, municipal elementary education had long been organized along confessional lines, with Catholic, Protestant, and Jewish schools.[100] As Polish school strikes paralysed education in Warsaw in early 1905, gymnasium students in Łódź, too, expressed their solidarity with the larger strike movement. However, specific demands for the 'Polonization' of education found less resonance in a city with such large Jewish and German populations.[101]

In January 1907, the Russian regime extended the right to national elementary education to its German citizens, as well as to Poles.[102] Shortly afterwards, a group of self-identified German citizens of Łódź, some of whom were members of the

---

[95] On labour organization in Łódź during the revolution, see Karwacki, *Związki zawodowe i stowarzyszenia pracodawców*.

[96] According to Polish sources, the party was known as the Constitutionell-Liberale Partei Deutschsprechender (Constitutional-Liberal Party of German-Speakers). The party, it was reported, committed itself to living harmoniously with other national groups as long as the rights of German-speakers, and their native language, were respected. See *Rozwój*, 1906, no. 15, p. 2.

[97] On the Constitutional-Liberal Party, see *Źródła do dziejów rewolucji 1905–1907 w okręgu łódzkim*, ed. N. Gąsiorowska, 3 vols. (Warsaw, 1957–64), ii. 39, 41–2; 'Niemcy w Łodzi', *Rozwój*, 1906, no. 64, p. 4. In both name and character, the party resembled the Baltic Constitutional Party established contemporaneously by ethnic Germans in Riga. See A. Henriksson, *The Tsar's Loyal Germans: The Riga German Community, Social Change and the Nationality Question, 1855–1905* (Boulder, Colo., 1983), 111.

[98] Quoted in Blobaum, *Rewolucja*, 174. On the school strikes, see ibid. 157–60; H. Kiepurska, *Warszawa w rewolucji, 1905–7* (Warsaw, 1974), 97–115.   [99] Blobaum, *Rewolucja*, 157–63, 172–81.

[100] E. Podgórska, *Szkolnictwo elementarne w Łodzi w latach 1808–1914* (Łódź, 1966), 20–54.

[101] Ibid. 127–8. On school strikes in Łódź during the revolution, see also J. Dutkiewicz, 'Strajk szkolny 1905 r. na terenie łódzkiego okręgu przemysłowego', *Przegląd Nauk Historycznych i Społecznych*, 6 (1955), 116–39.   [102] Podgórska, *Szkolnictwo elementarne w Łodzi*, 137.

Society of German-Speaking Foremen and Workers, petitioned the magistrate for the right to form a separate public school system and school board, with a budget independent of municipal funds and 'freed from the obligations of general municipal taxes'. In May 1907, the Russian Ministry of Education approved the request, creating two separate German and Polish school systems in Łódź, each with separate budgets and the power of taxation.[103]

The long-time mayor of Łódź, Władysław Pieńkowski, inaugurated the process with an advertisement in local newspapers: 'Those who wish to contribute to the German schools exclusively can submit appropriate requests . . . for their exemption from the common tax apportionment.'[104] By the end of 1908, this had resulted in waves of petitions and protests to the municipal and provincial authorities. When one Sofia Tauber followed the instructions as outlined in the newspapers, she received a form letter from the office of the mayor: 'In light of the fact that you belong to the German nation, the Łódź German School Commission . . . has not been able to fulfil your request regarding your exemption from the German tax apportionment.' Tauber responded with an angry petition to the governor of the province. Despite her German-sounding last name, she declared, 'I was born in this land and do not belong to the German nation . . . there's not a force on earth that could turn me, a Polish woman, into a German [*pol'ku zamenit'na nemku*].'[105]

Other letters of appeal argued that the formation of Polish and German schools left no room for the industrial city's other ethnic minorities: Czechs, French, English, Greeks, and Armenians. It also became clear that the 'division of the Łódź city schools according to nationality' did not solve the problem of religious difference.[106] By 1911, two additional school systems had been approved: one for Jewish and one for Mariavite (Catholic sectarian) children. By that year, almost all the different ethnic and religious groups were frustrated. A group of Polish residents of Łódź began their petition to the governor of the province with the assertion: 'In no city in the Russian empire is there such disorder, such Babel-like chaos with regard to education, as in the city of Łódź.'[107]

The issue at hand was not simply, as mayor Pieńkowski put it, 'the determination of the nationality of the taxpayer'. Equally at stake was the division of resources. Poles protested that the motivation for the German withdrawal from the common

---

[103] APŁ, Rząd Gubernialny WA, 13076, p. 30.

[104] As quoted in the petition of Sofia Tauber protesting the splitting of the school system. See APŁ, Rząd Gubernialny WA, 13076.

[105] This petition, as others to the provincial and municipal authorities, was written in Russian. The similarity in language among some petitions may indicate that the authors received assistance in writing. See APŁ, Rząd Gubernialny WA, 13076. Some of the requests sent to the municipality for tax payments to be made to either German or Polish schools are included in the following folders: APŁ, Akta miasta Łodzi, 2876, 2878, 4789.

[106] The category of 'German' schools, for example, expanded to include 'Russian Orthodox children' as well as 'Germans of all religious denominations'. See APŁ, Rząd Gubernialny WA, 13076.

[107] Ibid.

municipal school budget was the 'liberation from school-tax payments' for the benefit of schools whose students were from poorer Polish working families. The problem, in other words, was that 'the Polish element' alone, 'consisting primarily of industrial workers and craftsmen', was not financially equipped to maintain its own schools. While many individual industrialists rose above the fray, requesting that their tax contributions be divided equally between Polish and German schools, others raised the question of how industrial conglomerates were to be taxed. Ultimately, the municipality decided that joint-stock companies, banks, and lending associations were 'supranational' institutions and did not 'belong to any particular nation'.[108]

The discord in Łódź over the years 1907–11 was exacerbated by worsening Polish–German relations in Prussian Poland. On 26 November 1907, Chancellor Bernhard von Bülow placed a Colonization Law before the Prussian parliament: a project for the expropriation of Polish-owned lands in Poznania and West Prussia.[109] Though the Expropriation Act was not implemented immediately, it led to a storm in Polish public opinion. In a direct response to Bülow's action the Polish press in Russian Poland declared an economic 'boycott': 'the complete restriction of the sale of German goods in our country'.[110]

The use of the boycott as a means of Polish national warfare was not entirely a new phenomenon. As the Łódź newspaper *Rozwój* reminded its readers, the Polish press had first called for an 'economic struggle' against Germany in 1901, as a protest against Germanization in the realm of education.[111] Though the 1901 boycott had not received much attention, a relaxed censorship following the revolution allowed for marginally more coverage.[112] Now, once again, *Rozwój* emphasized 'the significance of producing and acquiring local goods':

The campaign that has currently been taken up by various spheres of Polish society should lead to the awakening and deepening of sentiments of economic patriotism—a factor just as

---

[108] See APŁ, Rząd Gubernialny WA, 13076. For requests from industrialists that their tax payments be divided equally, see APŁ, Akta miasta Łodzi, 2878.

[109] Buzek, *Historya polityki narodowościowej*, 361; Hagen, *Germans, Poles, and Jews*, 186–90; Blanke, *Prussian Poland in the German Empire*.

[110] 'Robotnik polski wobec bojkotu przemysłu niemieckiego', *Ziemia Lubelska*, 1908, no. 13. For other examples of use of the term 'boycott' to describe the campaign, see 'Bojkot', *Ziemia Lubelska*, 1908, no. 16, p. 3; 'Bojkot', *Ziemia Lubelska*, 1908, no. 19, pp. 3–4.

[111] According to *Rozwój*, it was the Warsaw daily *Gazeta Polska* that called for the 'economic struggle' in 1901. See 'Bojkot ekonomiczny Prus', *Rozwój*, 1907, no. 252, p. 2. The 1901 protest was in direct response to the 'Września affair': when Polish students in the town of Września (Wreschen) refused to say their prayers in German, they were beaten by their teachers. Both the court trial and the school strikes that followed became a rallying point in the Polish lands, mobilizing Polish intellectuals and writers. See L. Gomolec, *Strajki szkolne w Poznańskiem w latach 1901–1907* (Poznań, 1956); *Proces szkolny we Wrześni: Sprawozdanie szczegółowe na podstawie źródeł urzędowych*, trans. S. Dziewluski and J. Kucharzewski (Kraków, 1902); 'Sprawa Wrzesińska a Koło polskie', *Głos*, 1901, no. 50, p. 774.

[112] In general, limitations on coverage of events in the Russian empire led the Polish press to turn its attention to anti-Polish policy in Germany. See Jedlicki, *Suburb of Europe*, 276.

important as other forms of patriotism (speech, tradition, national culture) . . . We cannot allow ourselves to be reconciled to the demeaning state of economic dependence on enemies.[113]

The impact of the boycott on Polish–German relations within Russian Poland is not clear—if only because its advocates themselves were not entirely clear in their language. 'Germany', 'German goods', and 'German' (or 'Prussian') firms based in Poland all fell under the category of 'boycott'.[114] In Warsaw, proponents of the boycott formed a League for the Defence of Domestic Industry and Trade.[115] Reportedly, the boycott was also 'upheld strictly' in Polish towns close to the German border; in other parts of Russian Poland, it does not seem to have been as widely implemented.[116] Yet the significance of the boycott perhaps lay less in its reception than in the shift it signalled in Polish activism: nationalist leaders had begun to conduct economic politics even in the absence of a national state.

This reflected a parallel shift in Polish nationalist thought, a re-framing of the Polish question in geopolitical terms. Stefan Gorski's *Niemcy w Królestwie Polskiem* ('Germans in the Kingdom of Poland') of 1908 portrayed Łódź as 'the capital of New Germany' (Neudeutschland). Gorski pointed to the 'hand of Berlin' in Polish affairs: Germany, he argued, was not only attempting to colonize its own eastern territories but to occupy Russian Poland itself.[117] In the same year, the Polish nationalist leader Roman Dmowski, the leader of the Polish *koło* in the Duma, took it upon himself to articulate a new Polish foreign policy. In his pamphlet *Niemcy, Rosja, i kwestja polska* ('Germany, Russia, and the Polish Question') Dmowski asserted that Poland, once again, had become a question of international and geopolitical significance. With tensions between Russia and Germany steadily rising, Dmowski characterized German expansionism as a fundamental threat to Polish nationhood—while placing his hopes in Russia and its post-revolutionary democratization.[118]

The discourse about Polish economic dependence on outsiders could not avoid the 'Jewish question'. In its extensive coverage of the boycott, the Lublin newspaper *Ziemia Lubelska* had portrayed Jewish merchants as, at best, ambivalent about the campaign.[119] *Izraelita*, in contrast, under the pen of a Dr Arnsztajn, came out

---

[113] 'Bojkot ekonomiczny Prus', *Rozwój*, 1907, no. 252, p. 2.

[114] See e.g. 'Z Ziem Polskich', *Ziemia Lubelska*, 1908, no. 2, p. 2; 'Z kraju: Bojkot towarów niemieckich', *Ziemia Lubelska*, 1908, no. 5, p. 5; 'Bojkot', *Ziemia Lubelska*, 1908, no. 12, p. 3; 'Bojkot ekonomiczny Prus', *Rozwój*, 1907, no. 252, p. 2.

[115] 'W spawie [*sic*] bojkota', *Izraelita*, 1907, no. 49, pp. 1–2.

[116] 'Z Ziem Polskich', *Ziemia Lubelska*, 1908, no. 2, p. 2. *Ziemia Lubelska* reported that the Russian government had banned the boycott and associated activism, but that this had only further legitimized them. See 'Bojkot', *Ziemia Lubelska*, 1908, no. 16, p. 3.   [117] Gorski, *Niemcy w Królestwie Polskiem*, 29.

[118] On the geopolitical context for the pamphlet, see T. Wituch, 'Przedmowa do obecnego wydania', in R. Dmowski, *Niemcy, Rosja, i kwestia polska* (Warsaw, 1991), 5–9, 21–3.

[119] 'Z Ziem Polskich', *Ziemia Lubelska*, 1908, no. 2, p. 2; 'Bojkot', *Ziemia Lubelska*, 1908, no. 19, pp. 3–4.

as unequivocally in favour of it: 'The boycott of German goods must absolutely be carried out', and 'Jews cannot under any illusion shirk from taking part in this struggle'. German repressive legislation would only 'awaken a consciousness in Polish merchants and industrialists' and 'contribute to the creation of new branches of industry'.[120]

Arnsztajn went on to frame his argument within the larger context of debates regarding Jewish social integration: 'Much is said and written by us on the necessity of equal rights for Jews. But if we want to earn rights equal to those of the indigenous population, let us think about how to share its burdens equally.' The fact that 'both trade and industry are for a large part in the hands of Jews', Arnsztajn asserted, gave Jews a 'wide field of action'. He urged the Jews of Warsaw to 'call together a congress of the representatives of the most diverse branches of labour, trade, and industry, and they should plan out a campaign, and the provinces will join you, and the organized boycott will embrace the entire land'.[121]

Izraelita endorsed Arnsztajn's call for the boycott campaign against ethnic Germans in a subsequent editorial on the subject. However, its ties to Warsaw's economic elite undoubtedly led to the caveat that 'considering the complexity of economic life, [the boycott] will most likely not be carried out fully'. *Izraelita* therefore offered another option to its readers: 'it is not necessary . . . to wait for the organized action of anti-German leagues—on the contrary, each person can and should begin on his own the removal of the German language in favour of Polish'. 'The German language', *Izraelita* explained, 'is still used in social conversations, or in commercial correspondence, inside our country' by those who consider it to be 'evidence of education or a good upbringing'. Therefore,

it should not surprise us that society surrounding us looks with aversion at those who consider themselves citizens of the land . . . yet support the language of its fiercest enemy. And, after all, let us not forget that this same Germany has been a cradle of modern-day antisemitism—which even today exerts a stronger influence there than in any state of western Europe.[122]

Despite the efforts of *Izraelita*, Polish–Jewish relations generally did not improve as a result of the anti-German campaign. In Łódź, an economic crisis in 1912 led to the heightening of both social and ethnic tensions, especially among the working population.[123] Bad feelings remaining from the 1907–11 education conflict spilled over into debates on funding for a proposed Polish theatre in the city.[124] The populist *Lodzher togblat*, the new Yiddish-language newspaper in Łódź, purportedly opposed the project.[125] As elsewhere in Poland, a Duma bill to

[120] Interestingly, Dr Arnsztajn himself was from Lublin. See 'W spawie [*sic*] bojkotu', *Izraelita*, 1907, no. 49, pp. 1–2. [121] Ibid. [122] 'W sprawie bojkotu II', *Izraelita*, 1907, no. 50, pp. 1–2.
[123] W. Gajewska, 'Kampania wyborcza do IV Dumy Państwowej w Łodzi', master's thesis (Univ. of Łódź, 1967), 40. [124] 'Perfidya żydowska', *Rozwój*, 1912, no. 89, p. 1.
[125] On the rise of the Yiddish press in Łódź following the revolution of 1905–7, see L. Olejnik, 'Z dziejów prasy żydowskiej w Łodzi w latach 1904–1908', in W. Puś and S. Liszewski (eds.), *Dzieje*

introduce municipal self-government served as an additional cause for dispute, with each group jockeying for municipal representation.[126] Since the turn of the century, the proportion of Jewish merchants had increased significantly among the ranks of middling industrialists in Łódź—with a consequent impact on the city's demographic layout and electoral distribution.[127]

By the elections to the Fourth Duma in 1912, the Jewish vote in both Warsaw and Łódź bore a clear advantage. In Łódź, the physician Meir Bomash was elected to the Duma, the first Jewish delegate from the Kingdom of Poland.[128] Counting on this victory, Warsaw Jewish groups chose to cede to Polish interests and back the election of a Polish candidate in the Polish capital. They made clear, however, that they would only choose a candidate who supported equal rights for Jews. Roman Dmowski, of the National Democratic Party, predicated his candidacy on opposition to Jews. Jan Kucharzewski, the candidate of a bloc of Polish nationalist groups, adopted a more ambivalent position. While claiming to support Jewish rights, he also argued that Jews were numerically too preponderant in Poland and played too large a role in Polish economic life.[129]

As the 'Jewish question' became central to the electoral struggle, the Polish National Democrats began to publish a daily 'twopenny' newspaper, *Gazeta Poranna*, which asked its growing readership to 'buy only from Christians'.[130] By September 1912, newspapers across Poland were running the headline 'each for his own'.[131] When the elections were held the next month, Jewish electors failed to support Kucharzewski, choosing instead the socialist Eugeniusz Jagiełło. A Jewish political constituency that acted on behalf of its own interests had clearly emerged. In response, the National Democratic Party heightened its calls for a struggle against Jews.[132] The *Gazeta Poranna* published lists of Jewish-owned firms; a number of associations in Warsaw closed their membership to Jews, and there were reports of brawls on the streets of Warsaw.[133]

Żydów w Łodzi, 1820–1944: Wybrane problemy (Łódź, 1991), 140–56; M. Pawełek, 'Polskojęzyczna prasa żydowska w Łodzi do 1939 roku: Charakterystyka zewnętrzna', master's thesis (Univ. of Łódź, 1993).

[126] 'Stanowisko Niemców wobec samorządu', *Rozwój*, 1912, no. 81, p. 2. On the issue of municipal self-government in Poland as a whole, see T. Weeks, *Nation and State in Late Imperial Russia: Nationalism and Russification on the Western Frontier, 1863–1914* (DeKalb, Ill., 1996), 162–70.

[127] Pytlas, 'National Composition of Łódź Industrialists', 41–4.

[128] On Bomash's activism in the Duma, see GARF, f. 9458.

[129] Corrsin, *Warsaw before the First World War*, 89–96. See also Polonsky, *Jews in Poland and Russia*, ii. 108. [130] Corrsin, *Warsaw before the First World War*, 94.

[131] See e.g. 'Swój do swojego', *Goniec Częstochowy*, 1912, no. 241, p. 3. See also GARF, f. 240, d. 114, fos. 8, 17, 20–1.

[132] On the causal relationship between the development of modern Jewish politics and Polish antisemitism, see Polonsky, *Jews in Poland and Russia*, ii. 111.

[133] Corrsin, *Warsaw before the First World War*, 89–104; Blobaum, 'Politics of Antisemitism in Fin-de-Siècle Warsaw'; Golczewski, *Polnisch-jüdische Beziehungen*; Weeks, *From Assimilation to Antisemitism*, 163; GARF, f. 9458, d. 1, fos. 91–4.

The manifestation of open and organized antisemitism in Poland, in turn, contributed to the radicalization of Jewish politics. The ideal of Jewish social integration championed by *Izraelita* had seemingly exhausted itself; and after a period of internal factionalism, *Izraelita* collapsed in 1913.[134] Jewish nationalism, in contrast, in its various forms, enjoyed a new momentum. As early as June 1912, the populist *Lodzher togblat* had renewed calls of previous years for exclusively 'Jewish factories'.[135] By October of the following year, the tsarist police was reporting that lay-offs of Christian workers by Jewish factory owners in neighbouring Pabianice had led to strikes and violence.[136] In St Petersburg, the new Łódź Duma delegate, Meir Bomash, speaking over antisemitic interjections, delivered a bold political response to the Polish 'economic boycott'. Denouncing the campaign as an 'economic crusade' to 'displace Jews from their economic positions', he declared: 'we will fight for both human rights and political rights; you will not destroy with your fist our consciousness of our own human dignity'.[137]

It is well known that outside Warsaw the Polish struggle against Jews faced difficulties in its implementation—and Łódź was no exception.[138] The chief of the Łódź gendarme corps reported to his provincial superiors that in Łódź, 'owing to the particular conditions of local trade, which is located almost entirely in Jewish hands, the idea of a boycott of Jews has had no success whatsoever'. The 'boycott', he continued, was 'observed only in the intellectual sphere and manifested itself in the fact that Jews did not attend events of public entertainment organized by Poles and Poles did not attend the Jewish theatre, as well as in the refusal of the latter to participate in charitable fundraisers on behalf of Jewish institutions'.[139]

Nevertheless, discussions of Polish–Jewish relations continued throughout Poland for much of 1913—and they continued precisely regarding the concept of economic self-sufficiency. In a series of articles published in early 1913, the Łódź Polish nationalist newspaper *Rozwój* sought to distinguish between its own 'economic struggle' and what it characterized as calls by the Yiddish press for a 'boycott' of Poles. 'The current economic struggle', *Rozwój* editor Stanisław Łapiński wrote, 'is incorrectly called a boycott of Jews.' At its 'core' was rather the 'question of the defence and strengthening of the state of our propertied classes'. The slogan of 'each for his own', Łapiński argued, 'is a battle horn that summons Poles to work that is carefully organized, enduring, and unceasing'. Polish capital could only be created through the 'entrepreneurial spirit, which we have always

---

[134] Polonsky, *Jews in Poland and Russia*, ii. 111.

[135] 'A yudishe fabrik', *Lodzher togblat*, 1912, no. 138, p. 5; 'Af velkhe fabrikn arbetn yudishe arbeter?', *Lodzher togblat*, 1912, no. 140.

[136] GARF, f. 102, OO, 1913, 32, ch. 9, l. B, fos. 113–15.   [137] GARF, f. 9458, d. 1, fos. 91–4.

[138] GARF, f. 240, d. 114, fo. 19. The Warsaw Jewish satirist Dr Bim-Bom parodies the difficulties in implementing the boycott in his tract *Fir goyim; oder, megiles boykot mayses tsum lakhn* (Warsaw, 1913). See also Blobaum, 'Politics of Antisemitism in Fin-de-Siècle Warsaw', 302–3; Golczewski, *Polnisch-jüdische Beziehungen*, 113.   [139] GARF, f. 240, d. 114, fo. 19.

lacked until now; through private and social initiatives; through co-operatives and sensible saving'.[140]

At the heart of this struggle was Polish unity—and Łapiński criticized those whose zeal led them to demand of their neighbours that they 'boycott firms of Polish origin because they sold a certain part of their production to Jews'. However, he cautioned, 'to buy everything from foreigners that we could acquire amongst ourselves—that is a punishable act'. As an illustration, Łapiński asserted that 'for just furniture and upholstery alone, Łódź sends abroad annually, mostly to Prussia, 400–500 thousand roubles . . . when, in the meantime, we have our own upholstery firms in town'. Moreover, he informed his readers, 'Germans are planning to buy up the rich mines of beautiful Kielce marble—which the slogan of "each for his own" should decidedly prevent. It behoves us in this respect to develop a rescue campaign and, with its help, leave the Kielce marble mines in Polish hands.'[141] Remarks on Polish self-sufficiency could not avoid the question of Germany and Polish–German relations.

Yet why did Polish nationalist leaders in Łódź distance themselves from the concept of 'boycott' in particular? Later in the year, Łapiński elaborated on the term itself:

Every boycott—as an act that is, to a certain degree, a terrorist act—does not deserve recognition and support. Those people are reckless who call the current campaign for the nationalization [*unarodowienie*] of trade and industry . . . a boycott of Jews.

This is not a boycott and never was a boycott; it is a supremely justified struggle against the Jewish occupation [*zabór*], a fight for the economic autonomy of the country.[142]

In other words, Łapiński sought to emphasize that the 1912 campaign against Jews was part of a larger process of economic struggle that had begun several decades before, embracing ideas of economic self-sufficiency and movements for Polish co-operativism. The concepts both of the 'nationalization' of Polish industry and of a 'rescue campaign' with an articulated programme certainly had a more constructive connotation than a 'boycott'. But above all, they allowed for a certain degree of comparison between the struggle against Jewish and German economic power in Poland—equating the perceived expansion of Jewish financial influence with the old trauma of the Polish partitions and with ongoing geopolitical concerns about German imperial aims.

CONCLUSION

The development of modern nationalism necessitated not only a political but an economic re-evaluation of the relationship between Russia and Poland—and the ethnic minorities within them. As Łódź grew ever more rapidly—relying on

---

[140] 'Swoi do swoich', pt. 4, *Rozwój*, 1913, no. 9, p. 1. See also 'Kwestya żydowska', *Rozwój*, 1913, no. 8, p. 2.   [141] 'Swoi do swoich', pt. 4, *Rozwój*, 1913, no. 9, p. 1.
[142] 'Unarodowienie czy bojkot', *Rozwój*, 1913, no. 182.

imperial resources and contributing in turn to imperial textile production—it became central to this process. Moscow textile merchants and their pan-Slavist allies came to define imperial industry as exclusively 'Great Russian'; in their campaign against Łódź and Polish textiles, they targeted the contributions of ethnic German industrialists in particular. The resulting measures against ethnic Germans and competition from Łódź revealed the role of the state in enforcing a particular version of Russian modernization: one defined (and limited) by economic nationalism.

Ideas of economic nationalism, meanwhile, had already begun to evolve within the stateless context of the Polish partitioned lands. In the period following the uprising of 1863, discussions began in Warsaw regarding the economic relationship between Jews and Poles, and the place of Jews within the larger Polish social body. In Łódź, partly because of the linguistic and cultural affiliations of the German and Jewish elite, they led to comparisons of the economic and social roles of the city's Jewish and German populations. Łódź workers, suffering from cyclical economic crises (1892, 1899–1901, 1904–7, 1912), prompted communal and national leaders to address the question of working conditions and unemployment.

It was in Łódź, therefore, that national ideas were realized in concrete projects for economic self-sufficiency. The organization of 'Jewish factories' and the establishment of Polish worker co-operatives were both attempts at striving towards a particular national economic future predicated upon an improved working population. Whereas the theorists of Polish co-operativism strove towards a higher ethical stage in Polish social development, Andrzej Rogoziński explicitly linked this idea of moral or ethical progress with the struggle against Jewish economic power. Both Rogoziński himself and the workers of Jewish kerchief factories (at least as quoted by Łódź police reports) adopted the slogan 'one for all and all for one' to describe the national unity of their respective burgeoning organizations.

The liberalization that accompanied the Russian revolution of 1905–7 allowed ideas of economic self-sufficiency to develop into full-fledged movements. The revolution engendered the sort of nationalist organization that had already manifested itself throughout the partitioned lands: co-operativism, school strikes, and parliamentary activism. In Łódź, too, education now became a main arena for the expression of ethno-linguistic identity. The 1907–11 school affair revealed, of course, that the population of Łódź continued to define its identity in a variety of ways—social, national, and religious. But it also demonstrated the growing readiness of Łódź citizens to proclaim their allegiance to national institutions and to organize and mobilize on behalf of limited economic resources.

Another shift took place in the period following the revolution of 1905–7: Polish national activists began to cast Polish nationalism as a geopolitical question—and to conduct political activism accordingly. As economic nationalism transitioned from ideas to actual foreign policy, Polish leaders declared the first significant 'boycott' in response to German anti-Polish legislation. Polish nationalist activists did not distinguish between 'Germany' and 'ethnic German' citizens of Poland. The German expansionist threat embraced German goods sold in Poland, German firms, and the city of Łódź itself—'Neudeutschland' in Stefan Gorski's rendering. At the same time, Jewish intellectual and linguistic ties with German culture forced the Jewish question into the spotlight. In endorsing the boycott, and backing Polish commerce, *Izraelita* cut off ties with all things German, casting German anti-semitism in its own geopolitical context.

The 1912 boycott of Jews was thus the second major boycott of an ethnic group in Poland. It served as the climax of heightened national tensions that had emerged since the revolution of 1905–7 among those who identified as Poles, Jews, and Germans. Above all, as Łapiński suggested, it constituted the bookend of the development of ideas of economic nationalism that had their roots in the late nineteenth century. In this new era of mass consumption, a variety of groups asserted the significance of 'economic patriotism', characterized, as *Rozwój* put it, by self-sufficiency and 'economic autonomy'. In Russian Poland, modernity was defined not only by the large role of Jews and Germans in industrialization but by the formation of competing national visions of an economic future.

The Attitude of the Jews towards Poland's Independence

SZYMON RUDNICKI

TO UNDERSTAND the attitude of Jews towards Polish independence in general, as well as towards the actual re-establishment of an independent Polish state, we must delve into the historical background of the Polish–Jewish relationship. This attitude depended on a great many factors, the underlying one of which was the relations between Poles and Jews. The closer the Poles came to regaining and consolidating their independence, the greater the role played by current events. As a result, unresolved historical issues were deferred. An important factor was the degree of co-operation (or lack of it) between these two communities. Here I must immediately emphasize the diversity of both communities. It was never the case that, when Poles and Jews were under discussion, all members of either community could be included. For instance, the bulk of Jews were for the most part not involved in politics, nor did they identify with Polishness (*polskość*), though this did not mean that they were indifferent to who was in power. Therefore, when speaking about Jewish attitudes we usually mean those of the political camps and parties, or even the views of their leaders. Nascent feelings of nationalism complicated mutual relations. An element which significantly affected the Jewish street was the anti-Jewish propaganda conducted above all by the so-called national camp (*obóz narodowy*). A new element which played an important role was the appearance of a Jewish sense of national identity and its attendant aspirations. For nationally aware Jews, an important factor was the Polish state's readiness to fulfil their aspirations. These problems, here obviously identified summarily, are discussed in greater detail below.

Ezra Mendelsohn included the majority of Polish Jews in an east European model characterized by a relatively low level of assimilation and acculturation, by the retention of the Yiddish language and Jewish Orthodoxy, and by a specific economic structure.[1] Around 75 per cent of Jews lived in cities and small towns. The population in some small towns was almost entirely Jewish. In Warsaw, Jews

[1] E. Mendelsohn, *Żydzi Europy Środkowo-Wschodniej w okresie międzywojennym* (Warsaw, 1992), 27–9.

comprised about one-third of the inhabitants. This affected their professional structure. The overwhelming majority of the economically active Jewish population supported themselves by trade and business.

From the moment that the struggle to regain independence began, Polish Jews participated. In referring to the struggle for independence, I have in mind, above all, direct involvement in political activity against the partitions, as well as armed revolt. I am omitting a great number of other aspects, such as participation in commercial activity (which strengthened society's position vis-à-vis the partitioning powers), and the activities of Jewish publishers and booksellers, thanks to whom Polish books were distributed throughout Congress Poland and the territories directly incorporated into the tsarist empire, contributing to an awakening of national feeling. Jewish involvement in these activities was never widespread, but the same was true in Polish society.

Like other communities, the Jews did not constitute a monolith. The Haskalah, the Jewish Enlightenment, did not make the kind of inroads in Poland that it did in Germany or the Austro-Hungarian empire. As a result, the Polish middle class was not an attractive milieu for the Jewish middle class.[2] To all intents and purposes, almost the entire Jewish community was opposed to assimilation on both religious and nationalist grounds, though it is impossible to establish the number of people who did succumb to it.[3] However, even the moderate assimilationist processes were brought to a halt by the growing antisemitism propagated by the Polish nationalist movement (Narodowa Demokracja—National Democracy—also known popularly as Endecja). The phenomenon of acculturation had a much more extensive impact.

One line of demarcation was a person's attitude to Polishness and to Jewishness itself. The greater the links to Polish culture, the greater the involvement in Polish affairs. Part of the Jewish bourgeoisie was inclined to be conciliatory towards Russia, as were the Polish conciliators. Some of the young people who were assimilated became involved in the Polish underground movement whose goal was to see Poland regain its independence. The Orthodox and hasidic masses, like the peasants, were characterized by political apathy. Anxiety over a crust of bread also sapped any desire to get involved in anything beyond the daily struggle for survival. The relations of the Orthodox with the Poles also dissuaded them from doing so. Both communities lived their own lives and the majority on both sides were not inclined to change this state of affairs.

The goal of politically involved Jews was to obtain the rights of citizenship. This was above all the desire of the bourgeoisie and the intelligentsia. Together with the expansion of the intelligentsia, which was a vehicle of cultural change and self-awareness, Jews' involvement in Poland's struggle for independence also grew.

[2] H. Datner, *Ta i tamta strona: Żydowska inteligencja Warszawy drugiej połowy XIX wieku* (Warsaw, 2007), 27.

[3] W. Wierzbieniec, *Żydzi w województwie lwowskim w okresie międzywojennym: Zagadnienia demograficzne i społeczne* (Rzeszów, 2003), 28. The process of assimilation is discussed more fully in A. Landau-Czajka, *Syn będzie Lech...: Asymilacja Żydów w Polsce międzywojennej* (Warsaw, 2006).

Jews played an active role in the Kościuszko insurrection.[4] In September 1794, on the initiative of Józef Aronowicz and Berek Joselewicz, Jews began to establish an independent regiment of light cavalry, which was then commanded by Joselewicz. Among other engagements, this regiment took part in the fighting against Suvorov's army in Praga, during which almost all its men were killed. Jews also served in support services, and during the uprising they shouldered the lion's share of the finances. Jewish attitudes towards the insurrection which began in November 1830 varied. The intelligentsia, some of whom had already been educated in Polish schools, wanted to take part, and simultaneously mobilized the Jewish community to fight the partitioning power. The uprising was also supported by part of the Jewish bourgeoisie. The majority of the Jews, however, were for the most part indifferent towards the uprising, as were the peasants, who displayed open hostility towards the insurrectionary leadership's imposition of compulsory conscription.[5] The situation was not helped by the uprising's conservative leadership, which retained all the restrictions on Jews. Despite this, more than four hundred Jews served in the capital's National Guard (Gwardia Narodowa), while there were altogether 1,268 Jews in the City Guard (Gwardia Miejska).[6] It is difficult to calculate the number of Jews who served in regular military units. Jews also played an active part in the uprising which began in January 1863, although we do not know how many took up arms. But for the first time during an insurrection Jews even commanded some insurrectionary parties. They were also found in the central, as well as the local, leadership. Majer Bałaban claimed that hundreds, and maybe even thousands, of Jews lost their lives in the uprising or as a consequence of it.[7]

Many Jews struggled in their decision about which side to support. Attitudes were a function of local conditions, relations with officials, the extent of the influence of conservative Jewish elements, and the intensity of the insurrectionary movement, as well as of the attitude towards Jews of the insurgents, who did not always treat the Jewish population fairly. In the Kresy (Eastern Borderlands), the

[4] I discuss the role of Jews in the uprisings and the independence movement in S. Rudnicki, 'Żydzi w walce o niepodległość Polski', in J. Tomaszewski and A. Żbikowski (eds.), *Żydzi w Polsce: Dzieje i kultura. Leksykon* (Warsaw, 2001). I provide a discussion in it of the relevant literature.

[5] A. Barszczewska-Krupa, 'Polityka społeczna władz rządowych w Powstaniu Listopadowym 1830–1831', in W. Zajewski (ed.), *Powstanie Listopadowe, 1830–1831: Dzieje wewnętrzne, militaria, Europa wobec powstania* (Warsaw, 1980), 149.

[6] A. Eisenbach, *Wielka Emigracja wobec kwestii żydowskiej, 1832–1849* (Warsaw, 1976), 98.

[7] M. Bałaban, 'Żydzi w powstaniu 1863 r.', *Przegląd Historyczny*, 34 (1938), 582; *Żydzi a powstanie styczniowe: Materiały i dokumenty*, ed. A. Eisenbach, D. Fajnhauz, and A. Wein (Warsaw, 1963), 6–7. As a result of sentences passed by field courts, 396 insurgents were shot or hanged, including 25 peasants, 25 Jews, and 5 priests: J. K. Urbach, *Udział Żydów w walce o niepodległość Polski* (Warsaw, 1938), 181. For political reasons, propagandists for the National Democrats exaggerated the Jews' involvement, writing that their 'contribution to the events in Poland of 1861–4 was enormous', and that 'the Jews had their hands on the tiller during these events': J. Giertych, *Tragizm losów Polski* (Pelplin, 1937), 309, 310.

tsarist bureaucracy attempted to win over the Jewish population and pit it against the non-Jewish population.[8] In turn, insurrectionary propaganda did not always reach Jewish communities, which also affected their involvement in the uprising. Thus, the lower social orders for the most part remained politically indifferent.

In summing up Polish–Jewish relations in the nineteenth century, we can agree with Zygmunt Dreszer, a leading Sanacja figure, who stated that 'during periods of an outpouring of national feeling, such as the establishment of the Constitution of 3 May [1791] or periods of insurrection, a programme of assimilation and equality always came to the fore, while a current of antisemitism developed in the aftermath of a defeat'. He noted that antipathy towards Jews began to grow after 1908.[9] In the twentieth century, irrespective of political circumstances, this latter sentiment became increasingly dominant.

Religious and cultural differences, made sharper by both sides, hindered the creation of a feeling of community. The rabbinate tried to maintain this state of affairs. The anti-Judaism of the Catholic Church was also a significant obstacle. The Jews worked, in Marcin Kula's words, in 'intermediary professions', a situation which has always aroused suspicion, as for instance in the case of the Chinese in South-East Asia.[10] It should be added that the Polish middle class regarded Jews as competitors. Deprived of rights, the bulk of the Jews were above all afraid of authority, but reacted no less suspiciously towards non-Jewish society. For these reasons, they stayed aloof from political developments, although there were quite numerous exceptions to this rule.

'The twentieth century brought a new situation: the creation of modern Jewish society; in other words a society having its own goals and institutions.'[11] The attitude of the Polish political movements, with their stress on the Polish national character and their Catholicism, contributed to this outlook.[12] At the outset, nationalism, as a political movement, enjoyed a great deal of success. For those territories threatened either with Russification or Germanization, nationalism became the ideology of a great many Polish patriots. It was, by its nature, a movement which attacked, or at the very least excluded, ethnic minorities. An attitude of national and confessional exclusivism led to an ever more energetic campaign of anti-Jewish slogans. It was exacerbated by economic competition which was exploited in the political struggle.[13]

---

[8] D. Fajnhauz, 'Ludność żydowska na Litwie i Białorusi a powstanie styczniowe', *Biuletyn Żydowskiego Instytutu Historycznego*, 37–8 (1961), 27.

[9] Z. Dreszer, *Sprawa mniejszości narodowych w Polsce a program państwowej demokracji* (Warsaw, 1926), 26.   [10] M. Kula, *Uparta sprawa: Żydowska? Polska? Ludzka?* (Kraków, 2004), 196.

[11] Datner, *Ta i tamta strona*, 97.

[12] J. Holzer, *Dwa stulecia Polski i Europy: Teksty pisane w różnych porach wieku* (Poznań, 2004), 404.

[13] 'An important feature of the rise of active elements in society', wrote Roman Dmowski, 'is an economic movement in the Kingdom which is declaring war on small Jewish businesses. Irrespective of whether it merely acts in a positive fashion, by organizing autonomous Christian business, or whether it is accompanied by the whole apparatus, as it were, of antisemitism, playing on the baser instincts of the

The mere creation of political parties was something new in the Jewish tradition in eastern Europe and testified to the penetration into this community of the modernizing tendencies which Europe was experiencing in the nineteenth century.[14] The process of developing Jewish political parties lasted from the late nineteenth century until it basically came to an end during the First World War. As with Polish political parties, socialist organizations led the way. The first Jewish party was the General Jewish Workers' Alliance in Russia and Poland (Algemeyner Yidisher Arbeterbund in Rusland un Poyln), founded in 1897 and commonly known as the Bund. It had significant influence on the Jewish proletariat in Congress Poland and the Kresy. In many places, the Bund was the most powerful socialist organization. Józef Piłsudski wrote that 'among Christians the socialist movement has so far been developing slowly and has not made such great inroads among the people as it has among the Jews'.[15] Jews, and people of Jewish descent, were involved in all the revolutionary and socialist organizations operating on Polish territory. There was a Jewish Organization within the Polish Socialist Party (Polska Partia Socjalistyczna; PPS).

During both 1904 and 1905, a total of 417 Jews fought with the Military Organization (Organizacja Bojowa) of the PPS, representing 4.8 per cent of the force.[16] Jews also fought in the military structures of the Social Democracy of the Kingdom of Poland and Lithuania (Socjaldemokracja Królestwa Polski i Litwy; SDKPiL). The Bund's combat organizations, whose tradition of providing protection against pogroms began in the 1890s, had, like the SDKPiL, around eight hundred fighters.[17] They also took substantial casualties. According to official statistics of the Okhrana (the Russian secret police), during the fighting in Łódź in June 1905, 55 Catholics, 17 Protestants, and 70 Jews lost their lives.

However, the PPS did not recognize the Jews as a nation and questioned the Bund's legitimacy as an independent party. The principal accusation against the Bund was its refusal to accept as part of its programme the call for a free Poland. As one of the Bund's founders, John Mill, wrote:

For us the PPS position was unacceptable . . . We expected the liberation of the Jewish masses only as a result of victory by the socialist forces of the whole of Russia, including

masses, we should see in it above all the awakening in society of a healthy need to take control, through a native element, of one of the most important social functions and the growth of active elements in our middle orders, which are attempting to wrest economic levers out of the alien hands into which they have fallen': R. Dmowski, *Myśli nowoczesnego Polaka*, enlarged 3rd edn. (Lwów, 1907), 92.

[14] D. Engel, '"Masoret nega'im": he'arot al hamegamat hapolitiyot vehatarbut hapolit shel yahadut polin bein hamilḥamot ha'olam', in I. Bartal and Y. Gutman (eds.), *Kiyum veshever: yehudei polin ledoroteihem*, 2 vols. (Jerusalem, 1997–2000), ii. 650. Helena Datner has stressed that the rise of Jewish political parties created an alternative to assimilation: Datner, *Ta i tamta strona*, 79.

[15] J. Piłsudski, 'Kwestia żydowska na Litwie' (1903), in id., *Pisma zbiorowe: Wydanie prac dotychczas drukiem ogłoszonych*, 10 vols. (Warsaw, 1937–8), ii. 225.

[16] J. Pająk *Organizacje bojowe partii politycznych w Królestwie Polskim, 1904–1911* (Warsaw, 1985), 115.   [17] Ibid. 174, 184.

Poland . . . We could not adopt the PPS calls for an independent Poland as our rallying cry and separate ourselves from the general Russian socialist movement and become part of the PPS.[18]

The Bund never excluded the possibility of the rebirth of a Polish state, but did not agree to include calls for independence in its programme, tying its approach to developing events.

The Jewish political movement was characterized by considerable diversity. Essential differences could be seen in its tactics in the struggle for equal rights, and in its attitudes towards Polishness. The Jewish parties were also split by their vision of the character of the Jewish community: were they just a religious grouping or a nation? If they were a nation, should they not enjoy national autonomy? Only secular Jews spoke of national autonomy, which was expanded into a goal of cultural and national autonomy, as opposed to remaining a territorial minority. No form of autonomy was acceptable to the Poles. Moreover, a great many of them felt so strongly that both communities should retain their identity that they opposed the assimilation of the Jews. Here the Polish nationalists' interests coincided with those of most of the Jewish parties. The Jews also differed among themselves in their attitude towards a national homeland of their own; hence the division between Zionists and non-Zionists, but even the Zionists did not anticipate the complete destruction of the Diaspora.

Zionists, as well as the supporters of the Yidishe Folkspartey in Poyln (the Jewish People's Party in Poland, the so-called Folkists) and the Bund, all considered themselves to be a national movement. Leon Wasilewski, one of the leaders of the Polish socialist movement, wrote in 1913 about the origins of this nationalism: 'Amidst the stench of blood rising above pitiful Jewish dwellings plundered by the Russian mob was born nationalism, which opposed not only the hitherto-held view of the need to assimilate the Jews, generally accepted in the West, but the whole developmental process of this very same Jewry, as also of the societies within which these Jews live.' At the heart of this movement, which claimed that the Jews were a nation, lay more reasons than Wasilewski enumerated. However, his definition of Jewish nationalism is interesting; he, like the whole of the PPS, was opposed to it and was a proponent of Jewish assimilation. 'By Jewish nationalism', he wrote, 'I understand all those trends aiming to maintain Jewish nationality and combat assimilation.'[19] His use of the word 'nationalism' (*nacjonalizm*) thus differed from the accepted definition of nationalism in east-central Europe (which resembled rather 'chauvinism'), and was similar to the Anglo-Saxon usage that approximates to 'patriotism'.

The Zionists had the greatest influence. If in Galicia an independent party was

[18] G. Aronson et al. (eds.), *Di geshikhte fun bund*, 5 vols. (New York, 1960–81), i. 180, quoted by S. Bergman, 'Bund a niepodległość Polski', in F. Tych and J. Hensel (eds.), *Bund: 100 lat historii, 1897–1997* (Warsaw, 2000), 110.

[19] R. Wapiński, *Historia polskiej myśli politycznej XIX i XX wieku* (Gdańsk, 1997), 192.

formed from the outset, in the Russian partition it was initially part of the all-Russian movement, like the Bund. From the start it was a secular movement, although it recognized the role of religion in maintaining Jewish identity. The Zionists were never a homogeneous movement; they split into many parties and currents. A tendency towards socialism was always strong in the movement. It was only during the war that a religious branch of Zionism developed.

The First World War was a turning point in the history of Europe and the world. In the case of Polish territory no one had any doubt from its outbreak that there would be no return to the status quo ante. For the Polish political parties, the problem was whom to rely on. There were three key moments during the war: the occupation of the Kingdom of Poland by the Central Powers; the Act of 5 November 1916 that established a nominally independent Poland; and the revolution in Russia. In turn, the attitude of Polish society towards the Jews during the war had a direct correlation with the Jews' attitude towards the nascent Polish state. 'At the start of the war only rather narrow elites took part in the struggle for Poland', Andrzej Chwalba has written, and 'the masses were passive'.[20] The same was true of the Jews on an even larger scale.

Unlike the war in the West, the war on the territory of the former tsarist empire lasted not four years but six. It also precipitated the largest movement of Jews since the expulsion from Spain, including displacement from the Pale of Settlement and the flight of the Jewish population from eastern Galicia ahead of the tsarist forces. This was also a time of pogroms and plunder. Jews served in every army. Like the Jews in France and Germany, Jews from the Polish territories were loyal to their countries of residence. Galician Jews, like most of the Polish parties, came out in favour of an Austro-Polish solution. The Jews of the Kingdom on the whole also adopted a position similar to that of most of the population of Congress Poland, expressing support for Russia's war effort, but, after the German occupation of Warsaw, becoming reluctant to commit themselves further, fearing the return of the Russians. Immediately after the outbreak of war, Jews expressed hope for a better tomorrow, writing that

we are deeply convinced that the new state of affairs awaited by us with unshakeable faith will provide in Poland conditions of unfettered national existence and that its internal life will again be fully based on a foundation of unconditional justice. Then too will bright rays of social justice shine on the Jewish people, as they have on many occasions already shone on them through the generosity of free Polish culture.

As Konrad Zieliński, from whose book this quotation from the 'Declaration of the Polish Jews in Warsaw' is taken, rightly emphasizes, this was the official position. Unfortunately, it is unclear who was the spokesman for the Jews.[21]

---

[20] A. Chwalba, *Historia Polski, 1795–1918* (Kraków, 2000), 592.

[21] 'Deklaracja Żydów polskich w Warszawie', quoted by K. Zieliński, *Stosunki polsko-żydowskie na ziemiach Królestwa Polskiego w czasie pierwszej wojny światowej* (Lublin, 2005), 104.

The majority of Jews greeted the end of Russian rule with relief. They expected that, with a change in political conditions, they would receive the same rights as the Poles.[22] After the Kingdom was occupied by Germany and Austria, a sign of the new situation was the successive creation of a number of Jewish political parties, which was evidence of a break with the Jewish community's traditional model of behaviour.[23] This self-emancipation was not painless. Just as the appearance of Jews in the ranks of the Polish intelligentsia was met with hostility, so too was their participation in politics given a hostile or reluctant reception. At the time, the most pronounced example was the reaction to the behaviour of Jewish voters during the elections to the Duma in 1912.

The Folkists, whose party was founded in 1916, declared that the Jews' homeland was their country of residence. The Folkists rejected Zionist ideas as a pipe dream. They admitted the existence of the Jewish people, whose language, in their view, was to be Yiddish. They proposed a programme for the secularization of Jewish life, whose expression was to be the local commune created along national and not religious lines. The Folkists, taking up the cudgels from the start on behalf of Jews' national rights, stood for a free and democratic Poland. In their programme they demanded that 'all citizens, irrespective of gender, belief, or nationality, be equal before the law and that there be no privileges based on birth or social status'. Their main policy demand was to obtain cultural and national autonomy, which was to be achieved by means of the Jewish People's Council (Żydowska Rada Ludowa), as a body representing all Polish Jews.[24]

In March 1916 the Agudat Ha'ortodoksim (Organization of the Orthodox), called simply Agudah for short, was formed in Poland. It focused its attention on religious matters. The nationality problem did not arouse any great interest within it, although eventually it did recognize the Jews as a nation.[25] It was felt that until the Messiah opened the door to Palestine, Jews would continue to live in the Diaspora in harmony with the citizens of the countries in which they had settled.[26] One of Agudah's characteristics was its reluctance to become involved in political battles and its desire to be on good terms with the authorities. For Orthodox Jews,

---

[22] 'Deklaracja Żydów polskich w Warszawie', 105–6.

[23] Engel, '"Masoret nega'im"', 650; J. Frankel, 'The Paradoxical Politics of Marginality: Thoughts on the Jewish Situation during the Years 1914–1921', in J. Frankel, P. Y. Medding, and E. Mendelsohn (eds.), *Studies in Contemporary Jewry*, iv: *The Jews and the European Crisis, 1914–1921* (Jerusalem, 1988), 4.

[24] On the birth of the Folkspartey and its activities during the First World War, see M. W. Kiel, 'The Ideology of the Folks-Partey', *Soviet Jewish Affairs*, 5/2 (1975), 75–89; for the programme of the party, see A. Bełcikowska, *Stronnictwa i związki polityczne w Polsce: Charakterystyki, dane historyczne, programy, rezolucje, organizacje partyjne, prasa, przywódcy*, ed. J. Bełcikowski (Warsaw, 1925), 517–20.

[25] 'The Orthodox Jews, whom we have the privilege to represent, being loyal citizens of the Polish State stand for the belief in a Jewish national identity in which the leading role is played by religious and traditional elements': point 1 of a declaration made by Rabbi Avraham Tsevi Perlmutter, in *Sprawozdanie Stenograficzne Sejmu Ustawodawczego* (hereafter *SSSU*), 24 Feb. 1919, session 5, col. 181.

[26] Perlmutter, in *SSSU*, 27 May 1919, session 42, col. 5.

obedience to national authorities emanated from the dictates of their faith.[27] Thus, members of Agudah declared their loyalty to the Polish Republic and to every government. They saw Polish political life as irrelevant for Jews, so long as there was no threat to religious laws or deterioration in the conditions of Jewish community life.[28]

The so-called assimilationists represented a separate group. As *Wiadomości Polskie*, published by the military department of the Supreme National Committee (Naczelny Komitet Narodowy), wrote in 1917, 'The assimilationists represent amongst Polish Jewry the oldest camp, but unfortunately not the most influential one.'[29] They considered themselves to be Poles of the Mosaic faith. They continued to be Jews only in the eyes of the National Democrats; they were no longer considered such by other Jews. Some suffered from a split personality—found not infrequently in people of dual nationality. In the complex Polish situation they were forced to pick a side.[30]

By comparison with the behaviour of the Russian authorities and troops, a German occupation appeared to represent the start of a new life. Initially, the Germans tried to maintain a policy of friendship towards the Jews. On arriving, they even issued a proclamation announcing that they were bringing Jews justice, freedom, and civil and religious rights.[31] Furthermore, a number of German Jews took up the struggle for influence over the Jewish population in territory occupied by the Germans. Even before the war they had put forward a plan to create a kind of buffer state between Russia and Germany composed of many nations, in which the Jews would be granted autonomy. These utopian proposals were rejected by the German authorities, as well as by the Zionists.[32] After the Act of 5 November 1916 establishing a nominally independent Polish state, the Germans accepted the idea that the Jewish problem was an internal Polish matter.

[27] Typical of this position was Perlmutter's statement 'By following the law issuing from the lips of the authorities in power we are also following God's commandments': *SSSU*, 8 Mar. 1919, session 12, col. 549.

[28] J. Tomaszewski, 'Niepodległa Rzeczpospolita', in id. (ed.), *Najnowsze dzieje Żydów w Polsce w zarysie (do 1950 roku)* (Warsaw, 1993), 150.

[29] 'Żydzi w Królestwie Polskim', *Wiadomości*, 1917, no. 152, in *Żydowska mozaika polityczna w Polsce, 1917–1927: Wybór dokumentów*, ed. C. Brzoza (Kraków, 2002), 23.

[30] One of the Zionist leaders, Apolinary Hartglas, wrote: 'I have suffered all my life from a split personality since there is no power able to fuse these two separate souls. As a Jew, I was unable to forget the injustices suffered by my people in Poland (I had not personally experienced them), while as someone who had assimilated with the Poles I had to share a great many resentments towards Jews of the kind that even the very best Poles harbour. And this spiritual dichotomy has tormented me throughout my life and poisoned the best parts of my life': A. Hartglas, *Na pograniczu dwóch światów*, ed. J. Żyndul (Warsaw, 1996), 19. [31] M. Stecka, *Żydzi w Polsce* (Warsaw, 1921), 79.

[32] P. Wróbel, 'Wielka roszada: Syjoniści warszawscy pomiędzy Niemcami a Rosją w czasie pierwszej wojny światowej', in E. Bergman and O. Zienkiewicz (eds.), *Żydzi Warszawy: Materiały konferencji w 100. rocznicę urodzin Emanuela Ringelbluma* (Warsaw, 2000), 166–8. This issue is also discussed by M. Silber, 'The Development of a Joint Program for the Jews of Poland during World War I: Success and Failure', unpublished MS.

The change of occupying power brought the Jews hope for an improvement in their position. Moreover, they found it easier to communicate with the Germans than did the Poles, if only because of the closeness of Yiddish to German. However, the Polish parties perceived these contacts as an attempt by the Jews to obtain a privileged position.[33] Contact with the Germans also had a negative side. Towards the end of June 1916, the Germans themselves acknowledged that the Jews' economic position had deteriorated.[34]

The attitude of Polish political parties and society towards the Jews became a significant factor. The problem was complicated by the fact that, as Samuel Hirszhorn wrote in April 1915, 'In the case of the Jews, Polish political thought is in a state of total indecision, deals in hazy concepts, and if it does manage to come out with a definite statement, it is only ever in a negative sense.'[35] The war did not change attitudes towards the Jews and relations even took a turn for the worse.[36]

Jews of the Congress Kingdom demonstrated their attitude towards independence in 1916 during the first legal celebration of the holiday of 3 May, in which a great many of them took part. Jewish local communities presented declarations in support of Polish strivings for independence, and Jews joined parades. However, in some towns they were refused permission to do so.[37] At the same time, the Jewish press stressed manifestations of Polish–Jewish co-operation.

A great deal has been written about the participation of Jews in the legions established by Józef Piłsudski. We have no complete list of Jewish legionaries, but estimates vary from 4 to 10 per cent of the total number. As many as 15 per cent of the casualties were Jewish.[38] The largest percentage was in the First Brigade. Many of them were awarded the Cross of Valour and the Virtuti Militari. As Konrad Zieliński emphasizes, a higher percentage of young Jews than young peasants served.[39] In any event, by 1938 the Association of Jewish Fighters for Polish Independence (Związek Żydów Uczestników Walk o Niepodległość Polski) had about 6,750 members.

[33] Many years later, the National Democratic activist Tadeusz Świecki wrote: 'The attitude towards the Jews, everywhere hostile and ill-disposed, is exacerbated by the fact that under the present administration the Jews, as German-speakers, are able to take advantage of all sorts of concessions at the expense of the peasants': T. Świecki and F. Wybult, *Mazowsze płockie w czasach wojny światowej i powstania Państwa Polskiego* (Toruń, 1932), 208.   [34] Stecka, *Żydzi w Polsce*, 73, 75.

[35] S. Hirszhorn, 'Dzieje Żydów w Królestwie Polskim od 1864 do 1918 r.', in I. Schiper, A. Tartakower, and A. Hafftka (eds.), *Żydzi w Polsce Odrodzonej: Działalność społeczna, gospodarcza, oświatowa i kulturalna*, 2 vols. (Warsaw, 1932–3) i. 488.

[36] Piotr Wróbel quotes a letter from a Zionist leader in the former Russian partition, Yehoshua Heshel Farbstein, who complained in November 1916 that with every passing day the Jews were losing hope that it would be possible for them to settle relations with the Poles: Wróbel, 'Wielka roszada', 183. Wróbel does not indicate the basis for Farbstein's impressions.

[37] Zieliński, *Stosunki polsko-żydowskie*, 293–4.

[38] M. Fuks, 'Żydzi w zaraniu niepodległości Polski', *Biuletyn Żydowskiego Instytutu Historycznego*, 150 (1989), 37; id., *Żydzi w Warszawie: Życie codzienne, wydarzenia, ludzie* (Poznań, 1992), 269; J. Tomaszewski, *Rzeczpospolita wielu narodów* (Warsaw, 1985), 144.

[39] Zieliński, *Stosunki polsko-żydowskie*, 303.

An attempt to form a united bloc of Jewish parties prior to elections to the Warsaw city council met with mixed success. At the council's first meeting on 24 July 1916, the majority of the Jewish parties declared loyalty to and solidarity with the Poles. The Zionists made the following statement: 'The Zionist Organization in Warsaw associates itself with the demand for an Independent Poland, expressed in the declarations of the city councillors of the capital city Warsaw, as being also our absolute demand, and expresses an unshakeable conviction that a Free Polish Nation will guarantee Jews their just civil and national rights.'[40] Zionists were aware that a disharmony might develop between their striving for a Jewish state in Palestine and their loyalty to their country of residence. In answer to this kind of criticism, they would invoke the above resolution—that they wished to unite with the Polish nation 'on the basis of joint work for the good of the country and in defence of its interests'. However, in a proclamation published in both Polish and Yiddish, the Folkists wrote that 'the Jewish Committee expresses its solidarity with the Polish people in their struggle for Polish freedom and independence, and recognizes the Polish character of the country, but at the same time demands for Jews the rights of a national minority'.[41] However, the leader of the Folkists, Noah Prylucki, claimed from the start that only a peace conference could guarantee Jewish rights in Poland. Rabbi Dr Samuel Poznański preached a sermon in the synagogue similar in spirit to the Zionists' and Folkists' declarations.[42] Gabriela Zalewska's research suggests that 'as the German administrative machinery weakened, so too did the Polish side's tendency to compromise'. With the character of the future Polish state still an open question, and antisemitic propaganda on the rise, the Jewish side inclined increasingly towards caution.[43]

For Jews, it was not a question of Poland's independence, but of what sort of Poland it would be and how it would deal with Jewish issues. These concerns were expressed in the declarations of all the Jewish political parties in January 1917.

---

[40] *Organizacja Sjonistyczna w Królestwie Polskim w sprawie politycznego i narodowego uprawnienia Żydów* (Warsaw, 1918), 9–10.

[41] 'Zu di yidishe veler / Do wyborców żydowskich', *Varshever togblat*, 2 July 1916, quoted by M. Silber, 'Le'umiyut shonah, ezrahut shavah: hama'amats lehasagat otonomyah liyehudei polin bemilḥemet ha'olam harishonah', doctoral thesis (Tel Aviv Univ., 2001), 149. On behalf of the Folkists, Samuel Hirszhorn, underscoring the nation's Polish character, demanded an equal tax burden, a proportionate number of places in all institutions, freedom for Jewish schooling, and Saturdays off: K. I. Weiser, 'The Politics of Yiddish: Noyekh Prilucki and the Folkspartey in Poland, 1900–1926', Ph.D. thesis (Columbia Univ., 2001), 233.

[42] 'The hour of salvation approaches in which Polish freedom will be built, when the prophecy will be fulfilled and throughout our land there will be trust. A quotation from the Bible? In a free Poland there will no longer be those who have rights and those who have been deprived of them, first- and second-class citizens, for all will be equal, for justice and honesty, truth and peace are the bases on which the well-being and success of our Country will rest': 'Petiḥat mo'etset ha'ir', *Hatsefirah*, 26 July 1916.

[43] G. Zalewska, 'Społeczeństwo żydowskie Warszawy wobec kwestii niepodległości Polski', in M. M. Drozdowski and H. Szwankowska (eds.), *Warszawa w pierwszych latach Niepodległości* (Warsaw, 1998), 95.

The beginning of the functioning of the Provisional Council of State (Tymczasowa Rada Stanu) was the occasion for a renewed expression of a positive attitude towards the reconstruction of the Polish state. It should be noted that Jews were represented on the council by only one assimilationist.[44] Isaac Lewin has written that 'in this friendly atmosphere, where full understanding between Poles and Jews seemed possible, the newly formed Polish quasi-government began its work'.[45] This view, however, does not stand up to a confrontation with the facts.[46] Despite this, the Zionists and Folkists underscored their loyalty to Polish aims by taking part in demonstrations against the proposed detaching of the Chełm region from the German-created Kingdom of Poland under the terms of the Brest treaty between Russia and the Central Powers and the allocation of it to the newly established Ukrainian state.[47] Polish public opinion reacted to this stance with satisfaction in the Kingdom, but in Galicia the response was negative.[48] In many towns here anti-Jewish riots broke out.[49] This demonstrated the Jews' difficult position. Their every step upset someone. Furthermore, despite most Jews' expressions of Polish patriotism and their loyal stance, the confusion surrounding the treaty of Brest-Litovsk also had a negative effect on Polish–Jewish relations in the Kingdom. After the treaty, patriotic feelings increased, but so did xenophobia, while doubt was expressed as to the Jews' good will and as to the need to co-operate with them. News from Bolshevik Russia and the Jews' participation in the revolution there exacerbated these negative attitudes.[50]

Antisemitic statements in the press were also noted and there was conflict on certain town councils. However, Jews were hit hardest by the economic boycott, whose growth was seen most strongly in the Austrian zone of occupation,[51] although it was applied in the German zone too. Resolutions were even passed demanding the expulsion of Jews from specific localities. Jews were accused of all manner of abuses. They in turn accused various Polish institutions of discrimina-

[44]   P. Wróbel, 'Przed odzyskaniem niepodległości', in Tomaszewski (ed.), *Najnowsze dzieje Żydów w Polsce*, 133–5.

[45]   I. Lewin, 'The Political History of Polish Jewry', in I. Lewin and N. M. Gelber, *A History of Polish Jewry during the Revival of Poland* (New York, 1990), 15.

[46]   At the end of December 1917, the assimilated Jews met with representatives of the Polish government, including Stanisław Bukowiecki and Józef Mikułowski-Pomorski. They emphasized the need to repeal anti-Jewish laws and stated that discussions on equal rights would not be enough. In reply, the government representatives asked for support for emigration and even enquired about the possibility of the assimilationists emigrating to Palestine: 'A poylishe yidishe beratung vegn der yidn frage', *Haynt*, 31 Dec. 1917, and 'Tsu di poylishe yidishe beratung vegn der yidn frage', *Moment*, 31 Dec. 1917, both quoted by Silber, 'Le'umiyut shonah, ezraḥut shavah', 300.

[47]   'Polish Jews, when faced with the decisions of the Brest treaty, nearly always sided with the Poles': Zieliński, *Stosunki polsko-żydowskie*, 360.

[48]   Wróbel, 'Przed odzyskaniem niepodległości', 136.

[49]   F. Golczewski, *Polnisch-jüdische Beziehungen, 1881–1922: Eine Studie zur Geschichte des Antisemitismus in Osteuropa* (Wiesbaden, 1981), 170–1.

[50]   Zieliński, *Stosunki polsko-żydowskie*, 361.   [51]   Stecka, *Żydzi w Polsce*, 94–6.

tion against Jews.[52] They complained that assistance provided by the citizens' committees (*komitety obywatelskie*) was being unfairly distributed, which, given the widespread hunger, was especially painful.[53] A statement made in April 1916 by the head of the Warsaw Citizens' Guard that 'the Jews continue to display an exceptionally hostile attitude towards the Polish community and its public organs' is evidence of Polish sentiment.[54] He issued this statement after receiving a number of complaints about the ill-disciplined behaviour of the guard under his command in their dealings with Jews. There were similar complaints in Łódź.[55] The issue of concessions for restaurants, mills, and other economic enterprises also gave rise to a sense of grievance on both sides. A general deterioration in Polish–Jewish relations was observed.

Out of the 110 members on the Council of State (Rada Stanu), eight represented the Jews. Among them were representatives of all the main political currents, with a preponderance of assimilationists (three members) and Orthodox (two members). The Zionists entertained strong doubts about the Council of State, but were also critical of the Folkists, who were popular in Warsaw. Apart from the assimilationists, only the Orthodox unreservedly supported the Council of State, treating it as a branch of the Polish administration. However, even the Orthodox were disappointed when the prime minister, Jan Steczkowski, spoke in a policy statement of not regulating religious matters until they took over the reins of government from the occupying power.[56] Concern was expressed over the treatment of the Jews as only a religious group, and demands were made for equality. Educational changes that failed to take into account specifically Jewish factors also aroused some concerns. The method of awarding subsidies adopted by the Central Welfare Council (Rada Główna Opiekuńcza) created dissatisfaction. In February 1918 the council distributed aid to 102 private educational and charitable organizations in Warsaw, including fourteen Jewish ones, which meant that Jews received around 14 per cent of the total. At the time, Jews represented 40 per cent of Warsaw's inhabitants. Further, the council did not disburse the portion owed to the Jewish School Association (Żydowski Związek Szkolny).[57] Behaviour of this kind could not but arouse feelings of distrust and anxiety over the Polish authorities' policies in the future.

The lack of a clearly defined stance towards Polish statehood was a result not only of political agendas and events, but, as *Wiadomości Polskie* declared, 'it is like this first and foremost because in Polish society Jews have in the end been unable to

[52] Zieliński, *Stosunki polsko-żydowskie*, 224–7.

[53] Samuel Hirszhorn voiced the strongest accusations, writing: 'These committees were meant to bring assistance to every inhabitant of the country *without regard to religion or nationality*; in reality, however, they became agents of antisemitism': Hirszhorn, 'Dzieje Żydów w Królestwie Polskim', 489. He cites examples of discrimination by the citizens' committees and the Warsaw town hall. For instance, the Christian kitchens had to contribute 8% to the price of a lunch, whereas the Jewish ones had to contribute 44%: ibid. 497.   [54] Zieliński, *Stosunki polsko-żydowskie*, 228.

[55] Numerous examples are provided ibid. 228–9.   [56] Ibid. 323.   [57] Ibid. 329.

come up with a uniform political line'.[58] The editorial staff tried to understand the Jews' anxiety about Polish rule. In their opinion, this apprehensiveness was a consequence of equating the agitation by the anti-Jewish National Democratic press and its activists with the attitudes of the whole of Polish society. The editors concluded: 'In today's conditions no people, no nation can afford the luxury of applying hostile policies towards any sector of society.'[59] The paper illustrated this idea with the example of the Germans' ineffectual war against the Polish people. Unfortunately, this was an isolated point of view and from the outset the Polish state treated its Slav minorities with policies similar to those with which the Germans imposed Germanization. Relations with the Jews were different, but many elements of these policies dissuaded Jews from identifying completely with Polish statehood. In this same document we find an interesting opinion on positions taken by different Jewish parties towards independence. When writing of the Zionists, it held that each Zionist politician had a different point of view. Points of commonality were demands for national and, above all, citizenship rights. The position of the Folkists was described as the most intransigent, as they went much further than the Zionists, apparently demanding the transformation of Poland into a nation of nationalities. They compared their demands to those made of the partitioning powers by the Poles. Even *Haynt*, in a piece by Natan Szwalbe, levelled the accusation that 'the policies of the Folkists are very poorly presented, which has provided the Poles with an opportunity to prove that Jewish national aspirations are opposed to Polish aspirations'.[60]

During the First World War, Jews at first supported the creation of a multinational state in which they would not just be a minority amidst the Poles. They supported the creation of a strong state between Germany and Russia, or the attaching of the Congress Kingdom to the Austro-Hungarian empire by means of an Austro-Polish agreement. In the course of the war, seeing the ineffectiveness of their efforts, they changed their position and began to demand equal rights and personal autonomy in a multinational state.[61] When it became apparent that this plan too was unrealistic, they were prepared to accept a minimalist plan for cultural autonomy, or even to limit their demands to laws guaranteeing the Jewish minority protection against Polonizing trends and against limitation of their socio-economic rights.[62] The Polish side in turn accused above all the Folkists of seeking a solution to the Jewish issue in Poland on the international stage. The accusation was not without foundation. The Zionists and the Folkists, faced with a swelling tide of antisemitism and wishing to protect the Jewish population, recognized that only

---

[58] 'Żydzi w Królestwie Polskim', in *Żydowska mozaika polityczna w Polsce*, ed. Brzoza, 24.

[59] Ibid. 25.

[60] N. Szwalbe, 'Di poylishe parteyen un zeyer batsiyung tsu di natsyonale minderhaytn', *Haynt*, 9 Nov. 1917.

[61] On autonomy, see J. Żyndul, *Państwo w państwie? Autonomia narodowo-kulturalna w Europie Środkowowschodniej w XX wieku* (Warsaw, 2000).   [62] Silber, 'Le'umiyut shonah, ezraḥut shavah', 334.

pressure on the part of the Entente powers could guarantee them national and civil rights.[63] Following this line, they took advantage of the peace talks to raise the Jewish issue. This will be discussed later.

Poland was reborn as a nation state and to the very end opposed being regarded as a multi-ethnic one.[64] The question arose whether ethnic minorities had patriotic obligations towards a state which was limiting their rights: do a people's interests take precedence over the state's? In that case, would those who belonged to a minority display a greater loyalty to their own people, as the National Democrats maintained? For the Jews, these questions were more vital than for the Slav minorities, given the Endecja contention that Jews were only guests in Poland and not equal stakeholders.

During the period when the independent Polish state was being established the Zionists had the greatest influence among the Jewish political parties. On 21 and 22 October 1918, a conference of the party activists of the Zionist Organization (Organizacja Syjonistyczna) was held in Warsaw at which, in addition to resolutions on Palestine, a resolution was adopted on national politics in Poland. The participants, 'as Zionists and citizens', warmly welcomed the unification of Polish territory and the creation of an independent state. They expressed regret that Jews 'even now have not been drawn into the task of rebuilding the country', though they were as interested in it as any other citizen. They also expressed the hope that Poland would be built on democratic principles and unrestricted political and civil freedom, and that the Jewish people would be granted their appropriate rights.[65] For many of them, the establishment of Jewish national autonomy in Ukraine and Lithuania provided examples of how they should be treated.[66] In Ukraine, as early as 9 January 1918 the Central Council passed resolutions not only granting equal rights to all citizens, but also national and personal autonomy for all minorities. The same was true of Lithuania and the other Baltic states.

The real struggle to implement these demands began after the end of the First

[63] A. V. Prusin, 'War and Nationality Conflict in Eastern Galicia, 1914–1920: The Evolution of Modern Antisemitism', Ph.D. thesis (Univ. of Toronto, 2001), 179.

[64] As Przemysław Różański rightly points out, 'Poland's recently regained independence was not conducive to a stabilization or moderation of attitudes': P. Różański, *Stany Zjednoczone wobec kwestii żydowskiej w Polsce, 1918–1921* (Gdańsk, 2007), 65.

[65] Organizacja Syjonistyczna w Królestwie Polskim, Biuro Prasowe, Komunikat 25, Warsaw, 25 Oct. 1918: Archiwum Akt Nowych, Warsaw (hereafter AAN), PRM, cz. II, t. 35, fos. 14–15.

[66] On Jewish autonomy in Lithuania and Ukraine, see S. Gringauz, 'Jewish National Autonomy in Lithuania (1918–1925)', *Jewish Social Studies*, 14/3 (1952), 225–46; Š. Liekis, *A State within a State? Jewish Autonomy in Lithuania, 1918–1925* (Vilnius, 2003); S. I. Goldelman, *Jewish National Autonomy in Ukraine, 1917–1920*, trans. M. Luchkovich (Chicago, 1968); J. Frankel, 'The Dilemmas of Jewish National Autonomism: The Case of Ukraine, 1917–1920', in P. J. Potichnyj and H. Aster (eds.), *Ukrainian–Jewish Relations in Historical Perspective* (Edmonton, 1988), 247–80; N. M. Gelber, 'The National Autonomy of Eastern Galician Jewry in the West Ukrainian Republic, 1918–1919', in Lewin and Gelber, *History of Polish Jewry during the Revival of Poland*, 223. For the Folkists, autonomy in Ukraine became a model solution of the Jewish issue: Weiser, 'Politics of Yiddish', 262.

World War. It was then that a group of countries became established within whose borders lived a great many minorities, including Jews. The victorious powers were to decide on these countries' status and borders at a peace conference. Accordingly, the Zionists began a campaign to be granted the right to represent the Jewish diaspora; they demanded too that the conference guarantee the rights of minorities by signing special treaties with the new states. These would grant the minorities autonomy and should cover issues of religion, culture, education, schooling, and welfare, as well as the organization of economic life.[67] A resolution passed at the 4th Polish Zionist Conference, held on 18–22 August 1919, stated that 'the most urgent and most important objective of Zionist policy is the immediate implementation of civil and legal equality, as well as the granting of national rights, as recognized by a treaty between the Entente and Poland'.[68]

The independent Polish state was created as a democratic one. Its structure was, from a legal point of view, one of the most democratic in Europe. Regaining Polish independence was the fulfilment of a dream. However, Roman Wapiński has questioned whether the euphoria occasioned by Poland's recovery of independence was widespread. The majority, in his opinion, were preoccupied with the problems of daily life.[69] The minorities, not surprisingly, took a different view. From the moment that an independent Polish state was established, Ukrainians took up arms to create their own state. There were also nationalist tendencies among the Belarusians. The Jews, even before the restoration of independence, were demanding national and civil rights.[70]

For Jews, not much had changed. As early as 1917, in an anonymous pamphlet produced by the National Democrats, the possibility of anti-Jewish incidents was predicted,[71] and such incidents were not long in coming. The country's birth was accompanied by a wave of anti-Jewish violence. The 11th of November 1918 was a day of celebration for the Poles, and it was on this day that the first pogrom took place in Kielce. A wave of anti-Jewish disturbances rippled through the country, sometimes mutating into pogroms.[72] Such activities peaked in autumn 1918, but

---

[67] 'Rada partyjna syjonistów galicyjskich', *Nowy Dziennik*, 25 Aug. 1918.

[68] *Materiały w sprawie żydowskiej w Polsce*, ii: *Żydzi jako mniejszość narodowa*, pt. 1 (Warsaw, 1919), 99.

[69] R. Wapiński, 'Postawy i oczekiwania: Kilka uwag o zachowaniach społeczeństwa polskiego w pierwszych miesiącach niepodległości (listopad 1918–styczeń 1919)', *Kwartalnik Historyczny*, 1989, no. 3, pp. 9, 11. Likewise, Aleksander Hertz wrote that the overwhelming majority of native Poles had no sense that the new country was their own, and they did not identify with it: A. Hertz, *Żydzi w kulturze polskiej* (Paris, 1961), 194.

[70] S. Netzer, *Ma'avak yehudei polin al zekhuyoteihem ha'ezraḥiyot vehale'umiyot, 1918–1922* (Tel Aviv, 1980), 217.

[71] 'The Jewish question has become highly combustible amongst us so that flammable materials are being stockpiled, and these materials could lead to an explosion at the first opportunity, and since the war has made people harder, wilder, and more vindictive, this explosion could assume unexpected dimensions': *Żydzi podczas wojny* (n.p., n.d.), 12.

[72] This phenomenon has been observed by a number of scholars. Eugeniusz Koko's words are

continued throughout the first months of independence.[73] It is difficult to say how many Jews lost their lives.[74] We know even less about the numbers injured and material losses. Jewish protests were treated as part of an anti-Polish campaign.[75] These disturbances were not just the work of the mob. Often their instigators and participants were soldiers and policemen and the disturbances took place against a backdrop of the local authorities' passivity and a failure to react on the part of the central government. In Galicia, Jews were removed from government offices and from employment on the railways. Soon they began to be dismissed from the army. The Yiddish language was banned at rallies and meetings, as was its display on signs and announcements, as well as in inter-city telephone conversations.[76]

According to Zieliński, some Jews greeted the emergence of an independent Poland with hope. There certainly were such people. However, a more accurate view may be Aleksander Hertz's statement that there was nothing odd in the fact that the bulk of the Jews 'saw the fact of a Polish rebirth as something unexpected, somewhat incomprehensible, which they greeted suspiciously and doubtfully'.[77]

typical: 'From the moment of the Polish state's rebirth there was a sudden rise in tension between Poles and Jews, as seen in the numerous excesses and pogroms perpetrated on the Jewish population': E. Koko, *W nadziei na zgodę: Polski ruch socjalistyczny wobec kwestii narodowościowej w Polsce, 1918–1939* (Gdańsk, 1995), 45. The fact that pogroms were taking place in Poland was frequently denied. Ignacy Daszyński, for instance, stated that there were no pogroms, only anti-Jewish demonstrations: *SSSU*, 12 June 1919, session 48, col. 63.

[73] 'When the Poles saw their dream of independence close to coming true they lived as if in a state of collective nervous tension. One of the expressions of this tension was antisemitism': Lewin, 'Political History of Polish Jewry', 49. Konrad Zieliński writes of the demoralization of part of Polish society and its sense of impunity when attacking or robbing Jews: K. Zieliński, 'Od bojkotu do pogromu: O zajściach antysemickich w Królestwie Polskim jesienią 1918 r.', in K. Pilarczyk (ed.), *Żydzi i judaizm we współczesnych badaniach polskich*, iv (Kraków, 2008), 223.

[74] In his report published in October 1919 Henry Morgenthau, head of an American commission to investigate the situation of the Jews in Poland, estimated that there had been at least 280 victims. Norman Davies states that between 1918 and 1920 about 400 people died, as well as an unspecified number during the Polish–Bolshevik war: N. Davies, 'Great Britain and Polish Jews, 1918–20', *Journal of Contemporary History*, 8 (1973), 139.

[75] G. Radomski, *Narodowa Demokracja wobec problematyki mniejszości narodowych w Drugiej Rzeczypospolitej w latach 1918–1926* (Toruń, 2002), 43. The PPS, criticizing the anti-Jewish incidents and pogroms, simultaneously tried to play down their scale, 'especially in view of the great notoriety of these events in the international arena': Koko, *W nadziei na zgodę*, 45. Jędrzej Moraczewski, who served as prime minister during the first months of independence, tried to minimize the significance of the pogroms, attributing them to lawlessness and hasty demobilization: E.K. [J. Moraczewski], *Rządy ludowe: Szkic wypadków czasów wyzwolenia Polski do 16 stycznia 1919 roku* (Kraków, 1919), 16.

[76] For more detailed information, see S. Rudnicki, *Żydzi w parlamencie II Rzeczypospolitej* (Warsaw, 2004), chapter 'Sejm Ustawodawczy'.

[77] K. Zieliński, 'Żydzi polscy a niepodległość: Nadzieje i obawy', *Res Historica*, 22 (2006), 197; Hertz, *Żydzi w kulturze polskiej*, 194. Cf. Hertz's somewhat different later formulation: 'Without doubt there was no enthusiasm among the bulk of the Jews for a new Poland. There was a great deal of suspicion; there were fears. This fuelled antisemitism. Antisemitism in turn fuelled distrust on the part of the Jews': A. Hertz, *Wyznania starego człowieka* (1979; Warsaw, 1991), 163.

Those Jews in the Kingdom of Poland and western Galicia who were involved in politics acknowledged themselves at the outset as citizens of the new country. From the first sessions of the Legislative Sejm (Sejm Ustawodawczy) and throughout the twenty years of Polish independence, Jewish members of parliament declared their loyalty to the Polish state and concluded their parliamentary activity in September 1939 with just such a declaration of loyalty. If the issue of independence did not arouse doubts in the Jewish community, it was prepared to fight over the structure of the state.

Jews realized that they could become citizens with equal rights only in a democratic Poland. Thus, from the outset all Jewish political parties supported Piłsudski. As early as 12 November 1918, in the first declaration presented in the name of the Zionist Organization during an audience with Piłsudski, Yitshak Grünbaum stated: 'The whole of Poland sees in you, our Commander, a man who has been called to form a government. Likewise, we come with complete confidence to you with our demands.'[78] Representatives of the Orthodox and the Folkists who were present at the audience made similar declarations. Piłsudski, like the socialists, believed at the time in complete equality and in the need to assure full civil rights for ethnic minorities. Therefore, during the entire twenty years of independence, Jews found it easier to talk to the left, and thus, despite their traditional support for democracy (for only in that system could they achieve equality), were prepared to support Piłsudski's coup.

The alternative to government by Piłsudski was government by the National Democrats. Roman Dmowski, the unquestioned leader of the national camp, never made any secret of the fact that he was not a believer in liberalism or civil rights for minorities.[79] National Democratic propaganda monopolized discussion on what represented national values. It promoted the primacy of the nation in relation to the state, upheld the principle of national egoism, and assumed the inevitability of racial conflict.[80] Its slogan was 'Poland for the Poles'—hence its desire to assimilate Slav minorities and, when it came to the Jews, its policy of antisemitism. As early as 1895 Dmowski had written that 'The Jewish people are undeniably a social parasite in the countries where they reside.'[81] Another of the movement's leaders, Joachim Bartoszewicz, defined its attitude towards Jews as 'the natural reaction of a healthy

---

[78] I. Grünbaum (ed.), *Materiały w sprawie żydowskiej w Polsce*, i (Warsaw, 1919), 13.

[79] R. Dmowski, *Polityka polska i odbudowanie państwa* (Warsaw, 1925), 139.

[80] 'A nation, as a living organism, has the moral right to expand not only at the expense of passive, mindless, and socially formless nations, but even at the expense of other nations too, just so long as this expansion is natural and not based on brute force, coercion, or special laws': Z. Balicki, *Egoizm narodowy wobec etyki* (Lwów, 1902), 53.

[81] R. Skrzycki [R. Dmowski], 'Wymowne cyfry', *Przegląd Wszechpolski*, 15 May 1895, quoted by B. Porter-Szűcs, *Gdy nacjonalizm zaczął nienawidzieć: Wyobrażenia nowoczesnej polityki w dziewiętnastowiecznej Polsce*, trans. A. Nowakowska (Sejny, 2011), 10. The well-known poet and journalist linked to the nationalist camp, Zdzisław Dębicki, wrote in 1917: 'The fatal day when the first Jew stood on Polish soil is disappearing into the mists of time': Z. Dębicki, *Miasteczko* (Warsaw, n.d.), 51.

society, concerned for its development, against the destructive influences of an ever more tyrannical Jewry'.[82] The nationalist politician Stanisław Kozicki claimed that 'compromise between the aims of Jews and Poles was completely impossible'.[83] In consequence they aspired to isolate and then to remove the Jews from the country.

In the anonymous Endek pamphlet of 1917 previously mentioned, all the current grievances against the Jews were lumped together. The pamphlet began by claiming that the Germans had left the Poles at the mercy of the Jews, whom they had placed in every government office. This, it asserted, was due to the fact that all the banks and universities and the press, in both Berlin and Vienna, were in Jewish hands. The Galician authorities 'are powerless in the face of the Jewish deluge'. Piłsudski's legions were 'thoroughly permeated with Jewish influence' and they had entered Warsaw hand in hand with the Jews.[84] Morality had deteriorated.[85] Jews talked of equal rights, but failed to mention the need to raise the moral tone. The condition of Polish society had deteriorated.[86] 'In the struggle with the Jews, the Polish priest is perhaps the last activist who has not lost heart and has not let the opportunity slip away.'[87]

Calls for an economic and social boycott of the Jews increased. As early as the first months of Polish independence, there were instances when people were expelled from the Landowners' League (Związek Ziemian) for selling Jews not just land but also produce. On a number of occasions the central government, including the military, released information on widespread antisemitism that had sometimes turned into pogroms.[88] The authorities issued a number of circulars and directives aimed at preventing excesses, but this did not prevent anti-Jewish propaganda, while intervention in specific cases was rarely effective. Zieliński ends his book on Polish–Jewish relations during the First World War with the statement that 'there was a definite deterioration in Polish–Jewish relations, and this in large cities as well

---

[82] J. Bartoszewicz, *Podręczny słownik polityczny do użytku posłów, urzędników państwowych, członków ciał samorządowych i wyborców* (Warsaw, 1922), 31, quoted by M. Białokur, *Myśl społeczno-polityczna Joachima Bartoszewicza* (Toruń, 2005), 250; the image of the Jews in National Democratic propaganda 'also contained the message that Jewish anti-Polish behaviour was immutable'. Juliusz Zdanowski, too, wrote that 'As far as the mass of our people is concerned, antisemitism has been and still is the simplest formulation of nationalism, and even the watchword of the Catholic movement': J. Zdanowski, 'Diariusz', quoted by E. Maj, *Związek Ludowo-Narodowy, 1919–1928: Studium z dziejów myśli politycznej* (Lublin, 2000), 242.   [83] S. Kozicki, *Pamiętnik, 1876–1939*, ed. M. Mroczko (Słupsk, 2009), 429.

[84] *Żydzi podczas wojny*, 9.

[85] 'That ordinary Jew walking the Warsaw streets, his mind on business, has the face of a criminal': ibid. 27.

[86] 'Work on revitalizing the country has become paralysed; Polish solidarity organized in opposition to Jewish solidarity has been destroyed. The motto of buying from one's own has been forgotten': ibid. 13.   [87] Ibid. 30.

[88] *O Niepodległą i granice*, ii: *Raporty i komunikaty naczelnych władz wojskowych o sytuacji wewnętrznej Polski, 1919–1920*, ed. M. Jabłonowski, P. Stawecki, and T. Wawrzyński (Warsaw, 2000), 43, 52, 88, 108, 114, 117–18, 121, 138, 143.

as in rural and small-town settings, which hitherto had been relatively free of antisemitism and chauvinism'.[89]

For Jews, the most pressing issue was the structure of the state and the constitution. They hoped for the abolition of the legal restrictions inherited from the period of partition and for a legal guarantee of equal civil rights, as well as the rescinding of some of the anti-Jewish restrictions enacted by the Legislative Sejm and given effect in the workings of the state administration. The nature of the state was being decided by armed conflict, plebiscites, and the resolutions of the Great Powers.

The issue of the Minority Treaty of Versailles, the so called 'Little Treaty'—one of the most important international initiatives of these years—aroused and still arouses a great deal of controversy. Even during the war it was already being claimed, above all in the Zionist community, that, since it would be impossible to rely on the Poles to implement Jewish demands, the Jewish issue had to be internationalized. The Poles reacted by warning that demanding cultural and national autonomy and referring the matter to foreign governments would exacerbate Polish–Jewish relations. The demands which the Jews would make at the peace conference were anticipated in a note of 10 October 1918 drafted by Lucien Wolf on behalf of the Joint Foreign Committee, a body composed of representatives of American, British, and French Jewish organizations, which demanded equality for Jews and autonomy in the areas of religion and education.[90]

Representatives of Polish Jews who had come to Paris summed up their claims in a memorandum presented to the Polish Peace Delegation. They demanded, amongst other things, a constitutional guarantee of full equality, a guarantee of a share of the seats in the Sejm and in local government proportionate to the percentage of Jews in the population of Poland, democratically elected Jewish organizations of self-government which would deal with Jewish national issues as well as religious matters, and the creation of a Supreme Jewish Council as the highest representative body of the Jewish community in Poland. A memorandum presented to delegates to the peace conference took a similar line, though it laid out the issue of citizenship in greater detail.[91] Representatives of the Polish Zionists took an active part in the deliberations of the Versailles conference as affiliates of the Committee of Jewish Delegates to the Peace Conference, of which Leon Reich became deputy chairman. Reporting to Yitshak Grünbaum about meetings held with the Polish delegation, Leon Lewite noted that it was not taking 'an intran-

---

[89] Zieliński, *Stosunki polsko-żydowskie*, 427.   [90] Ibid. 390.

[91] 'Memoriał wręczony w Paryżu przez Delegatów Żydowskich Rad Narodowych w Polsce Polskiej Delegacji Pokojowej', in *Materiały w sprawie żydowskiej w Polsce*, ii/1. 23–8, also in T. Koźmiński, *Sprawa mniejszości na podstawie traktatu między głównemi mocarstwami sprzymierzonemi i stowarzyszonemi a Polską, podpisanego w Wersalu 28-go czerwca 1919 roku* (Warsaw, 1922), 149–56; 'Memoriał Komitetu Delegacji Żydowskich przy Konferencji Pokojowej, wręczony Ich Ekscelencjom Panu Przewodniczącemu i Panom członkom Konferencji Pokojowej', in *Materiały w sprawie żydowskiej w Polsce*, ii/1. 38–42.

sigent stance towards our national demands'; however, both Władysław Grabski, the chairman of these discussions, and Stanisław Kozicki emphasized that neither the Sejm nor the population 'is for it', i.e. in favour of the Jewish demands. Lewite remained optimistic up to the beginning of May 1919; Kozicki, however, suspected the Jews of undermining a strong and independent Poland.[92]

Many myths have arisen about both the Polish and the Jewish positions. In Poland, the role of Dmowski and his efforts to obtain favourable frontiers for Poland is remembered. On the other hand, he and his whole party accused the Jews of anti-Polish activity, supposedly in favour of the Germans and sometimes the Bolsheviks. Dmowski himself wrote of Lloyd George's adviser, Lewis Namier (whom he called 'a Galician Jew-boy'), as being the instigator of this activity.[93] However, in my view, neither understanding is correct. The Polish National Committee (Komitet Narodowy Polski) under Dmowski's leadership did indeed carry out a fine job in making the Allies aware of the newly forming state's problems and the border issues. However, we know that even his finest speech could not alter Britain's basic aims. Dmowski himself, who did not enjoy popularity in Britain, contributed to this failure.[94] Yet when it came to borders, the Jews were uninterested in Poland's western border, which was the subject of discussion in Paris. Therefore, the Polish failure in Paris was not the result of the Jewish lobby's activities.[95] In fact, it played a significant part in the adoption of the Little Treaty that protected national minorities. Besides, what interested Jewish activists was the east, where the masses of the Jews lived. However, it is true that the status of the Jewish minority was an important factor in the formation of public opinion on the new state in the international arena.[96] Poland's negative image was a result, above all, of the situation in Poland itself: news about pogroms and anti-Jewish incidents, often exaggerated, was reaching the West, primarily thanks to Jewish efforts, though the Allies also had their own sources of information.[97] Jews were

---

[92] Lewite's letters to Grünbaum of 29 Apr. 1919: Central Zionist Archives, Jerusalem, Yitzhak Gruenbaum archive, A127, t. 1058; S. Kozicki, *Sprawa granic Polski na konferencji pokojowej w Paryżu* (Warsaw, 1921), 56–7. Stanisław Głąbiński, who devoted a whole chapter of his memoirs to the subject —'Żydzi przeciw Polsce' ('The Jews Against Poland')—was in no doubt: S. Głąbiński, *Wspomnienia polityczne* (Pelplin, 1939).   [93] Dmowski, *Polityka polska i odbudowanie państwa*, 274, 383.

[94] David Kaufman's research shows that Dmowski annoyed the British establishment with his anti-semitic rhetoric: D. B. Kaufman, 'Polish–Jewish Relations during the Rebirth of Poland, November 1918–June 28, 1919', Ph.D. thesis (Univ. of Stirling, 2006), 52, 310. John Gregory, who handled Polish matters at the Foreign Office, stated that 'Dmowski . . . began doing his unconscious best to ruin the prospects of Poland at the Peace Conference, and had he continued alone in his vociferous demands for this and that we might have ended by witnessing a Fourth Partition': J. D. Gregory, *On the Edge of Diplomacy: Rambles and Reflections, 1902–1928* (London, 1928), quoted by Kaufman, 'Polish–Jewish Relations', 279.   [95] Kaufman, 'Polish–Jewish Relations', 213.   [96] Ibid. 64.

[97] Robert Lansing wrote to the US ambassador in Paris, William Sharp, on 2 December 1918, saying that 'The Department of State has received information through various sources of pogroms conducted against Jews in Poland. If these reports are true the sympathy of the American people for Polish aspirations will undoubtedly be affected': quoted by Kaufman, 'Polish–Jewish Relations', 110–11. In

accused of betraying Poland. It is true that the information on the situation in
Poland that appeared in the Western press, including the American, was often
exaggerated. On the other hand, the Poles in their statements tried to trivialize the
scale of the anti-Jewish incidents and even to deny their very existence.

The Jews' participation in the conference was criticized on the floor of the Sejm.
As early as May 1919, Ignacy Jan Paderewski claimed that 'the Jews . . . have
harmed us and are still harming us; they do not want any sort of Poland at all.'[98]
The negative attitude towards the treaty is evidenced by the fact that it was
published in *Dziennik Ustaw* (the official 'Journal of Laws') only on 6 December
1920,[99] a year and a half after its ratification by the Sejm. Only then did it become
legally binding.

Jewish public opinion was divided on the treaty. The assimilationists saw it is as
provocative; the Orthodox and the representatives of several trade organizations
were dubious as to its value. However, the majority of Jewish politicians and their
supporters were, at the moment of the adoption of the Little Treaty, convinced of
their success.[100] The treaty 'carries an olive branch of peace to the Jewish street',
wrote Leon Reich in his report from Paris to the Jewish National Council of
Eastern Galicia (Żydowska Rada Narodowa Galicji Wschodniej) on 29 June 1919.
He went on, however, to emphasize that the Jews had not achieved all their aims.[101]
As if responding to subsequent Polish charges, he declared that

in the new Poland, as a branch of the Jewish nation we want, in the manner of an ethnic
minority, to serve our own national interest and to spread our culture in accordance with the
rights granted by the treaty which Poland has signed. However, as Polish citizens, we want to
serve the aims of a free Poland and the development of the Polish nation's freedom. We
would like nothing better than that a free Poland should feel proud of its national-Jewish
population, which is conscious of its obligations as citizens and which enjoys the protection,
not of the League of Nations, but of the Polish state.

At the same time, he emphasized that 'it is essential that the government and the
people keep alive this faith by their behaviour towards us and by their actions'.[102]

Judging by articles that appeared in the press, people were under the illusion—or
readers were deceived into thinking—that this treaty would change the situation of

turn, Norman Davies claims that information on the situation in Poland was reaching the Foreign
Office from overseas Jewish press agencies and innumerable Jewish organizations in Britain: Davies,
'Great Britain and Polish Jews', 126. However, he subsequently writes of reports from the British
embassy in Poland and reports of special commissions dispatched to Poland: ibid. 129–30.

[98] *Archiwum Polityczne Ignacego Paderewskiego*, i: *1890–1918*, ed. W. Stankiewicz and A. Piber
(Wrocław, 1973), 152.   [99] *Dziennik Ustaw*, 1920, no. 110, item 728.

[100] Rudnicki, *Żydzi w parlamencie II Rzeczypospolitej*, 64; A. Polonsky, *The Jews in Poland and
Russia*, 3 vols. (Oxford, 2010–12), iii. 30.

[101] Letters of Leon Reich: Central Archives for the History of the Jewish People, Jerusalem, Nach-
man M. Gerber collection, P83 G 308. I should like to thank Marcos Silber, who made copies of Reich's
letters available to me.   [102] Ibid.

minorities and that international solidarity would not allow them to be persecuted. One of the treaty's architects, Louis Marshall, wrote on 11 February 1919 in a letter to a colleague that the treaty gave the Jews, as it did other minorities, the chance to live their own lives and to develop their own culture.[103] However, the countries on whose territories it was meant to be enforced were ill disposed towards it, or at least had serious reservations. They felt themselves discriminated against, as the treaty applied only to selected countries and not to the whole of Europe. They feared that the League of Nations might limit their sovereignty, and that minorities could organize themselves, becoming under certain circumstances an explosive internal factor. The Little Treaty of Versailles was, in their view, yet another tool in the hands of the minorities, allowing them to defend their rights, although there was no mention in it of any demands for international guarantees on creating cultural, let alone national, autonomy.

Unlike the Germans and Ukrainians, the Jews did not take advantage of the opportunity afforded by the Minority Treaty to have recourse to the League of Nations.[104] Jewish members of parliament adopted the principle of not raising Jewish issues in the international forum, including sessions of the Inter-Parliamentary Union.[105] However, on more than one occasion they would refer to its resolutions during debates in the Sejm. Yehoshua Farbstein retorted to criticisms of this behaviour that 'it is not he who invokes the treaty who is the guilty party, but he who creates the need to do so'.[106]

In Poland, opposition was greatest to the wording of article 1 of the Minority Treaty, in which Poland undertook 'that the resolutions embodied in articles 2–8 of this chapter will be recognized as basic laws, that no act, no directive, or any governmental action will contravene or run counter to these resolutions, that no act of parliament, no directive, or any governmental action in contravention of them will have the force of law'. Articles 3–6 regulated issues of nationality, whereas articles 2 and 7–8 guaranteed life and liberty, the free practice of religion, and completely equal rights. Article 7 guaranteed, amongst other things, the freedom to use one's own language in private, economic, or public matters; article 9 guaranteed freedom of school instruction in one's own language; and article 11 guaranteed observance of the sabbath. Finally, article 12 provided an opportunity to refer matters in dispute to the League of Nations.[107] In guaranteeing equal rights, the

---

[103] Polonsky, *Jews in Poland and Russia*, iii. 54.

[104] 'It is especially noteworthy that over the eleven-year life of the minorities treaty no Jewish issue from Poland has been tabled at the Council of the League of Nations. Yet it was the Jews themselves who were its spiritual fathers and that mainly on account of Poland, where the greatest number of them live': T. Katelbach, *Niemcy współczesne wobec zagadnień narodowościowych* (Warsaw, 1932), 30–1, quoted by Żyndul, *Państwo w państwie?*, 103.

[105] 'Przedstawiciele żydowscy na kongresie Unii Międzyparlamentarnej', *Nasz Przegląd*, 12 Nov. 1924.   [106] *SSSU*, 18 Dec. 1919, session 195, col. 32.

[107] Treaty between the Principal Allied and Associated Powers and Poland, in *Współczesna Europa polityczna: Zbiór umów międzynarodowych, 1919–1939*, ed. W. W. Kulski and M. Potulicki (Warsaw, 1939), 146–50.

treaty was above all favourable to the retention of religious and, to a lesser extent, national identity. To this day, historians argue about whether minorities gained or lost by the treaty and whether guarantees of their civil rights would have been ratified without the intervention of the Great Powers.[108] The fact is that the treaty was published in the *Dziennik Ustaw* only on 26 July 1920.

The Jewish members of the Legislative Sejm were allowed to vote for the first time on 24 February 1919 at the Sejm's fifth sitting. Declarations were made by representatives of all three factions of the Free Association of Members of Parliament of Jewish Nationality (Wolne Zjednoczenie Posłów Narodowości Żydowskiej; WZPNŻ) in support of a democratic Poland that would observe the principles of citizens' equality before the law and create conditions for the development of national minorities. A representative of the most powerful faction, Yitshak Grünbaum, declared that Jews 'are equal in rights and responsibilities', that they would play a part in building a just Poland, and that 'there can be not a shadow of doubt that the Polish state's cohesion and sovereignty are for us quite simply a political axiom'. He added that 'as a national minority, we demand the right to exist; in other words autonomy'.[109] Representatives of the other factions spoke in similar terms.

During the debate on the constitution, they pointed out that the drafts did not take into account the cultural and national rights of national minorities. As the Folkist Samuel Hirszhorn put it:

The constitution should assure all national minorities, including the Jews, self-government in the areas of culture, education in one's own language, social welfare, and charitable works; in other words national and personal autonomy. This should be an association of a public and legal nature, itself a legal entity, having as its local organ an ethnic commune with the same boundaries as the political district and at the head of which stands a Supreme National Council, elected by all the association's members on the basis of a five-point electoral law and without regard to gender.[110]

Jewish members of parliament also put forward amendments aimed at guaranteeing in the constitution the right to table legislative initiatives even for those political groupings with a limited number of members of parliament, opposing the view that the Sejm's standing orders should regulate such matters. They spoke here on behalf of all national minorities. Having no confidence in the position adopted by most of the Polish parliamentary clubs, they found it preferable that an appropriate regulation be inserted into the constitution. Representatives of the Polish Socialist Party (PPS), the Polish Peasants' Party—Liberation (Polskie Stronnictwo Ludowe — Wyzwolenie; PSL-W), and the National Labour Party (Narodna Partia Robotnicza; NPR) made similar representations, in opposition to the National Populist Union (Związek Ludowo-Narodowy; ZLN), which stood for a 'people's

---

[108] Rudnicki, *Żydzi w parlamencie II Rzeczypospolitej*, 65–6.
[109] *SSSU*, 24 Feb. 1919, session 5, cols. 190–1.   [110] *SSSU*, 13 May 1919, session 37, col. 66.

initiative' aimed at giving 100,000 voters the right to be able to table a legislative initiative.[111]

On the issue of a unicameral or a bicameral parliament, the Jewish members from the outset unhesitatingly supported the PPS and the PSL-W, who advocated a unicameral Sejm. They justified their stance by asserting that a senate would serve as a brake on social reform and would reduce the role of minorities. Grünbaum referred to the words of Edward Dubanowicz, who, during a meeting of the Constitutional Committee, had supposedly said that 'we should have a senate which will filter acts of parliament which have been passed as a result of foreign elements [*tych obcych*]'.[112] In the final voting at a plenary session of the Sejm on 16 March 1920, the Jewish parliamentary club (WZPNŻ) unanimously came out in favour of striking from the draft constitution the article calling for a second chamber.

They devoted the greatest attention to the articles in the draft constitution dealing with a citizen's rights and responsibilities, and in particular the civil freedoms of national minorities, including religious freedom. The cornerstone on which they based their political vision was the principle of equality for all citizens. In the end, they were unable to insert into the constitution a guarantee of cultural and national autonomy with complete freedom for minorities to develop within a state of nationalities (*państwo narodowościowe*). Every Polish political party represented in the Legislative Sejm was opposed. The Polish state became a nation state.[113] However, the constitution did include the clause that 'every citizen has the right to retain his nationality and nurture his own language and his national characteristics' (article 109, para. 1).[114]

Leopold Halpern, discussing the Jewish members' position on the constitution, wrote: 'On this issue, as on just about every other one, the Jewish members had their own specific point of view, based on Jewish national interests, and tried to reconcile them with the overall national interest.'[115] Yet not all Jews saw things the same way. If the Orthodox were satisfied with recognition of the Jews as a religious minority, the Zionists and the Folkists fought for recognition as a national minority. Unlike the other minorities, they were unable to demand territorial autonomy, so they sought cultural autonomy. It turned out that satisfying this demand was unrealistic, given the actual balance of power in the Legislative Sejm.

It would appear that the goal which the Jewish parliamentary club had set itself was best described by the Folkist Hirszhorn, who stated that 'when drawing up a constitution one should establish principles to protect people under the worst

[111] Y. Grünbaum, in *SSSU*, 24 Sept. 1920, session 167, cols. 33–5; S. Krukowski, *Geneza konstytucji z 17 marca 1921 r.* (Warsaw, 1977), 239–40. [112] *SSSU*, 28 Sept. 1920, session 168, col. 34.

[113] W. Komarnicki, *Polskie prawo polityczne: Geneza i system* (Warsaw, 1922), 215.

[114] Komarnicki pointed out that this was the only time that the constitution used the term—in his view incorrect—*narodowy* ('national'): ibid. 116. In fact, in the same article, para. 2, the related term *narodowościowy* ('to do with nationality') is also used, as it is in article 110.

[115] L. Halpern, 'Polityka żydowska w Sejmie i Senacie Rzeczypospolitej Polskiej, 1919–1933', *Sprawy Narodowościowe*, 14 (1933), 13.

circumstances. A constitution is drawn up for the worst eventualities so that the bureaucracy or the governing reactionary majority cannot persecute minorities.'[116] This explained the position of the Jewish members, who, in addition to a great many proposals of their own that aimed to give the constitution and the state a democratic framework, supported all proposals in a similar vein, from socialist, PSL-W, and NPR members.

One of the most significant problems in the Second Republic associated with its multinational character was to specify in the constitution the range of issues to which it would apply. There was a fundamental disagreement on the meaning of the concepts of 'nation' (*naród*) and 'citizen' (*obywatel*). In some articles the phrase 'Polish citizens' (*obywatele polscy*) was used, in others 'Poles' (*Polacy*) or 'persons of Polish nationality' (*osoby narodowości polskiej*). In the law of 17 June 1919 concerning the army officers' list, yet another term was introduced: 'a citizen of Polish nationality of the Polish State' (*obywatel Państwa Polskiego narodowości polskiej*).[117] This legal and terminological inconsistency led, according to members of parliament, to the exclusion of representatives of national minorities from the scope of the law, and all the more effectively by the insistence on a declaration that one was of Polish nationality when one applied for citizenship. During the discussion on specific articles, the Jewish members demanded in place of the accepted terms the introduction of a more precise definition of citizenship of the Polish state which would include all citizens.

The Jewish members of parliament saw equality before the law on three levels. First, the lifting of all restrictions which the laws of the partitioning powers had placed on the Jewish community, taking into account the differences between the partitions, as evidenced in this matter by the much greater discrimination against Jews practised in the Russian partition, and in addition by the far-reaching variations between the Kresy and the former Congress Kingdom, on the one hand, and the Austrian partition, where the basic restriction had in essence been the prohibition of the use of the Yiddish and Hebrew languages in official institutions and public life. Second, a guarantee of equality before the law passed by the authorities in independent Poland and finally enshrined formally in the Constitution of March 1921. Third, compliance with the law in force when it was being applied.

The Treaty of Versailles regulated the issue of citizenship. In practice, the definition of who had the right to Polish citizenship turned out to be very complicated, and this issue was continually raised in parliament throughout the duration of the Second Republic.[118] For Jews, the issue of citizenship was of prime importance for two reasons. First, it was important for inhabitants of the former

---

[116] *SSSU*, 11 Mar. 1921, session 218, col. 46.

[117] *Dziennik Praw Państwa Polskiego*, 1919, no. 50, item 325.

[118] J. Tomaszewski, 'Wokół obywatelstwa Żydów polskich (1918–1939)', in *Narody: Jak powstawały i jak wybijały się na niepodległość?* (Warsaw, 1989), 504–19; Rudnicki, *Żydzi w parlamencie II Rzeczypospolitej*, 68–72.

Congress Kingdom and the Kresy, because they were often unable to prove their national affiliation, or because the Polish authorities questioned their right to citizenship, since before 1914 a great many people had not bothered to regularize their legal status. They had omitted to record new places of residence on the appropriate rolls, feeling that this was superfluous because they continued to be inhabitants of the same country and because the procedure was often lengthy and expensive. Their families, and also even children born to them within the Kingdom, were thus considered part of the so-called transient population (*ludność niestała*).[119] Second, the issue of citizenship was important for those who during the First World War had found themselves in Russia, although they had previously lived on land that came to be incorporated into Poland by the Treaty of Riga of 1921. They were frequently unable to prove their former residence on the territory now included in the new Polish state, since all the marriage registers had been carried off by the retreating Russians. Despite the widely held popular conviction that after the revolution several hundred thousand Jews came to Poland, having never previously lived on territory that fell within the Polish state in 1921, the Ministry of Foreign Affairs assessed their numbers as no more than tens of thousands.[120]

On 31 July 1919 Jewish members of parliament tabled an emergency motion on the citizenship issue, appending to it a draft of a law. It was also signed by members of the PPS and the PSL Lewica (Left-Wing PSL), and by the German members.[121] The motion's proposers justified their initiative on the grounds that the terms of the Versailles Treaty applied only to a certain category of Polish citizen. They recognized the draft constitution, for its part, as being too general, although they did admit that overall it was in accordance with the Minority Treaty. In relation to the principles proposed in the draft constitution, the motion's supporters demanded an expansion of the group of people eligible for Polish citizenship. In their view, the cut-off date for residence should be 1914 and breaks in continuous residence caused by the war should have no influence on the granting of citizenship. The motion made no mention of the condition in the proposed law on citizenship of the Polish state prepared by the Ministry of the Interior and submitted by the government to the Sejm on 30 September 1919 that a Polish citizen had to have been entered on the roll of permanent residents of the former Kingdom of Poland, or had to have had permanent residence on the territories of the other partitions.[122]

At issue was the scope of the concepts 'permanent residence' (*stałe zamieszkanie*)

---

[119] In 1909, the last year from which we have data, the transient population and foreigners living in the Kingdom represented 18.6% of the total population: W. Grabski (ed.), *Rocznik Statystyczny Królestwa Polskiego: Rok 1914* (Warsaw, 1915), 38 (table 7).

[120] 'Rzut oka na stan sprawy żydowskiej w chwili obecnej': AAN, MSZ, Departament I, Wydział Ogólny, 9391, undated TS, fo. 23.

[121] 'Wniosek nagły posłów Hartglasa, Grünbauma i innych w przedmiocie ustawy o obywatelstwie (Druk 991)', in *Materiały w sprawie żydowskiej w Polsce*, iv: *Sprawa obywatelstwa polskiego* (Warsaw, 1921), 104–7.   [122] Ibid.

and 'settlement' (*osiedlenie*) used in the Versailles Treaty.[123] The Jewish members criticized the Constitutional Committee for recognizing only the permanent residence rolls of the former Kingdom of Poland, pointing out that a great many permanent residents had not been entered on them. The disagreement in the Sejm, however, focused above all on the residents of the western provinces of the Russian empire. The authorities included all of them in the category of 'refugees' from Soviet Russia and refused them citizenship. This had serious legal consequences. The overwhelming majority of urban dwellers were not registered at all on the rolls in their places of permanent residence. No general census of residents in urban districts in the North-Western Territory of the former Russian empire was conducted. The Jewish members spoke out against making confirmation of residence dependent on having been entered onto the permanent residence rolls in the Kingdom, or onto the rolls of urban or rural districts or of state organizations on the territory of the former Russian empire.

On 20 January 1920 the Sejm began its final deliberations on the draft of the citizenship law. An argument that was essentially of a legal nature led to a decision being taken that determined the fate of a number of inhabitants—not precisely calculable—of the reborn Republic. All the Jewish members' amendments were defeated and the law was passed with the votes of the ZLN and those of the peasant parliamentary clubs and the socialist club. After the coup of May 1926, the problem of citizenship was solved by conferring it on everyone to whom it had hitherto been denied. However, the National Democrats did not cease to demand that it should be withdrawn again. At the end of the 1930s, Sanacja members made similar suggestions, amongst other anti-Jewish legislative proposals.

Of the armed conflicts, the greatest one and the one which decided not only frontiers, but also the very existence of the state, was the Polish–Bolshevik war. The Communist Workers' Party of Poland (Komunistyczna Partia Robotnicza Polski), and hence its Jewish members, came out unanimously for the Bolsheviks. Some Jews thus found themselves alongside Poles, both on the Provisional Polish Revolutionary Committee (Tymczasowy Komitet Rewolucyjny Polski) and on individual revolutionary committees. They also formed a sizeable part of the people's militia.

The participation of Jews in the communist movement is a separate, extensive subject about which a great deal has already been written. To repeat the words of Jaff Schatz, 'before the war there were many Jews among the communists, but not many communists among the Jews'.[124] A few thousand Jewish communists out of some 3 million Jews was not a great number. It is true that the communists enjoyed greater support than their numbers would suggest, but one must take into account

---

[123] Komarnicki, *Polskie prawo polityczne*, 527.

[124] J. Schatz, 'Świat mentalności świadomości komunistów polsko-żydowskich: Szkic do portretu', in G. Berendt (ed.), *Społeczność żydowska w PRL przed kampanią antysemicką lat 1967–1968 i po niej* (Warsaw, 2009), 43.

the popularity of communist slogans in general, not just among Jews. Unfortunately, no public opinion polls exist in relation to the Polish–Bolshevik war, and in this and a great many other matters conclusions are based largely on somewhat deceptive, often tendentious, sources and on intuition, and without any reference to trustworthy numerical data.

The Bund took a much more ambiguous position than the communists. For example, one of its key leaders, Henryk Erlich, gave a speech at a meeting of the Warsaw city council on 8 July 1920 as the Red Army was approaching Warsaw. He claimed that Poland's independence and freedom were not under threat, and added that the Bund was opposed to invasion of any kind.[125] However, this view was not universally held in the Bund, and a split developed over its position vis-à-vis the communists.

For the majority of the Jewish population, who were deeply religious and socially conservative, communism, with its atheism and its mission to destroy the property-holding class, was unacceptable. After the Soviet government's peace notes of January 1920, the Jewish left-wing parties and middle-class groupings favoured a policy of peace.[126] Yet when the situation changed to Poland's detriment, widespread appeals were made to help the country in its struggle against the invader.[127] Religious leaders, representatives of economic organizations, and the leaders of political parties added their voices to the call. These appeals appeared in all the Jewish newspapers.[128]

The two most influential political forces came out strongly against communism:

---

[125] Bergman, 'Bund a niepodległość Polski', 112.

[126] The Jewish population's extraterritorial status, as well as the commercial nature of Jewish activity, undoubtedly had an impact on the mood for peace amongst the overwhelming majority of Jews: N. Szwalbe, 'Żydzi wobec pokoju', *Tygodnik Żydowski*, 6 Feb. 1920, p. 1.

[127] 'Our undoubted duty, the duty of Polish Jews, is to hasten with aid for the country and the state at this critical moment, to devote all our strength and abilities, to forget all past wrongs and insults, to demonstrate a willingness to show the highest degree of sacrifice': A. Hartglas, 'W chwili istotnego niebezpieczeństwa', *Tygodnik Żydowski*, 9 July 1920, p. 5.

[128] Some representative examples of appeals from *Tygodnik Żydowski*: 'Brothers, fellow believers! The hour has come. The Polish nation has been resurrected . . . Today, fellow citizens, it is our solemn and sacred duty to display unity with the Polish nation; for its misfortunes have been our misfortunes, its suffering has been our suffering, as we have not infrequently demonstrated, acting with determination, even laying down our lives to throw off a foreign yoke' (from an appeal by the Warsaw Jewish Community [Gmina Starozakonnych] and the Warsaw Rabbinate, *Tygodnik Żydowski*, 9 July 1920); 'W imię Boże!' ('In the name of God!'), an appeal from rabbis throughout Poland (ibid.); 'Jewish citizens, the duty of each of us is to subscribe to national loans' (from an appeal by the Merchants' Head Office, ibid.); an appeal by Shelomei Emunei Yisra'el (Agudah) (ibid.); 'Jews! Poland is in danger . . . Jews! Let us not forget what we owe this country in which we live and to whose rebuilding and development we have contributed . . . Jews! Fulfil your duties as citizens! Let each bring an essential donation, in both blood and life, as well as in worldly goods. Let no one shirk defending the Polish State's freedom and independence' (from an appeal by the National Parliamentary Club of Jewish Members of Parliament, the Provisional National Jewish Council, and a number of other organizations, *Tygodnik Żydowski*, 16 July 1920).

the Orthodox and the Zionists.[129] Although some Jews evaded conscription—and in this they were no different from the peasants—there were also those who volunteered in the struggle against the Soviets. As Janusz Szczepański notes, they represented 35 per cent of the volunteers at the Rembertów students' camp.[130] He also notes other instances of patriotic behaviour by Jews, who not infrequently saved the lives of Poles, even though they themselves were subject to repressive measures.[131]

However, propaganda, and not just of the National Democratic variety, saw Jews only as Bolsheviks.[132] This is a typical attitude of all nationalisms, which regard the 'outsider' (*obcy*) not as an individual, but as a member of a group. Thus the whole Jewish community was regarded as communized.

Even before the creation of an independent state, all left-wing political parties, Polish and Jewish alike, were treated as 'nests of Bolshevism in Poland'.[133] This view became widespread during the 1920 war. Statements of this kind can be found in the pronouncements of many Polish political parties, although the National Democrats led with this type of propaganda. The Catholic hierarchy and the rank-and-file clergy contributed greatly to this stance, and therefore deserve closer consideration. The problem of the national minorities was very rarely raised at episcopal conventions and conferences.[134] Of the two episcopal letters in which the Jews are mentioned, that of 10 December 1918 specifically enjoins the faithful not to assault Jews. But the bishops go on to say that 'we know and are aware of your accusations against them and we do not deny their validity or truth . . . We do not say this to criticize you. We know that Jewish agents in the pay of the Bolsheviks are themselves sowing the storm which is turning against them.' They write further that assaults on Jews are being perpetrated by criminals released from jail, as well as by Russian prisoners of war: 'Rumours reaching us strengthen our conviction that our community has had nothing to do with these painful incidents and the

---

[129] 'Under the influence of news of the Red Army's victories the wealthiest section of the Jewish community panicked. It was terrified at the thought of revolution and civil war': J. Szczepański, *Społeczność żydowska Mazowsza w XIX–XX wieku* (Pułtusk, 2005), 236.   [130] Ibid.

[131] The bishop of Łomża, Romuald Jałbrzykowski, claimed that most of those imprisoned by the Bolsheviks were Jews: ibid. 242.

[132] I. Kamińska-Szmaj, 'Słowa wzniosłe i gniewne u progu Drugiej Rzeczypospolitej', in A. Gabryś and M. Szewczyk (eds.), *Salon niepodległości* (Warsaw, 2008), 146. 'In order to manipulate public opinion the issue of Polish–Jewish relations was especially readily employed . . . The stereotype of the communist Jew and the freemason Jew, working always against the interests of the Polish people, was widely disseminated. The picture of the Bolshevik Jew was especially fearsome': M. Śliwa, 'W "krzywym zwierciadle" Drugiej Rzeczypospolitej', in Gabryś and Szewczyk (eds.), *Salon niepodległości*, 161; the author also quotes *Gazeta Warszawska* writing about the revolution: 'the whole Jewish nation and international socialism are responsible for this crime' (p. 162). E. Maj, *Komunikowanie polityczne Narodowej Demokracji, 1918–1939* (Lublin, 2010), 52.

[133] Statement by Jan Stecki, Minister of the Interior in the government of the Regency Council, quoted by Zieliński, *Stosunki polsko-żydowskie*, 340.

[134] Father S. Wilk, *Episkopat Kościoła katolickiego w Polsce w latach 1918–1939* (Warsaw, 1992), 389.

community joins us in condemning them.'[135] The bishops' message in this letter is clear, but it raises many questions. Here are but two of them, to which the letter gives no reply. If agents are responsible, why should the Jewish community suffer for their actions, and if they are criminals, why appeal to the whole nation? The bishops' appeal to international opinion went even further. Repeating antisemitic stereotypes along the lines of the *Protocols of the Elders of Zion*, they accused Jews of being a separate race aiming to take over the world.[136] The bishops and the clergy frequently made anti-Jewish statements in the years that followed. As a scholar of the episcopacy asserts: 'This phenomenon [antisemitism] was fairly widespread in Catholic circles and the clergy.'[137]

The attitude of the communists and, when all is said and done, of a relatively small group of young Jewish people was attributed by extension to the whole Jewish community. We have no evidence of mass desertions or specific espionage by Jews. However, mistrust of them and exaggeration of their 'crimes' led to concrete measures. This was especially painful for those who wished to take up arms in defence of Poland. On the orders of the Minister of the Army, a great many officers of Jewish faith were arrested. Some were removed from the army even after they had distinguished themselves in the fight for independence. Around ten thousand Jewish conscripts and volunteers were put in a camp at Jabłonna. The justification for this move was typical: 'The temporary creation of a holding station at Jabłonna was necessary so as to consolidate the excess in the percentage of rank-and-file Jews in order to process them with a view to further dispersal.'[138] The case of Jabłonna illustrates the army's general attitude towards Jews.[139] At the same time, the police

---

[135] Ibid. 393.

[136] 'Bolshevism is indeed moving to conquer the world. The race which directs it has already conquered the world through gold and banks, and today, inspired by the imperialist longings that have coursed through its veins from time immemorial, it is directly heading to bring about a final subjugation to the yoke of its rule': 'Biskupy polscy do episkopatu świata', in *Zwycięstwo 1920: Warszawa wobec agresji bolszewickiej*, ed. M. M. Drozdowski, H. Eychhorn-Szwankowska, and J. Wiechowski (Paris, 1990), 42.

[137] He describes as popular 'views suggesting that the Jews were aiming to assert control over every aspect of the country's social and economic life and create their own "Judaeo-Polish" state on the Vistula': K. Krasowski, *Episkopat Katolicki w II Rzeczypospolitej: Myśl o ustroju państwa. Postulaty, realizacja* (Warsaw, 1992), 176. Father Mateusz Jeż praised the clergy for its achievements in this area, asserting that in the villages, where the influence of the clergy was greater, there were fewer Jews, while in the towns 'those Catholics who are practising and are better Catholics, who regularly attend mass and listen to the sermons—they are greater antisemites': Father M. Jeż, 'Duchowieństwo polskie a żydostwo', *Rozwój*, 18 Oct. 1925.

[138] 'Likwidacja obozu w Jabłonnej: Komunikat Prezydium Rady Ministrów', *Chwila*, 12 Nov. 1920. After the war, it was stated that the reason for withdrawing Jews from the Warsaw garrison was their high proportion, which reached 40%. The Ministry of the Army had designated a norm of 10% of Jews in front-line units. Międzyministerialna narada w Prezydium Rady Ministrów, 1 Nov. 1920, confidential: AAN, MSZ, 9389, MS, fo. 15.

[139] A great many instances of anti-Jewish behaviour by soldiers were recorded, as well as the actions in Pińsk and pogroms in Lida and Vilna: Lewin, 'Political History of Polish Jewry', 142–53. Władysław

were carrying out operations against Jewish civilian organizations, especially
against the Bund.[140] Civilians were interned in camps at Dąbie, Strzałkowo, and
elsewhere. Jews were segregated, housed in separate huts, and treated worse than
other prisoners. The exact number of deaths that occurred there is unknown,
although they numbered in the hundreds.[141] Jabłonna and the shooting without
trial on 5 April 1919 of thirty-four participants in a Zionist meeting in Pińsk shook
the Jewish community and left a scar for many years. 'The tragedy of the events
of the second half of August and September 1920', writes Janusz Szczepański, 'lay
in the fact that the whole Jewish population was accused of collaboration with the
Bolsheviks.' In another book, devoted to society's attitude towards the war, he states
that 'contrary to widespread public opinion, fomented and sustained by the
National Democratic press . . . the majority of the Jewish population took part in
the fighting against the Bolshevik invaders to the best of their strength and
resources'.[142] A remark by Apolinary Hartglas probably sums up the mood of the
majority of the Jewish population: 'In 1916 both communities, Polish and Jewish,
shook hands and set off together. In 1920 the Polish community pushed away that
hand.'[143]

   A specific situation developed in the Kresy which the Poles sought to incorporate in the new state. This territory was of great interest to the Jews, and here
they constituted a group with a strong national identity.[144] The fate of hundreds of
thousands of Jews living there depended on the location of the border and the
Polish state's subsequent administration of this territory. It seemed that an opportunity for choice was opening up for the Jews. In reality, on the disputed territories
they were between a rock and a hard place. Each of the warring sides demanded
support for its aspirations. The Poles took no account of the Jews' expectations and
paid little attention to the propaganda that they themselves directed towards the
Jews. As Michał Sobczak has written, 'Basically, the Polish point of view came
down to this, that the Jews were always supposed to be on the side of the Poles.'[145]

Broniewski describes attitudes in the army as 'jingoism with savage antisemitism': W. Broniewski,
Pamiętnik, 1918–1922 (Warsaw, 1984), 41.

   [140] Davies, 'Great Britain and Polish Jews', 133.

   [141] Ibid. Davies refers to the report of a commission chaired by Ignacy Daszyński, which he defines
as 'the main historical source for the condition of Polish Jewry during the war': ibid. 135.

   [142] Szczepański, *Społeczność żydowska Mazowsza*, 243; J. Szczepański, *Społeczeństwo Polski w walce
z najazdem bolszewickim 1920 roku* (Warsaw, 2000), 391. Also, Tomasz Schramm has written that the
Jews' attitude provided no basis for calling into question their Polish patriotism: T. Schramm, 'Żydzi
wobec odradzania się państwowości polskiej', in *Przełomy w historii: Pamiętnik XVI Powszechnego
Zjazdu Historyków Polskich, Wrocław, 15–18 września 1999 roku*, ii/2 (Toruń, 2000), 204.

   [143] A. Hartglas, '3 maja 1916–3 maja 1920 r.', *Tygodnik Żydowski*, 14 May 1920, p. 4.

   [144] As Władysław Grabski wrote: 'The process of Polonization is going extremely slowly . . . The
Jews in the Kresy often feel more at home there than do the Poles': W. Grabski, *Idea Polski*, 2nd edn.
(Warsaw, 1935), 115.

   [145] M. Sobczak, *Stosunek Narodowej Demokracji do kwestii żydowskiej w latach 1914–1919* (Wrocław,
2008), 143.

Choice in favour of one side resulted in repression by the other. Meanwhile, Tobiasz Askenaze, a member of the Jewish Assistance Committee in Lviv (Lwów), declared that he had stood by the Polish flag his whole life: 'The overwhelming majority of the Jewish people is not and does not wish to be either Polish or Ukrainian [*ruski*]; it is Jewish and wishes to stay so.'[146]

As early as 27 October 1918, during a conference of Zionist delegates in Lviv, a dispute arose between the delegates from western and eastern Galicia. The former believed that it was necessary to side with the Poles, the latter were for strict neutrality.[147] When fighting broke out in Lviv four days later, they declared neutrality. Many other Jewish communes in eastern Galicia followed Lviv's example. On the whole, we tend to forget that the Orthodox and the assimilationists protested against this declaration, calling it dangerous for the Jews' future in Poland. When the Jewish councillors in Lviv came out in favour of incorporating Lviv into Poland, they joined the Polish National Committee.[148] In Jewish communities both in Galicia and, above all, in the Kingdom of Poland, the advantages extended to the Jews by the Ukrainians were received cautiously.[149] It is easy to forget that the majority of Jews in Lviv lived in a part of the city which had been occupied by the Ukrainians, and that as early as 10 November 1918 the Jewish safety council and the Polish military authorities had reached an agreement on 'zones of influence'.[150] Meanwhile, as a Ukrainian historian has written, 'the Jews were caught in the crossfire, with all the inevitable consequences'.[151]

The declaration of neutrality was well received by the Ukrainians, since for the leadership of the West Ukrainian People's Republic relations with the Jewish population were especially important.[152] They announced that all nationalities, including Jews, would receive a number of seats on the Ukrainian National Council proportionate to their numbers. At the same time, they recognized the Jewish National Committee (Żydowski Komitet Narodowy) as the legitimate representative of the Jewish population. There was more: the government of the West Ukrainian People's Republic created a Department of Jewish Affairs.[153] In practice, however, circumstances varied; at times the Jews were proclaimed, alongside

---

[146] W. Wierzbieniec, 'Żydzi w samorządach miejskich Lwowa, Przemyśla i Rzeszowa w latach 1918–1919: Wybrane aspekty', *Studia Judaica*, 27 (2011), 6.

[147] Gelber, 'National Autonomy of Eastern Galician Jewry', 210. The Zionist activist Dawid Schreiber wrote: 'The Jews living here do not have the right, and indeed do not want as a third nation, to interfere in a conflict between two other nations': *W sprawie polsko-żydowskiej: Przebieg ankiety odbytej w dn. 2, 3, 4, 9 i 16 lutego we Lwowie tudzież wnioski Komisyi wydelegowanej przez Tymczasowy Komitet Rządzący uchwałą z 1 stycznia 1919 r.* (Lwów, 1919), 16.

[148] Wierzbieniec, 'Żydzi w samorządach miejskich', 5–6.

[149] Zieliński, 'Żydzi polscy a niepodległość', 200.

[150] Prusin, 'War and Nationality Conflict in Eastern Galicia', 188, 190.

[151] O. Pawłyszyn, 'Żydzi wschodniogalicyjscy, w okresie Zachodnioukraińskiej Republiki Ludowej', in K. Jasiewicz (ed.), *Świat NIEpożegnany: Żydzi na dawnych ziemiach wschodnich Rzeczypospolitej w XVIII–XX w.* (Warsaw, 2004), 227.

[152] Ibid. 228.   [153] Gelber, 'National Autonomy of Eastern Galician Jewry', 234–5, 289.

the Poles, to be the Ukrainians' greatest enemies. Levies were imposed on them and there were instances of looting and even pogroms.

The Poles assumed it to be self-evident that the Jews should be on their side. Thus from the outset they treated the declaration of neutrality as a betrayal.[154] However, unlike the Ukrainians, who were ready to acknowledge Jewish national aspirations, they did not make the slightest effort to win over the Jews. Thus, an image of east Galician Jews as traitors was developed for domestic consumption. Yet a document presented at the time to the Anglo-French Military Mission claimed that 650,000 Jews stated themselves to be Poles,[155] and this was probably true. However, after the occupation of eastern Galicia by the Polish army, Jews were subjected to widespread repressive measures.[156]

The situation was different in the Kresy. The actual status of these territories was for a long time uncertain. Suffice it to say that Białystok was incorporated into Poland only in December 1919, and the Vilna area officially only in 1922. The Jews' situation was different too. In autonomous Galicia they were full citizens who dealt with the Polish authorities, whereas in Vilna and the Pale of Settlement they had long been subjects of the tsar. A significant proportion of the Jews in Vilna felt they had ties with Russian culture. Why then should they feel attached to Poland?—and all the more so since the Poles were doing nothing to encourage them, to prevent them from feeling excluded from Polish society. A member of the British mission to investigate anti-Jewish disturbances in Poland, Captain Peter Wright, mentioned in his report the accusation that Jews had taken Russia's side. But why, he asked, would they have done otherwise?[157] Józef Dowbór-Muśnicki's corps, and later the Polish army entering Lithuanian–Belarusian territory, did not by their behaviour inspire pro-Polish attitudes in either the Belarusian or the Jewish populations.[158] Despite this, the Zionist conference in Vilna in December 1918 came out in favour of neutrality. In Białystok there was a whole gamut of reactions, ranging from suggestions to turn Białystok into a free city, to protests against incorporating the city into the Polish state, to a proposal of neutrality, to a declaration of loyalty to the Polish state.[159] The National Democrats wanted to incorporate the Kresy as quickly and as tightly as possible into the Polish state, as evidenced, for example, by

---

[154] Gelber, 'National Autonomy of Eastern Galician Jewry', 186; Golczewski, *Polnisch-jüdische beziehungen*, 215–17.

[155] Memorandum on Eastern Galicia presented on 29 January 1919 to the Anglo-French Military Mission by the Committee of National Defence, quoted by Sobczak, *Stosunek Narodowej Demokracji do kwestii żydowskiej*, 146.   [156] Pawłyszyn, 'Żydzi wschodniogalicyjscy', 243.

[157] A. Czerniakiewicz, 'Ekscesy antyżydowskie wojsk polskich na Kresach Północno-Wschodnich RP (IV–VIII 1919)', in Jasiewicz (ed.), *Świat NIEpożegnany*, 580.

[158] Ibid.; J. Osmołowski, 'Wspomnienia z lat 1914–1921': Biblioteka Narodowa, Warsaw, akc. 6798, TS, pp. 309–10, 331–2. For pogroms perpetrated by the Polish army during the Polish–Bolshevik war, see *Kniga pogromov: Pogromy na Ukraine, v Belorussii i evropeiskoi chasti Rossii v period Grazhdanskoi voiny, 1918–1922 g.: Sbornik dokumentov*, ed. L. B. Milyakova (Moscow, 2007), documents 134, 135, 138, 139. See also the report of Sir Stuart Samuel's commission.

[159] K. Sztop-Rutkowska, 'Konflikty polsko-żydowskie jako element kształtowania się ładu

the emergency motion tabled by Stanisław Głąbiński on 1 July 1919 on behalf of the ZLN, which called for elections to be held urgently in the Nowogródek and Vilna regions. During the debate in the Sejm, Yitshak Grünbaum, speaking on behalf of the WZPNŻ, stated that the National Democrats, by trying to force through the incorporation into Poland of part of this territory, were aiming for a partition of Lithuania and Belarus, thus negating the appeal made by Piłsudski to the inhabitants of the former Grand Duchy of Lithuania. A partitioning of Belarus would 'create conditions in which the Belarusians will gravitate towards Russia. It is surely in Poland's interest from every point of view to detach this territory from Russia, which can be achieved only by supporting their aspirations to independence. Therefore, this is no time for elections as long as the future of this territory is undecided.'[160] Other Jewish politicians spoke in a similar vein. This position clearly followed the line of reasoning of Piłsudski, who at the time was a supporter of a federal solution.

Nor did the Jewish members of parliament change their point of view during the debate on the ratification of the peace treaty signed on 18 March 1921. Both the Zionists and the Folkists claimed that the Riga treaty did not respect the principles of national self-determination, nor did it safeguard minority rights. They emphasized, too, that it did not solve the issue of citizenship for the inhabitants of the former Russian empire. Contrary to the decisions of the Treaty of Versailles, the right to a national option was not guaranteed. As a consequence of these strictures, the Zionists decided to abstain, while the Folkists voted against the ratification of the treaty.

As regards the elections in Central Lithuania (as the Vilna region was also called) to a body which was to decide the future of these lands, leaders of the local Jewish community called on people not to take part. They made participation conditional upon a definition of the issues to be tackled by a future Vilna Sejm. In the opinion of the Lithuanian historian Šarūnas Liekis, this was a more conciliatory approach than that of the Belarusians and Lithuanians; it stood as a kind of declaration of neutrality.[161] As Jews represented the largest minority in the electoral constituency, the Polish authorities wanted to assure their participation in the elections. The Jews were prepared to propose their own list on condition that the Vilna region be guaranteed autonomy. In addition to general objections to taking part in the elections, Jews had serious local reservations too: they had more rights in Central Lithuania than in Poland, and would lose these in the event of incorporation. It was also emphasized that the Jews' cultural and economic interests did indeed lie more with Poland. The Ministry of Foreign Affairs tried to get the Jews to issue a declaration that they were not taking part in the elections because of their demand for a federation. This attempt failed. Despite their reservations, Jews did participate on

politiczno-społecznego w Białymstoku w latach 1919–1920 w świetle lokalnej prasy', *Studia Judaica*, 10–11 (2002–3), 136–8.

[160] *SSSU*, 31 July 1919, session 82, cols. 111–13.   [161] Liekis, *A State within a State?*, 162.

a committee preparing the opening of the Vilna Sejm and a rabbi took part in the actual ceremony.[162]

In the Legislative Sejm, the majority on the foreign affairs committee demanded the incorporation of Central Lithuania into Poland. In a motion tabled by the government, Piłsudski and Prime Minister Antoni Ponikowski called for the Vilna region to have autonomous status. Hirszhorn, speaking on behalf of the Jewish group, did not fail to point out that if an attempt had been made to put into practice Piłsudski's appeal to the inhabitants of the Grand Duchy of Lithuania, Lithuania would long ago have been united with Poland. He also directly accused the National Democrats of sabotaging this opportunity.[163] During debates on the matter in the Sejm, the Jewish members emphasized that it was impossible to build a nation state with 40 per cent minorities. They claimed that only a policy of toleration towards minorities could build a powerful Poland.

The Polish–Bolshevik war, and then the declaration of the Council of Ambassadors, put an end to the issue of borders. The constitution defined the shape of the new state. The Slav and German minorities aspired to detach themselves from the Polish state, and made efforts, including armed action, to move in that direction. The Jews never questioned the state's independence and territorial integrity. Quite the opposite: from the independent state's first days, the Jewish representatives declared their loyalty towards it, demanding in exchange that the Jewish community be treated as citizens with full rights. At the start of the Legislative Sejm's activity, and not waiting for the ratification of the constitution, Apolinary Hartglas prepared draft legislation on repealing legal restrictions on Jews. The March Constitution recognized the equality of citizens before the law. However, it did not lift the rules that had hitherto been in force. In this connection, the Jewish members on more than one occasion proposed motions and presented draft legislation on the matter. An example of this involved hospital fees. Jews using hospital services were not treated as members of the administrative district running the medical facilities in which the Jewish religious commune lay, which led to discrimination in the public health service. At the same time, members of the Jewish communal bodies paid the same local council taxes as other citizens, whose medical care was covered by the local council. There were additional regulations discriminatory to Jews in both civil and administrative law. Yet other forms of discrimination were practised against Jews living in the lands of the Russian partition, which before Polish independence had not been part of the former Kingdom.

Some restrictions were lifted during the process of ratification of more general regulations. Eventually, all regulations restricting Jews were abolished formally in 1931. However, soon afterwards proposals to reintroduce restrictions on Jews made their appearance. Some of them were passed in the form of acts of parliament.

---

[162] A. Srebrakowski, *Sejm Wileński 1922 roku: Idea i jej realizacja* (Wrocław, 1993), 67–8.
[163] *SSSU*, 15 Apr. 1921, session 224, col. 96.

The issue of national minorities was, alongside agricultural reform, the greatest problem facing the Second Republic. The language laws for Slav minorities represent an attempt at at partial solution. But up until the end Jews were not treated as a national minority. Their situation, especially in the second half of the 1930s, deteriorated. At one time, Jews had been urged to become members of the Polish nation through assimilation, but later the condition of conversion to Catholicism was added. Assimilated Jews were still tolerated, but by the end of the 1930s racist birth criteria were introduced.

To document this would require another essay, but in my opinion the second half of the 1930s was the most negative period of Polish–Jewish relations. The intensified antisemitism of the Endecja in the 1930s became an important part of their ideology, but also took the form of concrete acts against Jews. The Sanacja, too, changed its attitude towards Jews after Piłsudski's death. Essentially anti-Jewish draft legislation and legislation appeared; a wave of boycotts grew. Increasingly, fields of economic activity and professional advancement began to close. Antisemitic slogans appeared in Sanacja declarations. A policy of 'emigrationism' was adopted, which viewed emigration by Jews as a solution to the 'Jewish question'. An initial step was to be the isolation of the two communities.[164]

Such actions did not fail to influence the mood of the Jewish population, which was described by the senator Mojżesz Schorr: 'Within a short space of time, under a state constitution unchanged in both legal and economic terms, I have been demoted from a citizen representing the needs and aspirations of a sizeable proportion of the state's inhabitants to the rank of emigrant *in spe*, representing some ephemeral, transient group of Jewish incomers.'[165]

The Jews were among the first to recognize the dangers of Nazism. This was understandable, given the situation in Germany. In the face of the growing threat of war, Jews declared their complete loyalty to the state, took an active part in collecting subscriptions to provide weapons for the army, and joined its ranks when mobilization came. At the last sitting of the Sejm on 2 September 1939, held under falling bombs, Salomon Seidenman said: 'I declare yet again that the Jewish population of Poland is without reservation at the disposal of the Supreme Command,

---

[164] Referring to the racial differences between Jews and Poles, Michał Pawlikowski, a National Democratic columnist, wrote that the Jewish race 'has become a dreadful cancer on the body of civilization': P. Ponisz [M. Pawlikowski], *Sprawa żydowska w Polsce ze stanowiska narodowego i katolickiego* (Częstochowa, 1938), 22. Thus it was necessary 'above all to put every effort into isolating the Jewish race from the Polish one in order to sever the destructive influence of the Jews on the Polish psyche' (ibid. 53). 'No half measures will achieve the desired result. The cancer must be cut out with its roots down to the smallest infected tissue to prevent it growing back. Jewishness will grow from the last Jewish family in P[oland], if this family is allowed to remain as citizens' (ibid. 73). Further, the last sentence of a book by Władysław Studnicki, who was associated with the conservatives at the time that he wrote it, and who devoted it to the harmfulness of the Jews, reads: 'Removing the Jews from Poland is essential to the country's health': W. Studnicki, *Sprawa polsko-żydowska* (Vilna, [1936]), 123.

[165] *Sprawozdanie Stenograficzne Senatu*, iv, 5 Mar. 1937, session 22, col. 5.

and that it is ready to make every sacrifice that the moment demands.' Starting that month, they fought in the ranks of the Polish army in every campaign and on every front during the Second World War.

Translated from the Polish by Jarosław Garliński

Anti-Jewish Pogroms in the Kingdom of Poland

ARTUR MARKOWSKI

INTRODUCTION

AMONG the key questions posed in the rich literature devoted to pogroms are: who was to blame? who organized the pogroms of Jews?[1] While these questions are important and still relevant now, it is important to remember that they were already frequently posed in print soon after the pogroms, in anti-tsarist publications which used rhetoric such as 'who organized the pogroms in Russia?'[2] and 'of what use are pogroms?'[3]—the same questions which have been transformed today into subjects of academic inquiry. However, a basic problem is the fact that over the last hundred years the meaning of these questions has changed completely. At the start of the twentieth century they were posed in the first instance for political reasons. Today, however, we seek those responsible for the pogroms above all from a humanitarian perspective and out of concern for humanity's moral condition. We more rarely give them political meaning.[4] However, this transformation has not led to paradigm shifts in research. On the contrary, the paradigms have been reinforced by

I would like to thank Professor Marcin Wodziński, Professor Glenn Dynner, and Kamil Kijek for their valuable critical comments on this chapter. They have forced me to rethink some passages, have required greater precision and intellectual discipline in my thinking, and have stimulated me to do additional extremely interesting reading. The research for this article was supported by a Kwerenda grant from the Fundacja na Rzecz Nauki Polskiej.

[1] The most important works, now recognized as canonical, which deal with the pogroms of Jews in the Russian empire and which clearly pose the question of guilt are M. Aronson, *Troubled Waters: The Origins of the 1881 Anti-Jewish Pogroms in Russia* (Pittsburgh, 1990); S. M. Berk, *Year of Crisis, Year of Hope: Russian Jewry and the Pogroms of 1881–1882* (Westport, Conn., 1985); J. D. Klier and S. Lambroza (eds.), *Pogroms: Anti-Jewish Violence in Modern Russian History* (Cambridge, 1992).

[2] Yu. N. Lavrinovich, *Kto ustroil pogromy v Rossii?* (Berlin, 1909).

[3] M. Stogov, *Komu nuzhny pogromy?* (Petrograd, 1917).

[4] They take on such meaning only in a right-wing view of recent Polish history. The best example is the polemic surrounding Piotr Gontarczyk's book *Pogrom?* (Biała Podlaska, 2000), conducted between its author and Jolanta Żyndul from quite different philosophical standpoints. Another example could be the discussions on the occasion of the anniversary of the 1946 Kielce pogrom, and the proposition, advanced by right-wing columnists and scholars, that the pogrom had been instigated by

the results of research on pogroms committed during the Second World War. New discoveries and interpretations have been introduced into the public debate on responsibility for the Holocaust.[5]

The present study sets itself the goal of answering a series of lower-order questions, although they are no less essential to an understanding of those tragic events. In what follows I should like to examine and deal with some basic questions about pogroms in the Kingdom of Poland—to identify the geography of their occurrence, and the consequentiality (or not) of their development, and to study various social behaviours, including the activities of the representatives of the state apparatus, as well as their conduct when faced with pogroms. The answers to the questions thus framed will allow us to avoid the trap of the paradigms hitherto used in research on this issue, and will put behind us the whole context of a politically motivated interpretation of behaviour and statements; as a result, we shall also gain information as to who the perpetrators were and who are incriminated by the tragedy of these events.

WHAT LIMITS US AND WHAT CAN WE DO ABOUT IT?

Definitions

The basic methodological problem in studying events described as pogroms is how to define them. While western European scholars have expressed themselves more cautiously and less radically about the definition of a pogrom, Polish academics have managed to conduct polemics on the subject, which in point of fact have produced no results.[6]

A number of varied definitions have been introduced into the academic arena.[7] In his last book, John Klier made some subtle distinctions, coming to terms in a

the Jews themselves, or had at least been organized by the security organs. See J. Żyndul, 'If Not a Pogrom, Then What?', *Polin*, 17 (2004), 385–91; ead., 'It Was No Ordinary Fight', ibid. 397–9; P. Gontarczyk, 'Pogrom? The Polish–Jewish Incidents in Przytyk, 9 March 1936', ibid. 392–6.

[5] J. T. Gross, *Sąsiedzi: Historia zagłady żydowskiego miasteczka* (Sejny, 2000); A. Bikont, *My z Jedwabnego* (Warsaw, 2004).

[6] The importance of a definition has emerged in the above-mentioned exchange between Żyndul and Gontarczyk (see n. 4 above), as also in Dariusz Libionka's critical comments: D. Libionka, 'Poglądy historyków na pogromy w Rosji w latach 1881–1906', *Społeczeństwo i kultura: Rozprawy* (Warsaw, 1996), 263–4.

[7] Paul Brass has tried to sum up the older ones: see P. R. Brass, 'Introduction', in id. (ed.), *Riots and Pogroms* (New York, 1996), 33. Michael Aronson has defined a pogrom thus: 'The Russian word *pogrom* ("massacre", "devastation") came to be commonly used throughout the Western world to designate mob violence against Jews, no matter where it occurred and, even more broadly, mob attacks made against any minority group': Aronson, *Troubled Waters*, 4. Somewhat later John D. Klier, an eminent expert on the subject, stated: 'The word "pogrom" is Russian. Its usage became inextricably linked to antisemitic violence after the outbreak of three great waves of anti-Jewish rioting in the Russian Empire in 1881–2, 1903–6, and 1919–21': J. D. Klier, 'The Pogrom Paradigm in Russian History', in Klier and Lambroza (eds.), *Pogroms*, 13.

logical way not so much with the direct definition of a pogrom as proposed by various other writers, as with the underlying rationale, which in fact has had an enormous influence on the defining of the concept. In discussing the work of Hans Rogger,[8] Heinz-Dietrich Löwe,[9] and Michael Aronson, Klier demolished in turn the arguments that pogroms had an economic origin, and the interpretation of pogroms as violence directed at the Jews as capitalists.[10] At the same time he pointed to the contexts of 'carnival' as ways of analysing violence against Jews, indicating the real meaning of antisemitic convictions and symbols at the level of both folk culture and high culture; he also denied a religious basis for pogroms.[11] He finally came down on the side of seeing pogroms in terms of inter-ethnic violence,[12] adding also that at least the pogroms of Jews of 1881–2 were clearly an urban phenomenon.[13] Research on the reception of the word 'pogrom' also helps us to understand the complexity of the problem.[14]

However, it is important to realize that, by means of a single definition, writers are attempting to standardize certain phenomena—phenomena that are on the one hand alike, if we see at their heart group violence, manifested on a large scale against a group of clearly singled-out victims, but on the other hand distinct, if we examine a series of detailed, but no less important, issues.[15] After all, we must remember that the pogroms which took place in Russia during the second half of the nineteenth century and at the start of the twentieth varied considerably in many details, such as the social backgrounds of the perpetrators and the victims, their numbers, and the local context, understood in terms of inter-group relationships in

---

[8] H. Rogger, *Jewish Policies and Right-Wing Politics in Imperial Russia* (Berkeley and Los Angeles, 1986).

[9] H. D. Löwe, *The Tsars and the Jews: Reform, Reaction, and Anti-Semitism in Imperial Russia, 1772–1917* (Chur, 1993).

[10] J. D. Klier, *Russians, Jews, and the Pogroms of 1881–1882* (Cambridge, 2011), 64–5.

[11] Ibid. 68–9. [12] Ibid. 80.

[13] David Engel appears to be much more careful in the matter of definition. He has outlined the definitional parameters, and specifically the social and cultural conditions which led to pogroms: D. Engel, 'What's in a Pogrom? European Jews in the Age of Violence', in J. Dekel-Chen et al. (eds.), *Anti-Jewish Violence: Rethinking the Pogrom in East European History* (Bloomington, Ind., 2010), 19–37.

[14] The cultural and political histories of the word 'pogrom' have so far been investigated for two cultures. Lidiya Milyakova has shown how this concept has evolved in Russian culture (where it originates): L. Milyakova, *K voprosu ob istoricheskom znachenii slova 'pogrom' v russkom yazyke*: <http://mion.isu.ru/filearchive/mion_publcations/russ-ost/diaspr/9.html>; and Sam Johnson has analysed its implementation in Anglo-American culture: S. Johnson, 'Uses and Abuses: "Pogrom" in the Anglo-American Imagination, 1881–1919', in E. M. Avrutin and H. Murav (eds.), *Jews in the East European Borderlands: Essays in Honor of John D. Klier* (Boston, 2012), 147–66. The authors of the definitions are unanimous that the mythologizing of the phenomenon of group violence with which we are dealing, both in Russia and in the United States and western Europe, has resulted in the picture of pogroms becoming obscured. It has not only led to many of them becoming overgrown with legends, which not only differ considerably from the real events, but for years has also left our knowledge of them based on false premises. [15] S. Rudnicki, 'Pogrom siedlecki', *Kwartalnik Historii Żydów*, 233 (2010), 18.

the village or town. However, there is no doubt that what connects all these events is an antisemitic myth and a set of irrational anti-Jewish prejudices. This also served as the basis for, and an element in, other social or political behaviours that were not, however, connected with violence.

From the perspective of popular knowledge and its deep cultural roots, an event defined in a certain way was known as a pogrom, and it features under that name in literature, art, collective memory, articles in the press, political debates, and other cultural expressions (and also in gossip and legal testimony) at a period close in time to the events themselves. Of course, we must remember that there has never been full precision and uniformity in the lexical realm, and some creators of source material readily used other words and expressions in order to avoid the word 'pogrom', which at the end of the nineteenth and the beginning of the twentieth centuries was familiar and perfectly well understood in terms of crime and ill-treatment. The Russian term *besporyadki* ('disturbances', 'riots') can be recognized as basically a bureaucratic and official synonym for the word 'pogrom', if used in the context of violence directed against Jews.

If we accept the cultural attempt to define the events according to 'who took part', the list of pogroms will expand significantly. However, we shall then be speaking of occurrences which in reality differed enormously among themselves in scale, course of events, and consequences, and often also had differing immediate causes and a diverse genealogy. It was only in the popular imagination that they all coalesced into a uniform, seamless, sequential set of events, denoted by the name 'pogrom' or 'wave of pogroms'. The list of pogroms published in the *American Jewish Yearbook* in 1907 can serve as a splendid example.[16]

It should also be noted that, although today we restrict the use of the word 'pogrom' to manifestations of violence directed against Jews, we should not neglect the fact that the word appears in descriptions of completely different events too.[17]

In terms of a type of social behaviour, pogroms were never a specific phenom-

---

[16] 'From Kishineff to Bialystok: A Table of Pogroms from 1903 to 1906', *American Jewish Year-book*, 8 (1906–7), 34–89. Even a cursory glance shows that clashes between striking workers and police in Sosnowiec in 1904 (pp. 40–1) and Częstochowa in 1904 (pp. 42–3) were counted as pogroms. The strikes in Piotrków and Łódź (pp. 46–7) in the summer of 1905 were also called a pogrom, while the 1906 Białystok pogrom was described as three separate ones: in Białystok, Starosielce (today a district of Białystok, but earlier a small town near Białystok), and Bojary (then and now a district of Białystok) (pp. 64–5). A careful examination of the sources concerning the situation in Częstochowa reveals that in the second half of 1904 the strike movement in the town became significantly more active and was often brutally crushed by the police. However, shots were fired not at Jews as such, but at workers, among whom there happened to be Jews: see N. Gajda, 'Rewolucja 1905–1907 w Częstochowie', in J. R. Budziński and T. Matuszak (eds.), *Elementy społeczno-narodowe w rewolucji 1905 r.* (Piotrków Trybunalski, 2006), 56–7. Robert Blobaum points out the fear of a pogrom that was experienced by the Jews in Łódź in the summer of 1905, but he is writing of the bloody repression of workers' demonstrations: R. E. Blobaum, *Rewolucja: Russian Poland, 1904–1907* (Ithaca, NY, 1995), 98.

[17] For instance, the state authorities in Russia specifically referred to the collective attacks on the Mariavites as pogroms, or the violence directed against the Russian intelligentsia. In today's historical

enon, although if we examine the cultural and not the behavioural contexts they are clearly distinguished by a dimension of antisemitic convictions.[18] Group violence was one of the historical reactions to various forces that were breaking down the existing, traditional social structures.[19] The violence, however, required there to be a considerable cultural distance between the groups taking part in the pogrom; or, put otherwise, the fact of the violence was itself a proof of this distance. However, in terms of the number of incidents, and their frequency, repetitiveness, and effects, as well as their political consequences—an important point—pogroms of Jews represent without a doubt a separate research problem.

Sources

In order to break down the limitations imposed by definitions, I have searched for categories of sources which, on the one hand, record all possible occurrences of pogroms, while on the other refer exclusively to those which really did take place. I forgo all manner of speculation not only as to the fact of an occurrence, but also as to the course of its events, the number of its victims, and a depiction of the behaviour of the groups. To use the most popular and accessible source—the press—would be to miss the point. Attempts undertaken in Poland between the wars to write about pogroms on the basis only of selected press items are disappointing, for the flavour they convey is often in line with fashion or the paper's political views.[20] The press, both Jewish and non-Jewish, is in this case a source which is perfectly suited only to studying in what way impressions of pogroms were

literature the escalation of group violence against African Americans in the United States also goes by the name of pogrom, as do events in Indonesia. Attacks by socialists on brothels in Warsaw in 1905 are also called pogroms, and it was the word used earlier, in an anti-socialist pamphlet, in relation to the crushing of the socialist movement. See C. L. Lumpkins, *American Pogrom: The East St. Louis Race Riot and Black Politics* (Athens, Ohio, 2008); J. T. Sidel, *Riots, Pogroms, Jihad: Religious Violence in Indonesia* (Ithaca, NY, 2006); Blobaum, *Rewolucja*, 94; I. Poeche, *Fałszywe proroki; czyli, Pogrom socjalistów we wsi Rozumowie: Prawdziwe zdarzenie z naszych czasów* (Poznań, 1897).

[18] One need only consider, for example, peasants' behaviour in the Kingdom of Poland during the 1905 strikes, or earlier the so-called Galician massacre of 1846: J. Molenda, 'Walka o poprawę warunków materialnego bytu robotników rolnych poprzez przemoc grupową i rokowania w rewolucji 1905–1907 roku w Królestwie Polskim', in M. Przeniosło and S. Wiech (eds.), *Rewolucja 1905–1907 w Królestwie Polskim i w Rosji* (Kielce, 2005), 59–82. Jan T. Gross points out too the sort of anachronistic and destructive behaviour at one time popular among the peasantry: destroying anything different. The parallel drawn by Gross between the murders at Jedwabne and the Galician massacre is very apposite: Gross, *Sąsiedzi*, 89.

[19] This can be viewed in terms of the category of 'moral economy' set out by E. P. Thompson. The lower social orders lose their traditional social rank as well as their place in the social structure, and the mass disturbance described by Thompson as 'direct popular action' is an attempt to attain a position which in the popular imagination the group deserves. In the case of Jewish society in the Kingdom of Poland an analysis in terms of moral economy reveals above all a pent-up explosion of behaviour based on peasant's anti-Jewish conceptions. See E. P. Thompson, 'The Moral Economy of the English Crowd in the Eighteenth Century', *Past and Present*, 50 (1971), 78–9.

[20] J. Żyndul, *Zajścia antyżydowskie w Polsce w latach 1935–1937* (Warsaw, 1994).

created and how their social and cultural functioning developed. It shows the creation of legends and mythology, and permits a diagnosis of emotions and an examination of how pogroms did (and do) become an element of political debate.[21] Documents produced by those who experienced these events also have their defects. Memoirs display emotion and subjective opinions contributing little to attempts to discover what happened. Often they are written years later and are based on second-hand knowledge.[22] Memorial books belong to a similar category of materials, useful for studying collective conceptions and the stages of their development, but not the events themselves.[23]

In my view, then, the best materials are mid-level civil service and police documents, prepared in the Kingdom of Poland by provincial governors and the governor-general's private office, as well as by senior officers of the gendarmerie. I have been particularly interested in the correspondence between these offices and, to a lesser extent, in the direct correspondence of provincial governors with the Ministry of the Interior, but then only if it was classified as secret, or if it was not designed with the objective of creating public communiqués about pogroms. There are two reasons for this. First of all, neither the officials in provincial government nor those in the governor-general's office were directly involved in local matters. Inspection teams sent to the site of an incident were as a rule not involved in terms of finance, family, friendship, or patronage with any of the sides involved in a pogrom, unlike more junior officials, for they were not people from the local communities. All manifestations of the breach of public order were a threat to the rule of law throughout the country, for which the provincial authorities were responsible; hence it was in these authorities' interest to understand events, to uncover the reasons for them as well as their perpetrators, and also to take care of material damage and to calm emotions. The second reason is that at the provincial level officials had no cause to be secretive, deceptive, or neglectful in the event of a pogrom breaking out. Of course, one cannot rule out the possibility that a governor's antisemitic attitudes might result in the favourable treatment of those involved in a pogrom.[24] The same is true of materials produced by senior officers of the gendarmerie, and in that case I am more interested in the log of events in

[21] Sam Johnson has done this splendidly in her work *Pogroms, Peasants, Jews: Britain and Eastern Europe's 'Jewish Question', 1867–1925* (New York, 2011).

[22] An excellent example is provided by the memoirs of Apolinary Hartglas, written after the Second World War and remarkably similar in their account of the 1906 Białystok pogrom to a report on it by S. An-sky, which was published in 1910. Many years after the event Puah Rakovsky recalled the pogrom in Siedlce as having taken place supposedly in 1905, while she writes not a word of the pogrom in Białystok in June 1906, which was known worldwide, describing somewhat conventionally the two earlier ones of 1905: P. Rakovsky, *My Life as a Radical Jewish Woman: Memoirs of a Zionist Feminist in Poland*, ed. P. E. Hyman (Bloomington, Ind., 2002), 98.

[23] Andrzej Żbikowski, for instance, used them in this way: A. Żbikowski, *U genezy Jedwabnego: Żydzi na kresach północno-wschodnich II Rzeczypospolitej, wrzesień 1939 – lipiec 1941* (Warsaw, 2006), 71–4.

[24] Governors did behave in such a way in Kishinev and Odessa: E. H. Judge, *Easter in Kishinev:*

police records, or the personal details of those arrested, than in the information—in my opinion less trustworthy—on the behaviour of representatives of the internal security apparatus. The breadth of engagement with the issue of pogroms was not at all a consequence of the antisemitic attitudes of the tsarist civil service (although this is not the place for me to challenge this thesis, recognized in the academic literature), but of conscientiousness, or rather of the need, as part of its duties, to maintain public order in its area of responsibility. One other issue concerning sources emerges from this: the documentation that I have analysed does not adequately come to grips with the problem of anti-Jewish prejudice in representatives of the government and in society. This may stem either from a desire to conceal one's attitudes (in the case of officials), or because these attitudes were self-evident (in the case of society). Despite these limitations, documents of mid-level administrative and police authorities appear to be the best source for studying anti-Jewish pogroms in the Kingdom of Poland.[25]

WHAT HAPPENED?

In research done so far on pogroms in the Russian empire a chronology has been used which was established by Simon Dubnow, and only slightly modified later, and which is based on a division into so-called waves of pogroms. The first wave is identified as occurring in 1881–2 (1881–4), the second in 1903–6, and the third in 1918–21 (1915–21, or even lasting until 1924).[26] This framework automatically excluded from scholarly interest the events of 1829 (Warsaw) and 1878 (Kalisz), but more broadly also pogroms in Odessa, as well as a pogrom in Częstochowa in 1902, which did not fit into the accepted chronology. It dictated also a uniform scholarly approach to the pogroms of 1915, 1918, and 1920–1, even though they were carried out by quite different branches of the army.[27]

Anatomy of a Pogrom (New York, 1992), 63; R. Weinberg, 'Anti-Jewish Violence and Revolution in Late Imperial Russia: Odessa, 1905', in Brass (ed.), *Riots and Pogroms*, 70–3.

[25] Michael Ochs, the author of the first work written since the Second World War that deals systematically with the issue of pogroms in the Kingdom of Poland, also selected sources in a similar manner (although omitting the gendarmerie). He considered, however, that a definitive clarification of the authorities' role in the pogroms in the Kingdom of Poland (still that obvious paradigm of looking for guilty people!) depends solely on whether we are prepared to trust official documents, or whether we consider them as constructing a certain official, bureaucratic, fictitious version, so moderated as to conceal the involvement of representatives of the administration and the police in organizing pogroms. See M. Ochs, 'Tsarist Officialdom and Anti-Jewish Pogroms in Poland', in Klier and Lambroza (eds.), *Pogroms*, 177.

[26] The first article on pogrom chronology, and one with significant consequences, was S. M. Dubnov [Dubnow], 'Pogromnye epokhi (1881–1916)', in *Materialy dlya istorii antievreiskikh pogromov v Rossii*, i: *Dubossarskoe i kishinevskoe dela 1903 goda*, ed. S. M. Dubnov and G. Ya. Krasny-Admoni (Petrograd, 1919), pp. ix–xv.

[27] The outlines of these pogroms are discussed by Oleg Budnitsky in his *Rossiiskie evrei mezhdu*

The adoption of these chronological divisions in studies of pogroms led to an acceptance that they were a product of modern society at the end of the nineteenth and the beginning of the twentieth centuries, and resulted in the dark chapters of pogrom violence from an earlier time being sidelined; hence one rarely finds attempts to make comparisons, for example, with the Hep-Hep riots in the German Reich,[28] or comments on the longevity of cultural perceptions of the harmfulness of the Jews. Thus I believe it is essential to expand the period accepted by Michael Ochs for the study of pogroms in the Kingdom of Poland, extending it both backwards from 1881 and forwards from 1903, and to observe these phenomena from the creation of the Kingdom of Poland in 1815 to the outbreak of the First World War. The Great War not only changed social relationships, but also introduced new factors which made pogroms more likely.[29]

The first known pogrom of Jews in the Kingdom of Poland took place in Warsaw in 1829. It is definitely the most poorly documented. Neither police records nor local government files have survived, having been destroyed by fire in 1944 during the Warsaw uprising. We know of the incident only from the notes of Henryk Mackrott, one of the police agents that were deployed in Warsaw on the study of criminality. Małgorzata Karpińska, a researcher who has used this documentation, notes:

On 14 May 1829 there was a Jewish pogrom in the capital. Groups of young journeymen attacked followers of the Jewish faith near Bankowy Square, and the gendarmes moved in. It is difficult to establish the extent of these disturbances: Mackrott mentions many beaten Jews and a seriously injured Christian, who had been taken for an Israelite, since on that day he had been wearing a large round hat.[30]

It emerges from Karpińska's description that, as in an earlier pogrom that took place in 1804, this one was a spontaneous attack by Christian working men against Jews. It appears that in the first pogroms in Warsaw—in 1791, 1804, and 1829—perceptions of the Jews' economic harmfulness and of their anti-Christian prejudices played an enormous role. It is worth recalling that in 1804 the pogrom began when pieces of roofing shingle fell onto the canopy stretched over the Holy Sacrament which was processing by the Church of St Andrew. The Jews were

krasnymi i belymi, 1917–1920 (Moscow, 2005); see also O. Budnitskii [Budnitsky], 'Shots in the Back: On the Origin of the Anti-Jewish Pogroms of 1918–1921', in Avrutin and Murav (eds.), *Jews in the East European Borderlands*, 187–201.

[28] For more on these events, see S. Rohrbacher, 'The "Hep Hep" Riots of 1819: Anti-Jewish Ideology, Agitation, and Violence', in C. Hoffmann, W. Bergmann, and H. W. Smith (eds.), *Exclusionary Violence: Antisemitic Riots in Modern German History* (Ann Arbor, 2002), 23–43.

[29] A. Markowski, 'Rosyjski wizerunek konfliktu społecznego: Żydzi na pograniczu Królestwa Polskiego i Rosji w początkach Wielkiej Wojny', in D. Grinberg, J. Snopko, and G. Zackiewicz (eds.), *Lata Wielkiej Wojny: Dojrzewanie do niepodległości, 1914–1918* (Białystok, 2007), 148–63.

[30] M. Karpińska, *Złodzieje, agenci, policyjni strażnicy...: Przestępstwa pospolite w Warszawie, 1815–1830* (Warsaw, 1999), 104–5.

immediately blamed for an attack on the Christians and a spiral of violence was unleashed.[31]

The second Jewish pogrom in the Kingdom of Poland took place in Kalisz in 1878. It began in the context of a procession on the feast of Corpus Christi. In this instance too we have still not been able to reconstruct accurately the sequence of events, nor establish who the instigators of the incident were. The Polish-language press wrote about it extensively, embellishing and exaggerating facts with the aim of attracting readers and supporting its own ideological stance. Journalists reported that the spark which ignited it was a shout that Jews were destroying the altar at which the Corpus Christi procession was to stop. The local crowd taking part in the procession, and then peasants who had come in from the surrounding countryside, attacked the Jews with stones, flails, pitchforks, and sticks.[32] The tsarist authorities quelled the pogrom. During the investigation 140 people were questioned and eighteen charged. The gendarmerie reported that the cause of the outbreak was the local population's discontent at the economic exploitation practised by the Jews.[33] However, the proximity of a Christian festival permits us to look also for other reasons—especially ideological ones, or a social model for the disturbance.

The pogrom in Balwierzyszki (Balbieriškis) on 2 November 1881 broke out on All Souls' Day, which also coincided with a Jewish festival. Prior to the incident social relations had been excellent, and both Catholics and Jews had come out in numbers and were circulating through the streets of the small town. The pretext was a dispute between a Jew and a Christian. The result was the looting of several dozen houses, and several people injured. The pogrom was put down by the army.[34]

The most famous disturbances, on account of the sequence of events, were those in Warsaw from 25 to 27 December 1881. A pogrom broke out immediately after an incident in the Church of the Holy Cross, when a panic created during a service led to the deaths of twenty-eight people who were crushed by the crowd thronging to reach an exit. The direct cause of the pogrom was the accusation that Jewish pickpockets had caused the panic in order to cover up their thieving. A crowd composed of members of the lower social classes (journeymen and apprentices) went round smashing up Jewish houses and shops, going down Ordynacka, Czernichowska, Pańska, and Wiślana streets one after the other. The pogrom spread into neighbouring areas: Mokotów, Pruszków, Bródno, and Praga. The outcome was that altogether twenty-seven Jews were injured and one killed. Damage amounted to 1,228,931.50 roubles, and although this may have been exaggerated in order to obtain greater compensation, it clearly shows the looting dimension of the

---

[31] Gosudarstvennyi arkhiv Rossiiskoi Federatsii, Moscow (hereafter GARF), f. 110, op. 24, d. 1247, fo. 141.

[32] M. Iwańska, *Prasa pozytywistów warszawskich wobec Żydów i kwestii żydowskiej* (Łódź, 2006), 136–7.

[33] S. Wiech, *Społeczeństwo Królestwa Polskiego w oczach carskiej policji politycznej (1866–1896)* (Kielce, 2002), 211.   [34] Ibid. 214.

pogrom.[35] The disturbance lasted three days and was ended by the intervention of the military and the arrest of over 3,000 people—perhaps the largest arrest in the history of nineteenth-century Warsaw. Interrogations carried out by commissions lasted several weeks. The majority of the culprits were released, but several dozen were convicted, with punishments ranging from floggings to exile.[36] It is now much less often contended that these incidents were provoked by the Russian authorities. Surviving police and court documents clearly contradict such an interpretation. The pogrom broke out spontaneously, was not controlled by the authorities, and had no direct organizational links with similar incidents in other parts of the empire.[37]

At the beginning of April 1882 a pogrom broke out in Iłów, a small town in Warsaw province. After a church service a dozen or so young men attacked Jewish houses, breaking windows. A representative of the district watch (as the police was then known) arrested one of the culprits, Józef Dałkiewicz; the rest escaped. Altogether three people—a peasant, a worker, and a servant—were tried in the local court. The authorities reported that the culprits were mainly local peasants and that the police had prevented the crowd looting.[38]

Some three weeks later a pogrom broke out in Gąbin (where, incidentally, an earlier pogrom had been organized by Stefan Czarniecki's troops in the mid-seventeenth century). According to police documents the pogrom began with a quarrel on the square between a peasant and a Jew while some tobacco was being bought. The row attracted a group of idle onlookers from both groups. The numerical superiority of Jews in the town did not augur well for a Christian victory in a fight, so they sent for reinforcements to the neighbouring villages, lying to the peasants that the Jews were beating up the priest and the mayor. The mayors of the local villages rounded up the peasants and set off to support the townsfolk of Gąbin. The end result was that fifty-three out of the 158 Jewish houses in Gąbin were looted and destroyed. Four Jews and two Christians were injured, and the pogrom lasted all night. Not much was stolen (apart from strong liquor) and in this instance the crowd was bent more on destruction than expropriation. Order was restored by the army, which arrived the following morning. Twenty-five people were arrested.[39]

---

[35] GARF, f. 110, op. 24, d. 1247, fo. 17.

[36] Rossiiskii gosudarstvennyi istoricheskii arkhiv, St Petersburg (hereafter RGIA), f. 1405, op. 534, d. 1191, fo. 93.

[37] The 1881 Warsaw pogrom has possibly the greatest literature, which variously assesses culpability. However, there are no great differences in terms of the sequence of events. See A. Cała, *Asymilacja Żydów w Królestwie Polskim (1864–1897): Postawy, konflikty, stereotypy* (Warsaw, 1989), 271–7; S. Hirszhorn, *Historja Żydów w Polsce od Sejmu Czteroletniego do wojny europejskiej, 1788–1914* (Warsaw, 1921), 222–7; S. Kieniewicz, *Dzieje Warszawy*, iii: *Warszawa w latach 1795–1914* (Warsaw, 1976), 259; T. R. Weeks, *From Assimilation to Antisemitism: The 'Jewish Question' in Poland, 1850–1914* (DeKalb, Ill., 2006), 79–80; Klier, *Russians, Jews, and the Pogroms of 1881–1882*, 43–4; J. Shatzky, *Geshikhte fun yidn in varshe*, 3 vols. (New York, 1947–53), iii. 95–109.   [38] RGIA, f. 1405, op. 534, d. 1247, fo. 6[r–v].

[39] Ibid. 16–17[v]. Based on information from the gendarmerie, Stanisław Wiech states that in Gąbin fifty-five houses, three warehouses, and five shops were smashed up, and five Jews and four Christians

In the spring of 1882 a pogrom also broke out in Podlasie, in the small town of Janów (now Janów Podlaski). We know little about the course of events. Some drunken Christians left Finkelsztejn's tavern on the square and got into a quarrel with some Jews who were selling fruit on the square. The result was the destruction of stalls worth 300 roubles (hence not much), some beatings-up, and the theft of shoes that were for sale on the stalls. The culprits were handed over to the police.[40]

In June 1882, around the feast of Corpus Christi, a pogrom broke out in Czartowiec in the Lublin area as a result of a fire caused by children smoking cigarettes. In the village thirteen buildings were destroyed out of forty-eight. The Jews were blamed for supposedly selling cigarettes to the children. The Christian community decided to expel the Jews as an act of revenge. Jewish houses were looted, although the losses were minor (less than 20 roubles). Both sides to the conflict, Jewish and Christian, decided to come to an agreement involving compensation for the losses incurred.[41]

On 3 August 1882 a row broke out on the square in Preny (Prienai) while someone was buying apples. As in other such cases it grew into a pogrom. Depending on the version, between fifty-five and seventy Jewish houses were destroyed. About fifteen to twenty Jews were injured, and damage was estimated at 20,000 roubles. The culprits were peasants and the whole incident lasted three hours.[42]

In the autumn of 1902, there was a pogrom of Jews in Częstochowa.[43] It was sarcastically claimed that in fact it ended up being a pogrom of Christians, since the army, while putting down the rioters, killed two Christians with a volley. As in many such cases the pogrom started from a dispute on the market square. A Christian woman buying fruit claimed that she had been swindled by the Jewish stall-keeper, who had supposedly sold her produce that was not fresh. During the ensuing discussion the aggrieved woman's husband became involved, and the matter ended in rough pushing and shoving in which the woman was beaten up by the Jews and seriously hurt. In retaliation the woman's husband went to the church and began calling for revenge against the Jews, who, he claimed, had killed his wife, leaving their small children motherless. A crowd gathered and quickly seized on the issue, and a pogrom flared up. Initially stalls in the market were destroyed. Then Jewish streets, private houses, and shops were looted. Military patrols were successfully

were injured; he notes too that a pogrom broke out in Maków. However, local government sources do not bear this out. Wiech, *Społeczeństwo Królestwa Polskiego*, 216.

[40] RGIA, f. 1405, op. 534, d. 1247, fos. 20–24ᵛ.

[41] H. Bałabuch, 'Zajścia antyżydowskie w 1881 i 1882 r. na Lubelszczyźnie, w ujęciu władz gubernialnych', *Biuletyn Żydowskiego Instytutu Historycznego*, 167–8 (1993), 26.

[42] D. Staliūnas, 'Anti-Jewish Disturbances in the North-Western Provinces in the Early 1880s', *East European Jewish Affairs*, 34/2 (2004), 126.

[43] The governor of the Piotrków province gives a detailed sequence of events in a report on incidents in the province sent to the governor-general of Warsaw on 15 April 1903: Archiwum Główne Akt Dawnych, Warsaw (hereafter AGAD), KGGW (Kancelarja Generała-Gubernatora Warszawskiego), 1893, fos. 1–9.

dispersing the rioters to begin with, but at a given moment the crowd, revelling in the looting, turned aggressively on the troops. Shots were fired, and two people were killed and six wounded. According to the police authorities, the pogrom had been carried out by local workers; it lasted a day.[44]

POGROM OR PACIFICATION; OR,
THE 1906 SIEDLCE PROBLEM

The nature of the incidents in Siedlce in September 1906 has remained undisputed in public opinion.[45] No one has hitherto questioned that there was a pogrom in Siedlce, or that the local garrison carried out an operation of pacification.[46] Likewise, press reports immediately after the incidents in Siedlce, political commentary of the period, and present-day historical debate leave no room for doubt that a pogrom of Jews took place in Siedlce, although it was of a somewhat different nature than those elsewhere.[47] No doubt arises, then, if we accept the 'cultural' definition of a pogrom. In terms of public response, the consequences of this incident were identical to those in the pogroms in Kishinev in 1903, Odessa in 1905, or Białystok in 1906.[48]

However, if we are to provide answers to a series of questions connected not so much with an image of the culprit as with the structure of the incident and the contexts in which it arose, we must place a question mark after such an assessment. Documents of the provincial authorities discovered by Szymon Rudnicki permit a new interpretation. They consist of a series of reports from various institutions, and official correspondence constituting the findings of an administrative inquiry into the events in Siedlce.[49] It is worth noting too that in 1905–6 the social composition of the town was unusual. Edward Kopówka, Szymon Rudnicki, and Urszula Głowacka-Maksymiuk unequivocally point to the very active socialist circles in Siedlce, especially the Bund, but also the Polish Socialist Party (Polska Partia Socjalistyczna; PPS). All this intensive revolutionary activity directed against the tsarist authorities resulted in strikes, meetings, and several attacks in which

[44]   *Evreiskie pogromy v Rossiiskoi Imperii, 1900–1916*, ed. D. A. Amanzholova (Moscow, 1998), 36–7. The entire documentation devoted to the pogrom is in GARF, f. 102, delopr. 3, 1902, op. 100, d. 1508.

[45]   Just as after the 1905 pogroms, journalistic histories arose in Jewish circles that apportioned blame and discussed the martyrdom of the Jewish dead: *Megilat pera'ot shedlits bishenat 1906* (Tel Aviv, 1947), or the earlier A. Grünberg, *Ein jüdisch-polnisch-russisches Jubiläum: Der grosse Pogrom von Siedlce im Jahre 1906* (Prague, 1916).

[46]   Rudnicki, 'Pogrom siedlecki'; E. Kopówka, *Żydzi w Siedlcach, 1850–1945* (Siedlce, 2009) 41–51; Weeks, *From Assimilation to Antisemitism*, 137.   [47]   Rudnicki, 'Pogrom siedlecki', 18.

[48]   The press discussed these incidents at length, using rhetoric similar to that employed in the case of the 1906 Białystok pogrom: see 'Der khurbn in sedlits', *Naye tsayt*, 1906, no. 26, p. 1; no. 27, p. 1; no. 28, p. 1; 'Nokh vegn sedlits', *Naye tsayt*, 1906, no. 29, p. 1; 'Der pogrom in Siedlic', *Der Weg*, 1906, no. 197, p. 1 (and in every issue up to no. 200).   [49]   AGAD, KGGW, 2766.

representatives of the Russian authorities were wounded or killed.[50] The tsarist authorities' response was a tightening of control and eventually the introduction in the town of a state of emergency. In this connection authority was handed over to the military, the town was divided up in line with regional military pacification plans, and troops were placed on the streets. All writers emphasize—and townsfolk who were questioned soon after the pogrom did not deny[51]—that the incidents later called the Siedlce pogrom began when a number of shots were fired at uniformed policemen on the streets. No one has argued about the details of the sequence of events[52]—the differences merely concern which group of revolutionaries was doing the shooting: the Jews claimed that they were PPS activists, whereas the Russians pointed the finger at the Bund. The army stepped in and opened fire on buildings identified as being the source of the shots. Artillery was used, while the troops looted the Jewish quarter from where the shots had been fired at the uniformed police.[53] Kopówka claims that as a consequence of the incidents there were at least fifty dead, 100 injured, and around 500 arrested.[54] Altogether eighty-one houses were destroyed, while the total damage was estimated at 75,000 roubles.[55]

In a file discovered in the Archiwum Główne Akt Dawnych by Szymon Rudnicki, the first document is a dispatch sent from Siedlce to the governor-general of Warsaw on the day after the outbreak of the 'pogrom'. Three further documents are reports written by the acting governor in Siedlce describing events in the town. There is not even a hint in them that the incident had the marks of a pogrom and that Jews were the principal victims. A cavalry division staff officer sent in from Warsaw to make an inspection summed up his work in a report dated 1 September (Old Style) in which he used—as did the acting governor in Siedlce—a vocabulary and rhetoric consonant with the description of pacification measures in an unruly town. The enemy that the Russian army was taking on was the revolutionaries, while the cause of the attack was shots fired by persons unknown at representatives of authority.[56]

By contrast with the events in, for example, Częstochowa in 1902 or Warsaw in 1881, the word 'pogrom' appears nowhere in the 181 folios of official correspondence. The first time that the Russian word *besporyadki* (a frequent synonym for 'pogrom') appears is in the transcript of a deciphered telegram from St Petersburg discussing the secondment by the Minister of the Interior of a personal representative to report on the matter;[57] only then does 'pogrom' enter the rhetoric of the documents arising in the affair.

---

[50] Kopówka, *Żydzi w Siedlcach*, 34–44; Rudnicki, 'Pogrom siedlecki', 22; U. Głowacka-Maksymiuk, *Gubernia siedlecka w latach rewolucji, 1905–1907* (Warsaw, 1985), 67–115.

[51] AGAD, KGGW, 2766, fo. 4ᵛ.   [52] Rudnicki, 'Pogrom siedlecki', 27.

[53] It is worth adding that artillery was used in the Kingdom of Poland at least fifty-six times to put down revolutionary demonstrations: S. Kalabiński and F. Tych, *Czwarte powstanie czy pierwsza rewolucja: Lata 1905–1907 na ziemiach polskich* (Warsaw, 1969) 265.

[54] Kopówka, *Żydzi w Siedlcach*, 45.   [55] Rudnicki, 'Pogrom siedlecki', 33.

[56] All the reports are in AGAD, KGGW, 2766, fos. 8–23ᵛ.   [57] Ibid. 25.

Examining the details of the events in Siedlce, the authorities also assembled, in addition to reports, other material evidence. A set of photographs taken by the local photographer Adolf Gancwol-Ganiewski, most of which were used later in a pictorial piece in the *Tygodnik Ilustrowany*,[58] shows the physical impact of the pogrom: destroyed buildings with bullet damage on them, as well as a famous photograph— ideal incriminatory material—showing a building with a wall holed by an artillery shell.[59] On a map of Siedlce drawn by hand, but to scale, details of the movements of military patrols during the incidents have been marked in red ink. Also, as an addendum to a report, a table was compiled with details of the thirty houses from which shots were fired at the troops in Siedlce, and the names of their owners indicate that they belonged to Jews.[60] Nowhere else in the judicial papers on pogroms was documentation of this kind made use of in court cases and investigations of pogroms. On the contrary, the photograph, for instance, was used rather in publications with the aim of demonstrating the Russian authorities' culpability. The nature of the assembled documentation argues against the events in Siedlce having the character of a pogrom.

On the basis of the chronology of events, recreated in particular by Szymon Rudnicki, and surviving government papers, it might be safer to accept that the town was the site of an armed clash with the mainly Jewish revolutionary movement (the Bund), as a result of which the Jewish quarter was looted. A penetrating investigation brought to light cases of theft, for which soldiers were held responsible. It was conceded that some officers had exceeded their powers, although the authorities finally came to recognize that the whole operation had led to the calming of the town. Research paradigms that point to the authorities' culpability in organizing pogroms and to their anti-revolutionary disposition make it easy to term the events in Siedlce a pogrom. After all, it was mainly Jews who lost their lives (there were eight Christian casualties, hence far fewer than the Jews); the whole affair lasted three days (the same length of time as the best-known pogroms—in Kishinev in 1903, Odessa in 1905, and Białystok in 1906); and in June in nearby Białystok there had been a pogrom of Jews in which the army had participated and of which it was popularly (but falsely) believed to be the instigator.[61]

Despite this, the Siedlce pogrom should be seen more as the pacification of an unruly town: bloody, ruthless, and doubtless not free of anti-Jewish feeling among both the rank-and-file soldiers and their officers. I agree with the thrust of Rudnicki's article that the local authorities directed their activities against the Jews, but—and this is surely the key to a correct portrayal of these events—when they went on the offensive, what they had in their sights was above all the revolutionary

---

[58] *Tygodnik Ilustrowany*, 1906, no. 38, pp. 745–7.

[59] The photographs are kept in an envelope at AGAD, KGGW, 2766, fo. 31.   [60] Ibid. 18^{r-v}.

[61] For the Białystok pogrom and the controversies surrounding it, see A. Markowski, 'Pogromy, zajścia, ekscesy: Zbiorowe akty przemocy przeciw Żydom w Białymstoku pierwszych dekad XX wieku', *Studia Judaica*, 27 (2011), 23–44.

movement and its complete eradication in the town. It is difficult to expand on the causes of such drastic action, which at its peak exceeded the guidelines for military operations (this is confirmed by the later calling to account of a number of soldiers); perhaps the seizure of power in Krynki (Białystok province) by Jewish revolutionaries for three days in 1905 was enough of a precedent to force the authorities to take such extreme measures.[62] Perhaps the example of Białystok had an effect, where radical young people were daily attacking representatives of the authorities, making their work exceptionally dangerous.

Irrespective of the provenance of the surviving historical testimony, there are no traces of the involvement of the Christian population in the violence directed against the Jews in Siedlce. Rudnicki rightly observes that these incidents were closer in nature to the military pogroms of the First World War. In Siedlce, however, the situation lacked the elements of two enemy sides, betrayal, and demands for loyalty.[63] The sources do not unequivocally indicate informal encouragement to loot, although during the operations military discipline did fray. Attempts to compare the case of Siedlce to other pogroms of 1903, 1905, and 1906 do not succeed, for in all those cases it was to some extent Christian civilians who were on the offensive, at times in conjunction with the army and the police.[64]

From a cultural perspective the events in Siedlce remain (and rightfully so) a pogrom. After all, the legend surrounding this event developed in a schematic pogrom framework identical to those applied to Kishinev, Odessa, and other places. In the context of the paradigms of pogrom studies, the events in Siedlce are even better evidence of Russian agency, since there is direct proof of it—but this is on condition that we acknowledge the events to be a pogrom. If my interpretation has failed to convince, we should remember that what took place in Siedlce in 1906, although it had similar consequences to the instances of pogrom in Warsaw, Częstochowa, and other places, was conducted within a different social context (revolution) and by other instigators (the army). If the previously discussed incidents had certain traits in common, the one trait they shared with Siedlce was that the victims were Jews.[65]

---

[62] P. Korzec, *Pół wieku dziejów ruchu rewolucyjnego Białostocczyzny, 1864–1914* (Warsaw, 1965), 216–19.

[63] Markowski, 'Rosyjski wizerunek konfliktu społecznego'.   [64] Judge, *Easter in Kishinev*, 53–61.

[65] Further research is needed to clarify the events of 1892 in Łódź. Theodore Weeks labels them a pogrom, although the context of the incidents (an anti-tsarist demonstration) raises doubts about such terminology: Weeks, *From Assimilation to Antisemitism*, 107–8. Izaak Grünbaum took a similar line towards them: I. Grünbaum, 'Die Pogrome in Polen', in *Die Judenpogrome in Russland*, 2 vols. (Cologne and Leipzig, 1910), i. 151. Barbara Wachowska has also included these events in the category of pogrom: B. Wachowska, 'The Revolt in Łódź in 1892': <http://www.aapjstudies.org/manager/external/ckfinder/userfiles/files/Wachowska%2C%20Lodz%20Revolt.pdf>. In the light of the descriptions given by this trio of writers the events in Łódź followed more the lines of a regular battle involving firearms.

GEOGRAPHY AND CHRONOLOGY

An examination of the intensification of the incidence of pogroms in the Kingdom of Poland in the nineteenth century requires us to determine their geography and chronology. On the evidence of the surviving paperwork created by the provincial authorities, whether drafts of documents or internal correspondence, or papers provided for the central authorities (the Ministry of the Interior, the Ministry of Justice, the Department of Police), no fewer than ten pogroms broke out in the Kingdom of Poland between 1815 and 1914.[66]

The first known, though poorly documented, instance was in Warsaw in 1829.[67] The second time that events reached the level of a pogrom was in Kalisz on 23 June 1878.[68] A third pogrom broke out in Balwierzyszki on 2 November 1881,[69] followed by one in Warsaw on 25–27 December 1881.[70] Next, a series of pogroms took place in Iłów on 6 April 1882, Gąbin on 30 April 1882, Janów Podlaski on 19 May 1882, Czartowiec on 6 June 1882,[71] and Preny on 3 August 1882.[72] The last one before the First World War took place in Częstochowa on 11 September 1902.[73] As discussed above, the status of the incidents in Siedlce in September 1906 is debatable.[74]

Before 1881 there is no reason to speak of a 'wave of pogroms'. The events in Warsaw in 1829 and in Kalisz were isolated incidents and to a great extent a function of local causes. The intensification of such incidents in 1881 and 1882 is clearly evident, and the simplest thing would be to connect it with the first wave of pogroms of Jews in Russia. This is the one time when the parallel between events in the Russian empire and the Kingdom of Poland is clear and obvious. However, what is less clear is the nature of this 'wave': from Balwierzyszki (Suwałki province), to Warsaw and environs, then to Janów Podlaski (Lublin province), then again to Warsaw and Lublin provinces, and finally returning to the Lithuanian part of the Kingdom. This convoluted itinerary put forward by the pogrom theory arouses suspicion. While we can accept that the inspiration came from the east (though we shall never obtain irrefutable documentary proof), we cannot tie the sequential spread of this phenomenon to this line of thinking.

Documents dealing with the pogrom of December 1881 in Warsaw and testifying to the resonance of this incident, which I return to below, allow us to look differently at the spread of this phenomenon. It appears that the wave of pogroms

---

[66] Earlier, in the post-partition period, the sources note a pogrom in Warsaw in 1804: GARF, f. 110, op. 24, d. 1247, fo. 141; RGIA, f. 1405, op. 534, d. 1191, fos. 64–5.

[67] Karpińska, *Złodzieje, agenci, policyjni strażnicy…*, 104–5.

[68] Wiech, *Społeczeństwo Królestwa Polskiego*, 211, 216.

[69] Staliūnas, 'Anti-Jewish Disturbances', 126.   [70] RGIA, f. 1405, op. 534, d. 1247 and d. 1191.

[71] RGIA, f. 1405, op. 534, d. 1247, fos. 6–24.   [72] Staliūnas, 'Anti-Jewish Disturbances', 126.

[73] AGAD, KGGW, 2766 and 1893.

[74] In his 1910 article, Izaak Grünbaum wrote of six pogroms in the Polish lands (meaning the Kingdom of Poland) in the nineteenth century, among which he included the incidents in Siedlce of 1906: Grünbaum, 'Die Pogrome in Polen', 134.

in Russia had a purely ideological influence on events in the Kingdom of Poland. From an organizational point of view, the Warsaw pogrom was a local event, and it provided an example and a template for subsequent pogroms concentrated for the most part in Warsaw province, although it was neither the sole nor a necessary prerequisite for the outbreak of pogroms in the region. Without a doubt, however, the attitudes of the people and the anti-Jewish climate on the streets of Warsaw played an enormous part. Jacob Shatzky, describing the origin of the pogrom, also brought out the role of both modern antisemitism connected to the circles of the Polish intelligentsia close to Jan Jeleński, and the street propaganda reaching the city's inhabitants.[75] However, I believe that, in addition to this, broader problems of social transformation, which I discuss later, played a fundamental part, while events in Russia had created a precedent. Undoubtedly, the 1902 pogrom in Częstochowa also had a local character, but what is fundamental and different from the case of Warsaw is that it did not lead to further repercussions in the form of a wave of pogroms.

The chronology of the pogroms in the Kingdom of Poland clearly points to the importance of events in the capital for public behaviour in other places, especially during a period when the system of social communication was developing, when the press, the telegraph, and the possibility of speedy travel contributed to the dissemination of information that served as a basis for forming patterns of behaviour. Of course, faced with significant levels of illiteracy, local leaders played a key role in spreading by word of mouth in their immediate community news which they had read in the press, or had gleaned while travelling, or in some other fashion. Without a doubt, the city's status as capital, which in the nature of things set an example to be followed, was also a key factor here. The importance of example and pattern in the outbreaks of pogroms is also to be emphasized.

We cannot write about the geography and chronology of these events without highlighting two further issues. First, in 1881 and 1882 in some regions of the Kingdom there were physical clashes between the Jewish and Christian populations, sporadic destruction of property, and incidents of verbal abuse, all of which can definitely be interpreted in terms of pogrom tension, or simply as a prelude to mass disturbances. However, they did not develop along pogrom lines, owing to the actions of the administrative, police, and ecclesiastical authorities. Nevertheless, they did occur in both geographical and chronological proximity to the pogroms.[76]

The second issue is the lack of incidents which could be classified according to the old criteria as a second wave of pogroms. The Częstochowa pogrom has none of the traits associated with other, earlier incidents. It appears that there was no outside inspiration for it, either as regards the course of its events or in the form of propaganda. I should also like to suggest that, taking into account the sequence and character of the events in Siedlce of 8–10 September 1906, they should be classified

---

[75] Shatzky, *Geshikhte fun yidn in varshe*, iii. 96–7.

[76] Bałabuch, 'Zajścia antyżydowskie w 1881 i 1882 r. na Lubelszczyźnie', 23–36.

differently than they have been hitherto.[77] From a cultural perspective, we are with-out doubt dealing in this case with events which can be called a pogrom; and if we are analysing problems associated with the reaction to events, or with the reflection of them in art or literature, we must also include the case of Siedlce in this analysis. However, it must be emphasized that the surviving documents show that from the authorities' point of view this was more the pacification of an unruly town, which was presented and later interpreted as a pogrom. Needless to say, this does not diminish the tragic consequences of the incident.[78]

The period of the bloody pogroms of 1905 at the time of the intensification of revolutionary activity in the Russian empire was not marked in the Kingdom of Poland by such incidents. Of course, if we take into account street fighting put down in a bloody way by the tsarist army, it is often difficult to identify and cate-gorize events. Jews too were falling victim to the revolutionary fever. However, it is worth pointing out that at that time no measures specifically directed against Jews were recorded, although fear of such measures led to dozens of reactions by the political parties and the Church, calling for calm and efforts to prevent pogroms, which—as leaflets announced—the tsarist authorities wished to incite.

Interestingly enough, it turns out that what is far more important for the chron-ology of the pogroms is the fact that a significant majority of them took place about the time of important Catholic holy days, when the people had been stirred into activity (and sometimes formed into a procession), and were on the streets in festive mood and often in a state of religious fervour. The pogrom in Warsaw broke out on 14 May 1829, apparently without any connection to the religious calendar. However, the pogrom in Kalisz took place on 23 June 1878, on the Sunday three days after the procession on the feast of Corpus Christi, recalling the situation in Warsaw in 1804 when a pogrom broke out on the day of the procession itself.[79] The pogrom in Balwierzyszki was on All Souls' Day, 2 November 1881, which fell at the same time as a Jewish holiday. The best-known Warsaw pogrom, that of December 1881, occurred over Christmas. The Iłów pogrom took place on Maundy Thursday, when in the Easter services the words 'his blood be upon us and upon our children' are read—and Easter was a very dangerous time in Christian–Jewish relations.[80] The Gąbin pogrom broke out two days after Pentecost, the one in Janów the day after the feast of the Ascension, and the one in Czartowiec two days before the feast of Corpus Christi. The pogroms in Częstochowa and Siedlce have no connection with the religious calendar. However, Henryk Bałabuch has discovered

---

[77] Rudnicki, 'Pogrom siedlecki'; Kopówka, *Żydzi w Siedlcach*, 41; Grünberg, *Ein jüdisch-polnisch-russisches Jubiläum*; *Megilat pera'ot shedlits bishenat 1906*.

[78] In the literature produced so far on the subject writers have no hesitation in classifying the events in Siedlce as a pogrom. However, Szymon Rudnicki points out that it was a 'military pogrom', hence different from others known in other parts of the Russian empire at the start of the twentieth century and, in his view, similar to pogroms from the time of the First World War: Rudnicki, 'Pogrom siedlecki', 18.   [79] GARF, f. 110, op. 24, d. 1247, fo. 141.

[80] Klier, *Russians, Jews, and the Pogroms of 1881–1882*, 68.

that most of the attacks on Jews that took place in Lublin province in 1881 and 1882 also correlate with the dates of Catholic feasts: the Ascension, Whitsun, the Holy Trinity, and Corpus Christi.[81] It was not without reason that the feast of Corpus Christi appears to have been especially dangerous for Jews.[82] From an ideological perspective it is celebrated in conjunction with the establishment of the Holy Eucharist (on the Thursday) and is associated with the cult of the blood of Christ; it was associated too with the alleged desecration of the host by Jews, with the legend of using Christian blood in Jewish rites, and above all with the popular accusation that the Jews had killed the Son of God. In this sense, charges of ritual murder, or more broadly of using Christian blood, were traditionally linked to manifestations of aggression towards Jews. In such a context can we consider a pogrom as a type of ritualized revenge?[83] We should add too that any connection between the religious calendar and acts of anti-Jewish violence was probably indirect: government sources do not point to agitation by the clergy (although of course no texts of sermons preached in Polish have survived), while direct rhetorical elements of prayers and passages of the Mass read in Latin and for the most part not understood by the uneducated populace were not, in my estimation, influential. Key factors might rather have been deeply rooted anti-Jewish notions connected to the Christian faith, the stimulus of a religious festival, the mobilization of the people, and an exceptional feeling of religious distinctiveness on holy days.

It is worth mentioning in this context that in almost all the pogroms in the Kingdom of Poland some kind of triggering event is evident, most often a minor conflict, often with an economic basis. Therefore, we are dealing with the joint influence of a religious factor that energizes society in general and a specific economic factor that provides the immediate cause for the outbreak of physical aggression between whole communities. A business dispute turns into a quarrel, which then escalates into a conflict, no longer just between two directly interested parties but between two communities. Another kind of situation is one in which misfortune affected a whole community, and a pogrom was revenge against the Jews accused of causing it. In both situations a pogrom was a violent expression of the mood in a given location and proof of the climate of tension between the two communities. The events we are discussing also clearly indicate the very powerful social bonds obtaining within groups. The aggrieved Christian was able very quickly to gather around him a large number of members of his group for support; the same was true of the Jewish community, and an attack on a member of this community would mobilize especially the young men in an attempt to offer resistance, or at least

---

[81] Bałabuch, 'Zajścia antyżydowskie w 1881 i 1882 r. na Lubelszczyźnie', 27.

[82] At that time there were pogroms in other places in Russia too, e.g. Białystok in 1906; compare also the events in Lithuania: Staliūnas, 'Anti-Jewish Disturbances', 123.

[83] John Klier, however, unequivocally asserted that there was no strong link between accusations of ritual murder and pogroms: J. D. Klier, 'Krovavyi navet v russkoi pravoslavnoi traditsii', in M. V. Dmitriev (ed.), *Evrei i khristiane v pravoslavnykh obshchestvakh Vostochnoi Evropy* (Moscow, 2011), 203–4.

Pogroms of Jews in the Kingdom of Poland in the Nineteenth Century

○   Provincial centre

⌇   Provincial boundary

✳   Location of a pogrom of Jews

✕   Location of an event that counts as a pogrom from a cultural perspective

✛   Location of isolated demonstrations of violence against Jews or pogrom-like agitation

PRUSSIAN MONARCHY

RUSSIAN EMPIRE

9 ✳

12 ✛ ✛ 13   3 ✳

○ Suwałki

Łomża ○

14 ✛   ✛ 17

○ Płock

✳ 6   ✛ 16

15 ✛   ✳ 5

Warsaw ○ ✳ 1,4

○ ✕ 11

Siedlce

7 ✳

✳ 2

○ Kalisz

○ Piotrków

22 ✛   ○ Radom

✛ 24

○ Lublin

✳ 10

Kielce ○

✛ 18

✛ 23   ✛ 19 ✳ 20

8 ✳

✛ 21

AUSTRIAN EMPIRE

Locations and known dates

1   Warsaw, 14 May 1829

2   Kalisz, 23 June 1878

3   Balwierzyszki (Balbieriškis), 2 Nov. 1881

4   Warsaw, 25–27 Dec. 1881

5   Iłów, 6 Apr. 1882

6   Gąbin, 30 Apr. 1882

7   Janów (Janów Podlaski), 19 May 1882

8   Czartowiec, 6 June 1882

9   Preny (Prienai), 3 Aug. 1882

10   Częstochowa, 11 Sept. 1902

11   Siedlce, 8–10 Sept. 1906

12   Bierzyny, July 1881

13   Widgiry, Aug. 1881

14   Płońsk, 16 Jan. 1882 and 10 June 1882

15   Osmolin, 20 Apr. 1882

16   Wyszogród, 28–29 Apr. (or 30 Apr.) 1882

17   Nowe Miasto, 15 May 1882

18   Stojeszyn

19   Łabuński

20   Tyszowce

21   Krzeszów

22   Wieniawa

23   Szczebrzeszyn

24   Kurów

temporarily slow down the attackers. With time these instinctive social behaviours assumed the structure of self-defence groups, especially organized by Po'alei Tsiyon and the Bund, which were able to mount effective defence against pogroms using firearms.[84]

It is held that pogroms of Jews, especially in the 1880s, were an urban phenomenon, and that holds good for the Kingdom of Poland too. However, there was nothing odd about this: Jewish settlement in the second half of the nineteenth century was for the most part urban. Sporadic attacks on Jewish taverns, like those which took place in the provinces of Suwałki and Lublin in 1882, were very rare, and it is hard to include them in the category of pogrom. They were seen by the authorities more as brawls.[85]

The still poorly developed railway lines did not play an important part in pogroms in the Kingdom of Poland.[86] However, the accompanying map definitely has some similarities to the maps published by Klier, which show that the pogrom centres in southern parts of Russia were situated near larger cities, such as Elizavetgrad or Kiev.[87] In the Kingdom of Poland, Warsaw was a comparable centre, although less prominent than in other parts of the empire.

POGROM ATTITUDES

How can one describe the collective psychological state of mind accompanying pogroms? Fear was definitely dominant. Jews felt it; perhaps passive observers (Hilberg's bystanders) felt it too, and representatives of the authorities. The perpetrators were probably not immune either. However, everyone was afraid of something different. The Jews, as potential or real victims, were afraid of losing their property, their health, or even their lives. Observers were afraid of accidentally becoming victims, the authorities were afraid of losing control and of anarchy, and the perpetrators were afraid of being called to account and of punishment. It is hard to gauge this fear, and various efforts were made to deal with it, or to reduce the threat.

Another collective state was paranoia, which, especially after 1903, seized Jews and Christians alike, although its reality was very different for each group. It is defined as a response to false or exaggerated group convictions, which focus on being harassed, threatened, wronged, subjugated, persecuted, accused, and so on.[88]

[84] The most recent interpretations of the phenomenon of self-defence during the pogroms are given by Vladimir Levin in 'Preventing Pogroms: Patterns in Jewish Politics in Early Twentieth-Century Russia', in Dekel-Chen et al. (eds.), *Anti-Jewish Violence*, 99–103.

[85] Wiech and Bałabuch write more about these attacks: Wiech, *Społeczeństwo Królestwa Polskiego*, 214; Bałabuch, 'Zajścia antyżydowskie w 1881 i 1882 r. na Lubelszczyźnie', 25–6.

[86] Aronson attaches great significance to them in Russia: Aronson, *Troubled Waters*, 110.

[87] Klier, *Russians, Jews, and the Pogroms of 1881–1882*, pp. xxii–xxiii.

[88] R. M. Kramer, 'Paranoja zbiorowa: Nieufność między grupami społecznymi', trans. P. Sekuła, in P. Sztompka and M. Bogunia-Borowska (eds.), *Socjologia codzienności* (Kraków, 2008), 230.

It can arise in conditions of asymmetrical authority, when minority groups exist whose constituent elements have a sense of inferior status, or of being under surveillance. Such circumstances lead to a heightened sense of injustice in a community that is prey to paranoia, and to a tendency to overreact, seeing oneself as the target of the other group's negative behaviour.[89]

The fear felt by victims is movingly reflected in sources of a personal nature and in the press. In accounts and reports dealing with pogroms fear very often pushes descriptions of events into the background, or leads to serious distortions of them. The historian discussing today the tragic events surrounding pogroms must remember that every pogrom was seen by its victims as the introductory event to a cataclysm that could bring total destruction. The history of the Jews and the cult of suffering perceived in terms of religious experience was conducive to such a point of view. The pogroms of Jews in the Hellenic world and above all at the time of the First Crusade, then the tragic events accompanying Bohdan Khmelnytsky's uprising, were mainstays of a conception of Jewish suffering and its divine provenance. Life in the Diaspora, often in an environment unfriendly towards Jews, buttressed these fears with real examples of cyclical anti-Jewish behaviour and repression.[90]

Initial reactions to the Warsaw pogrom of 1881 in the Hebrew-language *Hatsefirah* and the Polish-language *Izraelita* emphasize above all that the collective emotional state of the writers, as representatives of the Jewish community, was one of fear.[91] At times it was also directly and clearly verbalized.[92]

The fear felt by the 'observers' (bystanders) manifested itself by their placing signs that they belonged to the Christian community on the houses occupied by them. During pogroms, or at times when there was a threat of them, crosses, images of saints, or icons would appear in windows. The fear felt by the authorities and the pogrom rioters materialized in the behaviour of these two groups, and I discuss this below when analysing their attitudes towards and conduct during pogroms.

A climate of fear is an adequate explanation of pogrom paranoia. If we apply a definition of collective paranoia to the situation of the Jewish community in the Kingdom of Poland, we easily discover that the illusory (although legally confirmed) emancipation introduced by ukase in 1862 raised unfulfilled hopes and in practice a sense of injustice, especially in centres of the Jewish intelligentsia.

[89] Kramer, 'Paranoja zbiorowa', 231–2.

[90] For more on the Jews' understanding of martyrdom and on its historiographical influences, see Y. H. Yerushalmi, *Zakhor: Jewish History and Jewish Memory* (Seattle, 1982), 37–52; J. M. Karlip, 'Between Martyrology and Historiography: Elias Tcherikower and the Making of a Pogrom Historian', *East European Jewish Affairs*, 38 (2008), 257–80; M. Rosman, *Jak pisać historię żydowską?*, trans. A. Jagodzińska (Wrocław, 2011), 52.

[91] *Hatsefirah*, 15/27 Dec. 1881, p. 386; *Izraelita*, 18/30 Dec. 1881, p. 409.

[92] A. Yedidya, 'Mikhtavim mivarshah: divuḥav shel ze'ev ya'avets al pogrom ḥag hamolad 1881 biyehudei varshah vehashlakhotav, yanuar–februar 1882', *Gal-ed*, 28 (2012), 175, 178. My thanks to Agnieszka Jagodzińska for bringing this source to my attention.

All that was needed was a dramatic trigger, working on the collective imagination in a mass fashion.

The examples of the Odessa pogroms, and perhaps of those which had taken place much earlier in the German Reich,[93] must have had a powerful effect on the consciousness of Jews in the Kingdom of Poland. Perhaps the tense situation between the Jewish and Christian communities also induced fear,[94] as witnessed by the letter written by Wulf Jakubson on 14 September 1877 to the governor of Warsaw in the name of the Jewish community of Mszczonów,[95] in which he requested that the army be sent in because rumours were spreading that during the night of 16–17 September, when the Jews would be celebrating Yom Kippur, the Christians would murder them. Similar requests were made by word of mouth at about the same time to county heads and municipal authorities by representatives of the Jewish communities in Nowy Dwór (16 September), Sochaczew (15 September), Skierniewice (15 September), Grójec (15 September), Żychlin (date missing), and Radzymin (13 September).[96] An investigation conducted by two gendarmes brought into Żychlin did not discover who had been spreading the false rumours. Nor were any of the fifty-six Jews questioned able to state that they had heard such threats from the mouths of Christians. Reporting to the governor of Warsaw, the head of the county of Kutno, betraying an anti-Jewish phobia, suggested that the panic had been caused by the Jews themselves with the aim of facilitating the amassing with impunity of gold and silver coins to be sent to Palestine during the confusion.[97]

The head of the county of Radzymin discovered, on the basis of conversations with Radzymin Jews, that the rumour had come from Warsaw and that it had also been confirmed by a peasant from a neighbouring village.[98] The report also contains an interesting story of a stranger, whom the peasant had met in a tavern, who intimated that a group of fifty people would shortly descend on the town and carry out a pogrom of the Jews. The official interrogated the peasants who were involved in the business, writing a report of their statements; however, he acknowledged that the stories had been made up in order to frighten the Jews, although he did put the local police on alert, just in case.[99]

It is difficult in this instance to judge whether in fact the stories that a bloody pogrom was being prepared were true. It is not even all that critical. For our purpose what is more important is that both several local Jewish communities and the authorities took the problem seriously. The governor, having collected reports on how the night of 16–17 September passed off in the 'dangerous' counties, reported on the matter to his superior, the governor-general in Warsaw, in a document

---

[93] Rohrbacher, '"Hep Hep" Riots of 1819'.

[94] Jacob Shatzky writes about this in *Geshikhte fun yidn in varshe*, iii. 96.

[95] Archiwum Miasta Stołecznego Warszawy, Kancelaria Gubernatora Warszawskiego, 15, fo. 1^{r-v}.

[96] Ibid. 4–11.   [97] Ibid.   [98] Ibid. 11.   [99] Ibid. 13–14.

several pages long; the authorities took steps to protect the Jewish population and on the critical night the district watch was out on patrol.[100]

Despite a lack of irrefutable proof, the authorities succumbed to pogrom psychosis and introduced a number of costly and time-consuming measures in order to uncover the originators of the rumours, but also to protect the Jews from a possible pogrom.

The pogrom of Jews in Kalisz in 1878 did not resonate among the public in the Kingdom of Poland. Apart from a few articles in the Warsaw papers, it did not make a large impact in the community and it did not lead to any obvious signs of a public response;[101] perhaps only in Wielkopolska did it give public opinion more of a jolt. However, the Warsaw pogrom of 1881 did resonate strongly in the surrounding area. This time a sense of fear spread widely, as did rumours of pogroms that were supposedly going to take place elsewhere. Suffice it to say that police reports and citizens' requests for protection flowing in from all sides filled a substantial file, and that they were meticulously analysed at the level of the Department of Police in St Petersburg. An examination of dozens of cases and petitions indicates unequivocally that the Warsaw pogrom had shifted a certain boundary in Jewish–Christian relations.[102] Immediately after it, society grew considerably more sensitive to antisemitic behaviour, both verbal abuse and attempts at physical violence. Nor can it be excluded that in circles unfriendly towards Jews the Warsaw pogrom was recognized as a precedent, and the number of such incidents did indeed rise, as is reflected in official documents. The Warsaw events were often exploited to threaten Jews with a pogrom, or to insinuate that one would break out shortly. However, matters fortunately never got beyond words. The civil and police authorities did nevertheless develop a sort of collective psychosis, treating seriously even the most absurd reports and checking all leads.[103]

Terror manifested itself particularly strongly after the pogrom in Kishinev in 1903. Jewish subjects of the tsar in the Kingdom of Poland continually reported to the authorities real or imaginary information that in dozens of places pogroms would soon break out.[104] For instance, in Warsaw on 7 April a Jewish woman by the name of Fredel Ejerweis met her subtenant, a Prussian subject, on Okopowa Street; describing the Kishinev pogrom, he told her that in Warsaw too the authorities had given permission 'to have some fun with you for three days'. The frightened woman reported the incident to the police; the culprit turned out to be in possession of a copy of the 'Marseillaise' and ended up in jail.[105]

The press, especially the underground press, reacted very rapidly to the Kishinev pogrom, accusing the authorities of carrying it out.[106] The atmosphere

[100] Archiwum Miasta Stołecznego Warszawy, Kancelaria Gubernatora Warszawskiego, 15, 10^r–v.

[101] Iwańska, *Prasa pozytywistów warszawskich*.

[102] Theodore Weeks correctly emphasizes this: Weeks, *From Assimilation to Antisemitism*, 85–6.

[103] GARF, f. 110, op. 24, d. 1247, fos. 186–365.   [104] AGAD, KGGW, 1932, fo. 7.

[105] GARF, f. 124, op. 12, d. 2717, fo. 1^r–v; AGAD, KGGW, 1932, fo. 1^r–v.

[106] H. Węgrzynek, 'Pogrom w Kiszyniowie (1903): Reakcje na ziemiach polskich i wpływ na

thickened by the day, especially in the large towns. Public tension was extreme. The antisemitism experienced by the Jews, the examples of earlier pogroms, and the tragedy in Kishinev had resulted in an acute sensitivity and a sort of pogrom paranoia secondary to the antisemitic paranoia, which was especially strong in circles of young Jewish people. In many places in the Kingdom of Poland there were clashes between Jews and Christians which went beyond verbal abuse, but yet did not have the symptoms of a pogrom.[107]

The psychosis which gripped the Jewish community sometimes placed it in the role of an aggressor. Fear of a pogrom, often incited by the press foretelling the start of a wave of pogroms, was so strong that it bred aggression. For instance, on 23 May 1903, in the village of Aleksota (Aleksotas) in Suwałki province, a crowd of Jews gathering by a bridge reacted aggressively to the police and some assembled Christians when ordered to disperse, showering them with stones.[108]

In this regard public behaviour—the collective paranoia which seized the inhabitants of the Congress Kingdom—did not differ from that in the empire's western provinces. For instance, in Chudnov in Kiev province in April 1903, some local Old Believers in their cups started a brawl in a tavern, calling for a pogrom. The Jews rang the fire bell and gathered outside the tavern armed with clubs. The drunken peasants fell into their clutches and were 'preventively' manhandled by this hastily assembled civil defence force.[109]

In this climate of great fear all sorts of myths about the Christians' anti-Jewish activities arose. Speculation that attempts were to be made to achieve the mass extermination of the Jews in Warsaw by poisoning them testifies to an apogee of fear. The rumour that Christians were handing out poisoned sweets and sugar to Jewish children resonated loudly. An investigation was conducted and dozens of witnesses were questioned, only to lead to the discovery that the accusation was mere speculation.[110] However, such a state of affairs shows just how extreme the tension was at that time between Jews and Christians. Public imagination, frayed by the threat of pogroms, willingly fed off the wildest nonsense, while the authorities, doubtless out of a sense of duty, meticulously checked every lead.

The pogrom in Białystok in June 1906 also aroused panic in the Jewish community. Both the Polish and the Jewish press fuelled fear, publishing bloody descriptions and images of events and foretelling a new series of pogroms. This time there was a different outcome—the flight of part of the Jewish population from a Warsaw gripped by pogrom panic.[111]

However, not every event was the product of frightened people's imagination.

postawy Polaków', in G. Borkowska and M. Rudkowska (eds.), *Kwestia żydowska w XIX wieku: Spory o tożsamość Polaków* (Warsaw, 2004), 456–61.

[107] AGAD, KGGW, 1932; the file contains several dozen reports of clashes between Jews and Christians from various locations in the Kingdom of Poland.   [108] AGAD, KGGW, 1932, fo. 2.

[109] GARF, f. 124, op. 12, d. 2715, fo. 1.   [110] AGAD, KGGW, 1932, fo. 126.

[111] Weeks, *From Assimilation to Antisemitism*, 137.

In May 1903 the police in Pułtusk discovered sixteen handbills put up around the town with the slogan 'Death to Jews today'.[112] Such events stoked even more fear and reinforced the Jewish community's conviction that a pogrom was only a small step away. They also directly demonstrate something which as a rule is missing from the rhetoric of police reports: a powerful anti-Jewish paranoia, compared with which the pogrom paranoia that we are discussing is secondary. This paranoia, which resulted from negative images of Jews and the depiction of them as aliens, and was strengthened by people's low social status, frustration, and disappointment with the transformation of feudal social structures into a modern society, revealed itself in verbal and physical violence directed towards Jews.

The year 1905 was pivotal, when in the autumn, after the tsar's October Manifesto, Russia was rocked by a wave of exceptionally bloody pogroms of the Jewish population.[113] In many towns the left sprang into action, publishing dozens of leaflets decrying the pogroms. We can read in many of these documents a clear message indicating tsarist or police instigation of the pogroms, which were classified as counter-revolutionary operations. They gave rise to a new type of paranoia —fear that the authorities and the government would use the police, the army, and criminal elements for their own reprehensible ends.[114] Initially picked up by Zionist and later by Soviet historiography, this came in time to create the paradigm for pogrom studies: the authorities as both executor and instigator of pogroms of Jews in Russia—a view fortunately now revised and rejected.

At times it appears that the revolutionary organizations used a pogrom as an incentive to direct against the authorities the aggression of the Jews and of the part of the population opposed to pogroms. For example, such is the nature of a pamphlet produced by the PPS in June 1905,[115] in which the author sees the 'rotten tsarist government's hand' behind the instigation of pogroms. Thus ways of manipulating knowledge about the pogroms and of exploiting the subject of pogroms in general appeared immediately. The alarmed Jewish community did not, however, easily succumb to such influences. Without a doubt there was a polarization of views here, but the evidence cited above of petitions to the authorities and reports about pogroms in the making confirms the failure of the policy of manipulation.

Efforts to help those affected during the pogroms also had a double significance. In addition to the intended result of aiding those injured, orphaned, or who had lost their property, they also prolonged fear by highlighting how tragic were the consequences of the crimes committed. It appears that, paradoxically, they may have reinforced collective fear, especially by sensitizing people not just to the real, but also to the supposed effects of violence. Many local communities collected donations to help the victims of the Kishinev pogrom. The Jewish theatres in Warsaw

---

[112] AGAD, KGGW, 1932, fo. 137.

[113] S. Lambroza, 'The Pogroms of 1903–1906', in Klier and Lambroza (eds.), *Pogroms*, 228.

[114] Biblioteka Narodowa w Warszawie, Dokumenty Życia Społecznego, sygn. IB Cim; under this shelfmark there are a dozen or so leaflets, mostly of the PPS. [115] A photocopy is in my possession.

competed with each other to raise the largest sums for the victims of the 1906 Białystok pogrom.[116] Each effort of this kind could not fail to affect the level of anxiety resulting from dramatic tales of the bloody victims of murder and robbery.

Everyone succumbed to collective paranoia. This was especially evident after the Kishinev pogrom, although it must be emphasized that even before the pogrom in Kalisz in 1878 local symptoms of it had been visible. The result was an increase in accusations that pogroms were being organized, aggression between Jews and Christians that was more than just verbal, and moving from place to place to look for a safer spot to live. It must be emphasized that the Russian authorities also succumbed to this paranoia, meticulously investigating each indication of a pogrom. Despite the fact that, especially after the 1903 tragedy in Kishinev, the tsarist authorities and police were accused in the opposition press of organizing the pogrom, the Jews unequivocally feared not the police and officials, but ordinary Christians. In paranoid and often invented reports of pogroms that were in the making, the local Christian population appeared as the potential perpetrators and the Russian authorities as the potential protectors.

The system of social relations in the Kingdom at that time shows this clearly, as does the fact that in the Jewish community's collective imagination the guilty parties and the perpetrators of pogroms were their non-Jewish neighbours, and not the police or the tsarist authorities, and that such ideas were the result of personal experiences and earlier incidents.

THE ATTITUDES OF THE AUTHORITIES

So far no clear and convincing proof has been produced that in the nineteenth century the Russian authorities organized and carried out pogroms of Jews within the Russian empire. The conviction that this was so, expressed during the deliberations of the First Russian Duma in 1906 by Prince Sergey Urusov, became a staple of one of the most important paradigms for studying this issue.[117]

In the case of all ten pogroms which occurred in the Kingdom of Poland in the nineteenth century both the civil and the police authorities introduced a number of measures targeted explicitly at the rioters. A pogrom was of itself a factor destabilizing the state's internal security and so it could not have been used, as some writers have contended, as a safety valve. During the critical period of mass public resistance to Russian rule, during the years 1905–6, there was no pogrom of Jews in the Kingdom of Poland carried out by the local inhabitants. Furthermore, the organization and perpetration of pogroms by the authorities was completely unnecessary in the Kingdom at the times and in the places where individual pogroms did break

[116] S. Ury, *Barricades and Banners: The Revolution of 1905 and the Transformation of Warsaw Jewry* (Stanford, Calif., 2012), 169–70.

[117] S. M. Galay, 'Evreiskie pogromy i rospusk I Gosudarstvennoi dumy v 1906 godu', *Voprosy istorii*, 2004, no. 9, pp. 32–3.

out. Their chronology shows no link with powerful social upheavals or conflicts on the fault line between society and authority. On the contrary, they aroused fear and led to a rapid and, for those days, competent response by the authorities. We do not know how the authorities in the Kingdom of Poland behaved in the face of the pogrom in Warsaw in 1829. In the remaining cases the authorities responding to the incidents were the civil administration, the police, and the Russian army. All the pogroms mentioned were ended by the actions of the civil or military authorities. They were followed by arrests and investigations, leading to prison sentences, fines, and occasionally exile. In Częstochowa in 1902, more rioters than Jews were victims when the troops fired a volley into the crowd, efficiently bringing the pogrom to an end.[118] After the pogrom in Warsaw in 1881 the city was engulfed by a wave of arrests, the like of which was not seen again until the Second World War. A special commission was set up, and in record time it brought the perpetrators to court, charging them with robbery, disturbing the peace, or grievous bodily harm—for after all the law did not recognize the notion of a pogrom or the penalties for such a crime.[119]

It is hard to fault the conduct of the governor-general of Warsaw, Petr Albedinsky, in the face of the pogrom. Historians accuse him of leaving the city, of responding sluggishly, and of not putting an end to the incidents.[120] Yet we should remember that, before taking any specific steps, he had to take stock of the situation (easier for a historian, much less so for an administrator in the Kingdom of Poland), and then by means of the appropriate procedure (the issuing of written orders) activate a military response. The Warsaw pogrom was put down by the army, not just by the police, of whom there were too few in the city. The governor-general's powers allowed him to use the army, but all this took time and required the appropriate bureaucratic steps. Contrary to historiographical opinion up until now, I believe that in this case the authorities used all available means. We should give full credit to the army for dealing with the pogrom without opening fire—by contrast with their later response in Częstochowa.[121]

In my opinion, it is also in the actions of the Russian authorities that we should seek the reason why there were no pogroms of Jews in the Kingdom of Poland in 1905. First, starting in 1903, when pogrom paranoia had gripped the country, the authorities demonstrated vigilance and foresight in forestalling a potential escalation of group violence, though this of course does not mean that there were no clashes between Jews and Christians. For example, in 1903 the authorities in Kalisz province were expecting a pogrom, mindful no doubt of earlier incidents in 1878, and they eagerly informed their superiors of measures taken to prevent a tragedy.[122] Secondly, in the tense atmosphere of 1905, when in many places the voices of

---

[118] GARF, f. 102, delopr. 3, 1902, op. 100, d. 1508, fo. 8^v.

[119] RGIA, f. 1405, op. 534, d. 1191, fos. 81–93.

[120] K. Lewalski, *Kościoły chrześcijańskie w Królestwie Polskim wobec Żydów w latach 1855–1915* (Wrocław, 2002), 138–9.

[121] GARF, f. 110, op. 24, d. 1247, fo. 136.   [122] AGAD, KGGW, 2196, fo. 11^v.

pogrom panic were raised, the Russian army already had a plan developed for the eventuality of a pogrom breaking out. A document is known that was sent to the Łódź police as a circular. It emerges from it that towns under threat had been divided into districts with designated military strongpoints, with operational areas for specific units, and with a complete emergency and intelligence-sharing plan.[123] There is no reason to doubt this document's veracity. On the contrary, we should recognize that good preparations by the authorities and the army, as well as effective deployment of the armed forces to crush the domestic revolution, contributed enormously to the fact that there were no pogroms of Jews in the Kingdom of Poland during the period 1903–7, which was when Russia was being convulsed by the so-called second wave of pogroms. The zeal shown by some officials in carrying out their duties to maintain law and order was sometimes astonishing. After the Warsaw pogrom one officer was accused of punishing some of the participants too vigorously with a whip. Permanently crippled, the mayor of a village outside Warsaw complained to the authorities that this officer had ordered that apologies be made to a Jew present at the whipping, and that the Jew's hand be kissed, and that when he refused, the officer ordered two private soldiers to beat him mercilessly, as accused of having taken part in the pogrom.[124] From surviving documents, particularly concerning pogroms of the 1880s and the Częstochowa pogrom, it clearly emerges that representatives of the authorities and the police feared the further development of the incidents, and were relieved when they succeeded in quelling a pogrom.

Of course, none of this meant that the authorities and the police were well disposed towards the Jews. Stanisław Wiech clearly points out that officers of the gendarmerie exhibited anti-Jewish attitudes. The deeply ingrained image of the Jew prevalent in the Russian administration contained a whole arsenal of elements of antisemitic propaganda.[125] Thus, in the authorities' actions and correspondence dealing with the pogroms one cannot detect any sympathy for the rioters, or any moral opposition to the pogroms or criticism of them. The style of these communications clearly indicates that the authorities made efforts to prevent pogroms and, once they had broken out, to stop them as effectively as possible, not out of sympathy for the Jews, but because of the criminal nature of such incidents. The governors, the governor-general, and the officers of the gendarmerie were interested in order and respect for the law, and thus in keeping the peace throughout the country; they were not interested in the Jews, or in the Christians' attitude towards them.

One should remember too that the Kingdom of Poland was a trouble spot in the Russian empire. It comprised much of its western border, it was an area that was ethnically non-Russian and often in revolt, and it was inhabited by victims of the tsars' imperialist policies—hence potential revolutionaries. Given such geopolitical

[123] GARF, f. 102, 1906, II otd., d. 550, fos. 307–8.

[124] RGIA, f. 1405, op. 534, d. 1191, fos. 97, 309–14.

[125] Wiech, *Społeczeństwo Królestwa Polskiego*, 201–21.

conditions, the authorities responsible for maintaining order had their hands full, and their actions required a resolute attitude in the battle for law and order. This emerged in particular during the 1905 revolution, when the Kingdom of Poland became one of its key sites.[126] Pogroms were even less welcome there than elsewhere.

The state authorities' efforts to prevent pogroms were supported by the religious hierarchies, often at the explicit request of the governors. The Catholic clergy expressed strong opposition to violence against the Jews in special pastoral letters and even personally.[127] It was condemned by the Catholic press[128] and from time to time by the Orthodox press.[129]

In this case the Catholic Church's authorities conducted a policy of changing tack. On the one hand, they attempted to support the civil authorities in combating pogroms, or rather to prevent them breaking out, labelling such behaviour un-Christian. On the other hand, when pogroms did take place they sought culprits among these same authorities, not accepting the idea that those guilty of murder and looting were Christians, and to a significant extent Catholics. The Orthodox Church appealed to higher moral and Christian feelings, avoiding the issue of guilt and not getting involved in the rhetoric of the state authorities' written pronouncements.

SOCIAL DETERMINANTS OF POGROMS

Pogroms as social behaviour can be examined from a number of angles: as a manifestation of social protest and dissatisfaction, as an attempt to gain economic compensation, as an expression of dislike of the alien (including a paranoid aversion to Jews among the antisemitic part of the Christian community), and finally as a manifestation of collective joint behaviour.[130] Of course, in practice all these aspects, although to varying degrees depending on the circumstances, played a key role in creating pogrom tension and then during an actual pogrom.

The particular concentration of instances of collective violence that occurred in the Russian empire during the second half of the nineteenth century can be linked with liberation movements. The slow-moving process of liberation for both the Christian peasantry and the Jews, led from the top by an administrative elite, could clearly not produce rapid cultural and social results. (I have in mind here a structural approach.) *De jure* emancipation often meant de facto frustration, fear, a feeling of unsatisfied need, or of outright disappointment, accompanied by a growing appetite for equality and its practical benefits. The feudal society that was clearly

[126] J. D. Zimmerman, *Poles, Jews, and the Politics of Nationality: The Bund and the Polish Socialist Party in Late Tsarist Russia, 1892–1914* (Madison, Wisc., 2004), 196.

[127] Lewalski, *Kościoły chrześcijańskie*, 128–9, 132, 136; S. Rudnicki, 'A Pastoral Letter Opposing Pogroms by the Apostolic Administrator of the Warsaw Archdiocese, May 1881', *Gal-ed*, 18 (2002), 43–57. [128] Lewalski, *Kościoły chrześcijańskie*, 140, 136–7.

[129] *Tserkovnaya gazeta*, 1906, nos. 20–1, p. 2. [130] Engel, 'What's in a Pogrom?', 24–8.

fading into history was thus not just a structure and a backdrop against which pogroms took place, but was also one of their causes. In the Kingdom of Poland the Jews were *de jure* granted equal rights in 1862, and the peasants were granted property rights (in other words partial emancipation) in 1864; both acts were flawed and aroused opposition among some Jews and among the peasants. Some former country-dwellers swelled the urban population, forming a group there from which were recruited unskilled workers, who stood lowest on the urban social scale, and sometimes also journeymen and apprentices, or even a criminal element.[131] The city was meant to be the promised land, whereas in fact it gave these people dozens of reasons to be dissatisfied. One of the most traditional ways for the peasantry to demonstrate this dissatisfaction was to cause mass disturbances and outbreaks of violence. The history of the eighteenth and nineteenth centuries recalls such behaviour on the part of the lower urban classes in the streets of Paris in 1789, 1830, and 1848. The peasants of Galicia expressed their dissatisfaction in 1846 by mercilessly murdering the gentry and plundering their estates. Peasants in the Kingdom of Poland plundered and attacked landowners during the agricultural strikes of 1905. Such brutal, bloody, spontaneous, and merciless manifestations of opposition often awoke fears of the 'dark', cruel mob throughout all of nineteenth-century Europe.[132] The general perception that the lower levels of the social pyramid had about their place in society, and about the privileges that accompanied it (privileges that were objectively of little consequence), lay at the heart of a group behaviour whose characteristic was an ostentatious demand that a lost sense of security be returned. This unexpected loss, which resulted from the social and economic reforms, could not fail to be discordant with their earlier expectations that nothing but good would come of the changes. A consequence of this specific moral economy was uncompromising violence as a social message, and its victim was a group seen to be inferior, superfluous, and outside the Christian construct of love. In this wild outpouring of feelings of dissatisfaction all that was needed was a suitable target, in line with the popular notion of 'scapegoat'. The Jews were ideally suited to this as a group alien in its culture and in its religion, in part differing on class grounds, and moreover portrayed since the mid-century by part of the elite as the cause of economic misfortune. It is fair to say that these kinds of social emotions were a good basis for the explosion of a terrible carnival of violence.

It should also be accepted that an increasingly greater social role was being played by modern antisemitic ideology, spread both by activists of the nascent nationalist and peasant movement (under the banner of Roman Dmowski and Father Stanisław Stojałowski) and by the lesser Catholic and Orthodox clergy. However, judging by the chronology of the pogroms in the Kingdom of Poland,

---

[131] Cf. Theodore Weeks's remarks on this in his *From Assimilation to Antisemitism*, 73.

[132] T. Kizwalter, 'Motłoch, tłumy, masy: Problem społecznego zakresu autonomizacji jednostki w XIX wieku', in W. Mędrzecki (ed.), *Autonomia jednostki w Europie i Polsce od XVII do XX wieku* (Warsaw, 2011), 51.

peasant antisemitism arising out of medieval ideas and religious prejudices was still a more important factor in them.[133]

The majority of pogroms that took place in the Kingdom of Poland also had a strong economic component to them. I do not mean economic and class differences, so much as the rather mundane mathematics of jealousy. The processes of emancipation were awakening egalitarian aims in this area too. The desire for possessions developed in a comparative context, and if it was difficult to satisfy one's needs and to raise oneself in the hierarchy of possession to a level equal to that of other groups (in this case the Jews), then those groups had to be brought down to one's own level by plundering part of their property or by destroying it. The 'plunder factor' can be seen in the case of the pogroms in Warsaw, Gąbin, Częstochowa, and Czartowiec. In the peasant and petty bourgeois economy of permanent scarcity, a pogrom was compensatory behaviour. In order for it to play such a role, however, it had to be directed against a group characterized in the imagination by two things: the possession of some wealth and a cultural strangeness.

The processes of building a collective group identity, or of building a notional community called a nation, were a huge factor in the social context of pogroms in the Kingdom of Poland. These processes were after all operating especially intensively at the time that pogroms of Jews were breaking out in Warsaw, Gąbin, and later Częstochowa. These processes encompassed separately, but almost in parallel, both Jews and the lower levels of Christians in the Kingdom of Poland. Supported by nascent political movements, as well as by the Catholic Church, they led to the creation of two large communities which differed in terms of culture, religion, and nationality, and which furthermore increasingly flaunted or indeed cultivated these differences. In the second half of the nineteenth century Polish and Jewish identity was often constructed in the context of mutual antagonism and in a dual relationship. The 'edges of the melting iceberg'—integrationist groups or the Polish socialist movement, which was relatively open to Jewish autonomy—did not have a significant impact on this process. The hostile attitude of some Polish groups towards the Jewish nationalist movement and autonomy, in competition with the positivists who accepted the idea of integration and the antisemitic National Democrats who utterly rejected it, completed the picture.[134]

Probably the only exception is the period of revolution in 1905 (up to the autumn), when the interests of both groups, and especially of circles associated with socialist ideas, were very close. However, there were no pogroms at that time in the Kingdom of Poland. Later an anti-Jewish mood increasingly developed, linked to the spread of National Democratic influences and accusations that the Jews had fomented the revolution, especially after its collapse,[135] but the threat posed by the

---

[133] Alina Cała discusses this in her *Wizerunek Żyda w polskiej kulturze ludowej* (Warsaw, 2005).

[134] J. Jedlicki, 'Intelektualiści oporni wobec fali antysemityzmu (Królestwo Polskie w latach 1912–1914)', in Borkowska and Rudkowska (eds.), *Kwestia żydowska w XIX wieku*, 462.

[135] Zimmerman, *Poles, Jews, and the Politics of Nationality*, 204.

so-called October wave of pogroms in Russia in 1905, and widespread opposition from public opinion in the United States, Great Britain, Germany, and Austria-Hungary, induced even the ideologues of the National Democratic movement to back away from such behaviour, and forced the authorities to keep a close eye on Christian–Jewish relations.

The collective dimension of violence during a pogrom made the rioters' task easier. In a crowd everyone felt untouchable and anonymous. The size of a group legitimized its actions, while a feeling of solidarity gave courage. The cultural distance noted earlier and the us/them dichotomy, not so critical in personal contact, reached new heights. It was a condition necessary if people were to assent to actions consciously recognized to be wrong. Unlike the well-known lynchings of African Americans in the United States (in that situation it was not a case of group violence on both sides, since often only a single victim was murdered), when the murderers delighted in having their picture taken with their dead victim, pogrom rioters avoided being identified, or having their handiwork recorded in photographs; sometimes, following the Galician model, they insisted on temporary assurances from the authorities that they had permission to 'beat up the Jews'.[136] Thus a strange situation arose in which a crowd respectful of religious norms and principles allowed itself to commit acts which it would not have permitted against its own group, recognizing the acts to be shameful and contrary to moral, religious, and legal precepts. Furthermore, the crowd committed acts which often individuals who were physically part of the crowd would not have committed on their own. This means that the group which was the pogrom's target had to be seen at least temporarily as not subject to the same principles and laws as members of one's own group, while numbers conferred a sense of public consent to commit a crime. This state of affairs brings to mind the massacre of cats in Robert Darnton's well-known essay.[137] The gulf between the microcosms of two social groups (in Darnton's case journeymen and the nascent bourgeoisie, in our case Jews and Christians from the lower social classes), a developed symbolism and peasant rituals not averse to violence or eliminatory practices, and a deeply ingrained sense of the justice and necessity of revenge or retribution—all these factors made it easier to undertake pogrom activity.

Nineteenth-century fears of the crowd assumed that the mob would uninhibitedly follow its urges, for instance its brutal and violent instincts, or its covetousness.[138] Thus, the crowd or mob (Polish *tłum, motłoch*; Russian *tolpa*) became a mass predestined to commit evil acts, and also one so anonymous and so ill defined that writing about it as the guilty party in a pogrom came easily and carried no weight.

---

[136] GARF, f. 102, delopr. 3, 1902, op. 100, d. 1508, fo. 15ᵛ; M. Soboń, *Polacy wobec Żydów w Galicji doby autonomicznej w latach 1868–1914* (Kraków, 2011), 245.

[137] R. Darnton, 'Workers Revolt: The Great Cat Massacre of the Rue Saint-Séverin', in id., *The Great Cat Massacre and Other Episodes in French Cultural History* (New York, 1984), 75–106.

[138] Kizwalter, 'Motłoch, tłumy, masy', 60.

Recognizing the problem of pogroms, the authorities took more trouble, however, and were not satisfied with the concept of the crowd as a direct perpetrator. Hence the descriptions of perpetrators in official documents, seemingly laconic, indicate rather clearly from which social groups pogrom rioters were recruited. In Często-chowa the pogrom had been carried out by 'riff-raff' (Russian *chern'*).[139] Earlier in Warsaw, for which we have a detailed social breakdown of the arrested rioters, the majority were members of the lower urban classes: day-workers, hired labourers, artisans.[140] They were poorly qualified, more often than not illiterate, and probably with a strongly developed sense of group identity based on religion and identifica-tion with a group of similar people. Their low economic status forced them to fight for every penny. Their desire for possessions and a sense of jealousy were also excel-lent fuel which, heated by anti-Jewish propaganda, formed a truly combustible mix. It is difficult to make an unequivocal judgement that these people as individ-uals were amoral and were ruled by base instincts; indeed, many of them were fervent practising Christians who tried to live in accordance with the Ten Com-mandments. As I have mentioned, the Catholic hierarchy was on the whole calling for calm, asserting that pogroms were contrary to the Church's ideals and the Christian faith. One could thus note that in specific social circumstances a new, or rather a double, group morality was emerging, not shared by members of the group individually, but expressed only collectively.

Surviving official documents say nothing about leadership, so eagerly empha-sized in the work of social psychologists. Must this indicate the involvement of the authorities? Not necessarily. In many cases leadership was anonymous in nature and was realized through an inciting and guiding of the crowd from the crowd, so that participants did not know who was speaking where. This was often self-appointed and short-lived leadership. The dynamics of events during a pogrom allowed not only for quick and easy changes of leader, but also for the operation at times of several centres of leadership. It is difficult to decide arbitrarily which of the rioters that come and go through the pages of Russian official documents can be identified as leaders. Is Kluk from Częstochowa one, who called for Jews to be beaten up near the local church? Can one identify as leaders the three inhabitants of Iłów men-tioned in the files, who were the first to be arrested by the police? It is also hard to see as a leader of a pogrom the Austrian subject and inhabitant of Lublin province, Osip Szlendak, whom the local police arrested on a charge of anti-government agitation, charging him also on the basis of witness evidence of inciting a pogrom against the Jews in Koźminek (Kalisz province) in the summer of 1903.[141] We should remember that participation in a pogrom was punishable, as was incitement to riot, thus attempts by the crowd's ringleaders to conceal their identity were hardly surprising.

[139] 'By reason of the Częstochowa riff-raff brutally settling scores with the Jews' ('povodom zhestokoi raspravy chenstokhovskoi cherni s evreyami'): AGAD, KGGW, 1893, fo. 1ᵛ.

[140] GARF, f. 110, op. 24, d. 1247, fo. 17; AGAD, KGGW, 1893, fo. 1ᵛ.

[141] AGAD, KGGW, 2196, fo. 11ᵛ.

Thus one essential social condition for the outbreak of a pogrom was significant social distance between the two groups. In this context ideas about the harmfulness of the Jews easily came to life, ideas that emanated from peasant antisemitism and that were latent and traditional in their meaning. However, they were not put into words as accusations of ritual murder, as was often the case in Russia (e.g. Kishinev), but were more widely understood through the prism of Roman Catholicism in the context of the foreign unbeliever and were, in my view, one of the more important causes of pogroms. Another cause arose from viewing economic differences in terms of traditional peasant needs and the assessment of other social groups, thus in essence it had a class character in the sense of a belief that the Jews possessed more and had become rich 'on the backs of Christians'. We should examine the escalation of violence in terms of group behaviour, which could be a means of turning round this state of affairs, and which could be used against a group explicitly judged negatively in moral terms. The key here is the previously mentioned dual morality, or a crowd morality more often than not different from the personal attitudes of individuals composing the crowd. Without a doubt it was the crowd that played the role of perpetrator in the tragic spectacles of pogrom.

CONCLUSION

Historians ascribe various dates to the beginnings of so-called modern antisemitism in the Kingdom of Poland. Theodore Weeks acknowledges the Warsaw pogrom of 1881 as the moment when the hitherto well-ordered relations between Poles and Jews broke down and as the beginning of the heyday of antisemitic ideology.[142] Joshua Zimmerman sees the dividing line in the 1905 revolution. He argues that the general strike politicized the masses and made it easier for the nationalist movement to penetrate the working class, giving rise to the development of antisemitism.[143] Irrespective of which dividing line we accept, pogroms of Jews in the Kingdom of Poland occurred earlier (before 1881) and did not occur later (in the period after the revolution). Of course, this does not mean that the phenomenon under investigation was divorced from the issue of antisemitism. On the contrary, it was an expression of it, but one limited to the display of a form of peasant antisemitism based on images and stereotypes connected with the ritual nature of the Christian faith, with the people's economic conceptions at the time, and with the overall make-up of the social structure of the Kingdom of Poland during a period of transformation. Significant too was the phenomenon, described by E. P. Thompson, of compensation, and of demands for the maintenance of the social order as traditionally understood by society's lowest layers. The imagination, fired by the festivities of Christian feasts, easily found a culprit for the current state of affairs and, reinforced by perceptions of the Jews' harmfulness and recognizing them as the object that was

---

[142] Weeks, *From Assimilation to Antisemitism*, 85–6.
[143] Zimmerman, *Poles, Jews, and the Politics of Nationality*, 204.

the focus of all the injustices and problems of everyday life, attempted to communicate its own grievances with force. The pogroms were essentially an expression of aggression resulting from the social frustration of the Christian population's lower classes, which easily found a collective 'culprit' physically to hand and one who was culturally distinct enough to have different moral standards applied to him.

The pogroms in the Kingdom of Poland, in terms of their chronology, were not a major part of this phenomenon in a European context. It is hard to establish whether the events in Odessa in 1821, 1859, and 1871,[144] or the Hep-Hep pogroms in the Reich in 1819,[145] became a model for them, although if we can speak at all about influences then we should do so more in terms of a precedent, that something like that had already taken place and that violence could be directed against Jews. We know too little about the number, geography, and chronology of pogroms in the period before the partitions to seek inspiration and models there.[146]

Some of the pogroms in the Kingdom of Poland took place when Jews were also being persecuted in Russia[147] and West Prussia.[148] However, it appears that here too the influences were only in the realm of ideas and of demonstrating the possibility of using collective violence against the Jews. The climate of acceptability of violence against the Jews present in Russian and German society definitely infected society in the Kingdom of Poland, although the columns of the press were filled more with Russian than German examples.

An important comparative observation is the lack of pogroms in the Kingdom of Poland during the revolutionary period 1905–7. (Even if we accept that the events in Siedlce were a pogrom of Jews, and not a pacification, there is no doubt that it was orchestrated not by the people but by the Russian army.) I would seek the cause of this state of affairs in two circumstances. First there was the enormous concentration of officials and military in the Kingdom of Poland, which was especially unruly, and of particular strategic importance, owing to its location on the frontier. It was here in particular that the Russian state apparatus was especially meticulous in putting down the revolution, leaving little scope for public lawlessness and unrest. The second reason why the Kingdom of Poland was free of pogroms during the period of revolution was the social situation, which was diametrically different from that of the 1880s. For one thing, powerful Jewish political groupings, capable of standing up to the pogroms not just ideologically, but also politically and physically, had made an appearance in the political arena and social structures. For another, during the period of revolution—at least up to the autumn of 1905—there was a spirit uniting Poles and Jews in their common struggle against the tsarist

[144] Klier, 'Pogrom Paradigm in Russian History', 15.

[145] Rohrbacher, '"Hep Hep" Riots of 1819'.

[146] Up to now we know the most about the pogroms in Kraków and Wrocław: H. Zaremska, *Żydzi w średniowiecznej Polsce: Gmina krakowska* (Warsaw, 2011), 456–77.

[147] On this, see Aronson, *Troubled Waters*, and Klier, *Russians, Jews, and the Pogroms of 1881–1882*.

[148] C. Hoffmann, 'Political Culture and Violence against Minorities: The Antisemitic Riots in Pomerania and West Prussia', in Hoffmann, Bergmann, and Smith (eds.), *Exclusionary Violence*, 82.

empire. Hopes of freedom effectively directed the energy of the masses towards the fight with the Russians and not among themselves.

The history of pogroms in the Kingdom of Poland is certainly not a history of tsarist terror directed against Jews and Poles. It represents yet another sad page in Polish–Jewish relations in the nineteenth century.

Translated from the Polish by Jarosław Garliński

Theology in Translation
Progressive Judaism in the Kingdom of Poland

BENJAMIN MATIS

INTRODUCTION

THE FIRST DECADES of the nineteenth century saw attempts in the Kingdom of
Poland to emulate the changes in ritual and doctrine which were being introduced
in the German-speaking lands. The relatively small numbers of reformers here
were, for the most part, strongly hostile to the rise of hasidism, finding its mystical
elements rebarbative and what they saw as its hostility to the non-Jewish world
alarming. They hoped through the achievement of legal equality and the modification of Jewish religious practice on the lines advocated by the Haskalah in Germany
that the appeal of hasidism would be undermined.

Accordingly they sought to make religious observance more orderly, to introduce
a sermon in German or Polish and establish the practice of having a choir to
accompany the cantor (*ḥazan*). In this way they hoped to respond to the call of the
authorities in the Kingdom of Poland for the Jews to transform themselves into
citizens differing from their compatriots only by their religion, which was to be
shorn of its 'medieval', 'fanatical', and 'anti-Christian' features. The changes in
religious observance also reflected a deeper philosophical position, which claimed
that Jewish religious practice had been modified continuously over the course of the
centuries and should now be brought into harmony with the increasingly secular
and science-based culture of the nineteenth century.

Even in German-speaking Europe, the introduction of these reforms had been a
slow process. The first 'reform' synagogue was founded by the businessman Israel
Jacobson in Seesen, near Kassel, the capital of Hesse-Kassel, in 1809 when it was
part of the Napoleonic Kingdom of Westphalia. It was Jacobson who introduced in
this synagogue confirmation ceremonies, choral music with instrumental accom-
paniment, and a modern sermon given in German, and as official head of the Jewish
community in Westphalia he thereby saw many of his ideas accepted into law and
general practice.[1] In 1814, after the defeat of Napoleon, Jacobson transferred from

---

[1] W. G. Plaut, *The Rise of Reform Judaism: A Sourcebook of European Origins* (New York, 1963), 27.

Kassel to Berlin and started a similar synagogue, which encountered resistance from the Orthodox community. Under pressure from it, in 1823 the Prussian government forbade choirs, sermons in German, and other innovations. Nonetheless, the 'new synagogue' movement continued, and found its centre in Hamburg, where Eduard Kley (1789-1867) and others, including Meyer Israel Bresselau and Seckel Isaac Fraenkel, established the Israelitischer Tempelverein (Jewish Temple Association). Services were at first held on Saturdays and Sundays, and later only on Sundays. Prayers were modified to remove references to Zion or to a personal redeemer, and an organ became a permanent feature of the liturgical music in this synagogue. The Prussian government ruling of 1823 which had laid down that there were to be no liturgical or religious changes in the Jewish religious sphere was relaxed only in the 1840s. In 1844 a maskil, Yehiel Michael Sachs (1808–64), was appointed third judge (*dayan*) on the rabbinical court and preacher in the main synagogue in Berlin. In the following year, Aaron Bernstein founded the Reform Society, out of which was to grow the Berlin Reform Congregation. Its synagogue, soon called a 'Temple' to suggest that the Jerusalem Temple did not need to be rebuilt, was the scene of far-reaching liturgical and doctrinal innovations. A less radical model was provided by Vienna, in particular by the Seitenstettengasse synagogue founded in 1826 and led by Rabbi Isaac Noah Mannheimer (1793–1865) and Cantor Salomon Sulzer. The details of what was referred to as the 'Wiener Ritus'—the Vienna Rite—will be discussed below. It was the Viennese model that would be adopted not only in various cities of the Habsburg empire, but even in the Kingdom of Poland.

It should be remembered that 'Reform Judaism' was by no means monolithic in the nineteenth century. Any change in the traditional liturgy, practice, or professed belief could be considered a type of reform, so that those who were quite radical in their changes to the liturgy (as in Hamburg) and those who made virtually no alterations (e.g. Mannheimer) are often lumped together. The debates within this very large reform camp were wide-ranging and at times called into question all aspects of Jewish life, including the liturgy and the prayer book. To quote Jakob Petuchowski, the only thing reformers could agree upon was 'the conviction that every generation has the right to introduce changes into the liturgical material inherited from the past'.[2] The leaders of these synagogues also sought to create a more professional rabbinate on the lines of that developing in Germany, a process which had become 'widespread and irreversible'[3] in the German lands by the 1840s. One of the goals of the Rabbinical School (Szkoła Rabinów) established in Warsaw in 1826 had been to train modern rabbis.

Polish Jews of the 'reform' persuasion who attended these synagogues con-

---

[2] J. J. Petuchowski, *Prayerbook Reform in Europe: The Liturgy of European Liberal and Reform Judaism* (New York, 1968), 348–9.

[3] I. Schorsch, 'The Emergence of the Modern Rabbinate', in id., *From Text to Context: The Turn to History in Modern Judaism* (Hanover, NH, 1994), 10.

sidered themselves 'Poles of the Jewish faith'. At the same time, particularly in Warsaw, they were highly influenced by German Jewry.[4] This seeming contradiction can be explained first by the fact that the integrationist desire to be accepted into Polish society was essentially based on the German Jewish model for the modernization of Jewish life that was part and parcel of the Haskalah, and secondly by the large influence of various reforms made to the synagogue liturgy in the German lands.[5] In addition, the congregation that ultimately became the Great Synagogue of Warsaw was founded by a Prussian Jewish immigrant to Warsaw in 1802, and the language of the congregation until the appointment of Rabbi Marcus Jastrow in 1858 was German, well into its second generation.[6] Moreover, all the preachers of the Daniłowiczowska Street synagogue and its successor, the Great Synagogue on Tłomackie Street, were educated, at least in part, in either Germany or Austria. These preachers—Abraham Meir Goldschmidt, Marcus Jastrow, Izaak Cylkow, Samuel Poznański, and Mojżesz Schorr—were well aware both of the more radical reforms espoused by Abraham Geiger and of the more traditionalist approaches of Isaac Noah Mannheimer in Vienna and Yehiel Michael Sachs in Berlin: the Daniłowiczowska Street synagogue used the Mannheimer prayer book, while Jastrow himself advocated a Polish-language translation of the very traditional Sachs prayer book.[7] They saw the adoption of the Polish language as an essential element in acculturation. In the words of one of the principal integrationists, Daniel Neufeld, by adopting the Polish language, one furthered the key aim of 'the amalgamation of individual autonomous races and tribes into one social structure'.[8]

LITURGICAL REFORMERS: TRADITIONALISTS AND MODERNISTS

Perhaps, then, it would be more helpful to think of the synagogue service as either following the 'traditional' prescribed, fixed liturgy referred to as *keva* from the point of view of halakhah (traditional religious law) or following 'modern' innovations that involved changes to the language of the liturgy itself—abbreviation, or the replacement of Hebrew or any other 'Judaic' language such as Aramaic by the vernacular. Almost all of what was and still is recited in the 'traditional' standard,

[4] On these developments, see particularly M. Wodziński, *Haskalah and Hasidism in the Kingdom of Poland: A History of Conflict*, trans. S. Cozens (Oxford, 2009); A. Jagodzińska, *Pomiędzy: Akulturacja Żydów Warszawy w drugiej połowie XIX wieku* (Wrocław, 2008).

[5] See M. Galas, 'The Influence of Progressive Judaism in Poland: An Outline', *Shofar*, 29/3 (2011), 55–67.

[6] See A. Guterman, 'The Origins of the Great Synagogue in Warsaw on Tłomackie Street', in W. T. Bartoszewski and A. Polonsky (eds.), *The Jews in Warsaw: A History* (Oxford, 1991), 181–211.

[7] See the unpublished complete version of Sara Zilbersztajn's MA thesis, in the collection of the Żydowski Instytut Historyczny, Warsaw; see also M. Galas, *Rabin Markus Jastrow i jego wizja reformy judaizmu: Studium z dziejów judaizmu w XIX wieku* (Kraków, 2007).

[8] Quoted in Wodziński, *Haskalah and Hasidism in the Kingdom of Poland*, 163.

fixed liturgy, with minor differences in wording that have more to do with regional custom (*minhag*) than modern changes, was essentially set during the talmudic era.

Changes made by the liturgical modernists were numerous and varied widely. Some simply involved the use of prayers in the vernacular instead of Hebrew or Aramaic; others were far more radical and based on ideology. The most far-reaching included removing any references to the messianic era, the physical resurrection of the dead, the return to Zion, the restoration of the Temple, a sacrificial cult of any kind, and even Jewish 'particularism', 'separateness', or 'chosenness'. Of great importance were the German translations or paraphrases that accompanied the Hebrew texts, or—just as significant—the lack of translation of certain phrases.[9] While there are many that could exemplify the liturgical-modernist camp, the most important was Abraham Geiger (1810–74). It was Geiger who would be most systematic in his ideas about liturgical reform, freely choosing to alter the Hebrew text of the prayers as well as excising some of them altogether. In the preface to his 1854 prayer book, Geiger wrote:

> The lamentation about the lost national independence of Israel, the plea for the gathering of the dispersed in Palestine and the restoration of the cult and priests—all that is relegated to the background . . . likewise the hopeful look into the future is directed to the messianic kingdom as a time of the universal reign of God, of a strengthening piety and righteousness among all men, but not as a time for the elevation of the People of Israel.[10]

Liturgical traditionalists made no such changes to *keva*, at least in Hebrew and on paper. The best-known and by far the most influential of these traditionalists or 'conservatives'[11] who did not wish to alter the Hebrew text were Isaac Noah Mannheimer and Yehiel Michael Sachs. Mannheimer's greatest change was the pruning of *piyutim* (liturgical poems) that had been inserted into the liturgy over the centuries since it had been fixed; Sachs included far more of the *piyutim* but had a marvellous gift for poetic translation that retained the meaning of the original. The two types of *piyutim* most often removed from the liturgy by the traditionalists were *yotserot* and *kerovot*—but even here qualifications need to be made. *Yotserot* are those insertions made in the blessings accompanying the morning Shema (the affirmation of the unity of God) between the first blessing after Barekhu (ending with 'yotser or uvore ḥoshekh . . . uvore et hakol': 'creator of light and darkness . . . and creator of all') and the first blessing before the Shema ('yotser hame'orot': 'creator of the heavenly lights'). *Kerovot* is the generic term for poetry inserted into the Amidah (lit. 'standing'; this set of silent prayers is the central portion of the liturgy), recited on special weekdays, sabbaths, and festivals, including the High

[9] J. J. Petuchowski, *Studies in Modern Theology and Prayer*, ed. E. R. Petuchowski and A. M. Petuchowski (Philadelphia, 1998), 184–5.

[10] D. H. Ellenson, *After Emancipation: Jewish Religious Responses to Modernity* (Cincinnati, 2004), 206.

[11] See Petuchowski, *Prayerbook Reform in Europe*; also *Abraham Geiger and Liberal Judaism: The Challenge of the Nineteenth Century*, comp. M. Wiener, trans. E. J. Schlochauer (Philadelphia, 1962).

Holidays (*yamim nora'im*).[12] *Kerovot* also include such popular *piyutim* as Tal (the prayer for dew) and Geshem (the prayer for rain), recited during the cantor's repetition of the Amidah in the *musaf* service on the first day of Passover (Pesach) and on Shemini Atseret, respectively. Mannheimer, who boasted in 1829 that 'we pray without any modification from *adon olam* [recited in the early morning preliminary service prior to Birkhot Hashaḥar] to *aleinu*, but we leave out all *piyyutim*',[13] made an exception for Tal and Geshem and others on the High Holidays, but generally omitted *yotserot*,[14] while the even more conservative Sachs included both *yotserot* and *kerovot* in his festival and High Holiday prayer books.

For these traditionalists, translations from the Hebrew were generally very close to the original. An occasional word might be changed, usually when it involved a negative reference to a non-Jew in order not to offend. Some texts, and in Sachs's case some very lengthy *piyutim*, are left untranslated but remain in the prayer book,[15] while other customary but not mandatory readings such as 'Bameh madlikin' were removed altogether.[16]

IZAAK CYLKOW AND HIS *MAḤZOR*: A TRADITIONALIST OF MODERN BELIEF

The *maḥzor* (High Holiday prayer book) for Rosh Hashanah of Rabbi Izaak Cylkow (1841–1908), who was appointed as rabbi to the Daniłowiczowska Street synagogue in 1865, is an excellent example of a decidedly creative and bold approach to theology in translation (though it may be noted that translation of the prayer book into Polish was certainly not new by the time Cylkow prepared his translations of the *maḥzor*).[17] Cylkow's Hebrew text is strictly traditional and the cuts in various *piyutim* are nearly identical to those of Mannheimer. Cylkow evidently had no intention of writing a simple translation, as he makes clear in his introduction. For him, the aesthetics of prayers could be as important as their actual content:

As far as the external form of these prayers is concerned, it carries the marks of the age in which they were created and cannot, at least for an adherent of Judaism, be the subject of criticism. The moment a sanctified form is considered rationally, it loses its lofty character and ceases to exist. As long as the liturgy keeps its age-old Hebrew garment—and for reasons of piety it must retain this—there can be no question as to whether or not it fits the

---

[12] I. Elbogen, *Jewish Liturgy: A Comprehensive History*, trans. R. P. Scheindlin (Philadelphia, 1993), 170–3. [13] Plaut, *Rise of Reform Judaism*, 43.

[14] *Maḥzor lemo'adei el: Festgebete der Israeliten*, iii: *Shalosh regalim*, ed. and trans. Rabbi Dr I. N. Mannheimer (Vienna, 1859).

[15] See M. Sachs, *Festgebete der Israeliten*, vi: *Schemini Azereth und Simchath Thorah* (Breslau, 1899), 182–8. [16] See *Gebete der Israeliten*, trans. J. N. Mannheimer (Vienna, 1857), 133.

[17] Earlier efforts included those by Yehezkel Hoge in 1822 and Henryk Liebkind in 1846, and three works by Daniel Neufeld: *Modlitewnik dla Żydów-Polaków* (1865); *Modlitwy dla dzieci izraelskich* (1865); and *Hagada szel Pesach; czyli, Wspomnienia o wyjściu Izraelitów z Egiptu* (n.d.).

taste, notions, or perceptions of the educated [modern person] . . . It is different, however, when we read a translation, especially a literal one, of the original text. Such a text may have many, sometimes jarring, characteristics which an uninitiated and, indeed, indifferent reader may not easily comprehend . . . there is the belief in the physical resurrection of the dead . . . and similar dogmatic concepts which are not always a relevant reflection of the beliefs currently animating enlightened Israelites . . . The only middle course for bringing the old form of the cult nearer to modern notions and aesthetic demands is the omission of certain passages which time itself has brought into disuse, and the insertion of some prayers in the national language, based on the underlying Hebrew, and, first and foremost, the moderate paraphrasing or elucidation of certain key passages [in the translation].[18]

Izaak Cylkow was born to a liberal-minded, Jewishly educated father, Mojżesz Aaron Cylkow, who was initially tutor to the children of Solomon Zalman Marcus Posner, a leading non-hasidic patrician and social activist in Warsaw who vigorously sought equal rights for the Jews of the Kingdom of Poland.[19] Moreover, Posner was also a 'modern, honourable, and enlightened talmudist' who added to a treatise relating that Christians were not idolaters a study that proved that 'contemporary nations (especially Christian ones) after they had rejected repugnant idolatry, worship the real God and follow praiseworthy morals'.[20] It is possible that Mojżesz Cylkow tutored his own son with Posner's sons. His influence on his protégés is clear: one of Posner's sons, Leon, later became a frequent contributor to the integrationist Jewish press, publishing articles in *Jutrzenka*.[21]

The Cylkow family moved to Warsaw from the Posner estates in Kuchary by 1854, as Mojżesz Cylkow had accepted a new position as teacher of Talmud to the upper grades at the progressive Warsaw Rabbinical School, where Izaak would be educated as well. Much has been written of the school itself, but in relation to Izaak Cylkow, of primary importance was the fact that the school was essentially considered a vehicle by which Jews became Poles of the Mosaic persuasion, an instrument of 'national integration'.[22] By the time Izaak Cylkow began there, the dynamic leader of the school, the radical integrationist Antoni Eisenbaum (1791–1852), had already died and been succeeded by the moderate integrationist Jakub Tugenhold. Aside from the dismissal of Abram Buchner, 'the most extreme of the assimilationists', in 1857, Tugenhold changed little at the school. Part and parcel of the education there was a thorough inculcation of Polish patriotism, for which Eisenbaum was well known; one of his pupils wrote years later that 'He taught the Jews to love the land on which they were born and to fulfill towards that

---

[18] *Machzor; czyli, Modlitwy Izraelitów na wszystkie święta*, pt. i: *Rosz Haszana*, trans. Dr I. Cylkow (Warsaw, 1910), pp. x–xiii; the English translations here and below are by Izabela Barry and Antony Polonsky.

[19] Z. Borzymińska, 'Izaak Cylkow — postać z "krainy snów uroczych"', in M. Galas (ed.), *Izaak Cylkow (1841–1908): Życie i dzieło* (Budapest and Kraków, 2010), 39–55.

[20] Wodziński, *Haskalah and Hasidism in the Kingdom of Poland*, 56–7.   [21] Ibid.

[22] A. Polonsky, 'The Warsaw Rabbinical School: Agency of National Integration' (unpublished text, copy in my possession), 3

land the duties of a grateful son.'[23] Eisenbaum himself believed that the synagogue was 'a major influence on the community. In it, sermons are delivered which exhort the followers of the Old Testament to shake off their outdated prejudices and to go forward together with the Christian Nations on the path of education and positive discoveries',[24] a philosophy that would be echoed years later in Cylkow's theological leanings. Upon graduating from the school, Izaak initially went to medical school, but subsequently went on to further education in Berlin on a scholarship of the Lomedei-Torah society that had been established by the members of the progressive Daniłowiczowska Street synagogue, the very same congregation that Izaak Cylkow was ultimately to serve.[25] One of the reasons for establishing this scholarship was to provide talented graduates of the Rabbinical School with religious education 'by sending them for a short time to foreign rabbis to prepare for their doctorates in theology and achieve a true preacher's routine, allowing them, from time to time, to appear at the synagogue as novices'.[26]

Cylkow was a member of the Polonized Jewish intelligentsia which began to emerge in the late 1840s, made up, in Marcin Wodziński's words, of 'the young followers of the Haskalah, the students of the Warsaw Rabbinical School, the liberal bourgeoisie, and the new representatives of the Jewish intelligentsia'.[27] It was this group that Hilary Nussbaum, another of its members, saw as responsible for the new currents which now emerged from the late 1850s within those sectors of Jewish society which favoured its transformation and reform. In his words:

Educational resources such as *Jutrzenka*, *Izraelita*, and the Jewish Orphanages run by the Warsaw Charitable Society marked new trends in the 1860s. However, the most spectacular, the most visible feature of this period, was the rise of the first generation of young Israelites—physicians, lawyers, biologists, philologists—who dedicated themselves to the specialist, higher-level, and honourable professions; they became the spirited citizens of the country, supporters of general education, and the most effective force for progress among the wider circles of their co-religionists.[28]

Certainly, the small modernizing circles were increasingly influential on the Jewish community board of Warsaw and their position was strengthened there by the founding in 1852 of a 'Polish' synagogue intended to challenge the 'German' orientation of that on Daniłowiczowska Street. The new Jewish intelligentsia, which showed its strength in the late 1850s in the conflicts over burial practices and inscription on tombstones in Polish, was strongly in favour of integration into Polish society. While a relatively weak group of traditional maskilim remained in existence and a group of radical assimilationists began to emerge, the dominant

---

[23] Ibid. 32.   [24] Ibid. 4.   [25] Ibid.

[26] Borzymińska, 'Izaak Cylkow', 51; English translation by Izabela Barry.

[27] Wodziński, *Haskalah and Hasidism in the Kingdom of Poland*, 154.

[28] H. Nussbaum, *Szkice historyczne z życia Żydów w Warszawie, od pierwszych śladów pobytu ich w tem mieście do chwili obecnej* (Warsaw, 1881), quoted by Wodziński, *Haskalah and Hasidism in the Kingdom of Poland*, 154.

element among the reformers was now a moderate group aiming at hegemony, who promoted pro-Polish acculturation while wishing to preserve Jewish religious traditions, albeit in a modernized and renewed adaptation. Their key members, such as Daniel Neufeld, Roman Kramsztyk, and the long-standing editor of *Izraelita*, Samuel Peltyn, were strongly in favour of maintaining a firm religious identity. Indeed, Peltyn's views on the preservation of traditional elements in any reformed version of Judaism, set out in the pamphlet published under the pseudonym Judaita and entitled *Projekt reformy w judaizmie ze szczególnem uwzględnieniem jego strony etycznej* ('A Proposal for the Reform of Judaism with Particular Reference to its Ethical Component'; Warsaw, 1885), had much in common with the views that Cylkow was to articulate.

It was to this group that Cylkow belonged. He returned to Warsaw in 1863 having completed his university studies, receiving a doctorate in philosophy and Semitic languages at the University of Halle. Within two years he was appointed Rabbi Jastrow's successor, having been chosen over Yehezkel Caro, who had been trained at the new Jewish Theological Seminary in Breslau and had also received his doctorate from the University of Breslau. Cylkow must have been highly impressed by what he saw and read in Berlin. Certainly he was aware of the conflicts provoked by the reforms that Geiger and others had tried to implement in the German lands and perhaps this served as reason enough for his comments in his introduction to his *maḥzor* for Rosh Hashanah: 'Changes introduced by foreign communities have brought only disorder to religious service, and often unwanted conflicts and disputes. Their benefits were always doubtful and did not alleviate the harm they brought.' After referring to the 'jarring characteristics' of the liturgy which 'an uninitiated and, indeed, indifferent reader may not easily comprehend', he goes on to mention 'the belief in the physical resurrection of the dead . . . and similar dogmatic concepts'.[29]

Cylkow's remarks are far more revealing than it first appears. It is not unreasonable to believe that he was referring to his own belief, or lack thereof, in these 'dogmatic concepts'. Certainly, in his description of the messianic era, Cylkow played down supernatural elements:

Yet another motif of Israelite prayers is the plea for the imminent affirmation of the kingdom of God [*malkhut shamayim*], or the coming of messianic times, the prophesied era of religious harmony and eternal peace. This era will bring with it better relations in the world, harmony, and the end of prejudice and superstitions. The one God, one justice, and one law will be solidified in all hearts and minds, and happiness and satisfaction will increase to immeasurable levels. This motif of the future rule of truth and the light recurs constantly, in diverse forms.[30]

Cylkow envisages here an age of reason, or a truly enlightened age, particularly in his suggestion that the era will bring about the end of prejudice and superstition,

---

[29] *Machzor*, trans. Cylkow, pt. i, p. xi.   [30] Ibid., pp. viii–ix.

the 'future role of truth and light' as opposed to the supernatural elements often alluded to in liturgy and espoused even by such a rationalist as Maimonides. Furthermore, he does not even mention the national elements of the messianic era, but relegates them, as well as the restoration of the sacrificial cult, to a brief mention at the end of his essay on prayer that makes up the bulk of his introduction to the *maḥzor*:

An often-repeating motif of prayer is *beḥirah*, the belief that God chose the people of Israel from among all the tribes and tongues of their time, made an eternal covenant with them, blessed them with His commandments, so that they would live according to the rules of truth, virtue, and mercy and cultivate all that is good and lawful in themselves. This is, more or less, the content of the Israelite liturgy, which is also permeated by a patriotic motif, a plea for the return of the scattered people to the old home of their forefathers, [as well as] the rebuilding of the Temple, the renewal of the primeval cult of sacrifice, [and] the resurrection of the priestly and levitic service in its original sumptuousness and radiance.[31]

Cylkow espouses a view that is far closer to German Reform than is suggested by his attitude to the content of the liturgy, and here is perhaps even bolder than Abraham Geiger, one of the fathers of German Reform. Geiger created a list of principles first articulated in his *Denkschrift* of 1869 while serving in Frankfurt am Main; there is a remarkable resemblance to the introduction to his 1854 Breslau prayer book. Interesting for us are the passages that could easily have been adapted by Cylkow for his introduction:

With all respectful retention of Judaism's historical elements, religious concepts which have had temporal validity but which have been displaced by a progressively purer conception, must not be retained in a one-sided and sharp accentuation. Rather must they be either totally removed or recast in a form which does not contradict the purer conception . . .

i. The prayerbook, by and large, should retain its customary character. It should continue to express in a precise form its connection with the whole history of Judaism. Consequently, in its essential components, the worship service remains in Hebrew.

ii. . . . the Hebrew text must be accompanied by a German *adaptation* . . .

iii. Highly materialistic descriptions of the deity, as they occur in the *piyyutim*, must be removed;

iv. The enumeration of the various angelic orders and the depiction of their activity cannot be admitted;

v. The belief in immortality must not content itself with the one-sided formulation of a physical resurrection . . .

vi. The national aspect of Israel must recede into the background . . . the look into the future should arouse the happy hope in the unity of all mankind, in truth, in justice, and in peace. However, wholly faded from our consciousness is the belief in the restoration of a Jewish State in Palestine.[32]

---

[31] Ibid., p. x.   [32] Petuchowski, *Prayerbook Reform in Europe*, 165–7.

Compare this extract from Geiger with what I have cited above and with the following quotation from Cylkow, keeping in mind that Cylkow had no intention of removing much of anything. Here he sets out in detail the 'jarring characteristics' of the traditional liturgy for those of modern religious sensibility:

First of all, there is the patriotic ethos which we have discussed above, the longing for the old cradle of the people, which is these days interpreted in many ways. There is also the belief in the physical resurrection of the dead, the existence of the choirs of angels, seraphim, and cherubim, and similar dogmatic concepts, which are not always a relevant reflection of the beliefs currently animating the enlightened Israelites . . . in translation, they become pale and colourless, and cannot be properly judged, or reach the hearts of those praying. Another characteristic of the form is the highly developed tendency to epitomize the forces of nature appearing under many names and populating the heavenly spheres: *ofanim, erelim, ḥayot,* etc.[33]

It is not too difficult from this passage to divine Cylkow's true thoughts in light of his education and his knowledge, including his knowledge of the German Jewish scene. It is entirely possible that Cylkow did not at all believe in the text of the liturgy that he was translating and was thus engaged in preparing a version that his congregation would accept. We are, however, left with a paradox: while Cylkow clearly seems to have had doubts about the literal truth of the liturgy he was translating, his determined insistence on maintaining both the form of the prayers and keeping Hebrew as the language of them 'for the sake of piety' does raise the possibility that he was likely more influenced by the more moderate liturgical reforms of Isaac Noah Mannheimer or Yehiel Michael Sachs, even if his personal theology was more akin to Geiger's in that he rejected the concept of a personal messiah or physical resurrection of the dead.

Yehiel Michael Sachs was a student at the University of Berlin from 1827 to 1835, and while there he directly experienced the bitter arguments that the reform controversy aroused within the Jewish community in that city. Margit Schad has described this conflict that had led to 'resignation and stagnation, the split of the community into hostile camps of traditionalists and supporters of reform, the "epidemic of baptism", and the growing indifference and apathy, especially towards the religious concerns of the community'. The young Sachs drew from this the lesson that one needed to find a third way between the 'insensibility' and 'passivity' of Orthodoxy on one hand and the 'arbitrariness' of a reform which would be capable of winning back those who were 'repelled by both extremes'.[34]

Sachs sought to avoid such a situation by a middle way that he established in part in his first pulpit in Prague, when he succeeded Leopold Zunz as the preacher at the Tempel. It was here that Sachs made use of the so-called Vienna Rite of Mann-

[33] *Machzor,* trans. Cylkow, pt. i, pp. xi–xii.

[34] M. Schad, 'The Problems of Moderate Reform: The History of the Berlin Liturgical Reforms, 1844–1862', in C. Wiese (ed.), *Redefining Judaism in an Age of Emancipation: Comparative Perspectives on Samuel Holdheim, 1806–1860* (Leiden, 2007), 170.

heimer, which kept the *keva* intact while removing most if not all of the *yotserot* and *kerovot* from the sabbath prayer book and retaining generally only a few selected ones on festivals and the High Holidays; additionally, the 'dignity and solemnity' of the religious service was enhanced by the musical innovations of Salomon Sulzer. The middle way that Sachs would subsequently espouse a few years later in Berlin came from a blend of Wissenschaft and real devotion to tradition, a realization that

(1) religious self-awareness, history, and law, on the one hand, and the 'legitimate' needs of the present, like that of a reform of the service on the other hand have always had and continue to have a living coexistence, and (2) that the current crisis must be blamed on the Zeitgeist ('nihilism, materialism, indifference, and selfishness') and not on historical Judaism. Sachs positioned his reform projects distinctly between the Reform movement and Orthodoxy. Radical reforms, he believed, destroyed the creative potential of self-understanding and self-cleansing; the Orthodox side, meanwhile, placed every tradition and custom as holy and inviolable in the way of living development . . . Thus, the principles of moderate reform were to restore what was pristine and original, 'give shape to the shapeless'. According to Sachs, the regeneration must occur out of its own substance, without the adaptation of alien forms that are not grounded in the nature and historical essence of the Jewish service.[35]

Cylkow is very similar to Mannheimer in his careful adaptation and editing of the liturgy itself, but the introduction to his *maḥzor* clearly echoes Sachs's reverence for tradition and his distaste for 'alien forms'. There are no changes in the wording of the prayers. The most popular of the *piyutim* remain, in the original Hebrew, without editing. Like Sachs, but unlike Mannheimer, Cylkow achieved translations that are particularly poetic and beautiful. However, it is in his translations and comments that he introduced some changes, and not only because he felt that the difficulty of the texts made them impossible to understand for the 'uninitiated' or 'indifferent' reader. It seems likely that Cylkow's insistence on prayer in Hebrew and his statements against 'foreign notions' of more radical change were indeed genuine and reflect his belief that it was too early to introduce openly the theological innovations of Geiger. Let us consider the following passages:

Prayer, which makes up one of the elements of 'eternity', the yearning for something loftier, unknown, and unreachable, which 'God implanted in the hearts of man' beside the irresistible pursuit of light and truth, good and beauty, found its sublime expression in the Psalms, originating partly in the age of David. Along with other works of religious poetry, contained in the synagogue liturgy, it has accompanied the Israelites through the ages, joined with their religious life, flowing from the source of their deepest convictions, desires, and hopes.[36]

Connected with this [i.e. prayer] are historical reminiscences, elegies on the destruction of God's tabernacle and city, a plea for mollification of anger and mercy for the humbled and mistreated remnants, cultural relics relating to age-old religious service, biblical passages

---

[35] Ibid. 172.   [36] *Machzor*, trans. Cylkow, pt. i, p. vii.

forming public addresses, symbols, traditions, the proverbs of our forefathers, which the Israelite renews in his soul, so that the ideals cultivated by the Jewish tribe and connected with its history do not die out and get lost.[37]

For this reason, the liturgy in Hebrew should not be altered, since it was so closely linked to the emotions which bound believers to their faith: 'The very words, evoking impressions of one's youth, the melody bringing back the echoes of long-forgotten memories, resurrected in the soul of the person offering prayer, make further reflection impossible.'[38]

All these statements read differently when one takes into account Sachs's general principle of liturgical reform grounded in historical tradition, and reflect Mannheimer's view that 'The basic prayer (tefillah) as a ritual act can remain in Hebrew. Not much will be gained by modifying the tefillah; in fact, a great deal may be lost in respect to popular appeal.'[39] Cylkow makes a compelling argument for the emotional ties to the liturgy itself, and makes it perfectly clear that sentiment *should* inform the editor of any prayer book. Reading Cylkow's introduction can leave us with two distinctly different impressions: (1) that Hebrew should remain the language of Jewish prayer and the prayers themselves should be part not only of Jewish national history but of the *personal* history of any Jew who has prayed in a synagogue; and (2) that whether or not the reader or the editor/translator of the prayer book believes in the literal content of the text is immaterial when considering both the historical and social significance of the text itself and the conflicts which would follow attempts at changing the text and customs of prayer. Custom (*minhag*), it is often said, becomes as powerful as halakhah, and that is as true for personal custom, the practice of the individual believer, as it is generally.

Cylkow's clear discomfort with some texts while retaining them for these reasons is admirably illustrated in his introduction to Kol Nidrei, the declaration with which the introductory evening service on the Day of Atonement begins, which makes possible the annulment of vows between the believer and God. While never stating explicitly that he wished he could remove the text, Cylkow forcefully echoed the arguments of Hai Gaon and other sages who disapproved of the text and was quite blunt when he wrote that 'This spoken formula that leads to false and slandering accusations has already been removed from the liturgy in many Israelite communities abroad.'[40] He was clearly echoing older arguments against the recitation of Kol Nidrei, particularly that a Jew could not be trusted;[41] indeed, throughout western Europe and the United States, the text had been removed for just this reason. It is worth presenting Cylkow's own words:

[37] *Machzor*, trans. Cylkow, pt. i, pp. ix–x.   [38] Ibid., p. xi   [39] Plaut, *Rise of Reform Judaism*, 43.

[40] *Machzor; czyli, Modlitwy Izraelitów na wszystkie święta*, pt. ii: *Jom Kippur*, trans. Dr I. Cylkow (Warsaw, 1934), 33; the English translations here and below are by Marta Krzemińska and Antony Polonsky.

[41] The *Jewish Encyclopedia* (New York, 1901–16) lists these references: J. C. Wagenseil, *Tela Ignea* [Altdorf, 1681], Disputatio R. Jechielis, 23; J. A. Eisenmenger, *Entdecktes Judenthum* (Königsberg,

It seems though, that in the course of time the whole formula has been abandoned altogether, because it lost its practical, religious foundation. Abdurhalim quotes the words of Hai Gaon, who says: 'In neither of the academies nor in Babylon is it customary to recite "Kol Nidrei" on the New Year or on the Day of Atonement; however, we have heard from our teachers that there are communities that do follow such a custom, of which we nonetheless do not approve.' In all events, what follows from all the rabbis' controversial opinions known on this topic is an adamant certainty that the formula pertains only to vows and oaths that an Israelite has sworn to God voluntarily. It does not in any way exempt him from the duties that have been imposed on him by the Covenant; duties towards God or fellow men, duties towards individuals, society, and nation, and above all from oaths already sworn, or those that he intends to take privately or in front of the court. This has already been stated by Rabbi Jeroham b. Meshullam in the volume *Toledot adam vehavah* written five centuries ago.[42]

Cylkow also took issue with the wording of Aleinu, the prayer at the conclusion of the daily service proclaiming the future establishment of the rule of the One God. His translation tries very carefully to avoid any possible confusion about the meaning of the text in its reference to idolatry that in the Middle Ages led the Catholic Church to censor part of it as a criticism of Christian belief. As Petuchowski has pointed out, while the prayer, as a whole, kept the balance between 'particularism' (of the Jewish people, expressed in the first paragraph) and 'universalism' (in the second paragraph), the form in which the 'particularism' was expressed was often disturbing to the liturgists of Liberal and Reform Judaism.[43] A literal translation of the text, with its strong accent on Jewish particularism, reads as follows:

It is our duty to praise the Master of all, to ascribe greatness to the Molder of primeval creation,

For He has not made us like the nations of the lands and has not emplaced like the families of the earth.

For He has not assigned our portion like theirs nor our lot like their multitudes,

But we bend our knees and bow and acknowledge our thanks before the King Who reigns over kings [literally, 'The King of King of Kings'], the Holy One,

Blessed is He.

He stretches out heaven and establishes the foundations of the earth,

The seat of His homage is the heavens above and His powerful Presence is in the loftiest heights.

He is our God and there is none other; True is our King, there is none beside Him

As it is written in His Torah: 'You are to know this day and take to your heart that YHWH is the only God—in heaven above and earth below—there is none other.'[44]

1711), vol. ii, ch. ix, pp. 489 ff.; J. C. G. Bodenschatz, *Kirchliche Verfassung der heutigen Juden* (Frankfurt and Leipzig, 1748), pt. ii, ch. v, §10; A. Rohling, *Der Talmudjude* (Münster, 1877), 80 ff.

[42] *Machzor*, trans. Cylkow, ii. 32–3.   [43] Petuchowski, *Prayerbook Reform in Europe*, 299.

[44] *The Complete ArtScroll Machzor: Yom Kippur*, trans. Rabbi N. Scherman (Brooklyn, NY, 1986), 152.

Cylkow himself in his poetic translation is very careful to limit Jewish 'chosenness', framing it in the past tense while at the same time providing an image of an enlightened future:

> May it indeed be our duty, in this congregation of His faithful servants,
> To praise the creator of the universe, to raise our grateful hands,
> That out of the tribes extinguished by the boundless flood,
> His light illuminated us, His truth has guided us,
> That he distinguished us from among the pagans, freed us from the bonds of darkness,
> Revealed to us His Covenant and the bright glow of His being.
> Oh, how beautiful is our role, how liberated are our souls,
> When the ties of sorcery and error do not restrict us any more;
> We were allowed to bow before the King, who Himself governs the world,
> To bend the knee and humble ourselves before His majesty,
> He who stretched out the skies, who laid the foundations of the earth,
> Revealed His teaching and proclaimed His will;
> So that it became imprinted deep in our minds,
> That He is alone on the earth and in the heavens above.
> As His word proclaims: 'In your heart you shall affirm,
> He is the only Lord, and there is no God apart from Him!'[45]

In addition, the phrase 'we were allowed to bow before the King' is translated in the past tense, as if to suggest that Jews were not the only ones *currently* to bow before God, a very major change from the original meaning of the liturgy—and one obviously made for the sake of those who wished to view Jews and Poles as brothers. Clearly, the articulation of Jewish specialness or particularism had been altered in Cylkow's version to view the Jewish people as enlightened earlier than other peoples of the world, but not the only people of the world to be so enlightened since.

Cylkow's paraphrase of Aleinu is a major theological statement in the guise of religious poetry. Cylkow's more enlightened conception was intended to replace an older, no longer valid vision and was recast into a form that does not contradict this purer ideal. He does seem here to be approaching the view of Geiger that in the messianic age, the difference between Israel and the Nations would disappear.

It is a sad irony of history that, even within Cylkow's lifetime, and certainly by his death in 1908, the long-hoped-for brotherhood was clearly failing. Those barriers would be built up all the more, beginning in 1881 with a wave of pogroms and ultimately climaxing with the modern antisemitism of Roman Dmowski and the Endecja. Support for integration remained significant within the Jewish elite but was increasingly supplanted by more modern 'isms', above all Zionism: Cylkow's successors at the Great Synagogue of Warsaw would be decidedly pro-Zionist, and indeed Rabbi Mojżesz Schorr was to be the president of the Polish chapter of B'nai B'rith.

---

[45] *Machzor*, trans. Cylkow, ii. 451.

CONCLUSION

Cylkow was an ardent integrationist who believed that the barriers between Jews and Christians had no place in his theology while at the same time remaining a liturgist of a decidedly traditional bent. His strong belief that the liturgy should remain in Hebrew and that no changes should be made in the traditional text was not only based on his view that the benefits of such changes had been outweighed by the conflicts that they had caused, but was also primarily because of the deep sentiments the traditional liturgy evoked in the worshipper. At the same time, Cylkow was capable of inserting very bold theological statements into his paraphrases of various prayers that revealed attitudes typical of Geiger and other followers of German Reform. The way Cylkow chose to frame Jewish 'particularity', and especially his understanding of the messianic future, was clearly based on the ideas of the Reform movement within German Jewry.

However, to describe Cylkow as a mere 'follower of Geiger in Mannheimer's clothing' would be a disservice to his efforts and, indeed, inaccurate. Petuchowski has argued that the Orthodox and the Reform Jew both took the words of the prayer book (*sidur*) in their most literal sense, the former accepting and the latter rejecting the text understood in this way. Neither group was able to see that the language of prayer was the language of poetry. In Petuchowski's view, if the tradionalists and modernists of the nineteenth century had understood this simple and fundamental fact, the whole history of Reform and Liberal Judaism might have been very different. This stress on theology meant that the imagery of the prayer book had to be read not poetically, but as prose, and the prayer book as a philosophical dissertation.[46]

Cylkow, however, seems to be have been able to navigate this issue differently. In accepting the sentimental need for tradition, he did not bind himself to the need to be dogmatic even when he clearly did not believe in the words of the traditional text. 'Relevance' in the understanding of most European Reform and Liberal thinkers meant the text had to appeal to the needs of the day and that its sense had to be taken literally: if they could not believe in what was expressed, they would not recite the prayers in which these ideas were embodied. Cylkow, on the other hand, found relevance in the need for the familiar, even when the literal meaning of the text was at odds with his theology. He clearly understood that the words of the prayer book were products of the period in which they were produced, but also appreciated their historical and cultural signficance. In this sense, Cylkow trod a narrow path between the traditionalists and the modernists, between the rational and the romantic.

[46] See Petuchowski, *Prayerbook Reform in Europe*, 348–55.

'Who Has Not Wanted To Be an Editor?'

The Yiddish Press in the Kingdom of Poland, 1905–1914

JOANNA NALEWAJKO-KULIKOV

A daily paper in Yiddish was for many a long year the dream and hope both of the Jewish masses, of the Jewish intelligentsia that had drawn closer to [those] masses, and also—or above all—of Jewish writers.   AVROM REYZEN[1]

The average Jew will have a growing need for a newspaper, a need which, given our Jews' cultural differences, is satisfied precisely by a paper in jargon [i.e. Yiddish].
                                                                                                ROMAN DMOWSKI[2]

THE PLACE FOR A JEWISH PAPER IS WARSAW

EFFORTS to obtain St Petersburg's agreement to the publication in Russia of works in Yiddish lasted more or less throughout the whole nineteenth century. The first such publication,[3] the weekly *Kol mevaser* edited by Aleksandr Tsederbaum, appeared in Odessa between 1864 and 1871. In 1867 the *Varshoyer yidishe tsaytung* appeared in Warsaw, and only later, in 1881, was permission granted for the publication in St Petersburg of the weekly *Dos yidishes folksblat*. In principle, however, 'jargon'[4] was seen as the greatest obstacle to 'civilizing' the Jews, and requests for

Gathering material for this study was made possible by research carried out in St Petersburg within the framework of an exchange between the Polish Academy of Sciences and the Russian Academy of Sciences. I should like to thank Professor Dmitry A. Elyashevich and Professor Rafail S. Ganelin for valuable advice, as well as my husband for help in translating archival sources from Russian.

[1] A. Reyzen, *Epizodn fun mayn lebn*, 3 vols. (Vilna, 1929–35), ii. 127.

[2] R. Dmowski, 'Kwestia żydowska', *Głos Warszawski*, 11 Nov. 1909.

[3] It is a matter of discussion whether we can consider Antoni Eisenbaum's *Dostrzegacz Nadwiślański/Der beobakhter an der vaikhsel* (1823–4), printed half in Polish and half in heavily Germanized Yiddish, to be a Yiddish publication. The very nature of the *Dostrzegacz*, which appeared thanks to government subsidies and which aimed to 'civilize' Jews, is also dubious.

[4] Even into the twentieth century Yiddish was commonly referred to in Polish as *żargon* (in Russian, *zhargon*), as it was considered to be basically a corrupt form of German.

permission to publish works, let alone daily newspapers, in the Yiddish language
were for the most part refused.[5] As Dmitry Elyashevich writes:

This attitude [of the tsarist authorities to the emergence of a Yiddish press] was always
decidedly negative, yet at various times there were various reasons for it, and a change in
these reasons can be seen as an indicator not only of a political shift in the narrow field of
censorship, but also of general ideological changes on the part of the tsarist authorities
towards the Jewish question.[6]

Such a change eventually took place at the turn of the century. It was linked to the
growing popularity of the Russian mass-circulation press (the so-called penny
press),[7] as well as to the appearance in the 1860s of modern literature in the Yiddish
language. The group of authors writing in Yiddish grew slowly—in Odessa to
begin with, and then in Warsaw, where a circle of writers formed around Yitskhok
Leyb Peretz:

By 1903 Warsaw had already become the main centre of modern Yiddish, and partly also
Hebrew, literature. *Der yud*, then *Di folkstsaytung* and the Progres publishing house, already
enabled young and old writers and poets to come to Warsaw . . . Kiev, which was something
of a centre of Jewish literature in the 1890s; Odessa, where Mendele himself lived and
worked, as did Y. Y. Linetski, Ahad Ha'am, Y. Kh. Ravnitski, and a very young Bialik; even
Vilna—the Jerusalem of the North—where the principal luminaries of Yiddish literature
lived and worked, such as Ayzik Meyer Dik and others, and of Hebrew literature, such as
Adam Hakohen—[all these] paled in comparison with the new light which arose in Warsaw. It was not surprising then that every young talent from these places headed for Warsaw,
which became the heart of Yiddish literature.[8]

Neither the fortnightly *Der yud*,[9] published in Kraków to avoid the tsarist censorship but distributed on the territory of the Russian empire, nor the literary almanacs
published by Sholem Aleichem and Y. L. Peretz (which served as de facto journals)
were able to satisfy this milieu's growing needs. It was even the case that Yiddish
writers, such as Sholem Asch and Avrom Reyzen, printed their works in Hebrew
translation in *Hatsefirah*, pretending that they had written them in Hebrew, while
the editors of *Hatsefirah*, according to Reyzen's memoirs, pretended to believe
them.[10]

However, such a situation could not continue indefinitely, the more so because
the new political forces which had arisen at the end of the nineteenth century in the

[5] For a discussion of the tsarist censorship's behaviour towards Yiddish publications, see D. A.
Elyashevich, *Pravitel'stvennaya politika i evreiskaya pechat' v Rossii, 1797–1917: Ocherki istorii tsenzury*
(St Petersburg and Jerusalem, 1999), 435–56.   [6] Ibid. 435.
[7] For more on this subject, see D. R. Brower, 'The Penny Press and its Readers', in S. P. Frank and
M. D. Steinberg (eds.), *Cultures in Flux: Lower-Class Values, Practices, and Resistance in Late Imperial
Russia* (Princeton, 1994), 147–67; L. McReynolds, *The News under Russia's Old Regime: The Develop-
ment of a Mass-Circulation Press* (Princeton, 1991).   [8] Reyzen, *Epizodn fun mayn lebn*, ii. 145.
[9] On the subject of *Der yud*, see R. R. Wisse, 'Not the "Pintele Yid" but the Full-Fledged Jew',
Prooftexts, 15/1 (1995), 33–61.   [10] Reyzen, *Epizodn fun mayn lebn*, ii. 106.

Jewish community—Zionism and the Bund—appealed to a base formed by the so-called *yidishe folksmasn*, whose language was above all Yiddish. If in the case of the Bund it was a central element in its own propagated ideology of *doykayt* ('hereness'), the Zionists had to approach the matter less dogmatically and more pragmatically. Ahad Ha'am wrote bitterly in a private letter a year after the First Zionist Congress:

In order to give you an idea of the current state of Hebrew . . . I need say only what friends in [the Warsaw publishing house] Ahiasaf have been telling me: of the two brochures which they published on the Zionist congress—the first one in Hebrew and written by *Herzl himself*, the second in jargon and written by Sholem Aleichem—the first sold only 3,000 copies, while the second one went to 27,000 copies![11]

Beginning in 1897–8 the avalanche of requests for permission to set up Yiddish daily papers and journals finally forced the Ministry of the Interior to revisit the issue of the Yiddish press.[12] This time there was eventually an appreciable result: in 1903 a group of Jewish intellectuals received permission to publish in St Petersburg the first Yiddish daily in the Russian empire, *Fraynd*, edited by Shaul Ginzburg.[13]

However, what worked against *Fraynd* was the fact that it came out in St Petersburg—a city almost devoid of a Yiddish base and in which most of the Jewish community was composed of wealthy, assimilated Russian Jews, who tended to read Russian Jewish publications such as *Voskhod* and Russian 'thick journals' (*tolstye zhurnaly*) rather than a Yiddish newspaper. Ginzburg himself admitted in his memoirs that typesetters for the paper had to be sought in Vilna, and contributors in Warsaw, and that basing a Yiddish daily in the Russian empire's capital raised all sorts of doubts among potential readers. 'During the whole time that I spent amongst Warsaw writers I heard complaints from all sides . . . the place for a Jewish paper was not amongst the Petersburg gentiles, but there in Jewish Warsaw!'[14] Yet if to begin with the very fact of producing a newspaper in Yiddish guaranteed its success with its readers, changes soon took place that meant that this was no longer enough. The trigger for these changes was the belated springtime of the peoples, in other words the 1905 revolution.

A FEW HOURS OF FREEDOM

In January 1905 a special committee, established to reform press law, began its work in St Petersburg, and already by the end of February the editors of almost every newspaper in the Kingdom of Poland, as well as book publishers, had demanded

---

[11] *Igerot ahad ha'am*, ii: *1898–1900* (Tel Aviv, 1956), 119 (emphasis original).

[12] Elyashevich, *Pravitel'stvennaya politika i evreiskaya pechat' v Rossii*, 452.

[13] For more on *Fraynd*, see S. A. Stein, *Making Jews Modern: The Yiddish and Ladino Press in the Russian and Ottoman Empires* (Bloomington, Ind., 2004).

[14] S. Ginzburg, *Amolike peterburg: forshungen un zikhroynes vegn yidishn lebn in der rezidents-shtot fun tsarishn rusland* (New York, 1944), 192.

the abolition of the pre-emptive censorship then in force.[15] The revolution began to bear its first fruit: on 1 August 1905 the first Yiddish daily in the Kingdom of Poland, called *Der veg*, appeared in Warsaw. The publisher, Tsevi Prylucki, had received a concession to publish it in St Petersburg; however, he had managed to arrange for this to be transferred to Warsaw. The first edition of *Der veg* caused a great stir among the Warsaw Jewish public: 'Wherever you went at that time, people were talking incessantly about the new *Kurier* or the new *Fraynd*, as many Warsaw Jews even many years later would always call every Jewish newspaper.'[16]

It was Prylucki's intention to make *Der veg* 'a general encyclopaedia compiled by a team of experts with a mission to educate the Jewish public',[17] and edited like Russian papers, that is with a leader on the front page. This layout appeared to be so immutable that even first-order news, such as the signing of a peace treaty in Port Arthur, was presented as if in passing and in second place.[18] The paper often waited for a piece of news to appear first in the Polish or Russian press. The Hebrew press also operated along similar lines at the time. According to Aron Gavze, one of the subsequent founders of *Haynt*,

The readers of *Hatsefirah* and other Jewish papers in Warsaw were accustomed to reading news reprinted from the Polish papers. When I once mentioned in *Hatsefirah* that the editor, Mr Nahum Sokolow, had survived a bomb explosion on his way through Grzybów, the editor, spotting this notice in the proofs, asked for it to be held back and reprinted only on the following day from the Polish papers.[19]

This way of presenting the news was soon to change; this was dictated by the rapid pace of revolutionary events, and the more so because, under their pressure, Tsar Nicholas II proclaimed on 17 October 1905 the October Manifesto on the freedom of expression, assembly, and the person. However, since the manifesto was not accompanied by any rules of an executive nature and it was unclear how to interpret the announced freedom of expression, representatives of the Warsaw press sent a petition to the governor-general in which they informed him that henceforth they would no longer be submitting material for pre-emptive censorship, since that would be in violation of the manifesto. The petition was signed by eight editors, including Eliasz Berman of *Hatsefirah* and Tsevi Prylucki.[20] The mere fact that their signatures could be found alongside those of Polish journalists is proof of the revolutionary attitudes of the time. Just a few years later this would have been impossible.

---

[15] Z. Kmiecik, *Prasa polska w rewolucji 1905–1907* (Warsaw, 1980), 19.

[16] D. Druk, *Tsu der geshikhte fun der yidisher prese (in rusland un poyln)* (Warsaw, 1920), 39.

[17] K. Weiser, *Jewish People, Yiddish Nation: Noah Prylucki and the Folkists in Poland* (Toronto, 2011), 50.   [18] Druk, *Tsu der geshikhte fun der yidisher prese*, 40.

[19] A. Gavze, 'Vi azoy mir hobn gearbet', in *Haynt yubiley-bukh, 1908–1928* (Warsaw, 1928), 4.

[20] S. Lev, *Prokim yidishe geshikhte: sotsyale un natsyonale bavegungen bay yidn in poyln un rusland fun 1897 biz 1914* (New York, 1941), 204; Druk, *Tsu der geshikhte fun der yidisher prese*, 43.

On 7 November 1905 the editors of Warsaw publications were informed officially of the lifting of pre-emptive censorship. As a modern Polish expert on the press has remarked, 'This was a turning point in the history of the Polish press.'[21] It was, however, even more of a turning point in the history of the Jewish press, since henceforth one can speak of the birth of a modern mass-circulation Yiddish press.[22]

The files of the Main Administration for Press Affairs of the Ministry of Internal Affairs held in the Russian State Historical Archive in St Petersburg allow us to follow the tsarist authorities' policies on issues dealing with the Yiddish press during the tumultuous first year of revolution. It was the custom for a potential publisher to submit to the Main Administration for Press Affairs a request for permission to publish a periodical, in which he outlined its general 'policy', or rather its structure. In almost every request this was the same, and it included amongst other things official information, socio–political articles, a review of the press, telegrams and correspondence, belles-lettres and literary criticism, articles on popular science, feuilletons, illustrations, and advertisements. The petitioner also provided more technical information: the proposed price for a single copy and for a yearly subscription, the address of the printer, and the names of the publisher and managing editor. The Main Administration for Press Affairs then approached the local authorities for the area where the request had originated (in the case of Warsaw this would have been the governor-general) for an opinion. If the local authorities voiced no objection and if the petitioner was not under suspicion for ever having engaged in anti-governmental activity, then the Main Administration for Press Affairs was supposed to grant permission. In reality, needless to say, practice varied. Let us examine several selected cases.

On 22 February 1905 Azriel-Meir Simkhelevitsh Braude from Białystok submitted a request to publish the daily *Di naye tsayt* (the paper itself was to be published in Warsaw and printed on the *Hatsefirah* presses). The request was rejected on the pretext that the sole censor in Warsaw who knew Yiddish was already overloaded with work (it may be noted in passing that they were fond of this argument and used it frequently). It was indicated as if incidentally that the petitioner, a former merchant of the second guild, had until the current year been the owner of a shop selling bedlinen and that he had never been involved with publishing.[23]

Braude's case shows that at least some potential publishers saw newspaper

[21] Z. Kmiecik, 'Prasa polska w zaborze rosyjskim w latach 1905–1915', in J. Łojek (ed.), *Prasa polska w latach 1864–1918* (Warsaw, 1976), 61.

[22] A characteristic of this period in the history of the Yiddish press is its development as a big-city phenomenon. This can clearly be seen in the surviving inventories of the Main Administration for Press Affairs (Glavnoe upravlenie po delam pechati). A pronounced majority of applications by publishers came from Warsaw, followed by Łódź, and beyond the Kingdom also Vilna, Białystok, and Odessa. However, there are no requests whatsoever to publish newspapers in the smaller towns and shtetls (in other words, something that was to be typical of the Jewish press in inter-war Poland).

[23] Rossiiskii gosudarstvennyi istoricheskii arkhiv, St Petersburg (hereafter RGIA), f. 776, op. 15, d. 44, fos. 1–9.

publishing not so much as a mission to inform, but rather as a way to make money.[24] But at the same time it is also witness to the enormous interest amongst the Jewish masses in a daily press. The petitioners themselves often provided this information. Thus, on 13 March 1905 Ayzik Elyashev (the publisher of the Hebrew daily *Hatsofeh*), residing in Warsaw at 20 Pańska Street, applied for permission to publish the daily *Der yud*, which he justified in this way:

The need for and the undoubted benefit of such an organ in Warsaw, where there are about 300,000 Jews, a great number of whom know only the spoken Jewish language [Yiddish], or who remain poorly oriented on the basic issues and occurrences of daily life, or who glean knowledge from unsubstantiated and sometimes illegal sources—this need is so obvious that it allows me to hope that my request will be granted.[25]

Elyashev's experience in the field of publishing undoubtedly worked to his advantage and his request might have been viewed positively had not the governor-general of Warsaw expressed reservations, when consulted as a matter of routine. However, in June 1905 the Department of Police warned the Main Administration for Press Affairs that

supporters of the revolutionary Jewish organization known as the 'Bund', with great persist-ence and working through various third parties, are trying to obtain permission to publish in the Jewish spoken language (jargon) a newspaper to be distributed among the masses of the Jewish people. Those who are assuming the responsibility for handling the matter will appear as completely fictitious editors, receiving for their efforts a previously agreed sum. To this end . . . a number of requests have recently been made by third parties, one of whom requests permission to publish a newspaper that is to appear with the title *Der Jude* [*sic*] ('The Jew').[26]

It is hard to establish whether this was true; it is not out of the question that it was, since the final surviving document in the *Der yud* file is yet another letter from Elyashev, this time requesting that the consideration of his request be suspended.[27] *Der yud* never saw the light of day.

However, Nahum Sokolow did receive permission to publish the daily *Der telegraf*. In a letter to the Main Administration for Press Affairs Sokolow presented himself as the publisher of *Hatsefirah*, which he described as 'one of the most seri-ous newspapers in this country', recently threatened, however, by competition from the Yiddish press: 'The competition created by these papers and the very fact of their existence is not a temporary, accidental phenomenon.' Sokolow wrote openly that Hebrew was accessible to only a narrow circle of readers (and completely incomprehensible to women), and that this circle was continuously shrinking. On

[24] The Russian scholar Aleksandr N. Bokhanov quotes in his work a comment from the early years of the twentieth century found in the archives (unfortunately, not identified more precisely): 'A news-paper represents the same capitalist undertaking as mining coal or producing alcohol.' A. N. Bokhanov, *Burzhuaznaya pressa Rossii i krupnyi kapital: Konets XIX v. – 1914 g.* (Moscow, 1984), 40.

[25] RGIA, f. 776, op. 15, d. 60, fo. 1.   [26] Ibid. 4.   [27] Ibid. 7.

the other hand, there was a large mass of Jews who did not know the language of the majority of local newspapers, in other words Polish ones.[28]

The editorial line proposed by Sokolow for the new paper did not depart from the norm. It was to include, amongst other things, government decisions and directives, news from Russia and abroad, articles on politics, literature, art, history, and socio-economic issues, belles-lettres, a law report, comic and sport sections, play reviews, a stock exchange report, obituaries, and advertising, as well as special supplements on major events.[29] However, the interesting thing is that in this case not only was the opinion of the governor-general sought (who emphasized the petitioner's many years of literary and journalistic activity), but also that of a colleague on *Hatsefirah*—a certain Isidor Fedorovich Gasfeld. In a letter sent to St Petersburg Gasfeld stated that there really was an enormous need for a 'jargon' newspaper in the Kingdom of Poland, but that few of the papers existing hitherto had gained any popularity, owing to their editors (who supposedly were 'unpopular' and 'intemperately inclined'). In his opinion, Sokolow was, by contrast, greatly respected among both the intelligentsia and the general public:

Mr Sokolow's word is law for the people, his voice is the voice of a prophet, and his moderate political views are in complete accord with government wishes, which all his work up till now confirms, as does personal confirmation by the local authorities, and therefore a newspaper edited by him will without question calm the minds of simple folk.[30]

On 11 October 1905 the Main Administration for Press Affairs permitted Sokolow to publish the daily, but the October Manifesto, which was proclaimed immediately afterwards, diametrically changed the situation of the press throughout the empire. This had long-term consequences for the Jewish population of the Kingdom of Poland, despite the fact that—as Dovid Druk, a journalist and contributor to *Der veg*, put it—'freedom in Warsaw lasted only a few hours'.[31]

AND WHO HAS NOT WANTED TO BE AN EDITOR?

The revolutionary liberalization of the press laws made it easier for anyone wanting to publish a newspaper to receive a concession. 'Anyone who wanted to be an editor (and who has not wanted to be an editor?) tried to arrange a concession for a newspaper', recalled Dovid Druk.[32] Many of these concessions were never taken up, and many publications were suspended after the production of barely a few issues, either from lack of funds, or because of some kind of harassment by the authorities. 'This all created such enormous chaos in the publishing world', writes Zenon Kmiecik, 'that even professional newsmen were unable to gauge whether a given publication had any chance of surviving for long, or whether it had no prospects at

---

[28] RGIA, f. 776, op. 15, d. 119, fo. 1. [29] Ibid. 2. [30] Ibid. 5.
[31] Druk, *Tsu der geshikhte fun der yidisher prese*, 43. [32] Ibid. 49.

all.'[33] New papers appeared on a daily basis, while others disappeared. In 1906 official statistics noted the appearance of 137 new titles (including Russian ones) throughout the Kingdom, of which as many as 100 were newspapers and magazines in Warsaw.[34] A considerable percentage of these were Yiddish publications. On 1 January 1906 the Warsaw Censorship Committee was reviewing as many as thirty-five applications for new Jewish publications (one in Polish, six or seven in Hebrew, and the rest in Yiddish). Even by then the list of managing editors already contained the names of people who would go down for ever in the history of the Yiddish press: Noyekh Finkelshteyn, Noyekh (Noah) Prylucki, Shloma (actually Shmuel) Y. Yatskan, Magnus Kryński, Mordkhe Spektor, and others.[35]

Most of the new publications which appeared on the wave of revolution did not stand the test of time (not excepting even *Der telegraf*, endorsed by Sokolow[36]), so let us recall only a few of them that have entered the annals of the Yiddish press. *Der veg*, already mentioned above, was suspended in October 1905 after three months owing to internal conflict on the board, problems with the censorship, and a generally difficult political situation, only to start up again under the same name at the end of the following month. The reconstituted daily did indeed make a better impression, was produced on better paper, and had an altogether richer content (for instance it began to print columns on the Jewish theatre, which was something quite new for the actors);[37] after the opening of the First Duma its circulation grew to 15,000 copies. However, the paper's financial problems began to multiply and its current backer pulled out. Neither the introduction of an evening edition (a first for the Jewish press!) nor the establishment of the Hebrew-language daily *Hayom*, whose profits were intended to save *Der veg* (it was hoped that after Sokolow suspended *Hatsefirah* in 1906, wealthy lovers of Hebrew would put their hands into their pockets for *Hayom*, so that Warsaw would not be left without a daily Hebrew newspaper)[38]—neither of these measures helped, and *Der veg* ceased to exist.

The final nail in *Der veg*'s coffin was the appearance of yet another daily newspaper, this time in a completely new format for the Jewish press. As has just been mentioned, in 1906 Nahum Sokolow suspended publication of *Hatsefirah*. As a result, a number of his colleagues decided to try their hand at publishing their own

---

[33] Kmiecik, *Prasa polska w rewolucji 1905–1907*, 33.

[34] Kmiecik, 'Prasa polska w zaborze rosyjskim w latach 1905–1915', 62. However, elsewhere Kmiecik attributes the number of 137 new publications rather to 1907, while in the previous year there had apparently been as many as 206 new publications: Kmiecik, *Prasa polska w rewolucji 1905–1907*, 33 (table 4).

[35] 'Sprawozdanie Warszawskiego Komitetu Cenzury na 1 stycznia 1906 r.', in M. Fuks, *Prasa żydowska w Warszawie, 1823–1939* (Warsaw, 1979), 296–7 (annexe 1). For the beginnings of the Yiddish mass-circulation press, in addition to the works by Lev and Druk cited above, see Weiser, *Jewish People, Yiddish Nation*, 43–72.

[36] *Der telegraf*'s lack of success can be explained by the fact that Sokolow himself, apart from putting his name to it, most likely took little interest in it.

[37] Druk, *Tsu der geshikhte fun der yidisher prese*, 46.

[38] Ibid. 48–9; Weiser, *Jewish People, Yiddish Nation*, 56–9.

paper, in Yiddish to boot. The idea came from Shmuel Yankev Yatskan, an enterprising, resourceful, and self-confident Litvak,[39] who brought into the project his editorial colleagues Avrom Goldberg and Aron Gavze, and also his friend of many years' standing Noyekh Finkelshteyn. On 28 May 1906 the first edition of the new penny daily *Yidishes tageblat* appeared. Aron Gavze recalled many years later that the four of them actually brought out the entire paper themselves; he was responsible for the Warsaw news round-up, news from the provinces, proofreading, and the paper's whole technical side, for a salary of 15 roubles per week. The editorial offices were at 38 Nalewki Street, in two rooms and a kitchen: 'The composition and stereotyping were carried out in the two rooms, while we set up the editorial office in the kitchen. There was a small table by the sink, and in the other corner—a lectern. These were the two editorial stations. My friend Goldberg sat at the table, while I wrote standing at the lectern.'[40]

Despite such spartan working conditions (although perhaps they were not especially worse than the working conditions for other editorial boards in the Warsaw of the time), within two weeks *Yidishes tageblat* had supposedly reached a print run of 70,000 copies.[41] The paper's great popularity was due to Yatskan, who had a fantastic feel for the market and saw what would catch on among a mass readership. The same year, he also began to publish a Yiddish weekly called *Yidishes vokhenblat*. As Kalman Weiser writes: 'Poland's largely traditional Jewish readers, accustomed to perusing religious texts at specified times, were still acquiring modern reading habits at this time, and Warsaw's Jews were little accustomed to reading Yiddish.'[42] Yatskan played above all on the informational and sensational content of the paper and on the speed with which it relayed news, and the readers, despite the lamentations and condemnations of an older generation of journalists, took the bait at once—although initially there was also no lack of those who were ashamed to put out their hand for a penny paper seen as 'not very intellectual'.[43] After only a few months, the editorial board was able to move to a town house at 8 Chłodna Street belonging to the father of Noyekh and Nekhemye Finkelshteyn and open its own printing works. This address would become one of the most important addresses on the map of Jewish Warsaw for the next thirty years and more.

[39]   The term 'Litvak' refers in Yiddish to Jews from the territories of the historical Lithuania, which included Lithuania as well as parts of Poland, Belarus, and Latvia. In Polish it refers to Jewish migrants from the western provinces of the Pale of Settlement (roughly present-day Lithuania and Belarus) who arrived in the Kingdom of Poland in several waves at the turn of the nineteenth and twentieth centuries. Having contacts with the Russian market and often speaking only Yiddish and Russian, they were perceived by Polish society as agents of the Russian authorities, aiming to Russify Poles, even though their migration to the Kingdom of Poland resulted directly from persecution they had experienced from the tsarist authorities.   [40]   Gavze, 'Vi azoy mir hobn gearbet', 4.

[41]   Ibid. According to the minutes of the Warsaw Censorship Committee for 1906, the circulation of *Yidishes tageblat* was 54,200 copies. See 'Sprawozdanie z czynności Warszawskiego Komitetu Cenzury w 1906 r.', in Fuks, *Prasa żydowska w Warszawie*, 298 (annexe 2).

[42]   Weiser, *Jewish People, Yiddish Nation*, 49.

[43]   Druk, *Tsu der geshikhte fun der yidisher prese*, 54–5.

Figure 1. The editors of *Yidishes tageblat* and *Vokhenblat* in Warsaw.
From *Tygodnik Ilustrowany*, 1907, no. 13, p. 271
(photo by Ł. Dobrzański)

In the history of the development of the Yiddish press the *Yidishes tageblat* was a remarkably significant step. In its tracks followed a series of publications, for instance the daily *Unzer lebn* founded in February 1907 by Mordkhe Spektor (editor) and Saul Hochberg (publisher), or another of Spektor's initiatives, the daily *Di naye velt* (1909). It was no longer an oddity but increasingly the norm to report current events rapidly, and to have one's own correspondents in politically important places such as the Duma (as, we may note, had already been the norm for many years in the Polish and Russian daily press).

THE BREAKTHROUGH OF THE YIDDISH PRESS

After *Yidishes tageblat* had been appearing for over a year its editors felt that the public was ready for something bigger:

Tageblat has been a colossal success and is educating tens of thousands of new Jewish readers, but at the same time it is clear that for many of these new readers *Tageblat* serves as a preparatory class, i.e. it teaches them how to read a newspaper for what it is; [but then] little *Tageblat* becomes too small for them and they want a bigger paper. Such a paper should be set up for *Tageblat*'s 'grown-up' readers.[44]

[44] A. Goldberg, 'Di entshtehung un der veg fun "Haynt"', in *Haynt yubiley-bukh*, 3.

Despite the fact that not everyone on the editorial staff shared this view, in December 1907 a request reached St Petersburg for permission to set up a new daily called *Haynt* ('Today'). The name—fully reflecting the editorial board's vision—had been thought up by Avrom Goldberg.[45]

Haynt's publishers, Yatskan and Noyekh Finkelshteyn, proposed the following rubrics for the new paper: '(1) telegrams; (2) leading articles; (3) city and general chronicle; (4) socio-political and scientific articles; (5) feuilletons; (6) letters; (7) review of the press; (8) illustrations and cartoons; and (9) advertising.' The paper was to cost 2 copecks for each edition, or 6 roubles for an annual subscription, and was to be printed on the presses at 8 Chłodna Street. A certain Khaim-Benyamin Tenenbaum assumed the responsibilities of managing editor.[46]

The new daily was supposed to start coming out on 1 January 1908, but because of work being carried out at the printing house it came out late on 9 (22 NS) January. In reality it was a continuation of *Yidishes tageblat*, but in a larger format. In the opinion of contemporaries, however, among them Dovid Druk—which is important, for Druk never worked for *Haynt* and wrote about Yatskan without much enthusiasm—this was a revolution in the Jewish press.[47] Ber Kuczer summed it up: 'the day on which *Haynt* was born was the day when the Jewish press broke through to the most distant and remote streets of the Jewish poor'.[48]

Haynt introduced into the Jewish press a new format for the front page, with a division into columns and headlines (the louder the better), with a consistent layout which allowed readers easily to establish the paper's contents, and with a differentiation of news items according to their importance. The first page of the first issue simply bombarded the reader with current affairs arranged under as many as five headings, suitably entitled 'Hayntige nayes' ('News of the Day'), 'Der hayntiger tog' ('The Present Day'), 'Kurtse yediyes' ('News in Brief'), 'Fun der letster minut' ('Stop Press'), and 'Vos tut zikh oyf der velt?' ('What's Happening in the World?'), to which should also be added a special lead story, in this case on the reopening of the Duma. The reader could then feel that he had his finger on the pulse of the most important events, both in Russia and abroad.

However, the real revolution, which in addition radically increased the paper's sales (from 15,000 to 35,000 copies[49]), was the introduction in the summer of 1909 of a novel in instalments called *In nets fun zind* ('In the Snare of Sin').[50] It was a move which, it appears, attracted to *Haynt* a section of the reading public not hitherto involved—women. Chaim Finkelstein, who later worked for *Haynt*, recalled:

[45] Ibid. [46] RGIA, f. 776, op. 22, d. 286, fo. 2.

[47] Druk, *Tsu der geshikhte fun der yidisher prese*, 86.

[48] B. Kuczer, 'Sh. y. yatskan—"Haynt" un "Hayntige nayes"', in D. Flinker, M. Tsanin, and S. Rozenfeld (eds.), *Di yidishe prese vos iz geven* (Tel Aviv, 1975), 65.

[49] Druk, *Tsu der geshikhte fun der yidisher prese*, 88.

[50] For some reason the story *Der anarkhist*, printed as early as 1908, had evidently not aroused readers' interest.

Several of my mother's lady friends have come round. Over a glass of tea they carry on a typical female conversation about clothes, men, and children. Then they dry up and there is a
silence. Mother is flustered: how should she entertain her guests, how to break the awkward
silence? Suddenly one of the ladies remembers a novel which is coming out in 'her' paper, in
Haynt, and begins to tell the story. It turns out that they are all reading the novel, that they
are all impatiently awaiting the next instalment, which they devour with bated breath even
before breakfast.[51]

These novels, sometimes written from scratch but more often modified for the
Jewish reader (or rather the female Jewish reader) from works which had come out
in one of the European languages, were usually written by Avrom Leyb Yakubovitsh.[52] However, it was not only women who read them. As Dovid Druk claims,
they also appealed to young hasidim, who were afraid to read 'real' novels since they
were forbidden by the religious authorities, but who could without difficulty
covertly read novels printed in instalments in a newspaper under the pretext of
reading the paper as such.[53] 'On the streets, in the shops, in the cafés—everyone
was talking about the novel's "heroes" as if they were real people. Quite honestly,
there was no hasidic house in which the story was not being secretly read.'[54]

Despite *Haynt*'s widely criticized sensationalism (more of which later), a great
many popular writers contributed to it (generous remuneration no doubt playing an
important part in recruiting them), amongst them Hillel Zeitlin, David Frishman,
Hersh Dovid Nomberg, and Sholem Asch. From 1912 to 1913 Yitskhok Leyb
Peretz had his own column called 'In mayn vinkele' ('In my Little Corner').[55]
Sholem Aleichem brought out in instalments the novels *Fun menakhem mendels briv*
('From Menahem Mendel's Letters') and *Der blutiker shpas* ('The Bloody Hoax').[56]
Bernard Singer's memoirs evoke the working atmosphere at *Haynt*:

Upon entering the ground-floor editorial offices—it was during the morning—I was overwhelmed by the shouting. In the first room a number of journalists were working, or rather
shouting over one another. The cantor from the synagogue was arguing with the music critic
about a review, while a music-lover was waiting in line, loudly complaining about the paper's
disparaging treatment of Wagner. In the other room a friend of mine was poring over piles of
German and French magazines. I could not understood how he could do any work; another

---

[51] C. Finkelstein, 'Der "Haynt" als varshtat fun arbeyt', in *Haynt yubiley-bukh*, 16.

[52] For Yakubovitsh's role in creating these trashy novels, see C. Shmeruk, 'Te'udah nedirah
letoledoteiha shel hasifrut halo kanonit beyidish', *Hasifrut*, 32 (1983), 13–33.

[53] Druk, *Tsu der geshikhte fun der yidisher prese*, 87.   [54] Ibid. 88.

[55] The title of the column has been interpreted as a sign of Peretz distancing himself from Yatskan's
methods. See A. Mukdoni, *Yitskhok leybush perets un dos yidishe teater* (New York, 1949), 21.

[56] *Der blutiker shpas*, built on the theme of the Beilis trial, contained numerous polemics with the
antisemitic views of the Russian press. See J. Nakagawa, 'Russkaya i evreiskaya zhurnalistika v romane
Sholom-Aleikhema "Krovavaya shutka"', in V. Mochalova et al. (eds.), *Materialy Pyatnadtsatoi
ezhegodnoi mezhdunarodnoi mezhdistsiplinarnoi konferentsii po iudaike*, ii (Moscow, 2008), 368–85. For
the controversies surrounding the title of the novel, see C. Finkelstein, *Haynt: a tsaytung bay yidn*
(Tel Aviv, 1978), 245–6.

journalist, who was taking clippings from American Jewish magazines, kept quarrelling with him the whole time.[57]

In addition to its strengths, *Haynt* had also some failings, which included a forceful, strident, at times aggressive tone, a ruthless fight for market share, and its widely criticized tabloid character and pursuit of sensationalism. This last feature in particular irritated both a great many readers and current or potential contributors. Therefore, Hillel Zeitlin, Dovid Druk, and Tsevi Prylucki—convinced that part of the Jewish intelligentsia still did not have its 'own' daily newspaper, although the market already seemed saturated, especially after *Der fraynd* moved from St Petersburg to Warsaw in December 1909—set up the daily *Der moment* in 1910. The name came from a popular column of political commentary written by Tsevi Prylucki in *Unzer lebn*.[58] The new daily, whose first issue appeared on the 5 November 1910, was planned as a 'middle-class newspaper, which soothed nerves, aimed to avoid making a clamour, and always sought compromise'.[59] *Haynt's* methods (including the printing of trashy novels) were renounced, although other devices were used: in 1911, for example, the editors of *Moment* announced a project to build a garden city in Miłosna near Warsaw. Readers were encouraged to collect coupons printed in the paper, which would let them take part in a draw for free plots. Nothing ever came of this project, but the aim was achieved: circulation rose to 20,000 copies.[60] The new paper also acquired part of the equipment of the defunct *Di naye velt*, including the printing presses.[61]

Kalman Weiser describes *Der moment's* general line as that of 'a non-partisan forum in which expressions of all Jewish political and cultural orientations were in principle welcome (with the exception of Assimilationism)'.[62] Admittedly, that could probably have been said of most, if not all, of the Yiddish papers of the day. But *Der moment* was undoubtedly characterized in general by a calmer tone than *Haynt*. In 1912, in addition to both Pryluckis, Druk, and Zeitlin, its editorial board included Mordkhe Spektor, Yisroel Khaim Zagorodski, Moyshe Yustman (known as B. Yeushzon), and Yosef Tunkel (known as Der Tunkeler).

The years 1910–12 became a period of fierce and ruthless rivalry between *Haynt* and *Moment*, in which the other papers simply ceased to matter and sooner or later ceased to exist. Up to the outbreak of the First World War both dailies to all intents and purposes monopolized the market for the Yiddish press in the Kingdom of Poland.

---

[57] B. Singer, *Moje Nalewki* (Warsaw, 1993), 209.

[58] Another reason for setting up *Moment* was a conflict with the publisher of *Unzer lebn*, Saul Hochberg. [59] Druk, *Tsu der geshikhte fun der yidisher prese*, 108.

[60] Ibid. 110–11; Weiser, *Jewish People, Yiddish Nation*, 65.

[61] Weiser, *Jewish People, Yiddish Nation*, 63. [62] Ibid.

WE HAVE NEWSPAPERS; WE DO NOT HAVE A PRESS

The social revolution that was the appearance of a Yiddish mass-circulation press awoke among people at the time a great many strong reactions, ranging from the extremely enthusiastic to the extremely critical.

For the milieu of Jewish intellectuals who knew and used Yiddish, the mass-circulation dimension of the press was irritating in every sense of the word 'mass'. Not only were the circulation figures of Yiddish papers much higher than those of reputable publications with a tradition,[63] their contents also suited perfectly the mass reader's none too refined tastes. M. Vanvild (the nom de plume of the columnist Moyshe-Yosef Dikshteyn) sounded the alarm in 1908: 'We have Jewish newspapers, but do we have a serious Jewish press?' He did not conceal his distaste for the mass-circulation press: 'The editorial offices of *Haynt* and *Unzer lebn* are ordinary little shops . . . where the Jewish reader is bought and sold.'[64] However, having got off his chest his dislike of Yatskan (in particular) and Hochberg, he unhesitatingly pointed the finger at those guilty for this state of affairs:

We have Jewish newspapers, a public consisting of tens of thousands, [we have] talented, exceptional journalists, first-rate columnists, real experts on the Jewish economic and social situation and on the Jewish nation's political and legal position, writers who thanks to many years of work know Jewish popular life—and yet we do not have a single serious newspaper. We have talented writers, while talented scribblers write in our papers; we have brilliant columnists, but in our papers—stupid bores; we have important ideological leaders, scholars, distinguished popular writers [*folks-shrayber*], yet in our papers . . . uneducated people, with no taste, with no education, and even with no brains. And yet, who is to blame for this? If someone were to say that the only guilty party for this state of affairs is our very own public it would not, I believe, be an exaggeration.[65]

Invoking the general reader's limited expectations did, however, produce the desired effect, and among the Jewish intelligentsia, accustomed to an ideal of elite culture, it created astonishment and indignation, and eventually a sense of threat. While disapproving of Yatskan's methods, they were not above employing similar ones themselves. Aron Gavze recalled the beginnings of *Haynt* thus: 'Day after day people kept ringing [us] up at the end of the working day to interrupt our work, and each time [we] were subjected to the most vulgar abuse and curses. Hanging up without answering did not help, since the phone would ring again and a fresh torrent of abuse and curses would rain down on us. This hindered and upset us dreadfully.'[66] One day Gavze recognized the familiar voice of the sister-in-law of the editor of 'a certain daily' (as *Haynt* used to refer to *Moment*) and the calls ceased.

---

[63] In 1906 the circulation figures were: *Yidishes tageblat*, 54,200; *Morgen-blat*, 18,000; *Der veg*, 9,000; *Hatsofeh*, 4,000; *Hatsefirah*, 3,000; *Izraelita*, 1,000. See 'Sprawozdanie z czynności Warszawskiego Komitetu Cenzury w 1906 r.', in Fuks, *Prasa żydowska w Warszawie*, 298 (annexe 2).

[64] M. Vanvild, *Di yidishe prese bay yatskan-hokhberg in di hent* (Warsaw, 1908), 6.   [65] Ibid. 3.

[66] Gavze, 'Vi azoy mir hobn gearbet', 5.

Much has already been written about the feelings which Yatskan himself inspired.[67] Not without reason did the term 'Yatskanism'—treating everything as a potential subject for cynical and shoddy journalism—arise in connection with him.[68] Examining the criticisms of Yatskan made by other journalists and publishers, Nathan Cohen sees in him 'an energetic individual with innovative, if not revolutionary, ideas, one who was not afraid to apply them, even at the cost of his reputation'.[69] Yatskan could indeed be accused of many things: treating people with disdain, having a more 'mercenary' than 'intellectual' attitude towards Yiddish culture, needless provocation. One thing of which he most definitely could not be accused was hypocrisy. Yatskan wrote what he thought, and it clearly never even occurred to him to consider whether or not it was appropriate.

Altogether—at some cost, which included even being arrested—he came out on top. Men of letters could brood, but at the end of the day *Haynt* never lacked for those wishing to have the paper print their work. Aron Gavze explained this simply: 'There arose the impression that *Haynt* was some kind of discretionary fund for every Jewish writer. Our publishers, the Finkelshteyn brothers, never turned anyone down and gave every writer without exception an advance, whether he brought them anything or not.'[70]

At this juncture it is worth stopping for a moment to review some exchanges between *Haynt* and the two writers that symbolize new Yiddish literature: Sholem Aleichem and Peretz. *Haynt*'s great coup was to secure exclusive rights to the former's literary output. As he wrote in a private letter: 'I have a contract with *Haynt* whereby I am not permitted to print a single line in Warsaw, either in a newspaper or in a magazine, except in *Haynt*; I can appear in print in a magazine (but not in a paper) in Vilna . . . And you raise the subject of *Moment* or *Fraynd*. Out of the question. Yatskan would slit my throat and have you shot.'[71]

It is clear that advantageous financial terms had induced the writer to conclude such an agreement. He never complained about his work with *Haynt* on that score, although he was forever seeking ways to publish more elsewhere and in such a way that Yatskan would not have grounds to slit his throat.

The relationship with Peretz was more complicated. No doubt Peretz never let Yatskan forget the latter's article on the official on the Warsaw *kehile* responsible for funerals and cemeteries who had supposedly refused to talk to a female customer in Yiddish and who had become angry with her for not knowing Polish. No names were mentioned, but the whole of Jewish Warsaw knew that Peretz himself was the

---

[67] See above all N. Cohen, '"An Ugly and Repulsive Idler" or a Talented and Seasoned Editor: S. Y. Yatskan and the Beginnings of the Popular Yiddish Press in Warsaw', *Jews in Russia and Eastern Europe*, 54–5 (2005), 28–53.

[68] Ibid. 44. Interestingly enough, Sh. Ts. Zetser had already used this term in 1904 in reference to Yatskan's earlier journalism, written still in Hebrew.   [69] Ibid. 50.

[70] Gavze, 'Vi azoy mir hobn gearbet', 5.

[71] *Briv fun sholem-aleykhem, 1879–1916*, ed. A. Lis (Tel Aviv, 1995), 569.

funeral director for the Warsaw *kehile*.[72] Yet despite this, the writer had agreed to work with *Haynt*. Aleksander Mukdoni believed that this was due to the pressure exerted by Helena Peretz and Yankev Dinezon.[73] Another version appears in the memoirs of Ber Kuczer, who cites the testimony of Froyim Kaganovski, one of Peretz's pupils, according to whom Peretz supposedly met all complaints with this reply:

I have realized that *Haynt* is on a mission. *Haynt* has found how to get to the reader. It is on the track of a better Jew, a Jew who is better educated, who comes to it from religious texts. And the one who comes . . . is a good reader. All the journalistic methods that Yatskan has been using to interest and find readers cannot harm me. It is for this very reason that I am starting up my own little corner[74] in *Haynt*. Through *Haynt* I shall find a whole legion of readers [*a breytn leyener-oylem*] with whom I can share my reflections and writing. I believe that I am doing great work in *Haynt*, work which I have done in no other paper.[75]

The fact remains that Peretz was the first significant personality from the milieu of Yiddish culture to stand up for the mass-circulation Yiddish press. In the article 'Di gele prese' ('The Yellow Press'), published in *Der veg* as early as 1905 or 1906,[76] Peretz drew attention to the extreme reactions of readers and suggested:

today's public, if it exists, values the man of letters either too much or too little, values each printed word either too much or too little. Either things are 'rubbish', 'fairy tales' [*mayse-bikhlekh*], laziness, or they are the opposite: holy writ, not to be changed, not to be challenged! . . . Today, when every boy can write, when things are being printed on every street corner, the public must learn to evaluate! Everyone must be allotted a place, trust should be granted sparingly, credit should be extended sparingly, and the public will attain a high level thanks to the yellow press! A child cannot learn to walk without taking a tumble![77]

The popularity of the Yiddish mass-circulation press also aroused distaste in the circles of assimilated Jews. Maria Kamińska, who came from the wealthy Eiger family, recalled many years later: 'I remember my parents' indignation when a newspaper came out in Warsaw in Yiddish. They felt that miserable political types were fuelling nationalist hatred among the Jewish masses and were trying to turn "jargon" into a literary language. All assimilationists took this position.'[78] The venerable *Izraelita* reacted similarly.[79]

---

[72] Kuczer, 'Sh. y. yatskan', 64.   [73] Mukdoni, *Yitskhok leybush perets un dos yidishe teater*, 21.

[74] An allusion to the title of his column, 'In mayn vinkele' ('In my Little Corner').

[75] Kuczer, 'Sh. y. yatskan', 64.

[76] I have been unable to locate this article in the paper itself, hence the uncertainty over its precise dating; I quote it from a reprint in an edition of Peretz's collected works. The term 'yellow press', borrowed from English probably via Russian, was used at the time to describe the mass-circulation press.

[77] Y. L. Peretz, 'Di gele prese', in id., *Ale verk*, 11 vols. (New York, 1947–8), vi. 259–60.

[78] M. Kamińska, *Ścieżkami wspomnień* (Warsaw, 1960), 188.

[79] See e.g. Lambda, 'Żargonowcy między sobą', *Izraelita*, 5 Jan. 1912.

WE ARE FREE PEOPLE

Polish public opinion was almost entirely approving of the stance taken by the assimilated community on the emerging Yiddish press,[80] the development of which aroused distaste and anxiety even among such people as Bolesław Prus or Eliza Orzeszkowa. According to Prus, 'So-called assimilation, in other words the integration of the Jews with the Polish population, has ended miserably, if not indeed laughably. The only Jewish newspaper in the Polish language, *Izraelita*, has folded, while the jargon papers multiply like yeast bacteria.'[81]

The Yiddish press, inaccessible to Poles owing to the language barrier, and more highly visible than the low-circulation and elitist Hebrew press, was perceived as the sinister invention of the detested Litvaks, who were inciting the Jewish 'ignorant rabble' against the Poles.[82] Furthermore, as Kalman Weiser has noted, 'The very notion of a modern Jewish culture in Yiddish was simultaneously oxymoronic and menacing, an open challenge to the supremacy of the Polish language and culture on Polish soil.'[83] Jewish editors and journalists became antiheroes in the Polish collective imagination, which was given full rein in countless articles, satirical poems, and even novels. In first place among these antiheroes was—who else?—Yatskan. He was the prototype of Juda Salomonowicz Suderow in Artur Gruszecki's antisemitic novel *Litwackie mrowie* ('A Swarm of Litvaks').[84] The profile of Suderow, as the founder of the first Warsaw daily in Yiddish, was drawn by the author in such a way as to leave no illusions about the hidden motives of the Yiddish press:

They were reading with great interest, and the movements of their eyes, head, hands, their cries, showed their great pleasure. From time to time they looked with respect at Suderow, who, with an expression of proud pleasure, answered each glance by inclining his head and smiling. They read the main story, glanced at the other headlines, and, folding the paper, looked enquiringly at its editor and publisher, who began: 'This daily paper "for our people"

---

[80] Grzegorz Krzywiec provides a penetrating discussion of attacks on the Yiddish press as an essential thread in an anti-Litvak campaign: G. Krzywiec, 'Prasa żydowska w zwierciadle polskiej opinii publicznej (1905–1914)', in J. Nalewajko-Kulikov with G. P. Bąbiak and A. J. Cieślikowa (eds.), *Studia z dziejów trójjęzycznej prasy żydowskiej na ziemiach polskich (XIX–XX w.)* (Warsaw, 2012), 267–98. For Polish–Jewish relations in general at that time, see T. R. Weeks, 'Poles, Jews, and Russians, 1863–1914: The Death of the Ideal of Assimilation in the Kingdom of Poland', *Polin*, 12 (1999), 242–56; J. Jedlicki, 'The End of the Dialogue: Warsaw, 1907–1912', in S. Kapralski (ed.), *The Jews in Poland*, ii (Kraków, 1999), 111–23.

[81] B. Prus, 'Dwa głosy', *Tygodnik Ilustrowany*, 30 Jan. 1909, p. 13. My thanks to Grzegorz Krzywiec for help in tracking down this quotation.

[82] For more on the stereotype of the Litvak, see F. Guesnet, 'Migration et stéréotype: Le Cas des Juifs russes au Royaume de Pologne à la fin du XIXᵉ siècle', *Cahiers du monde russe*, 41/4 (2000), 505–18.   [83] Weiser, *Jewish People, Yiddish Nation*, 71.

[84] The play on the initials S.J.J. (Szmuel Jankew Jackan) / J.S.S. (Juda Salomonowicz Suderow) is conspicuous.

will unite us, will bring us together, it will teach us where to go and what to do. Those who have been here for so many years, have they learnt how to unite, to band together to develop our native tongue? Now all right-thinkers will follow us, I shall lead them. They will be like us so that within a few years only the riff-raff, only the working-class cattle will speak Polish.'[85]

Leaving aside the dimensions of this anti-Litvak hysteria in the Polish press (it was of course one of the strands in the growing crisis in Polish–Jewish relations, which I shall discuss later), one can, however, state that the mass-circulation Yiddish press was created by and large by people from outside the Congress Kingdom. Yatskan was born in Vabalninkas (Wobolniki) in Lithuania, Goldberg and the Finkelshteyn brothers came from Brest-Litovsk, Saul Hochberg from around Białystok, Hillel Zeitlin from the Mogilev region, and the Prylucki family from Ukraine, as also Mordkhe Spektor. Could this have had an effect on their view of Poles and Polish affairs, if only in terms of the issue of Polish independence? It definitely could. They did not understand the dislike of Litvaks (especially in the context of Polish public opinion's emphasis on the existence of a Polish community outside the Kingdom of Poland), and they felt that it was absurd to treat Litvaks as agents of Russification.[86] In reply to the anti-Litvak campaign begun by the Polish press in the autumn of 1909, Noyekh Prylucki blamed integrationist circles for inciting dislike of Litvaks and treating arrivals from the depths of the Russian empire as 'Russians of the Mosaic faith':

[The assimilationists] did not welcome the unfortunate outcasts from Moscow and other cities with brotherly hospitality, but with bile and slander. Sensing in them *a healthy element, to whom the idea of assimilation was alien*, they would have given anything in the world, they would have abandoned their wives, diamonds and all, to prevent Russian Jews from entering Poland. From that time [when the Litvaks arrived], not a week goes by that they do not remind the Poles: 'We are who we were: your faithful slaves . . . we have nothing to do with this newly arrived rabble. They are strangers to us. We are Polish patriots; they are nationalists and Russianizers.'[87]

In the same text Prylucki explained the Jewish attitude towards Polish culture:

Rola or *Dzień*—we hate them. That's the truth and we don't deny it. But a Przybyszewski, a Kasprowicz, a Wyspiański, a Żeromski, a Wyczółkowski, a Lewandowski—never. They

---

[85] A. Gruszecki, *Litwackie mrowie: Powieść współczesna* (Warsaw, 1911), 215. I am grateful to Grzegorz Krzywiec for drawing my attention to this novel. See too F. Guesnet, '"Wir müssen Warschau unbedingt russisch machen": Die Mythologisierung der russisch-jüdischen Zuwanderung ins Königreich Polen zu Beginn unseres Jahrhunderts am Beispiel eines polnischen Trivialromans', in E. Behring, L. Richter, and W. F. Schwarz (eds.), *Geschichtliche Mythen in den Literaturen und Kulturen Ostmittel- und Südosteuropas* (Stuttgart, 1999), 99–116.

[86] See e.g. N. Prylucki, 'Tsi zenen di litvakes "rusifikatoren"?', in id., *In poyln: kimat a publitsistish togbukh (1905–1911)* (Warsaw, 1921), 156–72. A series of articles by Prylucki with the same title appeared in October 1909 in *Unzer lebn*.

[87] Prylucki, 'Tsi zenen di litvakes "rusifikatoren"?', 158 (emphasis mine).

delight us, as do all the great things in world culture . . . If only the Poles were capable of treating our culture with respect, just as we treat their great men and great works of art![88]

Haynt too was not indifferent to the intensifying Polish press campaign and it organized a survey of Polish–Jewish relations which addressed four points: (1) an opinion on the anti-Litvak campaign; (2) whether Russian Jews, seeing themselves only as Jews and not wishing to assimilate, could be good 'local citizens' (*landsbirger*); (3) possible limits to Jewish freedoms within the framework of the Congress Kingdom's request for autonomy; (4) the future for Jews in the co-operative movement on the Polish lands. 'The most respected representatives of the Polish nation'—that is, Bolesław Prus, Ludwik Krzywicki, Franciszek Nowodworski, Ignacy Baranowski, and Andrzej Niemojewski—were invited to take part in the survey. The survey, or rather a series of interviews usually printed on the paper's front or second pages, showed that 'even such old and widely respected Polish social figures and writers are not familiar enough with Jewish life, with our real hopes and aspirations'.[89] Indeed, reading the replies from the representatives of the then socio-political elite over one hundred years later, one can begin to wonder what the so-called simple folk of the time must have thought of the Jews. For instance, Ignacy Baranowski, presented by the editor as 'the greatest of philosemites', said:

The Jews are an unhappy people and have been mightily persecuted for several thousand years. I believe that that they are unhappier even than us Poles.

Filled with complaints and grievances for injustices and humiliations endured, the Jews must look to defend themselves, and at the same time they need to let out their bitterness and pour it over someone, either in word or in deed. It is easy to understand that in a crowd that is in pain it is not the idea of forgiveness that is uppermost, but the idea of revenge . . . To attack the Poles, to burden them with blame and sins committed and not committed by them: that is so easy and so cheap. Many a Jew will admit in his heart that much less harm has been done to him by the Poles than from another quarter; but to attack this other quarter is a risky business—so let the Poles have it![90]

If the Jews printed their newspapers in a language and a script not understood exclusively by them—ah, then there would be less suspicion, and fewer opportunities for it! But today all their denials crumble in the face of the impossibility of judging the truth of them . . . And in the Polish press there are publications trying to spread hatred of the Jews, but their number is small and their significance even smaller.[91]

[88] Ibid. 166.

[89] 'Shtimen fun poylishe folks-forshteyer vegn dem tsushtand fun der yidn-frage in poyln', *Haynt*, 4 (17) Oct. 1909, p. 1.

[90] 'Shtimen fun poylishe folks-forshteyer vegn dem tsushtand fun der yidn-frage in poyln, IV: Profesor Ignacy Baranowski', *Haynt*, 12 (25) Oct. 1909, p. 2. At Baranowski's request the editor printed his statement in Polish and with a Yiddish translation. The quotations here are translated from the Polish version.

[91] 'Shtimen fun poylishe folks-forshteyer vegn dem tsushtand fun der yidn-frage in poyln, IV: Profesor Ignacy Baranowski (ende)', *Haynt*, 13 (26) Oct. 1909, p. 3.

Bolesław Prus wriggled out of answering the question whether a Russian Jew could be a good citizen, but having listened to a journalist's description of the activities of traditional Jewish charitable societies, such as Linat Hatsedek, he warmly urged:

Write about all the Jewish associations, let the Polish people know who you are. We know the Jews—but do you realize which ones? We know the pickpockets, since they're the ones we see; they steal from us and they get caught. We know Jewish usurers, when they fleece us; but we don't know the real Jews. We think that a Jew is not capable of anything good. Show us then, really, introduce us to authentic Jews and their virtues.[92]

Ludwik Krzywicki felt that the Litvaks, not knowing Polish, 'are spreading the Russian spirit, language, and culture throughout Poland', although perhaps not altogether consciously. Nevertheless, he acknowledged without hesitation their right to become good citizens.[93] Franciszek Nowodworski (whose response to the survey was for some reason incomplete) regretted that central Russia was closed to Jews, which led to them all congregating in Poland.[94] The most negative and also extremely vague was Niemojewski, though it was nevertheless quite clear that he believed the Litvaks to be 'a foreign, impudent element'.[95]

The writer Eliza Orzeszkowa failed to respond to the survey. She refused to participate, explaining that the paper's representative who came to see her did not know Polish and she did not want to speak in 'the language he used' (presumably Russian).[96] However, she agreed to write an article on her attitude towards Zionism and the Jewish question in Poland, which appeared in *Kurier Warszawski* just after her death. In this article she took an extremely critical position on the idea of Yiddish as the Jews' national language, and so to a certain extent on the very notion of a Yiddish press:

From the argument, presented by Jewish nationalists, that jargon is the language of millions of people, one can only draw the conclusion that these millions need to be hauled up to a higher level of education so that they can sense the need for a better implement than broken German with which to express their thoughts and feelings, but one cannot draw the conclusion that it is the national tongue for these millions.[97]

Shortly after the survey, Yatskan published on the front page of *Haynt* an open letter to the editor of *Kurier Poranny* and Andrzej Niemojewski. He expressed

---

[92] 'Shtimen fun poylishe folks-forshteyer vegn dem tsushtand fun der yidn-frage in poyln', *Haynt*, 4 (17) Oct. 1909, p. 1.

[93] 'Shtimen fun poylishe folks-forshteyer vegn dem tsushtand fun der yidn-frage in poyln, II: Prof. Ludwik Krzywicki', *Haynt*, 5 (18) Oct. 1909, p. 1.

[94] 'Shtimen fun poylishe folks-forshteyer vegn dem tsushtand fun der yidn-frage in poyln, III: gevezener deputat Nowodworski', *Haynt*, 6 (19) Oct. 1909, p. 1.

[95] 'Shtimen fun poylishe folks-forshteyer vegn dem tsushtand fun der yidn-frage in poyln, V: Andrzej Niemojewski', *Haynt*, 18 (31) Oct. 1909, p. 2.

[96] E. Orzeszkowa, *O nacjonalizmie żydowskim*, in ead., *Pisma: Wydanie zbiorowe zupełne*, ix (Warsaw, 1913), 217.   [97] Ibid. 226.

disquiet in it that the anti-Litvak campaign was spreading to the most widely read Polish publications (such as *Kurier Poranny*) and protested against Niemojewski's opinion, expressed on its pages, that the Jewish press hated Poland and the Poles, and summoned them to a court of honour:

You gentlemen state as fact that the Jewish press in Poland demonstrates chutzpah in its attitude to Polish matters, is hostile and aggressive, and on this basis you conduct your whole campaign against the Lithuanian Jews.

I trust that, as the editor and publisher of two popular Jewish newspapers in Warsaw, *Haynt* and *Tageblat*, I have the right to demand of people such as yourselves, who are responsible for their words, indications in which issue, article, and line of my newspapers, which I have been publishing for four years, or even in all the other papers which are published in Warsaw and which I know well, one can find hatred or indeed an indecent tone when addressing Polish national issues.

If, Sir, you can point it out, I am ready to accept every moral and even financial punishment that Polish national institutions might impose on me.[98]

The letter was sent, in a Polish translation, to the editor of *Kurier Poranny*, who ignored it, a fact which Yatskan went on to mock on the pages of his daily paper.[99]

On the pages of *Haynt* Dr Noyekh Dawidsohn and Hillel Zeitlin commented on the replies collected in the survey. It was no accident that Dawidsohn—the descendant of a well-known and respected Warsaw family of patriotic tendencies— went first. The journalist who interviewed him emphasized that a flag hung in his study 'with a white Polish eagle, which Jewish soldiers bore during the Polish revolution of 1831 and which was subsequently hidden in the synagogue of his rabbi-grandfather',[100] and that he himself had no connections with Litvaks, and despite the lack of such connections he was one of the principal movers of the Jewish nationalist movement. Dawidsohn made a number of pertinent comments. First, 'The difference between conservative Poles and liberal Poles is merely that the former want to chase us out of the country, while the latter generously allow us to remain digested in the Polish stomach.'[101] Second, 'What would people say if someone tried to divide Poles into Poles from Poland and Poles from Galicia? Historically, Lithuanian Jews are Polish Jews too.'[102] The possibility that restrictions on Jews might be introduced in the event of the Kingdom being granted autonomy angered him, since Jews paid taxes just like any other citizens. In conclusion he said:

You ask . . . are there ways to combat this misfortune [the Jews' situation in Poland]? In my opinion, we must completely ignore the antisemitic campaign and not respond to their

[98] S. Y. Yatskan, 'A sof zol nemen!', *Haynt*, 21 Oct. (3 Nov.) 1909, p. 1.

[99] See S. Y. Yatskan, 'Dos vet nit geyen!', *Haynt*, 26 Oct. (8 Nov.) 1909, 1.

[100] 'Shtimen fun yidishe folks-forshteyer vegn der yidn-frage in poyln, I: Dr N. Dawidsohn', *Haynt*, 21 Oct. (3 Nov.) 1909, p. 1.   [101] Ibid.

[102] 'Shtimen fun yidishe folks-forshteyer vegn der yidn-frage in poyln, I: Dr N. Dawidsohn (ende)', *Haynt*, 22 October (4 November) 1909, 2.

attacks. Quarrels with them will achieve nothing. The one thing we can and should do is to inform the Jewish masses of the battle which is being waged against them and to awaken within them a sense of self-preservation by means of education and by setting up various co-operative Jewish associations.[103]

Dawidsohn's statement was clearly meant to be the start of a whole series of responses by representatives of the Jewish side, but for some reason this was abandoned. Perhaps his view on the pointlessness of trying to convince antisemites had been heeded, and a long article in several instalments by Hillel Zeitlin, 'Mir yidn' ('We Jews'), was published as a sort of replacement. To a present-day reader the title immediately brings to mind an article by Julian Tuwim, 'My, Żydzi polscy' ('We Polish Jews'). However, the overtones of Zeitlin's text were quite different. Despite the fact that he was addressing the Poles, as suggested by the subtitle of his series—'eyn entfer di poylishe folks-forshteyer' ('a reply to the representatives of the Polish people')—he was in fact also speaking to the Jews.

The very first sentence of his reply made things clear: 'We cannot assimilate, even if we wanted to and could.'[104] If the Jews could assimilate, they would have done so long ago, but they are organically incapable of doing so, which comes from their specific relationship with God. In Zeitlin's view, one did not have to be religious in order to perceive the exceptional nature of the Jewish race—which was proved by the fact that of all the ancient peoples the Jews alone had survived to the present day, despite a great amount of persecution.[105] The Jews' eventual assimilation would in any event not bring Polish society any benefit: those who assimilated were either idealists, dreaming of the universal brotherhood of man—and these were always only a few individuals—or they were social climbers. The latter 'say they are Poles, though they are no more Polish than they are Jewish'.[106] Like Prylucki, Zeitlin warned against treating 'Poles of the Mosaic faith' as the only model of Jewishness accepted by the Poles, criticizing again the stereotype of the 'Litvak-Russianizer' and pointing out that it was absurd to suspect Jews, who were deprived of full rights in Russia, of Russifying activity.[107] To the hypothetical accusation that perhaps the Jews' separatism might be more harmful to the Poles than calculated assimilation, he replied:

You are *Polish* nationalists. We are *Jewish* nationalists. So we both take more or less the same socio-historical position. We both recognize nationalism not only as something natural and essential, but also as something highly desirable . . . The difference between your view of nationalism and ours consists, however, in this:

You, in your opinions of Jews, start from national *egoism*. You see *yourselves* and *only*

---

[103] 'Shtimen fun yidishe folks-forshteyer vegn der yidn-frage in poyln, I: Dr N. Dawidsohn (ende)', *Haynt*, 22 October (4 November) 1909, 2.

[104] H. Zeitlin, 'Mir yidn (eyn entfer di poylishe folks-forshteyer)', *Haynt*, 3 (16) Nov. 1909, p. 2.

[105] H. Zeitlin, 'Mir yidn', *Haynt*, 5 (18) Nov. 1909, p. 2.

[106] H. Zeitlin, 'Mir yidn', *Haynt*, 8 (21) Nov. 1909, pp. 2–3.

[107] H. Zeitlin, 'Mir yidn', *Haynt*, 12 (25) Nov. 1909, pp. 2–3.

yourselves. That which really is only a certain lack of familiarity, or at worst a temporary unpleasantness, you see as something 'harmful' and 'dangerous' . . .

It is not only fear that has big eyes. Egoism does too. From every straw a mountain grows, from every passer-by—a frightening enemy . . .

We, however, perceive nationalism differently. In our eyes nationalism is a world principle [*velt-printsip*]. We are nationalists not from a narrow, egoistical love of ourselves, or from hatred or suspicion of others, but from a deep conviction that every nation without exception has the right to self-determination, that every nation must summon all its national strength, and that every nation can create cultural values only when living as a nation, having its own language, its own literature, and so on.

We hold that as Poles, Russians, Germans, etc. we create no value for ourselves or for the world, and that only by being good *Jews* can we also be good *people* . . .

We are *free people*.[108]

THE SOURCE OF EVIL

The dislike of *Haynt* as the embodiment of the worst features of the Jewish press appeared not only in press statements, both Jewish and Polish, but also in attempts to draw the authorities' attention to the paper's activities.[109] The writing of denunciations is a particular form of reader reaction, and it constitutes evidence that the game was thought to be worth the candle, in other words that *Haynt*'s influence was seen to be considerable.

In the files of the Main Administration for Press Affairs there are traces of a few inquiries carried out into *Haynt* in connection with reported accusations. In chronological terms the first one dates from 1911. An anonymous letter written by hand and in very shaky Polish claimed:

In the newspaper *Haynt*, comes out daily in Warsaw at 8 Chłodna Street, of 3/16 November 1911, no. 254, is an article entitled in Yiddish PRIZIVNIKES [conscripts].[110]
in this article the following is printed: ——
    that for the Old Testament Believers it is not worth doing military service, for after 4 years service they have no right to live all over like other Russian subjects, and the poor little Jews they are always worst and last in the whole empire ——
    I have put this whole article here.
    to my mind this newspaper must be banned at once for ever, for this is like a revolt.[111]

---

[108] H. Zeitlin, 'Mir yidn', *Haynt*, 13 (26) Nov. 1909, p. 3 (all emphasis original).

[109] I have found no trace of denunciations in the files concerning other Jewish newspapers, although unfortunately I have not seen the complete documentation created by the Main Administration for Press Affairs.   [110] This word is written in Yiddish in a style imitating printed type.

[111] RGIA, f. 776, op. 22, d. 286, fo. 8ᵛ. Given the difficulty of conveying in translation the flavour of the Polish original, it is worth reproducing it here:

'w gazeta Hajnt wychodzy co dzien w Warszawie ulice Chłodna No. 8 od 3/16-go Listopada 1911 r. No. 254 jest artykuł co się nazywa po żydowskiem PRIZIVNIKES
w tym artykułu jest drukowane następujące: ——

The incriminating passage was taken from an article by Yankev Pat, and it read: '. . . where you will be kicked out of, on the very day after your military service, there, where you are always the worst and the last'.[112] The censor of Jewish publications for Warsaw, Abram Greys, admitted in response to an enquiry from St Petersburg that the indicated excerpt could be interpreted as 'incitement to avoid doing military service'.[113] However, it appears that there were no consequences at the time, or at least they were not mentioned in the records.

In February 1913 a certain Mikhail Cherbakov, a member of the Union of the Russian People (Soyuz russkogo naroda, part of the Black Hundred movement), submitted a denunciation of *Haynt* in a letter addressed to the Minister of National Education. He wrote:

I venture to state that the time has come to look carefully at the currently appearing newspaper *haynt*,[114] which really is a source of evil. Indeed, where does hatred of one nation for another, i.e. the Jewish for the Russian, come from, as well as revolts and disturbances by pupils at the gymnasia and students, if not from the widely distributed and harmful newspaper *haynt*? Without going into its earlier anti-government articles, which were there to see before, I do no more than draw attention to the last article in no. 33 of the newspaper *haynt*, 'a reply from the Minister of National Education'. The paper states that the Minister of Public Education Novitsky supposedly said in the Duma after a speech by member of the National Duma Gurvitch that all Jews in Russia would be crushed. The question arises whether the editor of the newspaper *haynt* Yatskan has not twisted the Minister's words, and whether this phrase will not lead to quarrels and anger among the people. It is well known that Minister Novitsky, not only in his own name, let alone in the name of the government, would not say anything of the kind, which Yatskan knows, but he, Yatskan, in a premeditated manner and with a view to vilifying the Minister of National Education and inciting students to quarrel with the Minister, writes a little article which which [*sic*] does precisely vilify the Government, and for this article, clearly written with this aim in mind, the editor Yatskan must without doubt be called to account, and also the editorial offices of his newspaper *haynt* must be closed down once and for all.[115]

Since from the attached article one could deduce that the writer of the letter had misinterpreted its contents (doubtless someone had translated it for him, possibly incorrectly), the Main Administration for Press Affairs took the precautionary step

---

że dla Starozakonych się nie uplacie służycz w wojeno służby bo po służba 4 lata nie mają prawa mieszkacz wszędzie jak inny rosyjskich podanny i żydki oni sa w cały imperji zawsze najgorsze i ostatnych——
ten artykuł w całości położyłem tutaj.
podług mój rozum trzeba natychmiast zabronicz ta gazeta na zawsze bo to jest jak bunt'.

[112] '. . . fun vanen men vet dikh oyf morgen nokh dinst aroysvarfen, dort, vu du bizt shtendik der ergster un der letster': Y. Pat, 'Prizivnikes: bildlekh fun provints', *Haynt*, 3 (16) Nov. 1911.

[113] RGIA, f. 776, op. 22, d. 286, fo. 12.

[114] The title is written with a lower-case initial throughout.

[115] RGIA, f. 776, op. 22, d. 286, fo. 21. The writer is referring to the article 'Der gehilf-minister novitski vegn yidn in rusland', *Haynt*, 7 (20) Feb. 1913, p. 1.

of instructing the censor Greys to go through several issues of *Haynt* in some detail and express an opinion about the paper's overall line. At the end of March Greys sent to St Petersburg the requested opinion, in which he stated:

From the political point of view, as can be seen from the five issues presented, the paper takes a neutral line, but in the opinion of other Jewish newspapers appearing in Russia and abroad, the newspaper *Haynt* is a paper for simple folk and, in order to stimulate the interest of this section of the readership and increase its circulation, during the five years of its existence it has published sensational stories and feuilletons of an erotic nature, and pornographic novels, against which there have more than once been protests in the Jewish papers from parents, writers, and rabbis, declaring that the novels in the newspaper *Haynt* are contaminating young people's morals and represent 'literary poison'. However, the paper clearly does not go beyond approved bounds, since over the course of 1912 it was charged only once.[116]

Upon receipt of this opinion, the Main Administration for Press Affairs recommended that the Warsaw Censorship Committee pay special attention to *Haynt* on account of the said 'erotic feuilletons' and 'pornographic novels'. By return post from Warsaw came an opinion from another censor of Jewish publications, Anshel Erenberg, who declared that *Haynt* was not printing such material and explained:

Three years ago, before I joined the staff of the Committee (at the time I was an interpreter in the office of the Warsaw Chief of Police), the said paper was printing a sensational novel called *In nets fun zind*, but this novel's only sensationalism was its title; there was no pornography in the content. Nonetheless, the editors of another Jewish paper, *Unzer lebn*, no longer in existence, began printing protests against the novel supposedly from its subscribers, and it even printed a letter, signed by the widely respected rabbi of Warsaw, Perelmuter. It then turned out that the letter had been a forgery. Yet in reply to this letter the editors of the newspaper *Haynt* announced that they would award a monetary prize of 100 roubles to every person who could find just one passage in the novel that offended against morality.

No one replied to the advertisement by *Haynt*'s editors.

Haynt subscribers are for the most part people from the conservative element in the Jewish population and, if an article of an erotic nature had appeared in that newspaper, it would without doubt have led to a formal protest by the rabbis.[117]

Erenberg's common-sense opinion brought to an end the suspicions of the Main Administration for Press Affairs, and the denunciations did *Haynt* no harm. As early as 1911 its circulation had exceeded 100,000 copies, which was unheard of on the 'Jewish street' (though some time later *Moment* succeeded in doing the

---

[116] RGIA, f. 776, op. 22, d. 286, fo. 24. The censor's view of *Haynt*'s relatively 'right-thinking' character is confirmed by the list of Warsaw periodicals which were the object of legal action in the years 1906–16. Although there are Jewish publications on this list (including *Haynt*, *Głos Żydowski*, *Hatsefirah*, *Der telegraf*, *Der veg*, and *Der moment*), it does not appear that they were censored or punished more harshly than Polish periodicals. See RGIA, f. 776, op. 22, d. 457.

[117] RGIA, f. 776, op. 22, d. 286, fo. 30.

same).[118] *Haynt* was read not only in the Kingdom of Poland, but throughout the Pale of Settlement and even in Moscow—something, it appears, that *Moment* never achieved.[119]

It is possible to speak of a Jewish journalistic community in Warsaw already becoming consolidated around 1912. The mass-circulation Yiddish press had become an important element in Jewish life. These same journalists and editors began to see themselves as a separate professional group. That year at Passover a ball was held for Jewish journalists in Warsaw, which was the occasion for the appearance of a humorous one-off publication, *Der zhurnalist*. It was a little collection, illustrated by Leyb Brodaty, of satirical pieces written by fifty-two associates of the Yiddish press (not just writers and editors, but also, for instance, proofreaders). There are pieces in it by, amongst others, Sholem Asch, Der Tunkeler, B. Yeushzon (Moyshe Yustman), Shmuel Yankev Yatskan, Aleksander Mukdoni, Menahem Boraisha, and Nahum Sokolow. As an illustration, I shall quote from this collection one piece by Avrom Goldberg, 'Mayn tfile' ('My Prayer'), which in a humorous fashion says something both about relations between the press and its readership, and about relations between the journalists themselves:

May it be Thy will that in 'Arba pinot'[120] in *Haynt* there be no news about a new treatment for cancer, consumption, or any other illness, or else for days, weeks, and months life will be impossible on account of telephone calls, visits, and letters with questions about the name of the doctor, where he lives, and what he charges for a consultation.

May it be Thy will that Carnegie[121] establish no more literary or artistic foundations, or else we shall again be tormented with letters and requests for his address from young people who have made a lovely Star of David in the synagogue or a wonderful rattle for Purim and are artists, and from young people who write addresses [on letters] to America and are writers.

May it be Thy will that the Jews be granted equality and all rights and learn to stop 'giving' [i.e. bribing], and that when they come to the Jewish editorial office to ask for something to be 'fixed', and are told 'no', that they stop winking [knowingly] and asking: 'So how much then?' . . .

May it be Thy will that in *Hatsefirah* there appear no report of any nationalist board meeting, in *Moment*—no article by Noyekh Prylucki, in *Unzer lebn*—no interview with

---

[118] As far as I know, no other Jewish publication ever managed to repeat the success of these two. For the sake of comparison, in 1912 in Galicia the top circulation, at 40,000 copies, was that of the *Ilustrowany Kurier Codzienny* in Kraków. See J. Myśliński, 'Prasa polska w dobie popowstaniowej', in J. Łojek, J. Myśliński, and W. Władyka, *Dzieje prasy polskiej* (Warsaw, 1988), 51.

[119] According to a survey carried out in 1913 among Jewish students in Moscow, 16% of them read Jewish dailies (Hebrew and Yiddish), specifically: *Haynt*, 7%; *Hatsefirah*, 7%; *Fraynd*, 6%; and *Hazeman*, 3%. See A. E. Ivanov, *Evreyskoye studenchestvo v Rossiiskoi imperii nachala XX veka: Kakim ono bylo? Opyt sotsiokul'turnogo portretirovaniya*, ed. O. V. Budnitsky (Moscow, 2007), 375.

[120] 'Arba pinot ha'olam'—the title of a popular column in *Haynt* containing oddments from around the world.

[121] Andrew Carnegie (1835–1919), American industrialist, one of the wealthiest men in the world of his time, the founder of various cultural institutions.

Krupensky,[122] in *Fraynd*—no polemic with Kokovtsov,[123] or we shall hear of nothing else and draw attention to nothing else, and I, not to be an 'apostate', shall also have to read it.

May it be Thy will that all rabbis receive posts in large towns, all doctors of medicine—a practice, all doctors of philosophy—rabbinical posts or wealthy fathers-in-law, all leaders—places on boards, all melameds—good working conditions, all externs—good positions, all poets—Berdichev anthologies[?], all artists—benefit performances on a Friday night, all young people—something to do, all Zionists—new members for their action committees, and all organizations—the keys to the strong box of the Jewish Colonial Society. Then the postman will have less to lug to the editorial offices, and the dogsbody [less] to the editorial [waste-paper] baskets.

Almighty God, the God of our forefathers, Thou, who canst cause an earthquake and kill tens of thousands of people and who canst ensure too that one Jewish editor talk to another over the telephone, grant the wishes of Thy humble servant.[124]

A PROLONGED ILLNESS

The years 1912–14 brought a certain calm to the conflict between *Haynt* and *Moment* as a result of two incidents which sidelined the internal feuds and rivalry in the shadow of an external threat. These were the elections to the Fourth Duma and the Beilis trial.

It is well known that during the elections to the Fourth Duma the Polish press supported the candidature of the representative of the National Concentration, Jan Kucharzewski, who opposed Roman Dmowski. The mass-circulation Yiddish press, for its part, also actively encouraged Jews to take part in the elections:

Participation in the elections to the Fourth Duma is for me above all a symbol of our social awareness. Deprived of other rights, we do have the highest political right—the right [to vote] in elections to the national assembly. We must therefore hold on tightly to our little slice of emancipation . . . When Roman Dmowski ceaselessly attacks the Jews and wants to terrorize them to stay at home and stay out of politics, he is no better than a provincial Russian policeman . . . Shall we help him in this? Shall we behave as he demands? That would mean spitting in our own faces, putting a noose around our necks.[125]

The campaigning was effective; Jewish voters began to register en masse. Less than two weeks later Prylucki wrote elatedly: 'You feel like running out into the middle of the street on Nalewki, Franciszkańska, and Smocza and stopping every passing Jew and hugging him: "Bravo, my friends! *We are a nation! We are a people!*"'[126]

---

[122] This probably refers to Pavel Nikolaevich Krupensky (1863–1939?), a deputy to the Second and Fourth Dumas, a Russian nationalist activist.

[123] Vladimir Nikolaevich Kokovtsov (1853–1943), prime minister 1911–14.

[124] A. Goldberg, 'Mayn tfile', in *Der zhurnalist: a zamlung* (Warsaw, 1912), 5–6.

[125] N. Prylucki, 'Nit geyn tsu di valen iz a zelbst-mord!', *Moment*, 24 Sept. (7 Oct.) 1912, p. 2.

[126] N. Prylucki, 'A yosher-koyekh aykh, brider!', *Moment*, 4 (17) Oct. 1912, p. 1 (emphasis mine).

Proof of the scale of the success of the Yiddish mass-circulation press is the fact that the group of assimilationists supporting Kucharzewski—in the name of maintaining good relations with the Polish community—decided to produce its own daily newspaper in Yiddish. The instigator of this undertaking was Henryk Nusbaum. 'The assimilationists have been put to great expense setting up a jargon paper, which will compete with *Haynt* and company', reported Eliza Orzeszkowa in a private letter.[127] It was realized that campaigning in Polish was a wasted effort, or rather spoke to the converted. On 17 (30) April 1912 the first issue of a daily paper called *Nayes* appeared. It was edited by a certain Y. Slutski, later by H. Kershenbaum.

Two things strike a reader of *Nayes*: first, the lack of notable names among its contributors (moreover, the paper was rather more informational and with less socio-political writing than one might have expected); second, its popularizing of Polish literature by publishing in instalments translations of novels or stories by Aleksander Świętochowski (*Chawa Rubin*), Bolesław Prus (*Kamizelka*), and Maria Konopnicka, Eliza Orzeszkowa, Henryk Sienkiewicz, and others.[128] It is evident too that in response to the flowering of Yiddish literature, the assimilationists replied with the old positivist big guns. Unfortunately, in 1912 there was no chance of them winning anyone over, not least because of the ideological evolution of the classics of Polish positivism, which was no secret to anyone.[129]

Nayes's in-house journalism was also turning out rather bland and unconvincing. For instance, one of the leading articles, called 'Thoughts of a Polish Jew (ahead of the Elections to the Fourth Duma)', which was probably meant to convince the readers that an electoral alliance with the Poles was essential, if not for patriotic and civic reasons, then at least for anti-Russian ones, came across as weak and awkward (perhaps because of the censorship), while the absence of the writer's name did not help readers to identify with the proposed ideas.[130] The only article signed by Nusbaum that I have been able to unearth extolled the 'spirit of justice' which appears from time in individuals or also in whole nations and which leads to such events as the abolition of serfdom, or the emancipation of the Jews in the West. In order for them to achieve equal rights, Nusbaum recommended to the Jews 'love of one's neighbour, understanding, common sense'.[131] However, it appears

---

[127] E. Orzeszkowa, *Listy zebrane*, v: *Do przyjaciół: Tadeusza Bochwica, Jana Bochwica, Janiny Szoberówny*, ed. E. Jankowski (Wrocław, 1961), 250, quoted by Krzywiec, 'Prasa żydowska w zwierciadle polskiej opinii publicznej', 277.

[128] As a matter of interest, it is worth noting that at the same time *Der moment* was printing Sienkiewicz's *Ogniem i mieczem* in instalments, but without mentioning his name and with a note: 'prepared by G. Bagrov'.

[129] See e.g. T. Stegner, 'Przyczynek do ewolucji ideowo-politycznej Aleksandra Świętochowskiego', *Dzieje Najnowsze*, 17/3–4 (1985), 27–39.

[130] 'Gedanken fun a poylisher yid (far di valen in der 4-ter dume)', *Nayes*, 11 (24) June 1912, p. 1.

[131] Dr H. Nusbaum, 'Tsayt-gedanken', *Nayes*, 28 June (11 July) 1912, p. 2.

that in 1912, after the Polish press's anti-Litvak campaign, exhortations of this kind on the whole convinced no one.

The spirit of humility pervading the paper (one feels like saying 'of real Christian humility') also appeared in a series of leading articles titled 'Kempfen!' ('Fight!'), signed with the initial 'Sh' (*shin*). Judging by the year mentioned, which was when *Fraynd* was founded, the author was taking aim at the Yiddish press: 'It all began in 1903 and has done nothing but grow since then. We Jews suddenly became a nation of heroes, on the warpath, never a day's rest . . . We must fight! That is what our writers, our wise men—the real spokesmen for "our" opinions —say.'[132]

The author writes pityingly about the 'mitzvah of war' (*milkhome-mitsve*), a war supposedly being waged with everyone and about everything. In place of that he suggests to the Jews that they carry out personal work on themselves, which alone may produce the desired effect:

> And if we unceasingly carry out our personal work, an external blow will
>   not harm us ———
> To the spirit and its work a fist has never been a threat ———
> And perhaps ———
> Perhaps then external blows will thereby be weakened . . .[133]

It is hardly surprising that, spreading such an elevated moral programme, the paper folded in October 1912, immediately after the elections, which were in any case ignominiously lost by the assimilationist group.[134] Jewish electors, having a numerical advantage, had supported the socialist Eugeniusz Jagiełło, the only candidate to have clearly declared support for the idea of equal rights for Jews. It appears that Jagiełło's victory rather overwhelmed the Jewish columnists. After the initial enthusiastic reaction, they were faced, as was the whole Jewish community, with an appeal, announced by the Polish press, for an economic boycott of the Jews.[135] This meant not only a call to buy exclusively in Christian shops and to have business dealings with Christians, but also attempts to limit Jews' participation in such institutions as the Urban Credit Association (Towarzystwo Kredytowe Miejskie) or the Polish Cultural Association (Towarzystwo Kultury Polskiej).[136]

The Yiddish press meticulously noted all the manifestations of the boycott. It provided information in special sections, and writers also commented on it. Peretz recommended calm in the face of the boycott.[137] He felt that there was no

---

[132] Sh., 'Kempfen! (I)', *Nayes*, 16 (29) July 1912, p. 1.

[133] Sh., 'Kempfen! (II)', *Nayes*, 17 (30) July 1912, p. 1.

[134] For more on the elections, see S. D. Corrsin, *Warsaw before the First World War: Poles and Jews in the Third City of the Russian Empire, 1880–1914* (Boulder, Colo., 1989), 89–104.

[135] For more on this subject, see F. Golczewski, *Polnisch-jüdische Beziehungen, 1881–1922: Eine Studie zur Geschichte des Antisemitismus* (Wiesbaden, 1981), 106–20; R. E. Blobaum, *Boycott! The Politics of Anti-Semitism in Poland, 1912–1914* (Washington, 1998): <http://www.ucis.pitt.edu/nceeer/1998-812-19g-3-Blobaum.pdf>. [136] Corrsin, *Warsaw before the First World War*, 102.

[137] Y. L. Peretz, 'Boykot', *Haynt*, 14 (27) Nov. 1912, p. 3.

need to look for guilty parties and that the idea of a boycott had been germinating in the Polish community long before the elections:

Are we to supposed to bear a grudge that we have been allowed to *see* the hand that beats, to *hear* the lips that blaspheme? Are we to accuse those who introduced the *light*, and [blame them for the fact] that what people think and do about us has become revealed? . . . The elections are not the issue. The boycott will weaken, the harshness will diminish . . . But that which has come to light will not disappear. It will turn into a *prolonged* illness. A morass will appear. And if we do not defend ourselves, we shall drown in it.[138]

Hersh Dovid Nomberg wrote bitingly that in the absence of its own army and its own diplomatic service, 'Polish policy starts and ends with the boycott', since in essence the whole world was being boycotted: Russians, Germans, Jews, Ruthenians, Lithuanians, and everyone else. He pointed out that most 'patriotic' activities brought no quantifiable effects, and that there was a lack of constructive dialogue.[139]

Der moment, which in November 1912 published a whole mass of material on the boycott, also included an article in Polish. This was 'Nastroje chwili' ('Moods of the Moment') by Ludwik Sterling, addressed to the progressive element in Polish society, 'cultural Poland, humanitarian Poland'.[140] It was accompanied by the first in a cycle of articles by Hillel Zeitlin titled 'A yud tsu poliaken' ('A Jew to the Poles').[141] With his habitual patience Zeitlin explained: 'the actions of Jewish electors are unjustly linked to Jewish nationalism . . . With the exception of the assimilationist-antisemites there is not any Jew (he need not necessarily be a nationalist) who will vote to limit Jewish civil rights and for an economic battle with the Jews, i.e. for an economic battle *with himself*.'[142]

The other significant watershed for the world of the Yiddish press was the so-called Beilis affair. Its development was covered from the very beginning as it unfolded, but from the start of the trial in Kiev in October 1913 it became something more than sensational front-page news. As Avrom Goldberg emphasized, writing from the train to Kiev, 'it is clear that it is not just Beilis that is in the dock. He, and I, and you—all of us, all 12 million [Jews] will find ourselves in the dock in a few days' time.'[143]

Given the involvement of the Yiddish press, the Beilis affair did indeed become a personal issue for every Jew in Russia, and thanks to *Haynt* and *Moment*, a personal issue for every Jew in the Kingdom of Poland too. A typical issue of *Haynt* from that time consisted of four pages, of which three were devoted to reports on the trial. Not only was the actual trial described, but also the atmosphere behind the

---

[138] Y. L. Peretz, 'On kharote, on taynes', *Haynt*, 15 (28) Nov. 1912, p. 3 (emphasis original).

[139] H. D. Nomberg, 'Boykot', *Haynt*, 30 Nov. (13 Dec.) 1912, p. 4.

[140] L. Sterling, 'Nastroje chwili', *Moment*, 9 (22) Nov. 1912, p. 6.

[141] It was announced that *Moment* would also publish a Polish translation of it, but I have been unable to find it.

[142] H. Zeitlin, 'A yud tsu poliaken', *Moment*, 9 (22) Nov. 1912, p. 6 (emphasis original).

[143] A. Goldberg, 'Keyn kiyev tsum beylis-protses', *Haynt*, 23 Sept. (6 Oct.) 1913, p. 2.

scenes and in town was conveyed, and comments by the Russian press and reactions in Europe were reported, and so on. Both papers not only sent their own correspondents (several of them!) to Kiev, but more or less opened up offices there:

> *Moment* set up an office on the spot in the Kiev courtroom: Meir Grosman, Shloyme Yanovski, and the Russian Jewish journalist Mayzels were continuously in touch with the paper by telegraph . . . Only the correspondents of the two large Russian papers, *Russkoe slovo* in Moscow and *Rech'* in St Petersburg, telegraphed more words from Kiev than *Moment*'s correspondents.[144]

The Yiddish press's support for Beilis attracted the attention of the censorship. For instance, after the publication in *Haynt* of an article by H. D. Nomberg titled 'In di shvere teg' ('In Difficult Times'), an inquiry was opened, which led to the issue in question being destroyed, while the author was sentenced to a month in prison (though interestingly enough, the sentence was passed only in the spring of 1915).[145] Even earlier, in June 1912, the censorship withdrew from *Haynt* one of the chapters of Sholem Aleichem's new novel *Der blutiker shpas*, which turned on precisely the theme of the Beilis affair. Sholem Aleichem himself joked at the time that this was a punishment for the publishers of *Haynt*, since unlike the other novels published in instalments, *Der blutiker shpas* was administered by the editors 'with a coffee spoon, barely twice a week, for it bites!'[146]

Both the economic boycott and the Beilis affair were pushed into the background only after the outbreak of the First World War, which also deeply affected that part of Europe. However, it appears that Theodore R. Weeks is correct when he writes that 'the crisis in relations between Jews and Poles was to continue until the outbreak of the First World War and, in a sense, for much longer yet'.[147] It would later affect in a significant way the nature of the Yiddish press in newly independent Poland.

CONCLUSION

The outbreak of the First World War interrupted the Yiddish press's winning streak in the Kingdom of Poland. The majority of the newspapers coming out in 1914 did not survive the war (probably *Der moment* came through the war years the best; *Haynt* did so only with great difficulty). The next publications were born in a completely different political and geographical climate, while their editors and readers had to find their feet in the reality of a newly independent Poland.

Going through surviving issues of Yiddish-language periodicals from before 1914 it is not always easy to understand why some of them survived, while others folded. It appears that, in addition to an essential piece of luck—as always in such

---

[144] M. Mozes, 'Di ershte yorn fun varshever "Moment"', in Flinker, Tsanin, and Rozenfeld (eds.), *Di yidishe prese vos iz geven*, 74–5.   [145] RGIA, f. 776, op. 22, d. 286, fo. 41.

[146] *Briv fun sholem-aleykhem*, ed. Lis, 549.   [147] Weeks, 'Poles, Jews, and Russians', 256.

situations—a given periodical's clarity of image played an important part. This came about partly for obvious reasons (choice of subject matter and writers), and partly from the 'label' that readers attached to it. If people had not been generally convinced of *Haynt*'s scandalous and tabloid (thereby intriguing and different) nature, it might perhaps not have survived. Were it not for the reference point provided by the 'scandalizing' *Haynt*, perhaps *Der moment* might not have been born and survived.

The Yiddish press played a seemingly underestimated, but key role in the development of modern Jewish culture. To be sure, Dovid Druk claimed that just before 1914 the press had begun to devour Jewish literature, since the newspaper editors could dictate terms to the writers who depended on them.[148] Chone Shmeruk saw this same phenomenon from the other side: 'The growth of the Yiddish press established the economic base for a modern Yiddish intelligentsia and for the Yiddish writer.'[149] Doubtless, the instrument of the mass-circulation newspaper allowed writers to reach a wide market, which they would have been unable to do by any other means. Let us not forget too the bonuses that readers received, often in the form of books.

In a socio-political sense too the Yiddish press played a role, which it had assigned to itself: it prepared Jewish society for functioning in a modern nation state. As a result of the 1905 revolution, 'the center of Jewish community and politics had passed from the *gmina* building to the editor's desk'.[150] Editors and journalists became both spokesmen for, and teachers of, the Jewish masses. Quite possibly there would not have been such a flowering of Jewish life in the Second Republic had it not been for the heyday of the mass-circulation Yiddish press during the last years of the Kingdom of Poland.

Translated from the Polish by Jarosław Garliński

---

[148] Druk, *Tsu der geshikhte fun der yidisher prese*, 90.

[149] C. Shmeruk, 'Aspects of the History of Warsaw as a Yiddish Literary Centre', *Polin*, 3 (1988), 150.

[150] S. Ury, *Barricades and Banners: The Revolution of 1905 and the Transformation of Warsaw Jewry* (Stanford, Calif., 2012), 170.

Jews in the Kingdom of Poland, 1861–1914

Changes and Continuities

THEODORE R. WEEKS

JEWS IN POLAND AND THE EUROPEAN CONTEXT: EMANCIPATION AND THE JEWISH QUESTION

THE 'long nineteenth century', defined here as stretching from the final partition of Poland to the outbreak of the First World War, was a period of striking change for the Jews resident in the Polish lands. While the majority of Polish Jews remained Orthodox in religious practice, followed everyday lives quite different from those of their Christian neighbours, and spoke Yiddish as their primary tongue on the eve of the First World War, one could discern the beginnings of a thoroughgoing transformation that would become even more pronounced in the next generation (that is, by 1939). In 1848, Jews throughout Europe suffered from varying degrees of legal disability; by the end of the 1860s these restrictions had been mainly abolished, including in the Kingdom of Poland.[1] The only exception was within the Pale of Settlement (*cherta evreiskoi osedlosti*) of the Russian empire, where restrictive laws continued to be the norm.[2]

Even conceptually, the integration of Jews into surrounding societies only began in the late eighteenth century. That is to say, the population of old-regime European states can be seen as a collection of diverse legal communities or castes, not as a 'society' or 'nation' in which all individuals enjoyed the same rights and responsibilities. In the modern state, on the other hand, individuals are bound together in allegiance to state power, enjoying equal rights but also contributing equally to the

---

[1] For a classic analysis of the breakdown of barriers between Jews and their Christian neighbours, see J. Katz, *Out of the Ghetto: The Social Background of Jewish Emancipation, 1770–1870* (Cambridge, Mass., 1973).

[2] On the legal situation of the Jews in the Kingdom of Poland, see M. J. Ochs, 'St. Petersburg and the Jews of Russian Poland, 1862–1905', Ph.D. thesis (Harvard Univ., 1986); F. Guesnet, *Polnische Juden im 19. Jahrhundert: Lebensbedingungen, Rechtsnormen und Organisation im Wandel* (Cologne, 1998), esp. 177–250; and (for a historical overview) J. Kirszrot, *Prawa Żydów w Królestwie Polskiem: Zarys historyczny* (Warsaw, 1917).

maintenance of the state (taxes, military service, etc.). This banal fact is of striking importance for Jewish history: while the old regime tolerated and encouraged the Jews to live according to their own traditions and laws, speaking their own language, and dominating certain economic activities, the modern state's insistence on equal rights for all citizens meant *ipso facto* that significant cultural difference and the persistence of diverse legal standards presented, at the very least, a problem. The difficulty of integrating Jews into European societies can be seen in the antisemitism that in the late nineteenth century developed in Germany, France, and even Britain—but the problem of Jewish integration was far more difficult and perplexing for Poles, who lacked a state and among whom far greater numbers of Jews lived than in central or western Europe.

This is not to say that religious conceptions and prejudices against Jews were insignificant in this period. Indeed, one cannot understand the development of relations between Poles and Jews in this period without some consideration of the popular religious prejudices that both Jews and Poles harboured vis-à-vis their neighbours.[3] Furthermore, the key role of the Catholic clergy in Polish society, so important for a nation without a state, also influenced the direction of conceptions of how to integrate—or not—Jews into the Polish nation.[4] On a popular level, Jews tended to see their Christian neighbours as crude, unpredictable, violent, and following a religion that was fundamentally pagan, worshipping idols (images of saints). Poles, on the other hand, despised Jews as moneylenders and Christ-killers, while also fearing Jews as crafty, sly, and possibly even demonic: the 'ritual murder' legend was far from dead here.[5] While Catholic clergy did not advocate violence against Jews, the Church generally urged believers to have nothing to do with Jews. In short, religious beliefs emphasized and strengthened the maintenance of a large distance between Jews and Christian Poles.

THE JEWISH COMMUNITY IN POLAND: DEMOGRAPHIC CONSIDERATIONS

Throughout the nineteenth century and into the twentieth, the largest Jewish community on the Polish lands was that of the Kingdom of Poland. In 1816 over 200,000 Jews lived here, almost 8 per cent of the total population. As in Galicia, Jewish population in the Kingdom of Poland grew steadily in both absolute and relative terms. By 1865 more than 700,000 Jews lived here (13.5 per cent) and in 1897 some 1.2 million (14.5 per cent).[6] We must consider these figures with some

[3] A. Cała, *Wizerunek Żyda w polskiej kulturze ludowej* (Warsaw, 1987).

[4] On Catholicism and the Poles, in particular in the modern period, see B. Porter-Szűcs, *Faith and Fatherland: Catholicism, Modernity, and Poland* (Oxford, 2011).

[5] J. Żyndul, *Kłamstwo krwi: Legenda mordu rytualnego na ziemiach polskich w XIX i XX wieku* (Warsaw, 2011).

[6] An exceedingly useful set of statistical tables is included in A. Polonsky, *The Jews in Poland and Russia*, 3 vols. (Oxford, 2010–12), ii. 198–211.

suspicion as only the last of them was based on a fairly reliable modern census. Still, the growth of Jewish population is duly confirmed by other sources, including the increasing agitation expressed in the Polish press by the late nineteenth century that Polish cities were being overwhelmed by Jews. In part the growth of the Jewish population was natural, that is, due to a higher birth rate and (especially) lower death rate than among non-Jews, and in part it stemmed from immigration from the Pale of Settlement.

While Jews lived in towns throughout the Kingdom, the importance of Warsaw cannot be overstated. By far the largest city and largest Jewish community here, it was also the seat of government and, from the 1860s or so, the centre of industry and of the railway net in Russian Poland. Even after the Russian authorities shut down the university (the Szkoła Główna) after the January uprising of 1863, Warsaw remained the centre of Polish intellectual life and publishing, rivalled distantly by Kraków. For this reason the position of Jews in Warsaw was of key importance. Throughout the nineteenth century Jews made up a significant presence in Warsaw, some 12 per cent of the population in 1799 (7,688 of 64,829), over a quarter in 1856 (40,922 of 156,072), and over one-third in the first decade of the twentieth century.[7] The growing numbers of Jews in the 'Polish capital' was a cause for growing concern among many Poles by the late nineteenth century, who feared that the growing Jewish presence in Warsaw would weaken the Poles' ability to combat Russification measures coming from St Petersburg.

THE LEGAL POSITION OF JEWS WITHIN THE RUSSIAN EMPIRE

Significant reform for the Kingdom of Poland had to await the death of Tsar Nicholas I in 1855. His death in the midst of the catastrophic Crimean War marked a caesura in Russian history. The failure of the Russian armies in the Crimea laid bare the backwardness of the Russian state and made clear even to Russian conservatives (including the new tsar, Alexander II) that major reforms were necessary. The death in 1856 of the tsar's long-serving viceroy in Warsaw, Ivan Paskevich, underlined the end of an era.

In the Russian empire Jews lived in large numbers both within the Pale of Settlement and in the Kingdom of Poland (after 1861 known as the 'Privislinsky krai', the 'Vistula Territory'). The legal situation of Jews in each of these regions was quite distinct. Before 1862, Jews in the Kingdom of Poland were often subjected to even more stringent legal restrictions than their co-religionists residing in the Pale. In the Kingdom of Poland, thanks in great part to the efforts of the margrave Aleksander Wielopolski, Jews were granted legal equality (*równou-prawnienie*) in 1862. While some mitigation of Jewish legal disabilities within the

---

[7] Guesnet, *Polnische Juden im 19. Jahrhundert*, 34.

Pale did take place in the 1860s and 1870s, the legal situation in the Kingdom remained more favourable.[8]

It is important to keep in mind what 'legal equality' did and did not entail. Jews were now allowed to live anywhere in the Polish provinces; no towns were allowed to maintain the medieval *de non tolerandis Judaeis* statutes. Jews could, in principle, participate in education and public life on the same basis as their Christian neighbours. Jews could also purchase land (though not peasant land, but this was not a restriction specific to Jews). In essence the granting of 'equal rights' removed specific restrictions but it did not necessarily ensure that Jews would be treated on an equal basis with Christians. The most crass example of this was government service: very few Jews indeed were employed by the Russian administration at any level, with the exception of Jewish physicians (and this exception was significant mainly in the interior provinces of the empire where local organs of self-government, the *zemstva*, existed). It should also be remembered that while the Russian empire strove to become a *Rechtsstaat* in this period (especially with the legal reforms of the 1860s), in fact the gap between law and reality remained rather large.

POLES AND JEWS AGAINST RUSSIAN OPPRESSION: THE EARLY 1860s

The years before 1863 are usually remembered as a golden era in Polish–Jewish relations, symbolized by the young acculturated Jew Michał Landy who was killed by Russian bullets in April 1861 at a Polish patriotic demonstration. It is true that Jews and Christian Poles co-operated in these years to an unprecedented extent, with the patriotic Rabbi Ber Meisels even closing synagogues in solidarity with the closure of Catholic churches after an anti-Catholic outrage by Russian troops in October 1861. At the same time, one should not exaggerate the depth or breadth of this *zbratanie* ('fraternization'). After all, it had not been long since the so-called 'Jewish war' of 1859 when a Polish journalist had insulted and slandered assimilated Polish Jews in Warsaw for allegedly boycotting non-Jewish musicians. The nastiness of the ensuing debate indicated that all was not well between Poles and Jews. Still, it is significant that Poles and Jews found themselves on the same side of the barricades in the early 1860s.

Although exact numbers cannot be determined, many Jews responded positively to the Polish struggle and its commitment to equal Jewish civil rights. The funeral of the five Polish victims of a violent confrontation with government forces in

[8] On the background to and details of the declaration of Jewish equal rights, see A. Eisenbach, *The Emancipation of the Jews in Poland, 1780–1870*, trans. J. Dorosz (Oxford, 1991). For an argument as to why legal restrictions remained in place in Russia proper (the Pale of Settlement), see M. Hildermeier, 'Die jüdische Frage im Zarenreich: Zum Problem der unterbliebenen Emanzipation', *Jahrbücher für Geschichte Osteuropas*, 32/3 (1984), 321–57.

February 1861 soon turned into a massive public ceremony that included both Poles and Jews, an expression of inter-group solidarity beautifully memorialized by the Polish Jewish painter Aleksander Lesser. According to some historians, as many as a thousand Jews participated in the 1863 insurrection itself, of whom approximately four hundred were killed, wounded, or punished by the tsarist authorities. The Jewish supporters of the uprising included leading progressive Jews and maskilim, such as the rabbi and preacher of Warsaw's Progressive Synagogue, Marcus Jastrow; and representatives of traditional Jewish society such as Ber Meisels, who had become chief rabbi of Warsaw in 1856, came out publicly in favour of the Polish cause.

Not only the actual events of 1861–3 but the way they were subsequently recalled influenced Polish–Jewish relations.[9] For those Jews who yearned for a Polish–Jewish symbiosis, the events represented a key moment in those relations, one to which they could point in order to demonstrate Jewish loyalty and commitment to the Polish cause. Optimistic visions of solidarity and brotherhood notwithstanding, however, the defeat of the Polish insurrectionaries and the Russian government's subsequent steps to weaken the foundations of Polish national existence—including the closing of the university in Warsaw, restrictions upon use of the Polish language and dissemination of Polish culture, and measures to undermine the economic position of the nobility—represented critical blows to Polish efforts to achieve independence. Those blows caused many Poles to rethink earlier strategies. In the process of that rethinking, ideas about the place of Jews in the Polish community were also re-examined.[10]

THE PERIOD OF RUSSIFICATION

The post-1863 Russification policies were of course aimed mainly at Poles and Polish culture, but also had some effect on Jews. In particular the Russian authorities wished to prevent the adoption by Jews of Polish culture, but it is doubtful whether government measures had a significant impact on such processes. More significant was economic development, which, as we have seen, brought thousands of Jews into the Polish provinces while making knowledge of Russian an important tool for ambitious individuals, whether in the field of culture or in business. Still, the idea of assimilation, interpreted in various ways, remained a significant factor among Jews here. The weekly *Izraelita*, so to speak the flagship of the *asymilatorzy* ('assimilators'), appeared continuously from 1866 almost to the end of Russian rule. But lacking Polish-language secondary and higher schools, Poles in the Kingdom lacked basic tools for encouraging Jews to learn Polish and acculturate (this is

---

[9] M. Opalski and I. Bartal, *Poles and Jews: A Failed Brotherhood* (Hanover, NH, 1992).

[10] I have discussed Russification in its Polish context in T. R. Weeks, *Nation and State in Late Imperial Russia: Nationalism and Russification on the Western Frontier, 1863–1914* (DeKalb, Ill., 1996), 92–109.

in fundamental opposition to the situation in Galicia). Despite this fact, it is remarkable that thousands of Jews did learn Polish and to one degree or another adopt Polish culture.[11] Even a figure not normally considered a Polish patriot, Rosa Luxemburg (born 1871), grew up speaking Polish, not Yiddish, and felt herself at home in Polish culture.

The two generations between 1863 and the revolution of 1905 also witnessed the growth of a large (in relative terms) Polish-speaking Jewish community. This group was diverse, including businessmen such as Jan Bloch (despite his conversion to Protestantism he always considered himself a Jew), historians such as Aleksander Kraushar, and even the aforementioned Rosa Luxemburg. Despite the lack of a Polish state or a Polish school system, increasing numbers of Jews were learning Polish, reading Mickiewicz and Sienkiewicz, and in various ways beginning to feel Polish. The majority, of course, continued to follow traditional patterns of life, speaking Yiddish among themselves and remaining religiously observant. While some Polish Jews—Bloch, for example—learned Russian well, it is not possible to speak of assimilation to Russian culture among the Jews of the Kingdom of Poland, aside perhaps from rare individuals. Rather, Russian was learned for practical reasons, but in the Russophobic atmosphere of the Polish provinces, Jews feeling strong connections to Russian culture would almost inevitably move eastward.

The decades immediately following 1863 were dominated by the ideals of the positivists, stressing educational and economic work rather than politics to strengthen and develop the Polish nation. Strictly speaking, for the positivists the 'Jewish question' did not exist. Rather, they held that when Jews (like Poles) became educated and modernized, they would cease to follow backward religious practices and would be integrated into the general population. It must be noted, however, that the positivists tended to avoid mention of the Jews, preferring to focus on other issues. Still, a look at the portrayal of Jews in Polish society in the writings of two major positivists, Aleksander Świętochowski and Bolesław Prus, gives us a good idea of more general liberal attitudes towards the relations between Jews and Poles.

In 1877 Świętochowski published an article criticizing the Warsaw correspondent of the nationalist Russian daily *Novoe vremya* for a long article accusing Jews of economic exploitation. He rejected both the specific argument and the correspondent's claim that the Polish press underestimated the importance of the Jewish question, preferring silence to an open discussion of the matter: 'We are convinced that the Jewish question does not exist. There exists only the urgent need for compulsory education for Christians and Jews to pull them out of isolation and furnish them with habits of thinking and everyday life common to the rest of humanity.' Świętochowski denied that this issue deserved more specific attention in the press: 'We acknowledge openly that for us the Jewish question is neither the

---

[11] On these individuals who, like Kraushar, became Polish patriots of Jewish origins, see T. R. Weeks, 'The Best of Both Worlds: Creating the *Żyd-Polak*', *East European Jewish Affairs*, 34/2 (2004), 1–20.

most important nor the most terrible. We have far greater troubles.'[12] In the circumstances of political repression, severe cultural restrictions, and economic backwardness of Russian Poland in the 1870s, Świętochowski and his fellow positivists felt that energy needed to be directed towards general cultural enlightenment and economic development rather than being distracted by narrow ethnic and religious questions. While Świętochowski's attitude towards Jews was later to sour considerably, until 1905 or so he saw the integration of Jews into Polish society as a natural, unavoidable, and unremarkable process—one of many in the modernization of the Polish nation.

Bolesław Prus took a similar position.[13] One 'chronicle' from 1874 makes fun of a suggestion in the conservative weekly *Wiek* that Jews without visible means of support should be deported from Warsaw. Prus treats such an idea as utterly absurd and ridiculous, hardly to be taken seriously. Where would one put them all? The underlying message is clear enough: any such radical measure, besides being inhumane, would be infeasible and would in no way help improve Warsaw's economy.[14] Another short passage refers to the not always admirable business practices of Jewish moneylenders and *faktorzy* ('agents'). But a parable of a dispute between a Jewish moneylender, a Pole, and a wise rabbi makes clear Prus's aim here: to mediate between Pole and Jew, not to polemicize against one or the other. The column concludes: 'And the moral of the story? More warmth and light, less prejudice and arrogance—and both of you will be able to patch up your failings [*wasze braki połatać*].'[15]

Prus's *Kroniki* are full of slighting references to Judaeophobes and specifically to Jan Jeleński, whose case I shall consider below. For Prus this well-known antisemite was the epitome of a talentless careerist who seized on anti-Jewish slogans as a means of making a name—and a fortune—for himself.[16] As for the Jewish question itself, Prus characteristically played down its importance. In an article of 1878 entitled 'Kwestyka żydowska', Prus explained that his use of the diminutive form of *kwestia* stemmed from his belief that Jews did not represent a power (*potęga*) in Poland. Furthermore, he argued, no 'Jewish question' existed but only questions regarding 'peasantry, bourgeoisie, noblity, emigration . . . darkness, poverty, bigotry, inefficiency, lack of conscience, gullibility, etc.' All of these 'little questions' affect in one way or another all local residents, including Jews. The Jews' 'darkness' (*ciemnota*) was not exclusive to them: 'Darkness in our beautiful land prevails everywhere [*panuje wszechwładnie*], from cellars to roofs.' As for Jewish 'caste attitudes' (*kastowość*), 'Was it so long ago that a nobleman [*szlachcic*] was ashamed to take up commerce or an artisan trade?' To be sure, Jews differed from other

---

[12] A. Świętochowski, 'Nie tędy', *Przegląd Tygodniowy*, 6 (18) Feb. 1877, pp. 73–5.

[13] For more detail, see A. Friedrich, *Bolesław Prus wobec kwestii żydowskiej* (Gdańsk, 2008).

[14] B. Prus, *Kroniki*, i/1 (Warsaw, 1956), 94–6. This column was originally published on 30 May 1874. [15] Ibid. 212–13, originally published on 15 Apr. 1874.

[16] B. Prus, *Kroniki, 1875–1878* (Warsaw, 1895), 44, 185–6.

inhabitants of 'our beautiful land' by their 'jargon' (Yiddish), peculiar clothing (*chałat*), and at times unsavoury business practices. But all of this was a question of education and time, not a 'Jewish question'. Prus ends by noting that while critics of the Jews look only at Jewish vices at present, he looks both at the past (to understand how the present situation came to be) and to the future (when education and toleration will do away with these negative traits).[17] In this essay Prus exhibits his characteristic humour, irony, and tolerance. Despite certain lapses in later decades, this would be his prevalent attitude towards the Jews to the end of his life.[18]

Until the 1880s or so, and in many ways long after, the most widespread 'answer' to the Jewish question was 'assimilation'. But what did that mean? Alina Cała has pointed out that there were many different kinds of 'assimilation' in the post-1863 period.[19] Nearly all of these, aside from the 'total assimilation' that actually foresaw the disappearance of Jews as such, would fall under the rubric 'acculturation' or 'integration' in today's vocabulary. But one almost never finds such terms or their cognates in contemporary Polish or Russian (or German) discussions of the Jewish question. Given the presence of hundreds of thousands of Jews in the Polish lands, the idea of their actual disappearance, even in a cultural sense, would have seemed fantastic. And it should be recalled that even the most fervent *asymilatorze*, for example those Jews associated with *Izraelita*, constantly emphasized the need to retain some elements (religious and cultural) of Jewishness. Thus, ideally *Żydzi-Polacy* ('Jew-Poles') would both fit into the Polish nation and enrich it with their own cultural uniqueness. That was, of course, in principle.

The integration of foreign elements into a society—and Jews were undoubtedly perceived by most Poles as 'the other' in the nineteenth century—is always a complicated and many-sided process. First of all, the definition of 'Pole' and 'Jew' was not clearly fixed. Like many labels that 'everyone understands', actually discussing 'who belonged' often turned out to be far more complex than anyone had guessed. For acculturation (to use the modern term) to succeed, not only did Jews have to change somewhat, acquiring the Polish language and to some measure mixing in Polish society, but—and here is a key stumbling block—Poles had to accept these acculturated Jews as *nasi* ('ours'). To further complicate matters, by the late nineteenth century, many Jews were attracted to their own, Jewish nationalism. Some Poles, like Kazimierz Kelles-Krauz, pointed out that it was only logical for Jews to be as devoted to their nation as Poles were, and called for a compromise be-tween two nations.[20] Kelles-Krauz was an exception, however, even among socialists.

---

[17] Prus, *Kroniki, 1875–1878*, 407–10. The essay was originally published on 31 Mar. 1878.

[18] In the context of the Jewish question one must mention his 'Z powodu 12,000,000 guldenów', *Kurjer Codzienny*, vol. 25, nos. 307, 309, 315, 319, 321, 328, 331 (Oct.–Nov. 1889).

[19] A. Cała, *Asymilacja Żydów w Królestwie Polskim (1864–1897): Postawy, konflikty, stereotypy* (Warsaw, 1989); A. Jagodzińska, *Pomiędzy: Akulturacja Żydów Warszawy w drugiej połowie XIX wieku* (Wrocław, 2008).

[20] T. Snyder, *Nationalism, Marxism, and Modern Central Europe: A Biography of Kazimierz Kelles-Krauz (1872–1905)* (Cambridge, Mass., 1997).

As the ideal of assimilation faded in the final decades of the nineteenth century, it could have been replaced with a sober recognition of the need for Poles and Jews to compromise on equal-nation grounds: Kelles-Krauz's ideas. To some extent the Polish Socialist Party (Polska Partia Socjalistyczna; PPS) actually tried to implement such ideas, but much more common was another reaction: anger and hostility at Jewish 'betrayal' of the Poles.[21]

THE BEGINNINGS OF MODERN POLISH ANTISEMITISM

The pogroms of 1881 were a shock that affected everyone. In the wake of the Christmas pogrom in Warsaw, Świętochowski urgently called for a concerted and total assimilation of Jews into the Polish nation.[22] Another reaction, if one can call it that, was the beginning of publication of *Rola* in early 1883 (New Style). *Rola* was edited and to a great extent written by Jan Jeleński, who may fairly be called the father of modern Polish antisemitism. Still, it should be noted that Jeleński himself always rejected the label 'antisemite', claiming that he was merely trying to protect the Polish nation. Jeleński also always emphasized the Catholic religion, even though the Catholic hierarchy remained cool towards him. The real novelty of *Rola* was its consistent call to fight the Jews through economic organization, by setting up 'Polish' (i.e. non-Jewish) shops, warehouses, and trade. While he claimed to be a good Catholic, Jeleński's definition of Jew and 'Jewish commerce' was in practice close to racial. Whether Polish-speaking or not, Jews were the enemy.

Far more influential and far more famous than Jeleński, but in certain ways taking up his ideas, were the organizers of the National Democratic Party (Stronnictwo Narodowo-Demokratyczna, popularly known as the Endecja), chief among them Roman Dmowski. In the 1890s, their main enemy was positivism and anyone who advocated compromise and co-operation with the partitioning powers. In the first programme of the National Democratic Party (1897), 'Polishness' is nowhere defined and the Jewish question is passed over in silence. The sharpening of National Democracy's attitude towards non-Poles was reflected in the party programme of 1903, which delved into the Jewish issue in some detail. The National Democratic Party, it is stated, opposes any attempt to portray the Jews as a nationality; Jews are essentially alien residents of the Polish lands who must subordinate themselves to the Polish national interest. This being the case, when Jews league with the occupying powers or other enemies of the Polish nation, the National Democratic Party will fight them 'unconditionally' (*bezwzględnie*) and work for their expulsion. Those Jews who adopt a neutral position will be treated with tolerance, though the party will in any case work against Jewish domination in the

---

[21] J. D. Zimmerman, *Poles, Jews, and the Politics of Nationality: The Bund and the Polish Socialist Party in Late Tsarist Russia, 1892–1914* (Madison, 2004).

[22] T. R. Weeks, *From Assimilation to Antisemitism: The 'Jewish Question' in Poland, 1850–1914* (DeKalb, Ill., 2006), 82–3.

economy and the 'harmful influence of Jews' in social life. Finally, any Jewish individuals who identify themselves absolutely and unconditionally with the Polish
cause, even when it comes into conflict with Jewish interests, are to be accepted as
Poles.[23] While this is not, strictly speaking, a racial definition of Pole versus Jew, in
practice very few Jews could accept such terms in order to be accepted into the
Polish nation, in particular the explicit and insulting demand that they oppose
the community of their birth.[24] Thus, already by 1903 the later antisemitism of the
Endecja, while not yet fully developed, was present in outline form.

   The ideology of National Democracy is revealed in its name: it was national,
emphasizing the development of the Polish nation as a whole, and it was democratic, claiming to represent the best interests of the Polish people over narrow class
concerns. Against individualistic liberals like Świętochowski or Prus, the Endeks
insisted that the collective, the nation, came first. Unlike the positivists and most
previous Polish thinkers, the Endeks specifically excluded the Jews *as Jews* (even if
acculturated and Polish-speaking) from the Polish nation. Dmowski, indeed,
blamed the Jews (along with, to be sure, the Polish nobility) for creating the present
'unhealthy' state of the Polish nation with its underdeveloped middle class.[25] As
stated in the 1903 party programme, the future healthy development of the Polish
nation was contingent upon reducing 'Jewish influence', isolating and weakening
the Jews economically, and encouraging their departure from Poland. By refusing to allow any place for the Jewish masses in the Polish nation, the National
Democrats already at this early stage implicitly demanded their expulsion. Later
this implicit demand would become explicit.[26]

   Another outcome of the 1881 pogroms was the introduction of the so-called
'May Laws' of 3 May 1882 (Old Style). While these laws, which further restricted
Jewish rights of trading and residence, only applied to the Pale of Settlement
(i.e. not to the 'Vistula Territory', the Polish provinces), they affected Jewish life
throughout the empire. For one thing, increased harassment of Jews living in the
Pale encouraged them to migrate to the Kingdom of Poland, where economic
opportunities were in any case greater. It seems clear that the May Laws were not
consistently applied (this was, after all, the Russian empire), but the atmosphere of
insecurity among Jews in the Pale was surely felt in the Polish provinces as well.[27]
It is not surprising, given the administrative realities of the empire, that the new

---

[23] For the sections on Jews in the 1903 programme, see *Narodowa Demokracja: Antologia myśli
politycznej 'Przeglądu Wszechpolskiego', 1895–1905*, ed. B. Toruńczyk (London, 1983), 121–2.

[24] For a recent discussion of Dmowski in this key period, see G. Krzywiec, *Szowinizm po polsku:
Przypadek Romana Dmowskiego (1886–1905)* (Warsaw, 2009).

[25] In particular in R. Dmowski, *Myśli nowoczesnego Polaka*, 2nd edn. (Lwów, 1904).

[26] For a stimulating attempt to explain the course of Polish nationalist thought in the nineteenth
century, see B. Porter, *When Nationalism Began to Hate: Imagining Modern Politics in Nineteenth-
Century Poland* (New York, 2000).

[27] For an excellent overview of the condition of Jews in the Russian empire, see Polonsky, *Jews in
Poland and Russia*, ii. 3–39.

restrictions were not enforced consistently (corruption and inefficiency were endemic). Perhaps more remarkable is the fact that no new restrictions were introduced in the Kingdom of Poland. It is impossible to say with any certainty why this was the case. In his dissertation Michael Ochs suggests three reasons why the Russians did not restrict Jewish rights in the Polish provinces: there was no specific cause compelling enough, Russian administrators disagreed on whether to take such a step, and the economic consequences of further restrictions would have been negative.[28] To these quite convincing reasons I would add a more general one: the overwhelming bureaucratic inertia that reigned in the Russian empire, in particular as regards large and complex social issues.

Between 1863 and 1904, relations between Poles and Jews in the Russian empire became steadily more strained. Many factors were at play here: the restrictions on Polish culture and economic life, the immigration of Jews from the Pale of Settlement to the Kingdom of Poland, and the growth of Jewish national feeling, to name a few. By the end of the nineteenth century, there was a widespread perception among Poles that, despite the granting of equal rights to Jews (in 1862 in the Kingdom of Poland), the hoped-for assimilation of Jews to the Polish nation had not occurred. While this perception was almost certainly based on false premises and even factually incorrect, it was deeply felt. Thus many Poles found convincing the Endek arguments that Jews were stymieing and even actively opposing the cultural, social, and political development of the Polish nation. Before 1905, however, such feelings remained for the most part below the surface. It would take the revolutionary events of that year and even more the disappointments of failed expectations afterwards to bring the most passionate Judaeophobic sentiments out into the open.

WORSENING OF POLISH–JEWISH RELATIONS
AFTER 1905

The year 1905 is significant because it held out the promise of significant reform, perhaps even independence, for Poles, and ended in an almost total defeat of such hopes. During the actual revolutionary year Jews and Poles co-operated for the most part in the efforts to topple Russian rule. After the revolution's defeat, however, many came to believe the National Democrats' claim that Jews had conspired to set off the revolution to further than own aims against those of ethnic Poles. Despite the absurdity of these charges, the pain of disillusionment in the post-1905 years enabled the Endeks to use the label of 'Jew' to discredit any opponents, with very negative results for future Polish–Jewish relations. Ironically, the easing of censorship and the introduction of limited democratic elections (to the State Duma) served to exacerbate Polish–Jewish relations. The National Democrats used the

---

[28] Ochs, 'St. Petersburg and the Jews of Russian Poland', 81–5.

elections to brand any opponents traitors to the Polish nation and Jews or their hirelings.[29]

By 1912 relations between Poles and Jews in the Kingdom of Poland, and in particular in the centre of Jewish assimilation, Warsaw, were very strained. The very bitter electoral campaign to the Fourth Duma would lead to an almost total breakdown. In this campaign Dmowski's National Democrats were opposed by former allies who now, convinced that the Endecja had achieved nothing for Poles in the first three Dumas, formed the National Concentration (Koncentracja Narodowa) with the moderate candidate Jan Kucharzewski as their candidate for the Duma seat from Warsaw. Because of the split in the Polish camp and peculiarities of the electoral system, which favoured property-owners, Warsaw Jewish electors found themselves in the uncomfortable position of being forced to decide who would represent Warsaw in the Fourth Duma. When Kucharzewski refused to state explicitly that he would not back restrictions on Jews in future elected city governments, and after public threats designed to intimidate Jewish electors from putting forward a Jewish candidate, a relatively unknown elector from the PPS-Left, Eugeniusz Jagiełło, was chosen as Warsaw's representative to the Duma. Jagiełło received the support of all forty-three Jewish electors and no votes from either of the Polish nationalist organizations. The election of Jagiełło, labelled 'the Jewish delegate', led to a marked increase in tensions between Poles and Jews. Jagiełło himself was so frightened by the calls for physical violence that he actually went into hiding for several days.

The new National Democratic daily, *Gazeta Poranna*, and other papers responded to the embarrassing political defeat by calling for an economic and social boycott of Jews and Jewish-owned businesses under the catchy slogan of 'swój do swego po swoje' (roughly, 'stick to your own kind'). The Jewish journalist Bernard Singer recalled the unsavoury tactics resorted to as relations between Poles and Jews reached what seemed to be a new low: 'The paper unmasked Jewish shops which had Polish names and called for a boycott of Jewish doctors and lawyers.' While the exact impact of the boycott, which was accompanied by sporadic outbursts of anti-Jewish violence, is unclear, the campaign did little to improve the delicate state of relations between Jews and Poles in the Congress Kingdom. Singer further noted how 'walks [by Jews] into the Polish section gradually ceased. [Jewish] music-lovers stopped going to the Philharmonic . . . The Jewish public abandoned the Philharmonic. Gradually it also gave up the [Polish] theatre.'[30]

In this climate of hostility, there were some Polish liberals who publicly rejected the anti-Jewish boycott as counterproductive, un-Polish, and shameful. For them, the boycott represented a betrayal of the most cherished Polish traditions of tolerance, culture, and enlightenment. Perhaps the most famous Pole who protested the boycott was the linguist Jan Baudouin de Courtenay. Rejecting the division of

---

[29] T. R. Weeks, 'Fanning the Flames: Jews in the Warsaw Press, 1905–1912', *East European Jewish Affairs*, 28/2 (1998–9), 63–81.   [30] B. Singer, *Moje Nalewki* (Warsaw, 1993), 148.

the world into 'ours' and 'theirs', he refused either to love or to hate the Jews as a people, and dismissed with scorn the idea that Yiddish was somehow an inferior language or merely a 'jargon'. Arguing along rationalist, liberal, and anti-national lines, Baudouin de Courtenay condemned the boycott as the work of ignorant fanatics, cynical political manipulators, and fools. Polish traditions, political and economic progress, morality, and simple practical considerations demanded that Poles and Jews live together, if not in complete harmony, then at least without open conflict. Other prominent Poles, such as Ludomir Grendyszyński and Teresa Lubińska, protested against the boycott movement.[31]

These protests required a great deal of civil courage at a time when expressing reservations about the boycott was widely considered national treason. On the other hand, however, even these fervent opponents of the boycott often used anti-Jewish stereotypes and argumentation. Perhaps Baudouin de Courtenay came closest to accepting the idea of a 'supranational' Polish state that could deal equally with Poles and Jews. But his rejection of nationality as an ordering principle and his hyperrationality, which failed to consider the powerful feelings associated with a sense of national identity, prevented his ideas from finding broad resonance. Polish protests against the boycott rarely took seriously the demands of the Jewish national movement. In essence, all argued that relations between Poles and Jews should return to the (somewhat mythical) tolerance and 'enlightened' attitudes of the Wielopolski era. One may doubt whether such well-meaning suggestions had any possibility of influencing behaviour in the highly charged nationalist atmosphere of these years.

CONCLUSION

On the eve of the First World War, relations between Poles and Jews were tense, antisemitic rhetoric was widespread, and the previously prevalent ideal of assimilation found few open supporters. However, one needs to put this admittedly depressing situation into a broader context and avoid historical teleologies and stereotypes. After all, around the same time relations between Czechs and Jews were far from warm and there had even been anti-Jewish rioting by Czech nationalists in Prague. Yet in the inter-war period, Czechoslovakia was arguably the most liberal state in Europe vis-à-vis its Jewish citizens. We should also not lose sight of the fact that Jews were in fact becoming better integrated into Polish society. By 1914 young Jews were far more likely than a generation earlier to speak Polish, look like their Christian coevals, and to come into contact with Poles on an everyday basis. Thus, despite the negative attitudes between Poles and Jews that found expression in Jan Jeleński's *Rola* and the 1912 anti-Jewish boycott in the Kingdom of Poland, it

---

[31] J. Jedlicki, 'Resisting the Wave: Intellectuals against Antisemitism in the Last Years of the "Polish Kingdom"', in R. Blobaum (ed.), *Antisemitism and its Opponents in Modern Poland* (Ithaca, NY, 2005), 60–80.

would be ahistorical and false to argue that relations between Poles and Jews were irreparably damaged.

Among the factors that helped exacerbate relations between Poles and Jews were a general heightened level of nationalist feeling in the period, the lack of a Polish state, the large number of Jews, particularly in cities, and economic backwardness. Let us take these factors one by one. No one denies that nationalism was a strong and potent political, social, even cultural force in the half-century before the First World War. For Poles, with their memory of past greatness, a sophisticated high culture, but very little political power, nationalism was an obvious and reasonable reaction to the status quo. Among Jews, too, living in uncertain circumstances (legal, economic, social) and faced with apparently well-organized and growing anti-Jewish sentiments, nationalism was also a reasonable answer to the day's woes. One cannot say that 'antisemitism caused Zionism' or vice versa, but the historical record is clear that Zionism, Bund, and Polish nationalism—both in the generous form of the PPS and in the more narrow, aggressive National Democratic variety— were all developing together. After all, these parties all took shape in one form or another in the 1890s.

The relationship between nation and state is complex and not always properly appreciated. Indeed, in English and French it is often difficult to distinguish between *państwo* and *naród*. There can be no doubt, however, that everywhere the state was becoming vitally interested in defining and nurturing the 'nation', a process that would become far more developed in the inter-war period. Without a state, the Poles were at a distinct disadvantage in efforts to acculturate minority national groups like the Jews. While the Russian government could sponsor Russian-language schools, demand that civil servants use that language, and even enforce the use of Russian on the railways, Poles had no such possibilities. Thus while acculturation to Polish culture did take place among Jews, it was weaker than it would have been had a Polish state existed. Even more importantly, I think, Poles in the Prussian and Russian partitions feared for their own culture. While these fears were probably exaggerated, they made contemporary Poles far more sensitive to apparent 'treason' on the part of Jews who might speak some variety of Russian, for example, rather than Polish.

The simple number of Jews in the Polish lands was a major factor. When one-third of the population of Warsaw and Łódź was Jewish and this percentage appeared to be growing, it was not unreasonable for Poles to fear for their own status there. The obvious liberal answer, of course, would have been a more generous definition of 'Pole' to include Polonized Jews, but it must be said that liberal nationalists were rather unusual in this period. The large numbers of Jews in trade, banking, industry, and the professions made plausible the arguments that Poles required 'defence' from these intruders. To be sure, more sober, effective, and courageous political leaders could have pointed out—like Baudouin de Courtenay and others— that Poles and Jews were essentially fated to live together; hence some kind of sharing and mutual respect would redound to both groups' advantage. But, again, this is liberal ex-post-facto reasoning; the passionate anger and hatred of the immediate pre-1914 years were hardly open to sober, logical arguments.

Economic backwardness and the social structure of the Polish lands also worked against a calm, liberal answer to the Jewish question. Roman Dmowski and his party correctly pointed out that a healthy modern nation must possess a vibrant middle class. Jewish nationalists similarly argued that Jews needed to go back to the soil and become more 'productive'. Even Jan Jeleński's 'Christian co-ops' could be seen as progressive from an economic point of view, eliminating the middleman and delivering goods at lower cost to consumers (this was the theory though hardly the practice). The simple fact that any economic movement against middlemen and petty merchants would inevitably mean a movement against Jews certainly coloured the political discourse of the period. Thus in the Polish lands economic development was almost inevitably seen in ethnic and, especially, anti-Jewish terms. Jews were identified with capitalism, banking, railway building—in short, with modernity. While the Jewish community certainly suffered just as much as Christian Poles from these economic dislocations, the tendency to seek a scapegoat in the Jew was to some extent inevitable. Combine this with the cool cynicism of Roman Dmowski, who played the Jewish card to blacken the reputations of opposing parties and to gather political support, and it is hardly surprising that relations between Poles and Jews had reached a very low level by 1914.

During the nineteenth century the Jewish community in the Kingdom of Poland changed immensely. In many ways, these changes remained below the surface, with the older, more traditional generation still dominating everyday and religious life. The great majority of Jews here continued to speak Yiddish as a first language, to remain religiously Orthodox, and to have limited contact with their Christian neighbours. On the eve of the First World War, one must remember, Jews had enjoyed equal rights for barely a half-century in either Galicia or the Kingdom of Poland. In practice their rights were further diminished by prejudice and government practice restricting the hiring of Jews in many positions. Acculturation was limited by the limited number of Polish-language schools, which even after 1905 remained rare in the Russian partition. Thus in 1914 the Polish Jewish masses, while they had changed much over the past century, remained so to speak on the edge of modernity.

Feliks Perl on the Jewish Question

JOSHUA D. ZIMMERMAN

ONE OF THE MOST FASCINATING figures in the history of late nineteenth- and early twentieth-century Poland is that of the Polish Jew Feliks Perl (1871–1927). Perl is best known for his role in the founding of the Polish Socialist Party (Polska Partia Socjalistyczna; PPS) in 1892, a party that was not only led by Józef Piłsudski in its formative years but that also became the principal voice of Polish progressive politics throughout the first half of the twentieth century. As co-author of the party's founding programme (1892), editor-in-chief of its central organ, *Robotnik*, and representative in the Polish Sejm from 1919, Perl retained an eminent status during his lifetime. A committed assimilationist, he was considered by many Polish Jews as a zealous Polonophile. One leader of the Jewish socialist movement formed the following impression of Perl upon meeting him in the mid-1890s: 'Stiff and high-strung, he behaved more Polish than the Poles. The zealousness brought out by his Polish patriotism, his devotion to the [national form] of Polish socialism . . . often took a bizarre form.'[1]

Although characterized by Jewish political leaders as indifferent to Jewish concerns, Perl took an active interest in the so-called 'Jewish question' from the moment he entered political life. Yet despite his defence of Jewish civil rights and complete equality before the law, the figure of Feliks Perl has received little scholarly attention outside Poland.[2] Among Polish scholars, two historians have written full-length scholarly biographies of him.[3] Perl seems to have been largely perceived as a Pole by the Jewish community even if his Jewish origins were recognized. Thus in Jacob Shatzky's valuable three-volume history of the Jews in Warsaw Perl is mentioned in passing as 'the Warsaw Jew' who co-founded the PPS.[4]

---

[1] J. Mill, *Pyoner un boyer: memuarn*, 2 vols. (New York, 1946–9), i. 175.

[2] Perl does not appear, for example, in the standard English-language histories of modern Polish Jewry such as Antony Polonsky's celebrated *The Jews in Poland and Russia*, 3 vols. (Oxford, 2010–2012) or Ezra Mendelsohn's *The Jews of East Central Europe between the World Wars* (Bloomington, Ind., 1983). In Joseph Marcus's study *Social and Political History of the Jews in Poland, 1919–1939* (Berlin, 1983), 506, Perl is mentioned once as the most important Jewish leader in the Polish labour movement.

[3] M. Śliwa, *Feliks Perl* (Warsaw, 1988), and A. Uljasz, *Myśl polityczna Feliksa Perla* (Lublin, 2005).

[4] J. Shatzky, *Geshikhte fun yidn in varshe*, 3 vols. (New York, 1947–53), iii. 395.

Otherwise, interest in Perl in Jewish historiography is confined to obscure studies on the Jewish socialist movement in eastern Europe.[5]

The following study examines Perl's writings on the Jewish question in the Polish socialist press. It will also analyse articles that he wrote for the Yiddish press in the pages of the party's Yiddish organ, *Der arbeyter*. I argue that Perl devoted much thought to the future of Polish Jews. Although a committed assimilationist, he maintained that the struggle for Jewish equality was part and parcel of a broader campaign for the freedom of national expression, while stopping short of recognizing the Jews as a nation.

FAMILY BACKGROUND AND THE EARLY YEARS

Feliks Perl was born in Warsaw on 26 April 1871, into an affluent Polish-speaking Jewish family, to Dawid and Rozalia Perl.[6] His father had fought in the 1863 January uprising, for which he spent time in a tsarist prison. Perl was raised in an atmosphere of Polish patriotism and love of Polish culture.[7] A contemporary described him as the classic 'figure of the Jewish Pole [*Żyd-Polak*]—a patriot of the highest order who knew *Pan Tadeusz* by heart'.[8] At the same time, however, Perl grew up in the Jewish district of Warsaw at 21 Grzybowska Street in a home that kept to some Jewish traditions.[9] After graduating from a Russian gymnasium in Warsaw, he entered the School of Law at Warsaw University, and while attending it he joined illegal circles of socialists. In 1889 he became a member of the populist 'Second Proletariat' party (Socjalno-Rewolucyjna Partia 'Proletariat'). In 1890 he helped organize a May Day rally in Warsaw, co-writing the party's May Day circular.[10] Perl quickly moved up the ranks of the Second Proletariat, becoming a member of its central committee at the age of 20. On 24 March 1892 a wave of

---

[5] See, among others, M. Mishkinsky, *Reshit tunuat hapo'alim hayehudit berusyah* (Tel Aviv, 1981); id., 'Tenuat hapo'alim hayehudit berusyah vehatenuah hasotsialistit hapolanit', *Asufot*, 1 (14) (1970), 81–131; A. Gutterman, 'Assimilated Jews as Leaders of the Polish Labor Movement between the Two World Wars', *Gal-ed*, 14 (1995), 49–65.

[6] A. Uljasz, 'Poglądy Feliksa Perla na kwestię żydowską', *Annales Universitatis Mariae Curie-Skłodowska*, Sectio F, 57 (2002), 51.

[7] Śliwa, *Feliks Perl*, 12–13. For additional material on Perl, see Uljasz, 'Poglądy Feliksa Perla na kwestię żydowską'; J. Holzer, 'Perl, Feliks', in *Polski słownik biograficzny*, xxv/4 (Wrocław, 1980), 623–5; H. Piasecki, 'Feliks Perl — historyk i działacz PPS', *Biuletyn Żydowskiego Instytutu Historycznego*, 92 (1974), 59–70; B. Garfunkel, 'Feliks Perl', in N. Getter, J. Schalla, and Z. Schipper (eds.), *Żydzi bojownicy o niepodległość Polski* (Lwów, 1939), 67–70.

[8] Cited in Uljasz, 'Poglądy Feliksa Perla na kwestię żydowską', 52. Perl's love of Mickiewicz led him to publish a short study on the poet: Res [Feliks Perl], *Adam Mickiewicz* (London, 1898).

[9] Gutterman, 'Assimilated Jews as Leaders of the Polish Labor Movement', 15; S. Kieniewicz, 'Assimilated Jews in Nineteenth-Century Warsaw', in W. T. Bartoszewski and A. Polonsky (eds.), *The Jews in Warsaw: A History* (Oxford, 1991), 178.

[10] Piasecki, 'Feliks Perl — historyk i działacz PPS', 60. While preparing for the 1890 May Day rally in Warsaw, Perl met Teresa Reznikowska, a Russian Jew, who had arrived from Słonim in the Nowogródek area. Her Polish was weak but she knew Yiddish and Russian well. They began a relation-

arrests in Warsaw put a halt to underground socialist activity. Perl evaded arrest and fled to Germany in the following month.[11] Abroad, he completed his Ph.D. in 1895 at the university in Bern.[12]

When he crossed the border into Germany, Perl's political outlook was heavily influenced by the anti-national, populist orientation of the Second Proletariat. It was in Berlin that he learned of a shift in Polish socialist circles in London— led by Stanisław Mendelson (1858–1913)—to a pro-independence programme.[13] Perl went to Zurich at the end of May 1892, where he met other exiled socialists from the Kingdom of Poland. The circle of Polish exiles from Warsaw discussed Mendelson's views expressed in the pages of the London-based *Przedświt* ('Dawn'). Perl fell under Mendelson's influence. 'In Congress Poland, I had been a fervent adherent of the socialist-revolutionary party Proletariat', Perl recalled. But soon after settling in Switzerland,

I came to realize that the great days of the Proletariat had irreversibly diminished and that something new was needed for our movement. After some resistance I accepted the new programme, whose main architect was Stanisław Mendelson . . . I became convinced that the slogan of 'social revolution' could not replace a political programme, and that a galvanizing political programme must be based on the struggle against occupation—one that would properly take into consideration the Polish Question.[14]

Perl was invited to the founding convention of the PPS, which took place in November 1892 in Paris. There he argued for the primacy of the Polish state idea as well as the separation of the Polish and Russian revolutionary movements. Interestingly, the two leading proponents of Polish independence at the convention were Mendelson and Perl, the only participants of Jewish background of the eighteen that attended.

In the years 1892–1900 Perl served on the PPS's Foreign Committee in London, where he edited and wrote for several party newspapers. It was at this time that he became particularly interested in the history of the French Revolution and its approach to Jewish emancipation. His reading guided his vision of Polish state and society in general and of the Jewish question in particular. It was the slogan 'The Jews should be denied everything as a nation, but granted everything as individuals',[15] articulated in 1789, that Perl believed had to be applied to the Polish lands. That is, full social and cultural integration into Polish society and full equality before the law.

---

ship that resulted, ten years later, in marriage. She would later play a role in the PPS Yiddish press. See J. Holzer, 'Perlowa z Reznikowskich, Teresa', in *Polski słownik biograficzny*, xxv/4, 631.

[11] F.P. [Feliks Perl], 'Wspomnienia ze zjazdu paryskiego', *Jedność Robotnicza* (Warsaw), 1916, no. 26, p. 2; Śliwa, *Feliks Perl*, 31.　　　[12] Piasecki, 'Feliks Perl — historyk i działacz PPS', 60.

[13] Śliwa, *Feliks Perl*, 31.　　　[14] F.P., 'Wspomnienia ze zjazdu paryskiego', 2.

[15] 'The French National Assembly: Debate on the Eligibility of Jews for Citizenship (December 23, 1789)', in *The Jew in the Modern World: A Documentary History*, ed. P. R. Mendes-Flohr and J. Reinharz, 2nd edn. (New York, 1995), 115.

PERL'S UNDERSTANDING OF THE JEWISH QUESTION

It was in anticipation of the founding of the PPS that Perl first began to touch on the so-called Jewish question. In a letter he wrote from Zurich on 26 May 1892, he commented that any political agitation literature should include a condemnation of antisemitism. In another letter written in the summer of 1892 he cautioned against using Marx's position on the Jewish question, maintaining that it had become obsolete.[16] The PPS's first Yiddish organ appeared in December 1898. Printed in London, *Der arbeyter* had a print run of 1,500 copies for distribution in the Kingdom of Poland,[17] and was edited by Maksymilian Horwitz (1877–1937), a member of the PPS since 1896, who was the only intellectual party member at the time able to edit a Yiddish-language organ. According to Leon Gottlieb (1878–1947), who later worked as Yiddish editor and translator for the PPS, Horwitz himself smuggled the material for *Der arbeyter* out of the Russian empire, including the lead editorial, city chronicles, and factory reports.[18]

The first issue led off with an inaugural note, in Yiddish and Polish, by the central committee. Titled 'The Tsarist Regime and the Worker', it argued that civil and national liberation could only be attained by the break-up of the Russian empire into its 'natural parts'. The Jewish worker, it maintained, was obligated to combat the politics of Russification and to support the independence of Poland. 'We, Jewish workers in Poland,' *Der arbeyter* stated, 'undoubtedly share the same interests and needs as our Christian brothers in the same land. Their future is also our future, their aspirations, ours: an independent Polish Republic is therefore our political programme, for it is the only form of government that will give us the needed political rights for our class struggle.'[19]

In 1899 Horwitz was arrested in Warsaw. Signalling the importance the party attached to its Yiddish press, Leon Wasilewski (1870–1936), a non-Jewish Pole of aristocratic origins, took it upon himself to learn enough Yiddish in order to continue putting out *Der arbeyter*. Wasilewski recruited two Yiddish-speaking party members to aid in producing the second issue: Teresa Reznikowska-Perlowa

[16] Both letters are cited in Uljasz, 'Poglądy Feliksa Perla na kwestię żydowską', 54.

[17] Archiwum Żydowskiego Instytutu Historycznego, Warsaw, Archiwum Ringelbluma, 1183: Papers of Moses Kaufman, pt. 2, fo. 3; Ż. Kormanowa, *Materiały do bibliografii druków socjalistycznych na ziemiach polskich w latach 1866–1918* (Warsaw, 1949), 1. Pinkhas Shvarts claimed that issue no. 1 of *Der arbeyter* had a print run of 5,000, relying on the figure given by Władysław Pobóg-Malinwoski. See P. Shvarts, *Yuzef pilsudski: zayn batsiyung tsu der yidn-frage un zayn kamf kegn bund, 1893–1905* (Warsaw, 1936), 169; W. Pobóg-Malinowski, *Józef Piłsudski*, 2 vols. (Warsaw, 1935), i. 297. Because Pobóg-Malinowski did not cite a source for this figure, I am relying on Kormanowa's authoritative account of Polish socialist publications.

[18] [Leon Gottlieb], London, to the PPS Foreign Committee, London, 9 Jan. 1901, fo. 5: YIVO Institute for Jewish Research, New York, Bund Archives (hereafter Bund Archives), ME 21, folder 23.

[19] 'Di tsarishe regirung un di arbeter', *Der arbeyter* (London), 1 (Dec. 1898), 6: Bund Archives, microfilm division.

and Leon Gottlieb. Reznikowska-Perlowa (1871–1939) came from a lower middle-class Lithuanian Jewish family in Słonim, and had become active in socialist circles in Warsaw. She had first met Perl in Warsaw at the above-mentioned 1890 May Day rally, at which she was arrested. Once released, she went abroad, settling in London in 1900. It was in London that she began working as a compositor for the PPS organs *Przedświt* and *Światło*. During this time, Feliks Perl moved to London as well. The two married in the same year.[20]

While Perlowa improved the quality and style of the Yiddish, Perl agreed to write the feature article, which was translated into Yiddish by Gottlieb.[21] Perl began by proclaiming that autocratic Russia was the greatest obstacle in the way of the liberation of the working class, a regime that promoted inter-ethnic strife between the nationalities in order to prevent unifying alliances. 'The murderous Russian government is the greatest and most destructive antisemite,' stated *Der arbeyter*, 'so much so that Haman, may he rest in peace, was altogether a saint in comparison.'[22] The tsarist regime, *Der arbeyter* continued, used its power to inculcate hatred for Jews in other people, inciting the Poles, Lithuanians, and Russians. Moreover, the Russian government desired the Jews 'always to be sunk in the swamp of superstition and darkness' and did not intend to grant them civil rights.

But the anti-Jewish politics of the government should not be viewed in isolation. Rather, the Jewish question had to be seen within the broader context of the regime's nationalities politics in general, and the Russo-Polish conflict in particular. One of the greatest fears of the government, he wrote, was that the Jewish and Christian workers would combine into one party—the PPS. 'The despotic government wants the Jews to remain alien from everything . . . Polish—from all that concerns the Polish land—[to remain] a people apart [without] common aims with the Poles.'[23] The conscious effort of the government to undermine Polish–Jewish solidarity was reflected in its Russification programme, *Der arbeyter* argued. Unless Jews were acquainted with the Polish language and culture, alliances would be difficult to establish.

The Russian government restricted not only Jewish access to higher education but the movement of Jews outside the boundaries of the Pale as well. Government policy thus demonstrated, *Der arbeyter* maintained, that the tsarist regime sought to retard Jewish integration and had no intention of making Jews citizens. By way of comparison, the last king of sovereign Poland, Stanisław August Poniatowski, with

[20] A. Próchnik, 'Teresa Perlowa', *Kronika Ruchu Rewolucyjnego w Polsce*, 5/3 (1939), 17–18; Holzer, 'Perlowa z Reznikowskich', 631.

[21] Authorship is confirmed in internal party correspondence. See B. A. Jędrzejowski, London, to the PPS Aid Alliance, New York, 5 Mar. 1901: Archiwum Akt Nowych, Warsaw (hereafter AAN), 305/II/5, t. 4, fo. 295. For information on Gottlieb's role as translator, see B. A. Jędrzejowski, London, to C. Jakubowicz [Henoch Kowalski], Karlsruhe, 15 Jan. 1901, fo. 1: Bund Archives, ME 21, folder 23.

[22] [F. Perl], 'Di politik fun der rusisher regirung vegn yudn', *Der arbeyter* (London), 2 (Dec. 1900), 1.

[23] Ibid. 2.

support from Polish society, instituted reforms to modernize the Jewish population, 'to civilize them', and to transform them into full citizens of the country. But under Russian rule, the tsars propped up a fence of laws around the Jewish population that resulted in the persistence of Jewish alienation from Polish society. While avoiding mention of the Bund, Perl castigated Zionists for a political programme that sought to 'separate the Jews, severing them from the country's inhabitants'.[24] Thus, the only way to achieve liberation from tsarist rule was to create an anti-tsarist front with the Poles. 'In line with the Polish Socialist Party', Perl maintained,

we, Polish Jews, must fight for liberty, independence, and good fortune for the country in which we were born and in which we suffer from the capitalist yoke and the tsarist regime together with our brotherly Christian workers . . . Only in an independent Polish Republic will we obtain living conditions under which we will not be oppressed, and will have such political arrangements in which the working classes living in Poland [will be able to realize] . . . the socialist ideal. In this lies the only help, the only future for us, Polish Jews![25]

THE BUND'S HISTORIC DECLARATION ON JEWISH NATIONALITY, 1901

Meanwhile, the penetration of the national idea into the Jewish socialist camp led to a historic declaration in April 1901, when twenty-four delegates met in Białystok to convene the Bund's Fourth Congress.[26] Combining Karl Kautsky's position on the national question with the concept of extraterritorial nationality, the congress passed the following resolution:

The Congress resolves that a Social Democratic programme must not allow the oppression of one class by another, or of one nation or language by another. The Congress recognizes that a state such as Russia, which is made up of many different nations, will in the future be transformed into a federation of nationalities, and that each will have full autonomy independent of the territory in which it resides. The Congress maintains that the term 'nationality' should also apply to the Jewish people [*Der tsuzamenfor halt, az dem bagrif natsyonalitet darf men onvendn oykh oyfn yidishn folk*].[27]

---

[24] [F. Perl], 'Di politik fun der rusisher regirung vegn yudn', *Der arbeyter* (London), 2 (Dec. 1900), 2.
[25] Ibid. 3.
[26] The delegate count is given in the congress report: 'Der ferter kongres fun algemaynem yidishn arbeter-bund in rusland un poyln', *Der yidisher arbeyter*, 12 (1901), 97. The resolutions of the Fourth Congress were the first to be published as separate brochures in both Polish and Russian: *Czwarty Zjazd Ogólnego Żydowskiego Związku Robotniczego na Litwie, w Polsce i Rosyi* (London, 1901); *Chetvertyi s"ezd Vseobshchego evreiskogo rabochego soyuza v Litve, Pol'she i Rossii* (Geneva, 1901). For a complete Hebrew translation, see *Din veheshbon hava'adah harevi'it shel habund*, trans. T. Dolzhansky (Jerusalem, 1971).
[27] 'Der ferter kongres', 99. For a partial translation into English, see *Jew in the Modern World*, ed. Mendes-Flohr and Reinharz, 420–1.

A statement followed that revealed the hesitancy with which the congress as a whole endorsed the principle of Jewish national rights:

The Congress, however, regards it as premature in present circumstances to put forward the demand of national autonomy for Jews. The Congress maintains that, for the time being, we should only struggle for the repeal of all anti-Jewish laws; protest against the oppression of the Jewish nationality; and guard against inflaming national feelings, which can only obscure the class consciousness of the proletariat and lead to chauvinism.[28]

The resolution affirming Jewish nationality was adopted with both the PPS and the Zionists consciously in mind. If the restoration of Poland, the congress report asked, was to be based on historic rights, then would it choose boundaries from the sixteenth, seventeenth, or eighteenth centuries? 'It can be charged . . . that we recognize the present borders as an unalterable fact. In essence, [the Russian empire] was created by the help of fire and sword, swindle and the gallows. But were the so-called "historic" provinces of Poland . . . formed any differently?' The congress continued: 'We, social democrats, are generally not concerned with the state, and it is not our intention to alter its borders and carve out new ones. We are for total freedom and equality. With regard to national equality, its only guarantee is to be sought in national autonomy, not in territorial independence.'[29]

In addition to the resolution on the national question, the Fourth Congress decided to add 'Lithuania' to the Bund's name.[30] The new addition was significant in that it reflected the leadership's evolving conception of Lithuania as a territory distinct from Russia and Poland. The addition of Lithuania to the Bund's name also represented a changing regional perception. Henceforth, Russia receded in order. The Bund went from being 'The Jewish Social Democratic Group *in Russia*' (1893) to 'The General Jewish Labour Union *in Russia and Poland*' (1897) to 'The General Jewish Labour Union *in Lithuania, Poland, and Russia*' (1901). The late Moshe Mishkinsky has noted that the placing of the words 'Lithuania' and 'Poland' in the title reflected 'a factual shrinkage' of Russia to the southern Pale.[31]

PERL RESPONDS: A CRITIQUE OF
THE JEWISH NATIONAL IDEA

Following the Bund's Fourth Congress, Perl drafted the PPS's response. Perl had taken over as editor-in-chief of the party's central organ, *Robotnik*, after Józef Piłsudski's arrest in 1900. In its pages, Perl came out against the Bund's new position on the national question. He derided the Jewish leaders for what he

---

[28] 'Der ferter kongres', 100. For a full reprint of the resolutions and protocols of the Bund's Fourth Congress, see *Materialy k istorii evreiskogo rabochego dvizheniya* (St Petersburg, 1906), 111–28; N. Bukhbinder, *Di geshikhte fun der yidisher arbeter-bavegung in rusland* (Vilna, 1931), 104–12.

[29] *Czwarty Zjazd*, 10.   [30] 'Der ferter kongres', 100.

[31] M. Mishkinsky, 'Regional Factors in the Formation of the Jewish Labor Movement in Czarist Russia', *YIVO Annual of Jewish Social Science*, 14 (1969), 35.

described as an import into the Russian empire of a theoretical model for solving the national question in Austria-Hungary.

Perl's main critique, however, was that the Bund excluded Polish independence from its party platform. This omission derived, he argued, from a weak understanding of the national question in tsarist Russia. The faulty logic of the Bund's position, he maintained, derived from the idea that 'Russia, a despotic state . . . a conglomerate carved from [a host of] provinces, will transform itself into a . . . union of free nations. But Poland—no! Poland will oppress Jews, Germans, and Russians! Here, the influence of Russian government "science" appears, which always paints Poland in the darkest colours in relation to the glory of Russia.'[32] More importantly, the Bund's vision of a democratic federal republic was undemocratic in character, Perl argued, for under the Bund's plan, the nationalities of the western provinces and the Kingdom of Poland would be coerced into a federation ruled from Moscow. To Perl and his party, this position on the state reflected the political immaturity of the Bund's leadership. 'Unlike the Bund, we will not force anyone into a federation', Perl stated. 'We fully recognize the right of other nations to [either] an independent state or a *voluntary* union with Poland. The Bund's federation is not only impossible, but even if it were [possible], it would be a *forced* union.' In an effort to formulate a theoretical justification for its refusal to support Polish independence, Perl continued, the Bund had resorted to intellectual 'acrobatics' and 'prevarications'. How did the Bund arrive at such a position? Perl's answer is revealing: 'It derives from the Bund's original sin—its *all-Russian* position. In the country in which it is active—in Lithuania and Poland—the Bund has separated itself from the local population, neither shares its aspirations nor understands its interests, and does not sympathize with the exceptional predicament in which these subjugated people find themselves.' By linking the Jewish labour movement in Poland–Lithuania to Russia, 'the Bund plays a false and harmful political role'.[33]

Relations between Perl and the Jewish socialist leadership had always been polemical. Particularly after the Bund came out in favour of Jewish national rights, he publicly expressed concern that such a programme would inevitably lead the Jews into conflict with the Poles. Acting on this conviction, Perl would lead a right-wing current opposing any compromise. The official protocols of a conference of the PPS held in June 1903 refer to a discussion that took place on relations with the Bund. Two positions emerged, with one group arguing for non-recognition and the other, led by Piłsudski, favouring dialogue. Perl sided with the view that 'the Bund must either express its solidarity with us by entering [into the Jewish Section of the PPS], or struggle against us'.[34]

[32] [F. Perl], 'Bund o niepodległość Polski', *Robotnik*, 17 Sept. 1901, p. 2.

[33] Ibid. (all emphasis original).

[34] 'Sprawozdanie z konferencji C.K.R. odbytej w Wilnie 4, 5, i 6 czerwca 1903 roku': AAN, 305/III/3, podt. 3, fo. 7.

After the failed 1905 revolution, Perl resumed polemics about the Jewish question. The renewed interest was linked to a split in his own party. In November 1906 Perl helped found the PPS Revolutionary Fraction (PPS—Frakcja Rewolucyjna) or PPS Right. In March 1907 the PPS Right held its first congress. Probably on Perl's recommendation, the delegates came out against the rights of Jews to cultural autonomy. Instead, the PPS Right's programme included a statement guaranteeing 'the rights of national minorities in administration, schools, and courts', although this did not necessarily apply to Jews.[35]

CONSOLIDATION OF PERL'S THOUGHT, 1907–1914

The crisis that befell socialist parties in Russia in 1907 led to a total reorientation among Polish socialists committed to national independence. By 1908 the PPS Right's leadership and party press had relocated to Kraków. The party's dominant figure, Piłsudski, gave up hopes of unifying socialist parties in the Kingdom of Poland and, instead, devoted his energies to building the PPS's Fighting Organization (Organizacja Bojowa). Piłsudski had earlier played a major role in defining the party's attitude to the Jewish question.[36] After 1907 two figures reshaped the party's stand with regard to this question: Feliks Perl and Leon Wasilewski.

Otto Bauer's 1907 work on the nationalities question and social democracy appeared at a moment of great transition in Polish socialism.[37] The PPS had just split into two parties, and ideological lines between the two camps had hardened. The decision of the PPS's Jewish Section to join the PPS Left (PPS-Lewica) in November 1906 left leaders of the Revolutionary Fraction embittered. Jewish loyalty to the Polish national idea was now under question. The tense situation put Perl, the architect of the PPS Right's platform, on the defensive.

It is for this reason that Perl seized upon Otto Bauer's work to bolster his position. The task was made easier by the fact that Bauer's book appeared in Polish as early as 1908.[38] It was Bauer's analysis of the Jewish question that was particularly useful for Perl—a position that endorsed national rights for territorial minorities but only civil rights for Jews. As Bauer argued, 'national autonomy cannot be a demand of the Jewish workers'.[39] Bauer's seminal work appeared in the wake of a

---

[35] 'Program Polskiej Partii Socjalistycznej [Frakcji Rewolucyjnej]', repr. in *Polskie programy socjalistyczne, 1878–1918*, ed. F. Tych (Warsaw, 1975), 469–71.

[36] For an extended discussion of Piłsudski's attitude to the Jewish question, see J. Zimmerman, 'Józef Piłsudski and the "Jewish Question", 1892–1905', *East European Jewish Affairs*, 28/1 (1998), 87–107.

[37] O. Bauer, *Die Nationalitätenfrage und die Sozialdemokratie* (Vienna, 1907).

[38] O. Bauer, *Zagadnienie narodowości*, ed. M. Aleksandrowicz (Warsaw, 1908). It is interesting to note that, while the Polish edition was abridged, the section on the Jews was included in full: see pp. 83–94.

[39] O. Bauer, *The Question of Nationalities and Social Democracy*, ed. E. J. Nimni, trans. J. O'Donnell (Minneapolis, 2000), 306.

new current within the PPS, a non-ideological and pragmatic view favouring a new affirmation of Jewish nationality as a way of competing with the Bund. Maksymilian Horwitz, who had edited the first issue of PPS's *Der arbeyter* in 1898, had argued during the 1905 revolutions that the PPS must recognize Jewish national rights.[40]

In the pages of *Przedświt*, the organ (now based in Kraków) of the PPS Right, Perl raised serious questions about the practical applicability of Jewish national-cultural autonomy in imperial Russia. How would national-cultural autonomy function, he asked, in the army, in central state institutions, and in the relations between such institutions and local authorities? If, over the whole of the Russian state, each national language were co-equal, then the result would be a 'virtual Babel of linguistic chaos' that would render such a state of affairs impossible.[41] Besides, Perl wrote, Bauer had proved that the Jews did not constitute a nation in the modern sense of the word. The programme of national-cultural autonomy would only prolong Jewish separateness.[42] Polish Jewry could thus only base its future on immersion in 'a territorial nation'. Perl continued:

Both in their material struggle for existence and in their endeavour to achieve a higher spiritual culture Jews must use the language of the majority, and claim for themselves its intellectual property. They should work to multiply this wealth, and contribute to its growth and excellence. Jewish jargon will never serve the cultural needs of a higher level—it is only a temporary tool, an elementary guide to culture for the unenlightened masses. Together with the growth of culture, above all with the establishment of normal political relations, the language of the country's majority must take on an ever increasing meaning in the lives of the Jewish masses.[43]

Perl concluded with a summary of Bauer's 'correct' argument against Jewish national autonomy.[44]

Following the Bund's Eighth Party Conference in 1910, which had called for free Yiddish-language schools for Jews while continuing to 'struggle against assimilation', Perl responded forcefully. By contrast with earlier debates, he now contended with a new, Polish-speaking group of intellectuals within the Bund who had become prominent after 1905. More than any other figure, it was the Polish Jewish intellectual Bronisław Grosser (1883–1912) who represented a trend that Perl found alarming: the defection of Polish-speaking Jews, raised in Polonized families, to the Bund.

---

[40] Horwitz made this argument for the first time in the Warsaw-based PPS daily *Kurjer Codzienny*, and subsequently in his work *W kwestyi żydowskiej* (Kraków, 1907). See [M. Horwitz], 'W sprawie żydowskiej', *Kurjer Codzienny* (Warsaw), 6 Dec. 1905, pp. 2–4; [M. Horwitz], 'Di batsiyung fun der poylisher sotsyalistisher partey tsu der yudisher frage', *Der arbeyter* (Warsaw), 12 (15 Dec. 1905), 1–4.

[41] Res [Feliks Perl], 'W sprawie autonomii narodowej żydów', *Przedświt* (Kraków), 1908, no. 11, pp. 441–2.   [42] Ibid. 443, 446.

[43] Ibid. 446. For this passage, I have used the translation from M. Śliwa, 'The Jewish Problem in Polish Socialist Thought', *Polin*, 9 (1996), 25.   [44] Res, 'W sprawie autonomii narodowej żydów', 446.

Perl and Grosser came from similar backgrounds. Both were raised in assimilated households in the Kingdom of Poland, received a secular education, and held professional university degrees. But while Perl became passionately devoted to the pro-independence socialist movement, Grosser, twelve years younger, followed a different path. As a child and teenager, Grosser had fully identified as a Pole. His parents, although not converts, had severed their ties to the Jewish community to such an extent that Grosser had no knowledge of his Jewish origin until the age of 14 or 15.[45] Upon applying to the Warsaw gymnasium, he was shocked to learn that he was being subjected to a special Jewish quota arrangement.[46] Accepted into the gymnasium, Grosser joined an illegal group of young Polish socialists. But it was in high school that he began to wrestle with his identity, gradually moving away from the assimilationist spirit in which he was raised. After graduating from high school in 1902 he joined the Warsaw Bund and went abroad to Switzerland for university studies.

At the age of 19, Grosser met Vladimir Medem in Geneva. Medem recalled that when he first met Grosser,

> he knew scarcely a word of Yiddish. He was an artist in the realm of thought . . . enriched by a broad European, scientific, aesthetic, and political culture. But it was that Jewish mind which . . . was like a sensitive instrument that measured and weighed with the precision of a druggist's scale; a mind of steel-like sharpness, capable of penetrating issues and concepts, dissecting and analyzing them, identifying the smallest, most delicate elements.[47]

Medem stressed, however, that Grosser was 'impregnated with Polish culture that he loved'.[48] As Beynish Mikhalevich would later comment, Grosser was a true gift to the Bund,[49] editing the party's first Polish-language organs, *Głos Bundu* (1904–5) and *Nasze Hasła* (1906), while composing Polish-language circulars.

The presence of Grosser in the Bund as well as the Bund's Eighth Party Conference in 1910 led Perl to reflect further on the Jewish problem in the Polish lands. In 1911 both Grosser and Perl used the pages of their respective sister organizations in Galicia to debate with each other. In a reply to Perl, who had written an article critiquing the Bund's new programme, Grosser published a long article in *Der sotsyal-demokrat*, the Kraków-based organ of the Galician Jewish socialists, in which he argued the case for extraterritorial national-cultural autonomy for the Jews of Russia and Galicia.[50] Perl responded to Grosser in the Lwów-based

[45] B. Grosser, 'From Pole to Jew', in *The Golden Tradition: Jewish Life and Thought in Eastern Europe*, ed. L. Dawidowicz (New York, 1967), 435; M.M. [Moshe Mishkinsky], 'Grosser, Bronislaw', in *Encyclopaedia Judaica*, 17 vols. (Jerusalem, 1971–2), vii. 936; S. Dubnov-Erlich, 'Bronislav groser', in J. S. Hertz, *Doyres bundistn*, 3 vols. (New York, 1956–68), i. 319; B. Mikhalevich, *Zikhroynes fun a yidishn sotsyalist*, ii (Warsaw, 1923), 26–32.   [46] Mikhalevich, *Zikhroynes fun a yidishn sotsyalist*, ii. 32.

[47] V. Medem, *The Life and Soul of a Legendary Jewish Socialist*, trans. S. A. Portnoy (New York, 1979), 306–7.   [48] Ibid. 308.   [49] Mikhalevich, *Zikhroynes fun a yidishn sotsyalist*, ii. 28.

[50] Grosser's article, written under the pseudonym 'A.S.', appeared in *Der sotsyal-demokrat* (Kraków) on 24 Nov. and 1 and 8 Dec. 1911. Unfortunately, copies of *Der sotsyal-demokrat* from the year 1911 are unavailable.

socialist organ *Głos*, with a blow-by-blow refutation.[51] The problem with the Bund's programme, Perl argued, was that it placed Jews, a 'tribal-religious group devoid of territory', on an equal footing with 'modern authentic nations' who, like the Czechs in Austria-Hungary, possessed the objective conditions for independent development. By entirely overlooking the territorial aspirations of subjugated nations, Grosser misunderstood the fundamental basis of the national problem in eastern Europe:

In general, when comrade [Grosser] speaks at length about nations, about the nationalities question, one has the impression that all these nations . . . exist in the air. *Land* disappears from our view . . . Poland and the Czech lands do not exist; majorities and national minorities do not exist. It is in this mist that Jews appear and demand 'equal political rights for each nation'.[52]

Perl continued to write on the Jewish question in 1913. Having opposed the party's increasing emphasis on militarism at the expense of socialist principles, he played a role in founding the so-called 'PPS Opposition' (PPS-Opozycja). The new faction's platform, drafted in 1913, included an official position on 'the Jewish question and antisemitism'. The platform, composed by Perl, declared itself opposed to the programme of national-cultural autonomy for the following reasons: (1) the Jews lacked territory; (2) autonomy would lead to continuing Jewish isolation from Polish culture and society; and (3) equality for Yiddish in schools and administration would interrupt a natural process of Jewish integration into Polish culture. The party's goals regarding the Jews thus included 'removal of Jewish separateness, and joining the Jewish masses with the national-political interests of the country, particularly [in the realm of] proletariat solidarity in Poland without distinction of faith and origin'.[53]

Between 1908 and 1914, the PPS's position on the Jewish question crystallized into two camps. On the right, the PPS advanced an assimilationist position. Perl argued for full civil—but not national—rights for the Jews, a view deriving partly from the French model. With the lifting of all legal restrictions on Jews in France in 1791, social, political, and economic integration followed, Perl maintained. Indeed, under the party imprint, he published studies on the French Revolution and one on the 1848 revolution in France.[54]

Perl argued that the Bund's affirmation of Russia's territorial integrity worked directly counter to Polish national aspirations. A self-assertive Jewish nationality,

[51] Res [Feliks Perl], 'Na bezdrożach żydowskiego "renesansu"', *Głos* (Lwów), 6 Dec. 1911, p. 1, and 7 Dec. 1911, p. 1.   [52] Ibid., 7 Dec. 1911, p. 1 (emphasis original).
[53] 'Uchwały Konferencyi P.P.S. (opozycyi)', Jan. 1913: AAN, 305/III/41, podt. 3. Perl also discussed his views on the Jewish question in the organ of the PPS Opposition, *Walka*. See 'W sprawie żydowskiej', *Walka* (Warsaw), 1 (Oct. 1913), 7.
[54] See Res [Feliks Perl], *Krótka historja Wielkiej Rewolucji Francuskiej* (London, 1898), which was published in Yiddish as *Di groyse frantsoyzishe revolutsye* (London, 1905); and Res [Feliks Perl], *Rewolucja 1848 we Francji* (Warsaw, 1911).

consciously resistant to acculturation, would only foment anti-Jewish hatred on Polish soil, Perl maintained. In an important essay, J. S. Hertz observed insightfully that the dispute between the Bund and Polish socialists in late imperial Russia was to a considerable extent a reflection of 'the internal struggle among the various trends in Jewry'.[55]

PERL AS POLISH PARLIAMENTARIAN AND EDITOR-IN-CHIEF OF *ROBOTNIK*, 1919–1927

During the First World War, Perl never wavered from his assimilationist position.[56] In independent Poland, he remained engaged in Polish politics. During a session of the Constituent Sejm on 13 May 1919, he argued that cultural autonomy should not be extended to Polish Jews because Jews were not a national minority.[57] In his capacity as a member of the Polish Sejm, Perl consistently opposed the demand of Jewish parties for national-cultural autonomy.[58] While autonomy should be extended to territorial nationalities such as Ukrainians, Belarusians, and Lithuanians, Perl argued that Jews did not represent a 'nationality' and therefore could not be recognized as such.

Perl's entirely secular and rational approach to Jewish matters became apparent in November 1919 in the parliamentary debates on a universal Sunday rest day. Perl came out strongly in support of the bill in the face of Jewish objections on religious grounds. He based his position on rational grounds, stating that 'of course, in all societies, in which the big majority of the population traditionally rests on Sundays, only Sunday can be that day of rest'. He went further, however, stating that if a universal Sunday rest day forced Jews by economic necessity to work on the sabbath, then this would be a positive thing. 'If Jews will work on Saturday due to this [legislation]', he said, 'this will be no calamity! In any case this will be an escape from the "ghetto".'[59] Perl's position on the Sunday rest day was a reflection of his broader integrationist position on the Jews of Poland. As he had already argued much earlier, 'One has to seek the elimination of Jewish separateness and to link our Jews to the national-political interests of the country—to the solidarity of the proletariat without regard to differences of faith and origin.'[60]

---

[55] J. Hertz, 'The Bund's Nationality Program and its Critics in the Russian, Polish and Austrian Socialist Movements', *YIVO Annual of Jewish Social Science*, 14 (1969), 66.

[56] See Res [Feliks Perl], 'O nacjonalizmie żydowskim', *Jedność Robotnicza* (Warsaw), 1917, no. 11, pp. 1–3.   [57] Uljasz, 'Poglądy Feliksa Perla na kwestię żydowską', 66.

[58] Gutterman, 'Assimilated Jews as Leaders of the Polish Labor Movement', 16.

[59] Deliberations of the Polish Sejm, 20 Nov. 1919, cited in F. Golczewski, 'The Problem of Sunday Rest in Interwar Poland', in Y. Gutman et al. (eds.), *The Jews of Poland between Two World Wars* (Hanover, NH, 1989), 166.

[60] Res [Feliks Perl], 'W sprawie żydowskiej', *Walka* (1913), cited in Piasecki, 'Feliks Perl — historyk i działacz PPS', 68.

From 1919 until his death in 1927, Perl served as editor-in-chief of *Robotnik*, the PPS's daily newspaper. Despite his position as a founding father of the party, as co-author of the party's founding programme, and as editor-in-chief of the party's central organ, Perl's Jewish background made many uncomfortable. Thus, Jews regarded him as a Pole and Poles regarded him as a Jew.

Perl's marginality with regard to the Polish Jewish community continued in death as well as in life. When he passed away in Warsaw on 15 April 1927, at the age of 55, he was naturally to be buried in the Jewish cemetery in Warsaw. When his wife insisted on honouring her late husband's wishes for a strictly non-religious funeral, however, the Jewish communal authorities, under Orthodox auspices, refused. The issue evidently was resolved only when a section of the local PPS workers' militia approached Jewish communal leaders, who, under threat of force, backed down.[61] At the funeral, the eulogy was given by Ignacy Daszyński, then a member of the Sejm and a leading figure in the Polish socialist movement. Those attending included Piłsudski's wife, Aleksandra Piłsudska, and Stanisław Wojcie-chowski, who had just been forced to step down as the president of Poland after Piłsudski's *coup d'état*. Also attending were both the speaker of the Sejm and a former prime minister, as well as members of the cabinet, the Senate, and the Sejm. Senator Abraham Truskier, representing the Club of Jewish Deputies in the Sejm, also spoke.[62] The tombstone, which still stands today at the Jewish ceme-tery in Warsaw, reads: 'Feliks Perl: Creator of the Programme of Polish Socialism. Fighter for the Independence and Freedom of Poland.'

[61] Śliwa, *Feliks Perl*, 337–8.

[62] 'Felix Perl is Laid to Rest with Impressive Ceremonies in Warsaw', *Jewish Daily Bulletin* (New York), 21 Apr. 1927, pp. 1, 4.

Yiddish Language Rights in Congress Poland during the First World War

The Social Implications of Linguistic Recognition

MARCOS SILBER

INTRODUCTION

THE OFFICIAL RECOGNITION of Yiddish language rights in Congress Poland during the First World War had significant implications for a territory with a mixed ethnic composition. This essay focuses on the rights of the Yiddish-speaking community to use its distinctive vernacular in administrative procedures and schooling, in comparison with other ethno–linguistic groups in the same region. The concept of language rights here reflects the German notion of *Sprachenrecht*, which may be translated as the legal regulation of the use of a language in public life as part of broader inter-ethnic regulations in a multi-ethnic country.

The importance of language rights in a multilingual society is found at many levels. First there is the practical need to regulate communication between the bureaucratic apparatus and the individuals addressing it. Second, accepting language rights is a symbolic means of legitimizing the existence of a minority group by recognizing its vernacular. In contrast, non-recognition of its vernacular serves to exclude a group's ethnic identity altogether. Third, linguistic recognition affects a society's openness towards advancing or hampering the social mobility of the minority group.

This essay offers an analysis of the attitudes shown by the changing administrations towards the languages of non-dominant ethnic groups in Congress Poland during the First World War and the role these attitudes played in the state-building process. As Miroslav Hroch points out, linguistic demands by non-dominant ethnic groups emerged stage by stage, gradually and cumulatively. The highest stage was full equality, and involved the introduction of the non-dominant language into the administration, bureaucracy, and politics. The crucial point, Hroch explains, was when the demand for linguistic equality in administrative and political life endangered the monopolistic position of the state elites. Sooner or later, this demand turned into a struggle for positions in the administration. Under such circumstances, Hroch argues, the appeal for linguistic equality reflected more than mere national prestige or symbolic values: it contributed to the emergence of a nationally significant conflict of interests—an intrinsic part of the nation-building process.[1] In Hroch's argument, the non-recognition of a language symbolized strategies of exclusion.

In the same vein, according to Pierre Bourdieu, culture is, *inter alia*, a resource for domination in which intellectuals play key roles as specialists of cultural production and are creators of symbolic power.[2] In this respect, the recognition of certain cultural capital (in the present case, the languages of minority groups, and, specifically, Yiddish), or its exclusion, was a strategy to encourage or block the admission of certain groups into the 'state nobility', to use one of Bourdieu's concepts, referring to elites whose power stems from state recognition of their cultural capital as a legitimation of their claim to power in the state.[3]

This essay tests Hroch's and Bourdieu's contentions empirically regarding the recognition of various vernaculars in Congress Poland during the First World War by examining administrative measures intended, I will show, either to safeguard Jews from Polonization or from exposure to it, or to guarantee/exclude the status of Yiddish as a recognized minority language. Several of Hroch's basic premises provide a key to understanding the contradictory policies regarding the Yiddish language during the First World War and its aftermath, while certain modifications of these premises are needed in order to understand the linguistic policy towards the languages of other non-dominant groups.

The essay has three main parts. The first discusses the policies of the German authorities in the occupied areas until 1917. The second focuses on decisions made by the Polish administration established during 1917, which constituted the first steps of the Polish state in formation. The third part analyses the developments and inconsistencies outlined in the first two parts in light of the theoretical concepts presented there, and discusses their implications.

GERMAN POLICIES IN THE OCCUPIED AREAS UNTIL 1917

A New Era, New Policy, New Languages

The First World War was a time of pivotal importance to the national struggle for Polish independence, with the status of language constituting a cardinal issue in

[1] M. Hroch, *The Social Interpretation of Linguistic Demands in European National Movements* (Florence, 1994), 13–20; id., *Social Preconditions of National Revival in Europe: A Comparative Analysis of the Social Composition of Patriotic Groups among the Smaller European Nations*, trans. B. Fowkes (Cambridge, 1985), 175–91.

[2] D. Swartz, *Culture and Power: The Sociology of Pierre Bourdieu* (Chicago, 1997), 1–14, 189–246.

[3] P. Bourdieu, *La Noblesse d'état: Grandes écoles et esprit de corps* (Paris, 1989); in English, P. Bourdieu, *The State Nobility: Elite Schools in the Field of Power*, trans. L. C. Clough (Stanford, Calif., 1996).

this endeavour. In the main, the Polish national movement demanded exclusivity for the Polish language and culture and the entrenchment of this status in the laws of the Polish lands. The Polish national movement generally insisted that Jews adopt the Polish language in their educational institutions. In the same period, ensuring the status of their language was also a major issue in the Jewish struggle for recognition of their national rights in eastern Europe. The Jewish nationalist movement, in all its factions, demanded the recognition of Yiddish and / or Hebrew (the internal Jewish dispute over this issue is well known) and appropriate legislation guaranteeing its official status. This issue, which was raised before the war, led to an intense collision between the nationalist movements of Jews and Poles during the war.[4]

Both movements faced new conditions with the outbreak of the war. Congress Poland came under the occupation of the Central Powers—Germany and Austria —from 1915 to 1918. As part of German policy, the occupiers eliminated Russian as a 'societal language'. The concept of 'societal language', as defined by Will Kymlicka, refers to the value of a language recognized by the state and used in a wide range of state institutions, such as schools, the legal system, the economy, and the government.[5] The elimination of Russian and its replacement in Congress Poland by German, later to be followed by Polish, engendered and intensified the use of various vernaculars and led to an explosion of the politics of the vernacular.

That the general German aim was to bring central Europe under German control is well known. However, the means for establishing this control was a major source of contention between various officials and ministries within the German regime and administration, as, from the German point of view, there was no ideal solution to the problem of how to rule the area it had occupied. Some advocated direct German rule over Poland and substantial regions in western Russia (the supporters of this approach were mainly connected with *Junker* circles, most prominently General Erich von Ludendorff and Field Marshal Paul von

---

[4] For an excellent introduction to the rise of antisemitism and ethno-national tension in this period, see F. Golczewski, *Polnisch-jüdische Beziehungen, 1881–1922: Eine Studie zur Geschichte des Antisemitismus in Ost-Europa* (Wiesbaden, 1981). The literature on the growth of both Polish and Jewish nationalism is vast. On the rise of Polish xenophobic nationalism, see B. Porter, *When Nationalism Began to Hate: Imagining Modern Politics in Nineteenth-Century Poland* (New York, 2000); T. R. Weeks, *From Assimilation to Antisemitism: The 'Jewish Question' in Poland, 1850–1914* (DeKalb, Ill., 2006). Lastly, Frank Schuster and Konrad Zieliński have dealt with Jewish–Polish relations in Congress Poland during the First World War. See F. Schuster, *Zwischen allen Fronten: Osteuropäische Juden während des Ersten Weltkrieges, 1914–1919* (Cologne, 2004), esp. 251–7, 259–63, 265–82, 328–415; K. Zieliński, *Stosunki polsko-żydowskie na ziemiach Królestwa Polskiego w czasie pierwszej wojny światowej* (Lublin, 2005). For an introduction to the rise of Jewish nationalism, see Jonathan Frankel's seminal *Prophecy and Politics: Socialism, Nationalism and the Russian Jews, 1862–1917* (Cambridge, 1981); E. Mendelsohn, *On Modern Jewish Politics* (New York, 1993).

[5] W. Kymlicka, *Politics in the Vernacular: Nationalism, Multiculturalism and Citizenship* (Oxford, 2001), 25–7, 53.

Hindenburg, who headed the German forces in eastern Europe) by annexing vast territories to Germany or by transforming them into a quasi-colonial region.

However, the main drawback of direct rule, according to its opponents, was that annexing vast areas of the western part of the tsarist empire, including Congress Poland, to the Wilhelmist empire would flood it with masses of non-German peoples, mainly Poles and, additionally, Jews, whose loyalty to the German state was suspect. Moreover, this would bring about an unwelcome demographic shift in the structure of the German population generally and the Prussian population in particular, which could put the very stability of the empire at risk. Instead, they advocated indirect rule, proposing several options regarding structure and implementation. One was the Austro-Polish option: annexing large sections of Congress Poland to Austria. Another was joint Austrian–German control of Poland and the establishment of a large buffer state or, alternatively, smaller buffer states, which would be quasi-independent satellites of Germany. These options were meant to take effect after the more or less extensive annexation of portions of western and north-western Congress Poland, as well as parts of the districts of Kurland, Kovno, and Grodno lying north and east of Congress Poland.[6]

Ultimately, the German authorities were unable to agree on the manner of ruling the region or the extent of the areas to be annexed. During the course of the war, the pendulum swung in favour of one solution or another depending on circumstances, personalities, and political and belligerent constellations.

The Question of Language and Schools: The Case of Łódź

Until mid-1915, Łódź was the largest Polish city to fall into German hands. It was home to three major ethnic groups: Poles, Jews, and Germans. The percentage of Jews among the city's populace rose from 32.6 per cent in 1911 (167,100 Jews in a total population of half a million), to 40.1 per cent in 1918, despite the decline of the absolute number of the city's inhabitants due to the ravages of the war (137,200 Jews in an overall population of 341,800). During the same period, the proportion

---

[6] On the German war aims, see esp. L. Grosfeld, 'La Pologne dans les plans impérialistes allemands pendant la Grande Guerre 1914–1918 et l'acte du 5 Novembre 1916', in *La Pologne au Xe Congrès international des sciences historiques à Rome* (Warsaw, 1955), 327–56; I. Geiss, *Der polnische Grenzstreifen, 1914–1918: Ein Beitrag zur deutschen Kriegszielpolitik im Ersten Weltkrieg* (Lübeck and Hamburg, 1960), 41–114, 160–3; F. Fischer, *Germany's Aims in the First World War* (London, 1967), 96–110, 113–17, 179–83, 271–3 (abridged translation of his *Griff nach der Weltmacht: Die Kriegszielpolitik des kaiserlichen Deutschland, 1914/1918*, Düsseldorf, 1961); L. Grosfeld, *Polityka państw centralnych wobec sprawy polskiej w latach pierwszej wojny światowej* (Warsaw, 1962), esp. 54–127; E. Basler, *Deutschlands Annexionspolitik in Polen und im Baltikum, 1914–1918* (Berlin, 1962), 25–158, 385; W. Sukiennicki, *East Central Europe during World War I: From Foreign Domination to National Independence* (Boulder, Colo., 1984), mainly 118–22, 132–46, 240–8, 333–42. See also F. Fischer, 'Twenty-Five Years Later: Looking Back at the "Fischer Controversy" and its Consequences', *Central European History*, 21 (1988), 207–23; K. Jarausch, 'Revising German History: Bethmann Hollweg Revisited', *Central European History*, 21 (1988), 224–43.

of Poles in Łódź declined from 52.1 per cent in 1911 to 47.6 per cent in 1918. The German segment of the local population declined during the war years, stabilizing at 11–12 per cent of the populace.[7]

From the very beginning of the German occupation, the occupation forces tried to eliminate Russian as the societal language. Various regulations removed the Russian language from the public sphere: it was banned in all municipal institutions, the study of it or instruction in it was forbidden, and the use of Russian books in schools was made illegal.[8] Initially, the municipal council maintained the existing school system, but since Russian had been banned from the public sphere, Polish became the language of instruction and then the curriculum was also Polonized.[9]

In the spring of 1915, members of the Komitee für den Osten (Committee for the East, i.e. eastern Europe; KfdO)—a Jewish committee composed of Zionist leaders and other prominent Jews in Germany—visited Łódź to meet with important officials in the German administration and to propose a Jewish autonomist option as an alternative to the Polish one for backing German rule in the occupied territories.[10] The committee urged the occupation authorities to protect the Jewish population from the trend towards Polonization displayed by municipal authorities and their education department.[11]

The German occupation officials in charge of education matters, assenting to the idea that the Jewish population should be safeguarded against the movement towards Polonization,[12] forbade Jewish schools to use Polish as the language of instruction,[13] prohibiting it[14] on the basis of essentialist arguments ('Jews in Poland need not be Poles, nor can they be')[15] as well as instrumental ones ('only 200 Jews use the Polish language').[16] Rather, Jewish children would study German in their own segregated schools, since the occupation authorities decreed, in 1915, that each sector of the population would be educated separately.[17] This reflected a

---

[7] J. Janczak, 'Struktura narodowościowa Łodzi w latach 1820–1939', in W. Puś and S. Liszewski (eds.), *Dzieje Żydów w Łodzi, 1820–1944: Wybrane problemy* (Łódź, 1991), 47–8.

[8] 'Russisch verboten', *Die Zeit*, 3 Sept. 1915.

[9] Archiwum Państwowe w Krakowie (hereafter APKr), NKN 86: 'Sprawa szkolna w Łodzi'.

[10] Central Zionist Archives, Jerusalem (hereafter CZA), A15/VIII/13: Max Bodenheimer, 'Bericht über die im Auftrage des "Komitees fuer den Osten" im Mai–Juni 1915 unternommene Reise nach Russisch-Polen, Zweite Ausgabe, als Manuskript gedruckt' (n.p., n.d. [Berlin, 1915]), 1–6.

[11] CZA, A15/VIII/8: 'Bericht über das jüdische Schulwesen in Lodz', 21 May 1915.

[12] CZA, A15/VIII/8: 'Bericht über Unterredungen mit Herrn von Oppen, Graf Lerchenfeld, Rittmeister Stibel, von Kries (juni 1915)'; M. Hertz, *Łódź w czasie Wielkiej Wojny* (Łódź, 1933), 182–4.

[13] CZA, A15/VIII/9a: 'Notizen über die Tätigkeit des Herrn Justizrat Dr. Bodenheimer in Lodz (Zum Protokoll über die Sitzung vom 11.VI.15)'; Hertz, *Łódź w czasie Wielkiej Wojny*, 182–4.

[14] CZA, A15/VIII/9a: 'Notizen über die Tätigkeit des Herrn Justizrat Dr. Bodenheimer in Lodz (Zum Protokoll über die Sitzung vom 11.VI.15)'; 'Verordnung betreffend Regelung des Schulwesens', *Deutsche Lodzer Zeitung*, 7 Sept. 1915. See also Schuster, *Zwischen allen Fronten*, 360–1.

[15] APKr, NKN 86: 'Sprawa szkolna w Łodzi'.   [16] APKr, NKN 88: 'Sprawozdanie z Łodzi'.

[17] CZA, A15/VIII/2c: Moritz Sobernheim to Max Bodenheimer, 2 Sept. 1915; 'Verordnung betreffend Regelung des Schulwesens', *Deutsche Lodzer Zeitung*, 7 Sept. 1915.

curious policy of selective Germanization of the Jews, aimed at reinforcing German in the public sphere even though the population adopting it remained excluded from the German ethno-national sector. In late summer, on 24 August 1915, the occupation authorities issued a Regulation for the Organization of Schools (Verordnung betreffend Regelung des Schulwesens) aimed at reorganizing the education systems in the areas of Congress Poland on the left bank of the Vistula (occupied by Germany) in preparation for the start of the new school year.[18] The regulation established a religious criterion for school attendance, officially recognizing three religious groups: Catholics, Protestants, and Jews.[19] The ruling also stipulated that German would be the language of instruction in Protestant and Jewish schools.[20] This directive reflected the espousal of a thesis linking the national-cultural interests of the Jewish and Protestant minorities (the latter regarded as 'German'), placing both these population groups under the aegis of German culture and language.

The regulation was opposed by almost every segment of both Jewish and Polish society. The Polish press and the Polish establishment protested against separating Jewish pupils from their Polish counterparts, and demanded that Jews receive a Polish education. According to statements by various wings of the Polish national movement, the decision to have Jewish children study in the German language would turn the Jews into a tool for Germanization in Polish territory[21] and be an obstacle to fulfilling the movement's aspiration of establishing a universal school system with a Polish national orientation.[22] The Poles of the Mosaic Faith (Polen Mosaischer Konfession), an integrationist group, joined the Polish majority in this chorus of protest.[23]

[18] CZA, Z3/140: Zionistische Vereinigung für Deutschland to Kolenscher, 8 Sept. 1915; 'Verordnung betreffend Regelung des Schulwesens', *Deutsche Lodzer Zeitung*, 7 Sept. 1915. This regulation, though dated 24 August 1915, was not officially published until 30 August, appearing in the *Deutsche Lodzer Zeitung* only on 7 September (where it was reprinted on 10 September). On the regulation, see S. Hirszhorn, 'Żydzi Królestwa Polskiego podczas wojny światowej', in I. Schiper, A. Tartakower, and A. Hafftka (eds.), *Żydzi w Polsce Odrodzonej: Działalność społeczna, gospodarcza, oświatowa i kulturalna*, 2 vols. (Warsaw, 1932–3), i. 493–4.

[19] The contradiction between this religious criterion and the terms used in other parts of the regulation, reflecting nationality, was pointed out by the regulation's opponents. Politisches Archiv des Auswärtiges Amt, Berlin (hereafter PA AA), WK, no. 14a, Bd. 7: 'Seiner Exzellenz dem Kaiserlich Deutschen General-Gouverneur General von Beseler', 25 Sept. 1915.

[20] CZA, A15/VIII/2c: Sobernheim to Bodenheimer, 3 Sept. 1915; CZA, Z3/140: Z.A.C. to Julius Berger, 3 Sept. 1915.

[21] CZA, A15/VIII/9b: 'Protokoll der Unterredung der Herren Dr. Friedmann, Dr. Oppenheimer, Prof. Sobernheim, Kaplun Kogan mit dem Journalisten Herrn Feldmann und Herr Direktor Dr. Cohn am 10 Nov. 1915'.

[22] PA AA, WK, no. 14a, Bd. 7: 'Seiner Exzellenz dem Kaiserlich Deutschen General-Gouverneur General von Beseler', 25 Sept. 1915.

[23] See Ignacy Steinhaus's attitude as expressed in 'Die jüdische Schulfrage in Warschau', *Jüdische Korrespondenz*, 21 Oct. 1915 (Steinhaus was a member of the Polish Club (Koło Polskie) in the Austrian Imperial Council (Reichsrat) and the Galician Sejm); CZA, Z3/155: Ludwig Haas to the editors of

Among the Jewish national factions, Zionists, Bundists, Po'alei Tsiyon, and Territorialists opposed the regulation along the same lines as the Poles; all these groups also saw it as an attempt to Germanize the Jews.[24] Protesting the compulsory use of German in Jewish educational institutions, they demanded the preservation of Yiddish as the language of instruction for Jews on Polish soil.[25] The points they raised were practical (a lack of the technical wherewithal to change the language of instruction in the Jewish schools to Hochdeutsch, or the need to manage these schools in Yiddish during the transitional period until German could be introduced);[26] pedagogical ('It is ridiculous to teach in German when the Jewish children don't understand German');[27] and politico-cultural ('An attempt to Germanize the Jews will lead to their Polonization, owing to the Polonization pressures of the milieu. Thus, Germany will have lost its most natural ally in eastern Europe —the Jews',[28] or 'When the Germans leave Poland, the Polish people will direct their anger towards the Jews, who identified themselves as Germans'[29]). In actuality, their main demand was for the Jews to be acknowledged as a separate national group, which as such were entitled to preserve their language—Yiddish—without being subjected to either Polonization or Germanization.[30] Left-wing Jewish activists demonstrated publicly during September 1915 for Yiddish-language schools for the Jewish population.[31] A petition to this effect was signed by 30,000 Jews and submitted to the German local authorities in October 1915.[32]

To bypass the highly charged legal morass created by the education regulation, the Komitee für den Osten proposed the following legal tactic: Yiddish would be recognized as a dialect of German, thus enabling its use as a language of instruction in the schools. Curiously, the German occupation regime accepted this de facto solution and, consequently, Yiddish was allowed in the Jewish schools in the western area of Congress Poland, while Polish and German were to be used in schools where Polish had been the language of instruction prior to the war.[33]

Jüdische Rundschau, 9 Nov. 1915. See also J. Teitelbaum, 'Haḥinukh hayehudi hatikhoni bepolin bein shetei milḥamot ha'olam, 1919–1939', Ph.D. thesis (Tel Aviv Univ., 1994), 31–2.

[24] 'Die Schulfrage in Lodz', *Warschauer Tageblatt*, 27 Oct. 1915; CZA, A15/VIII/9b: 'Von den Mitgliedern des Legalisierungsausschusses des Jüdischen Schul- und Volksbildungsvereins in Warschau', Dec. 1915; Kh. Kazdan, *Di geshikhte fun yidishn shulvezn in umophengikn poyln* (Mexico City, 1947), 33–4; Teitelbaum, 'Haḥinukh hayehudi hatikhoni bepolin bein shetei milḥamot ha'olam', 33; CZA, A15/VIII/8: 'Zu der zionistische Resolution über die Schulfrage'.

[25] 'Die jüdische Sprache — ein deutscher Volksdialekt', *Kölnische Zeitung*, 20 Sept. 1915.

[26] PA AA, WK, no. 11, Adh. 2, Bd. 5: KfdO to Zimmermann, 11 Oct. 1915.

[27] CZA, A15/VIII/9b: 'Protokoll der Sitzung des KfdO am 8. Dez. 1915'.

[28] PA AA, WK, no. 11, Adh. 2, Bd. 5: KfdO to Zimmermann, 11 Oct. 1915.

[29] CZA, A15/VIII/9b: 'Protokoll der Sitzung des KfdO am 8. Dez. 1915'.   [30] Ibid.

[31] 'Dos lodzher lebn—a farzamlung vegn der yidisher folks-shul', *Lodzher folksblat*, 8 Sept. 1915.

[32] APKr, NKN 86: 'Sprawa szkolna w Łodzi'; Kazdan, *Di geshikhte fun yidishn shulvezn in umophengikn poyln*, 52–3; Y. Sh. Herts, *Di geshikhte fun bund in lodzh* (New York, 1958), 256.

[33] CZA, A15/VIII/2c: Kaplun Kogan to Bodenheimer, 25 Sept. 1915; CZA, A15/VIII/4: KfdO to Straus, 16 Dec. 1915. This solution suited the approach of the German occupation official in charge of

The pressure by Yiddish intelligentsia and Jewish political parties did not cease with this compromise, and these groups continued their efforts to obtain the recognition of Yiddish as the formal language of instruction in Jewish schools.[34] In summer 1916, with the approach of the new school year, the German authorities in Łódź relented and issued a ruling that set aside the fiction of the 'German dialect' and mentioned Yiddish as the language of instruction permitted in Jewish schools in the city, together with Polish and German.[35] The difference between the Regulation for the Organization of Schools of August 1915 and the new situation was that under the previous ruling, teaching was to be conducted in German, although in reality Yiddish was the language used, while now Yiddish was referred to explicitly as a recognized language, and as such was legally entitled to be used in schools.

This ruling was in force until September 1917, when new regulations regarding elementary school education in the Kingdom of Poland were issued. Until then, it was a source of consternation to the Poles that Yiddish was recognized as a language of instruction in the Jewish schools of Łódź, as they were making a concerted effort to accelerate the Polonization of the city's new official Yiddishist Jewish school system.[36]

The Question of Language and Schools in Warsaw

Warsaw, like Łódź, had a Polish majority, but the Jewish presence there was even more prominent. The percentage of Jews in Warsaw had grown from 33.4 per cent to 37.7 per cent in the period from 1882 to 1913, and in the first third of 1916, following the creation of Greater Warsaw (Wielka Warszawa), it reached 41.9 per cent. In the fifteen major neighbourhoods that comprised the municipality of Warsaw prior to the annexation of the suburbs in 1916, Jews accounted for about

Jewish affairs, Ludwig Haas. In his view, Yiddish was to be maintained as a language of instruction in schools founded after the German conquest, while the Jewish population would study in Polish in the schools where Polish was the language of instruction before the German occupation. CZA, A15/VIII/9b: 'Protokoll der Sitzung des KfdO am 20. Dezember 1915'.

[34] 'Der yudish-ovend in kontsert-zal', *Lodzher folksblat*, 16 Mar. 1916; 'Di farzamlung fun yudishn lerer-farayn', *Lodzher folksblat*, 9 Apr. 1916; 'Di grandioze farzamlung fun yidishn shul- un folks-bildung-farayn', *Lodzher folksblat*, 29 Apr. 1916; Herts, *Di geshikhte fun bund in lodzh*, 255–7; Kazdan, *Di geshikhte fun yidishn shulvezn in umophengikn poyln*, 54.

[35] 'Be'olamenu—sefat hora'ah bevatei-hasefer belodz', *Hatsefirah*, 10 Aug. 1916; 'Yidish als unterrikhts shprakh', *Varshever togblat*, 8 Aug. 1916; 'Di yidishe shprakh un di yidishe shuln', *Haynt*, 9 Aug. 1916; 'Di unterrikhts-shprakh in yudishe folks-shuln', *Lodzher folksblat*, 10 Aug. 1916. The Yiddish schools were to be run by the municipal school board, which was composed mainly of Polish Catholics or Polonized Jews seeking to Polonize the Jewish school system despite German regulations. The Folks-Bildung Farayn tried unsuccessfully to enlist some of its members who served on the municipal commission on Jewish schools to help open Yiddish schools: 'Di farzamlung fun yidishn shul farayn', *Lodzher folksblat*, 9 Aug. 1916. See also M. Bałaban, 'Raport o żydowskich instytucjach oświatowych i religijnych na terenach Królestwa Polskiego okupowanych przez Austro-Węgry' (1916), *Kwartalnik Historii Żydów*, 197 (2001), 54. [36] Hertz, *Łódź w czasie Wielkiej Wojny*, 163, 166–7.

44.9 per cent of the inhabitants. The prediction then (to be proved erroneous) was that in less than thirty years the city would lose its Polish majority, which was perceived in wide Polish circles as a threat. This prognosis, however, supported the autonomist demands by Jewish groups, especially the Yiddish intelligentsia.[37] Nevertheless, with the conquest of the city in August 1915, the Germans declared that they considered Warsaw a Polish city with no national issue whatsoever, that is, a city with no question about national minorities.[38]

In keeping with German policy, which granted the city council administrative responsibility for education, Warsaw's municipal council made education compulsory for the city's Polish-speaking children, while at the same time deciding that school attendance would not be compulsory for Jewish children whose parents did not want them to attend Polish schools. In practice, therefore, a decision was made to create a Polish-language state educational system. Jews who wished to do so could send their children to Polish schools, but, in contrast to the policy in Łódź, no parallel Yiddish system would be established.[39]

Following this decision, which accorded with German policy to preserve two separate educational systems for Jews and non-Jews,[40] the Warsaw city council divided the city's school-age population into two main ethnic groups: Jews and Poles–Catholics. The council, which was in charge of funding the elementary school systems of both groups, set up two school systems on a denominational basis, one Catholic and the other Jewish. However, while the council fulfilled this function dutifully with regard to Catholic children, it failed to provide an adequate Polish-language municipal elementary education system for Jews. The actual funding for the development of the Jewish schools came mainly from the Jewish community and was then transferred to the city treasury, while the Polish school system was funded entirely by the municipal treasury, by taxes from the entire population,

[37] Y. Leshtshinski [J. Lestschinsky], *Dos yidishe folk in tsifern* (Berlin, 1922), 42; B. Garncarska-Kadary, *Ḥelkam shel hayehudim behitpateḥut hata'asiyah shel varshah bashanim 1816/20–1914* (Tel Aviv, 1985), 75. The proportion of Jews cited by Piotr Wróbel for 1889 is 34.4%, reaching 39.2% in 1910: P. Wróbel, 'Przed odzyskaniem niepodległości', in J. Tomaszewski (ed.), *Najnowsze dzieje Żydów w Polsce w zarysie (do 1950 roku)* (Warsaw, 1993), 28–9. Although Garncarska's data are apparently more exact (owing to her sources), both point to the same tendency. This same trend emerges from Stephen Corrsin's data, notwithstanding differences in the figures. According to Corrsin, the percentage of Jews was 33.4% in 1882, 33.7% in 1897, and 38.1% in 1914. In the same period, the percentage of Poles declined from 58.1% to 55.7%, and in 1914 it was 55.2%: S. D. Corrsin, *Warsaw before the First World War: Poles and Jews in the Third City of the Russian Empire, 1880–1914* (Boulder, Colo., 1989), 145. Gabriela Zalewska proposes a datum for 1910 identical to that of Wróbel, and for 1914 identical to that of Corrsin: G. Zalewska, *Ludność żydowska w Warszawie w okresie międzywojennym* (Warsaw, 1996), 25.

[38] 'Warschau', *Deutsche Lodzer Zeitung*, 6 Aug. 1915.

[39] 'Der erste Beschluss des Warschauer Bürger-Komitees' and 'Zur Regelung der Judenfrage in Warschau', both in *Mitteilungen des polnischen Pressbüros*, 30 Aug. 1915. On the implementation of the obligatory education system in Łódź, see Hertz, *Łódź w czasie Wielkiej Wojny*, 164–6.

[40] Archiwum Główne Akt Dawnych, Warsaw, Niem. Władze okupacyjne na terenie byłego królestw. Pol., 17: 'Rozmowa Cleinowa z przedstawicielem prasy warszawskiej', 11 Aug. 1915.

Polish and Jewish alike. The city council thus systematically discriminated against the Jewish schools operating in Polish under its supervision and with the encouragement of the municipality.[41]

Immediately after the decision regarding compulsory education, a meeting was called by the Yidisher Lerer Farayn (Association of Jewish/Yiddish Teachers) in Warsaw to demand official Yiddish schools for Yiddish-speaking Warsaw Jews, in light of the relative success of the efforts made in Łódź. Yiddishists, Hebraists, Zionists, and Bundists banded together to insist on mandatory education for all children and for the recognition of Yiddish as an official language in the Jewish schools.[42] As in the case of Łódź, a petition was drawn up, and was signed by 32,645 people.[43]

In contrast to Łódź, however, and at the very same time, the German authorities did not respond favourably to this request and would not give Yiddish even de facto recognition as a language of instruction in the education system that was being established. The German authorities did not intervene in these issues in Warsaw, although in Łódź they were involved on a routine basis. At the same time, however, a liberal education policy introduced by the Germans led to unprecedented developments in *private* modern Jewish education for the secular and religious sectors, mainly in Yiddish.[44]

A Dual Policy

A dual policy thus emerged, in which distinctions were made between various regions. As explained by a leading member of the Komitee für den Osten, Adolf

[41] 'Di letste tsvey zitsungen in shtot-rat', *Varshever togblat*, 13 Aug. 1916; 'Fun der shabesdiker zitsung in shtot-rat', *Varshever togblat*, 14 Aug. 1916; 'Di Nowa Gazeta vegn di rekht fun yidish', *Haynt*, 15 Aug. 1916; 'Nowa Gazeta vegn a yidishe shule', *Varshever togblat*, 15 Aug. 1916. Polish progressive circles claimed that the municipal treasury should maintain the educational system in its totality and in an equitable way, including the Jewish system, on condition that the schools be supervised by the municipality and that the language of instruction be Polish. They did not, however, support the demand for Yiddish schooling. 'Zitzsungen fun shtot rat, donershtik un fraytik', *Haynt*, 13 Aug. 1916. These progressive circles were unable to enforce equal treatment of both school systems, and the city council continued to discriminate systematically against the Jewish education system in Polish. See 'Yeshivat-mo'etset ha'ir', *Hatsefirah*, 5 Nov. 1916; 'Devar-mah', *Hatsefirah*, 8 Sept. 1916; N. Prilutski [Prylucki], *Redes in varshever shtotrat* (Warsaw, 1922), 7–8.

[42] 'Di yidishe shulfrage in varshe', *Haynt*, 26 Aug. 1915; the article describes the meeting. It was widely quoted in the official local German press and in the semi-official Yiddish press in Łódź: 'Die jüdische Schulfrage in Warschau', *Deutsche Warschauer Zeitung*, 29 Aug. 1915; 'Di yidishe shulfrage in varshe', *Lodzher folksblat*, 27 Aug. 1915. The publication of such information in the official and semi-official press demonstrated the importance of the event to the authorities. See also Kazdan, *Di geshikhte fun yidishn shulvezn in umophengikn poyln*, 26–8; K. Weiser, *Jewish People, Yiddish Nation: Noah Prylucki and the Folkists in Poland* (Toronto, 2011), 127–39.

[43] Kazdan, *Di geshikhte fun yidishn shulvezn in umophengikn poyln*, 33–6; Weiser, *Jewish People, Yiddish Nation*, 137–9, 219–20.

[44] Kazdan, *Di geshikhte fun yidishn shulvezn in umophengikn poyln*, 13–43, 52–3; K. Weiser, 'German Policy and the Struggle for Yiddish Secular Schools in Congress Poland during the First World War', Yiddish Studies Master's Essay (Columbia Univ., 1996).

Friedemann, during one of his many trips to the German occupation zones, the differing policies regarding linguistic and education issues derived from 'political considerations regarding the future shaping of the occupied territories'.[45] In his view, the status of the Yiddish vernacular was treated as a political issue, with German authorities using the language question as a means of promoting geopolitical aims. Their policies reflected the broader plans and ongoing disputes within the German leadership regarding the future of the various regions.

Germany planned to rule over extensive areas in Poland. One region which was intended for annexation to Germany or for indirect German rule consisted of incompletely defined territories in the western and northern areas of Congress Poland (the *Grenzstreifen* or border strip). A substantial number of Germans already inhabited these regions, or would be brought there, although Germany sought to emphasize the multinational nature of the area.[46] The recognition of Yiddish in these areas signified the legal acceptance of the Jewish population as a separate ethnic group parallel to the Polish nationals and the German minority. By emphasizing a triad of languages and ethno-national equivalent groups living in defined boundaries, the German regime sought to de-Polonize Łódź and promote German rule in the region, either directly—by annexing the area (with or without its residents) to Germany—or by preserving it as a colonial or semi-colonial territory.[47] These measures helped put Greater Łódź, and a western belt of Congress Poland, under the aegis of the Reich without necessarily including the region's non-German population. The recognition of Yiddish in Łódź aimed to delegitimize (and then weaken) its attachment to any Polish political entity likely to arise.

The Jewish minority, and its demand for recognition of the Yiddish vernacular, was vulnerable to this kind of manipulation because its political claims mainly concerned cultural aspects and did not question the German aims of control and hegemony. Even the Jewish demand for national autonomy on a personal basis (or for some kind of minority rights) was not perceived as a threat to German dominance. Highlighting the lack of dominance by any one nationality worked in favour of German plans to gain indirect control over this area.

Still, the fate of Łódź was not completely clear in Germany's post-war schemes.[48] In German thinking, if the city were to be transferred to Poland, then retaining the Jewish population's existing vernacular would be better than to

[45] CZA, A15/VIII/2f: 'Bericht über die Reise Dr. Friedemann und Dr. Max Cohn zum Oberkommando Ost in der Zeit vom 8. bis 13. Mai 1916'.

[46] On the German plans for colonization and Germanization, see Basler, *Deutschlands Annexionspolitik*, 51–74, 385; Geiss, *Der polnische Grenzstreifen*, 78–106, 160–3.

[47] On the annexationist tendencies of the German Reich towards Poland, see Geiss, *Der polnische Grenzstreifen*. The German-speaking population in Łódź petitioned for the annexation of western parts of Congress Poland (including the city of Łódź) to Germany. See Z. Kulak, 'Memorandum of the Germans from Łódź Concerning the Annexation of Polish Territories to the Reich at the Time of World War I', *Polish Western Affairs*, 7 (1966), 388–403.

[48] Sukiennicki, *East Central Europe during World War I*, 146.

Germanize them, since the Germanization of the Jewish population, in such a case, would expose Germany to an unwanted stream of Jewish refugees. A cohesive local Jewish element, moreover, would balance out the Polish element and become 'a German control base'. In short, allowing the various ethnic groups to maintain their own vernacular supported the lack of dominance by any one nationality, and thereby undercut different claims for sovereignty over these areas and favoured German plans for indirect control.

If in the Łódź area the German regime favoured recognition of the Jewish national minority and their language, in the Warsaw area, and in central and eastern Congress Poland generally, German authorities used the language issue to lend support to the Polish character of the country. In these cases, they were willing to accept some of the demands by the Polish national movement for a Polish entity with its own language and culture, and thereby to recruit the movement to the German side in the overall German military effort. In Warsaw and central Congress Poland, therefore, the Germans found it expedient to disappoint the Jewish hope for autonomy in a Poland that would accept its linguistic and ethnic complexities, thereby undermining the Jewish minority's defence mechanisms.

The recognition or non-recognition of Yiddish was a tool for the German authorities, which they could use to show preference for one or another element of the population to suit their plans. The various means they employed to control, supervise, and redistribute the resource of the mother tongue as cultural capital point to the importance the Germans attached to this arena. Control over the use of the different vernaculars allowed them to shape the cultural world of the societies under their occupation, enabling them either to preserve or to change the social order according to their political plans. Moulding the educational system was a powerful means for achieving political purposes—a means whose importance was understood by the Germans, Poles, and Jews alike.

POLICY UNDER THE NEW POLISH ADMINISTRATION

The Provisional Council of State and the Recognition of the Vernaculars in the Municipal Domain

German political policy in the occupied territories shifted radically in 1916 to the goal of establishing buffer zones/authorities, or buffer states with limited sovereignty, between Russia and Germany. Towards the end of the year, this was translated into the formation of an independent German satellite state in Poland and the transfer of administrative responsibilities to newly established Polish governmental bodies. The first such framework was the Provisional Council of State (Tymczasowa Rada Stanu; TRS).[49]

One of the first issues to be discussed in the executive branch of the Provisional Council of State was the language question in Łódź.[50] The German authorities

[49] W. Suleja, *Tymczasowa Rada Stanu* (Warsaw, 1998), 11–49.   [50] Ibid. 159–60.

wanted to institutionalize the formal use of German in the municipal institutions, side by side with the Polish language, but the newly elected Polish city councillors were threatening to boycott the city council if it acknowledged both languages. In light of this, special deliberations were held to debate the status of both languages.[51] Because of the importance of the issue a special representative of the German occupiers attended the discussion besides the permanent representative of the German occupation regime. The regime drafted an ordinance recognizing the use of the German language in the municipality and in the city council.[52] Most members of the Provisional Council opposed recognizing German as an official language, despite the strong presence of the German language in the municipal space of Łódź since the German occupation, and in fact *because* of such a presence and even in spite of pressure from the German representatives during the discussion. Some arguments against such recognition reflected opposition to the German occupation's dictate.[53] Many others reflected fears that such recognition would reduce the legitimacy of the Polish state in formation in the perception of the Polish-speaking people ('making huge concessions to the German language would make a fatal impression in the country').[54] A special commission redrafted the ordinance, limiting the use of the German language in the city council, making it more acceptable: 'Initially equal permission was granted to the German and Polish languages; today we would not give such permission.'[55] But the very recognition of the German language provoked strong objections.

The argument presented by the prelate Fr. Henryk Przeździecki, a popular representative from Łódź, took the discussion a step further. He addressed the socio-economic consequences of recognizing any language other than Polish as official, arguing that to recognize German would transform bilingualism into a functional asset, which would simultaneously be disadvantageous to monolingual civil servants. He pointed to the possible dismissal of Polish-speaking civil servants who did not know German. To prevent putting ethnic or monolingual Poles at a disadvantage in the nascent state apparatus and endangering their position in the emerging bureaucracy, he opposed recognition of the German language. In this respect, he stated: 'We cannot accept any exception.'[56] Negating the recognition of the German language was thus a means to ensure the position of the monolingual Polish civil servants vis-à-vis the German-speaking municipal bureaucracy. Przeździecki's proposed amendment intended to exclude German, the language recognized in the rephrased ordinance, in order to regulate the implementation of an ethnically biased labour market policy. In this context, Przeździecki was the first discussant to point out that the denial of the *Sprachenrecht* of the minorities implied the exclusion of minorities from the resource of recognition of a societal language, thereby hampering minority groups in terms of recruitment to the public civil

[51] Archiwum Akt Nowych, Warsaw (hereafter AAN), TRS, Akt 7, Sprawy Samorządowe, 16 Feb. 1917. [52] Ibid., 23 Feb. 1917; 5 Mar. 1917. [53] Ibid.
[54] Ibid., 23 Feb. 1917. [55] Ibid., 5 Mar. 1917. [56] Ibid.

service and the concomitant social mobility. In fact, his proposition was consistent with discriminatory practices in employment as implemented in municipal institutions in Warsaw and other cities in Congress Poland where non-ethnic Poles (especially Jews) were discriminated against.[57]

The argument presented by Przeździecki spoke about German, but its subtext addressed Yiddish. This is clear from the response of Władysław Studnicki, a member of the Club of Polish State Partisans (Klub Państwowców Polskich)— a right-wing, pro-German political organization. He presented a very different perspective from that of Przeździecki. He claimed that the rephrased ordinance should mention non-dominant languages used in Łódź and in other cities in Congress Poland, in particular Yiddish. Studnicki argued:

> The common use of the jargon [Yiddish] could be useful when passing rules that apply to the population as a whole, as for instance regarding health or hygiene. In their [own] country, the Poles can be liberals because they are the landlords and their Polish language is the official language. The use of the languages that the minorities know must be allowed in the official institutions. When needed, it [the information] will be translated in both directions, into the official and into the secondary languages.[58]

Basically, Studnicki's position reflected a perceived need to facilitate communication between the bureaucratic apparatus and the individuals addressing it. His answer to Przeździecki essentially claimed that the other side of the exclusion of the languages of minorities would imply the waiver of council authority over these minorities. In other words, besides the ostensible pay-off from the rejection of the minority languages—i.e. reinforcement of the position of monolingual Polish civil servants—there would be a loss of authority over the minorities.

Studnicki's approach, however, was thoroughly rejected in formalistic and legalistic arguments which demanded the exclusive recognition of Polish in municipal institutions. Ludomir Grendyszyński, a leader of the National Work Group (Grupa Pracy Narodowej), contended that 'the jargon is unacknowledged and lacking any rights', and thus it should not be mentioned in the regulations.[59] Another influential member of the council, Franciszek Radziwiłł, asserted that it was 'absolutely necessary to eliminate bilingualism [Polish and German] in order to avoid any kind of precedent',[60] that is, the acknowledgement of Yiddish, which, linked so closely with the German-language question, would mean its recognition as a societal language and culture. The majority of the members of the council viewed the recognition of both the German and Yiddish languages as illegitimate, as undermining the building of a Polish state, and as endangering civil solidarity.

Nevertheless, the political circumstances dictated a compromise. Despite pressure from the German authorities, the decision was made in March 1917 that the

---

[57] Prilutski, *Redes*, 40–2; V. Shulman, 'In di yorn fun der ershter velt-milkhome', in *Di yidn in poyln fun di eltste tsaytn biz der tsveyter velt-milkhome* (New York, 1946), 875; Zieliński, *Stosunki polsko-żydowskie*, 279, 285–6.   [58] AAN, TRS, Akt 7, Sprawy Samorządowe, 5 Mar. 1917.
[59] Ibid.   [60] Ibid.

official language of the municipality and the city council of Łódź, as of other such bodies, would be Polish. However, as a concession to the pressure, a stipulation was added to the effect that in some cases the Łódź municipality would have the right to use German (only German; no mention was made of Yiddish) or to attach a German translation to correspondence with German authorities.[61] The members of the Polish faction in the Łódź city council did not accept this compromise and proposed to limit it as much as possible, 'with the goal of assuring the Polish character of the city's administration'.[62] They were particularly concerned with the highest positions in the city.[63] This statement amounted to the adoption of Przeździecki's point of view and reflected a desire to exclude minorities from the administrative apparatus.

The question of the status of the Yiddish vernacular arose again in July 1917 when the Provisional Council of State discussed proposed regulations for the district government drawn up by the Austrian occupation regime.[64] Regarding the language question, the Austrian proposal suggested a similar arrangement for Poland as for Galicia, recognizing the Polish language as official and providing minority rights to the German and Ukrainian languages. Ukrainian, which was widespread in eastern Galicia, was also relevant in the Austrian-occupied region of Congress Poland because of the large number of Ukrainians who lived there, primarily in the peripheral areas and especially in the Chełm region.[65]

In view of this, Studnicki, in accordance with his previously cited statement, argued that 'the rights of the minorities should be taken into consideration . . . in spite of the awareness that this contradicts the views of the executive of the Provisional Council of State'. The general attitude towards the rights of the minority languages was relatively open and tolerant during this debate. Jerzy Jampolski, a representative of the Austrian zone of occupation, emphasized that the provision in the proposed regulation allowing the possibility of permitting requests to the authorities and responses to them to be written in German and Ukrainian, as was the case in Galicia, was 'the minimal concession towards these national minorities'. Przeździecki stated that he was 'in favour of granting national-minority rights even

---

[61] Hertz, *Łódź w czasie Wielkiej Wojny*, 166–7; Suleja, *Tymczasowa Rada Stanu*, 160; W. Suleja, *Próba budowy zrębów polskiej państwowości w okresie instnienia Tymczasowej Rady Stanu* (Wrocław, 1981), 324.   [62] AAN, TRS, Akt 7, Sprawy Samorządowe, 27 Mar. 1917.   [63] Ibid.

[64] For a general description of the discussion concerning the regulations for the district government drawn up by the Austrian occupation regime, see Suleja, *Tymczasowa Rada Stanu*, 162–3. Surprisingly, Suleja did not develop in this monograph the language question which arose during such discussion.

[65] By the first decade of the twentieth century there was an increasing acceptance of the idea of a literary Ukrainian language based mainly on the Poltava region of Dnieper Ukraine but that also contained elements of east Galician vernacular, especially in its scientific and administrative vocabulary. 'Ruthenisch' ('Ruthenian') was the term officially used in Austria to refer to it. On the Ukrainian language question in the nineteenth century, see P. Magocsi, 'The Language Question as a Factor in the National Movement in Eastern Galicia', in A. S. Markovits and F. E. Sysyn (eds.), *Nationbuilding and the Politics of Nationalism: Essays on Austrian Galicia* (Cambridge, Mass., 1982), 220–38.

to 1 per cent of the population'. Stanisław Bukowiecki, another member of the Provisional Council, the director of the Department of Justice known for his view that there was a need to train a cadre of Polish officials, pointed out: 'It is natural that [different people] address the authorities in different languages. Actually, two petitions were made in the Czech language and they were accepted.' Jerzy Jampolski added: 'The petitions made in Czech or English [were accepted] as a matter of courtesy, but, after all, what is important is tolerance towards the minority languages.'[66]

Nevertheless, when it came to translating theoretical rights into practical regulations, the tone changed and other aspects were also considered. The first point of dispute revolved around the territorial scope of the rights of minority languages. Should a minority language's rights encompass the country as a whole or only certain districts? On the one hand, representatives of the Austrian-occupied region of Congress Poland supported the adoption of the Galician regulations at the territorial level. Ignacy Rosner, a leading figure in the Austro-Polish conservative group and a representative of the Austrian occupation regime, stated somewhat aggressively that 'from the political point of view it would be harmful if the Council of State were to remove precisely this point from the proposal', adding that 'the assurance of minority rights is a certain type of guarantee submitted to foreign nations by the Polish state'. Moreover, he doubted whether the acknowledgement of such rights at the district level only would be advantageous: 'If in Galicia freedom to take decisions in this issue had been given to the district authorities, the Ruthenian language would never have been recognized . . . In Congress Poland the situation would not be different.'[67] Józef Mikułowski-Pomorski added to this the argument that 'this question should be uniformly resolved for all the national minorities in Poland . . . not leaving vast freedom to the executive'.[68]

Against these views, on the other hand, most participants supported a regional approach to the language question, considering that the recognition of minority languages should be granted only at the district level. The different ethnic composition in each district, they claimed, dictated a different approach in each district. Discussions about the Ukrainian language, for instance, now centred on the question of how many Ukrainians there were and where they were to be found, as their numbers had fallen as a result of migration from the eastern periphery of Congress Poland to Russia in the wake of the ravages of the war. In this respect Bukowiecki stated that the recognition of the Ukrainian language should be very limited territorially, since 'after all the number of Ukrainians in the Lublin district is scanty'.[69]

A large proportion of the council members vigorously opposed recognizing the German language on the grounds that 'there are no Germans as a national minority in the Austrian occupation zone . . . [but only] in the German occupation zone.

---

[66] All quotations in this paragraph are from AAN, TRS, Akt 7, Sprawy Samorządowe, 7 July 1917.
[67] Ibid. Ukrainian was officially referred to as 'Ruthenian' in Austria: see n. 65 above.
[68] Ibid.   [69] Ibid.

[Therefore, the German language] should be discussed [only] when regulating the district government in the German occupation zone.' Nevertheless, the council members were aware that they could hardly avoid recognizing the German language in the Polish territory as a whole. Jampolski supported the proposal made by the Department of the Interior of the Provisional Council of State to 'leave the recognition of other languages to the district authorities'. Thus, for instance, 'if in a certain district there is a large percentage of Germans, the district authorities will certainly permit the presenting of petitions in that language'.[70] This position was broadly accepted.

To help persuade the council to adopt a positive policy towards minority languages, Ignacy Rosner, a strong advocate of the Austro-Polish solution, emphasized that 'the Polish borders are not yet determined, so [the recognition of minority languages] is a political issue, and since the Polish people are interested in a Poland [constituted] not only in its ethnographic borders . . . the affirmation of minority rights constitutes a kind of guarantee to foreign nationals in the name of the Polish state'.[71]

As a compromise, some council members suggested not naming the minority languages specifically, or even not raising the issue at all. Responding to this proposal, both Stefan Iszkowski and Jampolski expressed the opinion that

From the viewpoint of the interests of Poland, the two languages that should be permitted, i.e. Ruthenian and German, must be explicitly recognized, because only in this way will it be possible to prevent the use of the jargon, since it is, after all, impossible to claim in the regulation that the jargon is not a language. If we claim this is the case, we will have unending conflicts on theoretical grounds over the question of whether or not the jargon is a language.

But the mention of the languages to be recognized, as well as the omission of 'the jargon', should be done in a subtle way, because 'The most important side of the question is the political aspect, it is about the impact on foreign countries. After all, this will be the first time that the Council of State takes a stand on the rights of the national minorities; it should therefore speak out tolerantly.'[72] In other words, in implementing a policy regarding minority languages, the question of the Jewish vernacular, Yiddish, had to be taken into account, above all because of its international implications.

Following Iszkowski's and Jampolski's suggestions, Grendyszyński and Antoni Kaczorowski proposed to add to the German and Ukrainian languages two further languages: Belarusian and Lithuanian. 'In this way', the argument went on, 'we will prevent the jargon question from being raised.' As was the case with Ukrainian, a language used in the agrarian eastern periphery, so Lithuanian and Belarusian would be limited to specific and delimited districts, geographically peripheral. 'It is not possible that in Lublin, for example, a petition be submitted in Lithuanian or be answered in Lithuanian, as we cannot require that officials all over the country

---

[70] Ibid.   [71] Ibid.   [72] Ibid.

know Lithuanian.' A similar argument excluded any minority language from other big cities, since, 'for instance, in the statute of the capital city of Warsaw it is stated that the only official language is Polish'.[73]

The logic of denying the language rights of a non-dominant language in a city which did not have members of the population which spoke that language underscored the political aim of such denial in the case of the broad presence of speakers of a non-dominant language, Yiddish in this case, in the same geographical area. In this case, citing the languages permitted was clearly a strategy for rejecting the recognition of the Yiddish vernacular. This subtle manner of rejection was soon to be repeated.

The Provisional Council of State and the Recognition of Vernacular Languages in the School System

The language question arose again in the Department of Religions and Public Education (Departament Wyznań Religijnych i Oświecenia Publicznego) in a discussion of the proposal by the Austrian occupation authorities regarding the education of the Jewish population.[74] The status of the *ḥeder*s and the issue of language of instruction was a main topic in these deliberations. Józef Mikułowski-Pomorski, who headed the department, argued that the *ḥeder*s should not be recognized as state schools, since Yiddish was their sole language of instruction.[75] The use of the Polish language in Jewish educational institutions, he maintained, should be the criterion for granting them recognition as state institutions. By contrast, Studnicki, consistent with his statements on the issue of minority languages, came out in favour of granting state status to the *ḥeder*s, even if the children were taught in Yiddish, though his position was, as in the past, exceptional among the members of the Provisional Council. He contended that 'since the Jews constitute a large percentage of the population, their schools should be viewed as public schools'.[76] In areas with sizeable Jewish populations, he argued, Jews should be allowed to open Yiddish-language schools in which Polish would also be taught, along with Polish

[73] AAN, TRS, Akt 7, Sprawy Samorządowe, 7 July 1917

[74] Suleja, *Próba budowy zrębów polskiej państwowości*, 334. The Austrian authorities' proposal was based on a memorandum prepared by Mayer Bałaban, the consultant for Jewish issues in the Austrian occupation zone. On Bałaban's political activity during the war and its implications, see M. Silber, 'Me'ir balaban ufe'iluto hatsiburit-politit bepolin biyemei milḥemet ha'olam harishonah', *Shevut*, NS, 11 (27) (2002–3), 139–58. The memorandum was published by Frank Schuster, who wrote an interesting introduction to it. See F. Schuster, '"Lepiej jest wykonać w jednej części Polski całą pracę niż w całej Polsce połowę lub wcale": Uwagi dotyczące sprawozdania prof. dr. Majera Bałabana o wizycie w polskich gminach żydowskich w czasie I wojny światowej', *Kwartalnik Historii Żydów*, 197 (2001), 27–34; Bałaban, 'Raport o żydowskich instytucjach oświatowych i religijnych', ibid. 35–68.

[75] AAN, TRS, Sprawy Oświaty, Akt 11: Posiedzenia Wydziału Wykonawczego w d. 7.VII.17.

[76] Ibid. It seems that Studnicki's position was not exceptional among supporters of the Polish–German solution. Adam Ronikier's letter to Paul Nathan is a partial reflection of such a position: P. Nathan, 'Fortschritte in Polen', *Berliner Tageblatt*, 5 Apr. 1917.

history and geography.[77] In his view, the language of instruction in the school was not decisive for moulding loyal citizens of the Polish state. One could be a useful citizen of the Polish state without having a thorough command of the Polish language, or even without knowing it at all, he claimed, just as one could be fluent in Polish, yet be a harmful citizen of the Polish state.[78] These arguments, however, fell on deaf ears.

The Provisional Council discussed political guidelines not only for *ḥeder*s and other schooling for Jewish children, but for the educational institutions of other minorities as well.[79] Clearly, the members of the council were aware that recognizing the language of a minority group did not necessarily have an adverse effect on the status of the language they sought to promote—Polish—as is reflected in the rationale given for this policy decision:

In principle, the language of instruction in public schools shall be Polish. However, in exceptional cases, permission will be granted for teaching in Lithuanian, Ruthenian, and German. The communities must submit requests [in this regard], and the Department of Religions and Public Education must authorize them. Public and private schools with instruction conducted in languages other than Polish will be required to provide both oral and written instruction in the Polish language.[80]

This resolution was passed at the same time as the decisions regarding the *ḥeder*s, indicating the close connection between them. Notably, the decision regarding recognition of the minority languages used the same tactic of citing the recognized minority languages (Lithuanian, Ukrainian, and German) in order to avoid the question of Yiddish and to ignore the Yiddish vernacular.

The Transfer of the School System and the Question of Yiddish

While the protracted and exhaustive deliberations in the Department of Religions and Public Education over the education of the Jewish population were part and parcel of the discussions on education for national minorities, the Jewish issue was the last, and unresolved, topic in the negotiations between the German occupation authorities and the Provisional Council. The purpose of these discussions was to bring about an orderly transfer of administrative responsibility for the school system in Congress Poland from the occupiers to the council. The discussions on

[77] AAN, TRS, Sprawy Oświaty, Akt 11: Posiedzenia Wydziału Wykonawczego w d. 7.VII.17.

[78] 'Diskusyes vegn di yidn-frage', *Haynt*, 30 Apr. 1917. Studnicki's party adopted a resolution in accordance with his opinion: 'The evolution of all the cultures and nationalities that populate the Polish state will be guaranteed. All public positions and public posts will be open to all the citizens of the state without differentiation by religion or origin. The languages of the national minorities will be considered in the schools, in the administration, and in the courts.' 'Di poylishe parteyen un zeyer batsiyung tsu di natsyonale minderhaytn', *Haynt*, 9 Nov. 1917. Although Studnicki was supported by the German authorities, who exerted pressure on his behalf in the new state apparatus, his influence in the Provisional Council was minimal.

[79] AAN, TRS, Sprawy Oświaty, Akt 11: Posiedzenia Wydziału Wykonawczego w d. 17.IV.17.

[80] Ibid.

this matter went on for months, until September 1917.[81] The primary reason for the slow progress was the attempt by the German occupation officials to compel the Polish authorities to agree to an arrangement that was unacceptable to them. The sticking point concerned the division of responsibility between the Polish authorities and the minority schools, with the issue of education for the Jewish minority constituting a major stumbling block.[82]

The Provisional Council of State repeatedly threatened to resign over the German authorities' attempts to compel its members to agree to arrangements they considered unacceptable, namely the German insistence on the establishment of country-wide systems of non-Polish schools. Further, the Germans demanded that these national school networks have the authority to tax the populations they served and that these populations not be subject to double taxation. Alternatively, they proposed that the Polish government could subsidize these schools by means of a national subsidy that would reflect the relative proportion of minority students attending their respective schools.[83] According to the German proposal, the authority of the state over these networks would be only supervisory. The German occupation forces were thus supporting the establishment of a system of national educational autonomy for all the national minorities living in Polish lands.[84] Extensive propaganda efforts were made within the German national minority to encourage them to set up their own school systems, thereby confronting the Provisional Council with a fait accompli. The council, however, categorically opposed both demands—to establish minority school networks and to subsidize them proportionally ('It will create a state within a state').[85]

A month before the German occupation regime was to turn over responsibility for educational matters to the Polish authorities, two issues still remained unresolved: the problem of Jewish education, and the question of financial support and responsibility for supervision of the minority schools. While the German proposition's draft had already acknowledged Jews as a religious minority (a move that accorded with the wishes of the Polish authorities), the German proposal clearly put the rights of religious minorities (read: Jews) and national minorities (a clear reference to the German minority, which the occupation authorities were attempting to safeguard) on an equal plane. According to the German plan, these two categories were entitled to the same measures of security, supervision, and

---

[81] Suleja, *Tymczasowa Rada Stanu*, 171.

[82] M. Handelsman, 'Les Efforts de la Pologne pour la reconstruction d'un état indépendant', in id. (ed.), *La Pologne: Sa vie économique et sociale pendant la guerre* (Paris, 1933), 179–80; AAN, TRS, Sprawy Oświaty, Akt 11: Posiedzenia Wydziału Wykonawczego w d. 21.VII.17.

[83] AAN, TRS, Sprawy Oświaty, Akt 11: Posiedzenia Wydziału Wykonawczego w d. 16.VIII.17; CZA, A8/37/3: 'Bericht der Reise der Herren Dr. Adolf Friedmann, Dr. Franz Oppenheimer und Prof. Sobernheim nach dem östlichen Okkupationsgebiet im April/Mai 1917'.

[84] Handelsman, 'Les Efforts de la Pologne pour la reconstruction d'un état indépendant', 179–80; AAN, TRS, Sprawy Oświaty, Akt 11: Posiedzenia Wydziału Wykonawczego w d. 21.VII.17.

[85] AAN, TRS, Sprawy Oświaty, Akt 11: Posiedzenia Wydziału Wykonawczego w d. 16.VIII.17.

subsidy, whether their essential make-up was religious or national. The Polish proposal, by contrast, was clearly the outcome of a concerted effort to drive a wedge between these categories, giving priority to the national minorities (the code terminology denoting the German minority) over the religious minorities (i.e. Jews).[86]

The firm stand of the Provisional Council resulted in a compromise by the German authorities,[87] enabling the finalization of a regulation, drawn up on 12 September 1917, to transfer all responsibility for education to the Polish authorities.[88] The fundamental nature of the compromise was to create a distinction between the two types of minorities—national and religious—with a bias against the religious minority (essentially, the Jews) in comparison with the national minority (essentially, the Germans), who were given more rights. The occupation authorities agreed that private high schools would not receive state subsidies. The Polish negotiators, for their part, agreed to the creation of a system of officially recognized German elementary schools on a denominational basis (Protestant and Catholic). The two networks—one Protestant and the other Catholic—responsible for these schools would jointly present the budgetary requests of the German education network, and would be given government subsidies.[89]

Thus, official recognition for the Yiddish vernacular was sacrificed on the altar of a political compromise. The final regulation declared that Jews were solely a religious minority and that the state would establish parallel classes for Jews within Polish schools or in parallel schools where the day of rest would be Saturday. The *heder*s and *talmudei torah* were to be recognized as *private* institutions that would be required to provide a general elementary education in the Polish language. Public funding (by the local councils and municipalities) was to be provided for the classes taught in Polish. Notably, the stipulation concerning even this limited funding was included in the regulation only because of pressure from the German authorities, who insisted on it.[90]

Since the regulations formally stipulated that in the *heder*s and *talmudei torah* general subjects (including, of course, the Polish language) would be taught in Polish, and that these institutions would receive subsidies, it followed that Jewish

---

[86] CZA, Z3/146: 'Warschau den 17. August 1917—Entwurf der Schulabteilung—Entwurf des Direktors des Departements für Kultus und Unterricht—Gesetz über Berücksichtigung von Schulbedürfnissen der Minderheiten im Königreich Polen'. See esp. clauses 6–8.

[87] AAN, TRS, Sprawy Oświaty, Akt 11: Posiedzenia Wydziału Wykonawczego w d. 25.VIII.17.

[88] Suleja, *Tymczasowa Rada Stanu*, 172.

[89] Handelsman, 'Les Efforts de la Pologne pour la reconstruction d'un état indépendant', 180; K. Krasowski, *Związki wyznaniowe w II Rzeczypospolitej: Studium historycznoprawne* (Warsaw, 1988), 208, 210.

[90] AAN, TRS, Sprawy Oświaty, Akt 11: Posiedzenia Wydziału Wykonawczego w d. 25.VIII.17. Compare Archiwum Państwowe w Lublinie, Ces. Niemiecki Urząd Powiatowy w Łukowie, 200: 'Verordnungsblatt für das Generalgouvernement Warschau', 20 Sept. 1917, with CZA, Z3/146: 'Gespräch mit Herrn Vizekronmarschall v. Pomorski, über den Schutz der jüdischen Minderheit', 14 Sept. 1917; and see 'Das neue Stadium', *Jüdische Rundschau*, 19 Nov. 1917, p. 41; E. Zechlin, *Die deutsche Politik und die Juden im Ersten Weltkrieg* (Göttingen, 1969), 210.

children would study other subjects in another language. Naturally, that other language would be the vernacular spoken by the Jews—Yiddish. However, naming the language was avoided. Everyone in the council knew that Yiddish, the jargon, existed, and that it was vibrant and vital, but they refrained from mentioning its very existence for fear that in so doing they might be handing it formal, if only indirect, recognition. Moreover, the limited funding for the Jewish schools was to be allocated only 'so long as the children of the Mosaic faith are unable to attend state elementary schools', and so long as instruction in the general subjects 'shall be carried out according to the general [state] curriculum and under general [state] supervision'.[91] These regulations created an absolute separation between the two types of minorities and discriminated against the religious minority in comparison with the national minority, with the latter having more rights.

Strikingly, no reference was made to the relatively liberal educational policies introduced by the Germans in Warsaw, Łódź, and other provincial cities, which had led to unprecedented developments in modern Jewish education for the secular, religious, and ultra-Orthodox sectors, conducted mainly in Yiddish, and on a much smaller scale in Hebrew. With the transfer of control of the education system to the Polish authorities in September 1917, the Jewish population was free to develop its own educational system, but all education in Yiddish from then on was viewed as private. The Polish authorities systematically refrained from granting this network any public or state-related status, repeatedly stressing its status as a private system.[92] In September 1917, Yiddish was completely divested of any official connection to the state. Ironically, the Polish authorities now adopted the educational approach developed by the German occupation authorities in Warsaw during 1915–17, and extended it to the entire country which had refused to recognize Yiddish. For their part, the German authorities now sought to protect Yiddish, offering to the Jewish school system a status similar to that which was created for the German minority.

Finally, the Provisional Council guaranteed substantial cultural rights to the minorities in central Poland. The German occupation was thus effective in consolidating German educational institutions. German schools throughout the Government General of Warsaw grew at a brisk pace. By 1918 the number of German elementary schools reached its peak.[93] However, the policy of the new Polish authorities regarding Belarusian and Ukrainian schools was different. While the German occupation opened schools for them, from 1918 the Polish authorities did not act to develop them. Quite the opposite: in 1919 the new Polish authorities actually closed them.[94] The Polish authorities did not develop schooling for Jewish children

[91] AAN, TRS, Sprawy Oświaty, Akt 11: Posiedzenia Wydziału Wykonawczego w d. 25.VIII.17.

[92] Kazdan, *Di geshikhte fun yidishn shulvezn in umophengikn poyln*, 13–43, 52–3; CZA, Z3/146: 'Gespräch mit Herrn Vizekronmarschall v. Pomorski, über den Schutz der jüdischen Minderheit', 14 Sept. 1917.   [93] W. Chu, *The German Minority in Interwar Poland* (Cambridge, 2012), 122.

[94] K. Srokowski, *Sprawa narodowościowa na kresach wschodnich* (Kraków, 1924), 11; W. Paprocka,

even in Polish. Jewish representatives in Warsaw complained to the Warsaw city council in 1918 of a biased allocation of resources and budgeting. The number of places allocated to Jewish children in municipal schools was low and did not reach the minimal demands of the Jewish population.[95] These complaints were made to the city council since according to the regulations the municipality was responsible for providing such places.

BACK TO THEORY: YIDDISH AND OTHER VERNACULARS, A SOCIAL INTERPRETATION OF LINGUISTIC RECOGNITION

The official recognition or non-recognition of Yiddish was used as a tool by both the German and the Polish authorities to show preference towards one or other element of the population with the aim of achieving their political objectives. The various means of controlling and supervising the educational system employed by the administration point to the great importance attached to this arena. Control over education allowed the authorities to shape the cultural milieu of society and preserve or change the social order in accordance with their political goals. Thus, the shaping of the educational system was a powerful means for achieving political purposes. In effect, the Germans, Poles, and Jews all understood the importance of this arena and each attempted to exploit it.

Clearly, this is precisely what Germany did in the areas it conquered and administered as Ober Ost. The German occupation regulation of 24 August 1915 gave de facto recognition and de facto autonomy to Jewish education in Yiddish. In Vilna, moreover, Yiddish was recognized *de jure* as a language, and Jews were officially acknowledged as a nation.[96] In Warsaw, however, this was not the case. The local municipal authorities there did as they saw fit and refused to grant official status to Yiddish schools. The recognition of Yiddish as a language of instruction ended when responsibility for educational matters was transferred from the German administration to that of the Provisional Council of State in September 1917. With the start of the 1917/18 school year, the entire educational system came under Polish rule.

Once German policy changed, with the establishment of Polish governmental bodies to form the basis for an 'independent' state in Poland, the Polish authorities excluded Yiddish from the public sphere and defined Jewish education in Yiddish as private, although Jews were not denied the freedom to develop their own education system. The Polish authorities systematically refrained from granting

'Ludność białoruska a polska polityka mniejszościowa w okresie międzywojennym', *Etnografia Polska*, 39 (1995), 21.

[95] CZA, A127/386: 'Wyciąg ze stenogramu posiedzenia rady m. st. Warszawy dn. 24 czerwca 1918 r.'

[96] Š. Liekis, *A State within a State? Jewish Autonomy in Lithuania, 1918–1925* (Vilnius, 2003), 49–50.

instruction in Yiddish a public, state-related status, but repeatedly stressed its standing as a private system. Ultimately, Yiddish was divested of any connection to the state.

In addressing the issue of the official status of minority languages, the Polish administration recognized German, Lithuanian, and Ukrainian, but not the language of the Jewish population—Yiddish. The regulation that recognized Ukrainian, Lithuanian, and German confirmed that the new Polish state acknowledged an obligation to grant rights to minority cultures in the nascent state, which was at least partially multinational and multilingual. Such regulations generally acknowledged the special rights of minority languages, for example with guarantees that they would not be engulfed by the majority language and culture. However, in this particular regulation, these rights were not made universal. The regulation made a distinction between one minority—the Jews—and the others—Ukrainians, Germans, Belarusians, and Lithuanians. Why did the Polish authorities refuse to extend the same guarantees to the Jewish minority?

The issue was not entirely one of German coercion to recognize the languages of all the minorities, because while the German occupiers put pressure on the Poles to recognize German, they made no effort to compel them to recognize the Lithuanian or Ukrainian minorities and their languages.[97] Further, it was not purely an issue of territorial versus extraterritorial minorities, since the Germans were scattered throughout the country, while the Lithuanian minority, for example, was concentrated mainly in the north-east. Nor was it purely an instance of a distinction made between religious and national minorities, since in the case of the German national minority, educational autonomy was to be administered by two networks on a denominational basis.[98]

Likewise, it was not only a propaganda tool to gain control over areas to the east of Congress Poland, although a propagandistic element certainly existed, because the recognition of Yiddish in the eastern areas would actually promote support by the Jewish population for Polish claims. When at the beginning of 1918 the issue of recognizing the minority rights of the Jews in Lithuania as a tool to gain their support for the Polish cause was debated, Grendyszyński rejected it categorically because 'it will be a dangerous matter from the point of view of the relations in Congress Poland'.[99] When Lithuanians later used their recognition of Jewish ethno-cultural claims to strengthen Lithuanian claims to Vilnius, the Polish policy did not change.[100] In any event, these Polish expansionist plans were unrealistic in

---

[97] AAN, TRS, Sprawy Oświaty, Akt 11: Posiedzenia Wydziału Wykonawczego w d. 17.IV.17.

[98] Handelsman, 'Les Efforts de la Pologne pour la reconstruction d'un état indépendant', 180; Krasowski, *Związki wyznaniowe w II Rzeczypospolitej*, 208, 210.

[99] Lietuvos mokslų akademijos Vrublevskių biblioteka, Vilnius (hereafter LMAVB), Dept. of Manuscripts (Class DM), F79, vnt. 830: 'Narada w sprawie Żydów na kresach', Warsaw, 2 Jan. 1918.

[100] Z. Balshan, 'Ma'avakam shel yehudei lita al zekhuyoteihem hale'umiyot, 1917–1918', *Shevut*, 10 (1984), 80–2; Liekis, *A State within a State?*, 72–5.

late 1917, given the realpolitik of German hegemony in the second half of 1917 and its interpretation by key members of the Provisional Council.[101]

The refusal to recognize Yiddish was not based mainly on theoretical or normative grounds, as there was no Polish interest in embarking on a sincere discussion about whether Yiddish was a language, and the 'Provisional Council did not deal with theoretical considerations', as Józef Lewandowski ironically put it.[102] It is true that the view that Yiddish was a debased form of German was widespread among the public. This was similar to the disdain felt for Belarusian as a rustic and crude local dialect.[103] Yet political leaders' disdain for Belarusian (and Lithuanian) did not prevent the recognition of these languages in the periphery of the country, alongside the total denial of recognition to Yiddish.[104]

Moreover, this rejection cannot be mainly attributed to growing conflict between the Jews and the Poles, inasmuch as a similar intensification was taking place in the clash between the Polish and Lithuanian national movements at that time.[105] Lastly, antisemitic tendencies cannot be ignored, as they did indeed exist, but not to an extent that was greater than anti-Ukrainian fears or anti-German sentiment.

The decision made by the Provisional Council even stated that such rights should not be extended to nations that had 'immigrated' to the country as distinct from 'autochthonous' populations. However, minority rights were guaranteed to the Ukrainian population, which was expected to re-emigrate to the eastern peripheries of Congress Poland, and guaranteed to the German minority even in areas where it was considered as 'foreign', as shown above, but simultaneously denied to the local Polish Jews who had been present for centuries. In fact, the wording of the regulation explicitly stated that the Jews may not be considered as a group having national or linguistic rights.[106] My argument is that, undoubtedly, all the reasons cited above did deeply influence the exclusion of the Yiddish vernacular from the public sphere, yet they are insufficient to explain its total exclusion there and the simultaneous acknowledgement of the Slavonic and Baltic vernaculars in the eastern parts of Congress Poland.

I would like to add another dimension. According to my interpretation, another important reason why the Polish authorities refused to extend the same guarantees

---

[101] LMAVB, Dept. of Manuscripts (Class DM), F79, vnt. 830: 'Narada w sprawie Żydów na kresach', Warsaw, 2 Jan. 1918.

[102] J. Lewandowski, *Federalizm: Litwa i Białoruś w polityce obozu belwederskiego, XI. 1918–IV. 1920* (Warsaw, 1962), 50.

[103] W. Mich, *Problem mniejszości narodowych w myśli politycznej polskiego ruchu konserwatywnego, 1918–1939* (Lublin, 1992), 159–60.

[104] Ibid. See also J. Tomaszewski, 'Kresy Wschodnie w polskiej myśli politycznej XIX i XX w.', in W. Wrzesiński (ed.), *Między Polską etniczną a historyczną* (Wrocław, 1988), 38–9, 111.

[105] See e.g. P. Łossowski, *Konflikt polsko-litewski, 1918–1920* (Warsaw, 1996), 18–20, 22–4.

[106] CZA, A8/37/3: 'Bericht der Reise der Herren Dr. Adolf Friedmann, Dr. Franz Oppenheimer und Prof. Sobernheim nach dem östlichen Okkupationsgebiet im April/Mai 1917'; CZA, L6/106: Berger to Zentralbüro, 6 May 1917.

to the Jewish minority, and what underlay the seemingly disproportionate significance they attached to linguistic demands, may be understood from an analysis of
the socio-economic implications of linguistic recognition. Here I follow the argument presented by Przeździecki in the debate in the Provisional Council, who connected the *Sprachenrecht* of the minorities and the ethnically biased character of the
labour market.[107]

There were important structural differences between Jews and the Slavonic and
Baltic minorities which clearly affected the recognition of minority languages. Jews
were for the most part an urban minority, while Ukrainians, Belarusians, and Lithuanians were predominantly agrarian. My claim is that the economic structure,
conditions, and extant institutions at the disposal of a given minority group define
the extent to which it is able to take advantage of the legal and administrative
measures to safeguard it against the infringement of its culture and language by the
majority group and effectively implement the substance of official recognition as a
minority culture.[108]

Each of three minorities—Ukrainians, Belarusians, and Lithuanians—was con-
sidered mainly as a backward people not threatening the hegemonic power. As
Włodzimierz Mich has argued, Polish conservatives did not consider Belarusian
national demands as having any significant impact on the situation of the state.
They regarded the Belarusians or the Ukrainians in the eastern areas of Congress
Poland as no more than masses of peasants,[109] and granted recognition of their
rights only in a clearly delimited area, in order to be able to claim that the emerging
Polish state was meeting the cultural needs of its Slavonic and Baltic minorities.
The recognition of their linguistic rights would also ease communication with
populations considered almost exclusively agrarian and primitive, as well as facili-
tate their administration and supervision.

However, the minority rights conferred on the Slavonic and Baltic minorities
applied only in peripheral territories and preserved their situation of a rural minority there. The granting of such minority rights did not threaten the ethno-national
hegemony that the Provisional Council aimed to establish. In addition, schools
whose language of instruction was that of a minority were created slowly and ineffi-
ciently, and they were mostly based on those introduced by the German occupation
authorities; clearly they were kept marginalized.[110] Studnicki was later to claim,

---

[107] AAN, TRS, Akt 7, Sprawy Samorządowe, 5 Mar. 1917.

[108] On the connection between formal legal definitions and socio-economic conditions, see
N. Fraser, 'From Redistribution to Recognition? Dilemmas of Justice in a "Post-Socialist" Age', *New
Left Review*, 212 (1995), 68–93. Regarding the linguistic demands of a given minority and its social
structure, see Hroch, *Social Interpretation of Linguistic Demands*, 31–7.

[109] Mich, *Problem mniejszości narodowych*, 155, 157.

[110] J. Ogonowski, *Uprawnienia językowe mniejszości narodowych w Rzeczypospolitej Polskiej, 1918–
1939* (Warsaw, 2000), 22–3, 62–3. It should be mentioned that the rights granted to Jews studying in the
Polish schools, such as the exemption from writing on the sabbath, were scarcely implemented either: J.

when confronted with opposition to the new regulations, that Belarusian schools did not offer any professional training.[111]

This bears out Hroch's theory that the introduction of a non-dominant language into the administration, bureaucracy, and politics ensures the inclusion of the minority in the state apparatus and state elites, thus ensuring its equal access to state resources. In this case, however, these legal safeguards were granted to minorities living in outlying peripheral and agrarian districts, which was not the case for the Jews. The educational autonomy and linguistic recognition given to these groups kept them in the territorial (and cultural) periphery and thereby bound them to the economic system of the past. A priori, the opportunities for economic upward mobility within each of these agrarian societies were extremely limited in the newly emerging national states, while the educational autonomy that was granted to them limited these possibilities even further. By allowing schooling in minority languages, and the symbolic recognition of these languages in the countryside, the authorities, intentionally or unintentionally, bound Ukrainians, Belarusians, and Lithuanians to social and geographical peripheries blocking their access to the hegemonic institutions of the new state in formation. Moreover, the upward mobility offered to integrated Belarusians or Ukrainians in central and western Poland was through blue-collar jobs, for example as watchmen, janitors, or porters.[112] Instead of endowing the young people of these agrarian minorities with the socio-economic capabilities they needed to integrate successfully into the apparatus of power of the new state, this legislation in effect reduced their chances of doing so. At play was a strategy of the reproduction of the Polish literates, to use a concept developed by Bourdieu,[113] whereby non-dominant groups were forced to concede their positions to the preferred populace—ethnic Poles. An education system that preserved the language and culture of the hinterlands of necessity widened the gap between the populations of these areas and that in the centre, in favour of the latter. In this case, as opposed to the theoretical approach, the recognition of such a language constituted nothing less than a strategy of exclusion.

It is my contention that, indeed, this was precisely an important reason why the new Polish administration refused to recognize Yiddish as a societal culture and language. The structural positioning of the Jews was different. Jews were already positioned in the cities, or were considered poised to migrate there. In contrast to the Belarusian, Lithuanian, or Ukrainian peasantry, their presence in the urban middle class constituted a threat to various political groupings in Poland, who were extremely concerned about the growing Jewish preponderance in the cities.

Żyndul, *Państwo w państwie? Autonomia narodowo-kulturalna w Europie Środkowowschodniej w XX wieku* (Warsaw, 2000), 123; Zieliński, *Stosunki polsko-żydowskie*, 326–7.

[111] Mich, *Problem mniejszości narodowych*, 159.   [112] Ibid.

[113] P. Bourdieu and J.-C. Passeron, *La Reproduction: Éléments pour une théorie du système d'enseignement* (Paris, 1970); in English, P. Bourdieu and J.-C. Passeron, *Reproduction in Education, Society and Culture*, trans. R. Nice (London, 1990).

Although the socio-economic role of Jews in Polish society was varied and shifted over time, with great regional variations as well, the prevailing stereotype of the Jews as a 'middleman minority'[114] remained fairly stable, and it was precisely this stereotype that dictated Polish policy. More significantly, the role of Jews in this new urban society (characterized by a still deep cultural division of labour, as Michael Hechter described this concept[115]) was well known in Polish ruling circles. In short, the relationship between the Jewish population and the newly emerged Polish authorities was moulded by the prevailing stereotype of the Jews, and by the preponderant role of Jews as middlemen in the new urban economy. In the perception of the Provisional Council, Jews were a threat to the notion of a Polish national state-building project.

The recognition of Yiddish, as the Yiddish intelligentsia fervently demanded, would have established Yiddish literacy as a '*real entrance-card* to full citizenship and . . . social participation',[116] in Ernest Gellner's metaphor, or at least as a means of gaining access to the emerging state apparatus. The argument presented by Przeździecki in the debate in the Provisional Council clearly linked the *Sprachenrecht* of the minorities and their appointment as civil servants, a prominent theme in the discussion concerning the rights of Yiddish, as noted above.[117] The entrance card of Yiddish literacy would have given Jews full access to the state apparatus and turned their bilingualism into a functional asset.[118] The recognition of Yiddish might even have brought about the establishment of a dual 'state nobility' (Polish

---

[114] The term 'middleman minority' defines traits associated with various ethnic minorities noted for their commercial abilities; permanent middle-class minorities; and a large marginalization in the distribution of political power. See E. Bonacich, 'A Theory of Middleman Minorities', *American Sociological Review*, 38 (1973), 583–94. See also F. Barth, 'Introduction', in id. (ed.), *Ethnic Groups and Boundaries: The Social Organization of Culture and Difference* (Bergen, 1969), 9–38.

[115] M. Hechter, *Internal Colonialism: The Celtic Fringe in British National Development, 1536–1966* (London, 1975), 39–40.

[116] E. Gellner, *Culture, Identity, and Politics* (Cambridge, 1988), 16 (emphasis original).

[117] AAN, TRS, Akt 7, Sprawy Samorządowe, 5 Mar. 1917.

[118] For an excellent analysis of the multilingual system of one particular Jew, representative of a widespread pattern in Jewish life in inter-war Poland, see Batsheva Ben-Amos's insightful study of the multilingual diary of a young man from the Łódź ghetto, probably born immediately after the end of the First World War: B. Ben-Amos, 'A Multilingual Diary from the Ghetto', *Gal-ed*, 19 (2004), 51–74. Many Jews were bilingual (Yiddish/Polish) or multilingual, especially in intelligentsia circles, and employed what Itamar Even-Zohar calls a 'multilingual system', speaking different languages in different circumstances: I. Even-Zohar, 'Aspects of the Hebrew–Yiddish Polysystem: A Case of a Multilingual Polysystem', *Poetics Today*, 11 (1990), 121–30. As Ben-Amos pointed out ('Multilingual Diary from the Ghetto', 60–1), Shmeruk made use of the model developed by Even-Zohar and, referring to this aspect of Jewish life in inter-war Poland, emphasized the connections between the different languages in this multilingual polysystem: C. Shmeruk, 'Hebrew–Yiddish–Polish: A Trilingual Jewish Culture', in Y. Gutman et al. (eds.), *The Jews of Poland between Two World Wars* (Hanover, NH, 1989), 285–311. On the changing linguistic behaviour of the Jewish population, see I. Bartal, 'Midu leshoniyut masoratit leḥad leshoniyut le'umit', *Shevut*, 15 (1992), 183–94. The form of bilingualism so widespread in Jewish life (the dominance of the two main municipal vernaculars: Polish and Yiddish) was less present in non-Jewish society. Other forms of bilingualism (Polish–German) were present in

and Yiddish/Jewish), to use another of Bourdieu's concepts, referring to the elites whose power comes from state recognition of their cultural capital as an adequate source of legitimacy to their claim for power in the state.[119] The recognition of Yiddish would have introduced a dual administrative apparatus in the cities in two languages—Polish and Yiddish. Recognizing the Yiddish vernacular as a societal language would have turned the government apparatus in the city—the nucleus of the nascent state—into a bilingual entity; here we see the same factor at play as accounted for the attempt to exclude the German language in Łódź, as noted earlier. Such recognition would have given access to the Jewish intelligentsia, which in many cases had mastered both languages. The new Polish state institutions sought to block the Yiddish intelligentsia from access to the new arena of power—the emerging state apparatus, along the lines of Hroch's paradigm. By curtailing the upper mobility of the Yiddish intelligentsia in the cities, where their demographic presence was significant, the new urban professions of the nascent state apparatus could be reserved exclusively for the monolingual Polish intelligentsia.

However, not all members of the Yiddish-speaking community became bilingual. Quite the contrary, a large proportion probably did not,[120] and had to communicate with the newly formed state bureaucracy in Polish, a language only partially comprehensible to them. Approaching the authorities from a disadvantaged position, and using a non-societal language, they ended up in an inferior position even at the most basic practical level, with all the feelings of humiliation involved. Incompetence in the societal language gradually became a variable in hampering the social mobility of the Yiddish-speaking population. This obstacle would empower the Polish rural population, who were migrating to the cities at the time, while disabling the Jews, who were also moving to the cities then, or were already there.

The alternative offered by the authorities—permitting Yiddish in the traditional Jewish education system with a degree of exposure to the Polish language—was yet another means to control access to the new 'state nobility'. The traditional Jewish school system was less perceptive about the principle of equal treatment independent of ethno-linguistic attributions, an idea considered subversive by the new authorities because of its ethno-nationalistic paradigm. Moreover, the

some non-Jewish circles. See e.g. K. Radziszewska and K. Woźniak (eds.), *Pod jednym dachem: Niemcy oraz ich polscy i żydowscy sąsiedzi w Łodzi w XIX i XX wieku / Unter einem Dach: Die Deutschen und ihre polnischen und jüdischen Nachbarn in Lodz im 19. und 20. Jahrhundert* (Łódź, 2000), 127, 138. On social interaction between Jews and non-Jews in nineteenth-century Łódź which demonstrated other forms of bilingualism, see F. Guesnet, *Lodzer Juden im 19. Jahrhundert: Ihr Ort in einer multikulturellen Stadtgesellschaft* (Leipzig, 1997).

[119] Bourdieu, *La Noblesse d'état*.

[120] For a statistical analysis of the languages used by Jews based on the census of 1931, following over a decade of Polonization efforts by the state, see Y. Leshtshinski [J. Lestschinsky], 'Di shprakhn bay yidn in umophengikn poyln: an analiz loyt der folkstseylung fun 1931', *YIVO-bleter*, 22 (1943), 147–62.

traditional Jewish school system was less able to generate a 'state nobility', and as such did not constitute a source of competition with the Polish elite. Besides, it was a logical outcome to refuse the recognition of the modern network that might develop during the German occupation. Modern education could give students access to bodies of knowledge that could endanger the ethno-national vision of 'the new Poland' of the appointed Polish authorities. The same logic lay behind the underdeveloping of the Polish-language elementary education for Jews, its under-budgeting, and the discrimination against it.[121]

The alternative of assimilation was far from dependent on individual decisions, as access to the ranks of the ruling nation was not automatic. On the one hand, the Provisional Council was aware of the need to open the state apparatus to some educated members of the ethnic minorities,[122] yet it feared too large a mass of such candidates moving up from the lower linguistic strata into the mainstream and competing with the state nobility, as Przeździecki observed.[123] The minorities, therefore, were channelled to a peripheral out-group status even if they assimilated the dominant state culture.

In summary, the uneven division of the mother-tongue resource between the various ethnic groups in Congress Poland facilitated the formation of a social structure and a social hierarchy that the emerging Polish administration viewed as desirable. Their preoccupation with the distribution of this resource reflected a per-ceived threat posed by the Jewish minority, and especially by its Yiddish intelli-gentsia, which they viewed as undermining the ethno-national hegemony they sought to entrench and threatening the very legitimacy of the model of the state in formation. This was reflected not only in decisions of the Provisional Council regarding the structure of society and the distribution of salaries, but, more broadly, in the establishment of a hegemonic cultural capital. The policy established by the new Polish administrative authorities regarding selective linguistic recogni-tion allowed them to keep the Jewish minority from gaining access to positions that would enable them to undermine the existing order and use their status in the urban social structure to enter the political hierarchy. Simultaneously, the language policy was a tool used by the vulnerable Polish leadership in an attempt to insulate society from the infiltration of subversive ideas not only of the left wing, but involving civic notions of citizenship present even within the Polish national movement itself.

The legal system shaped by the Polish leadership, in seeking to give preference to the cultural capital of the Polish majority, tried thereby to curb the access of the Yiddish intelligentsia to the state nobility, or block any step that might enhance its position in Polish society. This was the reasoning behind its refusal to grant edu-cational autonomy to the Jews.

---

[121] CZA, A127/386: 'Wyciąg ze stenogramu posiedzenia rady m. st. Warszawy dn. 24 czerwca 1918 r.'

[122] Suleja, *Tymczasowa Rada Stanu*, 172–9; APKr, NKN, Szg. 11: Sprawy oświaty, 27 Feb. 1917.

[123] AAN, TRS, Akt 7, Sprawy Samorządowe, 5 Mar. 1917.

The Yiddish intelligentsia was bent on attaining rights for the Jewish minority, which would secure its status in the society and consequently establish its role in the political hierarchy. However, they were confronted with a special problem which they could not overcome: that these very demands worsened their already inferior political status vis-à-vis the Polish majority. The emerging state, by refusing to grant rights to the Jewish minority, would thus be able to give preference to the favoured element of society, which was in competition with the Jews. In the absence of a central government that might have shown an interest in cultivating the multi-national and multilingual aspect of the country, the Jewish population faced a cruel paradox. The combination of their urban lifestyle, specialization in occupations that were suitable to the new economy, and middleman social stratification, along with a distinctive cultural identity and a condition of political weakness, resulted in tragic, if well-known outcomes at the end of the First World War.

PART II

New Views

The Anti-Favus Campaign in Poland

Jewish Social Medicine

RAKEFET ZALASHIK

Parekh has existed among the Jews for so long already. It has spread, and we have all encountered it, and we are all familiar with this horrible disease, which covers the heads of the children and scars them for the rest of their lives. The children are laughed at and mocked because they look like monkeys. People distance themselves from them, and they are isolated and ashamed of their disease. And this feeling leaves in the children's souls the same trace as the disease on their heads.[1]

INTRODUCTION

Parekh was the popular name given to favus in Yiddish, indicating the centrality of the disease in the daily life of east European Jewry.[2] Favus ('honeycomb' in Latin), *tinea favosa*, is a dermatological lesion caused by a fungus. Another very similar disease is ringworm, in which various Tinea species damage the scalp. The two affected mainly children and young adults. In the nineteenth century, the mycotic aetiology of these skin infections was discovered. First, in 1837, the Polish physician Robert Remak, working at the University of Berlin, located hyphae in the crusts of the disease known as favus. In 1841, the Hungarian physician David Gruby went further, and discovered several different types of dermatophyte infections.[3] For decades, the treatment of favus was based on a painful, manual epilation of the hair and the application of various topical medications on the bald scalp, such as iodine, thallium salts, and nitrate of mercury. When it became evident that exposure to X-rays caused human hair to fall out, it was used also to treat favus and ringworm. X-ray epilation was introduced by Raymond Sabouraud in 1904,[4] and standardized by Robert Kienböck in 1907 and Horatio George Adamson in

---

[1] K.A., 'Favus (parekh) un der kamf kegn im', *Folks-gezunt*, 1923, no. 1, col. 21.

[2] A common insult among east European Jews was 'A yid, a parekh'. A colloquial term for a Jew in Polish was *parch*, 'scab', e.g. 'ty parchu!' ('you Jew!').

[3] L. Ajello, 'Natural History of the Dermatophytes and Related Fungi', *Mycopathologia et Mycologia Applicata*, 53 (1974), 93–110.

[4] 'Dr. Sabouraud's Address on the X-Ray Treatment of Ringworm', *Medical Electrology and Radiology*, 7/6 (1906), 121–2; G. Sichel, 'The X-Ray Treatment of Ringworm', *British Medical Journal*, 1906, no. 1, pp. 256–7.

1910.[5] X-ray therapy for favus and ringworm was widely adopted and was seen as a fast and safe method until the end of the 1950s.[6] It was only years later that a connection between X-ray irradiation of the scalp and cancer of the skin and brain was found, when an abnormal prevalence of such tumours was diagnosed in adults who were irradiated as children.[7]

Because of the visual manifestation of the disease, namely pinhead to pea-sized friable, umbilicate, yellow crusts, favus and ringworm have been related to other 'loathsome' diseases, such as trachoma, parasitic infections, and venereal diseases. Despite the relatively benign course of the disease, individuals who suffered from these ailments were highly stigmatized by society and, in the nineteenth and twentieth centuries in both Europe and the United States, the diseases were related to poverty and 'backwardness'.[8]

In the east European Jewish context, favus and ringworm were seen by Jewish physicians as a 'Jewish disease', common among deprived, poor, and ignorant Jews of the shtetl who did not undergo processes of enlightenment and neglected basic bodily hygiene. And indeed, in the 1920s, especially in towns and cities, poor east European Jews did live in crowded conditions, in small apartments, where the air was heavy and humid, and where they lacked basic hygiene.[9]

In a survey conducted by the Tsysho schools of the Polish Jewish Bund on the conditions of their pupils, it was found that 30 per cent of the families, with an average number of six members to a family, lived in one room; 25 per cent had but one window in their home; and only 8 per cent of the pupils had a bed all to themselves.[10] Many Jewish children in eastern Europe suffered from favus and ringworm of the scalp and some estimates even spoke about 26 per cent of Russian Jewish children suffering from favus.[11] According to a survey carried out in 1921 by Dr Irvin Michelin, there were 17,500 cases of favus in Poland.[12] Also, reports of

---

[5] R. Kienböck, 'Über Radiotherapie der Haarerkrankungen', *Archiv für Dermatologie und Syphilis*, 83 (1907), 77–111; H. G. Adamson, 'A Simplified Method of X Ray Application for the Cure of Ringworm of the Scalp: Kienböck's Method', *Lancet*, 173 (1909), 1378–80.

[6] M. E. Mottram and H. A. Hill, 'Radiation Therapy of Ringworm of the Scalp', *California Medicine*, 70/3 (1949), 189–93.

[7] R. E. Shore et al., 'Skin Cancer Incidence among Children Irradiated for Ringworm of the Scalp', *Radiation Research*, 100/1 (1984), 192–204; R. E. Shore et al., 'Skin Cancer after X-Ray Treatment for Scalp Ringworm', *Radiation Research*, 157/4 (2002), 410–18.

[8] On stigmatized diseases and the labelling of their subjects, see E. Goffman, *Stigma: Notes on the Management of Spoiled Identity* (Englewood Cliffs, NJ, 1963).

[9] S. E. Aschheim, *Brothers and Strangers: The East European Jew in German and German Jewish Consciousness, 1800–1923* (Madison, 1982); H. Markel, *Quarantine! East European Jewish Immigrants and the New York City Epidemics of 1892* (Baltimore, 1997).

[10] M. R. Eisenstein, *Jewish Schools in Poland, 1919–39: Their Philosophy and Development* (New York, 1950), 24.   [11] *Die Enstehung der Gesellschaft OSE und ihre ersten Massnahmen* (Berlin, 1925), 7.

[12] Of these, 3,000 cases were in Warsaw, 2,000 from elsewhere in Congress Poland, 2,500 in Vilna, 2,500 in Równe, 2,000 in Białystok, 2,000 in Brześć, 2,000 in Lwów, and 1,500 in Kraków. JDC Archives, New York, Dr J. J. Golub Collection (hereafter Golub Collection), Medico-Sanitary Department, Warsaw, 1921: report of Medical Commission Conference, Warsaw, 5 Dec. 1921, pp. 12–13.

the Society for the Protection of the Health of the Jews (Obshchestvo zdravook-hraneniya evreev; OZE) from across eastern Europe described the high rates of favus and ringworm among children, especially boys: only 20 per cent of patients were girls.[13] To mention just a few numbers: in Lithuania in 1922, 21 per cent of Jewish children were infected with ringworm;[14] in Bessarabia, 10,000 children with ringworm were counted by Jewish messengers;[15] and in Białystok and Vilna, one out of every six children in Jewish religious schools had favus, and in some cases whole schools were infected.[16]

During the period of mass emigration at the turn of the twentieth century, favus and ringworm belonged to the category of diseases that could, when detected, prevent east European Jewish immigrants from entering countries such as Canada and the United States.[17] Thus, the extent and the implications of favus turned it into a public health problem, a social disease akin to trachoma and tuberculosis, which confronted both east European communities and their brethren in western Europe and the United States.[18]

This study focuses on the anti-favus campaign carried out in Poland in the 1920s by the Society for the Protection of the Health of the Jews (OZE), the Society for the Protection of the Health of the Jewish Population in Poland (Towarzystwo Ochrony Zdrowia Ludności Żydowskiej w Polsce; TOZ), and the American Jewish Joint Distribution Committee ('the Joint', or JDC for short).[19] This was the first campaign conducted by these bodies and its success was the springboard for future collaborations between local Jewish medical organizations and the JDC. The infrastructure created for the anti-favus campaign consolidated TOZ and OZE in Poland as the central body that took care of the health of the Jews in the country and eventually dictated a long-term relationship between OZE/TOZ and the JDC. The anti-favus campaign was a starting point for wider hygienic reforms, not only because of the need to create local committees and to engage qualified medical staff, but also thanks to the establishment of nursing schools to spread education on

---

[13]   This difference was explained by contemporaries by the fact that boys were wearing hats, making the ground for fungus cultivation very comfortable, and by the fact that girls washed their hair more often and were in general cleaner. L. Wulman, *Tsen yor yidishe gezuntshuts-arbet in poyln: zum 10-yorikn yubiley fun toz* (Warsaw, 1933), 21.

[14]   *Die Entstehung der Gesellschaft OSE und ihre ersten Massnahmen*, 12.   [15]   Ibid. 14.

[16]   L. Wulman, 'OSE—its Achievements and Plans for the Post-War Period', *Harofé Haivri: The Hebrew Medical Journal*, 17th year (1944).

[17]   A. M. Kraut, *Silent Travelers: Germs, Genes, and the 'Immigrant Menace'* (Baltimore, 1995), 236–41.

[18]   E. Lederhendler, *Jewish Immigrants and American Capitalism, 1880–1920: From Caste to Class* (Cambridge, 2009), ch. 1; H. R. Diner, 'A Century of Migration, 1820–1924', in ead., *The Jews of the United States, 1654 to 2000* (Berkeley and Los Angeles, 2004), 71–111.

[19]   Founded in November 1914, the JDC is a non-political organization dedicated to helping Jews in distress all over the world. For an overview of its origins and history, see T. Schachtman, *I Seek my Brethren: Ralph Goldman and 'The Joint'. Rescue, Relief and Reconstruction—the Work of the American Jewish Joint Distribution Committee* (New York, 2001), 1–12.

hygiene and to the creation of other medical facilities in Poland. These needs evolved during the anti-favus campaign, revealing the necessity for the JDC to support a long-term and much wider campaign of preventive medicine.

Nevertheless, the campaign exposed constant tensions between OZE/TOZ and the JDC regarding aims, purposes, and roles. Whereas the JDC planned to give focused, limited help for this contagious ailment, OZE and TOZ saw this campaign as an opening for real reform in the field of hygiene among Jews in eastern Europe. The JDC wished to import the American social gospel to eastern Europe; although OZE and TOZ shared ideas of social and preventive medicine, they did not so quickly or unconditionally adopt this plan.

OZE and TOZ's double position as the beneficiary of Jewish American philanthropy—which demanded that they become self-sufficient—and as the benefactor of local Jewry—which demanded that local Jews become self-sufficient too—created social tensions between local agencies and the supporters of the anti-favus campaign. These tensions revolved around issues of class, medical authority, stigma, and the medicalization of Jews.

OZE/TOZ AND THE JDC

OZE was originally established in October 1912 in St Petersburg by Jewish physicians and prominent Jewish figures. Concerns about the status of Jews as a minority and professional worries motivated them to address the special health problems of Jews in the Russian empire, which were understood to be the result of poverty and poor hygiene. As Dr Moisey Gran, one of its founders, said: 'Jewry has been subjected in the course of its millennial history to varied and complex experiences . . . which manifested many weaknesses and unhealthy features when regarded from the viewpoint of hygiene, features demanding attention and special treatment.'[20] This was to be carried out by the implementation of Jewish social medicine, as another founder physician of OZE, Dr M. Schwarzman, clarified: 'Jewish public health must be fundamentally connected with other needs of Jewish life, it must be systematized, co-ordinated, and must base itself on a scientific study of the specific characteristics of the physical type and the nervous and mental constitutions of the Jews.'[21]

The goals of OZE, then, were to conduct research on contemporary health and social problems among the Jews and to improve their physical conditions by offering treatment and by seeking to gain control over public health facilities and services within the Jewish community.[22] More specifically, it wished to fight tuberculosis, reduce infant mortality, improve sanitary conditions in Jewish religious

[20] Quoted in Wulman, 'OSE—its Achievements and Plans for the Post-War Period', 185.
[21] Dr Schwarzman at the OZE conference in 1912, quoted ibid. 186.
[22] L. Epstein, 'Health and Healing', in G. D. Hundert (ed.), *The YIVO Encyclopedia of Jews in Eastern Europe*, 2 vols. (New Haven, 2008), i. 697.

schools, supervise Jewish rituals from a hygienic point of view, and carry out medical examinations and care of potential Jewish emigrants to America.[23]

OZE operated on the principles of social medicine and preventive medicine. Social medicine emerged as a concept during the nineteenth century in conjunction with the concept of nation-states and as part of health and social reforms in Germany and France which were concerned with developing the political role of medicine in creating egalitarian societies.[24] Social medicine articulated the fact that economic and social conditions have an impact on health and disease, and since the health of a population is a matter of social concern, societies should be responsible for promoting health through individual treatment and social means.[25] The idea of preventive medicine was based on the rationale that many diseases and social problems can be prevented if necessary means are taken on the individual and collective levels, including vaccinations, physical education, nutrition, etc. According to both ideas, health and illness are not only private concerns, but also public issues, and in the context of OZE's activities 'Jewish diseases' were a national issue.

During the First World War, OZE teamed up with the Jewish Committee for the Relief of Victims of War (Evreiskii komitet pomoshchi zhertvam voiny; EKOPO), organizing medical and sanitary relief and caring for orphaned and abandoned children, as well as transporting 40,000 refugees from various parts of Russia and operating hospitals, homes for the aged, soup kitchens, and orphanages.[26] Much of the activity of OZE during the war was financed by the JDC.

The JDC began to work in Warsaw in 1919, first as part of the American Relief Administration and then independently, organizing sanitary and medical aid, as well as child care. In 1918, OZE established a local branch in Poland. In 1919, OZE was banned in Russia, and it moved its headquarters to Berlin in 1922.[27] In 1921 TOZ was formed as a separate yet related organization.[28] It operated as a nation-

---

[23] This was realized through collaboration with Emigdirekt, an organization that helped Jews from eastern Europe to emigrate, mainly to the United States, by providing information about the immigration procedures, by helping them to learn new professions, and so on.

[24] G. Rosen, 'What Is Social Medicine? A Genetic Analysis of the Concept', *Bulletin of the History of Medicine*, 21 (1947), 674–733; D. Porter and R. Porter, 'What Was Social Medicine? An Historiographical Essay', *Journal of Historical Sociology*, 1 (1988), 90–106.

[25] See G. Rosen, *From Medical Police to Social Medicine: Essays on the History of Health Care* (New York, 1974).

[26] S. Zipperstein, 'The Politics of Relief: The Transformation of Russian Jewish Communal Life during the First World War', in J. Frankel, P. Y. Medding, and E. Mendelsohn (eds.), *Studies in Contemporary Jewry*, iv: *The Jews and the European Crisis, 1914–1921* (Jerusalem, 1988), 30.

[27] The organization in Russia was closed down partly because of problems with the Soviet regime and partly because of disagreements with the leadership of Jewish local communities (*kehilot*) that had gained autonomy under Soviet rule. See N. Shtif, 'Di tsen-yorike geshikhte fun "oze"', *Folks-gezunt*, 1923, no. 1 (suppl.), pp. 2–3.

[28] In Berlin OZE and TOZ functioned under one umbrella. In 1926 they united and operated for one year under the name OZE-TOZ. In 1927, TOZ took over the OZE institutions in Poland and Lithuania.

wide body, which could co-ordinate programmes, centralize information, supervise and control activities, raise funds, and receive funds from foreign relief agencies.[29]

Both OZE and TOZ operated on principles that promoted sanitary medical action through education, research, and propaganda.[30] The JDC, on its side, wanted to transfer 'American' liberalism and progressivism to the European context through science, the management of projects, and the rebuilding of Jewish communities. After July 1921, the JDC ceased giving general relief to the east European Jews and reorganized its work around the principle of functionality. This showed a transition from relief to constructive work and included two stages: first, identifying the problems and the needs of the local population through surveys and scientific investigations; and second, developing programmes specifically addressing these needs, conditioned by the co-operation of local agencies. The JDC sent a medical commission of eighteen medical professionals to Poland to obtain first-hand information about the health problems of the Jews and to locate professionals and a leadership that could carry out the programme.[31] Beginning in 1921, its medical department developed systematic means of fighting epidemics and supported OZE and TOZ, which gradually built up an effective system of health services for the Jewish population.[32]

PREPARING THE WAR AGAINST FAVUS

The idea to focus on favus had already occurred to the JDC in 1920. Dr Charles Spivak, the JDC special commissioner for health and sanitation, who toured Poland in 1920, wrote in his report that 'the eradication of favus in Poland will be the greatest boon to mankind and will be of lasting credit to the JDC'.[33] In other reports, the JDC explained that the fight against favus could improve the status of Jews in eastern Europe, describing the stigma related to the disease that should be overcome to allow Jews to emigrate more easily to Western countries. The focus on stigmatized diseases among east European Jews also has to be understood within the context of the self-image of American Jewry since the nineteenth century: American Jews focused on the stigmatized diseases of their east European brethren in part as a reflection of their desire to support the new immigrants and to keep immigration open, yet at the same time they concerned themselves with these medical issues because of their own anxiety in America and their desire to achieve

[29] Other Jewish medical organizations included Linat Hatsedek, Linat Holim, Bikur Holim, Tomekhei Holim, Ezrat Holim, and Beriut.   [30] Shtif, 'Di tsen-yorike geshikhte fun "oze"', 1.

[31] J. J. Golub, 'The J.D.C. and Health Programs in Eastern Europe', *Jewish Social Studies*, 5/3 (1943), 294–5.

[32] On the implementation of this pattern of operation in Lithuania, see R. Zalashik and N. Davidovitch, 'Taking and Giving: The Case of the JDC and OZE in Lithuania, 1919–26', *East European Jewish Affairs*, 39/1 (2009), 57–68.

[33] Golub Collection, Medico-Sanitary Department: confidential report from Dr Spivak to Dr Julius Goldman, 13 Apr. 1920, p. 18.

integration.[34] Moreover, from the First World War onwards, American Jews worked with west European Jews in order to reform east European Jews.

To fight favus in Poland, the JDC appointed in 1921 the Viennese Jewish anthropologist and physician Ignaz Zollschan (1877–1948) as the head of the X-ray division of the Medico-Sanitary Department of the JDC in Warsaw. Zollschan was one of the pioneers of radiology and was involved in organizing health services in the Polish capital. However, in January 1922, Zollschan quit his position,[35] clearing the stage for Dr Vladimir Altman, who originally was appointed as his assistant radiologist.[36] For Altman, the mission was clear:

> The aim is the practical eradication of favus, which is endemic among the Jewish population. That such eradication is possible is scientifically proved. The previous attempts in Paris and Hamburg to fight epidemics of *herpes tonsurans* [ringworm of the hair] with the same means were successful. It is worth noting that favus, with its much less contagious nature, would be much easier to fight.[37]

Yet for Altman, the infectiousness of the disease, even though it was lower than that of ringworm, meant that the success of the campaign depended on urgently solving the problem of consistency of action and unification of all organizational work. The campaign must move systematically from one area of Poland to another.

The preliminary plan of the JDC was to open X-ray stations in eight big cities in Poland with large Jewish populations—Warsaw, Łódź, Kraków, Lwów, Równe, Brest, Białystok, and Vilna—and some outside Poland in Riga, Kaunas, and Kishinev, to which children from the provinces would also be sent by parents and local medical professionals for treatment. At the same time, propaganda about the importance of the campaign was to be spread in Jewish newspapers, by flyers, and through leading figures in Jewish communities, such as rabbis and teachers, who were a source of authority and came into contact with many members, and also by public health nurses.[38] The JDC also planned to train X-ray specialists and dermatological favus nurses, who would travel from place to place, gather infected children, inspect Jewish homes, and educate Jews about hygiene.[39] Administratively, the operation was to be supervised by a central Anti-Favus Committee, and carried out by a hierarchy of committees in each district and province.[40]

The JDC assigned a total of $100,000 for the anti-favus campaign in Poland and

[34] G. Sorin, *The Jewish People in America*, iii: *A Time for Building: The Third Migration, 1880–1920* (Baltimore, 1992).

[35] Golub Collection, 371, Medical, Favus, 1922: letter from JDC to Altman, 4 Feb. 1922.

[36] Ibid.: letter from Waldman to Altman, 16 Nov. 1921.   [37] Ibid.: 'Allgemeine Plan der Aktion'.

[38] JDC Archives, 372, countries, Poland, Medical: letter no. 105, Dr Z. Syrkin to the direction of the Medico-Sanitary Department of the JDC, subject: Program for Public Health Education among Jews in Poland, 14 Dec. 1921.

[39] Golub Collection, 371, Medical, Favus, 1922: Vladimir Altman, 'Plan der Favusaktion', pp. 2, 4, 10–11.

[40] The Anti-Favus Committee comprised Dr Judt, Dr Markusfeld, Dr Sterling, Dr Wortman, and Dr Blay.

in other parts of eastern Europe: $80,000 for Poland (of which $24,000 was for the central offices in Warsaw and $8,000 for each of the other districts), and the rest for other countries.[41] In return, it expected the Jewish activists and population in Poland to mobilize fully to fight favus. As Morris Waldman, the director of organization of the work of the JDC, expressed it in a meeting with the local members of the special favus committee which took place on 19 May 1922 in Warsaw:

the people in America had done their share of help by raising sufficient funds and that $100,000 were assigned to this anti-Favus campaign, naturally to be carried out not only for Poland, but all over Europe. There was no reasons [*sic*] why there should be Favus in Poland any more than in Austria or Germany and it was felt that the local people should do their share in assuming the responsibility to do all possible to eradicate Favus from Poland.[42]

Besides the obvious attempts to promote Jewish self-improvement based on the Western model borrowed from assimilated and acculturated Jews in German-speaking countries,[43] the JDC's demand that Polish Jews take responsibility for their own health expressed a conceptual shift from help of the needy to self-help, which had begun to characterize twentieth-century philanthropy. In many ways, this shift perceived philanthropy as an investment: it had a limited duration, it aimed to stimulate self-help, and recipients had to prove they were capable of using the donation properly.[44]

One of the JDC's main operating principles was to build strategic alliances with other organizations that would take over responsibility for what the JDC helped to start. The natural partners in Poland were OZE and its local branch TOZ, which engaged in medical activity and hygiene education. In a meeting with TOZ members on 15 May 1922, Samuel Myer Schmidt, the assistant medical director of the JDC in Warsaw, stated that

we have now reached a point where we want to turn the work of [the] anti-Favus campaign to the local people, so that the local people will assume entire responsibility for the further organization and carrying on of this activity. While, up to now, the present local Favus Committee acted more or less in an advisory capacity to the JDC and the JDC organized the work and took the necessary steps to set the work in motion, we now want that the local people should actually carry on the work themselves and assume all responsibilities.[45]

Shneur Zalman Bychowski, a known Jewish neurologist, who was one of the TOZ Anti-Favus Committee members in its first days, thanked Schmidt for the trust that the JDC expressed in the local organization.[46]

---

[41] Golub Collection, 371, Medical, Favus, 1922: minutes of meeting of Anti-Favus Committee, 26 Sept. 1922, p. 1.   [42] Ibid.: extract of minutes of meeting held in Warsaw, 19 May 1922, p. 2.

[43] See Aschheim, *Brothers and Strangers*.

[44] J. Farley, *To Cast Out Disease: A History of the International Health Division of the Rockefeller Foundation (1913–1951)* (New York, 2004), 4.

[45] Golub Collection, 371, Medical, Favus, 1922: extract of minutes of meeting held in Warsaw, 19 May 1922, p. 1.

[46] Ibid. On Bychowski's work on 'Jewish diseases', see R. Falk, 'Nervous Diseases and Eugenics of the Jews: A View from 1918', *Korot*, 17 (2003–4), 23–46.

Trust, good will, and even the purchase of X-ray machines were not enough, however. According to the agreement between the two bodies offered by the JDC, the X-ray machines were the property of the JDC and were only lent out to TOZ for one year—the time period within which the anti-favus campaign should have been accomplished. The JDC representative was to work with local committees: all resolutions had to be accepted by this representative; the plan had to be carried out in co-operation with the representative; and the representative had to be the first person to whom the various committees appealed when they needed advice.[47] These terms were not fully accepted by the TOZ Anti-Favus Committee. First, they wanted the X-ray stations and the machines to remain in the hands of TOZ. The rationale was that since they were responsible for the entire campaign, they could not afford a situation in which the JDC would be able to take away the machines after only one year. Second, and more importantly, they determined that it was technically and epidemiologically impossible to accomplish the anti-favus campaign within one year.[48]

This dispute shows that the pattern of relations between the JDC and TOZ, between the philanthropists and the beneficiaries, was not so predictable and obvious. The fact that TOZ had space to negotiate indicates that the dependency was not solely one-sided. At least officially, TOZ was not willing to get involved in the campaign or to receive JDC money at any price. They wanted to negotiate the conditions of their agreement in order to maximize their sovereignty and independence as a local organization, or simply to protect themselves. Moreover, the dispute reflected the different roles each body had in this shared initiative: while the JDC had the money, the TOZ people had the local connections, and this was the basis on which they negotiated.

In August 1922, Altman contacted the JDC and complained that more than thirty employees at the X-ray division, including physicians and nurses, had not received their salaries because TOZ refused to spend the budget until its relationship with the JDC had been clarified. Under such circumstances, Altman warned, he could not continue his services.[49] In October of that year, the JDC agreed that TOZ could own the X-ray machines, and the full operation of the stations was formally transferred to the hands of TOZ.[50] Altman and the X-ray division were now the employees of TOZ.

Structurally, the role of various bodies and committees, as well as their spheres of authority, also needed to be clarified. The JDC gave the budget for the anti-favus campaign to TOZ in Poland and appointed it to be responsible for the entire campaign in all aspects. The budget was to cover the costs of the X-ray machines,

[47] Golub Collection, 371, Medical, Favus, 1922: letter from Altman to the director of the Medico-Sanitary Department, Warsaw, 'Organization of Favus Work', 15 May 1922.

[48] Ibid.: letter from TOZ Warsaw to the Medico-Sanitary Department of the JDC, 24 July 1922.

[49] Ibid.: letter from Altman to Schmidt, 'Schwierigkeiten in der Leitung der Favus-Aktion', 17 Aug. 1922, p. 2.   [50] Ibid.: letter from Golub to Alex Stawski, Councillor at Law, 17 Oct. 1922.

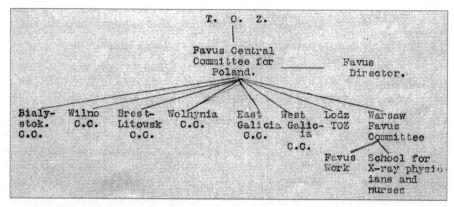

Figure 1. An organizational diagram prepared by Dr Jacob Golub: report of the second
meeting of the Favus Central Committee in Warsaw, 18 October 22.
JDC Archives, New York, Dr J. J. Golub Collection, 371, Medical, Favus, 1922

salaries for the administrative staff, rent for facilities, the maintenance of dormi-
tories for children who were coming from the provinces, ambulatory stations,
salaries for medical professionals, medications, and travelling expenses for nurses
and children. TOZ was responsible for the yet-to-be-established nursing school,
the Favus Central Committee (the Anti-Favus Committee), and popular hygiene.
The Favus Central Committee was in charge of the Executive Committee, which in
turn supervised the eight districts and all anti-favus activity. In addition to favus
work, the Warsaw district was also responsible for the Physicians' and Nurses'
School for dermatological, X-ray, and favus training (see Figure 1).

PROBLEMS OF IMPLEMENTATION

The campaign progressed at a relatively quick pace. In May 1922, X-ray machines
were brought from the Reiniger firm in Erlangen in Germany and from Siemens
in Vienna, and were assembled by specialists sent from the manufacturers. One
machine was put in a space rented from the Jewish community building at 19
Leszno Street in Warsaw. The other was placed at the Poznański Jewish hospital in
Łódź.[51] Another machine was brought to Riga, where two hundred children
underwent treatment, thanks to the qualified personnel at the station.[52] In August,
an X-ray machine was transferred to Dr Levin Gershon in Vilna and was put in the
hospital of OZE.[53] Already at the beginning of August, four patients per day were
being treated at the X-ray station in Warsaw, and the dermatological ambulatories

[51]   Golub Collection, 371, Medical, Favus, 1922: letter from Altman to Schmidt, 5 May 1922. The
Poznański Jewish hospital was built in 1885–90 by the Jewish industrialist and philanthropist Izrael
Poznański.   [52] Ibid.: letter from Altman to Michelin, 9 May 1922.
[53]   Ibid.: letter from Altman to JDC, 3 Aug. 1922.

in the city, which examined children's scalps, were also functioning. By the end of October, all the anti-favus stations nationwide were operating. They had examined 1,082 individuals, identified 138 for irradiation, and irradiated 313.[54] By the end of 1922, the first year of the campaign, 6,100 children in all had been cured.[55]

The campaign against favus and ringworm was an enormous logistical undertaking and was probably the biggest campaign against these ailments in the interwar period. The extent of the campaign and its complexity, as well as the poor, underdeveloped infrastructure, created various difficulties. The problem was not only the waiting for missing equipment, but also the lack of qualified and specialized personnel. In order to train medical staff to carry out the anti-favus campaign, TOZ established courses in Warsaw for physicians and nurses in roentgenology, dermatology, and hygiene. They were trained by Dr Sterling and Dr Markusfeld, both members of the Anti-Favus Committee. The training for nurses was four to eight weeks, and later they were sent to the provinces to support post-irradiation treatment and to spread propaganda on hygiene.[56] Since there were no local specialists in radiology, the lectures were given in German and were translated by the assistant physicians into Polish.[57]

Another problem was of communication between the main offices in Warsaw and other local committees, especially in the provinces,[58] and the systematic unity of operation in each of the districts, which was important from both a bureaucratic and administrative point of view and also a scientific one. Since OZE and TOZ were not only medical aid organizations, but also promoted research on the health of the Jews, their medical activity had to be systematized and documented. At a meeting of the Anti-Favus Committee held on 26 September 1922, 'in order to collect statistical data of the entire anti-favus action, the meeting decided to take the registration card of the Warsaw station as a model for individual stations, and to fill it out in Polish, or if needed in Polish and Yiddish'.[59] The decision to use Polish as the formal language on the registration cards indicates both the Polonization of the Jews and the way TOZ perceived itself and the anti-favus campaign: not only as an internal Jewish initiative, but as a national organization that was conducting a national campaign integral to general Polish society.

TOZ members had not predicted the nature of the main problem that the campaign was to face.[60] This was the lack of co-operation of the Jewish public. At a

[54] Ibid.: report on X-ray activities for October 1922.

[55] Golub, 'J.D.C. and Health Programs in Eastern Europe', 302; JDC Archives, 369, countries, Poland, Medical, TOZ: report from Golub to Kahn, 28 Sept. 1923.

[56] Golub Collection, 371, Medical, Favus, 1922: letter from Altman to Judt, 30 Aug. 1922.

[57] Ibid.: letter from Altman to Schmidt, 1 July 1922, p. 1.

[58] See letters from Syrkin to various bodies during September 1922: Golub Collection, 371, Medical, Favus, 1922: 'Organizacja akcji walki z favusem'.

[59] Golub Collection, 371, Medical, Favus, 1922: anti-favus TOZ meeting, 26 Sept. 1922.

[60] See, for example, a meeting in June at which it was decided after the installation of the X-ray machines to spread the information through flyers circulated among the 'houses of the poorest and

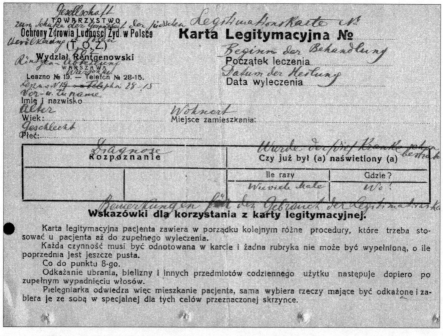

Figure 2. A patient registration card from the TOZ X-ray station in Warsaw.
JDC Archives, New York, Dr J. J. Golub Collection, 371, Medical, Favus, 1922

meeting of the Anti-Favus Committee that took place at the end of 1922, the topic
of the means of propaganda was discussed at length and it led to some disagreement among TOZ members. Dr Altman and Dr Gershon, the heads of TOZ, spoke
about the need to train more nurses to conduct door-to-door propaganda and to
locate potential children for dermatological examination. Dr Blay argued that this
would be a waste of money and instead suggested distributing flyers among poor
Jews and using the daily press to circulate information about the anti-favus
campaign. Dr Sophia Syrkin, the head of the education department in TOZ,
agreed with the former, claiming that Jews were not reading the flyers and that they
remained indifferent to written information. She said that the nurses must find
patients; otherwise, no one would apply for the treatment. She also argued that the
training of more nurses was essential for the success of the eradication of favus, not
only for propaganda purposes, but also for the maintenance of basic hygiene. Since
Jewish mothers had to work so hard, they did not have the time to deal with the

dirty Jewish streets' as well as in newspapers. Golub Collection, 371, Medical, Favus, 1922: Kommis-
sion zur Favusbekämpfung, TOZ, 6 June 1922. Retrospectively, Golub wrote in 1943: 'it was found that
ideas, practices and procedures brought from abroad were more readily accepted by the local people
when accompanied by attitudes and actions that were friendly, understanding and humble': Golub,
'J.D.C. and Health Programs in Eastern Europe', 296–7.

cleanliness of 'this child or another', and that was exactly what the job of the nurses should be.

In February 1923, the OZE committee published an announcement in their main popular newspaper in Yiddish, *Folks-gezunt* ('People's Health'), directed to 'the Jewish population from the area of Vilna, the administration of all Jewish organizations, communities, help committees, associations, societies, study halls [*batei midrash*], circles, which are active in the area of Vilna, to all the rabbis, teachers, civic activists, physicians, medical attendants, and midwives'.[61] In this announcement, they urged any sick people and their relatives or acquaintances to apply directly by letter to the OZE committee in Vilna or to talk to their community or to the committee of the shtetl to receive treatment against favus. In this announcement, the OZE committee also tried to encourage the rest of the population to take up their responsibility and to help with the favus campaign because of the contagious nature of the disease.[62]

Written propaganda that aimed to persuade the Jewish population in Poland to participate in the anti-favus campaign continued to appear in the newspaper's pages over the next few years. In 1924, Tsemakh Shabad, the head of OZE in Vilna and an important public and political Jewish figure, published an article entitled 'On Favus (*Parekh*)'. This article can be understood as a response to the general resistance of the Jewish population to treating favus, and perhaps even as a response to a certain resentment at the application of public health policies by a new Jewish organization such as TOZ.[63] In this article, common beliefs among the Jewish population about favus and its offered treatment were discussed. For example, apparently some Jewish parents believed that if a child had favus, he would not be drafted into the Polish army. Therefore, they did not send him for treatment. Another common belief was that X-ray treatment was dangerous (which was not yet known scientifically at the time), painful, and ineffective. It was believed that it did not fully cure the problem, and that the disease recurred. The last belief was that physicians and personnel in Poland lacked proper experience with the new treatment. Shabad concluded his article with a warning: 'Anyone who is not treated not only remains a cripple for his whole life, he also *remains infectious and brings misfortune on dozens of healthy people*—his sisters, brothers, and friends.'[64] Shabad's article indicates that favus was perceived as a real disability, which had to be treated not only because of the fate awaiting the individual, that is, becoming a 'cripple', but also because it endangered the patient's loved ones.

---

[61] Oze komitet, 'Vegn oysrotn di krankait "parekh" bay yidn', *Folks-gezunt*, 1923, no. 2 (suppl.), p. 1.

[62] Ibid. 2.   [63] Ts. Shabad, 'Vegn favus (parekh)', *Folks-gezunt*, 1924, no. 6, cols. 158–60.

[64] Ibid. 160 (emphasis original).

HEALING OR ERADICATION?
THE FAVUS CAMPAIGN AS SPRINGBOARD

In October 1922, only a few weeks after the anti-favus campaign was launched in all eight districts, questions about the purpose and the extent of it emerged. Local committees reported to TOZ that, with the available infrastructure, they could not offer treatment to the masses, but just to a small proportion of sick children. Some localities reported that they irradiated three patients at a time in the X-ray room—a method that prolonged the duration of the irradiation, but which enabled them to treat more patients every day.[65] The atmosphere among TOZ and OZE activists involved in the campaign was somewhat sceptical about meeting the goals; if one wished to eradicate favus among Jewish children in Poland, not only to heal a number of sick, one needed extensive means for doing so.

Dr Altman estimated that to treat 30,000 favus patients in Poland would cost two-thirds of a million dollars. Clearly, the $80,000 the JDC allocated for the campaign in Poland was not enough. Moreover, he thought that favus was the smallest problem the poor Jewish population faced. For him, what could have brought real change was a reform in hygiene education. Dr Gershon explained that more money should be invested in buying better and more X-ray machines; without them, eradication was not possible.

Representatives of the JDC explained that, when collecting money from American Jewry and transferring it to TOZ, they had thought about healing and not about the total elimination of the disease among Jewish children in Poland.

These preliminary worries proved to be invalid by the end of the first year of the campaign. A report submitted by Jacob Golub to Dr Bernard Kahn, the director of the Medico-Sanitary Department in Vienna, in September 1923, said that previous estimations about the prevalence of favus were too high, and that it appeared the actual number of individuals who suffered from favus and ringworm was not 25,000, but probably between 15,000 and 18,000. During the first year of the anti-favus campaign, 6,000 children had been irradiated. The rest could be cured within a period of two years. The success of the campaign in its first year would lead to the closing down of X-ray stations in western Galicia (Kraków) and eastern Galicia (Lwów).[66]

CONCLUSION

The year 1922 and the pilot of the anti-favus campaign were very crucial to future collaboration between the JDC and TOZ, as well as for establishing OZE/TOZ as a

[65] Golub Collection, 371, Medical, Favus, 1922: II Sitzung des Favus-Zentralkomitees in Warschau, 18 Oct. 1922, p. 5.

[66] JDC Archives, 369, countries, Poland, Medical, TOZ: report from Golub to Kahn, 28 Sept. 1923, pp. 3–4.

national, central body responsible for the health of the Jews in Poland. The success of TOZ in operating the anti-favus campaign led the JDC to close down its Medico-Sanitary Department in Warsaw in September 1923 and to transfer all its activities into the hands of TOZ.[67] This toook place under an agreement by which

the responsibility involved in the examination, x-raying and treatment of patients as well as the administration of the stations falls upon the TOZ and that local organization which directly conducts and supervises each station. In no case does the Joint Distribution Committee bear any responsibility for diagnosis, x-raying, treatment or interning of patients at the stations and detension [*sic*] homes. TOZ obligates itself to work on a monthly budget-basis for all of its stations, coordinating the work of all the favus stations on a uniform system of treatment as well as administration, the uniform bookkeeping and reporting system should be continued . . . In the event that the TOZ should be liquidated within a period of five years from the date of this contract, the supplies, instruments, drugs, furniture, x-ray machines and equipment and balances of the Joint Distribution Committee moneys could not be turned over to any other organization nor sold or otherwise disposed of without the consent of the Joint Distribution Committee.[68]

The JDC was very optimistic about the ability of TOZ to take over the mission, clarifying that 'the outstanding feature of the new organization, as it is spreading throughout Poland is the manner in which it includes in its central body existing and chartered organizations of Wilno, Bialystok, and Lemberg, doing work in the medico-sanitary field would lead to good work'.[69] At this point, the JDC had no plans about the future of TOZ when all of the JDC's funding was used up. Before closing down the JDC offices in Warsaw, Golub wrote: 'Organizing a national health organization in Poland is at best an experiment, new in the history of Polish Jewry; and as in all new experiments it is difficult to prophesy the future of the TOZ at the time when the organization is to face the problem of existing on its own resources.'[70]

TOZ continued to exist in Nazi-occupied Poland until the liquidation of the ghettos. It renewed its activities among the survivors in the immediate aftermath of the Holocaust. The anti-favus campaign, which began in 1922 and continued until the outbreak of the Second World War, proved to be a big success. In the first ten years of the campaign, 17,049 children and adults were treated, and 80 per cent of them completely cured; in total, the anti-favus campaign cured 27,760 cases.[71] The importance of the campaign derived not only from turning favus and ringworm from common infectious diseases into almost non-existing ones, but also from the

---

[67] Ibid. 1.

[68] JDC Archives, 369, countries, Poland, Medical, TOZ: agreement between the JDC and TOZ Executive Committee, 1 Sept. 1923, pp. 4, 5.   [69] Ibid.

[70] JDC Archives, 369, countries, Poland, Medical, TOZ: report from Golub to Kahn, 28 Sept. 1923, p. 3.

[71] Wulman, 'OSE—its Achievements and Plans for the Post-War Period', 188; Golub, 'J.D.C. and Health Programs in Eastern Europe', 302.

fact that it introduced education in hygiene and remedial means such as isolation and treatment of infected children. It also reflected the emergence of schools of medicine and medical care for children, which previously did not exist in eastern Europe among either Jews or Gentiles.[72]

[72] Wulman, 'OSE—its Achievements and Plans for the Post-War Period'.

Władysław Raczkiewicz and Jewish Issues

JACEK PIOTROWSKI

WŁADYSŁAW RACZKIEWICZ, the head of the Polish government-in-exile during the Second World War, could not avoid confronting issues concerning Polish citizens of Jewish nationality. As his own origins were in the Eastern Borderlands (Kresy Wschodnie), which for centuries had been home to a large Jewish population, he was conscious of the importance of this challenge. The war exacerbated any problems he had already faced as a high state official. Although he did not play a major political role and delegated a large part of his constitutional powers to the pre-September opposition, he continued to exercise influence as a symbol of the continuity of the state.

Raczkiewicz was born in the Caucasus and grew up in tsarist Russia. Before the war, he held ministerial posts, was provincial governor several times, served as speaker of the Senate, and was president of the World Union of Poles outside Poland (Światowy Związek Polaków z Zagranicy). He had travelled widely. By the standards of the days, he was a person open to the world, cultivated and free of national or racial prejudices (albeit holding clearly conservative and aristocratic views), and was an engaging conversationalist. Some elements of his public activities related to the Jewish minority.

From the moment he took over the office of president-in-exile, he needed to establish new relations with Jews or people of Jewish origin. It is noteworthy that the key negotiations for the so-called 'Paris agreement', which opened up the path to the presidency for him, were conducted with the well-known national politician Stanisław Stroński, whose own mother was Jewish. Raczkiewicz's interlocutor was even supposed to become the prime minister, but ultimately the leaders of the pre-September opposition who formed the political power base of the new government decided that General Władysław Sikorski would serve more effectively in that position. In any event, Raczkiewicz held key talks about taking over the office of head of state and about forming a government that would include a person of Jewish origin who, paradoxically, had earlier been generally regarded in Poland as one of the leading politicians of the antisemitic right.[1]

[1] S. Stroński, *Polityka Rządu Polskiego na Uchodźstwie w latach 1939–1942*, ed. J. Piotrowski, 3 vols. (Nowy Sącz, 2007), i. 25–6.

A significant, albeit behind-the-scenes, role in these negotiations was played by Anatol Mühlstein, councillor at the Polish embassy in Paris, who was related by marriage to the Rothschilds.[2] Mühlstein hoped to be granted the portfolio of Minister of Foreign Affairs. During the political contest between supporters of Józef Piłsudski and the pre-September opposition, Mühlstein used his social and political contacts among Frenchmen of Jewish origin. In negotiations to determine the shape of the Polish government-in-exile, he proved to be of great service to the opposition that aimed to take over the government:

They beg me to delay the French acceptance, in order to allow negotiations with Raczkiewicz to go ahead . . . I rush to see Champetier de Ribes. The minister tells me that he happens to be waiting for Łukasiewicz [the Polish ambassador in Paris]. I have arrived there first. Lucky coincidence. I introduce my proposal. Ch.R. frowns. He has had enough delays in this matter . . . Our negotiations will be more successful if Raczkiewicz is still not sure of his mandate. I promise that we will hurry. Taking this into account, he promises that he will not give Łukasiewicz a binding answer until 6 p.m.[3]

It is implicit in these words that people of Jewish origin in exile—where knowledge of languages and social contacts with local political elites mattered—had more clout than in Poland, and Jews, of different levels of observance or assimilation, participated in every Polish political trend of the time. For example, the well-known socialist Herman Lieberman was vice-president of the National Council (Rada Narodowa) in exile; Stefan Glaser, an eminent lawyer and professor at the Stefan Batory University, headed a department in the Ministry of Justice; and Władysław Neuman, a diplomat who for many years was Polish ambassador to Norway, was among Raczkiewicz's personal friends. Indeed, Neuman deserves special attention, as the president appointed him temporary head of the Civil Office during the political crisis of summer 1941, against the background of the Sikorski–Maisky agreement,[4] a fact which, in my opinion, is clear confirmation that Raczkiewicz had no antisemitic bias. Raczkiewicz generally treated national minorities with objectivity, as long as they were loyal to the state.

Surviving records of the activities of the president of the Polish Republic contain a number of references to meetings with people of Jewish nationality who were working in the apparatus of the Polish government-in-exile; here too no traces of prejudice against them appear. On the contrary, the president always displayed tact in his relations with such people. This lack of bias against Jews continued even when, in the winter of 1940, Raczkiewicz received the first information about the

---

[2] J. Łaptos, *Dyplomaci II RP w świetle raportów Quai d'Orsay* (Warsaw, 1993), 255.

[3] A. Mühlstein, *Dziennik: Wrzesień 1939–listopad 1940*, trans. D. Zamojska (Warsaw, 1999), 56.

[4] Concluded in London between the Polish and Soviet governments on 30 July 1941 under pressure from the British side. It restored diplomatic relations with Moscow (broken off on 17 September 1939 by Stalin) and announced an amnesty for Polish prisoners in the Soviet Union, but left unresolved the question of Poland's borders, thus provoking the opposition of some Polish politicians who sought the restoration of the pre-war borders.

Soviet occupation of eastern Małopolska. Raczkiewicz learned this news from Władysław Folkierski, a professor at the Jagiellonian University, now exiled in the West, who himself emphasized the role of Jews in the Bolshevik government and administration, a circumstance that had resulted in growing hostility towards Jews on the part of local Poles and Ukrainians. The president did not believe what he had heard, and we can only guess that he felt that Folkierski, a member of the right-wing National Party (Stronnictwo Narodowe), may well have been exaggerating the facts.[5]

Clearly, information on this matter, even though it gradually increased as time passed, did not affect Raczkiewicz's basic views. He continued to work with officials of Jewish origin, treating them with complete confidence. One such official was Dr Ludwik Rajchman, who was sent to the United States on a mission to establish personal contact with former president Herbert Hoover and to organize aid for Poland. Raczkiewicz had a position of authority in the deliberations held in the spring of 1940. In a discussion about the 'Jewish question' that he had with his close associate August Zaleski, the Minister of Foreign Affairs, they agreed that the issue was an internal Polish matter which the requirement for equal rights would sort out. They did stipulate, however, that this could not apply to the masses of Jews driven in by the Germans from other countries.[6] Evidently, they feared that the already large Jewish minority in Poland would multiply greatly owing to the immense scale of the resettlement carried out by the occupying forces.

The very day after these matters had been decided, Raczkiewicz met Izaak Ignacy Schwarzbart, the lawyer, Zionist activist, and former Sejm member of the Polish Republic (1938–9) at the president's seat at Pignerolles near Angers; Schwarzbart was a member of the National Council in exile from 1939 to 1945. Schwarzbart offered Raczkiewicz expressions of respect on behalf of the Jewish population and reassured him of their total commitment to reclaiming an independent Polish Republic. He wanted to lead a mission to the United States to lobby on behalf of Poland among American Jews.[7] Raczkiewicz accepted these assurances at face value, and promised to support the proposed trip in his talks with the Minister of Foreign Affairs.

Several months later, in the autumn of 1940 and now in the United Kingdom, Raczkiewicz again received Schwarzbart, who described his attempts to explain the situation in Poland to the Jewish community in England and the United States. These efforts, however, had produced few results. Schwarzbart noted that unfair accusations were frequently made against Poland. Raczkiewicz appealed to Schwarzbart's social conscience to intensify his efforts, as unjustified attacks had appeared in the Anglo-Saxon press at that time. According to Raczkiewicz, Schwarzbart's activities promoted the interest of both the Polish Republic and the Jews. Raczkiewicz emphasized that Poland was the first country in the war to take a

---

[5] *Dzienniki czynności Prezydenta RP Władysława Raczkiewicza, 1939–1947*, 2 vols. (Wrocław, 2004), vol. i, entry of 1 Feb. 1940.   [6] Ibid., 8 May 1940.   [7] Ibid., 9 May 1940.

stand against racist barbarity, even as the country suffered more than any others. He added that Poland, being on the side of world opinion that proclaimed humanitarian ideas, must in the future create conditions in which all its citizens could co-operate, regardless of religion or nationality. In order to achieve this, they had to work together now to create foundations for Poland that would allow it to play a fitting role in central Europe. Schwarzbart assured him that he would conduct his work on this basis.[8]

The next day the president met with Professor Olgierd Górka, an expert in nationality matters and head of the Nationalities Department. The meeting concluded by emphasizing the importance of the Jewish issue in obtaining peace conditions for Poland which would correspond to its justified aspirations.[9] Raczkiewicz found confirmation of such opinions in Minister Zaleski's reports; following his talks with the British, Zaleski had the impression that they were very interested in resolving the Jewish question.[10]

The president's main contact in Jewish matters continued to be Schwarzbart, who during meetings with Raczkiewicz reported on talks conducted with representatives of the press. In the spring of 1941, he underlined the immediate need for a specific settlement of the Jewish issue. The president pointed out that he had already spoken in support of full civil rights for Polish Jews, but that he thought that a decree was contraindicated because such legislative acts should be issued by a future Polish parliament. During discussions that focused on the opinions of radical émigré political groups who held views incompatible with those of the government on Jewish issues, the president advised restraint, as extremist groups were also to be found among some Jews whose opinions could damage the Polish cause. But he clearly wanted his interlocutor to use his influence with the Jewish community in the United Kingdom and the United States by emphasizing the Polish government's eagerness to co-operate with the Jews.[11]

The Jewish topic cropped up frequently at the president's numerous meetings, including his audience with Maksymilian Friede, the honorary consul in Peru and Ecuador. Friede indicated that, even as a Pole of Jewish origin, he considered the Jewish nationalists' demands unjustified; he stated that Jews could only have a positive influence on the system of future relations by demonstrating their best efforts to co-operate.[12] Similarly, in another audience, with a Mr Jaffe, Raczkiewicz was informed about German infiltration into Jewish organizations and the inadequate efforts of the Intelligence Service to counter such activity.[13] The president took seriously any warnings about nationalists and German agents when they were communicated by Jews themselves. He tried to remain objective about such contacts, but was unable to rise to their occasionally excessive demands. When on

---

[8] *Dzienniki czynności Prezydenta RP Władysława Raczkiewicza, 1939–1947*, vol. i, entry of, 9 Sept. 1940.   [9] Ibid., 10 Sept. 1940.   [10] Ibid., 29 Nov. 1940.
[11] Ibid., 6 Mar. 1941.   [12] Ibid., 17 Mar. 1941.   [13] Ibid., 7 May 1941.

6 February 1942 he received a delegation from the Jewish organization Agudah,[14] in the persons of Harry Goodman and Rabbi Abraham Babad, he was presented with a demand to appoint an Orthodox Jewish representative to the National Council. Raczkiewicz explained in great detail that this was impossible, as the council's make-up had already been decided; nonetheless, he agreed to inform the prime minister about the situation. He revisited the issue a month later, on 6 March 1942, during a meeting with Schwarzbart, who thanked him for his nomination to the National Council. Schwarzbart also expressed regret that an Agudah representative had not been appointed and said that until a representative of the Jewish right was chosen, he would act in that capacity. Raczkiewicz replied that, as a representative of Polish Jewry, Schwarzbart should strive to make Jews support Polish demands; the change in attitude would, he believed, serve to moderate the antisemitic tendencies which had intensified when Jews were seen to co-operate with the Soviet aggressor.

At about the same time, the first information reached Raczkiewicz about the extermination policy being carried out by the Third Reich in the occupied territories. According to the emissaries who transmitted this information, he reacted emotionally. One wrote: 'The president is struck with horror by the news about the barbaric terror perpetrated by the Germans, about Poles being deported to concentration camps, and about the creation of ghettos, which he asked me to describe.'[15] Though Raczkiewicz showed a great deal of empathy, he could take only symbolic action against the situation. A few weeks later, on 3 April 1942, he swore into office Szmul Zygielbojm, the newly appointed member of the National Council representing the Bund,[16] whom he then invited to a discussion. Raczkiewicz tried to maintain contact with all the currents of Jewish culture in exile; hence, no doubt, the meeting that he held later that month, on 29 April, with a delegation from a union of rabbis from Poland in the United Kingdom.

The president was by now deeply committed to improving relations with Jews. For example, when General Sikorski informed him on 15 August 1942[17] about a telegram from Moscow reporting that the Soviet government had threatened to halt the evacuation of the Polish army should it come to light that Jews were present among the evacuated civilians, he asked the prime minister to inform the Jewish members of the National Council of this fact immediately, so that they would not assume that the order to cease the evacuation of Jews came from Polish authorities. This was a matter of great importance, as the Polish ruling body learned a month

[14] Agudat Yisra'el: the world organization of Orthodox Jews, founded in 1912 in Katowice; it operated in Europe, the United States, and Palestine, and after 1948 mainly in Israel.

[15] K. Iranek-Osmecki, *Emisariusz Antoni* (Paris, 1985), 117–18.

[16] Bund: the popular name of the party of Jewish socialist workers, active 1897–1948 as the General Jewish Workers' Alliance.

[17] At afternoon tea with, among others, ministers, the executive committee of the National Council, and generals P. Dembiński, V. Malinowski, and B. Regulski. Polish Institute and Sikorski Museum, London: *Dziennik czynności Naczelnego Wodza*, xxxvii: *Sierpień 1942*, entry of 15 Aug. 1942.

later, when the American diplomat Wendell Willkie, after discussions with Jews in Palestine, made his support during forthcoming talks with the Soviet Union conditional upon the Polish government changing its attitude towards Jews of Polish citizenship in the Soviet Union, who had allegedly been refused assistance.[18]

In the meantime, Jews began to suffer an even more dire fate under German occupation. When Raczkiewicz saw Zygielbojm again in late 1942, Zygielbojm asserted that German policy was striving to completely exterminate the Jews, and he feared that the pronouncements by some extreme nationalistic Polish authorities might help them to carry out this plan. In his reply, the president pointed out that on many occasions the Polish government and recently the prime minister himself had stressed the principle of equal rights for all nationalities in Poland. He added that because the government was made up of representatives of all the most important trends of Polish political thinking, the Jews were guaranteed a place in that society. In order to improve the atmosphere, he suggested that the Jewish representatives in the National Council speak up more emphatically against the unjustified accusations being made against the Poles, for example about their negative attitude towards the departure from the Soviet Union of Jews of Polish citizenship.[19]

Raczkiewicz also appreciated receiving a new report from Schwarzbart about the latter's activities among Jews in the United Kingdom, in the campaign against the German barbarities being committed in Poland. Schwarzbart thanked the president for making known in the international arena that the Jewish population in Poland was being murdered by the Germans, and he asked that an instruction be sent to the ambassador in Kuibyshev to the effect that, if the opportunity arose for the further evacuation of Poles from the Soviet Union, Jews should be included among them. The president patiently explained that the government had already shown initiative in this matter during previous evacuations, and that it was only Moscow's intransigent attitude that had stood in the way. He said, however, that he would remind the Minister of Foreign Affairs of this request.[20]

Some tensions did arise in the president's relations with Jewish members of the National Council, in connection with demands that seemed to him on occasion unwarranted. During his meeting with Zygielbojm on 8 March 1943, for example, Zygielbojm—having been informed of the deaths in the Soviet Union of the well-known Jewish activists Henryk Erlich[21] and Wiktor Alter[22]—suggested that the

---

[18] *Dzienniki czynności Prezydenta RP Władysława Raczkiewicza*, vol. i, entry of 26 Oct. 1942.

[19] Ibid., 3 Nov. 1942.   [20] Ibid., 15 Dec. 1942.

[21] Henryk Erlich (Herz Wolf, 1882–1942) was a Jewish socialist activist and member of the Bund from 1903 to 1939. He served as a defence lawyer in political trials before the war. Erlich was in a Soviet prison from 1939 to 1941, and served with the Polish embassy in Kuibyshev in 1941. Subsequently he was arrested and committed suicide while in the custody of the NKVD.

[22] Wiktor Alter (1890–1941) was a Jewish socialist activist, journalist, and member of the Bund from 1905. During the war he was first incarcerated in a Soviet prison between 1939 and 1941; after his release he became a delegate to the Polish embassy in Sverdlovsk. He was then arrested and executed by the NKVD.

president issue a public expression of sympathy with the Jews. Apart from the fact that such an action could have further inflamed the already disastrous relations with Moscow, Raczkiewicz tactfully pointed out that as head of state he had hitherto never made public statements relating to any other specific acts of bestiality concerning prominent Polish representatives and therefore he did not think it possible for him to make a public statement about this particular instance. He added, however, that he was ready to address his expressions of sympathy to Zygielbojm, as the Bund representative.[23]

It was very likely their last meeting, as on 12 May 1943 the president was informed of Szmul Zygielbojm's death. The next day Raczkiewicz learned the details: Zygielbojm had committed suicide as a political protest against the world's apathy in the face of the mass murder of Jews in Poland. He had left a letter addressed to the president and the government. Raczkiewicz asked that the reasons for the suicide be made known and the contents of the letter disclosed, and on the evening of 13 May 1943, police from New Scotland Yard brought Zygielbojm's letter to him.[24] He entrusted to Professor Stanisław Grabski, the chairman of the National Council, the expression of condolence. Though he understood the tragic nature of this event, as a practising Catholic Raczkiewicz could not approve of suicide. Nonetheless, in his talks and meetings with the British, he frequently referred to the bestial methods used by Germans in the ghettos.[25] Unfortunately, we do not know if his statements at that time in London were considered accurate or intentionally exaggerated.

As head of the Polish government, Raczkiewicz faced insurmountable problems. The country he represented was under threat of occupation by an alleged 'ally', and so his absolute priority was to defend Polish territorial integrity and independence. This priority led him to some controversial decisions, such as declining to contribute to a publication on the occasion of the Jewish New Year unless the Jews took a clear stand on the matter of the Eastern Borderlands; he delegated the matter to the Minister of Internal Affairs instead.[26] Even the grim information brought out by emissaries from Poland did not change this basic requirement. One even maintained that 'the Jewish issue in Poland no longer exists, as no more than 10,000–20,000 Polish Jews have managed to survive the slaughter'.[27]

In early 1944, Raczkiewicz had a meeting with Dr Paweł Warszawski, who had escaped the Warsaw ghetto and had reached England. Warszawski recounted the liquidation of the ghetto, and stressed the great help given to Jews by Polish society. His own escape to London had been made possible by the Polish Socialist Party. Warszawski made the point that his dream to join the Polish army in order to fight the Germans had come true. The president expressed appreciation of his civic

[23] *Dzienniki czynności Prezydenta RP Władysława Raczkiewicza*, vol. ii, entry of 8 Mar. 1943.
[24] The letter was to be returned to the coroner.
[25] *Dzienniki czynności Prezydenta RP Władysława Raczkiewicza*, vol. ii, entry of 27 July 1943.
[26] Ibid., 27 Sept. 1943.
[27] Ibid., 22 Nov. 1943.

stance and stressed the importance of stating the truth about attitudes to Jews in Poland, as false insinuations were being circulated and wreaking havoc.[28] We can assume that Raczkiewicz was deeply convinced of what he was saying. He believed that instances of collaboration with the occupiers or 'racketeering' were entirely isolated incidents. As a person with no practical knowledge of occupation, beyond the routine information received from emissaries, he was not able to visualize the real conditions in Poland created by hunger, terror, and base instincts.

Just as Raczkiewicz was eager to believe his Western allies, so also did he trust accounts of the heroic conduct of Polish people under occupation. His mind was taxed by the Polish–Soviet situation, and he eagerly welcomed any support for the Polish position in the Eastern Borderlands dispute and for Polish sovereignty. On 11 January 1944, in a state of distress, he listened to the report of a monitored night-time broadcast by Moscow Radio, stating the Soviet government's official response to the Polish declaration. At this stage, Stalin was stipulating the Curzon Line as a future border with Poland. Because of this turn of events, Raczkiewicz was impressed by the immediate visit he received from Schwarzbart, who declared the solidarity of Polish Jews in defence of the Polish Republic and their readiness to support the position of the Polish government. In response to this gesture, the president emphasized the importance of publicizing this standpoint, and suggested that the prime minister be consulted about making the viewpoint known.[29]

These gestures of solidarity certainly improved the tone of their mutual relations. A month later Raczkiewicz enthusiastically accepted the proposal presented by Jewish representatives, led by Dr Sawielij Tartakower, to create an under-secretariat of state for Jewish matters. The Ministry of Internal Affairs did indeed wish to create a Council of Polish Jews with a permanent secretariat that would serve to liaise with the Council of Ministers, and a special Jewish unit in the Nationalities Department. Raczkiewicz felt that this was an appropriate move, and at the same time he remarked that the Jewish Council should play a part in making Jewish communities in the United States aware of the need to support Polish demands.[30] Raczkiewicz also had the opportunity to seek such support personally when he received Nahum Goldman, chairman of the World Jewish Congress in the United States, who offered greetings from the Jewish population. The purpose of his visit to the United Kingdom was to seek permission to send help to Jews in Poland via Sweden, which was agreed to by the Polish government. Goldman informed Raczkiewicz about actions undertaken by Jewish organizations to save Jews from the Soviet Union, where non-communist Jews were under persecution.[31] It seemed as if the two men had achieved real understanding.

However, a serious problem was affecting Polish–Jewish relations. The phenomenon of desertion from the Polish army by soldiers of Jewish origin dated back to 1942. It is estimated that in September 1942 there were some 4,300 Jews in the

---

[28] *Dzienniki czynności Prezydenta RP Władysława Raczkiewicza*, vol. ii, 3 Jan. 1944.
[29] Ibid., 11 Jan. 1944.   [30] Ibid., 25 Feb. 1944.   [31] Ibid., 2 Mar. 1944.

ranks of the Polish army, but that only about 1,000 remained by April 1944, which hints at a significant level of desertion. The main motives appeared to be their striving to remain in Palestine and the consolidation of local Jewish settlements. Some joined the British army. As long as this involved detachments of the Second Corps in Palestine, this situation was tolerated quite well by the Polish side.[32] Even if in individual cases of desertion sentences were pronounced, in practice they were not carried out.

The British, worried by the growth of the Jewish independence movement in Palestine, were not too pleased about the policy of 'shutting one's eyes' to these desertions. The trend increased as the departure for the Italian front drew nearer, and the desertions began to reach alarming numbers. In the spring of 1944, while briefing the president about the atmosphere in the army, commander-in-chief General Kazimierz Sosnkowski brought up the subject of the demoralizing number of desertions by Jews (in the United Kingdom too), which were sometimes due to communist agitation. Because some deserters cited manifestations of antisemitism in the army as the cause, the general gave orders that no obstacles were to be put in the way of Jews transferring to the British army; and returning deserters were to be accepted. Raczkiewicz supported this solution, although it was a far remove from the iron principles of army discipline in the context of a total war for survival.[33]

At the same time, Raczkiewicz underlined the necessity of establishing active contacts with parliamentarians friendly towards Poles in order to ensure protection against propaganda attacks intended to discredit the Polish war effort, as happened in the British parliament when an attack was launched on alleged antisemitism in the Polish army as a result of the desertion of a group of Jews.[34]

This thorny question, which was employed as propaganda against Poland, must have troubled the president. He clearly thought that it must have been Soviet-inspired. Not surprisingly, Raczkiewicz viewed this issue from the point of view of the Polish *raison d'état*. At the same time, in the spring of 1944, delegates from Poland insisted angrily that the Jews were neglecting to repay in kind the help rendered to them at the risk of Polish lives. According to the delegates, the fighting in the ghetto during its liquidation had been undertaken thanks to the Home Army divisions that had joined in to organize the fighting. Until then, the Jews had supposedly been passive and were even denouncing each other.[35] At the same time, however, these delegates confirmed that the systematic murdering of Jews by the occupying forces had resulted in a situation in which there were no more than 100,000 Jews left alive in Poland, including those in hiding among the Poles and in the forests.

The president was strongly affected by the anti-Polish press attacks and accusations of antisemitism. Knowing the true situation, he could judge the falsity and

[32] H. Sarner, *Generał Anders i żołnierze II Korpusu Polskiego* (Poznań, 1997), 144–5.
[33] *Dzienniki czynności Prezydenta RP Władysława Raczkiewicza*, vol. ii, entry of 3 Mar. 1944.
[34] Ibid., 19 Apr. 1944. [35] Ibid., 21 Apr. 1944.

tendentiousness of British press reports about a generalized antisemitism in the Polish army that caused Jews to desert, and about the allegedly severe sentences given to the deserters. He demanded that General Marian Kukiel, the Minister of Defence, issue an official corrective to counteract the hostile anti-Polish propaganda.[36] At Raczkiewicz's insistence, Kukiel duly took action against the campaign of defamation of the Polish army in connection with desertion by Jews, issuing a statement and ordering the investigation of several cases of reported antisemitism which were supposed to have occurred several months earlier. The subject arose again during a meeting between Raczkiewicz and General Sosnkowski, who was convinced that he was being deliberately targeted over the issue of Jewish desertion, in order to saddle him with responsibility for the alleged antisemitism in the army; he drew attention to the fact that deserters were committed for court martial in accordance with the requirements of the Minister of Defence.

The president was not satisfied with an approach that attempted to shift responsibility for this problem. He called in Kukiel to discuss a possible solution to the difficult situation created by the British press attacks; in response, the minister explained that he would hold talks with members of the British parliament, at which he planned to present a comprehensive picture, and he hoped that this action would contribute to clarifying the matter. The minister summoned the Chief of the Army Judiciary, Colonel Kazimierz Słowikowski, to discuss a sentencing policy and to investigate allegations of antisemitic statements made during the trials by people accused of desertion.[37]

This whole matter seriously disturbed Raczkiewicz. Because the government-in-exile lacked real military power, the only capital it possessed was its reputation as a defender of democracy. At the time, he was told by Jan Ciechanowski, the ambassador in Washington, that word of the sentences imposed on deserters was damaging the reputation of the Poles. The suggestion was made that those found guilty should be treated with clemency, even pardoned. However, that solution would have meant that those sentenced would have to lodge appeals for pardon, which would be an unlikely turn of events in light of their provocative conduct. There was also the fear that such a decision would cause another wave of desertions. Nevertheless, a reprieve would be seen as a gesture on the part of the army's commanding authorities. But it was essential to obtain a statement from the War Office that it would refuse to accept deserters into the British army. With instructions from the Minister of Defence, the Chief of the Army Judiciary launched an investigation of the matter.

The president again discussed the issue of Jewish deserters with the commander-in-chief, Sosnkowski. The general reminded him that he, the general, had advocated allowing Jews to transfer to the British army from the very beginning, when details of these desertions had first become known, but the British had refused

---

[36] *Dzienniki czynności Prezydenta RP Władysława Raczkiewicza*, vol. ii, 24–25 Apr. 1944.
[37] Ibid., 1 May 1944.

to accept this solution. According to the general, British agreement to this course should be sought. Raczkiewicz doubted that the British authorities would accept the policy; he told the general that it might result in an increase of desertion by such soldiers.[38]

At his next audience with the Minister of Defence, the president heard a report of a session of the National Council concerning this matter. General Kukiel's opinion was that suspension of punishment would be the best solution. The minister was planning to publish proof that the so-called antisemitic actions were limited to verbal abuse, a common occurrence among soldiers. He claimed that the infrequent cases that were reported to the authorities were always dealt with in accordance with the law. Raczkiewicz emphasized the need for the War Office to make a statement in Parliament about not accepting Jewish deserters from the Polish army into the British army and to remind public opinion that an order issued by the Polish Minister of Defence had been read out in all units, explaining the punishment for desertion specified in the code of laws.[39]

The next day the president and the prime minister Stanisław Mikołajczyk discussed the issue of Jewish deserters. Mikołajczyk did not reject the idea that those sentenced might submit an appeal for pardon. He thought it necessary to resolve this problem, as it reflected negatively on public opinion about Poland. Raczkiewicz, however, was disgusted by the Jewish soldiers' attitude, a feeling that could be sensed at his next meeting with Schwarzbart, who made a convoluted attempt to demonstrate that the Jews were in fact opposed to anti-Polish propaganda. Raczkiewicz was not convinced by the argument that neither Schwarzbart nor representatives of Polish Jews in exile were receiving any support, a fact that made it more difficult for them to counteract communist propaganda. The president was extremely ill disposed to the request that clemency should be shown towards deserters, accompanied as it was by the request that those guilty of antisemitic incidents in the army should be severely punished. Irritated, Raczkiewicz declared that he could not see any opposition from the Jewish side to the anti-Polish agitation, which had reached unbelievable proportions precisely in the context of the deserters' issue. He emphasized that sporadic cases of antisemitism in the army immediately provoked reactions by those in command, and he promised to become personally involved with this problem.[40]

Following this meeting, Raczkiewicz contacted Kukiel by telephone to summarize the above conversation. The general informed him that verdicts had been confirmed for nine out of twenty-one deserters. Eleven sentences had been suspended, and in the case of one other, the sentence had been sent for decision to the commander-in-chief. Kukiel also stated that those whose sentences had been suspended did not show remorse and had declared that they did not wish to serve in the Polish army.[41]

Another wave of attacks against the Polish government swept through the

---

[38] Ibid., 2 May 1944.   [39] Ibid., 3 May 1944.   [40] Ibid., 4 May 1944.   [41] Ibid.

leftist British press. These were led by the *Daily Worker* and *The Tribune*, while *Time and Tide* or *The Tablet* mediated in defence of the Poles. Raczkiewicz wanted more details and accordingly arranged a meeting for the next day with the Chief of the Army Judiciary Colonel Słowikowski, who submitted a report on the files of the Jewish deserters. These documents showed that they categorically refused to continue to serve in the Polish army, and revealed arrogant behaviour. In his view, foreign propaganda was involved. The soldiers deeply resented the deserters, but it was felt that their attitudes were not based on antisemitism. Admittedly, these files included approximately twenty cases that could be classified as involving antisemitic insults, but the files contained data from the whole four-year period in exile, and such cases were subjected to appropriate disciplinary action. Raczkiewicz felt reassured.[42]

This was why when he met with the British ambassador to the government-in-exile Owen O'Malley on 6 May 1944, Raczkiewicz expressed concern over the toleration of anti-Polish acts in the British press. In his opinion, the aim was to belittle Polish contributions to the war effort, to lower the prestige of the Polish authorities, and also to repeat Soviet propaganda, at the same time rendering clarification of the Polish position impossible. As an example, he cited the forbearance accorded to the unleashing of hostile action in the context of alleged antisemitism in the Polish army. He informed the ambassador that manifestations of 'antisemitism' were limited to a few cases of verbal abuse and were dealt with by those in command. But he considered unacceptable the toleration of certain articles in *The Economist* that referred to the Polish army as 'hooligans'.[43]

It should be emphasized that Raczkiewicz tried to be objective and to collect information from many sources when defending the Polish *raison d'état*. He discussed Jewish issues with Jews in his closest circle. Because he believed that Poland was being unfairly treated, he supported attempts to counteract propaganda about Polish antisemitism. The most difficult issue he faced with regard to national minority issues must have been the matter of Jewish deserters. It surely left a bitter taste, but at that time no one analysed it any further because of the much greater letdown by the Anglo-Saxon allies at the end of the war. The decisions taken in Yalta obscured the tensions with the Jewish communities, though it must be emphasized that after 1945, when Raczkiewicz tried to get some insight into who had actually been allowed by Moscow to govern the country, he was astonished by the dossier prepared by the Ministry of Internal Affairs. The make-up of the Warsaw government included individuals of Jewish origin, who formed the hard core of the new power apparatus of the contemporary ministries of Public Security, Propaganda, and Foreign Affairs. Unfortunately, we do not know what action Raczkiewicz took in response to this information.

All the evidence points to the fact that when Raczkiewicz was president, his

---

[42] *Dzienniki czynności Prezydenta RP Władysława Raczkiewicza*, vol. ii, 5 May 1944.
[43] Ibid., 6 May 1944.

attitude towards Jews was and remained influenced by their loyalty to the state which he represented. This was a pragmatic mindset, although one beset by severe problems throughout the war. The most serious problem concerned the mass desertions by Jews from the Polish army. Whatever the causes, Raczkiewicz perceived these as gross disloyalty to the Polish Republic on the part of his Jewish fellow citizens, all the more so as they happened on a massive scale at a time when the government-in-exile and he himself were under enormous pressure from the Allies, whose intention was to exact territorial concessions on behalf of Moscow and bring about voluntary subordination of the state to Stalin. In his view, the conduct of Jewish citizens at a time when the fate of Polish independence was being decided was nothing short of betrayal. Even allowing for cases of antisemitic verbal abuse, which in the army had probably been frequently ignored in the past, Raczkiewicz could not justify such conduct. As a former military man, he knew that armies had long tolerated strong language, scathing remarks, and even outright abuse. For him, such manifestations of antisemitism constituted a poor justification of a decision to desert at a critical time in the war. For many Poles, this was the time when the myth of the Polish Republic as a common home for many nationalities was finally laid to rest. A common state with Lithuanians, Ukrainians, and even Belarusians was now out of the question, not just because of the military power of the Red Army. During the war, the Bolsheviks succeeded in dividing these nations. Just as the desertions in the west adversely affected relations between the Polish government-in-exile and the Jews in the west, so in the post-war period the hoped-for Polish–Jewish co-operation was undermined by the participation of significant numbers of communists of Jewish origin in the post-war Stalin-dominated regime.

There is nothing to indicate that Raczkiewicz changed his attitude towards people of Jewish origin during the last years of his life. Rather, the opposite is true. As a cultured man and one open to the world, he never generalized any phenomena. His closest circle of acquaintances included many people of Jewish origin. The fact that some of them remained devoted to him until the end of his life is certainly an indication of this. A former consul of the Polish Republic who was of Jewish origin, Karol Poznański, helped to organize the funeral of the president of the Polish republic-in-exile. Sadly, the myth of the Polish Republic as a common homeland of various nationalities, a concept which Raczkiewicz strongly supported in his public activities, collapsed together with its independence.

Translated from the Polish by Aleksandra Hawiger

After *Złote żniwa*

An Attempt to Assess the Social Impact of the Book

ANTONI SUŁEK

A SHORT though heated debate took place in Poland in the first months of 2011, in reaction to three publications: *Złote żniwa* ('Golden Harvest'), by Jan T. Gross, with contributions by Irena Grudzińska Gross; *Judenjagd*, by Jan Grabowski; and *Jest taki piękny słoneczny dzień. . . .*, by Barbara Engelking.[1] The authors of these three books strongly challenge the widespread perception in Polish society of the Poles' relationship to the extermination of the Polish Jews by Nazi Germans. The writers present numerous examples, some new and some previously known to historians, of the participation of Poles in the murder of Jews and in the plunder of their property, demonstrating the scale of these acts and the methods and motivations of the actors. The authors show that the scale of the crimes committed by Poles against Jews was larger than had previously been thought, and they argue that these crimes outweigh the instances in which Poles gave help to Jews.

The debate was dominated by reaction to *Złote żniwa*, both because the book was deliberately meant to provoke shock and bring about a change in social awareness, and because it was the third work by this well-known author on a similar topic and with a similar message, following his groundbreaking *Sąsiedzi* ('Neighbours') and *Strach* ('Fear').[2] The question is: what was the social impact of *Złote żniwa*? Was it similar to that of *Sąsiedzi*, or did it have only a minimal impact, as did *Strach*? The

---

[1] J. T. Gross with I. Grudzińska-Gross, *Złote żniwa: Rzecz o tym, co się działo na obrzeżach zagłady Żydów* (Kraków, 2011), trans. as J. T. Gross with I. Grudzińska-Gross, *Golden Harvest: Events at the Periphery of the Holocaust* (New York, 2012); J. Grabowski, *Judenjagd: Polowanie na Żydów, 1942–1945. Studium dziejów pewnego powiatu* (Warsaw, 2011); B. Engelking, *Jest taki piękny słoneczny dzień… Losy Żydów szukających ratunku na wsi polskiej, 1942–1945* (Warsaw, 2011).

[2] J. T. Gross, *Sąsiedzi: Historia zagłady żydowskiego miasteczka* (Sejny, 2000), trans. as J. T. Gross, *Neighbors: The Destruction of the Jewish Community in Jedwabne, Poland* (Princeton, 2001); J. T. Gross, *Strach: Antysemityzm w Polsce tuż po wojnie. Historia moralnej zapaści* (Kraków, 2008), published earlier in English as J. T. Gross, *Fear: Anti-Semitism in Poland after Auschwitz. An Essay in Historical Interpretation* (Princeton, 2006).

question of the social impact of this book is especially legitimate as its target audience was society at large, not just professional or amateur historians.

An attempt to answer this question on the basis of opinion polls is presented in this chapter. Surveys designed by the author were carried out by TNS OBOP, the most experienced polling organization in Poland (established in 1958), in 2002, 2008, and 2011.[3] In order to examine the influence on mass beliefs of a stimulus such as a book, it is necessary to survey these beliefs both before the publication of the book and then again after the debate caused by it. It is also important to repeat the 'after' survey some time later so that both the immediate and the long-term effects may be examined.

In the case of *Złote żniwa*, it was impossible to carry out the survey before publication, because there was discussion of it in the media before it was published. The authors submitted the manuscript to the publishers at the end of 2010, but a popular television station had acquired an earlier version. The work then became the subject of a programme, in which the authors took part, that was transmitted on 3 January 2011 and was watched by 2.9 million viewers. Soon after, many interested commentators and historians came into possession of the typescript and a debate was sparked off in the media. By the time the final version of *Złote żniwa* was published on 10 March 2011 and the public could read it, the media debate had already reached its peak and indeed had lost momentum. Therefore, public opinion about the book was formed under the influence of the media, without direct contact with the book itself.[4] In this situation, the initial data would need to have been gathered not before the book was published but before its content unexpectedly appeared in the popular media. Naturally, this was impossible. A one-shot survey of the impact of *Złote żniwa* was conducted between 6 and 10 May 2011,[5] after the debate about the book had subsided, which made the measurement of its influence difficult, though not impossible.

---

[3] All the surveys analysed here were face-to-face interviews carried out with nationwide representative samples of about 1,000 people aged 15 or over. The maximum margin of error for a sample of this size is ±3.2%, with a confidence level of 0.95. The results of the surveys are set out in the research reports available at <http://obop-arch.tnsglobal.pl/archive>.

[4] Under the influence of the public debate on the typescript, the authors introduced some changes to the final version of the book. For instance, they markedly lowered the estimated number of Jews murdered or denounced by Poles from 'between 100,000 and 200,000' to 'a few tens of thousands'. The publishers stated in a note that future discussion should be based on 'the final version of the text of the book'. That is to say, up until at least 8 February 2011, when the publishers made available sample copies of the work, opinions expressed in the media about it were based on earlier versions of the text. See 'Ostateczna wersja książki Jana Grossa: Ważne zmiany', *Polska*, 9 Feb. 2011: <http://www.polskatimes.pl/artykul/366631,ostateczna-wersja-ksiazki-jana-grossa-wazne-zmiany-ws-liczby-pomordowanych-zydow,id,t.html>.

[5] TNS OBOP, *Po 'Złotych żniwach'* (2011): <http://obop-arch.tnsglobal.pl/archivereport/id/7913>.

ON POLES ENRICHING THEMSELVES AT THE EXPENSE OF JEWS

The first question is whether *Złote żniwa* revived society's memory of the issues discussed in the book. Did the book touch on matters imprinted on social memory but which had not been publicly discussed before because they constituted a taboo? The authors aimed to activate individual and collective memory. They argued that, during the war and immediately after it, many Poles gathered their golden 'harvest' not just metaphorically but also literally—that many people 'enriched themselves at the expense of Jews' ('wzbogacili się na Żydach'), stealing from them, murdering them, plundering their graves, or taking possession of their property in various ways. This message was in stark contrast to the image of a society which experienced not just unparalleled terror and repression during the German occupation, but also expropriation, impoverishment, and hunger.

In the survey the respondents were asked, without direct reference to the book, whether they had heard 'any people reminiscing or telling stories about anyone "enriching themselves at the expense of Jews" during the last war'. They were also asked more specifically if they had heard of anyone 'receiving gold from Jews for sheltering them', 'plundering or killing Jews and taking their possessions', or 'taking possession of the property of Jews murdered by Nazis'. These were the three main forms of enriching oneself at the expense of Jews as described in *Złote żniwa*. The digging of mass graves for Jews murdered in Treblinka and other death camps, to which much attention was devoted in the book, was a local phenomenon and was subsumed in the third form of enriching oneself at the expense of Jews. Table 1 contains the responses to these questions.

Table 1. Memories about people who 'enriched themselves at the expense of Jews' (2011)

Questions	Responses (%)	
	Yes	No
Have you heard any people reminiscing or telling stories about anyone 'enriching themselves at the expense of Jews' during the last war?	26	74
And have you heard of anyone receiving gold from Jews for sheltering them?	28	72
And have you heard of anyone plundering or killing Jews and taking their possessions?	22	78
And have you heard of anyone taking possession of the property of Jews murdered by Nazis?	23	77

Note: N = 1,000. For additional information relating to the survey, see text, n. 3.
Source: TNS OBOP, Po 'Złotych żniwach' (2011): <http://obop-arch.tnsglobal.pl/archive-report/ id/7913>.

Approximately one-quarter of the respondents had heard about people 'enriching themselves at the expense of Jews', so the phrase is known and understood quite well. Admittedly, we cannot tell from the survey how many of the respondents knew exactly what the expression implied—we can only tell what proportion of them had not heard of anyone who profited in such a way. Besides, the fact that someone was talked about as having profited at the expense of Jews does not mean that there was a basis for this rumour about him or her: the phrase was often just an expression of envious malice or an easy explanation for a person's sudden enrichment. However, the fact that such explanations were articulated and accepted shows that they had a basis in known or at least probable situations and that they were considered sufficient explanations. Further, the situations cannot have been particularly rare if a special expression was coined to refer to them, which has survived in the Polish language after many decades. However, the survey will not help us to determine just how often these events took place; that is for historians to discover through research.

Looking at the figures more closely, we see that between 22 and 28 per cent of respondents had heard of someone receiving gold from Jews for sheltering them, or of someone robbing or killing Jews and taking their possessions, or of someone taking possession of the property of Jews murdered by Nazis. A breakdown reveals the following:

> 13 per cent had heard about each of those kinds of behaviour;
>
> 9 per cent had heard about two of them;
>
> 15 per cent had heard about one of them;
>
> 63 per cent had not heard about any of them.

Therefore, in addition to the 26 per cent of the respondents who had heard the expression 'he enriched himself at the expense of Jews' applied to someone, a further 11 per cent had heard of behaviour that effectively falls under the same rubric. In total, then, 37 per cent of the respondents had heard about such behaviour and 63 per cent had not.

Because a nationwide representative sample is a set of individuals spatially dispersed, it is highly improbable that different respondents would be referring to the same people. Each of the respondents among that 37 per cent lived in a community in which it was held that someone had enriched himself or herself from Jews (whether or not the respondent used that expression); and either that someone was the only person referred to in this way in that community, or there might have been more. In any event, *Złote żniwa* does not deal with matters that no one in Poland has heard of or spoken about: many people—old and young, educated and uneducated, city- and country-dwellers—have heard about such incidents from personal narration. The authors of *Złote żniwa* and other books have transferred this knowledge from the private sphere to the public.

The public debate triggered by the book undoubtedly revived people's memories, encouraged them to talk and to exchange information on the issues raised in the book, and circulated the information among a broad range of social groups. During the interviews conducted in our survey, information until then stored in the recesses of a respondent's memory—about someone profiting from the extermination of the Jews—became more cognitively accessible. The respondents remembered more easily that they had heard of people enriching themselves 'at the expense of Jews' ('na Żydach'), of possessing something 'after the Jews [had had it]' ('po Żydach'), or of living 'on Jewish property' ('na żydowskim'). It is not possible to examine the extent to which people's memories were changed by *Złote żniwa*, as the topic had not been studied before the debate triggered by the book took place. However, all these interpretations are doubtless of interest to its authors.

ON MURDERING AND DENOUNCING JEWS

During the war, Poles murdered or denounced 'tens of thousands' of Jews to the Germans and the 'navy-blue police', consisting of Poles, that the Germans had formed. These actions were usually related to a greedy desire for Jewish gold. This is the thesis of the authors of *Złote żniwa*, and that is their estimate of the number of murdered and denounced Jews. Do present-day Poles share the same opinion as the authors of the book? They were asked the following question in the 2011 survey: 'Some historians write that during the occupation Poles murdered or denounced tens of thousands of Jews to the Germans and the police. From what you know, did that happen or not?' The answers are presented in the right-hand column of Table 2.

The degree of certainty of the answers turned out to be very low: only 9 per cent of the respondents said 'it happened', and 19 per cent said 'it did not happen'. However, it is difficult to expect ordinary people to express definite judgements about a matter that is so remote in time and shameful, and that has been passed over in silence until now—and, what is more, depicted in a variety of ways by the media. Negative responses are clearly dominant, though it is easier to be sure that something occurred than that something did not occur, for purely logical reasons. But this is not the entire story. A total of 32 per cent of the respondents chose the answer 'I do not know, but it could have happened', which was twice as many as the 16 per cent who responded 'I do not know, but it could not have happened'. Such answers are given not only because of a lack of certainty whether something occurred or did not occur. What these answers also involve is an acknowledgement that—in view of what one knows, has heard, or thinks about Poles, Jews, and Germans, and about people in time of war—some such event as betraying a person so that he is sent to his death, or some such event as Poles murdering so many Jews, might or might not be possible, can or cannot be conceived.

The meaning of the responses and the assessment of the book's impact are far

Table 2. Views on the responsibility of Poles for the death of Jews during the occupation and immediately after the war (2008, 2011)

The questions asked were:

(2008) 'Some historians write that about a thousand Jews were murdered in Poland immediately after the war. Do you think that happened or not?'

(2011) 'Some historians write that during the occupation Poles murdered or denounced tens of thousands of Jews to the Germans and the police. From what you know, did that happen or not?'

Available answers	Responses (%)		
	Jan. 2008	Apr. 2008	May 2011
I know that it happened	9	11	9
I do not know, but it could have happened	37	44	32
I do not know, but it could not have happened	16	15	16
I know that it did not happen	6	7	19
It is difficult to say	32	23	24
	N = 1,005	N = 1,005	N = 1,000

Note: For additional information relating to the survey, see text, n. 3.
Source: TNS OBOP, O Polakach i Żydach tuż przed 'Strachem' (2008): <http://obop-arch.tnsglobal.pl/archive-report/id/7664>; TNS OBOP, Efekt 'Strachu' (2008): <http://obop-arch.tnsglobal.pl/archive-report/id/7672>; TNS OBOP, Po 'Złotych żniwach' (2011): <http://obop-arch.tnsglobal.pl/archive-report/id/7913>. See text, n. 3.

from unambiguous, especially as two other books could also have contributed to the change we are attempting to assess—the well-documented monographs by Grabowski and Engelking. Among the categorical responses, those that disagree with the argument of the authors of *Złote żniwa* are clearly dominant, whereas among the other, less categorical responses it is support for their argument that is dominant. We do not know what people thought about this issue *before* the discussion took place; therefore, we also do not know the extent to which opinions *after* the debate are a consequence of the debate. However, it may be indirectly inferred that the debate about *Złote żniwa* did have some influence on the distribution of views.

Before the debate and the publication of the book, not even an approximate definition of the scale of the murder and denunciation of Jews existed in Poland in the social imagination or appeared in the space of communication. Even though such incidents were written about, they were not generalized into a phenomenon of such a large scale.

It is also important to look at the results of a similar study, carried out into the impact made by *Strach*, Gross's previous book, the Polish version of which appeared at the beginning of 2008.[6] In this survey, the question 'Some historians write that about a thousand Jews were murdered in Poland immediately after the war. Do you think that happened or not?' was asked at the time of the book's publication in January 2008, and again, after the debate about the book had ended, in April of that year.[7] During the months between the two surveys, the proportion of people who accepted that 'it happened' or 'it could have happened' increased from 46 per cent to 55 per cent, indicating an indisputable, though modest, effect brought about by the publication of the book (see Table 2). There is no reason why *Złote żniwa* should not have had a similar influence, though this is of course a weak argument. What needs to be taken into consideration as well is the probable *post factum* influence, of indeterminable magnitude, of earlier discussions in the Polish media caused by the appearance of the book's original edition as *Fear* in America in 2006, and the influence of the announcement that a Polish edition was going to be published. In any event, the view that very many Jews *could* have been murdered by Poles or with their help during the German occupation is no longer rare in Poland.

THE ATTITUDE OF POLES TOWARDS THE DEATH OF JEWS

The main controversy around *Złote żniwa* was not just about the facts—their occurrence and the scale of them. The dispute related mainly to their interpretation and their place in the image of Polish society during the war. Were these incidents common and socially accepted? For instance, was the murder of Jews really 'an acknowledged social practice in the countryside'? Was 'murdering Jews a phenomenon so common that the incidents were treated as a sort of shocking normality'? Was 'torturing and raping Jewish women a common practice then'?[8] Did these incidents just *take place* in Polish society under German occupation or do they *characterize* that society? Where should they be categorized in the picture of that society? Should they be at the very centre, because the extermination of the Jews was 'the biggest catastrophe of European civilization'?[9] Or should they be in a place that is conspicuous but not at the very centre, where the Polish underground state, society's resistance, and the armed struggle against Nazi Germany belong? It is to be noted that these latter phenomena were analysed by Gross himself in detail many years ago.[10]

The surveys' general questions about the attitude of Polish people towards the death of Jews touch upon the core of this problem. Here we do not need to limit

---

[6] It had been published first in English: see n. 2 above.

[7] TNS OBOP, *O Polakach i Żydach tuż przed 'Strachem'* (2008): <http://obop-arch.tnsglobal.pl/archive-report/id/7664>; TNS OBOP, *Efekt 'Strachu'* (2008): <http://obop-arch.tnsglobal.pl/archive-report/id/7672>.   [8] Gross and Grudzińska-Gross, *Złote żniwa*, 96, 104.

[9] J. T. Gross, 'Historia to nie księgowość', *Więź*, 2011, nos. 8–9, pp. 107–14.

[10] J. T. Gross, *Polish Society under German Occupation: The Generalgouvernment, 1939–1944* (Princeton, 1979).

ourselves to hypotheses in the examination of the impact of *Złote żniwa*—we can indeed measure it. We know what Poles thought in 2008, just after the debate on *Strach*, and because nothing that could significantly influence these views happened in Poland between then and the debate about *Złote żniwa*, it may be assumed that these views did not change. The final measurement after the examination of the impact of *Strach* constitutes the initial measurement in the examination of the impact of *Złote żniwa*.

Polish attitudes towards the extermination of Jews are a subject of public debate in which descriptions mix with generalizations and accusations with justifications. For the purposes of the research, four opinions on this issue were distinguished. They needed to be formulated in a simplified manner in the questionnaire, but they capture the essence of the matter: (1) 'Many Poles saved Jews and few persecuted them.' This is the defensive view, supporting the morally positive self-assessment of Poles; all the other opinions question this view to different extents. (2) 'Few Poles saved Jews and many persecuted them.' This is the accusatory view, contrary to the previous one. (3) 'Many Poles saved Jews and many persecuted them.' (4) 'Few Poles saved Jews and few persecuted them.' The difference between opinions (3) and (4) is partly a matter of the meaning of the words: what exactly is the difference between 'many' and 'few'? Notwithstanding, it would be hard to deny that both Poles who saved Jews and Poles who persecuted them constituted *proportionally* very small parts of the population. During the war, the majority of people were busy with their *own* lives and survival, and not with saving or murdering other people.[11] What views (3) and (4) have in common is a conviction that roughly the same number of Poles persecuted Jews as saved them.

Gross challenged the first, 'defensive' view and promoted the second, 'accusatory' view, in both *Złote żniwa* and *Strach*. Table 3 hints at the consquences of this. It turns out that the debate around *Złote żniwa*, as with that around *Strach* three years earlier, did not influence the most widespread and morally characteristic views of present-day Poles about the attitude of their wartime compatriots towards the death of Jews. The 'defensive' view that 'many Poles saved Jews and few persecuted them' has as many supporters in 2011 as it did before (47 per cent), and the small group of supporters of the accusatory argument closer to Gross's, that 'few Poles saved Jews and many persecuted them', has slightly diminished (the decrease, which may even be due to chance, is from 6 per cent to 4 per cent). The remainder of those respondents who expressed an opinion (31 per cent, no change) think that as many Poles ('few' or 'many') persecuted Jews as saved them. What is conspicuous here is not only the prevalence of Polish people's morally positive image of themselves. Almost 20 per cent of the respondents chose a view that they found difficult

---

[11] T. Szarota, *Okupowanej Warszawy dzień powszedni: Studium historyczne*, 2nd edn. (Warsaw, 1987), 594–611; A. Kłoskowska, 'Polacy wobec zagłady Żydów polskich: Próba typologii postaw', *Kultura i Społeczeństwo*, 1988, no. 4, pp. 111–27.

Table 3. Views on Polish attitudes towards the extermination of Jews (2008, 2011)

The question asked was: 'Every now and then there are disputes in Poland about Poles and Jews during the last war. Which of the following opinions is closest to yours?'

Available answers	Responses (%)		
	Jan. 2008	Apr. 2008	May 2011
Many Poles saved Jews and few persecuted them	43	47	47
Few Poles saved Jews and many persecuted them	3	6	4
Many Poles saved Jews and many persecuted them	17	19	18
Few Poles saved Jews and few persecuted them	12	12	13
It is difficult to say	25	16	18
	N = 1,005	N = 1,005	N = 1,000

Note: For additional information relating to the survey, see text, n. 3.
Source: TNS OBOP, O Polakach i Żydach tuż przed 'Strachem' (2008): <http://obop-arch.tnsglobal.pl/archive-report/id/7664>; TNS OBOP, Efekt 'Strachu' (2008): <http://obop-arch.tnsglobal.pl/archive-report/id/7672>; TNS OBOP, Po 'Złotych żniwach' (2011): <http://obop-arch.tnsglobal.pl/archive-report/id/7913>.

to accept—that many Poles saved Jews, and at the same time many persecuted them. However, *Złote żniwa* caused no increase in such views.

The general image that present-day Poles have of their compatriots' behaviour during the war is not very sensitive to the information provided in Gross's books. Some people continue to support this image, even though they possess, or at least have been exposed to, more detailed knowledge that contradicts those views. When the data from the 2011 survey are cross-tabulated they reveal that, while 70 per cent of those surveyed who denied that Poles murdered or denounced tens of thousands of Jews during the war accept the view consistent with this that 'many Poles saved Jews and few persecuted them', this positive image of Poles is also accepted by 34 per cent of those respondents who believe that Poles did indeed commit these disgraceful crimes. The knowledge of facts has not translated into generalizations —apparently the generalizations are based on something else.

WHY DID THE AUTHORS OF *ZŁOTE ŻNIWA* CONVINCE SO FEW POLES?

The social impact of *Złote żniwa* and the related debate proved to be complex. The book and debate no doubt revived the social memory of violence, robberies, and the murder of Jews. Probably they also convinced a small number of Poles that numerous incidents really did take place, and caused a significant number of Poles to think that such things at least 'could have happened'. However, the debate did not change the general and considered opinion about the attitude of Poles towards the killing of Jews. Why was this so, and why did a stimulus as strong as that book have much less of an impact than its authors had surely expected? First, we need to look for the answer in Polish people's attitudes and in the type of beliefs which *Złote żniwa* was to change; second, we need to look at the characteristic features of the book; and third, at the type of debate it caused.

Polish people's views on their relations with Jews are very resistant to change. The Polish national identity is very strongly tied to the experience of the Second World War; it was then that the self-stereotype of Poles as a 'nation of heroes and victims' was created. Polish people today still defend this stereotype, which shows them in a better light, and they unwillingly accept information that contradicts it. Jews are only reluctantly included as part of the common wartime suffering, especially in situations in which Poles themselves caused or collaborated in the suffering. Information that some of one's fellow countrymen behaved disgracefully, even if only a relatively small proportion of them, and even at a time as distant as the German occupation, is still treated as a threat to morally positive self-esteem. The national ego protects itself, and such information is not eagerly accepted. And when it is accepted, the consequences for the image of one's own nation are not accepted. Another obstacle is the fact that the crimes were committed against Jews, and Jews still constitute an object of antipathy and resentment to some Poles.[12]

Some of the characteristics of *Złote żniwa* that were stressed by historians and journalists in the opinion-forming media may have thwarted the authors' expectations by hindering rather than helping to break down the cognitive and emotional reluctance of some readers to accept the message of the book. Some academic historians of the era, while not in the least denying the incidents described in *Złote żniwa*, and while acknowledging the authors' merit in reminding the public about them, criticized their one-sided narrative, weakly justified generalizations, and the forming of opinions detached from the social context of war and occupation.[13] Some of the judgements expressed in the book were also criticized. In encouraging the public to read the book, the publishers claimed on the cover that the authors 'do not avoid sharp moral and historical judgements, and an expressive, direct use of language; they do not hide their emotions'. This characteristic of the book must have discouraged many readers. For example, the director of the Auschwitz-Birkenau museum summed up the debate about *Złote żniwa* by stating that, in his opinion, the book was 'full of judgements and generalizations which did not stimulate further debate, owing to the disheartening simplifications on which they

[12] A. Sułek, 'Ordinary Poles Look at the Jews', *East European Politics and Societies*, 26/2 (2012), 425–44; M. Bilewicz, M. Winiewski, and Z. Radzik, 'Antisemitism in Poland: Psychological, Religious, and Historical Aspects', *Journal for the Study of Antisemitism*, 4/2 (2012), 423–42.

[13] M. Zaremba, 'Biedni Polacy na żniwach', *Gazeta Wyborcza*, 15 Jan. 2011; P. Machcewicz, '"Złote żniwa", historia zaangażowana', *Gazeta Wyborcza*, 12 Feb. 2011.

are based', and that today, ten years after the publication of the groundbreaking *Sąsiedzi*, different books are now needed: 'this is not the place for facile writing, brutal judgements, and rhetorical generalizations'.[14]

In response, supporters of the book argued that it is not a monograph on the subject in the traditional sense, but a historical essay, in tune with the 'modern' way of writing history, and that its critics follow an outdated 'narrow positivism' and have a 'barbarian' lack of understanding of what a historical essay is, with its own type of narrative and criteria of accuracy and evidence. Without a doubt, both monographs and essays are equally legitimate methods of writing history, and perhaps even many of the criticized features of *Złote żniwa* do fall into what can be defined as an essay, but such a form also has its price: it tends to move rather than convince, especially over issues of great importance, on which the readers firmly stick to their opinions. If the genre chosen by the authors clashed with the Polish historians' conventions regarding history, then it necessarily clashed even more strikingly with what the broader audience was accustomed to. The literary genre of the book helped to introduce its content into the space of communication, but they did not help it to become accepted by the general public. From this point of view, its literary characteristics proved counterproductive. The outcome of the shock education turned out to be more of a shock than an education.

Złote żniwa is similar to *Sąsiedzi* and *Strach* in certain respects, such as subject matter, message, conventions, and language. The reaction to Gross's book was also played out in accordance with a certain schema, as if it were a realization of a script of some sort, encoded in the public discourse. Making public disputes phenomena of the media has the consequence that to an even greater extent they become subject to a predictable exchange of established communicative idioms. It is not just the types of standpoint that are predictable—typologies elaborated for the analysis of the debate about *Sąsiedzi* are used for the analyses of Gross's later books too. Sometimes it is even possible to predict who will react with deep indignation and crude attacks on the author, and who will show strong support and justify every weak argument with the justness of the cause it serves. The debate becomes confrontational and lacks what Marek Czyżewski, a sociologist at the University of Łódź, calls 'mediatory work—an effort to reconcile the standpoints'.[15] It leads to the strengthening of contrary positions rather than to the working out of a multi-faceted representation that would win over more people than at present, perhaps even the majority of society.

However, a new motif appeared in the schematic debate surrounding *Złote żniwa* by comparison with the previous debates. This time, the division of opinions in the media that formed mass opinion was not only between the respective supporters of the affirmative and the critical histories of Poland, but also between the opponents

[14] P. M. A. Cywiński, 'Inne czasy, inne pytania', *Więź*, 2011, no. 7, pp. 45–6.

[15] M. Czyżewski, 'Polski spór o książkę *Strach* Jana Tomasza Grossa w perspektywie "pośredniczącej" analizy dyskursu', *Studia Socjologiczne*, 2009, no. 3, pp. 5–26.

and supporters of 'Polish–Jewish dialogue'. In my opinion, the most serious critiques of the book were published in the daily newspaper *Gazeta Wyborcza*, an advocate of critical history of Poland, and in the monthly *Więź*, for many years an advocate of dialogue. Adam Michnik, the editor-in-chief of *Gazeta Wyborcza*, even intended to write a 'polemical afterword' to the book (as Gershom Sholem did to Hannah Arendt's *Eichmann in Jerusalem*), but he changed his mind because he 'did not want to appear in the company of those strange characters who criticize Gross'.[16] With that explanation, Michnik showed how strong a certain type of political correctness was in some circles in the discussion about *Złote żniwa*. Perhaps —though the argument for this is not so strong—there are different types of 'correctness' in other circles that distorted the public expression of personal opinion, and shaped public opinion in the opposite direction.

The fruits of the 'harvest' of *Złote żniwa* discussed so far are direct and immediate effects which occurred—or failed to occur—within a few months. However, the impact of the book has not been limited to minor changes in people's opinions. The book broke another taboo of public debate and permanently added to the space of communication a content that had previously been absent from it. This impact is unquestionable and irreversible. Naturally, no one can predict its possible future consequences, but they may be anticipated by analogy with the known impact of *Sąsiedzi*, the first book of Gross's trilogy.[17]

The most important theme in the debate about *Sąsiedzi* was the role played by the local Polish community and the officers of the Nazi German state in the crime perpetrated in the town of Jedwabne.[18] In the opinion surveys conducted in 2002 and 2011, this complex problem was addressed in the form of a simple question with a choice of short answers for the respondents.[19] Five answers were arranged to reflect decreasing participation of Poles and increasing participation of Germans. In answer to the question 'Who, in your opinion, murdered the Jews in Jedwabne?', the responses 'Poles encouraged by Germans' and 'Germans with the help of Poles' are closest to the true situation as depicted by historians. The answers 'local Poles, without Germans participating' and 'only Germans, without Poles participating' are indisputably false, and the answer 'Poles forced by Germans' is essentially false, though there were elements of force in the actions of the Germans. The answers 'local Poles, without Germans participating' and 'Poles encouraged by Germans' blame the Polish side; 'only Germans, without Poles participating' and 'Poles

[16] A. Michnik, 'O milimetr od antysemityzmu' (interview by Z. Nosowski), *Więź*, 2011, no. 7, pp. 29–41.

[17] A. Sułek, 'Pamięć Polaków o zbrodni w Jedwabnem', *Nauka*, 2011, no. 3, pp. 39–49.

[18] P. Machcewicz and K. Persak (eds.), *Wokół Jedwabnego*, 2 vols. (Warsaw, 2002); D. Libionka, 'The Debate around the Jedwabne Massacre', in F. Tych and M. Adamczyk-Garbowska (eds.), *Jewish Presence in Absence: Aftermath of the Holocaust in Poland, 1945–2010* (Jerusalem, 2014), 847–96.

[19] TNS OBOP, *Polacy o zbrodni w Jedwabnem* (2002): <http://obop-arch.tnsglobal.pl/archive-report/id/1345>; TNS OBOP, *Po 'Złotych żniwach'* (2011): <http://obop-arch.tnsglobal.pl/archive-report/id/7913>.

Table 4. Views on the responsibility of Poles for the death of Jews during the occupation and immediately after the war (2008, 2011)

The questions asked were:

(2002) 'There was recently a debate in Poland about the crime committed against the Jews in Jedwabne. Who, in your opinion, murdered the Jews in Jedwabne?'

(2011) 'You probably remember or know that ten years ago there was a debate in Poland about the crime committed against the Jews in Jedwabne. Who, in your opinion, murdered the Jews in Jedwabne?'

Available answers	Responses (%)	
	2002	2011
Local Poles, without Germans participating	1	5
Poles encouraged by Germans	9	13
Germans with the help of Poles	14	10
Poles forced by Germans	17	11
Only Germans, without Poles participating	9	15
I do not know exactly	44	34
I have not heard about it	6	12
	N = 1,008	N = 1,000

Note: For additional information relating to the survey, see text, n. 3.
Source: TNS OBOP, Polacy o zbrodni w Jedwabnem (2002): <http://obop-arch.tnsglobal.pl/archive-report/id/1345>; TNS OBOP, Po 'Złotych żniwach' (2011): <http://obop-arch.tnsglobal.pl/archive-report/id/7913>.

forced by Germans' blame the German side; and 'Germans with the help of Poles' blames both sides. Table 4 presents the results of the surveys.

Over the course of the decade from 2002 to 2011, the percentage of people who spontaneously said, in various ways, that they did not know who murdered the Jews in Jedwabne decreased, from 44 per cent to 34 per cent. Such answers are not surprising, as the question is difficult and requires respondents to possess both information and motivation. In such types of situation, some of the respondents with less information and motivation will save themselves the effort of formulating an answer. For some people, the massacre in Jedwabne in 1941 is not an issue important enough for them to make an effort to work out who caused it, given that the media present multiple opinions on the subject. However, about half of the respondents—50 per cent in 2002 and 54 per cent in 2011—*did* have an opinion on this matter. People are gaining knowledge extremely slowly, almost imperceptibly, but nevertheless their knowledge is increasing.

In 2011, just as in 2002, the German occupiers were considered the main direct perpetrators of the crime much more often than local Poles. There has been an important change, however. In 2011, 26 per cent of all respondents, exactly as many as in 2002, thought that the Germans were the *main* perpetrators ('only Germans, without Poles participating' plus 'Poles forced by Germans'). By contrast, in 2002 a total of 10 per cent ascribed this role to Poles, while by 2011 18 per cent of the respondents considered Poles to have been the perpetrators. Opinions on who the perpetrator was are becoming more and more defined, categorical, and schematic. There has been a decrease in the number of answers ascribing blame to both sides ('Germans with the help of Poles'), and the remaining answers are now more polarized. More respondents blame only Germans (an increase from 9 per cent to 15 per cent) or only Poles (an increase from 1 per cent to 5 per cent). This is how memory works—the essence remains and the details slip.

Perhaps in a few years, maybe ten, more Poles than at present will accept that many of their compatriots plundered and murdered Jews under the German occupation. However, the process of change will be slow, retarded by the loss of social memory. Its pace will mostly depend on broader changes within Polish identity and on further historical research and public debate on the relations between Poles and Jews.

Translated from the Polish by Anna Tilles

Righteousness and Evil

Jedwabne in the Polish Theatre

KATHLEEN CIOFFI

I can't even think . . . Everything falls apart . . . There's nothing in life that connects with this . . . double revelation of righteousness and evil.   NATHAN KAPLAN

ALTHOUGH EVERYONE KNOWS that life is complicated, almost never black and white, and all humans have the potential within them for both good and evil, it is still not easy to fully comprehend this duality when one is confronted with it head on, as was Nathan Kaplan during filming of the documentary *Shtetl*, directed by his friend Marian Marzyński.[1] Just as Kaplan, a Jewish American from Chicago, was shocked at learning of the combination of both goodness and badness in the wartime behaviour of the natives of Brańsk, his parents' home town, so too was much of the entire Polish nation flabbergasted by the revelations in *Neighbors*, Jan Tomasz Gross's book about another small town in north-eastern Poland, Jedwabne.[2] *Neighbors* revealed that during the Second World War, Poles—not Germans—had killed their Jewish neighbours in Jedwabne and in some other towns and villages. But more than that, it began a process of questioning what I have elsewhere called 'the Polishness narrative', that is, the story of heroism and victimhood that Poles tell themselves about themselves.[3] This process has also affected the theatre.

During the communist era, the theatre functioned as what Ewa M. Thompson calls 'a substitute location for commemorating the traumas and glories of the nation'.[4] Although it was subject to censorship, and some productions were banned, many producers and theatre companies in the decades from the 1950s to the 1980s

---

[1] *Shtetl*, directed and produced by M. Marzyński, Marz Associates, in association with WGBH/ Frontline (Boston, 1996).

[2] J. T. Gross, *Neighbors: The Destruction of the Jewish Community in Jedwabne, Poland* (Princeton, 2001); originally published as J. T. Gross, *Sąsiedzi: Historia zagłady żydowskiego miasteczka* (Sejny, 2000).

[3] K. Cioffi, 'Introduction', in K. Cioffi and B. Johnston (eds.), *The Other in Polish Theatre and Drama*, special issue of *Indiana Slavic Studies*, 14 (2003), 3.

[4] E. M. Thompson, 'Ways of Remembering: The Case of Poland', in T. Trojanowska et al. (eds.), *New Perspectives on Polish Culture: Personal Encounters, Public Affairs* (New York, 2012), 226.

still managed to stage plays that audiences interpreted as defiant commemorations of anti-Russian or anti-communist resistance. Such plays ranged from Romantic and neo-Romantic classics—such as *Dziady* by Adam Mickiewicz or *Noc listopadowa* by Stanisław Wyspiański—to satiric plays by Sławomir Mrożek and productions by alternative theatre groups such as Poznań's Teatr Ósmego Dnia (Theatre of the Eighth Day). Although this function of theatre as a location for memorializing and catharsis has diminished as it has become less necessary since 1989, the tradition of serious theatre that acts in this way still very much exists in post-communist Poland. Even so, it took some time for the Polish theatre to come to grips directly with the *Neighbors* phenomenon.

The earliest theatrical reaction to the revelations in *Neighbors*, albeit an indirect one, was Krzysztof Warlikowski's 2003 production of Shakespeare's *Tempest*.[5] Warlikowski himself has stated that his production was very much influenced by the Jedwabne controversy:

at the moment when I staged *The Tempest*, the so-called 'Jewish question' appeared in Poland with the emergence of Jedwabne . . . At the end of the play, when Prospero meets with the Neapolitans and the Milanese, there can be either forgiveness or resentment. It's similar to the situation that unfolded in Poland two years before with Jedwabne, which created a lively polemic . . . At the time of Jedwabne, there was a remembrance ceremony . . . It was the largest Jewish political event in post-war Poland, in the presence of the Polish President, who said: 'Forgive us' . . . To return to *The Tempest*, there was thus this meeting with people who had caused harm to others, and who had even wanted them dead. Like this memorial day in Jedwabne: everyone was there for forgiveness.[6]

Warlikowski claims that only his staging of the reconciliation scene in *The Tempest* was inspired by the 2001 memorial ceremony commemorating the sixtieth anniversary of the Jedwabne massacre and says, 'we didn't try to point directly at Jedwabne, not at all'.[7] But in fact more than that one scene is permeated by the sense that a resonant past incident has cast a long shadow over the present events of the play. In this rather unconventional interpretation of *The Tempest*, Prospero's having been cast out of his kingdom casts a pall similar to the one that the massacre that occurred in Jedwabne in June 1941 cast over the zeitgeist in Poland after the release of Gross's book.

It was not until 2008, however, that Polish plays dealt directly with the Jedwabne massacre and the controversy surrounding it. In that year, *Burmistrz* ('The Mayor'), by Małgorzata Sikorska-Miszczuk, was given a reading at Teatr na Woli (The Theatre in Wola) in Warsaw in May, and *Nasza klasa* ('Our Class'), by Tadeusz Słobodzianek, received its first reading in October at the International Festival 'Theatrical Confrontations' (Międzynarodowy Festiwal 'Konfrontacje Teatralne'),

---

[5] *Burza*, dir. K. Warlikowski, premiere 2003, filmed 2008 (DVD; Warsaw, 2009).

[6] K. Warlikowski, in conversation with F. Arvers and P. Gruszczyński, with a response by M. C. Steinlauf, 'Re-imagining the Jewish Legacy in Post-Communist Poland: Dialogues', *Polish Theatre Perspectives*, 1/1 (2010), 90–1.   [7] Ibid. 91.

an annual festival in Lublin, which that year was devoted to the theme 'Jews in the Theatre'. The two plays differ in style, genre, and tone, as well as in the aspects of the controversy they choose to engage. While *Nasza klasa* concerns itself both with the massacres that occurred in Jedwabne and the nearby town of Radziłów and with the post-war suppression of knowledge about the annihilation of the region's Jews, *Burmistrz* reflects more on the post-*Neighbors* controversy over the pogrom and the memorial ceremony for the sixtieth anniversary. However, both plays in very different ways are at least as concerned with what Sławomir Grünberg calls 'the legacy of Jedwabne'[8]—the battle for memory between those who basically accept Gross's narrative and those who completely reject it—as they are with the massacre itself.

BURMISTRZ: TWO SURREALIST TAKES ON THE CONTROVERSY

Burmistrz is more overtly concerned with this battle. It was inspired by Anna Bikont's reporting in *Gazeta Wyborcza* in 2002 about the tribulations of the mayor of Jedwabne, Krzysztof Godlewski. Godlewski told Bikont, 'When I read *Neighbors*, I saw something had to be done.'[9] He tried to get a school renamed after Antonina Wyrzykowska, a local woman who had saved seven Jews; he talked on local television about his dreams that the Jewish cemetery in Jedwabne would become a place of pilgrimage; and he spoke at the memorial ceremony. However, he was completely unable to move his constituents in Jedwabne, and eventually not only resigned his post as mayor but also emigrated to the United States. Sikorska-Miszczuk turned what Bikont called the mayor's 'desperate search for something positive'[10] into her own brand of absurdist theatre.

Sikorska-Miszczuk's aesthetic is anti-realistic; as Dara Weinberg points out in an article about a reading of the play in Los Angeles, 'With so many other writers searching for factual accounts relating to Jedwabne, Sikorska-Miszczuk's work takes a different tack: it makes frequent use of surrealism, breaking the fourth wall, self-referentiality, and acerbic irony.'[11] Characters in the play include 'The Mother of God', 'A Penitent German', and 'A Beauty Queen'. Some scenes of the play take place in a 'cemetery that is not there', where the 'Mayor Before' sees a town that used to be there but no longer exists. In the climax of the play, the townspeople, who

---

[8] *The Legacy of Jedwabne*, documentary film produced and directed by S. Grünberg, Log In Productions (Spencer, NY, 2005).

[9] A. Bikont, *My z Jedwabnego* (Warsaw, 2004), 230. All quotations from this book come from the English translation by Alissa Valles, forthcoming from Farrar, Straus, and Giroux, which Valles has generously shared with me. Page numbers refer to the Polish edition.   [10] Ibid.

[11] D. Weinberg, 'Two Readings by Playwright Małgorzata Sikorska-Miszczuk', *Culture Spot LA*, 27 Nov. 2011: <http://culturespotla.com/2011/11/two-readings-by-playwright-malgorzata-sikorska-miszczuk/>.

firmly reject the mayor's attempt to acknowledge the dead, carry the town's jewel-encrusted monument—which represents not only the old Jedwabne monument that attributed blame for the massacre to the Germans, but also the town's refusal to see the truth—to the cemetery, where the Mayor Before speaks to them:

I know the Truth is hard to bear. Hear me out: this isn't easy, but I see a slow change taking place in some of you! We need time. Hear me out, Townspeople of my Town. You're under fire even though you've not committed this crime. It's hard to bear such a burden. Time—give it time! Don't do this! Townspeople, it's me, your Mayor! Don't do this! It's me! It's me![12]

Then the townspeople set the monument down on him, and he becomes the 'Mayor After'. The Beauty Queen, who has witnessed this act, turns to stone.

This play was well received in Poland: it was a finalist for best play at the 2010 Festival of Polish Contemporary Plays R@port (Festiwal Polskich Sztuk Współ-czesnych R@port) in Gdynia and was broadcast on the Polish radio programme *Scena teatralna* ('Theatrical Stage') in June 2011. Nevertheless, Sikorska-Miszczuk came to feel that her play was 'too cryptic' and she decided to retell the story, explaining, 'I was looking for a less mythical space in which to place my characters.'[13] So, shortly after the radio broadcast of *Burmistrz*, she wrote *Burmistrz, część II* ('The Mayor, Part II'), in which 'Professor Jan T. Gross' is actually a character. However, although this retelling incorporates dialogue taken straight from Bikont's book and also from news accounts of the memorial ceremony, it is obviously not intended as a docudrama or even as a realistic fictional drama: for example, the book *Neighbors* itself is also a character, along with 'God from the Town', 'God from Jerusalem', and 'God from New York'. The climax of this version is the memorial ceremony, to which a character called the 'Townsperson' reacts sceptically, saying 'I'm out of here'.[14] In the denouement, the members of the town council continue to reject the Mayor, saying, 'You could have been our Mayor, not theirs . . . You did what the Jews wanted, and now they've left you.'[15] The Townsperson curses the Mayor, who emigrates to America, where he meditates on his fate:

Was I alive only to learn that I'm stubborn? That's what I keep asking myself as I wander the empty sidewalks along your broad streets. It's this European habit: walking. I hear a language that isn't mine. I'm scared of places I don't know, customs I don't understand. I'm a stranger. I will never belong anywhere anymore. Fear is always with me, I say it, I repeat it, garbling your words. I keep thinking that I was stubborn, very stubborn. And that I found

---

[12] M. Sikorska-Miszczuk, *Burmistrz*, in *Notatnik Teatralny*, 56–7 (2009), 319. All quotations from this play and *Burmistrz, część II* come from the English translations by Artur Zapałowski, which appear in slightly different form in *(A)pollonia: Twenty-First-Century Polish Drama and Texts for the Stage*, ed. K. Duniec, J. Klass, and J. Krakowska (London, 2014), 58–121. Thanks to Jon Lawrence Rivera of Playwrights' Arena, Los Angeles, for sharing the English translations with me. Page numbers refer to the Polish editions.   [13] Quoted in Weinberg, 'Two Readings'.

[14] M. Sikorska-Miszczuk, *Burmistrz, część II*, *Dialog*, 56/12 (2011), 193.   [15] Ibid. 194.

the strength to stand by myself and my truth. That's something to be proud of, something big. But the loneliness, the loneliness.[16]

Much like the real Krzysztof Godlewski, the Mayor in Sikorska-Miszczuk's play leaves Jedwabne with only his pride intact: he has stood up to his constituents but his 'desperate search for something positive' comes up empty.

NASZA KLASA: A THEATRICAL GRAPPLING WITH THE CAUSES AND THE AFTERMATH OF A MASSACRE

Nasza klasa is more ambitious than either of Sikorska-Miszczuk's plays, in that it tries simultaneously to reflect on, personalize, and generalize the pogroms of June 1941, as well as to reveal the complexities of the pre-war, wartime, and post-war history of the Jedwabne region. Słobodzianek, in the English edition of *Nasza klasa*, acknowledges drawing 'knowledge and inspiration' not only from *Neighbors*, but also from another book edited by Gross and his ex-wife, Irena Grudzińska Gross, that collects letters written by Polish children who were deported to Siberia during the period of Russian occupation of eastern Poland at the beginning of the Second World War; from the report by the Instytut Pamięci Narodowej (Institute of National Remembrance) summarizing the investigation into the Jedwabne massacre; from Anna Bikont's reportage about Jedwabne and Radziłów; and from films by Marzyński, Paweł Łoziński, and Agnieszka Arnold.[17] He uses the source material in an imaginative way: rather than precisely reconstructing the massacres in the two towns, he fashions a kind of amalgam of Jedwabne's and Radziłów's stories and of truth and fiction. For example, of the ten characters, eight are based —some fairly closely, some much less so—on real people who lived in either Jedwabne or Radziłów. However, he transforms their stories into something more universal that tries to explore how people who grew up together and knew each other intimately could turn on each other, and how they could live with themselves afterward.

The play follows the fates of ten classmates from their schooldays through the Soviet occupation at the beginning of the Second World War, the subsequent German occupation, the massacre, the post-war period, and right up to and beyond the sixtieth anniversary of the massacre in the barn. Five of the classmates are Jewish, five are non-Jews. This roughly reflects the population distribution in Jedwabne: although at one time there were more Jews than non-Jews in the town, by

---

[16] Ibid. 195.

[17] T. Słobodzianek, *Our Class*, adapted by R. Craig from a translation by C. Grosvenor (London, 2009), 5; published in Polish as T. Słobodzianek, *Nasza klasa* (Gdańsk, 2010). Books and films Słobodzianek acknowledges are Gross, *Neighbors*; J. T. Gross and I. Grudzińska-Gross (eds.), *'W czterdziestym nas matko na Sybir zesłali...': Polska a Rosja, 1939–42* (London, 1983); P. Machcewicz and K. Persak (eds.), *Wokół Jedwabnego* (Warsaw, 2002); Bikont, *My z Jedwabnego*; *Shtetl*, dir. Marzyński; *Miejsce urodzenia*, dir. P. Łoziński (Łódź, 1992); *Sąsiedzi*, dir. A. Arnold (Warsaw, 2001).

the 1930s non-Jews slightly outnumbered Jews. Jews and non-Jews did, in fact, go to school together in Jedwabne and Radziłów; by contrast with some shtetls in Poland, there was no separate Jewish school in Jedwabne, and the Jewish school in Radziłów was too expensive for most Jews to attend. Słobodzianek has mentioned that he was inspired by a pre-war school photograph of one of the Jedwabne survivors (Szmul Wasersztajn) standing next to one of the alleged perpetrators (Jerzy Laudański), both smiling.[18] Among the classmates in the play, three are perpetrators of the massacre, two are victims, two are rescuers, two are survivors, and one leaves town for America before the massacre occurs.

The play is set in a nameless town; the words 'Jedwabne' or 'Radziłów' are never mentioned. Słobodzianek depicts pre-war relations between Jews and non-Jews as being relatively friendly until the death in 1935 of Marshal Józef Piłsudski, who had pursued a policy of toleration towards Jews and other ethnic minorities. During a rehearsal of a choral recitation of a poem lamenting his death, one of the classmates, Heniek, inserts his own words:

> The Marshal's a prick with a circumcised dick
> Who only loved women and jewels
> He married three times and committed his crimes
> And sold all us Poles to the Jews![19]

Heniek's words reflect the atmosphere in the late thirties in the Jedwabne region, which was a hotbed of antisemitic sentiment stirred up by the National Democratic Party (Stronnictwo Narodowe, or Narodówka, as it was popularly known) and by the Church. Anna Bikont documents the local climate in the first chapter of her book *My z Jedwabnego*, entitled 'Lord, Rid Poland of the Jews'.[20] In the play, after Piłsudski's death, things immediately become worse for the Jewish classmates, who now must sit at the back of the class during Catholic prayers. One of them, Menachem, gets bullied and beaten up by his non-Jewish classmates.

Then the war starts and the characters describe the arrival of the Soviet army. The town, especially the Jews, welcomes the Soviets. Two classmates, Jakub Kac (spelt Katz in the English edition) and Menachem, are put in charge of a new cinema created by the Soviets from the former Catholic club. Everyone, including local Jews, quickly becomes disillusioned with communism, however, and four non-Jewish classmates form an 'underground resistance movement' to fight against the Soviets.[21] One of them is arrested and severely beaten by the NKVD (the Soviet secret police, forerunners to the KGB). All these details closely track facts that Słobodzianek has gleaned from his source materials, including Gross's *Neighbors*.

---

[18] Press materials, Wilma Theater, Philadelphia, Oct. 2011. The Wilma presented the US premiere of *Our Class*, 12 Oct.–13 Nov. 2011. For my review of this production, see K. Cioffi, 'The Ghosts of Memory', *Theater*, online edition: <http://theatermagazine.org/our-class>.

[19] Słobodzianek, *Our Class*, 14.   [20] Bikont, *My z Jedwabnego*, 30.

[21] Słobodzianek, *Our Class*, 27.

For example, Jedwabne did actually have an anti-Soviet underground, as pointed out by Gross: 'In one respect the *gmina* Jedwabne had a history unlike those of most places under the Soviet occupation. A vast anti-Soviet underground organization had been established there early on, and in June 1940 it was tracked down by the Soviet secret police, NKVD, and destroyed.'[22] Polish critics of Gross's book tend to dwell on the twenty-month period of Soviet occupation of eastern Poland, a time of arrests, shortages, and deportations to Siberia, and imply that Jewish collaboration with the Soviets during that time somehow explains the massacres at Jedwabne and elsewhere in the region.[23]

Słobodzianek disposes of the Soviet occupation period in only two scenes, which examine how the atmosphere of fear and entrapment created by the occupation combined with pre-existing antisemitism to lead to a kind of moral decay. For example, Zygmunt, a classmate who goes into hiding when his father is deported for displaying an illegal Polish flag, discovers that the Soviet constitution forbids holding children responsible for the crimes of their fathers, so he writes a letter to Stalin to complain. This gets him an interview with the NKVD, which results in his collaboration with them under the code name 'Popov' and his subsequent betrayal of Rysiek, one of his classmates in the resistance cell. It is the terrified Jakub Katz, however, who is the one who gets blamed for the betrayal, when the NKVD officers bring him to identify the beaten-up Rysiek. The somewhat absurd details of Zygmunt's involvement with the NKVD (right down to the letter to Stalin and code name) are mainly derived from Bikont's interviews with a man named Zygmunt Laudański, who was one of the people convicted after the war of the Jedwabne crime. And the blaming of the Jewish Jakub Katz for the betrayal illustrates one of the points that Gross makes in *Neighbors*: that the Polish characterization of Jews as collaborators with the Soviets has been based not on fact, but on stereotypes 'confirmed' by happenstance.[24]

The atrocity itself takes up three scenes in the play. In the first, Jakub Katz is beaten with fence-posts by Rysiek, Heniek, and Zygmunt, before Rysiek finally crushes his head with a large paving stone. In the second scene, Rysiek and Zygmunt rape Dora, a Jewish classmate. And in the third, Rysiek participates in the killing of Jewish men inside the barn, while Zygmunt orders the Jewish women, including Dora, into the barn, where they are burned to death. Meanwhile, Menachem escapes the killing spree by running to Zocha, a non-Jewish classmate, and begging her to hide him in her barn. Władek, another non-Jewish classmate, hides the Jewish Rachelka in his family's attic.

The mixture of fiction and non-fiction is particularly intriguing in *Nasza klasa*. Menachem and Zocha are partly based on Szmul Wasersztajn and Antonina

---

[22] Gross, *Neighbors*, 47.

[23] See e.g. T. Strzembosz, 'Collaboration Passed Over in Silence', in A. Polonsky and J. B. Michlic (eds.), *The Neighbors Respond: The Controversy over the Jedwabne Massacre in Poland* (Princeton, 2004), 220–36.   [24] See Gross, *Neighbors*, 46–7.

Wyrzykowska, the woman who saved him. Like Zocha, Wyrzykowska was married to an older man and probably had an affair with Wasersztajn (although she never admits it to Bikont). However, unlike Zocha, who is afraid to help Dora or her child, Wyrzykowska actually hid not only Wasersztajn, but six other Jews as well, and was assisted in helping the Jews by her husband. Władek and Rachelka are modelled on Stanisław Ramotowski and Rachela Finkelsztejn from Radziłów: as in the play, Ramotowski hid Rachela and persuaded her to convert to Christianity and marry him. However, unlike Władek in the play, who makes no effort to help Rachelka's family, Ramotowski did try, unsuccessfully, to save the rest of the Finkelsztejns.

It is the fictional details that Słobodzianek invents that illustrate the mixture of righteousness and evil in Polish–Jewish relations that he is trying to illuminate. For example, the real Jakub Kac, a 73-year-old man rather than the young know-it-all depicted in the play, was murdered on 25 June 1941, just after the German invasion, an indication that the motivation was score-settling for his behaviour during the Soviet occupation. In the play, his fate symbolizes the tragic consequences of the mistaken *żydokomuna* (Judaeo-communist) stereotype, a stereotype taken advantage of by the duplicitous Zygmunt. The completely fictional Dora and Rysiek, on the other hand, represent the intertwined fate of Polish Jews and non-Jewish Poles. Earlier in the play Rysiek writes a valentine to Dora, but during the pogrom, he rapes her. Dora protests against her rape, but she must still be attracted in some way to Rysiek because when he rapes her she says, 'I felt a pleasure I'd never known.'[25]

In the second half of the play, the consequences of the massacre on the survivors, rescuers, and perpetrators are shown. Immediately after the massacre, Rachelka (now called Marianna as her Christian name) must confront the barely veiled antisemitism of her neighbours and the memory of her fellow Jews who have been killed. On the way to her combined baptism and marriage ceremony, she muses on her fate:

> riding through the town . . . where there wasn't a single Jew left. And in the Jewish houses the new owners now stood . . . in their doorways and by their windows and on their porches . . . and they glared at me as I drove past, their faces filled with hate. I didn't have to close my eyes to see the former residents standing there beside them. Tears fell down my face and for the first time I felt there was no reason to live.[26]

When they get drunk at Władek and Marianna's wedding, Rysiek hallucinates, seeing Dora, and Zygmunt sees the ghost of Jakub Katz. Later, Władek kills Rysiek when Rysiek tries to take Marianna away to the ghetto; as Rysiek dies, he sees Dora's ghost again. Władek and Marianna go into hiding in the forest, where Marianna gives birth to their baby, who dies soon after birth. Many of these details—including the taking away of Marianna by a Polish betrayer and the death of their newborn while they were in hiding—closely follow the story of the Ramotowskis

---

[25] Słobodzianek, *Our Class*, 43.   [26] Ibid. 58.

from Bikont's book; however, the Rachelka/Marianna of the play is far more ambivalent about Władek than Marianna Ramotowska seems to have been about her husband: compare Słobodzianek's Marianna ('To be honest I never thought much of Władek')[27] with Bikont ('For the next sixty years they [the Ramotowskis] didn't part for even a split second').[28] The fictional character is also far more self-reflective than the rather reticent woman Bikont interviewed.

Słobodzianek mixes even more fictional elements into his characterizations of Menachem and Zocha than those of Władek and Marianna. Although Menachem is based on Szmul Wasersztajn, upon whose testimony Gross based many of his assertions in *Neighbors*, and Wasersztajn was prone to lies and exaggerations,[29] Menachem is an even more ambiguous figure. In the early scenes, he appears to be basically sympathetic, albeit cowardly, but after the war, he becomes consumed by revenge, joining the secret police and obtaining confessions (including one from Zygmunt) through torture. Zocha is also less sympathetic in the play than the real-life Wyrzykowska: after emigrating to America she gets a job working for a Jewish family, but leaves it, saying, 'Was I to be a skivvy for Jews the rest of my life?'[30] In real life, Wyrzykowska acted with admirable courage during the war and later in life seemed mystified by her countrymen's antisemitism: she told Bikont, 'I had the pleasure of saving Jews' lives. But people look at you askance for it.'[31]

Słobodzianek has been criticized for the even-handedness with which he deals with the Polish Jews and the non-Jewish Poles in the play. For example, Agnieszka Arnold, the documentary film-maker whose film *Sąsiedzi* inspired Jan Gross to write his book, told Blanka Zizka, the director of the US premiere of *Our Class*, 'In the play, they are all equal in their behavior . . . The play tries to explain Evil through psychology. But the reason for the pogrom was pure and simple Polish anti-Semitism.'[32] Others have criticized the play for exactly the opposite reason: that it is too eager to ascribe the causes of the massacre to 'pure and simple Polish anti-Semitism'. For example, Dominic Cavendish in an article in the culture section of the London *Daily Telegraph* writes, 'The conclusion you could easily come to, watching *Our Class*, as many of the reviewers have, is that Poles were just itching for the German invasion as the excuse to give violent vent to their deep-rooted anti-

---

[27] Ibid. 104.   [28] Bikont, *My z Jedwabnego*, 66.

[29] See ibid., ch. 11. Bikont makes clear in this chapter that many of the incidents that Wasersztajn claimed in his testimony to have personally witnessed were not, in fact, witnessed by him. She also makes several wry remarks about his tendency to exaggerate his own exploits, especially in the memoir that he dictated to a Spanish-speaking journalist.

[30] Słobodzianek, *Our Class*, 81.   [31] Bikont, *My z Jedwabnego*, 256.

[32] B. Zizka, 'Agnieszka Arnold, Documentary Filmmaker—Part One': <http://www.wilmatheater. org/blog/agnieszka-arnold-documentary-filmmaker-%E2%80%93-part-one>. Henryk Grynberg, in his review of the Washington, DC, production, also criticizes the play for what he calls its 'assumption of symmetry', and he also objects to Dora's reaction to her rape. H. Grynberg, '"Our Class" by Tadeusz Słobodzianek in Washington: A Fascinating Show but Not about Jedwabne': <http://www.aapjstudies. org/index.php?id=179>.

Semitism.'[33] But Słobodzianek's mission as a dramatist is neither to expose evil as a documentarian might nor to dig into the details of the massacre as a historian would; rather, he is trying to explore imaginatively the mindsets of people thrust into situations that they could never have prepared for.

Although Słobodzianek does not directly explore the role that religion played in the towns of Jedwabne and Radziłów, he does touch on it through the two clerical characters in the play: Heniek, who becomes a priest, and Abram, who leaves the town for America before the war starts, and becomes a rabbi. Of the two, Abram, based on Rabbi Jacob Baker, who, like his fictional counterpart, emigrated to America from Jedwabne before the war's start, is characterized as the more generous of spirit. Heniek, who is based in part on Father Edward Orłowski, the parish priest in Jedwabne who opposed the building of a new monument in Jedwabne to replace the old one that had laid the blame for the massacre on the Germans, comes off very badly. First, he (unlike Orłowski, who did not grow up in Jedwabne) helps to perpetrate the massacre, and later it is implied that he is also involved in the sexual abuse scandals that have rocked the Church in recent years. Abram, on the other hand, is mainly represented by his letters to his remaining classmates, which highlight early on his obtuseness about what is going on in his home town. Later, however, his letters provide two of the play's emotional high points: first, when he recites in his letter to the Polish government the names of all the relatives he lost in the massacre in the barn, and in the final scene when he lists in his letter to Marianna the even more numerous names of all his descendants.

In fact, Abram is the only character in the play who seems to find fulfilment in his life. All the others—whether survivors, rescuers, or perpetrators—seem to be cursed by the events of that day. Zygmunt, for example, loses his son in a tragic accident, as does Menachem. Zygmunt seems to feel remorse for his deeds: 'Something strange happened to him before he died. He started quivering and trying to fling himself out of bed. Tears were streaming down his cheeks.'[34] Zocha, estranged from her children, overdoses on sleeping pills in her nursing home. Heniek dies while hallucinating that the Jews who died in the pogrom surround him. As Władek dies, he sees Rysiek and the baby that died in the forest. Marianna spends the end of her life watching nature documentaries on television. These sad fates do not bear much resemblance to the destinies of the actual people that Słobodzianek based the characters on; the real Zygmunt Laudański, for example, answers Bikont's question about whether he regrets anything he did with 'Nothing whatsoever'.[35] However, they do accord with local lore in the Jedwabne area, as reported by social historian Marta Kurkowska-Budzan, who grew up in Jedwabne: 'People [in Jedwabne] talk about "God's punishment".'[36]

---

[33] D. Cavendish, 'Is Our Class at the National Theatre Really Such a Reliable History Lesson?', *Daily Telegraph*, 9 Nov. 2009.   [34] Słobodzianek, *Our Class*, 95.

[35] Bikont, *My z Jedwabnego*, 95. On the other hand, Ramotowski says of the Radziłów murderers, 'Those who killed later didn't have an easy death themselves': ibid. 64.

[36] M. Kurkowska-Budzan, 'My Jedwabne', in Polonsky and Michlic (eds.), *Neighbors Respond*, 205.

In general, *Nasza klasa* has been well received in Poland. For example, it won the prestigious Nike Award, which is conferred annually for the best book written in Polish and published in the previous year. Although the award is open to books in all genres, prior to the prize for *Nasza klasa* awarded in 2010, it had never been given to a play. The production at Teatr na Woli (where Słobodzianek is now artistic director) has received some excellent reviews, such as the one in *Metro* that begins, 'Everyone should see *Nasza klasa* at the Teatr na Woli.'[37] Kalina Zalewska, who reviewed the Theatrical Confrontations festival in 2008 for the monthly magazine *Teatr* in an article entitled 'Landscape after Gross', considered the reading of *Nasza klasa* to be the highlight of the event:

It seems that the author was able to touch on [the characters'] secret. This involves crudity of motivations, but also a terrible tangle of historical circumstances surpassing their human potential. The catastrophe recounted in the play is like the most ordinary story in the world, yet the marvel of the event turns out to be the intimacy of the victims and their persecutors . . . He also shows a terrible era in which people were fraternizing with death. They reckoned with the fact that someone would knock on the door with the intent to murder, and that this could be a neighbour.[38]

The points that Zalewska brings up about *Nasza klasa*—the 'terrible tangle of historical circumstances' and the 'era in which people were fraternizing with death'—highlight Słobodzianek's achievement in creating a theatrical work that attempts to grapple with such a complicated and painful issue as Polish–Jewish relations before, during, and after the war.

However, not everyone agrees that *Nasza klasa* deserves its laurels. In an article entitled 'Our Class Not an A+', for example, a theatre critic reviewing the presentation of the play at an international festival in Łódź criticizes it for 'its purely ethnic and ideological treatment of the subject undertaken':

The performance employs the ethnic patterns of the town both to shatter them and legitimize them. So, all the events and confrontations of the show play out on the level of Pole–Jew, and not Jakub–Zygmunt. And since everything is a question of nationality and the effect of twentieth-century ideologies in conjunction with religion, we see figures who fit the theses of the author moving around the stage, rather than living characters with a multiplicity of human experiences, feelings, motivations, choices.[39]

This critic is objecting, essentially, to a lack of realism in the play, and Słobodzianek told Zizka that this was a common criticism made by members of the audience in

---

[37] E. Błaszczk, 'Lekscja z "Naszej klasy"', *Metro*, no. 1943 (19 Oct. 2010): <http://www.e-teatr.pl/pl/artykuly/104380.html?josso_assertion_id=9C6E3C8AB2532D1E> (my translation).

[38] K. Zalewska, 'Krajobraz po Grossie', *Teatr*, 2008, no. 12, p. 8 (my translation).

[39] Ł. Kaczyński, 'Teatr Powszechny: Nasza Klasa nie na "piątkę"', *Polska Dziennik Łódzki*, 8 Mar. 2011: see <http://www.dzienniklodzki.pl/artykul/377393,teatr-powszechny-nasza-klasa-nie-na-piatke,id,t.html> (my translation). The Seventeenth International Festival of Plays Pleasant and Unpleasant (XVII Międzynarodowy Festiwal Sztuk Przyjemnych i Nieprzyjemnych) in Łódź was hosted by Teatr Powszechny.

Poland: 'When the play doesn't comply with their expectations, some of the audience members get angry and attack the production not necessarily for the content but for its form.'[40] Słobodzianek's background includes stints as a director, literary manager, and playwright in several puppet theatres, including the avant-garde Wierszalin Society. *Nasza klasa*, while it is far more realistic than productions he created in collaboration with Wierszalin, can hardly be described as a realistic play. Its structure requires the actors to switch constantly between narration, where they are speaking directly to the audience in the third person about events as they happen to their characters, and more traditional dramatic dialogue with other characters; in general, the use of these so-called story theatre conventions is often criticized for two-dimensionality.[41] However, in this play, one could make an argument that it is particularly appropriate since it echoes the voices of actual witnesses to the Jedwabne and Radziłów massacres who were quoted by Bikont or Gross speaking in the third person.

CONCLUSION

Neither *Nasza klasa* nor *Burmistrz* (either part) makes the events of July 1941 the climax of their actions. As Zalewska points out in her review of *Nasza klasa*, 'the drama does not focus on the catastrophe, does not make it the turning point through which time is divided into before and after. On the contrary, it seems to disappear from view under the pressure of new events and problems.'[42] In this way, the plays differ from Holocaust dramas such as those one might see on the New York or London stages, which foreground the catastrophic fate of the Jews. In fact, some reviewers of the London and Toronto productions of *Our Class* criticized the play precisely because they felt that the second half, which takes place after the burning of the barn, was anticlimactic.[43] However, both Słobodzianek and Sikorska-Miszczuk are as interested in the effects of 'the catastrophe' on non-Jewish Poles as on Polish Jews.

But what are those effects? Sikorska-Miszczuk shows us a man whose life is changed, and not for the better, by finding out the truth about the Jedwabne massacre, while Słobodzianek shows us a group of survivors and perpetrators, all of whom are haunted by it. While both authors, like the investigators from the Instytut

---

[40] B. Zizka, 'Arriving in Warsaw—Part One': http://wilmatheater.org/blog/arriving-warsaw-part-one>.

[41] For example, the American director Mary Zimmerman, who specializes in story theatre adaptations, has been called 'a creator of animated pop-up books for adults': B. Weber, 'Theater Review: If Leonardo Had Had Access to PowerPoint', New York Times, 30 June 2003.

[42] Zalewska, 'Krajobraz po Grossie', 8.

[43] See e.g. M. Billington, 'Our Class, Cottesloe, London', *Guardian*, 23 Sept. 2009; R. Ouzounian, 'Review: Our Class Offers Powerful Acting in a Perplexing Play', *thestar.com*, 8 Apr. 2011: see <http://www.thestar.com/entertainment/stage/2011/04/08/review_our_class_offers_powerful_ac ting_in_a_perplexing_play.html>.

Pamięci Narodowej, appear to have, in the main, accepted Jan Gross's conclusions about the events in Jedwabne, those conclusions remain far from being accepted by all segments of Polish society. In fact, shortly before the US premiere of *Our Class*, the new monument erected in Jedwabne to memorialize the massacre was defaced with swastikas and graffiti.

This raises the question of whether plays like *Nasza klasa* and *Burmistrz* are inducing an unwarranted complacency in their audiences. Theatre critic Witold Mrożek feels that *Nasza klasa* lets the intellectual urbanites in the auditorium off the hook too easily:

The stream of the plot also deftly avoids issues—notwithstanding the play's title—of class. All Poles here—after Goldhagen almost—suckle antisemitism with their mother's milk, so that sometimes it manifests itself in silly taunts and sometimes in someone's head being broken with a rock. But what kind of people are these 'all'? Not those with whom the 'cultured' theatre audience can identify. Our class is not their class. Oh, the trash from Poland 'C', the ignorant mob, the rabble.[44]

Mrożek refers to the divide between the so-called Poland A, Poland B, and Poland C groups that seems to have widened after 1989. He thinks that the play lets its audience (relatively affluent theatregoers from Poland A) believe that antisemitism is something that only peasants from Poland C feel. However, according to Irena Grudzińska Gross, polls have shown that antisemitism 'has become significantly less common in Poland since the publication of the first Gross book'.[45] While complacency is never warranted, it does seem as if the discussion that Gross initiated with *Neighbors* and has continued in *Fear* and *Golden Harvest* has brought about a transformation, at least among elites, in the thinking of non-Jewish Poles about the Others who were once in their midst.[46] Although plays such as *Nasza klasa* and *Burmistrz* may not themselves help this change reach non-elites, I believe they should be regarded as signs that an improvement, and a big one, has taken place.

[44] W. Mrożek, 'Czytanka o Jedwabnem', *Krytyka Polityczna*, 24 Oct. 2010: <http://www.krytykapolityczna.pl/Serwiskulturalny/MrozekCzytankaoJedwabnem/menuid-305.html> (my translation).

[45] K. Zimmerer, 'People Dealt this Fate to People: Katarzyna Zimmerer Talks to Irena Grudzińska-Gross and Jan Tomasz Gross', *Biweekly.pl*, 18 (2011): <http://www.biweekly.pl/article/2130-people-dealt-this-fate-to-people.html>.

[46] J. T. Gross, *Fear: Anti-Semitism in Poland after Auschwitz. An Essay in Historical Interpretation* (Princeton, 2006); published in Polish as J. T. Gross, *Strach: Antysemityzm w Polsce tuż po wojnie. Historia moralnej zapaści* (Kraków, 2008); J. T. Gross with I. Grudzińska Gross, *Golden Harvest: Events at the Periphery of the Holocaust* (New York, 2012); published in Polish as J. T. Gross with I. Grudzińska-Gross, *Złote żniwa: Rzecz o tym, co się działo na obrzeżach zagłady Żydów* (Kraków, 2011).

From Brzeżany to Afula: A Child's Journey from Pre-War Poland to Israel in the 1950s

A Conversation with Shimon Redlich

GABRIEL N. FINDER

INTRODUCTION

ALTHOUGH A GENERATION separates us, Shimon Redlich and I became close friends when he became aware of and encouraged my scholarly interest in *Undzere kinder* ('Our Children'). Now a professor emeritus, Redlich, then 13 years old, starred in *Undzere kinder*, the last Yiddish-language feature film produced in Poland in 1948–9. In it he plays a Jewish child hidden by a Polish family. Since Redlich and I first met, we have made it our mission to bring this little-known but fascinating film to a wide audience. Together we have introduced *Undzere kinder* to a general audience of filmgoers in Munich and to academic audiences in London, Jerusalem, and Salzburg. Redlich opens our joint presentation of *Undzere kinder* with personal reminiscences from the making of the film, including his recruitment for its cast, his preparation for his role, and his interaction with the film's director, Natan Gross, and its stars, the famed Yiddish comedians Szymon Dzigan and Yisroel Shumacher. For my part, I situate *Undzere kinder* in its historical context, emphasizing the horrific fate of Polish Jewish children during the Holocaust—only 3 per cent survived—and, for this very reason, the symbolic importance attached by the post-war Jewish community in Poland and elsewhere to the child survivor, which is poignantly reflected in the film.[1] In Salzburg, at an international

---

[1] For my analysis of the film—it is not without its flaws in my opinion—see my article 'Überlebende Kinder im kollektiven Gedächtnis der polnischen Jüdinnen und Juden nach dem Holocaust: Das Beispiel *Undzere Kinder*', in C. Bruns, A. Dardan, and A. Dietrich (eds.), *'Welchen der Steine du hebst': Filmische Erinnerung an den Holocaust* (Berlin, 2012), 47–64; the English version will appear as 'Child Survivors in Jewish Collective Memory in Poland after the Holocaust: The Case of *Undzere Kinder*', in N. Baron (ed.), *Nurturing the Nation: Displaced Children, State Ideology and Social Identity in Eastern Europe and the USSR, 1918–1953*, forthcoming.

conference called 'Children and War: Past and Present' that was held in September–October 2010, we not only introduced and screened *Undzere kinder* but also conducted a conversation the next day in front of an audience of conference participants; the subject of our conversation was Redlich's childhood and adolescence.

Shimon Redlich was born in 1935 in Lwów (Ukr. Lviv) and spent his pre-war childhood in Brzeżany (Ukr. Berezhany), a town in eastern Galicia, then part of Poland, now located in Ukraine. With the outbreak of the Second World War, Brzeżany came under Soviet rule in September 1939. After the German invasion of the Soviet Union in June 1941, the Nazis established a ghetto in Brzeżany. When they initiated the deportation of Jews from the ghetto, Redlich and his family hid in the attic of their home, but when remaining in hiding there later became unsustainable, Redlich and his mother Chana fled and found refuge in the nearby village of Raj, where they were hidden by a courageous Ukrainian family until the end of the war. In 1945, Redlich and his mother settled with remnants of their family in Łódź (in Yiddish, Lodzh or Lodz), which was then evolving into a centre of Jewish life in post-war Poland. He and his mother emigrated to Israel in 1950.

After his absorption in his teenage years into Israeli society and the completion of his military service, Redlich embarked on an academic career. He obtained a BA in history and literature from the Hebrew University in Jerusalem in 1960, an MA in Russian studies from Harvard University in 1964, and a Ph.D. in Jewish history from New York University in 1968. From 1970 until his retirement in 2003 he taught modern Jewish history at Ben-Gurion University in Beer Sheva, Israel. Over the course of his career, he served in various administrative capacities, including chairman of the history department, director of the Center for East European Jewish Studies, and for many years the director of the Rabb Center for Holocaust and Redemption Studies.

Redlich's area of expertise is the history of the Jews in twentieth-century Poland, Russia, and the Soviet Union. He is the author of numerous highly regarded books and articles in this field. A large share of his research has been devoted to the study of Soviet Jewry during the Second World War, with special emphasis on the activities of the Jewish Anti-Fascist Committee (Evreiskii antifashistskii komitet). His most notable publication on this topic is *War, Holocaust and Stalinism*.[2]

Since the 1990s, Redlich's scholarship has taken a new, more personal turn. In three successive volumes he examines the history of the Jews in pre-war, wartime, and post-war Poland and in Israel in the 1950s, seen through the prism of his own life. From the dual vantage point of an eyewitness to history and a trained historian, Redlich has developed a distinctive style in his approach to an exploration of these years, which correspond to the years of his own childhood and adolescence; it is based in part on his own memory, in part on documentary evidence, and in large

---

[2] S. Redlich, *War, Holocaust and Stalinism: A Documented History of the Jewish Anti-Fascist Committee in the USSR* (Luxembourg, 1995).

part on oral interviews with other protagonists, Jewish and non-Jewish alike, in the dramatic events in which he himself took part. The first two volumes of this trilogy are *Together and Apart in Brzezany*, published in 2002 (which has been translated into Polish, Ukrainian, and Hebrew), and *Life in Transit*, published in 2010 (which has likewise been translated into Polish).[3] *Together and Apart* has provoked both admiration and disparagement because of Redlich's relatively positive portrayal of the interaction of his fellow Jews and their Polish and Ukrainian neighbours in pre-war eastern Galicia, and, moreover, his sympathetic depiction of several noble Ukrainians who risked their lives to help him and his family under Nazi occupation. His account thus largely upends the conventional wisdom about Polish–Jewish and Ukrainian–Jewish relations, which, according to the attitudes and perceptions that prevail among the majority of Jews in Israel and the Jewish diaspora, have been characterized by immutable distance, friction, and outright hostility. In the view of the Polish sociologist Kaja Kaźmierska, Redlich's unorthodox approach has placed him on the margins of academia.[4] Redlich concurs with this assessment, appro-priating the label of 'marginal historian' for himself with pride. In his opinion, precisely because of his liminal position in the profession, he is uniquely situated to be an 'intermediary among different and conflicting groups and societies', no small matter since 'such intermediary work is significant and important for a better future'.[5] He is currently at work on the last volume of the trilogy, which will deal with Israel in the first decade after the establishment of the state; the book's point of departure will be his own tortuous integration as an adolescent survivor of the Holocaust from Poland into fledgling Israeli society.

The story of the young Redlich—that of a Jewish child living in Poland on the threshold of the Second World War and under Soviet and Nazi occupation during the war, surviving the Holocaust, and starting a new life first in post-war Poland and then in the nascent state of Israel in the aftermath of the war—encapsulates the major themes treated at the 'Children and War: Past and Present' conference: the lives of children in the shadow of war, in the throes of war, and in the aftermath of war, be they children who died in or endured the Second World War or other conflicts, not only in Europe but also in Africa, the Middle East, and elsewhere around the globe. In Redlich's case, he is, moreover, a representative of an ageing generation of surviving children of the Holocaust, among them hidden children, who are the last living witnesses to this unparalleled moment in twentieth-century Europe's cataclysmic history. Redlich and other child survivors of his generation represent a link between the past and the future, inviting us not only to contemplate the consequences of war for children but also, by dint of his and their inspiring

[3] S. Redlich, *Together and Apart in Brzezany: Poles, Jews, and Ukrainians, 1919–1945* (Blooming-ton, Ind., 2002); id., *Life in Transit: Jews in Postwar Lodz, 1945–1950* (Brighton, Mass., 2010).

[4] K. Kaźmierska, *Biografia i pamięć: Na przykładzie pokoleniowego doświadczenia ocalonych z Zagłady* (Kraków, 2008), ch. 6.

[5] S. Redlich, 'Some Remarks on the Holocaust by a Marginal Historian', in J. Ambrosewicz-Jacobs (ed.), *The Holocaust: Voices of Scholars* (Kraków, 2009), 109.

example, to forge a new beginning in the aftermath of the Second World War, to harbour hope in a transformative future.[6]

The following interview is based on our public conversation in Salzburg.

INTERVIEW WITH SHIMON REDLICH

FINDER You were born in a hospital in Lwów, in eastern Galicia, which was then part of Poland in 1935, but your family lived in Brzeżany, which was not far from Lwów. Brzeżany, where you spent your childhood, is the focal point of your book *Together and Apart in Brzezany*. Would you describe the demographic structure of the town?

REDLICH I've always perceived Brzeżany as an ethnic and religious triangle, the three sides of which were Poles, Jews, and Ukrainians, in that order. This is also clearly reflected in the title of my book. Consider the demographic data. In the 1930s, on the eve of the Second World War, the total population of Brzeżany was between 14,000 and 15,000. More than half of the town were Poles, more than a third Jews, and around 20 per cent Ukrainians. It should be pointed out that this was also the proportion in many other medium-sized towns throughout eastern Galicia in the Polish Eastern Borderlands [Kresy Wschodnie].

FINDER How would you describe your childhood home before the Second World War? Did you come from a religious Jewish family? What did your parents do for a living? Which languages were spoken at home? Did your family identify to any extent with the Polish state and with Polish culture?

REDLICH Ours was a quite typical middle-class, urban Jewish family in eastern Galicia. It was basically religious, but not hasidic or ultra-Orthodox. I recall distinctly that at age 3 to 4 I would recite Jewish morning prayers such as 'Moide Ani Lefunekhu' (as it sounds in the pronunciation of the east Galician Jews). I must have learned it from either my grandpa Fishl or my father Shlomo. I also recall going on Saturdays, the Jewish sabbath, with my father and grandpa Fishl to the Brzeżany Great Synagogue, the largest in town. For years I even retained in my memory the image of the *bimah* [raised platform in front of the congre-

---

[6] The last paragraph of Hannah Arendt's *Origins of Totalitarianism* is poignantly apropos here: 'But there remains also the truth that every end in history necessarily contains a new beginning; this beginning is the promise, the only "message" which the end can ever produce. Beginning, before it becomes a historical event, is the supreme capacity of man; politically it is identical with man's freedom ... This beginning is guaranteed by each new birth; it is indeed every man': H. Arendt, *The Origins of Totalitarianism* (1951; New York, 2004), 616. For a stimulating exploration of the transformative political implications of this concluding passage from Arendt's magnum opus, see A. Eshel, '"Hannah Arendt's Politics and Poetics of Insertion', in A. Eshel and U. Baer (eds.), *Hannah Arendt und die Geisteswissenschaften*, forthcoming. Redlich's personal journey from Brzeżany to the present, ever punctuated by new beginnings, is now the subject of the 2014 documentary *Shimon's Return*, directed by Sławomir Grünberg and Katka Reszke.

gation from which the prayers are recited and the Torah scroll is read] and the arch above the niche in which the Torah was kept, adorned with images of lions. The house was of course kosher. I recall the Jewish holidays, mostly Purim, since this was particularly fun for a child. I remembered for years the *purim-shpilers* who would appear in the door and sing a tune: 'Pirem iz haynt, morgn iz oys, git mir a gratser un varft mikh aroys' ['Today is Purim, tomorrow it's over, give me a coin and throw me out']. When I look at the old photos of my parents and grandparents taken in the 1930s, I notice that grandpa Fishl, with his white beard, is wearing a hat, a *kapelush*, whereas my father's head is uncovered. Before marrying into my mother's family, my father was a *yeshive bokher* [a student in an academy for the study of Jewish law]. This change in my father's appearance might indicate some changes that occurred in his life as far as religion was concerned.

Our family's main and only source of income in the 1930s was our cloth store, which was placed right opposite the town hall in the main market, in the centre of town.

As far as languages are concerned, my parents and grandparents spoke Yiddish among themselves, but they spoke to me, a member of the younger generation born in the 1930s, in Polish. They apparently made an effort to teach me proper spoken Polish, and even today (so I'm told by my Polish interlocutors) my pronunciation is good. They would speak Polish in public, for example in the store to customers, and even more so Ukrainian, since most of the customers were Ukrainian peasants from nearby villages. I also had a Ukrainian nanny, who apparently spoke to me somewhat in Ukrainian. For many years I remembered some humorous rhymes in Ukrainian about Toska-Kaposka. Thinking back now some seventy years, I would say that as a boy aged 3 to 5 I already had a feel then for three languages. The most Polish-educated member of our family was Malcia, my mother's younger sister and the youngest of my mother's siblings, who was born in 1914. She was a graduate of the Brzeżany classical-type gymnasium, with Greek and Latin. Although multilingual, the Brzeżany gymnasium —which was named after the town's most notable native son, Edward Rydz-Śmigły, the Inspector General of the Polish Armed Forces and, from November 1936, Marshal of Poland, who was commander of all Polish forces when the Germans and then the Soviets invaded Poland in September 1939—was a bastion of Polishness.

As for my own memories of official ceremonies, I distinctly recall that on some Polish state holidays we would adorn our small balcony with the white-and-red Polish national colours. As a child I was fascinated by military parades on such occasions, especially by the music and sounds of the military band. Only decades later did I learn that the 51st Regiment of the Polish infantry was permanently stationed in our town, which explains the frequency of those parades and the ubiquity of the marching tunes I used to listen to.

FINDER In *Together and Apart in Brzezany*, you and the people whom you interview for your book—Jews, Poles, and Ukrainians from Brzeżany and villages in the surrounding countryside—tend to have happy memories from the late 1930s, including happy childhood memories. One reads accounts of antisemitic unpleasantries and relatively rare outbursts of antisemitic violence directed at individuals, but they are depicted as exceptions to the rule of a state of equipoise between Jews, Poles, and Ukrainians. It is not what your readers might have expected from a book on relations between Jews and non-Jews in eastern Poland on the eve of the Second World War. They would have expected to see many more manifestations of friction and animosity between Jews and non-Jews, if not more eruptions of antisemitic violence. How do you explain your rather benign description of Jewish–non-Jewish relations in pre-war Brzeżany and its environs? Why is your description of them positive in comparison with most accounts—both by historians and by those who lived through this period—of life in Poland in the 1930s?

REDLICH You should keep in mind that for me Brzeżany is not only history but also personal memory and perhaps even a certain dose of wishful thinking. I did record in my book a number of antisemitic incidents in the town, as they were recounted to me by my interviewees. There was a certain degree of antisemitism in the local gymnasium, there was a partial boycott of Jewish stores, but these incidents never reached extreme proportions as in some other Polish towns. It is important to conduct research of specific regions in inter-war Poland and look in them for differences in Polish–Jewish relations. In Brzeżany, situated in eastern Galicia, with its Habsburg-era *Gemütlichkeit* and its tradition of some degree of tolerance, inter-ethnic relations were not as bad as in other places in Poland. Another element in Brzeżany is the fact that at times Polish–Ukrainian relations were much more tense than Polish–Jewish relations. Please keep in mind that my purpose in writing my book was to bring to life the ethnic triangle in Brzeżany and to discuss as even-handedly as possible all three groups. Perhaps if I had focused on Brzeżany's Jews only, I would have dealt more with antisemitism.

FINDER Did Jewish children interact with Polish and Ukrainian children in pre-war Brzeżany? Can you personally recall any interactions with Polish and Ukrainian children?

REDLICH There was apparently some interaction, but it wasn't extensive. One of my interviewees, Karol Codogni, told me that in his specific neighbourhood Polish and Jewish children used to play together and he even learned some Yiddish as a child. I assume that poor and religious Jewish children in Brzeżany kept completely apart from non-Jewish children. There was a large number of middle-class Jewish families in Brzeżany, but there were very few assimilated or assimilating Jewish families. This perhaps explains why even middle-class

Jewish kids tended to play mainly with their Jewish counterparts. I personally do not recall playing with non-Jewish children before the war.

FINDER Can you recall from your childhood memories any substantive inter-actions between Jewish and non-Jewish adults?

REDLICH No.

FINDER On the basis of your childhood memories, those of your Jewish, Polish, and Ukrainian interlocutors, and your subsequent historical research, do your perceptions of the triangular relationship between Jews, Poles, and Ukrainians in Brzeżany yield a larger historical significance for our understanding of relations between Jews and non-Jews in the pre-war period?

REDLICH My pre-war childhood memories are rather irrelevant, except for the fact that I had a Ukrainian nanny and I assume that this wasn't an isolated case. As for my historical research and the numerous interviews I conducted with Brzeżany Jews, Poles, and Ukrainians, they do yield wider historical significance for our understanding of the specific region of eastern Galicia, since many other towns in that region were quite similar to Brzeżany in their demographic make-up and as far as inter-ethnic relations were concerned.

FINDER In September 1939, eastern Poland, including Brzeżany, was occupied by the Soviets. From the standpoint of a child, according to your recollections, did the Soviet occupation, which lasted until the Nazi invasion of the Soviet Union in June 1941, change the dynamics between Jews, Poles, and Ukrainians in Brzeżany?

REDLICH This is too complex a question for childhood memories of a boy aged 4 to 6. However, looking in retrospect from an adult's point of view, I might say that the very fact that before the war I started attending a *ḥeder* [Jewish ele-mentary school devoted to learning Bible and religious tradition], while during the first Soviet occupation of Brzeżany I attended a Soviet-style kindergarten, means that I must have met non-Jewish children there as well. I do not have any authentic personal recollection of other children from that time.

FINDER What happened to you and your family when the Soviets took over?

REDLICH As I mentioned already, I started attending a Soviet-style kindergarten. I explicitly recalled for years that on its walls there were large pictures, images, or posters of Soviet leaders, and particularly one impressive image of Stalin and Voroshilov. Another authentic childhood memory from that short-lived Soviet period is that of a Red Army officer, a Jew, who would visit our apartment from time to time. I recalled for many years not so much his face but rather certain parts of his uniform—the cap with the dark red Soviet five-pointed star and his leather belt and harness, which I can still smell even today.

FINDER The next turning point in your life was the Nazi invasion. Would you describe the fate of the Jewish community of Brzeżany under Nazi occupation?

REDLICH Persecutions of Jews in Brzeżany started with Ukrainian anti-Jewish outbursts in the immediate weeks following the German occupation of the town in early July 1941. The first substantial round-up (in German, *Aktion*) took place on the eve of Yom Kippur in early October of that year. About 600 Jews were executed on the outskirts of the town and buried in a mass grave. The next mass murder of Brzeżany Jews took place in mid-December 1941 during the Hanukah holidays. The Brzeżany ghetto was established in mid-January 1942. In September 1942 there was a massive round-up and 2,000 Jews were transported to [the extermination camp] Bełżec. The next two round-ups, with transports to Bełżec, took place in October and December 1942. The next wave of round-ups was in March–April 1943. The last round-up and the liquidation of the remaining Jews in Brzeżany was in mid-June of that year, when close to 2,000 Jews were shot and buried in the old Jewish cemetery. That spelled the tragic end of the centuries-old Jewish community of Brzeżany.

FINDER How did the Nazi occupation affect relations between Jews, Poles, and Ukrainians in the town? Do you have any personal recollections of relations between Jews on the one hand and Poles and Ukrainians on the other under Nazi occupation?

REDLICH This is a very complicated issue. It is described in my Brzeżany book. On the whole, inter-ethnic relations within Brzeżany's Polish–Jewish–Ukrainian triangle deteriorated considerably, and tensions and violence became quite prevalent. The pre-war triangle, already shaken badly under Soviet rule in 1939–41, actually came apart. Each group became separated from the others and the worst (but also some good) in human beings came to the surface. The unusually harsh and inhuman conditions of Nazi rule and behaviour brought out the worst in human nature.

FINDER As you've mentioned, there was a ghetto in Brzeżany. Would you describe it? How did you and your family survive in the ghetto?

REDLICH The ghetto in Brzeżany was located right in the middle of the town not far from the market and the town hall. I recall that most of the time we lived in a three-storey building that used to be a hotel before the war. Instead of our four- or five-room apartment, our entire family now lived in one small room. I do not recall hunger during that time.

FINDER What do you personally remember from this period in the ghetto?

REDLICH I have kept several events in my memory. I recall hazily the various round-ups, not so much the details as the prevailing atmosphere of fear. I recall voices and sounds. On one occasion, while I, with other members of our family, was in a hiding place, my mother didn't succeed in entering that place and remained on the outside. I recall the Germans' voices and hearing shrieks, and later my mother told us that she had been kicked by a German in the chest, but luckily she wasn't taken away to be killed. I recall various bunkers prepared by the Jews living in our building, including an underground bunker that even had air and light. Our last hiding place, just before the final round-up in June 1943, was a clever double-walled space in the attic of our house. One could only either sit or lie down in it, even a boy of 8 like myself.

FINDER You left the ghetto before the Nazis' final liquidation of it. Would you describe how you escaped from the ghetto? Who was with you? Where did you go?

REDLICH Not so. We remained in that attic hideout for about half a year after the liquidation of the Brzeżany ghetto, between the summer of 1943 and the winter of 1944. Our food was provided by the Polish family of Stanisław and Karol Codogni, friends of my grandpa Fishl. We were lucky that all that time our house in the former ghetto remained unoccupied. Once a Polish family moved in, we couldn't stay any longer. We contacted my aunt Malcia, who was hiding with her husband Vovo in the house of a Ukrainian peasant woman in the nearby village of Raj (which is the word for 'paradise' in both Polish and Ukrainian). This noble woman agreed to take us into her house.

FINDER What do you personally remember of your escape from the ghetto?

REDLICH Today I'm not sure any more what my authentic memories are and what are the stories I heard from other members of my family. Actually, when I visited Brzeżany in the early 1990s for the first time since leaving it in 1945, I asked Tanka Kontsevych, our Ukrainian rescuer, now an old woman, how we made it to her place. A few years earlier when I met Karol Codogni, I conducted a long interview with him, during which I asked him how he had helped us escape from Brzeżany to Raj. From my memories and those of my family and from Karol's and Tanka's memories, I can piece together that fateful event. It was a cold and snowy winter evening, the streets were empty. My mother and I left our attic bunker and went down the stairs to an inconspicuous corner somewhere along the street where Karol Codogni was waiting for us. Then he led us to some other corner where Tanka was waiting. She took my limping mother by her hand, and since I could hardly walk as my leg muscles were atrophied, she placed me on her back, and this strange procession marched for hours in a roundabout way to her house in Raj.

FINDER What, in your view, motivated your Ukrainian rescuers to hide your family?

REDLICH   This is a very complex story. A number of elements, the most significant being the simple human compassion of an illiterate Ukrainian peasant woman. Then there was the love affair between Tanka and my good-looking uncle Vovo, his promise that after the war he would divorce my aunt Malcia and marry Tanka. Tanka could have told him, as happened in similar cases, that she would only hide him alone. However, she agreed to keep Malcia and then later myself, a child, and my mother. She even agreed to hide my old grandpa and grandma, but they were discovered on their way to Tanka, imprisoned, and eventually executed. We were extremely lucky that these two old people didn't reveal the truth in spite of being questioned, apparently, by the Germans.

FINDER   What do you remember from your time in hiding? Do you remember your thoughts, feelings, and fantasies from this period?

REDLICH   It is very difficult for me to differentiate between my authentic memories as an 8- to 9-year-old boy and memories repeated over the years by the adult members of my family. Still, some moments stand out, either the very pleasant and the highly exciting or the extremely frightening ones. For instance, one sunny morning I'm looking out into Tanka's garden from our hiding place in the tiny attic of her house. I see grass and trees and I can feel the warmth of the sunshine. I imagine how pleasant it will be once the war is over. On one occasion, during daytime, as German soldiers horsed around with Tanka downstairs, we sat in the attic just above them with bated breath. The tinest creak could have been fatal. I wetted my pants, right there, in utter silence, like an animal. One afternoon while Tanka was out, two German soldiers walked in demanding straw. The straw was stored right near us, in the attic. Anya, Tanka's 10-year-old daughter, started screaming and didn't let them climb up into the attic. Then Tanka returned, climbed the ladder, and started throwing down the straw to the Germans. I supplemented my sporadic memory of those frightful moments when I interviewed Anya half a century later. Since Malcia and Vovo, a young couple, were so close to me day and night and since I also sensed the existence of the relationship between Vovo and Tanka and knew that German soldiers were chasing after Tanka, from time to time I had some sensual and sexual fantasies. I also recall that the four of us were constantly playing endless card games to pass the time.

FINDER   The Red Army liberated eastern Poland in the summer of 1944. How do you remember feeling once the Red Army arrived and you were able to emerge from hiding?

REDLICH   To tell the truth, I do not recall any specific day or moment of our liberation by the Red Army. I do recall, however, that year when we lived in Brzeżany after the liberation from the summer of 1944 to the summer of 1945. For me it meant life back to normal. I had a few close friends who survived in hiding like myself. We used to play and talk. We were fascinated by the Red Army soldiers, their uniforms, their guns. We learned from them and from the loud-speakers installed in the centre of town various Russian wartime melodies and songs, which I cherish to this day. There were also very impressive daily announcements by Radio Moscow, which started with the exciting and dramatic words 'govorit Moskva' (Moscow speaking). The speaker (years later I learned that he was Yury Levitan) announced the progress of the Red Army and the capturing of various cities on the way to Berlin. These announcements were always followed by heavy gun volleys coming from Red Square, near the Kremlin, that celebrated Soviet military victories. I remembered for years Soviet military funerals in Brzeżany, with the marching soldiers, their uniforms, the band, and, most of all, the open Soviet-style caskets with the upper part of the body and the face of the deceased in full view. Stuck in my mind from the first year in Brzeżany after liberation is the hanging of a man in the market square. I remember standing near a window facing the market. It was snowing. There was a small crowd. A small truck appeared and stopped in the middle of the crowd. From the platform of the truck, where a few people were standing, someone seemed to read something from a piece of paper. After a few minutes, the truck departed, but one person from the truck's platform remained, hanging, his body dangling from side to side. I was told that the man was a *banderovets*, a Ukrainian nationalist partisan.

FINDER You and your family left Brzeżany and moved to Łódź in 1945. Why?

REDLICH That was part of the general population movement at the time. Almost all Polish citizens in the region, including the few Jewish survivors, were repatriated from the Soviet Union to post-war Poland. This I know today, of course. But then, as a 10-year-old boy, I didn't ask any questions. For me this was sheer adventure. We spent the last few weeks prior to our departure from Brzeżany camping outside along the railway station. It was summer and very hot. While the adults gathered and talked, the kids played and had a good time. It was like a vacation. Finally, we were loaded, with our meagre belongings, onto an open freight train. It would be forty-six years before I would see Brzeżany again.

FINDER What are your personal recollections of this move?

REDLICH The train rolled slowly through the picturesque countryside. Occasionally, we were caught in a violent midsummer rainstorm. For me, it was fun, but it wasn't much fun for the adults. My aunt Malcia was in the last weeks of her pregnancy, and my uncle Vovo secured a seat for her in one of the passenger cars. My aunt and uncle got off the train before we reached Łódź, on the Polish side of the new post-war border, because she was due any day, and they didn't want her to give birth on the train. I have no recollection of the remaining part of the voyage, but it must have taken a week for the train to reach Łódź. I don't recall my arrival in Łódź, but I know from family stories that while I was left in Łódź, my mother continued the long journey to western Poland, where many residents of Brzeżany settled.

FINDER When you arrived in Łódź, you were 10 years old. Who lived with you? Where did you live? Which school did you attend? Did you participate in any extracurricular activities? What do your remember about your life in Łódź? Did you interact with Poles who were your age? Were these happy years for you?

REDLICH For the first few weeks I lived with relatives of ours who arrived in Łódź some time earlier, the family of Dr Lipa Wagszal from Brzeżany. Then for four and a half years I lived with my mother, my aunt Malcia, and my uncle Vovo in a ground-floor apartment, in a house on the corner of Gdańska and 1go Maja [First of May] streets in the centre of Łódź, which was in the heart of Jewish Łódź in the post-war years. All Jewish institutions and schools in post-war Łódź were located near each other; so I had a ten- or fifteen-minute walk to my Zionist-oriented Hebrew school and a twenty-minute walk to the Hashomer Hatsa'ir [Young Guard] Zionist youth movement, which I was a member of during our stay in Łódź. Actually, our apartment, the Hebrew school, and Hashomer Hatsa'ir were the three locations around which my life centred during my Łódź years. Most of my memories of these places are good and happy memories. I was an outstanding student at the Hebrew school and recall my teachers' positive attitudes, praising me, selecting me for plays and recitations. I had some very close friends both at school and in the youth movement. Since most of my milieu was Jewish and Zionist, I recall a constant feeling of belonging, being part of the surrounding society.

I do not recall a prevailing atmosphere of antisemitism in post-war Łódź, as some of my Łódź friends and schoolmates do. That said, a few unpleasant incidents of an antisemitic nature remain in my memory. I'm walking home one afternoon; it's almost dark. Suddenly, two Polish boys, older and bigger than me, appear out of nowhere and push me into the entrance to a building. They slap me and disappear. I don't recall any words being spoken or shouted, though they must have called me names. On another occasion, on a bright summer afternoon, I'm walking along 1go Maja, when two or three Polish boys surround me and start calling me names. This time, for some reason, I'm not afraid. Feelings of anger and rage overcome me instantly. I reach into my pocket, pull out a penknife, and draw the blade. They run away, and I chase them. Overall, I hardly interacted with Poles. I lived in a 'Jewish Łódź' during the first post-war years.

I attended extracurricular activities, but not too far from my family. My mother and relatives didn't allow me to go to summer or winter camps with Hashomer Hatsa'ir; they always wanted me to be close by. This was caused, apparently, by the fears and worries of the recent past—the war and the Holocaust. Besides, I had always been, even during the worst times of the war, a pampered child, a *ben yokhid* [only child]. My mother never remarried, and most of her attention and worries were centred on me. The only extracurricular activities I recall were short day trips to nearby forests with Hashomer Hatsa'ir or with my Hebrew school. There were only a few weeks one summer when I was put in the Jewish children's home in Helenówek, on the outskirts of Łódź. My memories from these few summer weeks are very mixed. This was the first time in my life that I was separated from my small family and living with my peers.

FINDER   While you were in Łódź, you appeared in the film *Undzere kinder*, which was filmed in Helenówek. What do you remember about being recruited to appear in *Undzere kinder* and appearing in it?

REDLICH   This was one of the most exciting times for me as a 13-year-old youngster in post-war Łódź. I had been selected to play the part of a Jewish child survivor in that film by our music teacher Israel Glantz, who co-operated with Natan Gross in the production of *Undzere kinder*. The film is a Yiddish-language film, and since I hardly spoke Yiddish, which is written with Hebrew characters, Glantz copied my whole part from the script in Polish letters, which I then learned by heart. I recall our trips to Helenówek and the long hours of shooting the same scenes, but it was still fun for me and for the other kids who appeared in the film. I never made the connection then in my mind between the scene I acted in as a Jewish child living in hiding and my real past in Brzeżany and in Raj during the war and the Holocaust as a Jewish child who survived hidden. We kids hardly ever mentioned among ourselves our respective wartime experiences, especially those of us who survived in Nazi-occupied Poland. By contrast, those who lived and survived the war in the Soviet Union used to tell us about those years in such exotic places as Uzbekistan. They even remembered some Uzbek words.

FINDER   You and your family emigrated from Poland to Israel in 1950. Do you recall the journey from Poland to Israel?

REDLICH   Yes, I do. But not in detail. I recall leaving by train from the Łódź Fabryczna railway station on a cold winter day of 1950. We travelled south via Czechoslovakia and reached northern Italy. I recall seeing for the first time in my life dark-skinned and black-eyed people who were not Jewish. They were Italian. We stayed for a couple of weeks in a transit camp for *olim* (Jewish émigrés) on the island of Poveglia, just off Venice. I recall meeting in that camp two good-looking dark girls from Egypt. This was the first time I met non-Ashkenazi Jews. Then came the week of travelling by ship from Venice to Haifa. Another adventure. The boat was owned by the ZIM company and its name was *Galilah*. There was a storm on the way and I, like most of the *olim*, threw up and felt miserable. But most of the time it was fun. I recall distinctly the Hebrew songs emanating from the loudspeakers, particularly those sung by the very popular singer Yaffa Yarkoni. I must have known at least some of them from my Hebrew school in Łódź and from Hashomer Hatsa'ir. Actually, my Łódź adolescence at school and in Hashomer Hatsa'ir had prepared me for this moment in my life. My mother and I (aunt Malcia and Vovo still remained in Łódź for a while) were very excited in expectation of meeting shortly the Israeli part of our family whose names I had kept hearing within the family for many years. One morning we heard shouts that you could see Mount Carmel and Haifa. In a few hours people started calling our names. When we went up on deck, we were told that a man in a motor boat nearby was looking for my mother and me. It turned out that this was my mother's younger brother Ze'ev (Volcie), who had made *aliyah* (immigrated) in the early 1920s and lived in Afula, in the Jezreel Valley. The next morning we disembarked and here he was again waiting for us, accompanied by Pnina, my mother's younger sister, a founder of Kibbutz Merhavya, not far from Afula.

FINDER When you arrived in Israel, you were a 14-year-old adolescent who had survived the Holocaust. There was a strong emphasis in the nascent State of Israel, which was established in 1948, to mould Jewish youth, to create a 'new Jew' who differed from his stereotypical Diaspora counterpart. Unlike the latter, the new Jew was to be self-reliant and tough. How would you describe your personal absorption into the rhythm and fabric of Israeli life? How do you remember the transition from being a Polish Jewish child survivor of the Holocaust into an Israeli teenager? Do you recall being treated differently or feeling different from other teenagers, in particular sabras, those born in Israel? Was this a happy period in your life?

REDLICH I am working now on what I hope to be the third and last part of my part-autobiographical, part-historical trilogy, the volume following *Together and Apart in Brzezany* and *Life in Transit*. Its tentative title is *A New Life in Israel, 1950–1954*. It will centre on my first years in Israel. I'm still in the process of rethinking that period in my life. Let me offer some preliminary remarks. I wasn't only a Polish Jewish child survivor. During the more than four years of my adolescence in Łódź, I was educated and groomed to become a future *oleh* to Erets Yisra'el, by both my Hebrew school and the Zionist-Socialist Hashomer Hatsa'ir youth movement. On the other hand, even after the few initial years of my life in Israel, I did not become a sabra-like teenager. The answers to these questions are quite complex. Let's go into some of the basic details of my absorption into Israeli society in the early 1950s.

Although my mother and I were taken in by family (my uncle in Afula), within a few weeks of my arrival in Israel I was placed in Kibbutz Merhavya of Hashomer Hatsa'ir, near Afula. Even there I was not part of a peer group of new immigrants, as most arrivals of my age usually were. Since my aunt Pnina was one of the founders of Merhavya and since I already knew Hebrew quite well,

I joined a *kevutsa* (a grouping of youth) that consisted mostly of Merhavya-born sabras. This unique situation was both good and bad for me. I integrated very rapidly into the Israeli Hebrew youth culture. I spoke fluent Israeli Hebrew within months of my arrival. I went for hikes across Israel with my *kevutsa* and very quickly got to know Israeli landscapes 'through the soles of my shoes'. At the same time, I didn't feel comfortable socially and psychologically. For the first time in my life, I was sharing a room with two boys and two girls my age, 14 to 15. This was part of *linah meshutefet* (boys and girls sharing the same dormitory room), which was one of the cardinal principles of Hashomer Hatsa'ir kibbutz life for youngsters of that age. Some of my peers still practised *miklaḥat meshutefet* (common showering) as well. I tried to avoid it. I must have felt inferior at least to some of the boys in the group, who were physically more developed and more influential. Seemingly minor but very meaningful for me was the practice of nicknames. Almost every youngster had a nickname. I hated my derogatory nickname, or, to be more precise, nicknames, which hinted at the fact that I was a new *oleh*. I was an excellent student in the classroom but was quite poor and inefficient in performing physical labour and at sports. After less than two years I left Merhavya and lived for the next three years in Afula with my mother, who received a very modest *shikun olim* (a subsidized apartment for new *olim*). There I completed my education at the local high school. Here, too, I faced name-calling, even among the 16- to 18-year-olds. Although I was friendly with youngsters my age, both boys and girls, my best friend during those years was another *oleh*, a classmate from Romania, which says something about my social absorption.

FINDER Finally, I would ask you to reflect on the role of memory in your life. In *Together and Apart in Brzeżany*, you write that you repressed your memories of the Holocaust for a long time. Perhaps you also repressed certain memories of the post-war years, when you evolved into adolescence first in Łódź and later in Israel. Memory clearly plays a central role in your recent publications. When, in your case, did memory return? Why, in your view, did it return when it did?

REDLICH The fact is that not only I but many other child survivors did not discuss their wartime fates and experiences in the immediate post-war years. A good example of this can be seen in Joanna Michlic's interview with the writer Henryk Grynberg.[7] Young Hershek never told his friends at the Helenówek children's home about his recent past. Children at my Łódź school and in Hashomer Hatsa'ir hardly ever spoke about their former lives. Nor was Israel of the 1950s and 1960s a place that encouraged memories of the war and the Holocaust. It seems that there are two major elements that either encourage or discourage memory: one is the specific stage or circumstances of one's life, the other is the attitudes towards memory within the surrounding society. My mental energies

---

[7] See J. B. Michlic, 'Bearing Witness: Henryk Grynberg's Path from Child Survivor to Artist', *Polin*, 20 (2008), 324–35.

were apparently centred on building a new life in Israel: high-school studies, army service, higher education, and the first stages of my academic career, then getting married and starting a family. It was only sometime in the mid-1970s that I started dealing with my past. The trigger was a course on the Holocaust that I taught as a visiting assistant professor of Jewish studies at the University of Pittsburgh in 1975–6. I was then 40, in mid life. I started looking back. In the 1980s I started searching for my Polish and Ukrainian rescuers, whom I succeeded in finding and renewed contacts with, contacts that had stopped in 1945, when I was a child. There was also a significant psychological moment: I had a strong urge to revive and reconstruct the place of my happy and normal childhood, namely, Brzeżany of the years before the Second World War. Another important factor in my return to the past was the momentous changes in eastern Europe which took place in the late 1980s and early 1990s. They enabled my physical return to the places in my past: Poland, Ukraine, Brzeżany, and Łódź. As for Israeli society, it is by now a known fact that Israelis started confronting the Holocaust in a more personal and intimate manner (as opposed to the former ceremonial, selective, and general approach) following the Eichmann trial and increasing steadily thereafter. Survivors in Israel, from being shunned and looked down upon, became in time 'heroes' of sorts. To be a survivor became almost an honour. This change of attitudes must have affected me as well. One more point that I'd like to make is that memories start fading with age. If I hadn't written my Brzeżany memories, scant and sporadic as they were, ten years ago, some of them would have been lost for ever. I felt obligated to write them down before that happened.

FINDER Thank you for sharing your thoughts with me and with others.

REDLICH You're welcome. It was my pleasure.

Obituaries

Jakub Goldberg
1924–2011

On Tuesday, 15 November 2011, Jakub Goldberg, Professor Emeritus of History at the Hebrew University of Jerusalem, and one of the moving spirits in the revival of Polish Jewish historical research after the Holocaust, passed away in Jerusalem.

He was born in Łódź in 1924 to a Polish-speaking family, hearing Yiddish only from his grandparents. His mother died when he was but ten years old—a trauma which lived with him throughout his life, even despite the horrors he endured during the Holocaust. At the outbreak of World War II, he moved to Warsaw with his father, though he soon decided to come back on his own to Łódź, to be with his grandmother who had remained there. Incarcerated in the ghetto, the teenage Goldberg found work in the administration and so was able to survive. In later years, he would say that he had picked up his fluent German during his years in the ghetto. In 1943, he was sent to work as a slave laborer in the Skarżysko munitions factory. Marched westwards in April 1945, he ended up in Buchenwald—a slave laborer in the ammunition factory at the Meuselwitz sub-camp.

The young Goldberg then returned to Poland, which he saw as the only place he would be able to receive a full academic education in the difficult post-war years. Studying under Bohdan Baranowski, he received his doctorate from the University of Łódź in 1960 with a thesis entitled 'Stosunki agrarne w miastach ziemi wieluńskiej w drugiej połowie XVII i w XVIII wieku' ('Agrarian Relations in the Towns of the Wieluń Region in the Second Half of the Seventeenth and the Eighteenth Centuries'). It was his work on the small towns of the Wieluń district that led Goldberg to research on the history of the Jews in Poland since they figured so prominently in small-town life in that period. He thus became one of the small band of Jewish scholars who continued to write on Jewish topics in Poland despite the very difficult atmosphere of the fifties and sixties.

Under pressure from the censor, he, like all his colleagues, was forced to adopt a Marxist approach to writing history. Years later, with the benefit of hindsight, he admitted that as a young man he had been genuinely excited by the interpretative possibilities which the Marxist approach seemed to open up.

This obituary was first published in *Acta Judaica Lodziensia*, 1 (2011), and is reproduced here by permission.

During these years, Goldberg visited Israel, making his first contact with the scholarly establishment there. He also became deeply involved in the project of microfilming sources for Jewish history from Polish archives. Under his direction, hundreds of reels of microfilm with tens of thousands of documents, including much material on the history of the Jews in Łódź, were sent to Jerusalem for scholars there to use.

In 1967, anticipating by less than a year the antisemitic purge that was to come, Goldberg left Poland for Israel. He left behind a long chapter on the history of Pabianice as part of a multi-authored history of Łódź to be published in his absence. He was shocked to learn that in the difficult atmosphere of 1968, it was published under someone else's name! It came with a sense of some vindication in 1990, when that historical wrong was finally righted, and his study, *Dzieje Pabianic w XVII–XVIII wieku* ('The History of Pabianice in the Seventeenth and Eighteenth Centuries'), was published under his name as a separate booklet.

In Israel, Goldberg soon befriended other historians of Polish Jewish background, such as Jacob Talmon of the Hebrew University in Jerusalem and Raphael Mahler of Tel Aviv University. He was a given a post in the History Department of the Hebrew University, where he worked until his retirement in 1992.

During his early years in Israel, Goldberg was deprived of access to Polish libraries and archives, but determined to continue his work on Polish Jewish history. He developed his, then radical, vision of Polish Jewry as deeply embedded in their social, economic, and political surroundings. More than a decade before the social turn swept American Jewish historical scholarship, he coined the aphorism which was to become the touchstone for all his future research: 'There is no history of Poland without the history of the Jews, and no history of the Jews without the history of Poland.'

He developed this approach through a wide range of articles, books, and source publications. Most prominent among them was his three-volume edition of sources for the history of early modern Jewish institutions entitled *Jewish Privileges in the Polish Commonwealth: Charters of Rights Granted to Jewish Communities in Poland–Lithuania in the Sixteenth to Eighteenth Centuries*, published by the Israel Academy of Sciences from 1985 to 2001. Other topics whose research he pioneered included Polish–Jewish relations in early modern Poland–Lithuania, the roles of Jewish communal institutions in Polish–Lithuanian society, and the history of Jewish tavern-keeping.

Of particular importance was his work on the question of Jewish converts to Christianity in the Polish–Lithuanian Commonwealth. He published not only a series of articles in Polish, but also a Hebrew-language monograph on this subject. Once again, he developed a highly original point of view. In previous studies, the convert had often been seen as a traitor to his or her religion, and was treated negatively. Goldberg proposed viewing the act of conversion not as exemplifying the gap between Polish and Jewish society, but as a connection between them. In this view, the convert could be seen in a totally new light as a form of bridge between the two.

Goldberg's Jerusalem home became a place of pilgrimage for the young generation of scholars who began to take an interest in Polish Jewish history in the 1970s and 1980s, and his own doctoral students in the 1990s. He treated the issue of working with graduate students with the utmost seriousness, devoting much time and effort to giving them the tools necessary for the complex task of research in the field and to shaping their academic approach in general.

With the warming of relations between Poland and Israel in the 1980s, he was deeply involved in the academic contacts that preceded the opening of formal diplomatic channels. One of the founders of the Center for Research on the History and Culture of Polish Jews at the Hebrew University, he directed it in the early 1990s, among other things, overseeing and editing the Hebrew translation of Meir Bałaban's monumental history of the Jews in Kraków and Kazimierz, first published in the 1930s.

During all these years, he retained his connections with those Jews born in Łódź and survivors of the ghetto who were living in Israel. When his *Festschrift* was published in 1998, it came out with the active support of various members of this group.

As the newly re-established democratic Poland began to come to grips with its difficult past—and especially with the issue of Polish–Jewish relations—Goldberg was increasingly viewed there as a pioneer in the field and his work gained a new popularity in academic circles. In 1992, he was granted an Honorary Doctorate by the University of Warsaw and in 1998, he was appointed a foreign member of the Polish Academy of Arts and Sciences in Kraków.

In 2005, he was appointed a foreign member of the Polish Academy of Sciences in Warsaw. These, and other similar awards, were a source of special pride to him. His achievements were also recognized by the Polish State authorities, which twice bestowed high awards upon him. At the very end of his life, he renewed his connections with his *Alma Mater*—the University of Łódź, giving his help, support, and advice to the Center for Jewish Research there. In 2010, he traveled back to Łódź to celebrate the fiftieth anniversary of his doctorate with a special—and very moving—ceremony of renewal.

Kuba, and his beloved wife Olga (also a professor at the Hebrew University), kept an open house in Jerusalem for his students, friends, and visiting colleagues from Poland. Though he retained a highly critical approach to matters academic, his close circle always enjoyed his generosity and warmth. With his passing, we have lost not only a dear friend and colleague (and in many cases, mentor, too), but also a highly original scholar, and one of the last living connections to the vibrant world of Polish Jewry from before the Holocaust. Sadly, he did not live to see the massive volume of Polish-language sources for the history of the Council of Four Lands, which he compiled over more than twenty years. Published by the Wydawnictwo

Sejmowe in Warsaw just a few weeks after his death under the title *Sejm Czterech Ziem: Zródła*, it will surely be a fitting monument for his life's work.

   Yehi Zikhro Barukh!

ADAM TELLER

Hasidism without Romanticism

Mendel Piekarz's Path in the Study of Hasidism[1]

WHEN I first read one of Mendel Piekarz's books (I believe it was *Biyemei tsemiḥat haḥasidut*), I imagined the author as a slight, stooped-over, grave-countenanced, elderly man, sitting in a tiny, dimly lit room, its tall walls lined floor to ceiling with yellowing first editions of Musar and Drush books, while, pencil in hand, he assiduously underlined key phrases. Many years later, I met Piekarz in person at his home in Jerusalem; it was our only meeting. I was surprised to find out how close my imaginary figment had been to reality. Almost every detail was accurate, except for his countenance: Piekarz was pleasant and soft-spoken; not grave at all.

Dr Piekarz was one of the greatest scholars of hasidism of the latter generation and, it should be added, one of its most unusual scholars.[1] He was born in 1922 in the town of Pułtusk in Poland (the province of Warsaw), studied at *ḥeder* and in yeshivas, and was an alumnus, among other institutions, of the radical Musar yeshiva of Novhardok. At a certain phase in his life, he abandoned religious observance and adopted a secular-Zionist-socialist world view. During the Second World War, he fled to the Soviet Union, and later returned to Poland. He immigrated to Palestine on the *Exodus* (1947), served in the army, and until 1954 was a member of Hashomer Hatsa'ir's kibbutz Gal On. In 1954, he took up the study of Yiddish and Hebrew literature at the Hebrew University. His outstanding teachers were Dov Sadan and Isaiah Tishby.

In 1958 Piekarz began to work at Yad Vashem, and in this capacity he published comprehensive bibliographies on the reflection of the Holocaust in the Hebrew-language press and in Hebrew literature. He simultaneously continued his university studies in the field that interested him above all—hasidism. His master's thesis was on Bratslav (Breslov) hasidism—a topic that continued to interest him through-out his life. His first book, *Ḥasidut braslav: perakim beḥayei meḥolelah uvikhetaveiha* ('Bratslav Hasidism: Chapters in the Life of its Creator and of its

---

[1] The biographical survey in this chapter is based mostly on the instructive essay by David Assaf, in his blog 'Oneg Shabat': <http://onegshabbat.blogspot.com/2011/08/blog-post_24.html>.

Writings'), was published by the Bialik Institute in 1972.[2] From this point onwards, he published many of his books with the same publishing house.

In the early 1970s Piekarz began to work on his doctoral dissertation, 'Theological Trends in the Drush and Musar Books in Eastern Europe during the Emergence and Early Spread of Hasidism'.[3] Simultaneously, he devoted himself to creating an edition of Joseph Weiss's personal collection of works on Bratslav hasidism.[4] At that time, Piekarz, who was already recognized as a scholar of this hasidic group, did not limit himself to standard editing, but also critically annotated and supplemented Weiss's articles. Some scholars were taken aback by this approach, but Piekarz received a warm and complimentary letter of approval from the supreme authority on matters concerning kabbalah and hasidism—Gershom Scholem.

Scholem continued to encourage Piekarz, even when the latter disagreed with him. In his doctoral thesis, Piekarz sought to prove that some of the ideas promoted by hasidism had already been developed in the Drush and Musar literature of the seventeenth and eighteenth centuries. He was referring, *inter alia*, to the radical notions of *averah lishmah* (sin for Heaven's sake) and *averah tsorekh teshuvah* (a sin required for repenting). Scholem thought that these ideas had originated in Sabbatianism, while Piekarz criticized that view and argued that no link could be found between the persons who promoted these ideas at that time and the Sabbatian movement and its offshoots. Before completing his work, Piekarz published some of his findings in articles in the journal *Molad*.[5] Scholem, who received one of the articles that criticized his view, wrote a fascinating letter to Piekarz in which he defends his opinion but expresses deep appreciation for Piekarz and for his research, and wishes him success on his thesis. The thesis was indeed completed the following year (1977), and a year later it was published by the Bialik Institute under the title *Biyemei tsemihat hahasidut* ('The Beginning of Hasidism').[6]

Piekarz worked at Yad Vashem until retirement. During all those years, although he was not affiliated with any university or research institute that enabled him to pursue his study of hasidism, he consistently published books and numerous articles on this topic. He also published critical reviews of others' research.

[2] M. Piekarz, *Ḥasidut braslav: perakim beḥayei meholelah uvikhetaveiha* (Jerusalem, 1972); id., *Ḥasidut braslav: perakim beḥayei meholelah, bikhetaveiha uvisefiḥeiha*, 2nd, expanded, edn. (Jerusalem, 1996).

[3] M. Piekarz, 'Megamot ra'ayoniyot besifrei derush umusar bemizraḥ eiropah biyemei tsemiḥat hahasidut vereshit hitpashetutah', doctoral thesis (Hebrew Univ. of Jerusalem, 1977).

[4] J. Weiss, *Meḥkarim baḥasidut braslav*, ed. M. Piekarz (Jerusalem, 1975).

[5] M. Piekarz, 'Avot hahasidut beḥibur shel darshan lita'i, 5541 [1781] (r. aharon ben r. yeshayah kregloshker)', *Molad*, NS, 4 (1971), 298–303; id., 'Radikalizm dati biyemei hitpashetut hahasidut: torat "kaf remiyah" bekhitvei eli'ezer lipman mibrodi', *Molad*, NS, 6 (1975), 412–37; id., 'Hate'udah harishonah bidefus letorat hahasidut: shenei ma'amarim me'et hamagid mimezerich bishenat 5538 [1778]', *Molad*, NS, 7, (1975), 183–6.

[6] M. Piekarz, *Biyemei tsemiḥat hahasidut: megamot ra'ayoniyot besifrei derush umusar* (Jerusalem, 1978).

From the beginning of the 1980s Piekarz began to turn gradually to the study of later hasidism, and many view these researches as his most significant contribution. Focusing chiefly on the perception of the *tsadik* and of his authority, his research during this phase dealt mainly with the transformation that hasidism underwent from a radical movement with daring messages to a conservative and 'heteronomous' movement. The pinnacle of this research phase is his book *Ḥasidut polin* ('Polish Hasidism').[7] Even before publication, Piekarz provoked a sharp controversy because of an article he had written about Rabbi Aharon of Belz's escape from Budapest to the Land of Israel, and about the farewell sermon by his brother, Rabbi Mordecai (the father of the current Belzer Rebbe), in which, in the name of the rebbe, he promised peace and tranquillity to the Jews of Hungary.[8] Rabbi Nathan Urtner, who described the rebbe's flight and published the sermon in a censored version, without the 'problematic' passage, responded to Piekarz,[9] and Piekarz continued this discussion in his book.[10] Some time later, Esther Farbstein also addressed this issue, and noted that at the time of the rebbe's escape from Hungary, the Nazis had not yet invaded the country, and that the invasion, which occurred shortly after, came as an utter surprise. Therefore, she concludes, the sermon was censored not because of moral discomfiture at the actual act of escaping, but rather because it exposed the fact that the rebbe had erred.[11]

In his later years Piekarz suffered a stroke, from which he recovered. He passed away on 21 August 2011, at the age of 89.

*

Piekarz wrote a series of important books on the history of hasidism. Although he was also a Holocaust scholar, he will no doubt be remembered as the scholar of a movement that he did not like, to say the least. He covered nearly the entire corpus of literature this movement produced, from its inception to the Holocaust, in almost every region in which it flourished (with the exception of Hungarian hasidism, which has been almost entirely ignored by scholarship). This fact should not be taken for granted: the founding generation of researchers of hasidism was interested almost exclusively in early hasidism—the first three generations, and until 1815 especially.[12] These scholars viewed this era of the movement as its time of ascendancy, innovation, and bold religious radicalism, while the following period

---

[7] M. Piekarz, *Ḥasidut polin bein shetei hamilḥamot uvigezerot 700–705 [1939–1945] ('hasho'ah')* (Jerusalem, 1990).

[8] M. Piekarz, 'Gezerot polin umenuḥah veshalvah liyehudei hungaryah biderashah ḥasidit belza'it beyanuar 1944 bebudapest', *Kivunim*, 11 (1981), 115–19.

[9] Rabbi N. Urtner, 'Al derashah ḥasidit belza'it', *Kivunim*, 14 (1982), 145–9.

[10] Piekarz, *Ḥasidut polin*, 424–34.

[11] E. Farbstein, *Hidden in Thunder: Perspectives on Faith, Halachah and Leadership during the Holocaust*, trans. D. Stern, 2 vols. (Jerusalem, 2007), i. 67–153.

[12] D. Assaf, *The Regal Way: The Life and Times of Rabbi Israel of Ruzhin*, trans. D. Louvish (Stanford, Calif., 2002), 8–11.

was viewed as one of decline, atrophy, and decadence.[13] Therefore, they took for granted that the period of the movement's emergence was worthy of study, while the later period was uninteresting. If any interest was evinced in the established rebbes from the mid-nineteenth century onwards, the focus was on those figures, such as Rabbi Mordecai Yosef of Izbica, who in the view of these scholars preserved the movement's essential vitality, its audacity and originality. By way of contrast, contemporary hasidic scholarship is more prudent in its approach: it continues to pay attention to the first stage, but also extends its gaze to the later generations. It does so with a less judgemental cast of mind, sometimes emphasizing the fact that it was during the movement's later period that it consolidated and achieved most of its public influence. Piekarz was a fierce supporter of the 'decadence thesis', and in this respect, he was essentially a member of the 'old school' of research. However, his view of later hasidism as decadent did not prevent him from studying it. On the contrary, he devoted long years of labour to its study.

Why did Piekarz choose to study this supposedly 'uninteresting' period? Characteristically, this scholar did not provide a personal account of his motives and theoretical concerns, and scarcely engaged in questions of an abstract nature. However, it seems one can easily conjecture what his response to this question might have been: on the contrary—it is precisely the processes of decline and decadence that are interesting; and, just as it is interesting to understand how leaders justify a revolutionary change, so it is interesting to see how they justify the conservative reaction which retreats from the earlier transformation. The leaders of later hasidism, in his view, were not interesting as theologians or spiritual figures, but rather as 'advocates who resent that name, and for the most part even wily spokesmen for their prejudices' (to use Nietzsche's phrase),[14] and as leaders who influenced their flocks of followers. And so he spent many years poring over hundreds of books by the hasidic leaders of the nineteenth and twentieth centuries, great and small, and with extraordinary assiduity collected countless sources that to his mind indicated the trends that were characteristic of later hasidism, and which gained in strength over time: 'a retreat to the heteronomous foundations of religion', 'vulgar tsadikism', opposition to innovation, and sanctification of Galut (exile).[15]

But Piekarz also had another veiled motive—an ideological one. He shared the conviction that the trends exemplified by the hasidic rebbes were responsible for the passive attitude and anti-Zionist positions of the pre-Holocaust era. The combination of a conservative outlook and hasidic optimism encouraged, even in the midst of the genocidal process, an attitude of acquiescence, which sought to find

[13] M. M. Buber, *Or haganuz* (Jerusalem, 1977), 35; R. Mahler, *Haḥasidut vehahaskalah* (Merhavia, 1961), 9; id., 'Maḥaloket sants-sadigurah: shetei shitot baḥasidut hashoka'at', in *Proceedings of the Fourth World Congress of Jewish Studies*, ii (Jerusalem, 1969), 223–5; Piekarz, *Ḥasidut polin*, 50, 181.

[14] F. Nietzsche, *Beyond Good and Evil: Prelude to a Philosophy of the Future*, trans. W. Kaufmann (New York, 1989), pt. i, aphorism 5.

[15] Piekarz, *Ḥasidut polin*, 50, 121; M. Piekarz, *Hahanhagah haḥasidit: samkhut ve'emunat tsadikim be'aspaklaryat sifrutah shel haḥasidut* (Jerusalem, 1979), *passim*.

even in extreme suffering signs of light and good and the seeds of an imminent redemption. Piekarz, who did not experience the death camps himself but lost many of his loved ones in the Holocaust, wished to show how some of the failures of the hasidic leadership were rooted in the world view that they had cultivated. His great book (and to some, his most important work) *Ḥasidut polin* is oriented to such views. No reader of this work can escape the impression that its first chapters, which survey in great detail the ideological process that Polish hasidism underwent from the end of the nineteenth century until the Holocaust, are nothing but a rich body of evidence leading to the guilty verdict of the book's final chapters—a verdict which, so Piekarz believed, was shared even by some members of the hasidic movement itself.[16] Indeed, Piekarz continued the battle of secular Zionism against the ultra-Orthodox establishment, and promoted the old thesis that claimed that the Holocaust was proof of the accuracy of the Zionist prognosis and of the failure of exilic outlooks. Such claims, which are broached now and again even in contemporary discussions, are marred by factual imprecision and sometimes also by lack of intellectual integrity, but this issue cannot be elaborated here. The main point is that for Piekarz, such claims emerged from a profound and poignant sensibility that found expression in his unique style of scholarship.

*

If later hasidism was perceived by Piekarz as 'decadent', we might expect him to have viewed early hasidism as a fresh breath of air, as did most of his predecessors who supported the decadence thesis. But this was not the case. Piekarz did indeed describe early hasidism with less of a judgemental tone, but with it too he refused to fall in love. His comprehensive study *Biyemei tsemiḥat haḥasidut* aimed to demonstrate that the early hasidic teachers had scarcely innovated a thing, and that most of their ideas were already widespread among *darshanim* and Musar thinkers, mostly forgotten and overlooked preachers who were active in eastern Europe on the eve of the Ba'al Shem Tov's appearance. He considers the Torah teachings of the early *tsadikim*—like those of the rebbes of later hasidism—as full of contradictions and hyperbole. Even in one of his most important and famous articles, that on the concept of *devekut*, Piekarz seeks to extinguish his readers' enthusiasm with a dose of cold water.[17] While Gershom Scholem argued that the concept of *devekut*— mystical communion with God—was the chief innovation of hasidism in the field of Jewish mysticism, Piekarz, with typical meticulousness, attempted to show that this was not the case: first, the concept had been developed long before the Besht, and second, even in early hasidism, this concept was replete with non-mystical

---

[16] In his opinion, that is the way one should understand the responses of R. Klonimus Kalman of Piaseczno, the Rebbetzin of Stropkov, and R. Isachar Shlomo Teichthal: Piekarz, *Ḥasidut polin*, 373–424.

[17] M. Piekarz, 'Haḥasidut—tenuah ḥevratit-datit bire'i hadevekut', *Da'at*, 25 (1990), 127–47; English version, M. Piekarz, 'Hasidism as a Socio-Religious Movement on the Evidence of *Devekut*', in A. Rapoport-Albert (ed.), *Hasidism Reappraised* (Oxford, 1996), 225–48.

connotations, alongside the mystical ones to which Scholem had drawn attention. Instead, Piekarz viewed the theory of the *tsadik* as hasidism's main innovation—the theory that in his opinion (shared also by a number of his predecessors) was also the root of the movement's decadence in later generations, especially after the succession of leadership began to follow a dynastic principle.

And yet, the heritability of leadership was not the only bane of hasidism. Bratslav hasidism, which did not follow a dynastic principle, underwent, according to Piekarz, its own processes of decadence. Indeed, Piekarz had written his master's thesis about this movement, and this was also the topic of his first book and of the collection of Joseph Weiss's research papers that he edited. However, while Weiss focused on the existential wrestling in Rabbi Nahman's thought and on his theology, Piekarz focused more on the question of Nahman's perception of himself and of his role as a *tsadik*, on the messianic aspects of this conception, as well as on the paths of concealment and transmission of Bratslav literature. Weiss evinced empathy for Nahman's entangled soul, while Piekarz was much more detached in his approach. He appreciated Weiss's engagement and identification, but cautioned against 'all sorts of fashionable writings' that pinched out 'fragments and shreds in order to stitch them together with trendy psychological and mystical threads'.[18]

Eventually Piekarz turned to investigate the later manifestations of the movement and of its messianic spirit, in his article about the new Bratslav in Israel of the 1960s.[19] This study was apparently his only research project that extended to post-Holocaust hasidism—and one of the first studies ever that turned its attention to this topic. Piekarz also regarded the later Bratslav movement, that of the 'Bratslavizers and Nahmanizers' ('hamitbraslavim vehamitnahmanim'),[20] as decadent in comparison with that of its founder (although he was not especially enamoured of the figure of Rabbi Nahman, either). It would seem, therefore, that the slide into decadence was not, in his view, intrinsically tied to the existence of a living, highborn *tsadik*.

*

One of the outstanding forebears of the 'decadence thesis' was Martin Buber.[21] Piekarz, as has been noted, adopted this thesis, and similarly viewed the heritability of the office of rebbe as the mother of all evil, but his approach to hasidism was very different from that of Buber. Buber took a nostalgic view of early hasidism, as a movement with a profound religious message of dialogue with God, a message that he hoped to enliven in ways that were compatible with modern times. Piekarz had no such religious yearnings, and frequently regarded this kind of nostalgic view of

---

[18] Piekarz, *Ḥasidut braslav* (1996), 6.

[19] M. Piekarz, 'Misipurei ḥasidut braslav', *Da'at*, 8 (1982), 95–108; repr. as 'Hamifneh betoledoteiha shel hameshiḥiut haḥasidit habraslavit', in T. Baras (ed.), *Meshiḥiyut ve'eskhatologyah* (Jerusalem, 1984), 325–44. See also his *Ḥasidut braslav* (1996), 199–218.

[20] Piekarz, *Ḥasidut braslav* (1996), 199.   [21] Buber, *Or haganuz*, 35.

hasidism as romantic whimsy that utterly misconstrued and missed the true spirit of the movement.

In truth, the decadence thesis is itself no less at fault for its romantic valorization of whatever is prior, young, rebellious, and daring. The premise that anyone who abandons the young spirit of daring rebellion and turns to the path of institutionalization or to a reactive traditionalism is necessarily 'decadent' and 'in decline' is in itself a romantic notion, at least in a certain respect. This romantic outlook ignores the fact that great religious movements are not designed only to be a platform for youthful adventures of innovative youngsters, or to inflame the imagination of modern intellectuals who glorify antinomian boldness. Such movements are meant chiefly to provide a responsible and supportive framework for the lives of individuals and communities, and in the present case—also to serve as a framework for the preservation of traditional values, in the face of challenges to tradition. The romantic expects a religious movement to be all *Sturm und Drang*, devotion and enthusiasm, and is disillusioned when these elements are on the wane. Therefore, by adopting the decadence thesis, Piekarz betrays the same expectation and disappointment, proving that he too was affected by the same romantic spirit that he castigated.

The decadence thesis is coloured, undoubtedly, by tendentious value judgements. What early students of hasidism, including Piekarz, viewed as 'decadence', could by the same token have been regarded *sine ira* as processes of routinization of charisma, in Max Weber's terms.[22] According to Weber and his followers, such processes are typical of innovative religious movements. Weber himself remarked upon the instability of charismatic authority[23] and the fact that it is appropriate mostly for the revolutionary phases of religious movements.[24] He even noted the connection between heritability and institutionalization, remarking that

As soon as charismatic domination loses its personal foundation and the acutely emotional faith which distinguishes it from the traditional mold of everyday life, its alliance with tradition is the most obvious and often the only alternative . . . In such an alliance, the essence of charisma appears to be definitely abandoned, and this is indeed true insofar as its eminently revolutionary character is concerned . . . In this function, which is alien to its essence, charisma becomes a part of everyday life.[25]

---

[22] M. Weber, *Economy and Society: An Outline of Interpretive Sociology*, ed. G. Roth and C. Wittich, trans. E. Fischoff et al., 2 vols. (Berkeley and Los Angeles, 1978), i. 246–54, ii. 1121–3; R. Bendix, *Max Weber: An Intellectual Portrait* (New York, 1962), 301–7. On the possibility of acquiring a type of impersonal 'family charisma', see ibid. 308–14. For the application of this theory to hasidism, see the illuminating article by S. Sharot, 'Hasidism and the Routinization of Charisma', *Journal for the Scientific Study of Religion*, 19/4 (1980), 325–36; for an online version of the same, see <http://www.jstor.org/stable/1386127?seq=9>. [23] Weber, *Economy and Society*, ii. 1114. [24] Ibid. 1115–17.
[25] Ibid. 1122–3. Still, even Weber, who was so aware of the deterministic necessity of this process, appears to bemoan it: 'Every charisma is on the road from a turbulently emotional life that knows no economic rationality to a slow death by the suffocation under the weight of material interests: every hour of its existence brings it nearer to this end': ibid. 1120.

One may examine the processes of institutionalization of a movement with the expectation that it may stay for ever young, rebellious, and bold, and even express feelings of rage or disappointment when it fails to meet these expectations, but such processes may also be viewed in a less judgemental manner, similar to the way that one observes the maturation of a young person. Children are more vivacious and charming than adults, but part of their charm is due to the fact that a young person is burdened with a lesser degree of responsibility. Therefore, an adult who continues to behave like a child will no longer be regarded as delightful, but rather as infantile. Such too is the fate of religious and other types of movements which are characterized by high religious tension. The process of institutionalization of such movements is none other than their process of maturation. Institutionalization of this kind can take on different forms, and in hasidism, the heritability of the office of rebbe is a case in point. There is no doubt that the dynastic principle entailed not a few unsavoury consequences, but such outcomes can be found at the margins of any strong institutionalized movement, and they do not appear to be more widespread in hasidism than elsewhere. On the contrary, it seems as though even in its later period the movement was populated by not a few figures who were far removed from any such corruption, who led deeply religious lives, and who carried the burden of public office with devotion and perseverance. But there is a more important point to be made. Institutionalization is an outcome not only of fatigue and feebleness, but also of changing needs: a movement composed chiefly of the young and newly mobilized is unlike a movement that must look after community and educational institutions and care for the livelihoods of its members, while also defending itself against perils from the outside. A movement of the first kind may indulge in leaders whose chief virtue is their capacity for ecstatic prayer and the spiritual ascent to higher worlds; a movement of the second type requires a leadership which is much more in touch with down-to-earth realities, despite the price and alongside the advantages of such earthliness. Therefore, the expectation that hasidism would for ever persevere in its childhood phase and never grow up is not only unrealistic, but also morally indefensible.

*

Piekarz was a harsh critic not only of hasidism and of its leadership, but also of its scholars. He did not mince words when it came to critiquing many of his colleagues, and from time to time he wrote reviews of their books in Israeli daily newspapers. A large number of these reviews attacked what he perceived as the romanticizing of hasidism. He viewed Arthur Green's book *Tormented Master* as an attempt to portray Rabbi Nahman as a religious existentialist and thus construct him as a 'Tzaddik for the modern man'—a phrase that Green himself had used in his book,[26] and which Piekarz viewed as a key to understanding his overall approach.[27]

---

[26] A. Green, *Tormented Master: The Life and Spiritual Quest of Rabbi Nahman of Bratslav* (Woodstock, Vt., 1992), 330.   [27] Piekarz, *Hasidut braslav* (1996), 219–46.

The pioneering book by David Assaf on Rabbi Israel of Ruzhin, which many hasidim viewed as too critical of its subject, Piekarz criticized for being too favourable towards him, mainly because Assaf attempted to describe the rebbe's ostentatious 'regal way' not only as a personal orientation, but also as a 'path of worship', while Piekarz viewed it only as blatant megalomania and unrestrained corruption.[28]

Piekarz made minimal use of his colleagues' research. His books come across as bundles of citations and references—almost all from primary literary sources, either hasidic or darshanic. Academic scholarship is only scarcely cited, even where it might have supported Piekarz's conclusions; literature in languages other than Hebrew or Yiddish is altogether absent. Testimonies and memoirs, whose reliability he doubted,[29] were also hardly ever referenced. There is also scant discussion in his writing of the historical developments that surrounded the cited texts. More abstract analytical or theoretical models are similarly non-existent. He draws all of his generalizations or essential conclusions entirely from his own reflection on the material, by means of a spare and minimalist analysis, which often is dwarfed by the sheer mass of sources and minutiae. This manner of writing is far removed from current academic convention. A student submitting a seminar paper in such a style —not to mention a master's or doctoral thesis—would be severely condemned. But this was not the case with Piekarz. Although everyone recognized these shortcomings of his writing, the outstanding value of the research was immediately acknowledged, and his books were mostly published by the distinguished Bialik Institute press. This was not because of charity or leniency, but rather owing to the recognition that the contribution of these books was so great that they could not be passed over, despite faults of one nature or another. Moreover, it was precisely Piekarz's focused approach that endowed his work such great persuasive power, as if he were saying to the reader: such and such is my argument; here are the sources in support of it; *quod erat demonstrandum*.

All of the above characteristics made Piekarz an exceptional figure in the academic scene, to which he never completely belonged. A regular position in an academic institution was never conferred on him (he made a living as a researcher at Yad Vashem), and he also scarcely lectured at academic conferences. When he did attend a conference, he usually sat with the crowd as an auditor, and is often remembered for his vocal and acerbic remarks to the speaker. Even though a great many professors honoured him and made extensive use of his books, he himself was never awarded the title of professor, and actually did not pursue any academic career. It is hard to say whether he was pained by this, but it is clear that he was

---

[28] M. Piekarz, 'Lu ratsiti, yakholti letsavot la'ets la'avor mimekomo lemakom aḥer', *Haaretz Book Review*, 16 Jan. 1998 (review of Assaf's *Derekh malkhut*, the original Hebrew version of *The Regal Way*).

[29] M. Piekarz, 'Al sifrut ha'edut kemakor histori ligezerot "hapitron hasofi"', *Kivunim*, 20 (1983), 129–57.

unwilling to make any concessions just to become a part of that world. 'He was a Novhardoker,' Elhanan Reiner said to me once in conversation: 'utterly loyal to his own truth, showing no partiality to anyone, and truly disdainful of titles and honours.' There is much truth in this characterization, especially in light of the fact that in his youth Piekarz was indeed a student at the radical Musar yeshiva of Novhardok. He preserved these traits, indicative of the spirit of the Musar movement, despite having distanced himself from its religious universe.

Indeed, if at first I had imagined Piekarz as a serious person, it was chiefly because his writing was all gravity. He never took pity on his readers. His books were meant not to entertain, but to teach, and to advance science. If one wishes to learn, one must deign to delve into the minute details. The detail-oriented nature of his writing frequently leaves the reader with the sense that the forest cannot be seen for the trees. And yet, a reader who manages to complete one of Piekarz's books will find an uncommon satisfaction in having done so, as one who has completed an arduous journey, and says: it was hard, but I learned something. The gravitas of his oeuvre is first and foremost a reflection of the seriousness with which he treated the requirement to prove his argument. This too, perhaps, was an expression of the stringent ethos of a *musarnik*.

Piekarz bequeathed to the next generation a body of research marked with stylistic shortcomings and a minimum of scholarly dialogue, and sometimes coloured by ideological and emotional biases, but always replete with extraordinary, innovative knowledge (in terms of both content and research orientation) and characterized by impressive thoroughness. These positive attributes not only compensated for the shortcomings but turned them into a challenging stimulus—the challenge of ploughing through the books, despite their density, the challenge of understanding the argument, not only in its own terms, but vis-à-vis other scholarly literature, and the challenge of identifying the ideological 'bent' of the author, and neutralizing it. In this sense, Piekarz rendered himself not only as a teacher who transmits content to his students and readers, but also as a teacher who hones and exercises their critical and scholarly faculties. Beyond doubt, this scholarly oeuvre has established a place of honour for its author in the increasingly growing and flourishing body of hasidism scholarship.

BENJAMIN BROWN
Translated from the Hebrew by Ilana Goldberg

Paula Hyman
1946–2011

'DESPITE ALL OBSTACLES, our [women's] movement progressed because we knew that you have to take power, that no one gives it to you voluntarily. And that you can take it only if you know how to educate.' This bold assertion about Jewish women's rights in Poland by the Zionist activist Puah Rakovsky over a century ago captures the indefatigable spirit of Paula Hyman, who introduced the former's memoirs to a new generation of readers.[1] It was my privilege to meet her early in my career and to co-edit a volume of *Polin* devoted to 'Jewish Women in Eastern Europe' with her.[2] When Hyman passed away after a courageous struggle with cancer on 15 December 2011, she left behind a prodigious volume of groundbreaking scholarship, students whom she had mentored with immense generosity, and dedicated feminists with whom she had laboured for gender equality in Judaism, as well as numerous devoted friends and family.

Paula Hyman was the Lucy G. Moses Professor of Modern History at Yale University. As a young graduate student at Columbia University (where she earned her doctorate in 1975), she observed the 'absence of women from all that [she] was studying' and set out to place their stories into the broader narratives of Jewish modernity. Not only did she seek to 'reclaim the experience of Jewish women', as she once wrote, but also to explore how gender as a category of analysis could elucidate social relationships and power relations in Jewish history. As a social historian, Hyman was especially interested in Jewish migration, encounters between cultures (especially between 'East' and 'West'), conflicts between social classes and generations, and the construction of modern Jewish identities. She brought those at the margins to the fore of scholarly inquiry, challenging the hegemony of certain master narratives at the expense of others.

Her first book, *From Dreyfus to Vichy*, established Hyman as a specialist in French Jewish history. Rejecting the image of French Jewry as a moribund community that had grown complaisant after its attainment of emancipation, she traced how immigrants from eastern Europe, so despised by native French Jews for their foreignness and poverty, infused the community with new vitality and strength.

---

[1] P. Rakovsky, *My Life as a Radical Jewish Woman: Memoirs of a Zionist Feminist in Poland*, ed. and intro. P. E. Hyman, trans. B. Harshav with P. E. Hyman (Bloomington, Ind., 2002).

[2] *Polin*, 18 (2005).

Reversing the native–migrant narrative, Hyman showed that Jewish immigrants not only gradually acculturated into French culture on their own terms, but also fostered the emergence of 'a broader conception of Jewish identity, which included the ethnic and cultural elements formerly discarded as the price of assimilation'.[3] Her next major project on French Jewry, *The Emancipation of the Jews of Alsace*,[4] has been described as 'social history at its best and most persuasive'. In this study, Hyman brought the experience of rural Jews in Alsace to the centre of the story. Their tenacious devotion to tradition, as Hyman illustrated through their occupational structures, marital and family practices, religious rituals, and folk culture, challenged conventional wisdom about rapid assimilation as the inevitable consequence of emancipation. At the same time, her study also showed the disruptive impact of migration to the urban centres and the transformative nature of French education on those who left the rural environment. Hyman drew all these key themes together in a brilliant synthesis in *The Jews of Modern France*, a 'two-hundred-year odyssey' through French Jewish history.[5]

For Hyman, one of the important marginalized groups in history was Jewish women. Their exclusion from the narratives of both Jewish and general histories was not simply an academic problem but a deeply personal matter. Her long-time friend Deborah Dash Moore recalled that when Hyman visited her at Vassar College in the mid-1970s, they exchanged ideas about her participation in the annual Berkshire Conference of Women Historians 'to make sure that Jewish women were not excluded as subjects of women's history'. Among other things, they discussed a recent op-ed in the *New York Times* by Herbert Gutman that mentioned the kosher meat boycott by Jewish immigrant women in New York. 'Out of those conversations emerged her brilliant article "Immigrant Women and Consumer Protest"',[6] reminisced Dash Moore. 'She went back to Yiddish newspaper sources, to the census records, to court documents, in order to narrate a form of activism unaccounted by historical scholarship to that point.' That article—read widely in university classes and reprinted numerous times—indeed revealed Hyman's 'biting humor and feminist insight'.[7] It demonstrated how housewives from the Lower East Side to Williamsburg and Harlem could transcend boundaries that divided the secular from religious and radical from liberal—all for a common cause in the face of rising food prices and soaring rents.

Dash Moore and Hyman would later co-edit the highly acclaimed two-volume *Jewish Women in America: An Historical Encyclopedia*, which 'provides the first standard reference work on the lives, history and activities of Jewish women in the

[3] P. Hyman, *From Dreyfus to Vichy: The Remaking of French Jewry, 1906–1939* (New York, 1979), 233.

[4] P. E. Hyman, *The Emancipation of the Jews of Alsace: Acculturation and Tradition in the Nineteenth Century* (New Haven, 1991).   [5] P. E. Hyman, *The Jews of Modern France* (Berkeley, 1998).

[6] P. E. Hyman, 'Immigrant Women and Consumer Protest: The New York City Kosher Meat Boycott of 1902', *American Jewish History*, 70 (1980), 91–105.

[7] Deborah Dash Moore, email correspondence, 4 Oct. 2012.

United States . . . from the arrival of the first Jewish women in North America in 1654 to the present'.[8] The entries in this encyclopedia were integrated into Hyman and Dalia Ofer's larger *Jewish Women: A Comprehensive Historical Encyclopedia*. In their introduction, the authors echoed Puah Rakovsky's ambitions for educating women through knowledge so that they could take control over their own lives: 'Believing that knowledge empowers, we were particularly eager to provide this and future generations of Jewish women [with] the tools to become, as much as possible, agents of their own situations. We also recognize the importance of this knowledge for Jewish men.'[9]

When she was invited to deliver the Stroum Lectures in Seattle,[10] Hyman decided to focus on issues of gender 'because they not only highlight the regularly overlooked experiences of women but also pose new questions about male behavior'.[11] This project provided the perfect opportunity to compare the gendered projects of assimilation in several comparative contexts: in western Europe, east-central Europe, and America. Based on previously neglected memoirs, diaries, and letters of Jewish women (as well as previous studies by Marion Kaplan and others), Hyman argued that in the West, the bourgeois division of public and private spheres produced gendered patterns of assimilation: whereas bourgeois culture rewarded Jewish men who abandoned traditional study of sacred texts in favour of secular education and professional life, it linked women to spirituality and familial sentiment. Relegated to the domestic sphere, Jewish women became the guardians of ritual practices in the home.

In eastern Europe, by contrast, the ideals (though not the reality for all) prescribed an arrangement that allowed the husband to study Torah and gave the wife the task of earning the livelihood. According to Hyman, this inverted structure of work and the exclusion of women from religious study 'facilitated women's assimilation through their work patterns and access to secular education' and radical movements of the late nineteenth and twentieth centuries.[12] Bringing the story full circle to America, she posited that women's roles as agents of assimilation in eastern Europe allowed them to embrace the new consumer culture and leisure practices that shaped American Jewish families. Moreover, Hyman highlighted observations by social reformers that Jewish immigrant women were more 'attuned to political questions and far more convinced of their right to act politically than were their immigrant neighbors'.[13] In other words, actions such as the kosher meat boycott emerged out of a specific milieu in which women believed they had the right to defend their daily existence. At the same time, Hyman pointed out that

---

[8] P. E. Hyman and D. Dash Moore (eds.), *Jewish Women in America: An Historical Encyclopedia*, 2 vols. (New York, 1997), cover.

[9] P. E. Hyman and D. Ofer (eds.), *Jewish Women: A Comprehensive Historical Encyclopedia* (Jerusalem, 2006), preface.

[10] These were published as P. E. Hyman, *Gender and Assimilation in Modern Jewish History: The Roles and Representation of Women* (Seattle, 1995).   [11] Ibid. 12.   [12] Ibid. 71.   [13] Ibid. 112.

immigrant women also served as 'buffers against the disruptive influences of the new society'.[14]

In her introduction to *Gender and Assimilation in Modern Jewish History*, Hyman graciously thanked her graduate and undergraduate students for stimulating her thinking. Beth Wenger, who is now a distinguished professor of history at the University of Pennsylvania, described Hyman as follows: 'She was a generous mentor who combined impeccably high standards with genuine compassion. A creative and productive scholar, she was also a role model to me and so many others. Her commitment to feminism not only broke down barriers but impacted the way she treated students and colleagues on a daily basis.'[15] When I visited Yale University to give a lecture soon after her passing, Hyman's orphaned graduate students described her generosity and willingness to share her time and wisdom. Shari Rabin and her cohort related a story that reflected their mentor's deep sense of responsibility to junior scholars like myself. Hyman told them about the final decision regarding our co-edited *Polin* volume: she had insisted that my name (Freeze) appear before hers (Hyman) on the cover of the volume. 'She needs the credit much more than I do', she remarked, refusing to budge on the issue. As I sat in her office before my lecture, with her piles of unfinished papers and well-worn books around me, I recalled the first time I met her. Hyman had made it a point to come to my first Association for Jewish Studies (AJS) talk and, as terrifying as it was to take a question from her, it made me feel like I really belonged to the scholarly academic community.

For many of us, Hyman was a model of what it means to be a feminist scholar. She lived by the second-wave feminist rallying cry 'the personal is political'. Her close friend and colleague Marion Kaplan remembered their meeting at Columbia University and political activities together: 'We noticed each other at Columbia Women's Liberation and pamphleted against the war in Cambodia in Park Slope, Brooklyn, not the Park Slope of today but a very nationalistic pro-war area. We pamphleted together, we were scared!'[16] Hyman was one of the founders of Ezrat Nashim, which called on the Conservative movement for 'equal access to positions of leadership and religious participation from which Jewish women were excluded because of their gender'. Specifically, Ezrat Nashim demanded that women be counted in a *minyan* and be ordained as rabbis. Marion Kaplan aptly remarked that Hyman 'had her strong opinions, but she also chose friends and a spouse with strong opinions'. Without these strong opinions, change would never have taken place.

It was Paula Hyman's strength of spirit and fierce determination to persevere that we will all remember. At the AJS presentation of her Festschrift volume, *Gender and Jewish History*, so lovingly compiled by Marion Kaplan and Deborah

---

[14] P. E. Hyman, *Gender and Assimilation in Modern Jewish History: The Roles and Representation of Women* (Seattle, 1995), 97.   [15] Beth Wenger, email correspondence, 5 Oct. 2012.
[16] Marion Kaplan, email correspondence, 1 Oct. 2012.

Dash Moore,[17] when Hyman stood up to accept our tribute of admiration and appreciation, there was not a dry eye in the room. Before us stood a bold pioneer of Jewish women's and gender studies. Like Puah Rakovsky, who created the monthly journal *Froyen-shtim* ('Women's Voice') 'to conduct enlightenment work among Jewish women, because the doors of the Yiddish press are for us women closed with seven locks', Hyman has left behind a legacy that will help unlock those doors that still remain closed.

CHAERAN FREEZE

[17] M. A. Kaplan and D. Dash Moore (eds.), *Gender and Jewish History* (Bloomington, Ind., 2011).

Vitka Kempner-Kovner
1920–2012

VITKA KEMPNER-KOVNER is known primarily as the life partner and soulmate of Abba Kovner (1912–87). There are several photographs displayed in her living room, including one of her close friend Rozka Korczak (1921–88), but the most striking image of all is the towering portrait of Abba Kovner. We see him there, long white forelock and all, staring straight at the camera with a pensive, serious look in his eyes, his prominent position on the wall epitomizing the place he occupied in Vitka's life. During our numerous conversations, Vitka repeatedly emphasized that she never sought 'liberation' from the label 'wife of Abba Kovner', poet and fighter, a founder of the FPO (Fareynikte Partizaner Organizatsye; United Partisan Organization) in the Vilna ghetto and the designer of its famous poster calling for resistance. 'I lived in Abba's shadow', Vitka admits, 'and it was good to be there, because he was the most interesting man I have ever met in my life.'[1]

Vitka avoided personal recollections of the Holocaust era for many years. She only began her book about the heroic acts of that era long after the fighters and partisans—some of whom were no longer among the living—had already submitted their testimony and published their own books.

Since the 1980s, victims' memories and survivors' stories have increasingly supplanted the tales of heroism documenting the battles in ghettos and forests, as reflected in the Yad Vashem Shoah Victims' Names Project (launched in 1989) and in the publication of numerous autobiographies of Holocaust survivors, including some published privately.[2] The complexity and difficulties expressed in individual stories of survival became the focus of Holocaust Remembrance Day ceremonies and events. Organized trips to Poland for young people also emphasized the personal element, as groups were accompanied by survivors, who described everyday life in the ghettos and camps visited.[3]

[1] Author's conversations with Vitka Kempner-Kovner, 2003–7.

[2] D. Porat, 'Hasipur od lo supar', *Haaretz*, 22 Jan. 2007; D. Gutwein, 'The Privatization of the Holocaust: Politics, Memory and Historiography', *Israel Studies*, 14/1 (2009), 36–64. This development is the result of changes in Israeli society as of the 1980s, with its increasing emphasis on personal achievement, as contrasted with the admiration for collective accomplishments that typified the early years of the State of Israel. Gutwein calls this era 'the period of privatized memory'.

[3] See, for example, *Hope Is the Last to Die: A Coming of Age under Nazi Terror* (Armonk, NY, 1996), the autobiography of Halina Birenbaum (b. 1929), who spent her childhood in the Warsaw ghetto, was

Focus on the collective memory of the survivors' struggle for life evoked reactions among former underground fighters and partisans, some of whom even expressed feelings of guilt because the battle stories merited most public attention in the early years of the State of Israel. Such sentiments were clearly reflected in the words of Fredka Mazia of Kibbutz Haogen, who had participated in the underground at the Sosnowiec ghetto in south-western Poland:

They turned us into heroes, but I am not certain we deserved it. They [the fighters] were prepared when they set out, equipped with cover and communications, while women from the ghetto went out just like that, with no help, seeking bread for their children. Who suffered the harshest conditions? I don't know. Today, it appears that all those mothers and older people who tried to survive all the horror and retain their human dignity were the true heroes. I know that I'm speaking heresy, but ultimately neither the fighting nor anything else did any good. It was simply another reaction, perhaps an easier one from a moral point of view. It is much more difficult for a young person to accompany his parents to the camps, knowing that he cannot let them go alone. That was great heroism, at least as great as ours, if not greater.[4]

In any event, although the tales of heroism had top priority, Vitka Kempner-Kovner did not attract any special attention, even though her acquaintances retold her story at gatherings, in recorded testimony, and in interviews. For example, when Vitka's friend Rozka Korczak met with senior Labour Zionist officials and Yishuv (pre-state Jewish community) officials on her arrival in Palestine in 1945, she extolled Vitka's bravery and courage, as well as the activities of other women in the underground.[5] On the witness stand at the Eichmann trial, Abba Kovner himself spoke about her courage.[6] During the 1960s and 1970s Vitka participated in group interviews together with Kovner and Rozka Korczak,[7] but hardly spoke and barely expressed her views about the events in which she had been involved. The dominant figure in those interviews was Abba Kovner, who reconstructed the period and even expressed his views of those events. Vitka never expressed any reservations about Kovner's having served as spokesman for the three of them under such circumstances.

Other fighting women, including Warsaw ghetto fighter Zivia Lubetkin, Białystok resistance figure Chaika Grossman, and Rozka Korczak, published books and

---

sent to Majdanek, Auschwitz, and Ravensbrück, and participated in the death marches. It was first published in Polish in 1967, and a Hebrew translation came out in 1982.

[4] *Ma'ariv*, 24 Apr. 1987.

[5] R. Korczak-Marle [Korczak], 'Do'aḥ ruzkah korchak beva'ad hapo'el shel hakibuts ha'artsi began shemu'el: haḥaverot bigevuratan', in ead., *Ruzkah: leḥimatah, hagutah, demutah* (Tel Aviv, 1988), 87–106.

[6] Abba Kovner's testimony at the Eichmann trial: <http://www.snunit.k12.il/shoa/kubnr1.htm>.

[7] Group interviews of Kovner, Korczak, and Kempner, Yad Vashem Archives, Jerusalem, 3882/03. They were interviewed by Yitshak Arad in 1974 and by Yehoshua Sobol—at Kovner's home in Kibbutz Ein Hahoresh—in 1982.

were invited to speak at memorial ceremonies and on radio programmes. Rozka was a founder of Moreshet—the Mordechai Anielevich Memorial Holocaust Study and Research Center—which commemorates the heroism of fighters in ghetto uprisings and the anti-Nazi underground. Grossman, a Hashomer Hatsa'ir leader during the war, was elected to the Knesset representing the Mapam faction. By contrast, Vitka chose to continue maintaining a low profile, considering the key functions she fulfilled during the Holocaust and the Brikhah, the movement organized to bring survivors to western Europe and from there to British-controlled Palestine. She never published her memoirs or autobiography. It appeared as if she preferred not to draw any attention to the courageous acts she performed during the Holocaust era.

Vitka, born in Kalisz, near the Polish–German border, was 19 when the Second World War broke out. The conquering German soldiers tortured and murdered the town's Jewish residents. In winter 1940, she escaped to Vilna, which had recently become the capital of the Lithuanian Soviet satellite state. After the German invasion of the Soviet Union in June 1941, the Vilna ghetto was set up and implementation of the Final Solution began immediately thereafter. About 40,000 of Vilna's Jews were slaughtered at Ponary up to early 1942. In response to the murders, the FPO was set up in January 1942, uniting several hundred youth-movement members in Vilna. Vitka was a fighter and courier in the underground and operated outside the ghetto as well. She became the first woman in occupied Europe to participate in combat against the German army when she placed an explosive charge on a railway track. This operation, launched before partisan units began organizing in the forests of Lithuania, required much courage, as she had to spend days outside the ghetto until she found a suitable place to plant the mine. Some time earlier, she had dyed her hair blonde to disguise her Jewish origins.

As the September 1943 date for destruction of the ghetto drew nearer, the underground command decided to mount an escape. Vitka led the last group that left the ghetto for Rudniki forest, where she commanded a scouting unit that left the partisan base daily to find appropriate sites for operations. She and her comrades also participated in numerous actions against the Germans, including the well-known explosion at the transformer and water pump in Vilna. In another operation, she rescued dozens of Jews from the Kailis labour camp near Vilna and brought them to a partisan base.

In summer 1944, Vitka participated in the conquest of Vilna. Her scouting unit was the first to enter the city, making sure there were no pockets of resistance left. Several months later, Vitka left for Poland with a group of survivors and partisans who had organized the Brikhah movement. She was also a member of the Nakam organization, which sought to avenge the slaughter of Jews by conducting mass sabotage operations on German soil, such as poisoning water sources. After several failed attempts of this type, Vitka and the rest of the group reached Palestine in June 1946.

Vitka came to Palestine in Operation Biria, involving two 'illegal' immigrant ships carrying Holocaust survivors.[8] The first ship, known as the *Haganah*, left La Ciotat, near Marseille, on 23 June 1946. On 28 June it met up with the *Biria*, a ramshackle freighter that had sailed from Marseille earlier, on the high seas. The next day, the immigrants were transferred from the *Haganah* to the *Biria* by rowing boat, to avoid the risk that the mechanically superior and faster ship might be seized by the British as they neared the shore. Vitka attests that the *Biria* was built to accommodate only 150 people, not the thousand refugees and survivors crammed onto its decks. There was not enough food and water for all the passengers and their voyage was

a simulation of hell. If it exists, this is what it looks like . . . People sat next to one another with no way to move . . . I volunteered to hand out water. I had one bottle and everyone got a small cup. They kept cursing me and screaming at me: 'You Kapo! You're behaving worse than they did in the concentration camps. You're drinking all the water! You're not giving us anything to drink.'[9]

The *Biria* began listing to one side because of the excess weight. The crew radioed appeals for help and the British dispatched an auxiliary force, but it offered no water or food to the passengers and did not tow the ship. On 1 July the *Biria* reached the port of Haifa, where it was secured to the quay. This is how Vitka reached the destination she had longed for, her strength drained, after long years of struggle. She and Abba Kovner established their home at Kibbutz Ein Hahoresh.

In the 1960s, Vitka studied psychology at Bar-Ilan University, devoting her energies to personal development in her profession. Her diagnostic and treatment methods met with success among her patients and gained esteem among her professional colleagues. Generations of students followed in her footsteps and Vitka herself continued working as a psychologist until the age of 87.

Vitka's concern with her personal memories of the Holocaust began after the 1986 premiere of *Partisans of Vilna* in New York. This film, produced by Aviva Kempner, was one of the first English-language documentaries to describe the Jewish armed struggle against the Nazis, focusing on Jewish resistance in Rudniki forest in Lithuania. It was based on interviews with about forty underground fighters and partisans living in the United States, Israel, and Lithuania, and also contained rare original footage. Following the screening, Vitka was interviewed in the United States by the American Jewish feminist magazine *Lilith*. This personal interview, the first to address her activities in the underground, was conducted from a gender-oriented point of view. Vitka told her interviewer, editor Aviva Cantor, that women were sent to carry out dangerous operations because it was easier for them to hide. She described the inferior status of the women fighting in the forests, contrasting it with her own role: 'I was the only woman in all the forest

---

[8] Operation Biria was commanded by Palyam officer Bezalel Drori (Palyam was the naval branch of the Palmah). See <http://www.palyam.org/English/Hahapala/hf/hf_Biria>.

[9] Vitka's conversations with Avraham Atzili, 1989 (private, limited, publication in Hebrew).

who was an intelligence scout. There were only five scouts. I was the commander of the little group of five scouts. We go out every day, to look for good places to make sabotage; to work for espionage, to seek information from the peasants, to find out where are the Germans stationed, what are they doing.'[10] This was also the first time that Vitka mentioned the loneliness and fear she felt during scouting operations among hostile peasants, on the snowy roads and in the dense forests. She did not express any opinion, however, regarding the controversial events that occurred in the Vilna ghetto and after the war, such as the surrender of partisan commander Yitshak Wittenberg, escape to Rudniki forest in September 1943, and the activities of the Nakam group.

Vitka explained that the immediate danger facing the men, coupled with an uncompromising desire to fight the Germans, turned the women into fighters against their will. Women were sent out of the ghettos to carry out dangerous operations because it was easier for them to hide their Jewish origins in the event of a body search. Nevertheless, the title 'courier', used to describe many of the fighting women, was one indicator that women were not considered to be 'real' fighters. In subsequent interviews, Vitka again expressed her objection to the term 'courier', emphasizing that 'they only made young women into couriers there; they called young women couriers . . . We [in Vilna] called them emissaries, never couriers. I heard the term for the first time when we met with people from the Warsaw ghetto here [in Israel] . . . We called them emissaries, people who were sent out on a mission. I do not like the concept either. What is a courier?'[11]

Vitka told Cantor about the difficulties she faced as a fighting woman in the underground and among the partisans, emphasizing the difference between the status of women in the partisan battalion she joined and in other fighting groups in the forests of Lithuania. In her battalion, women filled important and dangerous roles. It was only in Rudniki forest that women merited egalitarian treatment because they were serving in a separate Jewish battalion, commanded by Kovner, who appreciated their operational skills. Jewish women were not readily accepted into the Russian and Lithuanian partisan units in eastern Europe and most suffered humiliation and disrespect. The partisans felt that women were unsuitable for combat and that their presence had a deleterious effect on the men's ability to fight. It was widely believed that women diverted the men's attention from combat. In any event, there were numerous instances in which Jewish women were banished from partisan battalions and replaced with local women. Only a few Jewish women succeeded in joining Russian fighting units, thanks to their husbands or boyfriends,

---

[10] *Lilith*, 16 (1987), 24.

[11] Vitka is quoted in S. Geva, 'Yitsugan shel nashim basho'ah basiaḥ hatsiburi bishenot haḥamishim uviyemei mishpat eichman', Ph.D. diss. (Tel Aviv Univ., 2008), 37–8. In any event, despite the glorification of revolt and battle in public discourse of the 1950s and 1960s, that women joined fighters' groups in the ghettos and among the partisans was presented as 'lack of choice'. Regarding the courier's function, see also L. J. Weitzman, 'Living on the Aryan Side in Poland: Gender, Passing and the Nature of Resistance', in D. Ofer and L. J. Weitzman (eds.), *Women in the Holocaust* (New Haven, 1998), 203–4.

who rendered their own service contingent on the women's inclusion. Some Jewish men saw to it that their wives were housed with local peasants, who protected and supported them. At times, Jewish partisans agreed to join fighting battalions without their wives, whom they provided with support and sustenance at nearby family camps. There were Russian commanders who exploited their position and compelled young Jewish women to marry them. Refusal in such cases was nearly impossible and could even result in death. Jewish women in partisan groups were usually involved in cooking, baking, laundering, or nursing, trying to prove how necessary they were to the partisans, given the prevailing conditions. Young Jewish women on kitchen duty performed their jobs devotedly and were commended in the orders of the day issued by various female commanders. They also worked as clerks, typists, and translators at battalion, brigade, and regimental headquarters. Some young women distributed material in villages and nearby localities.[12] After the war, Vitka was awarded the Order of the Red Star, one of the Soviet Union's highest decorations for valour.

Other interviews with Vitka were conducted as part of a gender-oriented study of the Holocaust. American and Israeli researchers, such as Judith Tydor Baumel, Dalia Ofer, Joan Ringelheim, and Lenore Weitzman, began examining women's experiences and coping strategies during the Holocaust era, inaugurating a significant field of study at universities and research institutes in Israel and throughout the world. One conclusion derived from these pioneer gender studies declared that during periods of crisis and instability, including the Second World War era, women adjusted to what were ordinarily perceived as 'male' combat roles, attempting to adapt to the inhumane conditions of war. They proved themselves and demonstrated their endurance by coping with family matters and protecting their children.[13] This gender-oriented outlook, which assessed the women's unique response to the struggle for survival during the Holocaust, provided insights that enabled Vitka to write her memoirs and analyse her actions accordingly.

Vitka also began publicizing her version of the battle against the Nazis in response to critical remarks about Kovner voiced shortly after his demise. Kovner's views and actions met with some disfavour during his lifetime as well, especially in the early 1980s. Although he generally refrained from responding to his accusers, Kovner did mention them in a conversation with Levi Arye Sarid, published as an article after his death.[14] In early 1988, some of Kovner's movement colleagues published press articles, literature, and theatrical works, commenting disparagingly about his decisions and behaviour during the Holocaust. Yehoshua Sobol's play *Adam*, performed by the Cameri Theater in 1989 and 1990, and Amala Einat's

---

[12] Korchak-Marle, 'Do'aḥ ruzkah korchak'; M. Kananowitz, *Milḥamot hapartizanim hayehudim bemizraḥ eiropah* (Tel Aviv, 1954), 329–34; author's conversations with Kempner-Kovner.

[13] See J. T. Baumel, '"Ḥagerah be'oz motneiha": giborot hasho'ah bazikaron hakolektivi', *Dapim leḥeker hasho'ah*, 13 (1996),189–201; Ofer and Weitzman (eds.), *Women in the Holocaust*; J. Ringelheim, 'Women and the Holocaust: A Reconsideration of Research', *Signs*, 10/4 (1985), 741–61.

[14] 'Teshuvat aba kovner lemastinav', *Yalkut moreshet*, 47 (1990), 96–7.

novel *Dibah she'ein bah kalon* ('Libel without Disgrace') criticized the decisions Kovner made in the ghetto as a member of the underground leadership.[15]

In an article in the Israeli periodical *Iton 77*, Hashomer Hatsa'ir member Yitshak Zohar accused Vitka of collaborating with the *Judenrat* and turning Jewish fighters over to the Germans to save herself and the underground command.[16] Vitka sought to respond, defending her own name and Abba's, but chose not to take on her accusers directly, preferring to present her own testimony regarding events that took place during the ghetto period. She was interviewed repeatedly by Kovner's biographer, Dina Porat, whose book *The Fall of the Sparrow: The Life and Times of Abba Kovner* garnered much praise and offered a thorough description of events involving the partisans of Rudniki forest.[17] Vitka felt that the book constituted an appropriate response to Kovner's antagonists.

Vitka played a major role in commemorating Holocaust-era resistance. Besides being interviewed by Porat, she spoke with one of Rozka's cousins, Rich Cohen, whose book *The Avengers* was published in the United States in 2001. Cohen interviewed Vitka extensively after Abba and Rozka died. At Vitka's initiative, he met with former Nakam members, who told him how events unfolded in Europe after the war.[18] *The Avengers* does not purport to constitute historical research; rather, it is based on long-term acquaintance with members of the Korczak-Marle and Kovner families. The story, part fact and part fiction, describes the activities of Rozka, Vitka, and Abba in the ghetto, the forest, and the Nakam group, with no attempt to conceal the author's admiration for their accomplishments. The book received excellent reviews in respected American newspapers, such as the *New York Times* and the *Boston Globe*. Following its publication, Vitka was interviewed by Larry King, describing her unique situation as a fighting woman in the ghetto underground and among the partisans.

I first met Vitka Kovner during a Holocaust Remembrance Day ceremony at Beit Berl College in 2003. Over the next five years, I interviewed her several times and listened to her Holocaust-era stories. Our meetings blossomed into a special

---

[15] *Adam* was written in Paris between February and April 1988. The play describes the story of an imaginary figure named Nadia, an old woman living in Israel of the late 1980s, said to be Yitshak Wittenberg's lover. Adam asks Nadia to tell her story because all the others have already told theirs (Sobol thus hints at the various versions of the Wittenberg affair published in memoirs and history texts). Nadia claims that she does not remember the details of the affair precisely, but tells her story nonetheless. Her version is based on testimony that was first published in *YIVO-bleter* (the journal of the YIVO Institute for Jewish Research) in 1947. In the play, Abba Kovner appears with the name Lev, a pale figure with no backbone who aspires to replace Wittenberg so that he can enjoy the privileges afforded by the position of head of the underground. In Amela Einat's *Dibah she'ein bah kalon* (1994), Rivka Baumel describes Moshe Lerman (Kovner) as the object of her love and one of the most admired commanders of the Jewish underground movement in the Holocaust. Forty years after the war, the book attempts 'to reveal and present the truth with all its weaknesses'.

[16] *Iton 77*, 23–5 (1990).

[17] D. Porat, *Me'ever legashmi: parashat ḥayav shel aba kovner* (Jerusalem, 2000).

[18] R. Cohen, *The Avengers: A Jewish War Story* (New York, 2001), 3–10.

friendship that went beyond interviewee–interviewer relations. Vitka asked me to join her at a ceremony marking the donation of Abba Kovner's pistol to the new Yad Vashem Museum. This was the pistol that Kovner used as commander of the Vilna ghetto underground and of a partisan unit in the forests of Lithuania. It was of considerable personal and symbolic significance to Vitka.

As our meetings became more frequent and the barriers fell, Vitka began to share her thoughts, feelings, and views with me and did not hesitate to describe the difficulties she faced in those days. She spoke to me on a personal level and not as the representative of some ideology or movement. Her training as a psychologist enabled her to explain and analyse the reasons for her courage. She believed that her spontaneity and ability to make snap decisions, as well as her powerful desire to overcome any obstacle she encountered, shaped her reactions to the Holocaust. She never denied the difficulties, however, nor did she conceal the personal price she paid: 'I carried out dangerous operations by myself during the war and felt very much alone', she stressed. 'I felt far more confident when I went out on a mission together with the group.' 'There were moments when I almost broke, but I felt that I had no choice', she added.[19]

Our interviews laid the groundwork for writing Vitka's biography. In our conversations, Vitka recalled what had happened in the Vilna ghetto and Rudniki forest, as well as the activities of the Nakam group. The biography does not detail new facts, but rather reassesses events from the point of view of Vitka Kovner, who was present when they took place. As we continued conversing, I wondered whether testimony submitted during the early years following the Holocaust was more relevant historically because the events were still ingrained in memory. On the other hand, perhaps time and distance enabled Vitka to address her memories in a more forthright manner. Historian Yoav Gelber claims that although people commonly believe that memories of distant past events are flawed and selective, there are essentially no substantive differences between testimony given a few months or years after an event occurred and memories recalled decades thereafter. Furthermore, he maintains, selective memory is already evident a short time after a given event.[20] While I cannot draw any general conclusions from my meetings with Vitka, I can attest that in her particular case, the passage of time added something to her testimony. It was only at the beginning of the twenty-first century that Vitka allowed herself to describe the incidents as a woman and an individual and not as a member of Hashomer Hatsa'ir. Even in our initial conversations, she stressed that membership in the movement was not of any major significance to her. Similarly, she felt free to express her opinions and recall her feelings about the ghetto, the forest, and the Nakam group.

Our conversations raised yet another question: was Vitka capable of reconstruct-

---

[19] Author's conversations with Kempner-Kovner.

[20] Y. Gelber, *Historyah, zikaron veta'amulah: hadistsiplinah hahistorit ba'olam uva'arets* (Tel Aviv, 2007), 271–2.

ing the series of events in which she participated without being influenced by previously submitted testimony and extensive writings about the period by Abba Kovner and Rozka Korczak? Could she contradict the testimony and descriptions of the people closest to her, the ones she loved? This question is particularly acute because interpretation of events is no less significant than the events themselves.

The discussions I held with Vitka Kempner-Kovner took place as a kind of extended or open interview whose progress and content were in no way structured or defined in advance. We had a friendly conversation and exchange of ideas, occasionally digressing to unrelated topics as well. We developed mutual trust that enabled free flow of information. Vitka felt our conversations were important to her and looked forward to them. The relaxed atmosphere of the open interview made it easier for Vitka to recall details from her past and enabled her to clarify controversial events that had various interpretations.[21] Thanks to the unique quality of our interaction, when Vitka told me her story, when she evoked her memories, she was not only remembering events of the past but also interpreting them. She was not only a witness but also a historian, while I, as the interviewer, shared in this dialogue and participated in creating the testimony of my 'historical source'. Because of the interaction that developed between us, my questions and comments undoubtedly influenced the description of events and their analysis.

Partisan and poet Hirsch Glick, who wrote the lyrics to the 'Partisans' Anthem' in 1943,[22] also wrote 'Hymn to the Partisan Woman' in 1942, which he dedicated to Vitka. The song glorified her unique character, which helped assure the success of the FPO's first operation—attacking a train carrying German arms and soldiers.

The harsh struggles that Vitka faced during the war revealed her abilities as a human being and as a woman, as well as her courage, moral values, and modesty. Vitka Kempner-Kovner possessed rare character traits that were manifested under the impossible conditions of war.

MIRI FREILICH

[21] Regarding open interviews, see A. Yeheskel (Friedler), *Le'erog et sipur haḥayim: reh-biografyah shel nitsolei sho'ah* (Tel Aviv, 1999).

[22] Hirsch Glick (1922–44) was a poet and partisan in Vilna. When Vilna was conquered by the Germans in late June 1941, he joined the FPO. Throughout the war years, he continued to write. He was in the group that was captured and sent to a work camp in Estonia on 1 September 1943. In summer 1944, he tried to escape from the camp with several other inmates, but all were killed. In 1943, Glick wrote the words to the 'Partisans' Anthem' while in the Vilna ghetto, dedicating it to the memory of the Warsaw ghetto fighters and his comrades in arms who perished.

Roman Totenberg
1 January 1911–8 May 2012

ON 8 MAY 2012 the world lost one of the greatest Polish violinist-virtuosos, whose career spanned nine decades, at the tender age of only 101. He was born on 1 January 1911 (1/1/11). I was hoping he would live at least to 111 or until 120 (as per the Jewish joke and/or wish: 'May you live until 120'). A remarkable man and personality.

I was blessed to know this compassionate, generous, kind, soul. He was always a close friend of the Fitelberg family. He made his concert debut under the baton of the prominent Polish composer-conductor Grzegorz Fitelberg at age 11, and he left an indelible impression on everyone whose heart, mind, and soul he touched. He was also responsible for playing the premiere of Jerzy Fitelberg's Concerto for Violin and Orchestra.

Once when I flew to Boston to visit Totenberg for a documentary film concerning Grzegorz Fitelberg (who himself was a violinist and pedagogue), I had the unique opportunity not only to film him but to receive an impromptu personal concert which was unforgettable and unique. He was also teaching a group of his illustrious students and hosting a luncheon for them. Though not feeling well that particular day, he had no thought of cancelling our appointment or his teaching engagement. Roman Totenberg recalled Grzegorz Fitelberg candidly and humbly: 'In Warsaw I often played with Gregor Fitelberg: Brahms's concerto and many other works.'

His affiliation with Szymanowski, Rubinstein, and Fitelberg also extended to the maestro Grzegorz Fitelberg's son Jerzy Fitelberg. He shared a story about Szymanowski and Jerzy Fitelberg with me:

I remember Szymanowski very well. He was very tall, elegant, handsome, and reticent, only saying much when it was one-to-one. In 1933 or '34 in Paris I played some of his compositions and he liked it so much that he offered to play a concert with me. We played a recital there and later went to Italy, England, and Scandinavia for about two years of concerts. I was surprised by how well he knew music. When I played a Brahms sonata or something else, he knew exactly what it was and its construction. The son of the conductor Gregor Fitelberg

This is a revised version of an appreciation previously published online at <http://www.aapjstudies.org/index.php?id=156>.

was composing modern music and I helped him with a work, which I brought over to Szymanowski, who said, 'Jerzy knows his Stravinsky, doesn't he?'

I believe Totenberg was referring to the *Canzone pour violon et piano* (arrangement pour violon par Roman Totenberg) by Haendel-Fitelberg. This was published in Paris by Éditions Max Eschig.

On one occasion he shocked and surprised me by presenting me with a vary rare concert programme from Paris, in which he had played a piece of music by Jerzy Fitelberg for violin.

Totenberg had many positive attributes that endeared him to all those who were blessed, honoured, and privileged to have known him personally. Charismatic and charming. Generous. Hospitable. Inspirational. Patient. These are but a small sampling. He was a genius. His smile, sense of humour, and sensitivity infected you with his warmth.

My adopted brother and good friend, Polish violinist Hubert Pralitz, recalls Totenberg fondly and with great reverence: 'I once met Roman Totenberg in Gdańsk. I was a young violinist. It was truly remarkable that he let me play his Stradivarius. This was the first and only time I ever had the opportunity to play on such a fine instrument.'

One cannot mention all the accomplishments and life history of Roman Totenberg in a limited space and time, but three events are worth noting in this special tribute. In 1983 he was named Artist Teacher of the Year by the American String Teachers Association. In April 2007 he was honoured with the New England String Ensemble's Muses and Mentors Award for his great artistry and significant contributions to string education. In 1988 the Polish government awarded him the highest honour, the Order of Merit, for his lifelong contributions to Polish society.

When he was in hospital after he had turned 100, a nurse came to check up on him. He asked her, with his sense of humour as quick as ever, 'What's wrong? I'm not dead yet!' Miraculously, even at the age of 101, his mind was still sharp.

According to his daughter Nina Totenberg, he had 'a remarkable death' at the end of his earthly existence. One episode of this time epitomizes his personality. From a hospital bed in his Newton home, he is teaching one of his many students, Letitia Hom. He listens to her playing the Brahms Violin Concerto. 'Slow down here', he murmurs. 'Slow down.' His kidneys are shutting down. At 101 years of age, the legendary violinist—a man who hung out with Stravinsky and Copland, Menuhin and Rubinstein—is finally dying. But he's still teaching. He murmurs something Hom can't hear. 'What?' she says. He repeats himself, but she still can't hear. She bends over his bed, putting her ear to his mouth. Totenberg says, perfectly clearly: '*The D was flat.*' Nina Totenberg adds, 'He's not going to go quickly —he has work to do.'

This maestro of magic and music will be missed by all who knew him.

His legacy of music lives infinitely in our hearts, minds, and souls.

God gave us a gift.
Roman Totenberg.
A man of music.
Virtuoso violinist.
Roman Totenberg, I believe, is now on special assignment, playing solo only for God and the angels.

GARY FITELBERG

Zenon Guldon
1936–2012

PROFESSOR ZENON GULDON, a historian, organizer of academic life, and academician, was born on 24 November 1936 in a working-class family. He studied for the degree of MA in the Faculty of Arts of the Mikołaj Kopernik University in Toruń in the years 1953–7. Having worked in various historical disciplines under such major figures as Professors Stanisław Hoszowski, Franciszek Paprocki, Bronisław Włodarski, and Leonid Żytkiewicz, he acquired a practical knowledge of their research techniques. This made it possible for him to tackle a wide range of subjects using various research methods.

He launched his academic career with the publication of his brilliant master's thesis *Walka klasowa chłopstwa polskiego od XII do połowy XIV wieku* ('Class Struggle of the Polish Peasantry from the Twelfth to the Middle of the Fourteenth Centuries'; Toruń, 1958) and four years later he obtained a Ph.D. from the same university with his thesis *Rozmieszczenie własności ziemskiej na Kujawach w II połowie XVI wieku* ('Distribution of Land Ownership in the Kujawy District in the Second Half of the Sixteenth Century'; Toruń, 1964). He successfully submitted his habilitation thesis, *Związki handlowe dóbr magnackich na prawobrzeżnej Ukrainie z Gdańskiem w XVIII wieku* ('The Commercial Links of Noble Estates in Right-Bank Ukraine with Danzig in the Eighteenth Century'; Toruń, 1966), at Toruń in 1967. He was 31 at the time. From 1957 he had also been working as a teacher at the Mikołaj Kopernik University in Toruń, where he was ultimately promoted to associate professor.

These were the circumstances that shaped the pattern of his later long-term investigations and academic research. These included Polish history of the sixteenth to the eighteenth centuries, encompassing Kujawy, the Dobrzyń land, and the Wielkopolska region, as well as Ukraine and Belarus and—after 1970, having become associated with Kielce—also the Kielce and Małopolska regions. Occasionally he would go beyond these subjects and included the Middle Ages and the nineteenth century. From the earliest days of his academic research he also focused on wider interests, which were by no means disparate or random but were concentrated around one single, uniform subject matter. These included economic history, particularly the history of trade and cities, historical geography, the history of settlement, and the historical demography of the Old Polish period. During the

1970s he also took up the methodology of regional research and taught history in higher educational institutions.

From the start of his academic career, he also wrote on many levels, ranging from strictly scholarly papers conforming to a rigorous formal discipline and supported by an abundance of erudite material, to more popular texts. The latter not only provided a clearly presented overview of the current state of knowledge, but were also enriched by the results of his own research conducted specially for a particular text. He readily took on methodological and source-book research, testifying to an editorial expertise that he acquired under the tutelage of outstanding teachers. He did not avoid critiques, polemics, or reviews of research, but he preferred the form of studies and debates, which always, under his pen, strove towards a synthesis.

The essential value of Zenon Guldon's early, pre-1970, output was further enhanced by the introduction of a number of hitherto underestimated sources, including customs registers and oaths, and by a fundamental knowledge of archival resources in Poland and an expertise related to such resources in Russia and in Sweden.

The ability to follow up enquiries, to read sources carefully, and to place his discoveries in a wider context attracted graduate students. Among those who completed their habilitation under his direction were Professors Maria Bogucka, Józef Burszta, Nikolay Krikun from Ukraine, M. Dosman, Irena Rychlikowa, and Władysław Serczyk. Among those scholars who favourably reviewed his monograph *Podziały administracyjne Kujaw i ziemi dobrzyńskiej w XIII–XIV wieku* ('Administrative Boundaries of the Kujawy District and the Dobrzyń Land in the Thirteenth–Fourteenth Centuries'; Warsaw and Poznań, 1974) were Professors Antoni Gąsiorowski, Marceli Kosman, and Andrzej Wędzki. Historians also praised his three-part *Lustracje województw wielkopolskich i kujawskich, 1628–1632* ('Surveys of the Wielkopolska and Kujawy Provincial Administration Offices, 1628–1632'; Wrocław, Bydgoszcz, and Poznań, 1967–9) for the wide range of sources it included and the high quality of its editorial skill.

In 1970 he was appointed lecturer and researcher in the newly created (1969) Higher Teachers' College in Kielce, later renamed the Higher Pedagogical Institute. This presented him with new challenges. Admittedly, he did not neglect his research related to the economic history of the Kujawy and Wielkopolska regions, but from the early 1980s onward, the number of publications devoted to them began to diminish. This gap was filled by studies on the Kielce and occasionally the Małopolska regions. Along with this territorial shift, new subjects made their appearance in Professor Guldon's publications. He devoted a number of studies, papers, and articles to the economic life of the Old Polish Industrial Region. The high point of this research turned out to be his *Górnictwo i hutnictwo w staropolskim okręgu przemysłowej w drugiej połowie XVIII wieku* ('The Mining and Iron Works in the Old Polish Industrial Region in the Second Half of the Eighteenth Century';

Kielce, 1994), co-authored with Jacek Kaczor. He concentrated on production, trade, and transport in the towns between the rivers Vistula and Pilica and between the Kingdom of Poland and the East. This can be seen in his book *Z dziejów handlu Rzeczypospolitej w XVI–XVIII wieku: Studia i materiały* ('The History of Trade in the Polish Republic in the Sixteeenth–Eighteenth Centuries: Studies and Materials'; Kielce, 1980), co-authored with Lech Stępkowski.

From the mid-1970s, he turned his attention to what were, for him, new demographic, social, and economic problems connected with the issues of ethnic minorities such as Scots, English, and Jews in the Polish Republic. He began with the history of settlement and population numbers of these minorities in the Kielce region and the part they played in the economic life of the towns, particularly in commerce. In time, he expanded the field of his observations and included Polish–Jewish conflicts between the sixteenth and eighteenth centuries against a religious background and the functioning of Jewish autonomous communities in the towns of the Kingdom of Poland. He devoted many articles and studies to these subjects, which had hitherto been taken up by historians only sporadically, and he continued to work on them until the end of his active professional life. He also published several short works which arose from his research, including *Żydzi i Szkoci w Polsce w XVI–XVIII wieku: Studia i materiały* ('Jews and Scots in Poland in the Sixteenth–Eighteenth Centuries: Studies and Materials'; Kielce, 1990); *Ludność żydowska w miastach lewobrzeżnej części województwa sandomierskiego w XVI–XVIII wieku: Studium osadniczo-demograficzne* ('The Jewish Population of the Left-Bank Part of the Sandomierz Province in the Sixteenth–Eighteenth Centuries: A Study of Settlement and Demography'; Kielce, 1990), co-authored with Karol Krzystanek; and *Procesy o mordy rytualne w Polsce w XVI–XVIII wieku* ('Ritual Murder Trials in Poland in the Sixteenth–Eighteenth Centuries'; Kielce, 1995), co-authored with Jacek Wijaczka. English versions of the last two of these studies later appeared, making them available to the international academic community.[1] He also co-authored several English-language works with Waldemar Kowalski.[2]

---

[1] Z. Guldon and K. Krzystanek, 'The Jewish Population in the Towns on the West Bank of the Vistula in Sandomierz Province, 16th–18th Centuries', in A. Polonsky, J. Basista, and A. Link-Lenczowski (eds.), *The Jews in Old Poland, 1000–1795* (London, 1993), 322–39; Z. Guldon and J. Wijaczka, 'The Accusation of Ritual Murder in Poland, 1500–1800', *Polin*, 10 (1997), 89–140.

[2] Z. Guldon and W. Kowalski, 'Between Tolerance and Abomination: Jews in Sixteenth-Century Poland', in R. B. Waddington and A. H. Williamson (eds.), *The Expulsion of the Jews: 1492 and After* (New York, 1994), 161–75; Z. Guldon and W. Kowalski, 'The Jewish Population of Polish Towns in the Second Half of the Seventeenth Century', in A. Teller (ed.), *Studies in the History of the Jews in Old Poland in Honor of Jacob Goldberg* (Jerusalem, 1998), 67–81; Z. Guldon and W. Kowalski, 'The Jewish Population and Family in the Polish–Lithuanian Commonwealth in the Second Half of the Eighteenth Century', *The History of the Family*, 8/4 (2003), 517–30; Z. Guldon and W. Kowalski, 'Jewish Settlement in the Polish Commonwealth in the Second Half of the Eighteenth Century', *Polin*, 18 (2005), 307–21.

Living in the Kielce Province, Professor Guldon would not have been a proper historian had he failed to take up the problems related to its regional issues, which had been much discussed since the beginning of the twentieth century. This is why, between 1977 and 1984, he voiced his opinions with great expertise and concision on such matters as the concept of region and regionalism in general, the specifics of the Kielce region in particular, and regionalism in matters related to teaching history. He reactivated a regional research which continues to this day. Professor Guldon also published source texts in Kielce, including sources related to industrial history and population statistics, registers of births, marriages, and deaths, other registers, taxes, inventories, and regulations. These, no less than the deeper regional thinking that he initiated, were indispensable to the creation of a workshop for a team of young historians who, inspired by him, continue to carry out research into Polish economic history between the sixteenth century and the present. On several occasions he published methodological guides for history students, as he was convinced that a rationally constructed research workshop would be of service to them, and not just during the time they were studying.

During the Kielce period he was also extremely active as a member of learned societies, such as the Polish Historical Society (from 1958 onward, becoming president in 1971, then vice-president of the Kielce Branch of the Polish Historical Society), the Bydgoszcz Learned Society, and the Toruń Learned Society. During 1973–4 he was director of the Learned Society of Kielce and remained a member of its establishment. He participated actively in the work of the Society of Friends of Mining, Iron Works, and Industry in the Old Polish Industrial Region, collaborated in the compilation of the *Słownik historyczno-geograficzny ziem polskich w średniowieczu* ('Historical and Geographical Dictionary of Polish Territories in the Middle Ages') issued by the Polish Academy of Science, and was a member of the Kraków Branch of the Historical Commission of the Polish Academy of Science and the Historical Geography Commission of the Polish Academy of Science Committee for Historical Sciences.

He also took on many administrative responsibilities at the Higher Teachers' College in Kielce. Following his appointment there he created and organized the Independent History Workshop, which later became the History Institute. During 1976–80 he became deputy director of scientific research and, more than once, director of scientific research units in the Institute and a member of collegiate bodies of the College. During 1982–3 he carried out the duties of director of the Main Library of the Higher Teachers' College, which its staff remember with gratitude. He was frequently awarded both state and departmental honours and prizes. But it was not until May 1980 that he was promoted to full professor in the Higher Pedagogical Institute in Kielce.

He ceased to work at the Higher Pedagogical Institute in Kielce at the beginning of the 1991/2 academic year, but continued to hold a central position not only in local, but also general Polish economic history of the sixteenth to eighteenth centuries. Suffice it to say that between 1992 and 2008, when his last publications appeared, he had published nearly 150 texts.

Professor Zenon Guldon died in Kielce on 25 July 2012.

MARTA MEDUCKA

Translated from the Polish by Theresa Prout

Notes on the Contributors

RICHARD BUTTERWICK-PAWLIKOWSKI is Professor of Polish–Lithuanian History at the School of Slavonic and East European Studies, University College London. He is the author of *Poland's Last King and English Culture: Stanisław August Poniatowski, 1732–1798* (Oxford, 1998) and *The Polish Revolution and the Catholic Church, 1788–1792: A Political History* (Oxford, 2012). His research focuses on the Enlightenment and its critics, the Catholic Church, and the monarchy and parliamentarianism in the Polish–Lithuanian Commonwealth.

KATHLEEN CIOFFI is a book editor at Princeton University Press, as well as a drama critic and theatre historian who writes frequently about Polish theatre. The author of *Alternative Theatre in Poland, 1954–1989* (Amsterdam, 1996), she has also published articles, interviews, and reviews in *Theater*, *TDR*, *Slavic and East European Performance*, *Contemporary Theatre Review*, the *Polish Review*, and several anthologies. She is also the series editor for PIASA Books, the publishing arm of the Polish Institute of Arts and Sciences of America.

GLENN DYNNER is Professor of Religion at Sarah Lawrence College and the 2013–14 Senior NEH Scholar at the Center for Jewish History. He is the author of *Men of Silk: The Hasidic Conquest of Polish Jewish Society* (New York, 2006), and *Yankel's Tavern: Jews, Liquor, and Life in the Kingdom of Poland* (New York, 2013). He is also editor of *Holy Dissent: Jewish and Christian Mystics in Eastern Europe* (Detroit, 2011).

GABRIEL N. FINDER is an associate professor in the Department of Germanic Languages and Literatures and Ida and Nathan Kolodiz Director of Jewish Studies at the University of Virginia. His research interests lie in central and east European Jewish history and culture, the Holocaust, trials ensuing from the Holocaust, memory of the Holocaust, the reconstruction of Jewish life after 1945, and post-war relations between Jews and non-Jews in central and eastern Europe with an emphasis on Poland. He is contributing co-editor of volume 20 of *Polin* ('Making Holocaust Memory', 2008) and of two forthcoming publications: *Jewish Honor Courts: Revenge, Retribution, and Reconciliation in Europe and Israel after the Holocaust*, with Laura Jockusch; and volume 29 of *Studies in Contemporary Jewry*, with Eli Lederhendler ('Humor in Jewish Culture').

FRANÇOIS GUESNET is Sidney and Elizabeth Corob Reader in Modern Jewish History in the Department of Hebrew and Jewish Studies at University College London. He specializes in the early modern and nineteenth-century history of Polish and east European Jewry. His publications include *Polnische Juden im 19.*

Jahrhundert: Lebensbedingungen, Rechtsnormen und Organisation im Wandel (Cologne, 1998) and more recently an anthology of non-fictional Polish writings about the Jews of Poland, *Der Fremde als Nachbar: Polnische Positionen zur jüdischen Präsenz. Texte seit 1800* (Frankfurt am Main, 2009). He has edited volumes on Jewish historiography, Jewish–Lithuanian relations (with Darius Staliūnas), a comparative investigation on antisemitism in post-communist Poland and Hungary (with Gwenyth Jones), and on the history of Warsaw as a Jewish metropolis in the nineteenth and twentieth centuries (with Glenn Dynner). He currently serves as chairman of the Executive Group of the UCL Grand Challenge on Intercultural Interaction.

AGNIESZKA JAGODZIŃSKA is Assistant Professor at the Department of Jewish Studies at the University of Wrocław, Poland. She is the author of the prize-winning monograph *Pomiędzy: Akulturacja Żydów Warszawy w drugiej połowie XIX wieku* (Wrocław, 2008) and editor of two other books: *W poszukiwaniu religii doskonałej? Konwersja a Żydzi* (Wrocław, 2012) and *Ludwik Zamenhof wobec 'kwestii żydowskiej': Wybór źródeł* (Wrocław, 2012). Her main academic interest is the history of Polish Jews in the nineteenth century, in particular Jewish acculturation and integration, and Christian missions and conversion of Jews. Currently she is working on the topic of the missions of the London Society for Promoting Christianity amongst the Jews in Poland.

YEDIDA KANFER received her Ph.D. in Russian, East European, and Jewish history from Yale University in 2011. She subsequently served as a research scholar at the Kennan Institute of the Woodrow Wilson International Center for Scholars. Yedida is interested in themes of Polish–Jewish relations, empire, nationhood, religion, gender, and memory.

ARTUR MARKOWSKI is Assistant Professor at the Department of History of the University of Warsaw. His principal interest is the history of Jews in the tsarist empire in the nineteenth century. He is director of the programme on anti-Jewish pogroms in the Polish lands in the nineteenth and twentieth centuries. He is the author of *Między wschodem a zachodem: Rodzina i gospodarstwo domowe Żydów suwalskich w pierwszej połowie XIX wieku* (Warsaw, 2008) and co-editor (with Wojciech Śleszyński) of *Sztetl — wspólne dziedzictwo: Szkice z dziejów ludności żydowskiej Europy Środkowo-Wschodniej* (Białystok, 2003) and (with August Grabski), *Narody i polityka: Studia ofiarowane Jerzemu Tomaszewskiemu* (Warsaw, 2010).

BENJAMIN MATIS was educated in music and musicology at the Peabody Conservatory and Queens College of the City University of New York. He then went on to study Jewish music and liturgy while earning a Master of Sacred Music diploma at the Jewish Theological Seminary of America, where some of his teachers in liturgy included Rabbis Morton Leifman and Debra Reed Blank as well as the renowned Menachem Schmeltzer. He is preparing for his Ph.D. work under

Michał Galas at the Jagiellonian University and currently serves as cantor at the Shelter Rock Jewish Center in Roslyn, New York.

JOANNA NALEWAJKO-KULIKOV is an assistant professor in the Institute of History, Polish Academy of Sciences. She is the author of *Strategie przetrwania: Żydzi po aryjskiej stronie Warszawy* (Warsaw, 2004) and *Obywatel Jidyszlanda: Rzecz o żydowskich komunistach w Polsce* (Warsaw, 2009) and co-editor (with Grzegorz Bąbiak) of *Trudny wiek XX: Jednostka, system, epoka* (Warsaw, 2010) and (with Grzegorz Bąbiak and Agnieszka Cieślikowa), *Studia z dziejów trójjęzycznej prasy żydowskiej na ziemach polskich (XIX–XX w.)* (Warsaw, 2012).

ALEKSANDRA ONISZCZUK is a Ph.D. student in history at the University of Wrocław, preparing her thesis on the politics of central and local governments of the Duchy of Warsaw towards the Jews. She received her MA in history from the University of Warsaw (on the Jewish community in Kalisz in 1815–1914) and a MA in law from the University of Wrocław (on the status of Jerusalem after 1948 in international public law). She also graduated in Jewish Studies at the Centre for the Culture and Languages of the Jews, University of Wrocław. Since 2010 she has worked at the Educational Research Institute, Warsaw.

JACEK PIOTROWSKI is a professor in the Faculty of History at the University of Wrocław specializing in history and political science. Among his books are *Aleksander Prystor, 1874–1941: Zarys biografii politycznej* (Wrocław, 1994), *Generał Stefan Hubicki: Żołnierz, polityk, lekarz (1877–1955)* (Wrocław, 2009), and a monograph, *Piłsudczycy bez lidera: Po 1 września 1939* (Toruń, 2003). He is the editor of the multi-volume collection of documents *Dzienniki czynności Prezydenta RP Władysława Raczkiewicza, 1939–1947* (Wrocław, 2004) and of Stanisław Stroński, *Polityka Rządu Polskiego na Uchodźstwie w latach 1939–1942* (Nowy Sącz, 2007). His books have received prizes from the Rektor of the University of Wrocław, the Fundacja na rzecz Nauki Polskiej, and the weekly *Polityka*.

SZYMON RUDNICKI is Professor Emeritus of Contemporary Polish History at Warsaw University and specializes in the history of Poland. He is the author of several monographs and many articles about the Polish nationalistic and right-wing political movements and Polish–Jewish relations. Among his most important books are *Równi, ale niezupełnie* (Warsaw, 2008), *Żydzi w parlamencie II Rzeczypospolitej* (Warsaw, 2004), and *Obóz Narodowo-Radykalny: Geneza i działalność* (Warsaw, 1985).

MARCOS SILBER is a senior lecturer in the Department of Jewish History and chair of the Department of Multidisciplinary Studies at the University of Haifa. He is the author of *Different Nationality, Equal Citizenship! The Efforts to Achieve Autonomy for Polish Jewry during the First World War* (Hebrew; Tel Aviv, 2014) and editor with Szymon Rudnicki of *Stosunki polsko-izraelskie (1945–1967): Wybór dokumentów* (Warsaw, 2009; Hebrew version: Jerusalem, 2009). He has published numerous articles in the *Simon Dubnow Institute Yearbook*, *Journal of Israeli History*, *Tsiyon*, *Gal-ed*, *Shevut*, *Michael*, *Iyunim bitekumat yisra'el*, and *Journal of Baltic Studies*.

ANTONI SUŁEK is a professor at the Institute of Sociology of the University of Warsaw. His interests encompass the history of sociology, sociological methodology, and public opinion research. In the years 1994–8 he served as the president of the Polish Sociological Association, and in 1999–2001 as Chief Adviser on Social Affairs to the prime minister of the Republic of Poland.

THEODORE R. WEEKS is Professor of History at Southern Illinois University, Carbondale. He is the author of *Nation and State in Late Imperial Russia: Nationalism and Russification on the Western Frontier, 1863–1914* (DeKalb, Ill., 2008), *Across the Revolutionary Divide: Russia and the USSR, 1861–1945* (Oxford, 2011), and *From Assimilation to Antisemitism: The 'Jewish Question' in Poland, 1850–1914* (DeKalb, Ill., 2006). He is presently completing a history of Vilnius as a multicultural city, 1795–2000.

MARCIN WODZIŃSKI is Professor of Jewish Studies at the University of Wrocław. His special fields of interest are the social history of the Jews in the nineteenth century, the regional history of the Jews in Silesia, and Jewish sepulchral art. He is the author of several books, including *Haskalah and Hasidism in the Kingdom of Poland: A History of Conflict* (Oxford, 2005) and *Hasidism and Politics: The Kingdom of Poland, 1815–1864* (Oxford, 2013), both published by the Littman Library. He is the editor of the Bibliotheca Judaica and Makor/Źródła series. He is vice-president of the Polish Association of Jewish Studies and editor-in-chief of its periodical, *Studia Judaica*. In 2011 he was awarded the Jan Karski and Pola Nirenska Prize by the YIVO Institute for Jewish Research.

RAKEFET ZALASHIK is the Israel Studies Scholar at the Moses Mendelssohn Center, University of Potsdam. She is the author of two books: *Ad Nafesh: Immigrants, Refugees, Newcomers, and the Israeli Psychiatric Establishment* (Hakibuts Hame'uhad, 2008) and Das unselige Erbe: Die Geschichte der Psychiatrie in Palästina, 1920–1960 (Frankfurt am Main, 2012). Her current research focuses on TOZ (Towarzystwo Ochrony Zdrowia Ludności Żydowskiej) as a case study of health and minorities in inter-war Europe.

JOSHUA D. ZIMMERMAN is Associate Professor of History at Yeshiva University in New York. He is the author of *Poles, Jews and the Politics of Nationality: The Bund and the Polish Socialist Party in Late Tsarist Russia, 1892–1914* (Madison, 2004) and the editor of both *Contested Memories: Poles and Jews during the Holocaust and its Aftermath* (New Brunswick, NJ, 2003) and *Jews in Italy under Fascist and Nazi Rule, 1922–1945* (New Brunswick, NJ, 2005). In the 2011/12 academic year, he was Miles Lerman Center for the Study of Jewish Resistance Research Fellow at the US Holocaust Memorial Museum in Washington.

Index